CU00895166

A Policeman's Paradise?

*The History of Policing
in New Zealand,
Volume Four*

A Policeman's Paradise?

Policing a Stable Society
1918–1945

Graeme Dunstall

The Dunmore Press
in association with the
Historical Branch, Department of Internal Affairs

©1999 Crown Copyright

First published in 1999 by Dunmore Press in association with the New Zealand Police and with the assistance of the Historical Branch, Department of Internal Affairs, Wellington.

Australian Supplier:
Federation Press
PO Box 45
Annandale 2038 NSW
Australia
Ph: (02) 9552-2200
Fax: (02) 9552-1681

ISBN for complete set of 5 volumes 0-477-01346-5

ISBN 0-86469-356-7

Text: Times New Roman 10.8/12
Printer: The Dunmore Printing Company Ltd
           Palmerston North

Contents

Figures

Preface

This is the fourth volume in a series on the history of policing in New Zealand commissioned by the New Zealand Police. In contrast to the era covered in the previous volumes by Richard Hill, the years from 1918 to 1945 were a distinctive period of stability in New Zealand policing. By the early 1920s, a pattern of police organisation and administration had been established that lasted until the early 1950s. So, too, the nature of police work in the inter-war years was relatively unchanging. Stability in policing mirrored a high degree of social cohesion and order despite the impact of technological change, economic depression, and war.

This account attempts to meet two objectives. The first was implicit in my original commission: to provide a narrative administrative history of a government department. The second objective reflects my inclinations: a social history of police work which examines thematically the various patterns of policing within a broader context of continuity and change in social behaviour. Befitting a centralised police force, the discussion has a country-wide focus while trying to be sensitive to regional differences. This overview is complemented by the many regional histories of policing that have been produced in recent years. From the outset I had in mind three types of reader: present and past police personnel, my academic colleagues, and my family, representing curious lay people who knew little about police and policing (but who have come to live the subject for a long time). In attempting to meet different interests, I have risked satisfying none.

The focus on police work relies to a considerable extent on the recollections of former policemen and policewomen. When the project began there were still a significant number of retired police who had joined during the inter-war years and were willing to be interviewed or to reflect on questions I asked while writing their reminiscences. In part, then, this is their history; it is shaped (not uncritically) by the memories of the survivors: those who had careers in the Police Force and generally thought well of it, though they were often critical of many aspects of administration and working conditions.

A paucity of police administrative files for the period covered by the book reinforced the reliance on oral history and a close reading of newspapers. Key exceptions to the gaps in police archival resources are the case files and station records now in National Archives, and Police surveillance files held by the Security Intelligence Service. These sources have been used selectively.

This is a work of many hands. Over a long period, I have received considerable assistance from more people than I can acknowledge individually here: past and present police personnel; archivists and librarians; colleagues and students. Most of those who provided information and assisted with research are acknowledged in the bibliography; I regret any omissions. For assistance over a long period and crucial work in the final production of the book, some must be singled out. Former Chief Inspector Sherwood Young, the mainstay of the project as the Police history liaison officer, was generous in his assistance, advice and patience. I have had complete freedom to express my own opinions. Former Senior Constable Barry Thomson provided key non-archival sources and insights, and Richard Hill some challenging perspectives. Chris Connolly provided salutary comments on a draft of the first chapter, while Michael Bassett improved the last two. Sue Upton's photograph search turned up many that have been used. Michael Davies of the New Zealand Police drew the maps. Patricia Sargison compiled the index. Successive chief historians of the Historical Branch of the Department of Internal Affairs have shown forbearance in monitoring my progress, with Claudia Orange overseeing the last stages of writing and publication. At the Historical Branch, Bronwyn Dalley gave necessary support and a critical reading of the draft, as did David Green while editing the text sensitively and making it a better book.

Working on this book (and also on the succeeding volume) in conjunction with the demands of other university work has taken longer than I wish anyone to remember. It would not have been completed without periods of study leave generously granted by the University of Canterbury, and the sustained support of Kathy, Emily and Esther, and of my parents.

NORTH ISLAND POLICE DISTRICTS IN 1918

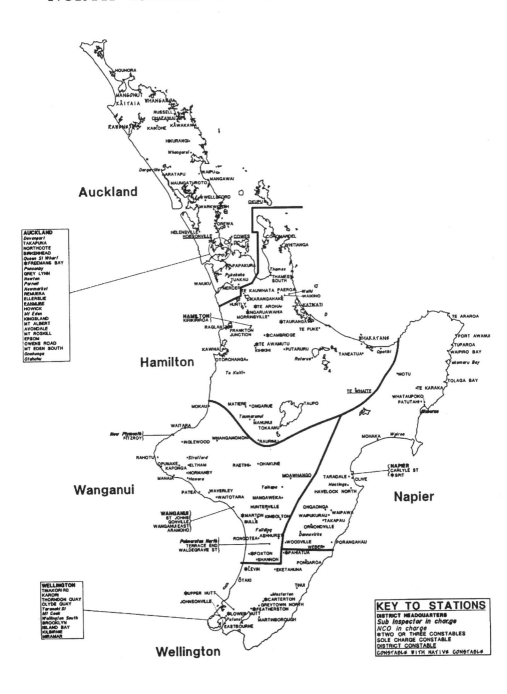

SOUTH ISLAND POLICE DISTRICTS IN 1918

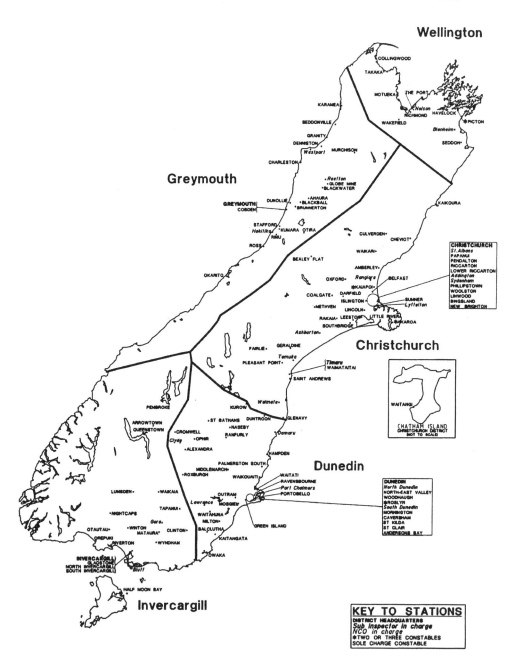

NORTH ISLAND POLICE DISTRICTS IN 1939

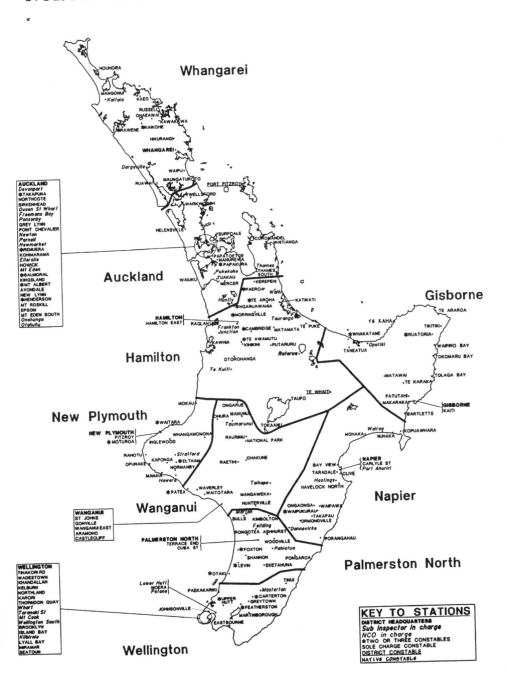

SOUTH ISLAND POLICE DISTRICTS IN 1939

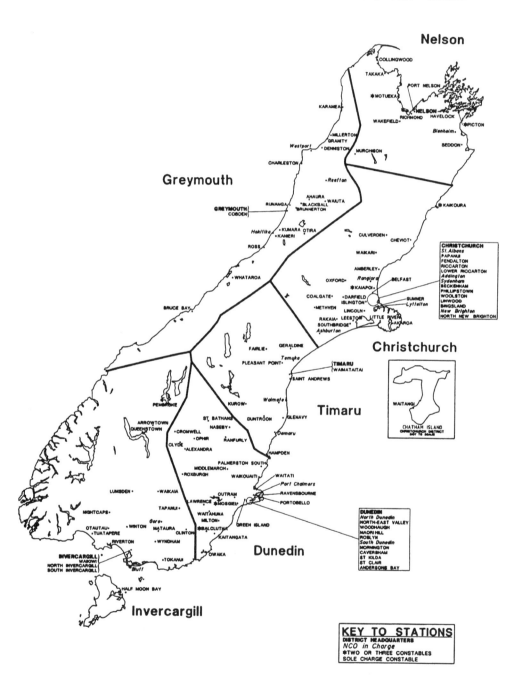

Introduction
Patterns Set

Taking a long view of the history of New Zealand policing, the period from the 1920s to the 1940s can be seen to be distinctive in its stability – in both the organisation and patterns of policing and the degree of social cohesion and tranquillity. Taking the short view, the years between 1918 and 1945 encompassed ongoing social and technological changes, economic instability, depression and war, during which the Police Force remained a largely unchanging institution in its attitudes, priorities and methods.

During these years enduring expectations of the efficacy and neutrality of New Zealand preventive policing were established, built on the modes of police work in small towns. But there were tensions between expectations of effective and impartial policing and the capacities and methods of police in the suburbanising, increasingly motorised cities, especially Auckland. To some critics, the Police Force seemed to be stagnating, falling behind the times. To others who challenged the political or economic status quo, or state-desired norms of behaviour, police were seen as agents of the state (or of those perceived to influence its policies) rather than as neutral servants of the law.

The years between 1922 and 1955 were preceded and followed by extended periods of administrative change in policing. By contrast, a pattern of administration was established by the early 1920s that endured for 30 years at least. In this period, for example, the number of staff at Police Headquarters in Wellington remained small, symbolising the continuity of a particular mode of administration.[1] Between 1898 and 1922, the number of police districts had grown from seven to fourteen; they were only modified during the next 44 years by the addition of the Nelson District in 1928. Similarly, the number and distribution of stations were broadly stable during the inter-war years; so too was the ratio of police to population (averaging about 77 per 100,000), which was significantly lower than the ratios 50 years earlier or later (figure I.1). The main innovation was the advent of the New Zealand Police Association in 1936, although this body's influence on working conditions and patterns of administration was not to be fully felt until well after the Second World War.

Patterns of police work were also relatively unchanging during the

Figure I.1: New Zealand Police Numbers 1878–1954

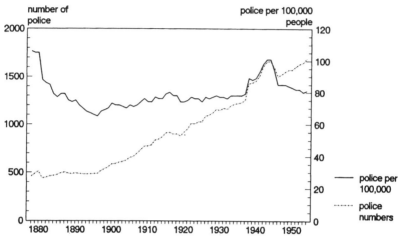

Source: Annual Reports.

inter-war years, with an emphasis on regular patrolling and surveillance. There were distinctive modes of city and small-town policing by uniformed men, complemented by small numbers of detectives who often worked alone and relied on their skills as interrogators rather than on technical aids. By 1920 the rudiments of professionalisation had appeared in New Zealand policing, along with a developing sense of a distinctive occupational community amongst men who had to remain aloof and detached from their communities.

Shaping the predominant mode of uniformed policing was the long-term shift which had occurred since the 1860s from order imposition to order maintenance. The overtly coercive paramilitary policing of often turbulent Pakeha and Maori males evolved into a more benign system in which the local constable was a 'peace officer' symbolising the coercive potential of the state and facilitating the production of order in stable communities that were essentially self-policing.[2] The inter-war years saw the heyday of a small-town society with its large core of stable families, its variety of institutions for social interaction, its strong pressures for conformity, and its sustained inculcation of desired norms. Such communities desired the presence of a local constable as a resource if needed, and a visible deterrent to criminals, rather than an intrusive agent of the state. The relatively small number of police in comparison with Australia and Britain epitomised official perceptions of increased social stability. Though the number of police in 1920 (916) was double that in 1878, the number of police *per head of population* had fallen by nearly a third.

The rate of prosecutions for violence (figures I.2, I.3) and for public order offences associated with drunkenness (figure I.4) also fell,

Figure I.2: Reported Assaults 1878–1954

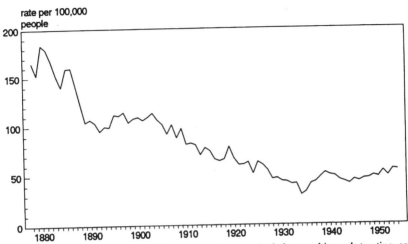

Source: Annual Reports. Note: The category does not include assaulting, obstructing or resisting constables, or indecent or sexual assaults.

Figure I.3: Reported Homicides 1878–1954
(three-year moving average)

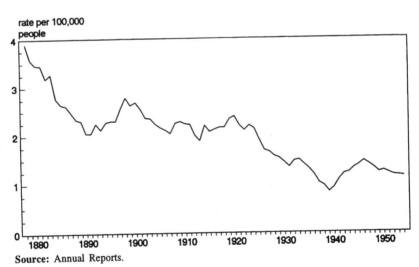

Source: Annual Reports.

especially between the wars. Pakeha males (who constituted the great majority of those prosecuted) apparently become much more orderly, in public at least. Reported assaults per head of population fell by over 60 per cent between the late 1870s and the early 1920s; they continued to fall and reached their lowest point in the early 1930s (roughly a quarter of the rate of 50 years earlier), before beginning a long-term rise,

Figure I.4: Arrests for Drunkenness 1878–1954

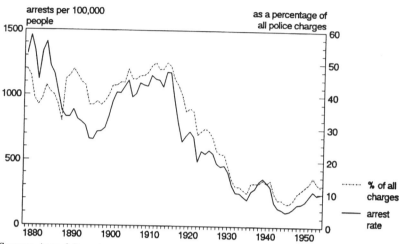

Source: Annual Reports.

slowly at first, and then more steeply from the 1960s. Broadly in tandem, the homicide rate[3] fell by 80 per cent during the 60 years to 1940. Ostensibly, New Zealand communities were more tranquil, more socially cohesive, between the wars than at any other time since the beginning of European settlement. The declining rate of prosecutions for violence also suggests more benign policing, with local constables exercising discretion and dealing informally with disputes and complaints of assault, especially where these arose within families.

In fact the workload of police did not diminish. Between 1919 and 1939, the total number of offences prosecuted (a crude measure) rose from 23,312 to 43,162, a greater increase than that in population or police numbers. By the early 1920s, an increasingly interventionist state had applied an ever more complex mesh of restraints on behaviour – most notably on alcohol consumption and gambling, the policing of which did not slacken significantly during the inter-war years despite or, more accurately, because of widespread resistance to state-imposed norms. Similarly, systematic peacetime political surveillance of 'revolutionary organisations', along with prosecutions for 'seditious offences', began in 1919, despite the absence of any real threat to public order or constituted authority during the inter-war years. Also from the 1920s, the growth of motorised traffic added a new dimension, and a mounting number of files, to police work. To a significantly greater extent than hitherto, Maori communities felt the effects of more intrusive state policing in this period, with rates of prosecutions of Maori males for both assault and theft rising further above those of Pakeha.

More fundamentally, perhaps, the balance between police-recorded violence and theft altered significantly between the turn of the century

Figure I.5: Reported Thefts 1878–1954

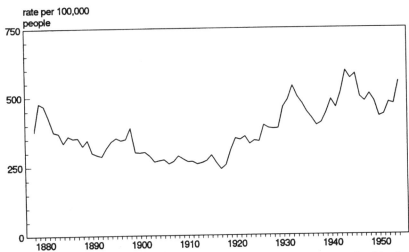

Source: Annual Reports. Note: Theft includes all categories of 'simple theft' listed in the Police statistics. It does not include the unlawful taking of property associated with burglary, robbery or fraud.

Figure I.6: Reported Burglaries 1878–1954

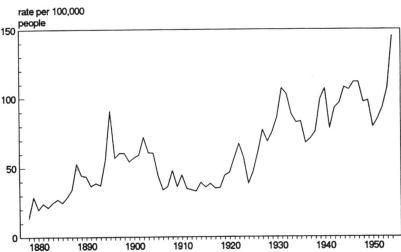

Source: Annual Reports. Note: Burglary is breaking and entering with intent to commit a crime. Burglary in this graph includes attempted shop and housebreaking and being in the possession of housebreaking implements.

and the 1930s: though reported assaults decreased, reported thefts and burglaries increased substantially in a series of waves during the inter-war years (figures I.5, I.6). In the first years of the century about two and a half times as many thefts as assaults were recorded by the Police; by the end of the 1930s the ratio was more than 10:1. In common with other European and settler societies, by the early twentieth century New Zealand had moved to a 'modern pattern' in which recorded violence was relatively low compared to property crimes.[4] Though communities might be more orderly, they were not necessarily more law-abiding; the reckless, the risk-takers, and the resisters to pressures to conform remained, especially amongst young males, and greater social stability did not necessarily mean a lessening of anxieties about crime, especially in the cities. What then was the relationship of the Police Force to the state in the inter-war years, and what was the nature of its self-defined role as a preventive police?

Servants of the state and the law

Speaking in the Legislative Council in 1922, Sir Francis Bell, concerned at the threat of sedition, declared that 'the most valuable servants of the Crown in active service are the police'.[5] Similarly, to the wartime Prime Minister Peter Fraser in 1940, 'There was no more valuable Government Department than the Police Department'.[6] In the few crises of public order this century, the New Zealand Police played a crucial role in 'maintaining law and order' – and in effect protected particular governments from those who challenged their policies in the streets. But the Police have been much more than just defenders of the status quo. For successive governments, the Police have carried out many functions not conventionally thought of in terms of 'law and order'. As Fraser put it, policemen 'had not merely the duty of repressing people or safeguarding life and property; they had social services to perform'.[7] For countless individuals, the department was (and is, in more modern parlance) the only '24-hour social service', responding to a wide range of calls for advice and assistance.

   Such a variety of roles was typical of police forces in Australia, North America and Western Europe. Indeed, in broad outline, the history of the New Zealand Police this century parallels the development of uniformed, paramilitary, 'preventive' police forces in other modern urban-industrial societies, and especially Australia.[8] Similar patterns of social change were at work. Moreover, from 1898 at least, the New Zealand Police as a national force was consciously modelled on London's Metropolitan Police, created in 1829 – an identification symbolised by the constable's uniform from 1912, when a helmet and tunic with pockets replaced a military-style shako and patrol jacket.[9] Yet the nuances of changing uniforms suggest that parallels should not be pushed too far.

   Distinctive features of its history mark off the New Zealand Police from similar forces elsewhere. From 1878, police were no longer routinely and visibly armed (though arms were available and sometimes carried);[10] by the 1930s the Force had shed much of its responsibility for traffic control; in 1957 it lost its Special Branch and, ostensibly at least, its concern with political surveillance. Also distinctive was the fact that, following the abolition of the provincial governments in 1876, the provincial forces were amalgamated with the central government's Armed Constabulary into the New Zealand Constabulary Force under the Minister of Defence. (In 1886 this Force was split into the colony's standing army and the New Zealand Police Force.) Such centralisation into a single unified police force paralleled prior developments in each of the Australian colonies,[11] but it contrasted markedly with the localism of American policing, the large number of separate borough and county forces in Britain (before the 1960s), and the combination of a national force with municipal forces in Canada. After the formation of the Commonwealth of Australia in 1901, New Zealand stood virtually alone in having a single national force. To some (but not all) commentators on the British tradition of policing, a single centrally controlled police force could potentially be a 'tool of government' and lack 'independence' in exercising its powers[12] – a view that was not shared by New Zealand administrators.[13] Certainly, by the 1920s the notion of police independence had come to be established in New Zealand as strongly as it was held in Britain. In summary, change in the organisation of New Zealand policing was not merely imitative of the British model; it was induced and moulded by local circumstances.[14] And it has also to be viewed as part of wider changes in the New Zealand public service.

In broadest outline, the history of the Police from the 1880s as a central government department mirrors the evolution of the public service as a whole.[15] For all government departments, including the Police Force, the long depression of the 1880s was a time of retrenchment. With the advent of the Liberal government in 1891 came a period of bureaucratic growth and change lasting until the First World War. Twelve new departments were created by 1912, others were amalgamated, and civil servants increased in number from 9,369 to nearly 24,000 in twenty years.[16] During this period the ranks of policemen virtually doubled, more than keeping pace with the growth of population. Its growing size and diversity forced changes in the management and control of the public service. These years saw mounting pressure for the replacement of recruitment and promotion through political patronage by the principle of a career service. Culminating with the Public Service Act of 1912, the bureaucracy was classified into grades with regular procedures for recruitment, discipline, promotion, and retirement on superannuation. Day-to-day responsibility for staff management was transferred from political control to departmental heads or to the Public Service Commissioner established in 1912.

Here, in some respects, the Police led the way, along with Railways and the Post and Telegraph Department. For the Police it was a slow and difficult process involving three Commissions of Inquiry and two resignations by Commissioners between 1898 and 1909, and a general reluctance by Liberal governments to relinquish ministerial control of personnel management.[17] Even so, the period between 1898 and 1912 saw moves (especially under two Commissioners recruited from the London Metropolitan Police, J.B. Tunbridge and Walter Dinnie) to professionalise the Force in terms of both greater independence from political control and greater efficiency and consistency in police practice. In 1898 a Training Depot was established in Wellington with more rigorous standards for recruits. The following year a police pension scheme (the first in the public service)[18] was introduced along with compulsory retirement at age 65. These measures removed blockages to promotion, which gradually became more consistent and merit-based (examinations which were a prerequisite for promotion were introduced in 1913). Except for a few rural men, policing became a full-time occupation which recruits increasingly saw as a life-long career, a view symbolised by the appointment in 1912 of John Cullen as the first Commissioner of the Force to rise from the ranks.[19] (Henceforth governments were reluctant to breach this precedent.) New Police Regulations issued in 1913 encapsulated the moves since the turn of the century towards improved supervision of the rank and file and greater discipline in dress and behaviour. It remained for Commissioner John O'Donovan to articulate an ideal of police service in 1920. By then an enduring pattern of administration had been established.

Despite mounting pressures for economy, the growth of the public service continued in the 1920s. Depression in the early thirties again brought retrenchment. Rapid expansion resumed following the election of a Labour government in 1935. This was accompanied from 1945 by a new emphasis on training and education, organisation and methods in the public service. Change continued after Labour's loss of power in 1949; indeed the pace quickened from the mid-fifties.

Viewed more closely, individual departments show variations from this broad pattern of development, and the Police are no exception. For one thing, the relative position of the department within the bureaucracy changed. In 1876/77 the New Zealand Constabulary Force comprised about a fifth of all central government staff; 35 years later police were only one in every 26 state servants.[20] In 1912 the department was still the fourth largest (after Railways, Post and Telegraph, and Education, including teachers), and it remained fairly sizeable in relation to many others. But in terms of both personnel and expenditure it was increasingly overshadowed by the rapidly growing public service. For the Police (by contrast, for example, with the education and health services, or the Labour Department from 1936),[21] the period 1918 to 1945 was essentially one of administrative stagnation. Certainly police numbers kept pace with the growth of population. Indeed in the early 1930s the Police did not feel the government's pruning knife as severely as did other departments. Yet the pay and working conditions of police personnel were in many respects inferior to those of other public servants.[22] According to the political scientist Leicester Webb in 1940, the renewed growth of the public service in the late 1930s had produced 'a healthy tendency to self-criticism and constructive thinking on the problems of public administration'.[23] Little of this was to be seen in the Police Department. Rather, a perception of the Police as the 'Cinderella Department'[24] grew in the inter-war years and persisted after 1945 as conservative police administrators and frugal governments responded only slowly to changing circumstances.

In fact, certain features of organisation marked off the Police from other government departments. As the political scientist (and former public servant) K.J. Scott commented, police 'are most often thought of, perhaps illogically, as a separate organ of government outside of the public service.'[25] By tradition and ethos the Force was (and is) a paramilitary organisation subject to a discipline that was more strict than that applied to most other state agencies. As late as 1963 Commissioner C.L. Spencer maintained that 'the police are in a real sense a fourth "fighting" service – the primary one in fact for internal law, order, and security, albeit that they seek to wage their wars without lethal weapons'.[26] Uniforms and rank structure (and, by the 1960s, the four services' sports tournaments) emphasised the affinity of the Police with the military rather than with the civil service. More specifically, the insignias of the upper Police ranks followed the Army pattern, and at times ranks in the Police Force were equated with those in the Army for determining rates of allowances and pensions.[27] In this period 85 per cent of the Police Force were constables, supervised by NCOs (13 per cent) and 20 or 30 commissioned officers. During the inter-war years, each of the armed services came to be administered by a board chaired by the Minister of Defence.[28] By contrast, control of the Police – both operational and administrative – was vested in the Commissioner alone.

Furthermore, unlike the armed services, the Police could be seen as being a 'social service' both in its broadly defined role in preventing lawbreaking and disorder and in providing aid in everyday emergencies. From 1958, such a distinction was emphasised by the dropping of the word 'Force' in official usage. Yet as a 'social service' the Police differed from the education and health services in particular, not just by its discipline and its coercive power, but also by its degree of centralisation. The latter feature also distinguished the organisation of policing from that of traffic control until the 1970s at least.[29] According to Police Regulations issued in 1919, it was the duty of the officer in charge of a district to 'superintend and control' his men 'in accordance with Acts, regulations, and departmental directions, subject to the approval of the Commissioner in all instances'.[30] In theory, all administrative decisions and policies of any consequence were made at the centre; there was a national system of enforcement with little scope for local variation. Yet the limitations of transport and communications in this period meant that operationally the control of policing was effectively decentralised. In practice, policemen at all levels exercised initiative and discretion: they could be sensitive to local attitudes and conditions. Ultimately, however, the exercise of discretion was subject to tight administrative control by the Commissioner and his senior officers. There was no formal or even indirect control by the local community over enforcement policies and priorities.

By contrast, control of primary education was divided between a central government department and locally elected school committees and education boards from 1877. Similarly, the management of hospitals was placed in the hands of a multiplicity of locally elected boards from 1885.[31] There were no comparable institutions controlling police, who from the outset (as in Australia) had been a 'state-authorised imposition' rather than a community innovation controlled by local magistrates.[32] Decentralisation of control to provincial governments in the 1850s reflected the fragmentation of settlements and the balance of power in the two-tier system of government; centralisation reflected the reverse. From the mid-1860s, central governments recognised the importance of having full control of police – especially with a new Armed Constabulary on the racial frontier in the North Island. Moreover, policing became a function which only the most prosperous provinces could afford without central aid; centralisation would bring economies and greater efficiency in policing a mobile population. Though the principle of centralisation was widely accepted in the General Assembly by the early 1870s, there was reluctance to implement it fully before the provincial governments were themselves abolished.[33] By 1877, then, the concept of the local policeman as a state official rather than a local community appointee was well established. In the longer term, continuing acceptance of this concept depended on police being responsive to local opinion while not appearing to be partisan – being seen as servants of the law as well as of the state.

As a centralised, national system of administration, the Police could be seen as paralleling the Post Office. Staff of both organisations were spread extensively throughout the country. In 1922 there were 327 police stations, of which 239 (nearly three-quarters) were one-man stations. There were over two thousand country postmasters and postmistresses.[34] Postmasters might be more numerous, but in theory no area of the country was not subject to the purview of police. From their inception, both departments were key agents of public administration for the colonial state, and they continued to be looked to by both central and local authorities for service between the 1920s and the 1940s. So much was this so that O'Donovan complained in 1919, 'Every Department in the Public Service seems to consider it has the right to first call for the assistance of the police to carry out their business. Public bodies and Hospital Boards consider they have a right to demand the assistance of indefinite numbers of police'. The 'extraneous duties' then included (varying with location) registering births, marriages, deaths, aliens, electors, and pensioners; collecting agricultural and pastoral statistics; inspecting factories, fisheries, weights and measures, hotels and licensed clubs; licensing firearms; and acting as kauri gum and Crown lands rangers, customs officers, receivers of gold revenue and mining registrars, agents for the Public Trustee, clerks of courts and hotel licensing committees, bailiffs, probation officers, gaolers, and court orderlies.[35] Moreover, 'public men and public officers seem to be under the impression that whole squads of detectives and plain-clothes men are kept in reserve awaiting their call, like fire-brigade men.' O'Donovan warned that should the Police continue to be 'the "handy men" of the whole Government services', many more would be required – and the cost would have to borne by their clients.[36]

But unlike the Post Office, the Police Department was patently not a business enterprise. Where the Post Office derived from its agency services a significant revenue which could support a rapidly increasing staff during the inter-war years,[37] the Police did not normally charge for services rendered. Here, the notable exception was traffic control, where the Department's attempts to recover its costs led to local authorities taking responsibility from the mid-1920s.[38] Country constables themselves rather than the Department were paid for certain duties they performed for other departments. Again, by contrast with the Post Office, the revenue generated by law enforcement went into the Consolidated Fund; it was not earmarked for investment in improved police facilities (such revenue would not have been sufficient for this purpose in any case). Contrasts in the architecture and convenience of post offices and police stations not only reflected differences in the nature and scale of the services provided, they were redolent also of contrasting methods of financing. Policemen might be the 'most valuable' public servants, but they were also expensive in the eyes of cost-conscious politicians during the inter-war years. Successive governments were generally reluctant to spend lavishly on improving stations and facilities. And so, after a period of general improvement in facilities before the First World War, an ethos of penny-pinching pervaded the Department between 1918 and 1945.

The feature which above all else marks off the Police within the state services has been its relative autonomy from both external bureaucratic and ministerial control since the First World War. Like the Railways, defence forces, and the Post Office (from 1919),[39] the Police Force was not subject to the provisions of the Public Service Act 1912. Hence the Force did not come under the purview of the Public Service Commissioner.

The freedom of the Force from control by the Public Service Commissioner was seriously challenged neither in 1912 nor subsequently. Yet the reasons for the exemption were not immediately obvious at the time. As 'servants of the Crown', police could be (and were) seen as part of the executive, along with other employees of central government.[40] One of the main objects of the 1912 Act, according to its author, the Reform government's Minister of Justice A.L. Herdman, was that 'patronage should be destroyed, that political influence should be done away with, and the power of making appointments [be] intrusted to experts, who shall be responsible not to Ministers, but to [Parliament].'[41] Sir Francis Bell, introducing the bill in the Legislative Council, conceded that the Police Force was 'by no means free from the suggestion that political influence does obtain there'.[42] Another object of the bill was to bring uniformity to the staffing of the public service. Herdman hoped to 'make it impossible for any Department to glorify itself .... to work out its destiny as if it were distinct and apart from all the rest of the service'.[43] Such a comment could apply as well to the Police as to any of the other departments. Indeed Premier John Ballance's abortive Civil Service Bill of 1892, which sought to classify all departments in a unified service, included the Police Force.[44]

So too did the 'Hunt' Commission of Inquiry into the unclassified departments in 1912, though the Commission was initially uncertain as to whether its brief extended to the Police and Defence Forces.[45] This Commission had been appointed by the Mackenzie ministry in May 1912. By the time it reported in August the Liberal government had fallen and been replaced by Reform under W.F. Massey. Herdman had long been an advocate of public service reform.[46] He introduced his Public Service Bill into the House before the Commission's report was tabled in September. In many respects – but not all – the bill (Herdman claimed) 'anticipated' the findings of the Hunt Commission.[47] Why then were the Police exempt from its provisions?

To Bell, the Police Force had 'always stood in a position different from the ordinary public service'. Both he and Herdman stressed the affinities of the 'semi-military' Police with the defence forces. The Public Service Commissioner 'would be ... more unsuited' than the government to make appointments to these 'disciplined' organisations. Essentially, the government wanted to keep 'direct control' of the Force.[48] Herdman spelt this out a year later when introducing a bill to replace the 'obsolete' Police Force Act of 1886: 'it is absolutely necessary in the interests of the public, in the interests of the Force, and in the interests of discipline that Ministers of the day should have unfettered control of the Force'.[49] Recent experience (notably, the exposure of indiscipline that had culminated in the forced resignation of Commissioner Dinnie in 1909)[50] had made politicians sensitive to the character of the men who led the Police. It was inexpedient to relinquish control over senior appointments. And mounting industrial unrest in 1912–13, with signs of this infecting the police rank and file, made direct control of a reliable force even more vital. (In 1913, Herdman and Cullen quashed the formation of the first New Zealand

Police Association, seeing it as a threat to discipline.)[51] More generally, the large size and distinctive character of the Police Department, like the Railways and the Post Office, seemed to make it difficult to assimilate into any broad scheme. In 1912 the focus of reform was on the plethora of smaller departments: to establish a unified career service free from political patronage, and to promote efficiency and economy.

Underpinning the concept of a unified public service in 1912 was a belief in the essential homogeneity of bureaucratic work: skills and experience could be readily transferred from one department to another. Police Commissioners successfully resisted this view. Policemen of all ranks were seen as requiring special attributes, training and discipline. Within the public service there appeared to be no comparable work relevant to the determination of salaries and grades. Though such a view did not apparently shape the findings of the 'Hunt' Commission in 1912, it was implicitly accepted by the later Royal Commission on the State Services, which paid little attention to the Police when it reported in 1962. This was surprising, since the occupational distinctiveness of the Police was not unique within the public service. The 1962 Commission noted that since the 1930s the ranks of specialised technical and professional staff had grown faster than those in the clerical grade. By the early 1960s the state services largely consisted of 'a wide variety of such occupational groups which often have little affinity one with another'.[52] In fact, the extent to which work done by the Police could be 'civilianised' and brought under Public Service Commission[53] control became a thorny issue from the 1950s.

The fundamental justification for the relative autonomy of the Police Department came to be expressed in constitutional terms. This was implied in Bell's cryptic comment in 1912 that a policeman was 'hardly a public servant'.[54] In fact, the constitutional status of the New Zealand Police was not then or later clearly spelt out by statute.[55] By 1912 it rested more on the perceived original powers of a constable in English common law (a judicial construction from the late nineteenth century) and local conventions which were still evolving in the relationships between Ministers and Commissioners. In New Zealand, between 1898 and the First World War, there began an erratic shift from direct ministerial supervision and control towards the 'modern fiction'[56] that the Police were the servants of the law rather than of the state. New Zealand Commissioners of Police, from Tunbridge onwards, had a hand in establishing the concept of their 'independence' from ministerial direction.[57] In doing so they drew upon the degree of managerial autonomy apparently achieved by the early Commissioners of the London Metropolitan Police and the doctrine of police independence of the executive espoused later by the courts.[58]

By the 1970s, the Department's view reflected the position established some 50 years earlier: police officers were 'not, in ordinary parlance, servants of the Executive but holders of a public office'.[59] Clearly enforcement of the law and the maintenance of order were basic functions of government, which had to provide the means for them to be achieved. But the manner in which the law was enforced and order maintained was the responsibility of the Police. In performing this role the Police exercised 'original authority, not one delegated by the Executive'. And so in matters of law enforcement, the Police were answerable not to the government of the day but to 'the law' – or more concretely, to the community through the courts. Governments therefore could not direct the Police on when and how to enforce the law; yet they clearly had an interest in the cost and efficiency of the Department. In 'matters of administration' Ministers could 'quite properly control the Police to a certain extent'.[60] Though the relative autonomy of the Police Force had been established by the 1920s, the dividing line between matters of administration and enforcement remained moot.

The ambiguous constitutional position of the Police within the state services was reflected in the Police Force Act 1913 and the regulations made under it. All members of the Force had to take the prescribed oath binding them to serve the sovereign, to 'see and cause His Majesty's peace to be kept and preserved; ... [to] prevent to the best of [their] power all offences against the same; ... [and] to the best of [their] skill and knowledge discharge all the duties thereof faithfully according to law'.[61] In the eyes of the Force and of the courts, this oath reinforced the 'original authority' which police officers possessed in common law as constables.[62] In fact, the autonomy and discretion of individual constables, whatever their rank, was limited by their belonging to a hierarchical and disciplined organisation: their 'first duty' (according to the 1919 Regulations) was 'perfect obedience to [their] superiors'.[63] Constables could be, and were, instructed to arrest or not to do so. Much then depended on the position of the Commissioner and his relationship with the Minister. By the Police Force Act 1913, it was the Governor (in effect, the Cabinet rather than the Minister alone),[64] and not the Public Service Commissioner, who appointed the Commissioner of Police, who was to have 'the general control of the Force'.[65] Potentially, from 1913 a Commissioner had a greater degree of authority than his predecessors had enjoyed; henceforth a Minister could not, it seemed, circumvent a Commissioner and exercise direct control of the Force.[66] When contrasted with the powers of 'control and direction' explicitly given later (for example) to the Ministers of Education and Health,[67] the provisions of the 1913 Act could be seen as underlining the relative autonomy of the Police.

Yet in 1913 Herdman did not see himself as fettered in his control. The Police Force Act empowered the Minister to assign Superintendents and Inspectors to police districts and to order an inquiry into their conduct if necessary.[68] Moreover the 1919 Police Regulations (in force until 1950) contained the important qualification that the Commissioner's 'superintendence and control of the Force' was 'subject to the directions

of the Minister'.[69] The precise import of these Regulations is difficult
to establish, but it is clear that the Police were not independent of the
executive. The Minister was given a general authority to consult the
Commissioner and to seek his cooperation if need be, not just in matters
of departmental administration, but also regarding the manner in which
the Police performed 'their duties'.

Ministerial authority was given added point by the insecurity of the
Commissioner's tenure of office. In effect, the Commissioner and all
other police officers held office 'during the pleasure of the Crown'.
Though the 1913 Act provided procedures for inquiries into misconduct
and for appeals, police officers could, nonetheless, be dismissed with
no grounds stated, and without the right of appeal or to take action for
wrongful dismissal.[70] 'Moreover', as Prime Minister Fraser pointed out
in 1947, 'they would not want to retain office if not working in harmony
with the Government. That would be an invidious position'.[71] In fact
no Commissioner has been dismissed, though two (outside the period
covered by this book) have been called upon to resign under threat of
dismissal.[72] Potentially then, the Police Force was subject to ministerial
control; police were the servants of the state as well as of the law. And
Commissioners recognised this in their dealings with Ministers.

On matters of departmental administration, Ministers could, and
did, intervene. In June 1930, J.G. Cobbe, responding to public pressure,
appointed a special committee to review Commissioner W.B.
McIlveney's dismissal of a Sergeant from the Force – to the chagrin of
McIlveney, who took early retirement because he saw the tribunal as
lacking statutory authority and thus making it 'impossible for me ... to
carry on the general control of the Force vested in me by statute'.[73]
Nonetheless, by the 1920s Ministers were no longer involved in the
routine affairs of the Department. To some extent this reflected a broader
shift in the relationship of the public service with the political executive
after the advent of the Public Service Commissioner. By the early
1930s it had become a dictum that a Minister was 'expected to be
concerned with departmental policy and not with departmental
administration'.[74] Practicality reinforced principle. Ministers with a
number of portfolios were in no position to exercise an extensive and
continuous attention to administration. (E.P. Lee, the Minister in charge
of the Police in 1920, was also responsible for the Prisons Department,
and had the portfolios of Justice, External Affairs, and Industries and
Commerce.) Yet there was often no precise distinction between policy
and administration.[75] And clearly there were differences in this respect
amongst departments: in Public Works and in Education, for example,
Ministers tended to be much more involved in the minutiae of
departmental affairs than was the case with the Police. In December
1963, Commissioner Spencer spelt out what seems to have become
established as the usual practice by the 1920s: ·

in comparison with many other Permanent Heads, I do not have a great number of dealings with my Minister on the day to day functioning of my department. The fact is that so long as the Commissioner of Police does not exceed the bounds of his authority and exercises reasonable judgement the ends of justice are best served when there is no attempted political interference in his activities. This is how it has been throughout my term of office. I do not mean from this, however, that I fail to keep my Minister informed on major police activities. Practically all policy involves finance .... there are some matters falling within my financial authority on which I seek Government approval before proceeding. These are matters on which there is likely to be public controversy involving the Government.[76]

Ultimately the relationship between a Minister and a Commissioner depended (as it did for other departments)[77] on the experience of individuals, force of personality, and the extent to which issues were politically contentious. Herdman, the Minister in charge of the Police until 1918, worked cooperatively with Cullen until 1916 when the Commissioner retired;[78] his successor, O'Donovan, gained even greater managerial autonomy. Ministers might intervene, but few major administrative changes were forced on the Police between 1918 and 1945. More typically, the Minister became the Department's advocate, defending it from criticism and putting forward the Commissioner's views on matters of legislation and administration. Indeed, through their Ministers from the turn of the century, Police Commissioners had an influence on law-making as they sought increased powers to deal with perceived problems of policing (and in the process added to the growing mesh of restraints on behaviour).[79] Shortly before his retirement in 1921, O'Donovan paid a warm tribute to the Ministers he had worked with,

for their confidence, support, and assistance in all matters appertaining to my work. It is pleasing – indeed, it is due to them – to put on record that they have maintained in practice the fine ideal which all authorities on the subject contend for as regards the relations of the Minister to the chief executive police officer – viz., that the latter should be supported in the proper execution of his duties and held responsible for efficient administration, but otherwise without interference. At the same time, no blind trust was imposed in me – every act, every proposal was carefully scrutinised by the Minister, and his counsel was readily given in every difficulty. It is unnecessary to stress the effect this attitude had in maintaining the authority of the Commissioner and promoting the discipline of the Force.[80]

The evidence suggests that Ministers rarely intervened in individual cases of law enforcement during the inter-war years – a notable exception being the Massey Cabinet's decision to prosecute Bishop Liston for sedition in 1922 (thereby taking a politically contentious issue out of the hands of the Police).[81] Clearly Commissioners were sensitive to the attitude of the government of the day on issues of public order and policies of law enforcement. Given the lack of policy files for the inter-war years, direct instructions are hard to find; but instances (albeit infrequent) can be found of Ministers suggesting or even laying down policies on how the law should be enforced. Fraser, as Minister in charge of the Police and then wartime Prime Minister, was probably more interventionist than his predecessors between the wars. On 9 April 1949, for example, he effectively instructed the Police not to take action against unchartered clubs selling liquor on the West Coast until after they had applied for charters; unchallenged, this immunity from prosecution lasted for about five years.[82] Even so, Commissioners were jealous of the image of their independence. In 1935, Commissioner W.G. Wohlmann brought a case for criminal libel against the editor of *Farming First*, who had alleged that the Commissioner had 'shielded' a Minister from prosecution in a gaming case. Giving evidence, the Minister in charge of the Police, Cobbe, said: 'if the Commissioner thinks a prosecution is justified, he takes it. I may venture an opinion.' In this case, Cobbe declared, the Commissioner had made his own decision and he 'did not interfere with it.' For his part, Wohlmann affirmed his independence and his discretion; in this case 'it seemed obviously wrong to prosecute innocent persons on technical grounds .... the ends of justice would be met by the prosecution of the two principals.' The editor withdrew any imputation against the Commissioner and pleaded guilty, to be convicted and fined £25.[83] Though Ministers, when pressed like Cobbe, might reiterate that the Police were free from political control, they did not generally 'resort to notions of police independence to avoid answering questions' in Parliament.[84]

The relative freedom from both political and external bureaucratic control which the Department enjoyed had long-term effects on its position within the public service. In particular, exemption from the provisions of the Public Service Act allowed the development of different personnel policies: different age and other qualifications for recruitment; different policies for promotion; different levels of education and patterns of training.[85] It also meant that the Police did not automatically benefit from any improvements in pay and conditions for the staff covered by the Act. Attempts were made by means of a Uniformity Committee to keep a broad consistency in conditions across the state services. But the Police Department was not represented on this committee, and marked disparities in conditions of work and service emerged, to the increasing concern of the Public Service Commissioner.[86] Being autonomous had its costs as well as its benefits. Until the mid-1950s, police officers were poorly paid in comparison with other state servants.

Improvements in pay and conditions depended on pressure from the Police themselves – from both rank and file and leadership. But in contrast with other central government employees, there was no staff association for police officers until 1936.[87] Much thus depended on the leadership of the Police Force.

From 1912 Police Commissioners were promoted from the ranks. Except for a period between 1955 and 1958, occupational expertise rather than simply administrative skill was the criterion for police leadership.[88] In this the Department was not alone. Within the public service as a whole, the prominent public servant J.K. Hunn observed, it was 'taken for granted that any organisation with a technical name requires a technical head'.[89] The Police also shared with the rest of the public service an antagonism towards the principle of an 'administrative' class on the British model: specially recruited leaders were not welcomed. Nor was the Department open to the arrival of able administrators from elsewhere in the public service. Being outside the purview of the Public Service Commissioner meant that there was no interchange of personnel, apart from a very small number of 'civilian' staff in the 'clerical' grade. Essentially the Police had their own career structure based on seniority for those who passed their exams. Drawn from the ranks of the most senior officers with no more than half a dozen years to serve, Commissioners were aged, inbred and sometimes inert. The political scientist Leslie Lipson commented of the Police in 1948 that the 'administrative system of this department could not be described as progressive'.[90]

Regular external reviews of administrative efficiency might have prevented such a state of affairs. Certainly the Audit Office and Treasury exercised financial control over the Police, but this was rarely a stimulus for 'progressive' administration. The Public Service Commissioner had the responsibility of promoting and maintaining departmental efficiency and economy. To this end departments under his jurisdiction could be periodically inspected – but again, this did not apply to the Police. And in any case, before the 1950s at least, it is debatable how effective such inspections were in promoting innovation and improvement.[91] All in all, there was no effective provision for regular external review of the Police Department. (This stood in contrast to Britain, where Inspectors of Constabulary had existed since the mid-nineteenth century to monitor the efficiency of the English and Scottish forces.) Essentially, for police between 1918 and 1945, the efficiency and quality of their activities were not subject to direct ministerial or external bureaucratic control.

What oversight was provided by the courts? Not surprisingly, an eminent judge, Sir Thaddeus McCarthy, whose legal career began in 1931, believed that his peers had 'not generally been timid in exercising their right to comment adversely if in their opinion a police officer has acted illegally, unfairly or even unwisely'.[92] Between 1918 and 1945, Ministers instituted Commissions of Inquiry into police conduct and methods following adverse judicial comment in two cases; both inquiries cleared the police involved.[93] Generally, magistrates and Supreme Court judges expressed confidence in police integrity. By the 1920s, police preparation of their prosecutions was shaped with an eye to close judicial scrutiny, and police prosecutors came to be respected by local magistrates. The percentage of theft charges resulting in convictions increased in both Magistrates' and Supreme Courts during the inter-war years; and the percentage of convictions for common assault charges, and for assaulting or obstructing police, increased consistently in the Magistrates' Courts from the turn of the century until the 1930s. The trend was not so clear for serious assaults or homicides in the Supreme Court, where judges and juries were harder to convince.[94] Yet much police activity did not result in charges being brought before a court, and was thus not subject to judicial review. Where cases were brought to court, only pleas of not guilty allowed the actions of individual police to be scrutinised; most cases in Magistrates' Courts involved guilty pleas. Thus later commentators have expressed a pessimistic view of the degree of legal accountability of the servants of the law.[95]

In practice, by the 1920s, the most significant restraints on police behaviour were public criticism in newspapers and the hierarchical system of discipline over which the Commissioner had 'general control'. Adverse publicity could stimulate parliamentary questions and ministerial inquiry, and thus threaten the managerial autonomy of Commissioners. Sustained criticism threatened the public standing of the Police Force and made consent to its authority more fragile, less freely given. Accordingly, Commissioners monitored public comment closely, calling for reports and applying sanctions where necessary. More intangibly, an ideal of police service, inculcated in the Training Depot, reinforced by supervision, and increasingly a part of the occupational culture of those who saw policing as a career, also acted as a crucial (if immeasurable) constraint.

The Police Department was thus in a distinctive position within the public service. Police officers could be seen as being servants of both the state and the law. Potentially there was a tension in this dichotomy. Some New Zealanders, probably a majority, during the inter-war years saw the distinction as non-existent or insignificant. To the strikers and their families at Waihi in 1912, however, the police came to be seen as 'Massey's Cossacks' being used to support the 'employing class' – indeed the 'Waihi affair cast a long shadow' over former Red Feds' views of the police during the inter-war years.[96] Similarly, to Rua Kenana and his followers, the armed police who came to arrest the Tuhoe prophet for sedition in 1916 were soldiers of a Pakeha government determined to assert Pakeha law – amongst the people of Maungapohatu, memory of the 'The War' of 1916 remained 'as bitter as gall'.[97] Such views of police as agents of a partisan state persisted. Indirectly, governments could and did influence the activities of police by their willingness or unwillingness to provide resources. More directly, governments clearly had an interest in how the law was enforced and order maintained. Commissioners could not but be responsive to the views of the executive. Even so, the concept of 'independence', and with it an image of impartiality, was seen by successive Commissioners from 1918 as being crucial if the Police Force was to carry out its role of 'maintaining law and order'. In practice the Department had a high degree of autonomy in the way it defined its role and sought to carry it out.

Preventive policing

During the inter-war years, the phrase 'maintaining law and order' summed up government, police, and popular conceptions of the essential role of the Police Force. Under the Police Force Act 1913 constables were appointed 'for the preservation of peace and order, the prevention of crime, and the apprehension of offenders against the peace.'[98] The Act went no further in spelling out the functions and objectives of the Force, leaving it to conventional wisdom, the law, and ultimately to the police themselves to define their role in practice. At its core by the 1920s was the notion of preventive policing to keep public order and control crime. Even so, how closely did the official definition of the Force's role accord with the reality of policing between 1918 and 1945? And, indeed, was the concept of 'law and order' unambiguous?

To most politicians and police, the expression 'law and order' conveyed a concept that was absolute, clear-cut, and widely perceived and accepted. According to this view there was a consensus as to what constituted crime and disorder: all recognised such behaviour when they saw it. Many in their communities shared a similar conception. But, in different ways and degrees, not all did so. Unionists denied the possibility of 'peaceful picketing', Maori seeking to acquire liquor on the same terms as Pakeha, and gamblers who perceived a class bias in the framing and enforcement of the gaming laws – all discerned an inequality before the law which was inconsistent with 'the rule of law'. Unfounded fears of civil strife in 1919 and 1920, the variable policing of demonstrations in the early 1930s, the widespread tolerance of illicit after-hours trading by pubs in country districts, and the more circumspect policing of family violence by contrast with the close controls on behaviour in public spaces all suggested that notions of law and order were in fact abstract, relative, and varying, perceived in different ways by individuals and communities according to their circumstances and sensibilities. The idea of 'law and order' could be problematic, raising the questions: whose concept of law? whose notion of order?

As a definition of the role of the Police, the concept of 'maintaining law and order' was unsatisfactory in another way. It suggested too little and also too much. Too little, for the role of the Police was much wider than this. By the 1920s, as noted earlier, police performed a wide range of official tasks: from inspecting factories and collecting agricultural statistics to registering aliens and chasing up those who failed to maintain their wives and children. Between the 1920s and the 1940s, the Police Force was unable to shed much of its routine work for other government departments. Certainly, Commissioners were reluctant to take on new tasks which might mean a diversion from an increasing emphasis on a more narrowly defined priority of preventing and detecting crimes against people and property; they avoided, for example, increasing their responsibilities in traffic control. However, both official and popular conceptions of the police role in protecting life and property encompassed not just criminal acts but also other contingencies, including accidents, civil emergencies arising from floods and earthquakes, search and rescue, and the restraint of those who were a danger to themselves. 'To illustrate the demands made insistently and urgently upon the police', O'Donovan – impatient with such a broad concept of police responsibility for order maintenance – in 1919 cited the case of

> a hospital surgeon in a town where only six police are stationed [who] requisitions for three of them to take charge of a refractory or suicidal patient. He insists it is the duty of the police to look after such patients. Under pressure of necessity, established by precedent only, the police furnish the necessary guard, to the absolute neglect of all other police requirements.[99]

Concern with public safety was but one aspect of the 'social service' role of the Police which Peter Fraser saw as exemplified (in by-now conventional 'ideal-type' terms) by the country constable who was 'the guide, philosopher, and friend of the whole community'.[100] Though the expanding numbers and role of child welfare officers after the Child Welfare Act 1925 reshaped formal police involvement in child welfare issues,[101] informal guidance (and physical punishment) of young males by suburban, small-town, and country constables continued, often in lieu of prosecution. In reality, then, police were expected to do much more than preserve 'law and order' in the narrowly conceived terms of prosecuting lawbreakers and suppressing disorder.

Yet the concept of 'maintaining law and order' can also suggest too much: that without the so-called 'thin blue line' society would dissolve into disorder and lawlessness. 'Primarily the police force is the community's first line of defence against those internal dangers from which it can never be wholly immune', declared the *Dominion* in 1919, after the killing of Constable Vivian Dudding on duty: 'In proportion as the work of the police is conscientious and efficient, lawless violence is excluded from the life of the State, and the weakest are secure from harm.'[102] Reflecting on the Melbourne police strike of 1923, the *Otago*

Daily Times warned that society depended 'for its existence on the stability of certain institutions, the institution which represents law and order above every other.'[103] Modern urban-industrial societies had long become used to the idea of visible paramilitary police forces as the seemingly crucial element in maintaining social cohesion. Uniformed policemen symbolised 'the presence of the state in everyday life'; they affirmed the maintenance of order.[104] The popular belief in their effectiveness was underlined by the Liverpool and Boston police strikes in 1919, and that four years later in Melbourne, which were associated with riots and mob looting. Although 'stereotypes of "anarchy" and "lawlessness" have prevailed', the actual level of violence and disorder appears to have been less than the legends of the strikes suggest.[105]

Clearly, police contributed to the maintenance of law and order; they had assisted in the 'taming' of the colonial frontier, and as a result, by the 1920s both governments and communities had high expectations of their coercive role, albeit this was increasingly symbolic. Yet an assessment of the impact of police in shaping the nature of colonial social relationships depends on determining how far nineteenth-century Pakeha and Maori were 'self-tamed' – how disorderly they were in reality, and how strong were other influences in producing social tranquillity.[106] Ostensibly, police were the 'first line' of formal social control; but they were not the only 'line of defence', as the *Dominion* acknowledged in 1919. And so the question remains: how crucial was the Police Force between the 1920s and the 1940s? No conclusive answer can be given here, for this would require an appraisal of all the complex mechanisms that lead people to obey rules, and that secure order in New Zealand society. Broadly and speculatively, it seems that levels of disorder and lawlessness (however defined) depended fundamentally on the policies and authority of governments and on a variety of social and economic conditions, with the presence of police reinforcing the informal mechanisms of control within communities. By the 1920s the New Zealand Police Force had become in essence a social fire-brigade service whose activities could be, amongst other things, preventive.[107] It responded to a wide variety of calls for assistance, sought to ensure the orderly settlement of disputes, and attempted to identify, contain and regulate those whose behaviour challenged the prevailing notions of law and order. Rather than being the *first*, it could more properly be seen as a *last* line of defence when other usually effective mechanisms to secure order had failed.

This was not how the role of the Police was officially defined by the 1920s. Following the precepts of the London Metropolitan Police, Commissioner Tunbridge had asserted in 1898 that 'the primary duty' of a Police Force was 'to prevent crime' rather than to react to events. To Tunbridge, 'offences against property are as a general rule admitted to be preventable crimes', and the 'rise or fall in the number' of such offences was 'generally accepted as a fair criterion of the inefficiency or efficiency respectively of a Police Force'.[108] The notion of a 'preventive police', as it developed in Britain in the early nineteenth century, had two senses. In its broader sense the role of the Police was seen as being to deter would-be lawbreakers, and to preserve the peace. Deterrence would be accomplished by creating a belief in the coercive power of the Police and in the certainty of capture resulting from either the presence of the Police or their ability to detect offenders after the event. However the popular conception of the role of the Police by the 1920s seems to have been narrower and simpler than this: the visible presence of a vigilant policeman deterred offenders and preserved the peace. 'To my mind', an English judge declared in a late nineteenth-century 'Address' still imbibed by New Zealand policemen in the 1920s:

> the Constable who keeps his beat free from crime deserves much more credit than the man who only counts up the number of convictions he has obtained for offences committed within it. It is true the latter makes more show than the former, but the former is the better officer. The great object of the law is to prevent crime; and when many crimes are committed in any particular district one is apt to suspect that there has been something defective in the amount of vigilance exercised over it.[109]

In its narrow and simple sense, then, a 'preventive police' controlled crime 'by preventing it from occurring instead of merely detecting it after the fact.'[110]

According to this belief, successful prevention depended on certain features of organisation. In particular, it depended on 'coordination and collective effort – the central direction of the police rather than reliance on officers who were more like entrepreneurial private detectives than public officials.'[111] In theory the New Zealand Police conformed to the model. It was a highly centralised department organised on paramilitary lines. In fact the coordination and control of their men (no policewomen were appointed until 1941)[112] remained a continuing problem for Commissioners. Despite the hierarchy of supervisors and strict discipline, front-line police still possessed a considerable degree of autonomy.

The second characteristic of a 'preventive police' was its pervasiveness. In the cities and large towns there had to be regular day and night patrols, and elsewhere enough men to cover whole districts, recognise the local residents and subject them to surveillance if necessary. In New Zealand during the inter-war years, most constables were patrolmen; in 1922 only 4 per cent of the Force were detectives who specialised in catching offenders after the event (figure I.7). Dispersal of the population meant that there were two kinds of 'preventive police'. In 1922 about 80 per cent of police were potentially patrolmen – either as 'local' men (country or suburban constables at one-man stations) or as beat men based at the main city stations. In theory the whole country

Figure I.7: Police Districts and Male Staff in 1922 and 1945

	1922			1945		
	Uniform Branch	Detective Branch	Total	Uniform Br	Detective anch	Total Branch
WHANGAREI	29	1	30	39	2	41
AUCKLAND	175	10	185	305	36	341
HAMILTON	64	2	66	88	4	92
GISBORNE	29	1	30	38	2	40
NAPIER	46	2	48	61	5	66
NEW PLYMOUTH	30	1	31	51	3	54
WANGANUI	38	1	39	53	3	56
PALMERSTON NORTH	40	2	42	57	2	59
WELLINGTON	182	8	190	254	28	282
NELSON	-	-	-	38	2	40
GREYMOUTH	43	1	44	43	2	45
CHRISTCHURCH	111	8	119	172	18	190
TIMARU	39	1	40	45	3	48
DUNEDIN	95	4	99	118	11	129
INVERCARGILL	44	1	45	53	2	55
HEADQUARTERS	7	-	7	8	2	10
TOTAL	972	43	1,015	1,423	125	1,548
PERCENTAGE	96	4		92	8	

Source: Annual Reports, 1922 and 1945. **Note:** Numbers at 31 March, including District and Native Constables, but excluding staff on leave prior to retirement or without pay, police 'lent' to other agencies, Police Matrons, and (in 1945) 33 female constables.

was under the surveillance of policemen. The inner-city areas were divided into beats patrolled 24 hours a day, while the active suburban or country constable was expected to be constantly travelling around his district. And so another feature of a preventive force was its visibility: not just because policemen patrolled, but also because they wore a distinctive uniform which was instantly recognisable – both by citizens needing assistance and by criminals who would be deterred. The focus of policing was on public spaces, especially streets, where – it was widely believed – potential offenders would be deterred by preventive policing. Common sense and the experience of street policing seemed to confirm this.

However the effectiveness of the preventive police (according to the nineteenth-century notion) depended on some assumptions which were increasingly challenged by experience in twentieth-century New Zealand. This may be illustrated by the following example. In 1921 the Christchurch *Star* complained that 'though the city is almost full of various kinds of vagrants and undesirables, there were only two constables on actual beat duty' during the day. Court reports showed 'plainly' that property offences were 'increasing at an alarming rate'. A local magistrate commented that 'a race of thieves seemed to be growing up in the Dominion'. During the last week (according to the *Star*) 'an influx of bad characters' had 'set in from the North Island, ostensibly looking for work', and they were still arriving. Times were 'too hard' in Auckland and Wellington. 'They are seeing what can be picked up in Christchurch'. But 'we cannot look after them', declared a local police officer – the Force was below strength and work was 'heavier than ever'. And so, the *Star* concluded:

> it is hardly any wonder that crimes against property are reported every day, and many of the offenders go unpunished. Scores of small sneak thefts ... are never reported to the police. Raids on washing and fowlhouses and vegetable gardens go on without interruption. Bicycles vanish from private stands, and motor-car parts are lifted in broad daylight. Conditions are growing worse instead of better. On all sides there is a demand for increased police protection.[113]

This vignette reveals a number of long-standing assumptions about the 'preventive police'. The first was that a growth in property offences could be explained by the presence of identifiable 'vagrants' and 'bad characters', a relatively small number of people who should be the focus of preventive policing. Such an assumption was based on the notion of a 'criminal class' that had been widely held in the nineteenth century but was losing its force by the 1920s. Certainly there were still safe-blowers and sneak thieves, pickpockets and 'spielers', frequenting the main centres or crossing the Tasman in search of opportunities.[114] Each year detectives from other centres were sent to Christchurch during its Show week in November to keep their 'own city criminals under observation and to point them out' to local police.[115] But the notion of a particular social group as a potential threat to order and property that was implicit in the *Star*'s comments was broader than this. It encompassed some at least of the shifting population of unskilled casual labourers who moved from centre to centre, from town to countryside and back again, in search of work. These transients – 'swaggers' or the 'rough' in nineteenth-century terms – generally haunted the pubs. And when numerous, rowdy, or apparently loafing, they were often seen as a threat to order and property by 'respectable' residents. The *Star* reported police fears that if 'a big row occurred in the daytime near the Square, or the railway station, or any of the main streets, only two constables would be free to join in'.[116] Certainly, the census conducted in April 1921 revealed that farm and other labourers comprised about a third of the 11,000 males then unemployed, nearly half of whom had been out of work for more than a month.[117] A sharp recession in 1921– 22 (and also deepening depression from 1929) saw men take to the roads in search of work. However, no 'big row' occurred in Christchurch during 1921–22. Overall, fewer thefts were reported and arrests for public order offences made in the Christchurch District in 1921 than the year before; and in 1922 there was a further substantial decrease in the number of arrests for drunkenness, though reported burglaries and thefts from dwellings did increase.[118] Unskilled labourers, whether or not they were itinerant, were relatively fewer in number[119] and more orderly than 30 years earlier.

Much of the reported offending could not be explained by reference to a 'criminal class', however broadly defined. O'Donovan was at a loss to explain the 'extraordinary number of cases of homicide' (26) in 1920: the 'circumstances in which the crimes were committed indicate that they were not preventable by any police measures.'[120] The *New Zealand Herald*, reviewing 'crime in Auckland' for 1921, believed that although there had been 'many cases' of theft and burglary where 'large amounts' were involved, 'there have been no signs that organised bands of criminals have been operating'.[121] That many crimes against property were apparently opportunist was epitomised by the recently created offence of car or bicycle 'conversion'.[122] In the 1920s, it seems, most of those apprehended and prosecuted by police were not known to have offended previously. And, in common with patterns of arrests at other times and places, they were disproportionately youthful, male, working-class,[123] and (from the 1920s) Maori.[124] This pattern partly accounts for the 'wide interest' which the *Herald* noted was aroused in 1921 by the prosecution of an Auckland solicitor for the theft of trust monies. Such a case signalled that lawbreakers were not necessarily confined to a distinct social group, but were to be found in all walks of life.

Crucial to the effectiveness of a 'preventive police' was an assumption that most potential offenders (those not constrained by conscience) were rational: that they had the ability and the willingness to calculate the risks of being caught and would thus be deterred. In 1921 the Christchurch *Star* assumed that the local 'vagrants and undesirables' would be deterred from theft if they perceived the police to be ever-present. They (and others) might well have been. During the inter-war years, however, the growing number of those prosecuted for offences against property suggested that many calculated poorly, if at all, the risk of apprehension. Moreover, by the 1920s, certain categories of offender – 'sexual perverts',[125] drunkards,[126] and 'juvenile delinquents' – were seen as being neither willing nor able to calculate the risks. In the early 1920s the number of sexual offences reported was small, but they were seen to be 'steadily increasing'.[127] Concern mounted. A Committee of Inquiry into Mental Defectives and Sexual Offenders recommended in 1925 that the courts be empowered to give indeterminate prison sentences to such offenders.[128] Clearly the risks of arrest were not seen as a deterrent. In the case of drunkenness, the numbers arrested were large – 8,671 in 1921. While police did contain petty disorder in the streets using drunkenness charges, there was a high degree of recidivism amongst those they dealt with. Generally, in the early 1920s, over a third of the males and nearly two-thirds of the females charged had previous convictions.[129] Alcohol contributed to violence and disorder – and hence to much police business. But while the craving for drink might impair rationality, the criminal justice system rarely admitted diminished responsibility in such cases. Rowdies and impecunious drunkards were in and out of jail.

By contrast, diminished responsibility was increasingly admitted in the case of youthful offenders.[130] By the Crimes Act of 1908 no child under the age of seven could be convicted of an offence; nor could any under fourteen unless they knew they were doing wrong. Led by J.A. Beck from 1916, reformers in the Education Department sought to ensure that no child was regarded as criminal. A child welfare branch and children's courts dealing with all children under the age of sixteen years were established by the Child Welfare Act of 1925. Though these new courts held children accountable, they were seen as having a reformative or 'readjustment' rather than a punitive function. Symbolically the Child Welfare Branch sought, with incomplete success, to exclude uniformed policemen from the children's courts. Children were seen as not yet ready, through innocence of the law or faulty upbringing, to calculate fully the risks of lawbreaking. Their misbehaviour was labelled 'juvenile delinquency' and they were usually admonished by magistrates or deemed to require 'preventive' supervision by child welfare officers rather than other sanctions. Local constables might be construed as 'bogeymen' by parents seeking to control their children,[131] but the deterrent effect of this cannot be measured. Increasing appearances of young males before the children's courts from the mid-

1930s, especially for property offences, suggested not just a shift towards greater formality in dealing with youthful misconduct,[132] but also that juvenile delinquency was not necessarily susceptible to 'preventive policing' as this was defined in the inter-war years.

For those able and willing to calculate the risks, how pervasive and visible were the Police in the 1920s? Fifty years later police and public alike cherished fond myths of the ever-present man on the beat, or the local constable who knew the people of his patch intimately.[133] The reality was probably rather different, especially in some of the districts of suburban constables. In the expanding suburbs the continuing turnover of population[134] often made it difficult for the local constable to get to know his residents well – particularly those likely to give him the most work. Constable C.H. McGlone at Mt Albert, for example, had a rapidly growing number of residents in his district, with a total population of more than 11,000 in 1921.[135] Furthermore local constables, especially country men, had large areas to work. The district of the mounted constable based at Culverden covered 2,362 square miles.[136] In 1921 the constable stationed at Taradale was not alone in finding it impossible to 'efficiently supervise' his area, which contained seven hotels (the furthest 60 miles from the station), five new soldier settlements, and several railway camps of over a hundred men.[137]

Country and suburban men might go on patrol; more often they were out and about following up phone calls, serving summonses and completing files sent from other stations. True, their visibility gave a sense of security to many residents. 'I may say "that we sleep calmly in our beds" knowing that our lives and property are secure on account of the protection of the Police', wrote the mayor of Cambridge to O'Donovan after Constable James Dorgan was killed on duty at Timaru in August 1921.[138] Yet local constables discovered few crimes and were often far from scenes of disorder. In practice, their role was ostensibly reactive: they depended on the public for their knowledge of crime, responded to calls for assistance, and were often not available immediately when required. Local police might defuse disputes, contain disorder, and catch some offenders, but the extent to which their presence (at a distance) deterred misbehaviour because of fear of apprehension remains a matter for debate.

Nor was the uniformed patrolman always present in the inner-city areas. Here many beats were laid out, but the number regularly worked seems to have been small. The square mile of central Christchurch, within the four avenues, was patrolled in September 1921 by eight men at night and by two during the day. A further fifteen would have been required to fill all the beats as well as do point-duty. Twenty men were needed to walk the empty beats surrounding Queen Street in Auckland. Provincial towns were in similar straits. Except for Superintendent S.P. Norwood at Wellington, all the officers in charge of districts asked for more men. Because of leave, sickness, and the demands of other work it was sometimes difficult to provide even one man for daytime street duty in Hamilton and Palmerston North. At Timaru there were 'insufficient men on street duty, especially when overseas steamers are in port'. New Plymouth and Stratford each needed another constable for there to be 'a more efficient night patrol'. The shopkeepers of Hastings (where there were six constables in 1921) had since the 1890s employed a nightwatchman to supplement the vigilance of the constable on night patrol. Along the North Island main trunk railway line and in Waikato, towns such as Te Kuiti and Morrinsville needed more men for patrols and to be at the station when the trains arrived.[139] Yet even when beats were worked, a constable could be difficult to find when wanted, and might be off his beat for considerable periods.

Were then the numbers of New Zealand police in the 1920s adequate to give practical effect to the theory of 'preventive policing'? Clearly the Christchurch *Star* thought not, pointing to an increase in 'preventable' offences against property; and it was not alone. London, the exemplar of the theory, had 421 citizens to every policeman in 1891.[140] By contrast, the number of people per policeman in New Zealand's four main centres ranged, in 1921, from 757 in Wellington to 1,174 in Christchurch; and New Zealand's overall number of citizens per policeman (1,310) was more than double the figure for England and Wales.[141] Clearly, the great differences in scale between Britain, with much of its population densely packed into conurbations, and small-town New Zealand in the 1920s, rendered this sort of comparison rather meaningless. 'Inadequacy must be relative. The whole population of New Zealand is not much more than that of Glasgow', Commissioner Wohlmann observed in 1934.[142]

Contemporaries continued to make comparisons nonetheless, especially with police forces across the Tasman. In the 1920s and 1930s, the ratio of population to police was far higher in New Zealand than in New South Wales and Victoria; in 1921 it was almost double that of Queensland and Western Australia (figure I.8). A marked disparity remained until the early 1970s, even when traffic officers are included in the numbers. Yet such a disparity was accepted by politicians and Police Commissioners, during the inter-war years at least. It was seen as reflecting differences in both society and topography. As Wohlmann put it in defending the adequacy of the existing police facilities:

We have to bear in mind, in addition to the relatively small population of New Zealand, its geographical conformation, its absence of large cities, its relatively uniform diffusion of population, and its insular position.

The problems in New Zealand differ from those in largely populated countries. The inauguration of mobile squads [which New Zealand then lacked] in London, ... Melbourne and Sydney, were to meet the menace of organised gangs of criminals, which we have not in this country.[143]

Figure I.8: Population per Policeman in New Zealand Urban Areas[a] and Australian States 1911–1941

Urban Area	Years					
	1911	1916	1921	1926	1936	1941
AUCKLAND	941	874	992	1,012	866	636
WELLINGTON	828	756	757	800	807	678
CHRISTCHURCH	1,079	1,019	1,174	1,185	1,102	933
DUNEDIN	921	929	1,004	851[b]	986	802
HAMILTON	1,140	898	986	788	668	658
GISBORNE	1,338	1,055	1,314	924	776	689
NAPIER	929	796	781	785	709	662
HASTINGS	1,750	1,224	1,624	1,607	1,181	1,108
NEW PLYMOUTH	1,075	1,088	1,265	1,138	1,011	878
WANGANUI	1,016	976	1,176	1,089	937	852
PALMERSTON NORTH	744	824	889	939	921	803
NELSON	986	1,107	1,181	1,306	968	799
TIMARU	1,134	1,055	862	935	990	801
INVERCARGILL	1,047	1,051	961	950	988	920
NEW ZEALAND	**1,333**	**1,258**	**1,310**	**1,299**	**1,283**	**1,084**
NEW SOUTH WALES	685	737	787	786	729	744
VICTORIA	809	817	886	884	810	822
QUEENSLAND	607	624	673	723	749	716
SOUTH AUSTRALIA	983	780	894	902	738	639
WESTERN AUSTRALIA	594	642	684	715	802	791
TASMANIA	803	874	908	915	838	832

Sources: Annual Reports, *New Zealand Census*. **Note:** (a) 'Urban Areas' as defined by the census; (b) this figure reflects the extra police transferred to Dunedin for the Dunedin and South Seas Exhibition of 1925–26. In 1927 the ratio was 1:1,130.

The national ratio of population to police was published in the annual reports of the Police Force each year until 1950. Its minor fluctuations during the inter-war years reflected an ad hoc policy on police manpower, a shifting balance between specific requests from officers in charge of districts and what the politicians would allow. Before 1956 there was no formally established national ratio to be maintained. Police administrators clearly took account of population changes. They asked for more men, and redeployed them, not with any specific ratio in mind but on the grounds of increasing workloads (involving not merely the reporting of more offences) and the potential demands of special circumstances, such as the proximity of a port, the number of hotels, the nature of the workforce, and the distance between stations.

Cities were conventionally seen as the hotbeds of crime. Yet in the early 1920s Christchurch had a ratio of population to police which was not significantly lower than the national one. The Christchurch *Star* claimed that 'the country districts are always clamouring for more protection, and occasionally they are served at the expense of the cities'.[144] Indeed, apart from Wellington, many smaller towns and country areas may well have received a disproportionate share of the country's police, in the 1920s at least.[145] Among the 25 provincial towns with more than 3,000 people, just five had more people per policeman than Christchurch, and only eight had ratios higher than Auckland's in 1921. Of the 55 small towns with 1,000 to 3,000 inhabitants, 24 apparently had less population per policeman than Auckland, Christchurch, or Dunedin. Consistent with the concept of surveillance that was inherent in preventive policing, the ratio of population to police tended to be lower in country districts with scattered settlements. During the inter-war years some of the largest provincial towns continued to have fewer people per policeman than Auckland, and most had less than Christchurch. Over the country as a whole, and in three of the four main centres especially, the New Zealand Police were relatively thin on the ground in the inter-war years.[146]

Given the relatively small number of men, how were they to act effectively as a 'preventive police'? Edwin Chadwick, who did much to elaborate the concept of a 'preventive police' in England, pointed out in 1868 that the very existence of a 'force known to be immediately available of itself operates as a preventive'. The 'rowdies' had to be taught that it was 'not the single policeman alone who was to be considered, but the large indefinite force that was behind to back him'.[147] This was the lesson taught by the police expedition to arrest Rua Kenana in 1916. It was also the message sheeted home to many others who resisted the authority of individual constables on city streets.

Yet in practice this message was not always so clear. For the 239 constables at one-man stations in 1922, as well as for many constables on beat duty, a 'large indefinite force' was generally *not* immediately available. Jostled by a Christchurch crowd in May 1918, for example, Constable E.T. Bosworth was forced to release a prisoner who had assaulted him.[148] Constable William Fisher, patrolling Timaru streets early one morning in October 1921, was attacked and injured by two men who then escaped – though they were later captured by other policemen.[149] However, the burglar who had shot Constable Dorgan outside a Timaru shop at 1.30 am two months earlier was never identified. A policeman working alone at night was 'a marked man', observed a local newspaper.[150] But a constable did not have to be alone to be isolated. Bystanders in Morrinsville refused to help the local constable assert his authority in two violent episodes in 1925.[151] Much more was involved in the acceptance of a constable's authority than his possession of coercive power. As Chadwick noted, a 'police force ... must owe its real efficiency to the sympathies and concurrent action of the great body of the people'.[152] Its coercive power had to be accepted by a substantial majority in the community. How was this to be achieved, especially in the circumstances of social conflict experienced by Pakeha New Zealanders in the 30 years before 1920, with a growing wave of temperance sentiment, recurring cycles of 'sectarian epilepsy',[153] and mounting industrial unrest from 1906?

From the 1890s at least, New Zealand Police Commissioners sought to legitimate police power by drawing on the British tradition. They followed closely the strategy of legitimation devised by the first Commissioners of the London Metropolitan Police. In 1920 Commissioner O'Donovan set out many of the key ideas in his 'Address to the New Zealand Police Force' which was published in the so-called 'Black Book' containing the acts, regulations, and instructions governing the Police.[154] For the next 30 years all constables were issued with a copy of the 'Black Book', and thus the ethos of O'Donovan's 'Address' endured into the late twentieth century. It summed up the strategy of legitimation adopted, or at least aspired to, by the leadership of the Police Force, which set out actively to secure public acceptance of its authority. Essentially, in O'Donovan's view, public confidence in police would be secured by a belief in the independence and impartiality of the Force: they were servants of the law, not arbitrary agents of government. Such a belief in police neutrality would be based on three things: on the subordination of the police to the law, on the manner in which they enforced the law, and on the conduct of each policeman.

The identification of police as 'agents of the legal system' enabled them to 'draw from a reservoir of symbolic ... power'.[155] To O'Donovan, the laws were 'the highest secular expression of the moral standards of the nation'. For him, as for many, the criminal law was based on a moral consensus; it 'favours no party', and police were called upon by oath to enforce it without 'favour or affection'.[156] When, for example, the threatening behaviour of a crowd of Europeans forced some Indian immigrants to leave the small town of Carterton in July 1920, O'Donovan immediately issued instructions that Indian immigrants were 'entitled to the protection accorded to all law-abiding citizens. The police must, therefore, suppress all acts of hostility contrary to law against such persons, and, where the law has been infringed, ... [prosecute those] deemed to be the culprits. This order applies to the case of all Asiatic people in the Dominion'.[157]

As servants of the law, police should expect public cooperation. Yet in reality the New Zealand Police Force was a government department. It was difficult for police officers in certain circumstances not to be seen as acting as agents of a particular government to enforce a particular conception of order. The policing of industrial disputes and demonstrations was a case in point; prosecutions for 'seditious offences' were another. Furthermore, some laws were not accepted by substantial sections of New Zealand society: in the early 1920s liquor licensing and gaming laws stood out in this regard, as did the Tohunga Suppression Act of 1908 in the eyes of many Maori.[158] More broadly, in New Zealand as elsewhere, the impact of policing fell disproportionately on particular individuals, families, and sections of the population, who could be expected to regard police warily, with suspicion if not hostility. How then could the Police Force create and maintain a public image of independence and impartiality? Appealing to the abstract authority of the law was necessary, but of itself insufficient.

For one thing, it was necessary to create a belief in the constitutional independence of the Police. To O'Donovan at least, this had been largely accomplished by 1920. In the maintenance of order, in which governments clearly had a strong interest, O'Donovan saw the role of the Police as defending not a particular government but abstract constitutional authority:

> We now come to a time when organised bodies of the community, bent upon obtaining rights or advantages, and impatient with constitutional or moral methods, seek to gain their ends by disturbance, violence, and illegal means. The conflicting parties divide into hostile camps. Our duty in such a condition is to preserve peace and protect life and property. We take up our stand unmoved on 'No man's land', and compel the conflicting parties to retire to the constitutional trenches and to have recourse only to legal and moral measures.[159]

Here, with his eye on the recent past as well as current tensions, the Commissioner laid claim, as would his successors, to the middle ground between contending parties. To establish the legitimacy of police authority, such a position was necessary in theory; but was it tenable in practice? In the political surveillance carried out by the Force between 1919 and 1956, police practice was perceived by many on the Left in New Zealand as serving partisan ends. This was (to reiterate) also the case with the Police role in the industrial confrontations of 1912 and 1913, when government policy had influenced the way police (under Commissioner Cullen) handled the disputes[160] – a fact long remembered in the lore of militant trade unionism. O'Donovan sought to make police practice in dealing with industrial disputes and demonstrations more circumspect by establishing an ethos of restraint. Also influential in shaping police practice were limitations of resources. Given the small numbers of police and their geographic dispersal, there were severe limits to the coercive power of the Force. In fact the maintenance of public order in the streets depended not on police power so much as on the unwillingness of individuals and crowds to challenge it. Clearly the discipline of strikers and demonstrators over the succeeding years was, in part, testimony to a belief in the myth of police power. But it was testimony also to the success of the strategy of legitimation. Between 1918 and 1945 police power was accepted by many (but not all) because it was usually applied with a minimum of provocation and violence. In New Zealand, as in Britain, the Force 'evolved a technique of restrained power for handling demonstrations'.[161]

Techniques of crowd control reflected a wider ethos of restraint in the administration of the law. Indeed the manner in which the Police sought to enforce the law and maintain order was seen as being crucial in gaining public acceptance of police power. Here again O'Donovan articulated the ethos eloquently:

> The letter of the law may appear rigorous, but the administration of it may be beneficent. We keep a baton, but seldom use it; when we do its application should be scrupulously proportioned to the need. Consistency and firmness without harshness should be the guiding principle, but indiscreet leniency is calculated to do more mischief than a degree of harshness. Both should be avoided.[162]

The Police then should not act arbitrarily, but rather with due regard for legal authority and procedure. Restraint also meant that the Police should enforce local by-laws (breaches of which 'are not in themselves criminal or wrongful') in 'a manner to effect their purpose without unnecessary irritation'. As O'Donovan put it: 'While discrimination of classes should be avoided, a rigid rule that all breaches must be prosecuted should not be followed. A wise discretion should be exercised, and warnings given in suitable cases'.[163]

Instances can of course be found over the years of arbitrary action by policemen. There are also examples of what, in retrospect, seem over-strict enforcement of the law or an apparent lack of discretion. The prosecution in 1927 and 1928 of those promoting euchre tournaments in apparent breach of the Gaming Act provides a good example. The Supreme Court upheld these prosecutions. This raised an outcry from Canterbury school committees and social clubs. Successive Ministers of Justice saw fund-raising euchre tournaments as harmless but refused to give any clear direction to the Police, whose policy of strict enforcement apparently continued until the law was changed in 1933.[164] By contrast, in the case of the six o'clock closing of public bars introduced in 1917, a very much larger section of the community was involved and there was no change in the law for 50 years. In these circumstances country and small-town policemen generally displayed what the locals would have recognised as a 'wise discretion'.[165]

Ultimately it was the behaviour of individual policemen that was crucial in establishing public acceptance of police authority. O'Donovan recognised this:

> Our prestige as peace officers depends more upon personal character and conduct than even upon the law with whose authority we are clothed. This view of conduct must not be confined to the official and public side of life; it must be carried into all the affairs of private life also: even in this we cannot divest ourselves of the character of our office.[166]

The Commissioner sought policemen who would personify independence, impartiality, and moral rectitude. No man with 'a moral standard inconsistent with truth and honour' would suit. Similarly, the 'crank' and the 'agitator' had no place in the Force: 'they will be weeded out when their propensities are discovered'.[167] To express any political or sectarian sentiments was a disciplinary offence.[168] This view was long maintained, although serving policemen were to seek election to local authorities and Parliament from the 1950s. 'If a constable wants to stand for Parliament, the best thing he can do is to resign', affirmed Fraser in 1947. 'There is a vast difference between a constable and a member of the Public Service'.[169] This was also true of other aspects of a policeman's private life. 'Behaving in a scandalous or infamous manner, or being guilty of profane, immoral, or disgraceful speech or conduct' was punishable. A member of the Force had to be mindful of his associates and of his financial affairs. He could not be under any 'obligation' to 'any person interested in the liquor trade'; he was not allowed to keep racehorses or company with bookmakers, nor to gamble or be found drunk. He could not marry without permission.[170] '[A]bove all things', declared O'Donovan, 'it is essential that no unauthorised influence outside the Force should be allowed to act upon your conduct in the discharge of your duties .... [When] your independence is bartered, ... the confidence of the public is lost'.[171]

And so, in theory at least, the policeman had to remain aloof, detached from the community. His authority was to be essentially impersonal. This was particularly true of the beat constable, who had (in O'Donovan's view) the greatest opportunity of impressing the public for good or ill. He is constantly in the eye of the public. His manly, upright deportment, his gravity of demeanour, his calm alertness, emphasized by a scrupulous attention to the proper condition of his uniform dress, make the first favourable impression. These are the silent witnesses of training and discipline; lack of them produces the opposite effect.[172]

Not all constables of course conformed to the ideal stereotype – but most of those persistently unwilling or unable to conform had to go. Discipline was strict. And as a result, the Force did succeed in creating an image of impersonal authority, particularly in the cities. Such an image was caught well, albeit with tongue in cheek, by one observer in 1934, to whom policemen on street duty 'are even more remote than cenotaphs, though to the sight almost as familiar .... [No one ever sees] a policeman acting under any strong emotion. They are not for hire. They just stand about and appear to be friendless'.[173]

Yet this sense of separation from the community depended on circumstances. An image of impersonal authority fitted the inner-city beat constable better than it did the local man in the country or small town, or even the suburbs. The authority of the constable in his one-man station was inevitably more personal than that of the man on the beat. By the 1920s the myth of the effective local policeman was already established: he was a man locally well-known and respected; a man (in the words of one obituary) who was 'kind', 'impartial', and 'always more eager to settle a case out of court than in court'; a man who dished out 'fatherly advice' – and probably also some summary justice, especially to youths.[174] Essentially the efficient local constable was seen as maintaining law and order on his patch, not by going strictly by the book, but rather by developing a personal authority over and rapport with the local community. Such an authority was prized. When a country constable went to the city on promotion as a sectional Sergeant, he became 'a cog in a wheel', according to Superintendent John Lander looking back on his career in 1939; and he had 'not nearly the same standing as when he was running his country station and had the respect and friendship of the people round him'.[175]

In the public mind then, there were at least two broad styles of police behaviour: that of the man on the beat and that of the country constable. Both styles were part of the Department's ethos of an independent, impartial force. And it seems that from the 1920s the Police Force was successful in creating and maintaining a large measure of acceptance of its authority. One 'index of the public's tolerance' is the rate of offences reported for assaulting, resisting, or obstructing the Police. These figures (like all police statistics) need to be interpreted with care – they are 'not a simple measure of the standing of the police'. Nonetheless, there is a significant long-term trend which closely parallels experience in Britain and Australia.[176] At the turn of the century the rate hovered near 40 offences reported per 100,000 population. By 1920 it had fallen to 20, and by 1930 it was below 10, where it remained (except for 1931 and 1938–42) until the mid-1950s. From this point the rate began to rise sharply, reaching 40 per 100,000 again in 1972 and peaking at 132 in 1981.[177] By the 1920s, it seems, the Force had succeeded in creating high expectations in the community about the quality of police behaviour and its ability to maintain order and prevent crime. These expectations would continue to rise.

Did this mean that the New Zealand Police was effective as a 'preventive force'? In 1920 a commentator on European and American policing asserted that 'even were we to secure 100 per cent efficiency in our patrol and detective work, most crimes would still go unhindered'. But he admitted that such a view would be 'a matter for surprise'[178] – it did not accord with the prevailing expectations. The logic of the theory of 'preventive policing' suggested that there was a direct relationship between police activity and the amount of crime, and that police 'efficiency' could thus be measured. Accordingly the Police Department kept statistics of its most important business: the number of offences reported, and the number of offences for which someone was subsequently arrested or summoned. The trends, patterns, and possible significance of this very ambiguous data will be examined in chapter four. But, whatever the meaning of police statistics, they reveal little about overall police effectiveness in maintaining order and preventing crime. Indeed this is probably impossible to measure. Though 'crime' meant for police breaches of the criminal law, societal concepts of crime have been variable, not absolute. And even if universal agreement existed on what behaviour actually was criminal and disorderly, it would still be very difficult to assess 'how much crime and disorder a community produces, or how much would be produced if the police functioned differently (or not at all)'.[179]

Even so, from the 1920s there was a growing tension between the expectations and realities of 'preventive policing'. In part at least this tension contributed to the perception of the Police as a stagnating 'Cinderella Department' in the early 1930s.

PART ONE

Continuities

CHAPTER 1

A Time of 'Stress and Difficulty' (1918–21)

The years immediately following the Great War of 1914–18 stood out in the mind of Commissioner O'Donovan as a time of 'exceptional stress and difficulty'.[1] Viewed more broadly, the years 1919–21 saw a transition between much longer periods of change and then stability in the development of the Police Force. As we have seen, a process of change in its organisation had been under way since 1898. Issues of administration, working conditions and rank structure raised in the years before the war remained to be settled in 1918. Questions unresolved by 1921 generally remained so until the late 1930s at least. In these years too the Department faced the legacy of war in its shortage of staff and facilities, as well as the social stresses of the transition to peace.

Much then rested on the Commissioner and his Minister. Thomas Wilford, a Liberal member of the wartime National ministry, became Minister in charge of the Police in February 1918, succeeding Alexander Herdman, who joined the Supreme Court bench. Like Herdman, 'Tom' Wilford's experience of 30 years as an advocate in criminal cases, 'fighting the Police Force ... in the Courts of the country', had given him considerable respect for its men.[2] And like Herdman, but unlike many of his successors, Wilford was no mere cypher in the affairs of the Police. He was less preoccupied than either of his immediate successors, Prime Minister W.F. Massey and E.P. Lee, with the demands of other departments. Like his predecessor, however, Wilford worked with a Commissioner who sought to retain the initiative and his 'independence' in the administration of the Force.

When the Armistice was signed in November 1918, John O'Donovan had been Commissioner for nearly two years. At 60 years of age, he no longer kept good health. The stresses of wartime administration had led to him taking 'protracted sick leave' in 1918.[3] Even so his reputation as a competent administrator was to be enhanced in the next three years. Irish-born and Catholic, like five of the other nine top officers then in the Force, O'Donovan was nonetheless marked off by personality and background. A carefully trimmed goatee gave an air of distinction to 'a man of gentle manner and fine sensibilities'.[4] Where his compatriots in the Force usually had little formal education and had been labourers before joining, O'Donovan had been a pupil teacher and became a qualified solicitor while a constable. Wide reading enriched a natural eloquence which claimed the respect of politicians. His 'Address to the New Zealand Police Force' gave enduring expression to its ethos; his funeral oration at the graveside of the murdered Constable Vivian Dudding moved a wider public.[5] His fine words suggested 'a remarkably able and fair-minded man – one of the most gentlemanly officers in the Public Service'.[6] But some constables might well have formed a different impression from their dealings with the Commissioner.[7] The extent to which O'Donovan was flexible in meeting demands from the rank and file owed something to Wilford, and to the nature of the problems they faced in 1918–19. For O'Donovan and successive Ministers, the key issues of administration were the morale and the adequacy of the Force.

By 1918 there was a growing restiveness in the Force about longer working hours and deteriorating working conditions. There had been a sharp rise in the cost of living, but no wage increase since April 1914 apart from a small 'war bonus'. More men than ever before resigned in 1917. Growing numbers joined the Public Service Association, membership of which had been permitted in 1913. But the right of the PSA to represent constables remained undetermined. Pressure for official recognition mounted in 1918, in the face of procrastination by Wilford and O'Donovan.[8] That other long-standing issues were unresolved also rankled. There was the question of the relative status, pay and promotion prospects of the Uniform and Detective Branches. And beat constables, especially in the cities, had long wanted a day shift of eight hours, instead of one that was 'practically thirteen hours' long – four hours on duty, four off, four on again, and travelling time.[9] Housing was a growing problem. Beat men needed to live within walking distance of the station, while constables on transfer looked for decent dwellings at reasonable rents. Wartime attempts to control rents had failed to prevent their sharp rise in the cities, and had indeed discouraged house building.[10] For its part the Department was inadequately accommodated in many places. Failure in the past to buy or build sufficient premises meant that the Force was 'obliged to rent unsuitable houses' for stations. In some places it was 'now homeless' and retained its stations 'only by the special favour of the owners, or on payment of exorbitant rents'. Such was the state of police accommodation that the 'satisfaction of members of the Force with their lot and with their actual situation is very much bound up with this matter', O'Donovan warned Wilford in 1918.[11]

Pay was the first priority however. A spur to action may well have been the strike of 6,000 London Metropolitan Police on 30 August 1918 which had quickly secured them the promise of a substantial pay rise.[12] On 11 September Wilford announced an increase of 1s 6d a day for NCOs and constables, backdated to 1 April. At the same time he conceded that a 'considerable number' of other administrative matters 'would have to be settled'.[13] It was another month before he finally decided that there should be a ballot of all policemen to determine the position of the PSA. Given three choices, 34 men were not in favour of any union, 87 wanted their own police association, and an overwhelming 697 voted for representation by the PSA. A majority of the rank and file feared what Wilford and O'Donovan probably wanted – a docile organisation easily influenced by the Police administration. Though the results were announced at the end of November, the mechanics of representation were not finally settled until January 1919. The Police Regulation prohibiting 'combinations' of members of the Force was amended to permit membership of the PSA.[14] However, in representing the views of policemen, the executive of the PSA was constrained in a number of ways. Different 'sections' of the Force had to be represented on the executive, and all policemen should be able to comment and vote on all matters raised. Until May 1921, meetings of PSA members in the Force needed the permission of the officer in charge of their district. Furthermore the Minister reserved the right 'to limit and define' the matters discussed, and to 'require any safeguards for the preservation of discipline' that he saw as necessary.[15]

Early in February 1919 four policemen joined the PSA executive, and remits flowed in from the districts. Already, however, Wilford had moved to circumvent PSA pressure. He announced the terms of a Committee of Inquiry into pay and conditions which would focus on the relationship between the Detective and Uniform Branches. The Committee would also consider the feasibility of introducing an eight-hour day shift for beat men. So that it could be properly assessed, such a shift would also be trialled in Wellington. The Committee's personnel remained to be announced. Rank and file opinion in Wellington wanted its members to come from outside the Force 'to ensure an absolutely impartial investigation'.[16] On 1 March the British government established a parliamentary committee under Lord Desborough to review police pay and conditions of service. In New Zealand, however, the inquiry was to be an internal one with a panel of four commissioned officers chaired by the Wellington magistrate, W.G. Riddell. In theory at least the different interests of detectives and uniformed men were represented: Superintendent Nicholas Kiely in charge of Auckland District and Superintendent Arthur Wright of Dunedin had made their way in the Uniform Branch (Wright through the District Office, Kiely on the front line); Inspector Joseph McGrath from Napier and Sub-Inspector Charles Broberg at Headquarters had spent most of their careers as detectives – Broberg had risen rapidly to commissioned rank, while McGrath had been overtaken by more junior men from the Uniform Branch. The committee was appointed in late February, but it was to be another month before it toured the country to hear submissions.[17]

Figure 1.1: Male Police Numbers and Wastage 1911–1945

Year ending 31 March	Total Police	Retired or Died	Resigned Voluntarily	Resigned Compulsorily or Dismissed	Wastage (% of Total Police)
1911	788	22	24	14	7.6
1912	835	18	27	10	6.7
1913	846	16	30	1	6.1
1914	870	13	34	4	6.4
1915	911	12	19	12	4.7
1916	916	18	30	7	6.0
1917	898	14	41	5	6.7
1918	901	21	34	5	6.7
1919	878	24	30	8	7.1
1920	916	18	39	3	6.5
1921	950	11	42	5	6.1
1922	1,009	19	21	9	4.9
1923	1,003	14	50	5	6.9
1924	1,027	20	39	6	6.3
1925	1,026	20	37	8	6.3
1926	1,085	11	21	13	4.1
1927	1,096	14	37	14	5.9
1928	1,117	23	29	14	5.9
1929	1,155	18	20	10	4.1
1930	1,146	18	15	21	4.8
1931	1,169	13	8	2	2.0
1932	1,157	14	6	5	2.2
1933	1,195	23	8	7	3.2
1934	1,211	20	6	1	2.2
1935	1,219	13	9	5	2.2
1936	1,226	20	4	7	2.6
1937	1,255	16	12	5	2.6
1938	1,428	16	14	5	2.4
1939	1,439	24	16	1	2.9
1940	1,457	24	36	10	4.9
1941	1,509	30	52	13	6.3
1942	1,599	28	18	12	3.6
1943	1,640	12	15	18	3.0
1944	1,634	20	32	17	4.4
1945	1,565	31	50	8	6.1

Source: Annual Reports. **Note:** The data does not include District or Native Constables, Police Matrons, or the policewomen appointed from 1941. 'Wastage' includes those who retired on superannuation or medically unfit, or who died, resigned or were dismissed.

In the meantime discontent was reported amongst the rank and file in the capital, and the rate of resignations increased.[18] Police morale became part of a larger issue: the adequacy of the Force. Between 1916 and 1919 the rate of 'wastage' of men from the Force had increased sharply (figure 1.1). More than resignations was involved. Retirements doubled in 1917/18, while the number of deaths in the service rose to an all-time high in 1918, with Senior Sergeant J. Burrows and fourteen constables falling victim to the 'Spanish' influenza epidemic which swept the country from October. Sickness drastically reduced the available manpower. An average of 80 men (9 per cent of the Force) were off duty through sickness or on leave during the year. In Auckland alone 65 men, nearly two-thirds of the city force, were laid up at one time with the 'flu.[19] The rate at which men were leaving the Force was similar to that before the war, but the losses of front-line staff were not made up. From December 1916 O'Donovan had abstained from recruiting men liable for military service. Even when the war ended recruits were hard to attract. The pay increase of September 1918 (16.6 per cent for newly appointed constables) was not enough to keep up with the sharply rising rates for unskilled labour outside the Force. And so by March 1919, there were 52 fewer constables than three years earlier. A depleted staff, O'Donovan complained, was burdened with much work for other departments, to the 'neglect of the legitimate requirements of the public in respect of purely police protection and attention'. *'Where are the Police?'* became the editorial refrain, in Auckland particularly.[20]

Such a question betrayed a growing sense of insecurity. Taking the long view this may be seen as partly the result of rapid population growth and change, especially since the turn of the century.[21] In the twenty years to 1921 New Zealand's population increased by more than half to over 1.2 million. Most of the cities and larger provincial towns had grown at a much faster rate. By 1921, a third of the population lived in the four main centres. With its rapidly expanding suburbs, Auckland was by far the largest city. In the years 1921–36 it was to grow by nearly 53,000, Wellington by 42,000, Christchurch by more than 26,000, and Dunedin by only 9,500 – this last a slower rate of growth than most of the largest provincial towns.[22] Contrasts in city growth rates and in their population per policeman[23] were reflected in different perceptions of public tranquillity during the 1920s: Auckland newspapers were more worried about crime than was the *Otago Daily Times*.

Viewed from the closer perspective of 1919, the sharp rise in complaints of assault, 'mischief' (vandalism), theft and burglary pointed to an unsettled social climate in the aftermath of war.[24] It was 'an open secret', the *Timaru Post* commented later, that the Police anticipated 'a considerable increase in crime throughout the country' with the soldiers' return – 20,000 came home by December 1918, the main body from the

Figure 1.2: Police Pay Rates 1918–1945

Rank	1918 1 April	1928 1 April	1937 1 May	1945 28 March
	per annum	per annum	per annum	per annum
Superintendents	£460 to £520	£570 to £615	£606 to £641	£700 to £720
Inspectors	£380 to £440	£500 to £560	£526 to £586	£620 to £660
Sub-Inspectors	£330 to £360	£450 to £480	£476 to £506	£550 to £575
	per day	per day		
Senior Sergeants (and Senior Detectives from 1919)	16/- to 17/6	21/- to 22/-	£409 to £427	£465 to £490
Sergeants (and Detective Sergeants from 1919)	13/6 to 15/-	19/- to 20/-	£372 to £391	£420 to £445
Constables (and Detectives from 1919) on permanent appointment:				
under 3 years' service	10/6	15/-	£299	£335
3 and under 6 years	11/-	15/6	£308	£335
6 and under 9 years	11/6	16/-	£318	£360
9 and under 14 years	12/-	16/6	£327	£375
14 and under 20 years	12/6	17/-	£336	£385
over 20 years' service	13/-	17/6	£345	£400
			per day	
Probationary Constables	9/-	11/-	11/-	£230
Women Police: under three years				£290
over three years				£300
		(allowance from 1 Oct)	(allowance)	
Chief Detectives	18/- to 19/-	3/-	3/-	
Senior Detectives		3/-	3/-	
Detective Sergeants	16/6 to 17/6	3/-	3/-	
Detectives	13/- to 16/-	3/-	3/-	
Acting Detectives		1/6	1/6	
Plain-clothes Constables attached to a Detective Office		1/-	1/6	
	per annum	per annum	per annum	
Matrons	£120 to £156	£150 to £180	£180 to £210	£230 to £300
Surgeons	£120	£150	£150 (in 4 centres, £25 elsewhere)	£200 (in 4 centres, £25 elsewhere)

Source: *New Zealand Police Gazette.*

following February.[25] Symptomatic of this were police concerns at the growing number of incidents involving firearms, and that more people than ever were carrying revolvers or 'automatic' pistols – a belief reinforced on 6 October 1919 when Constable Dudding, called to a Wellington domestic dispute, was shot by a wharf labourer with an 'automatic'.[26] The 'Revolver Menace', as one magistrate called it in May 1920, heightened the fears of those disturbed by the rhetoric of militants in the labour movement that 'disloyal and lawless elements' would use arms in 'future strikes and riots'.[27] The 'cost of living, the hampering of industries and commerce, and the dislocation of labour' caused 'a certain amount of apprehension and unrest', O'Donovan observed. Yet in his annual report written in mid-1919, he was more sanguine than he had been a few months earlier or was to be a year later. 'The good sense of a community enjoying the most liberal constitutional privileges', he wrote, 'has asserted itself in every emergency and promises to prevail at all times over passions'.[28]

There had been signs early in 1919, however, that a major industrial stoppage might soon occur,[29] and this prospect had underlined for the government the need to ensure an adequate and reliable police force. The 'gravity of the situation' impressed a committee of Ministers who reported to Cabinet early in April. Cabinet accepted its recommendation that an increase of 1s 6d per day be granted from 1 April to constables and Sergeants, and that the house allowance for married men be increased. The rest of the public service could not expect a corresponding increase, for the Police were a special case: public order 'could not be preserved' unless a 'sufficient number' of suitably qualified and trained men were maintained 'in a state of contentment and complete discipline'.[30] Commissioned officers (who had missed out on the 1918 pay increase), Senior Sergeants and detectives had to await the results of the Committee of Inquiry. Wilford received its report at the end of May. The Committee rejected the claims of the Detective Branch for a separate rank and career structure. It recommended instead a common seniority list for promotion purposes, the interchange of men between the branches, and 'equal pay for equal ranks' – with the unusual work and expenses of detectives being recognised by special allowances.[31] In the light of the Committee's findings, Wilford announced new pay scales for officers and NCOs which established greater margins between the ranks.[32] For his part O'Donovan implemented the Committee's recommendation that the 'eight-hour system' for beat constables be trialled in the four main centres for a further twelve months.

Recruitment certainly picked up. By April 1920, 127 new constables had been appointed and the Force had regained its peak strength of four years earlier. To secure recruits, O'Donovan now accepted twenty year olds.[33] Ex-constables who had served in the Expeditionary Force were reappointed to their former position on the seniority list. Their superannuation rights were preserved by the Police Force Amendment Act passed in November 1919.[34] To get men onto the street as quickly as possible, O'Donovan postponed reopening the Training Depot, which had been closed when recruiting dried up in 1916.[35] To this end also, authority granted in wartime to appoint recruits as temporary constables on probation was made permanent by the 1919 Amendment Act. By this means O'Donovan could retain 32 men recruited during the war who were now too old or otherwise deemed unsuitable for permanent appointment. But such a move was criticised by Labour members of the House, echoing feeling amongst the rank and file of the Police in Wellington. Temporary constables implied a dilution of entry standards; they might be used as 'a lever' against pressure to improve pay and conditions; and (a fear merely hinted at) they might be rapidly recruited 'in time of industrial trouble', becoming 'specials' with uniforms on. Prime Minister Massey, by now in charge of the Police, denied any such ulterior motives: the measure was wanted by the Commissioner ('a man who knows his job and does it well') simply to 'obviate inconvenience'.[36]

The Labour MP Peter Fraser acknowledged that there had been 'considerable improvements' in police pay and conditions during Wilford's term of office.[37] And, despite friction between the Commissioner and the PSA, negotiations had continued. Any suggestion of rank and file militancy in 1919 thus came to nothing, in stark contrast to the police strikes in London and Liverpool on 31 July, and in Boston during September. Yet restiveness remained. Changes sought by the police members of the PSA in June – notably a detailed syllabus for police exams, appeal rights paralleling those of public servants, a weekly day off, and retirement at 60 – were not conceded.[38] O'Donovan did adopt the recommendations of the Committee of Inquiry in the new set of Police Regulations which came into effect on 1 October. But the hard face of Force discipline endured. Annual leave, for example, was 'a privilege' rather than a right; the assistance of counsel was not permitted in disciplinary inquiries; and the new regulations regarding 'sick pay' seemed ungenerous. 'Many of the rules and regulations', wrote a reporter, were felt to 'indicate a desire on the part of the department to make every man keep a watch on his neighbour'.[39]

More critical for constables in the cities and largest towns were housing difficulties about which the Department could do little, in the short term at least. Increased house allowances were still insufficient. And they were no answer to the sheer shortage of houses. The predicament of Constable Dorgan typified the plight of many married beat men. In October 1919 he applied to transfer from Timaru because the 'housing problem' had 'become so acute'. Nine months later O'Donovan replied that the problem was no more acute at Timaru than elsewhere: 'I cannot transfer men about for that cause'. Nonetheless he asked how Dorgan was placed now. Since October the Constable had been forced to shift twice. In July 1920 he received notice to quit his third house and move – with his epileptic wife, two young children and by now 'considerably damaged' furniture – to a small four-roomed one, 40 minutes walk from the police station. All the Commissioner could do was to hope that Dorgan might 'lawfully retain possession' of his present house, offering to obtain advice from the Crown Law Office.

'The same difficulties', O'Donovan responded, 'confront all classes of the community who cannot purchase residences'.[40]

Rising rents were part of the continuing pressure of the cost of living as a fragile post-war boom continued until early in 1921. By 1920 the cost of living had increased by at least 60 per cent since July 1914, but the basic pay for a constable had risen by only a third. And as the two pay rises for constables and NCOs since March 1914 had been flat-rate increases, those further up the scale had lost ground even more. During March 1920 Police branches of the PSA pressed for a substantial pay increase of 6s a day. 'New hands' were particularly unsettled by the thought of higher wages outside the Force. 'Dissatisfaction with the rate of pay, however, ... extends to all ranks', Superintendent McGrath reported from Dunedin. In Christchurch, a policeman commented that older men were keeping the younger men 'quiet'; but if things did not change the 'Government might find them aligned with the revolutionaries if trouble did break out'.[41]

With an eye on the deteriorating economic climate, the government took some months to make up its mind.[42] This time the Police were not a special case, despite continuing anxieties about labour militancy. An increase of 3s a day (25 per cent for a 'new hand') was given, in line with that to public servants and railwaymen. Resignations fell sharply and the problems of recruitment eased – a trend reinforced by mounting unemployment in 1921. At last, in May 1921, O'Donovan was able to reopen the Training Depot in Rintoul Street, Wellington, with a class of 25 men. There were to be no more public complaints by officers about the appearance and indiscipline of some raw recruits on the street.[43] In the two years to March 1922, the number of uniformed constables increased by 83. Yet still the issue of police numbers remained. O'Donovan's apparent aim of merely restoring the pre-war ratio of police to population was unacceptable to the *New Zealand Herald*, for which the ratio had been inadequate before the war, and was even more so after it: 'To-day there is a larger population to protect, the criminal element is no smaller and is apparently more aggressive, and more officers are engaged on such extraneous duties as traffic control, so that the effective strength is even lower than the figures indicate'.[44]

In fact traffic control was not an 'extraneous duty' but a long-standing one which, like arms control, made new demands on the Department in the immediate post-war years. Policemen had long dealt with accidents and breaches of the municipal by-laws involving pedestrians and horse-drawn traffic. 'Neglecting to give proper attention to the regulation of vehicle traffic' was a disciplinary offence for a beat constable.[45] This responsibility assumed a new dimension with the growing number of motor vehicles from the turn of the century. Estimates of their number by 1918 vary from 30,000 to 60,000. When registration began in 1924 there were 106,449, including over 71,000 cars.[46] Traffic censuses revealed that in Christchurch car usage increased threefold between 1915 and 1922, and had doubled again by 1926.[47] Fatal motor accidents averaged 60 a year by 1922/23 and had nearly trebled in number by 1928.[48] Just before the war, both the Auckland and Wellington city councils had made arrangements to employ policemen on permanent point duty; Christchurch followed suit in 1921. Wilford scoffed at suggestions that such men in Wellington were an 'absolute redundancy'; the men on duty 'at the corner of Manners Street and at Stewart Dawson's corner' were 'very necessary'. And so all probationers in the newly reopened Depot were instructed in 'traffic work'.[49] Though the Department recouped some of the cost, the demands of traffic control represented a drain on manpower. Perhaps because of this, the Department escaped the task of registering and licensing motor vehicles that was planned in 1921 and introduced three years later by the Motor Vehicles Act.

With arms control, however, the Police carried the full burden of administration. This increased substantially when the Arms Act passed in August 1920 came into effect the following January. For O'Donovan the passage of this Act had become a matter of some urgency. Pre-war legislation was effectively a dead letter, and so the Commissioner sought to make permanent the wartime restrictions on the carriage, possession, and importing of firearms, and to extend their scope. An already prepared bill was redrafted shortly after Constable Dudding's death in October 1919 to outlaw automatic pistols; it had not been introduced because of the pressure of parliamentary business. In the meantime Police anxiety mounted. Incidents with revolvers continued: in Christchurch, an escaped prisoner produced an automatic pistol when about to be rearrested; a Maori youth was killed by a revolver bullet near Raetihi; at Runciman, the post office was held up.[50] The most dramatic event was the cold-blooded killing of the Ponsonby postmaster on 13 March 1920. Three revolvers were later found and traced to Dennis Gunn in what was the first New Zealand conviction for murder on fingerprint evidence.[51] The incidence of death and injury by firearms seemed to be increasing. In the two years to 30 June 1920 there were eight murders or attempted murders, 60 suicides, and 70 injuries known to the Police to have been caused by firearms – fifteen of them by automatic pistol. Returns from retailers indicated that 173 automatics had been sold in this period, while a further 376 were still in stock. But it was feared that the bulk of the revolvers in circulation were war trophies brought back by soldiers. In fact there was a sharp increase in the number of firearms imported during 1920 – some 20,500, a quarter more than the previous peak of imports in 1912 (figure 1.3).[52]

The new Arms Act sought to 'make Better Provision for the Public Safety'. For the Attorney-General, Sir Francis Bell, this meant preventing 'factions being armed against each other'.[53] Fears of armed rioters were reflected in clauses enabling the proclamation of areas where the

Figure 1.3: Firearms Imported for Civilians 1880–1939

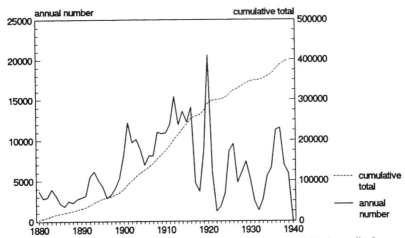

Source: *Review of Firearms Control in New Zealand*, Wellington, 1997, Appendix 2.

possession of arms, ammunition and explosives was prohibited, and empowering the Police to search for arms and to seize those held by dealers.[54] For the Police the most significant provisions were not new, but they represented a more effective application of control – and consequently 'entailed an extraordinary amount of work'.[55] Dealers had to be licensed, all firearm owners registered, and permits issued for the purchase and sale of all firearms (and ammunition for them) except shotguns. Permits were also needed to carry a revolver and for returned soldiers to retain automatic weapons as souvenirs. Anyone else possessing an automatic had to destroy it, export it, or hand it over to the Police by 1 April 1921. For O'Donovan the pressure was on in the last four months of 1920 to draw up comprehensive regulations and have them vetted by the Solicitor-General, printed, promulgated, and circulated to districts along with the necessary forms and registers. At the same time and continuing into 1921 the Commissioner faced a stream of anxious queries. Dealers wanted to simplify transactions amongst themselves; mine managers to escape 'impracticalities' in the permit system for explosives; rifle clubs to be exempt from permits in buying ammunition; and individuals to retain automatics as curios. Amendments to the Act thus had to be made in 1922.[56] For staff in the districts the Act meant further 'extraneous duties' as 200,000 arms were registered within a year. In Auckland alone 17,000 arms were registered, 600 automatics handed in, and over 300 applications to retain such pistols received by April 1921.[57]

Such were the pressures of administration, and the shortage of manpower, that the establishment of new police districts decided upon in 1918 took nearly three years to complete. O'Donovan believed that the subdivision into smaller districts would 'have an immense effect upon the efficiency of the Force.' Officers in charge would be able to give 'greater attention' to supervising their stations and men, whereas 'the volume of correspondence now received at the District Offices practically engrosses [their] whole attention'. With smaller districts even the burden of files would be more manageable. However the 'difficulty of sparing men from general duty for the office staffs' delayed their creation.[58] And once established, all the new districts quickly joined the chorus of claimants for more men on beat duty. The number of police districts increased from nine to fourteen between August 1918 and January 1921.[59] Their boundaries were later adjusted, but the basic divisions were to be substantially altered only by the creation of Nelson District in December 1928 and Rotorua in April 1966 before a major recasting into six regions with 28 districts in 1988. Even with the subdivision that had occurred by 1921, considerable variation in the size of districts remained – they ranged from 30 men each in Whangarei and Gisborne to 190 in Wellington and 185 in Auckland in 1922. Problems of supervision also differed. Stations varied in size from one to 74 men in 1919. In the Whangarei, Wanganui, Greymouth and Invercargill districts over 80 per cent of the men were in one-man stations that were widely scattered and poorly served by roads, especially on the West Coast and in North Auckland. At the other extreme were Auckland and Wellington, which had their share of sole-charge stations alongside large inner-city stations containing detectives and sections of beat men.[60]

Superintendents controlled the four largest districts, Inspectors the remainder. They were served by a small and overworked staff. There were five in the Wellington District Office in 1919 – Senior Sergeant M. Gaffney as District Clerk and four constables. Staff numbers had not changed since well before the war. Yet the number of files handled had nearly doubled in six years, and warrants had more than trebled.[61] When ex-Constable T.F. Smith returned from the war with an artificial leg, he was rejected by O'Donovan. But with his typing skills, Smith was quickly accepted for office work when he came to the notice of Superintendent Norwood of Wellington.[62] The 'slaves of the office desk' usually worked from 8.30 am to 5 pm, but often came back to work at night for an hour or two.[63] Essentially they were policemen acting as file clerks and typists. Until May 1921, all files went to the officer in charge of the district, through the commissioned officers assisting them in the case of the four main centres.[64] In addition to 'such events as may affect the public peace', criminal files, personnel matters, and complaints from the public, 'strict and constant attention' was to be paid to 'economy' by the officer in charge. All accounts and returns were to be examined and 'authenticated by his certificates of approval'.[65]

In May 1921 O'Donovan sought to rearrange the duties of commissioned officers in the four largest districts. Henceforth Inspectors would be the ' "corresponding" officers of the district'. On them would fall the 'burden of the great bulk of correspondence' that had hitherto preoccupied Superintendents, whose 'primary and most urgent duty', declared the Commissioner, 'is to supervise the police and their duties in the Headquarter cities'. Superintendents had to apply themselves to maintaining 'an effective Force' and to building up 'reserves in each branch sufficient to reasonably meet defections' through wastage, leave or other duties. While Inspectors remained 'continuously in charge at the District Office and Headquarters Station', Superintendents were to visit and inspect the remainder. This included stations in neighbouring districts over which their jurisdiction was extended – though the 'full responsibility' of the Inspectors in charge was 'not diminished'. By creating four 'Divisions' supervised by Superintendents, O'Donovan tried to ensure the coordination of districts in the face of their subdivision. The paramilitary hierarchy of command was maintained on paper at least. Experienced officers could watch over those recently promoted to control new districts. In fact such supervision and advice was probably minimal, given the more immediate concerns of Superintendents and the slowness of communication. Certainly the number of files sent by Inspectors directly to the Commissioner for decision or comment did not diminish.[66]

At Headquarters in 1919 there was a staff of fourteen, comprising six 'civilians' and eight policemen – a Sub-Inspector, two Senior Sergeants, four constables and the Commissioner. Civil service staff had been introduced into Headquarters following the report of the Royal Commission of Inquiry into the Police Force in 1909.[67] But with one exception, R.F. Madden, they remained essentially file clerks and typists. 'Dick' Madden was appointed as clerk in 1910 and promoted to Chief Clerk three years later. Some of the correspondence from the public he dealt with in the name of the Commissioner. Even so he was still lowly ranked in the public service classification in 1919.[68] Most of the routine administration was ultimately the responsibility of, and indeed done by, policemen. This reflected a deeply ingrained bias against civilians within the Police Department which the strictures of the Royal Commissioner in 1909 had failed to remove. Essentially it was a question of trust and control. The Department had its own administrative practices and dealt with records 'of an essentially confidential nature'. Policemen, 'having been tried, can be implicitly trusted', was how Sub-Inspector (later Commissioner) A.H. Wright put it in 1909.[69] And above all, policemen were subject to the Commissioner's discipline, while from 1913 civilians were ultimately under the control of the Public Service Commissioner. Such a concern was shown in the changing status of E.W. Dinnie, fingerprint expert and photographer at Headquarters since 1903. In 1915 he was transferred from the civil service to the Police as head of the Criminal Registration Branch with the rank of Senior Sergeant.[70] Another NCO was in charge of the Police Store. Constables assisted

Dinnie and the Storekeeper, and another edited the weekly *Police Gazette*.

Assisted by Sub-Inspector C.R. Broberg,[71] the Commissioner was immersed in day-to-day administration. O'Donovan apparently saw most of the files that came in from the districts, frequently making detailed comments on them in his copperplate hand. Instructions were issued, advice offered. No stations could be opened or closed, or men moved, without his sanction. Personnel matters had to be dealt with – transfers, promotions, leave, discipline, rewards. He read closely the monthly and other special reports on 'revolutionary organisations' and industrial matters which streamed in from 1920. Similarly he cast an eye over the criminal files that came to Headquarters. All expenditure – including the renting and maintenance of police premises – required his approval. Parliamentary questions as well as letters to Ministers needed replies drafted. On top of all this, legislation had to be prepared and regulations drawn up. Delays, such as Constable Dorgan experienced in getting a reply to his request for a transfer, were to be expected. Small wonder also that the Commissioner was largely desk-bound. Except when the 1919 Committee of Inquiry convened in the main centres, O'Donovan found little time to visit the districts. Nor was there time to plan for changes in facilities and methods – even if money had been available. And it was not.

On 1 March 1918 Police Headquarters moved from the Government Buildings to the new Wellington station in Johnston Street. Completion of the new premises was not a sign of things to come. Rather it represented the end of an era so far as expenditure on stations was concerned. Since the turn of the century the Auckland Central station in O'Rorke Street had been opened and added to. Christchurch Central had been greatly enlarged by the construction of a two-storey brick block in 1906. Dunedin police had moved in 1915 into a massive brick pile, reminiscent of New Scotland Yard, that had already for twenty years been the local prison. New stations had also been built in the provincial towns and country districts. Even so, much remained to be done in 1918. Of the 327 stations, many were dilapidated older buildings at the end of their 'useful life' and virtually beyond repair. O'Donovan painted a gloomy picture of police premises, and urged a sustained building program when the war ended. But 1918 saw a sharp fall in spending on police buildings, and expenditure in the next 30 years, though sometimes greater in money terms, did not match that of the preceding twenty years in real terms (figure 1.4).[72]

Between 1918/19 and 1920/21, money spent on police stations from the Public Works Fund did increase fivefold – three times faster than total spending from the Fund. Yet scarcity of labour and 'abnormal' building costs rendered large-scale improvements impossible. Premises were purchased rather than built. 'A satisfactory beginning has been made', the Commissioner reported in 1920; 'but a great deal more must

Figure 1.4: Expenditure on the Police Department from the Consolidated and Public Works Funds 1911–1945

Year ending 31 March	Total Government Expenditure from Consolidated Fund (in £ million)	Police Department Expenditure from Consolidated Fund		Police Expenditure as % of total Government Expenditure from Consolidated Fund	Cost per Inhabitant*	Expenditure from the Public Works Fund on Police Stations
		Amount (£)	% Change			Amount (£)
1911	9.3	179,106		1.92	3/4	9,030
1912	10.3	185,065	+3.3	1.80	3/5	19,817
1913	11.0	202,100	+9.2	1.83	3/8	18,423
1914	11.8	214,834	+6.3	1.82	3/9	14,094
1915	12.3	235,424	+9.5	1.91	4/1	19,122
1916	12.4	245,121	+4.1	1.98	4/3	25,484
1917	14.0	244,297	-0.3	1.74	4/3	21,147
1918	15.1	261,324	+7.0	1.73	4/6	18,814
1919	18.6	302,478	+15.7	1.63	5/2	6,157
1920	23.7	306,684	+1.4	1.29	5/-	24,944
1921	27.9	398,978	+30.1	1.43	6/5	36,843
1922	28.4	411,056	+3.0	1.45	6/4	22,544
1923	26.2	377,788	-8.1	1.44	5/8	6,298
1924	26.1	386,919	+2.4	1.48	5/9	12,838
1925	27.3	399,289	+3.2	1.46	5/9	18,553
1926	23.5	408,035	+2.2	1.74	5/9	16,594
1927	24.3	410,506	+0.6	1.69	5/8	7,411
1928	24.9	417,975	+1.8	1.68	5/9	5,561
1929	24.1	444,970	+6.5	1.85	6/2	6,925
1930	25.2	452,883	+1.8	1.80	6/1	8,442
1931	24.7	456,672	+0.8	1.85	6/-	8,360
1932	24.8	413,821	-9.4	1.67	5/5	2,535
1933	22.5	426,988	+3.2	1.90	5/6	1,022
1934	24.2	427,344	+0.1	1.76	5/6	74
1935	24.4	435,545	+1.9	1.78	5/7	2,754
1936	25.8	453,890	+4.2	1.76	5/9	6,710
1937	30.6	496,978	+9.5	1.62	6/3	7,149
1938	35.2	601,482	+21.0	1.71	7/6	11,086
1939	35.7	607,390	+1.0	1.70	7/6	77,745
1940	37.6	627,502	+3.3	1.69	7/8	60,664
1941	38.7	649,715	+3.5	1.68	7/11	24,343
1942	39.5	677,353	+4.2	1.71	8/3	**
1943	38.2	716,125	+5.7	1.87	8/10	**
1944	46.5	777,372	+8.5	1.67	9/5	**
1945	53.0	759,193	-2.4	1.43	9/1	**

Sources: Annual Public Accounts, *AJHR*, 1911–1920, B-1; Annual Financial Statement, *AJHR*, 1921–1941, B-6; Annual Reports on the Police Force, *AJHR*, H-16; Public Works Statement, *AJHR*, 1923 and 1941, D-1.

*   A contemporary calculation made in shillings and pence. The amount has been rounded to the nearest penny.

** Comparable data lacking

be done to house and equip the Department and its members'. And the circumstances of many like Constable Dorgan called for 'special attention'. A 'comprehensive scheme' was urgently needed to house married men near to their stations in the cities and large towns. This would also serve the interests of the Force, since men living in the suburbs were 'difficult and slow' to mobilise in emergencies. In 1918 O'Donovan had already requested an immediate 'extension of the functions and powers' of the Labour, Public Works, or Advances to Settlers Department to either house policemen at reasonable rents or assist them to buy. He recognised that renting was more 'practicable' than purchase, given 'the constant changes in residence caused by transfers'. In the event the Police Department had to use its portion of the Public Works vote to provide residences for staff. And its Minister made clear the government's priorities: the demands on workmen and materials for 'workers' dwellings' were such that 'building-work' for the Police had to be kept to the 'lowest minimum'. Sufficient houses were acquired only to meet the needs of officers and NCOs who took charge of districts and stations. Married beat constables had merely the prospect of relief following recent increased recruiting. Some at least could be transferred to country stations as the 'large number of young unmarried men' now in the city barracks issued onto the streets.[73]

As recession deepened in 1921, O'Donovan refrained from 'urging anything but what is absolutely essential'.[74] His restraint applied not just to the improvement of police premises, but also to the development of other facilities – especially those providing mobility and communications. When Wilford visited Christchurch during Show week in 1918, he was driven out to the races at Riccarton each day in a taxi hired by Superintendent John Dwyer. The Minister noted that the Police lacked a car; 'you must have one', he told Dwyer, 'so apply for a motor car straight away as I may be leaving the Ministry any day now'.[75] Although Dwyer was 'a bit tardy' in putting in the application, Wilford left authority for the car before going to the Opposition benches. During 1918/19 the Force had acquired its first motor vehicles. Four vans were built to the Department's specifications, two for Auckland, and one each for Wellington and Christchurch. These replaced horse-drawn prison vans and were 'also quite suitable for ambulance work'. A 'touring-car' was supplied for the use of the Commissioner, the Wellington Superintendent and their staffs based at Johnston Street. O'Donovan recognised that one could also be 'placed with advantage' at each of the district headquarters and at other 'important towns', in order that officers might more readily visit and supervise outlying stations.[76]

But beyond this no need for cars was envisaged. The system of patrol was still essentially by foot; occasionally by bicycle in the case of suburban constables, or by horse in country districts and on the fringes of cities. City policemen setting out on inquiries used public transport where necessary. Beat men with difficult drunks hailed a taxi

– and hoped the drunk would pay the fare. Except for the four main centres, and especially Auckland and Wellington, the towns remained fairly compact. And the 'criminal classes' were still basically pedestrians, at least in the eyes of the Police. Railway stations rather than roadsters needed to be watched. Car ownership in the early 1920s was confined largely to the affluent and the respectable.[77] Even so the problem of 'speeding' was becoming important. Moreover, in the suburbs there were just not enough men to maintain the traditional pattern of beat patrol, and in country areas horses were increasingly seen as costly to maintain and too slow for inquiry work. Thus in 1919 'some' motorcycles were bought. In Auckland intermittent motorcycle night patrols of residential areas began. The Palmerston North District received two motorcycles to offset the shortage of men available to undertake inquiries in the country. One was based at Feilding and the other at Palmerston North, where the troop-horse was disposed of. On the grounds of 'economy and efficiency' the Commissioner also encouraged country men to use their own cars (for which they would receive an allowance) rather than police horses.[78] But in city and countryside alike, Superintendent Wright warned in December 1921, 'motor-cars must not on any account be hired for special trips where there is a regular motor service or other means of transport which can be used at much less cost'.[79]

Considerations of cost also moulded police administrators' attitudes towards the rapid advances that were occurring in telecommunications. By 1919 there were some 72,000 telephones in New Zealand; a decade later there were 157,000 and the four main centres had automatic exchanges. Per head of population the provincial towns had more phones than the cities.[80] On this basis the total number of telephones was still quite low – six per hundred people in 1919. Potentially, however, the accessibility of policemen to the community – and with it, expectations of police service – was radically enhanced in the years following the war. For its part, the Police Department in 1921 had 298 of the 2,002 telephones in government department offices, and seven of the 415 private telephones paid for by the state.[81] But this did not mean that suburban and country constables could always be reached by telephone. Some country stations were not yet connected to an exchange, and many had only a partial service. Devonport and Northcote stations on Auckland's North Shore, for example, had no connection at night until 1923.[82] At Waipawa, there was for some years a telephone in the station but not in the police house. This was not satisfactory to the local settlers, who argued that policemen should be able to be reached 'at any hour of the day or night as their services were required.'[83] For this reason also, Superintendent McGrath pressed (unsuccessfully) for another man at the Dunedin South station, where there was no one in the watch-house at night to answer the urgent phone calls coming in from this 'large, thickly populated district'.[84] Yet even with an extra man, the staff at Dunedin South could not have responded quickly to most calls, because they lacked a car and were constrained in hiring taxis.

Despite advances in technology, the time was far from ripe for fundamental changes in methods of policing. For one thing the technology available was still primitive. It would be more than twenty years before the deployment of radio-controlled cars was practicable in New Zealand.[85] More importantly, an overriding concern for 'economy' reinforced conservative attitudes towards organisation and methods. The injunctions against the use of toll calls (and against the hiring of cars, as already noted) exemplify this. Amongst the public, telephones were increasingly used in place of telegrams during the 1920s.[86] For Police administrators, however, 'bureau' (or 'toll') calls were a costly and insecure means of passing information – and difficult to monitor. Files could be commented on; but the import of phone calls might not be recalled accurately, if at all. In May 1924 the constable at Culverden noted a District Order issued by Superintendent W.H. Mackinnon in Christchurch: 'In future the telephone is not to be used by any member of the Force for a bureau call for the purpose of conveying information that could be sent through the post in the ordinary way. The practice of using the telephone bureau on trivial matters must cease'. To this Inspector Stephen Till added a rider for the Sergeant at Rangiora emphasising that 'the use of the telephone bureau is to be strictly limited to cases of absolute necessity. In most cases a telegram will answer the purpose much better than telephone communication.'[87] Successive Commissioners held similar views. Long after 1926, when the North and South Islands were linked by cable and long-distance toll calls became possible, Commissioners used telegrams – often in code – when sending urgent messages. Toll calls were only to be made when 'absolutely necessary' and a 'verbatim record' of them was to be kept, Commissioner McIlveney reiterated in 1929.[88]

In 1921 a period of quite substantial change in the Police Force came to an end. In the circumscribed use of telephones and cars, for example, as in many other features of departmental organisation and administration, the pattern set by the end of 1921 was to endure for at least 30 years. Commissioner O'Donovan's retirement in December marked the turning point. After 42 years' service he had another eighteen months to go before compulsory retirement at the age of 65. 'Officially' he was going so as 'to ease the pressure on those below him and make way for their promotion'.[89] In fact 'a period of exceptional stress and difficulty' had taken its toll on his health. Nonetheless O'Donovan clearly felt his job was done. He expressed a justifiable 'satisfaction' that the 'foundations of a very fine Police Force' had been laid, and that 'its full development and perfection as a highly efficient executive instrument of government, of the first importance in promoting the safety, comfort, and happiness of the community, are assured.'[90]

In shaping the 'foundations', O'Donovan had exercised considerable influence as both architect and builder. Yet it would be too simple to see his passing alone as bringing a change in the fortunes of the Force. Other hands were also at work, as O'Donovan himself recognised in paying tribute to his Ministers. They for their part recognised O'Donovan's force of personality.[91] But such influence as O'Donovan exercised was greatest when it coincided in 1919 with both a sense of crisis and a favourable economic climate. Such a combination of personality and circumstances was not to reappear until 1955. Indeed, more potent than personality in moulding the development of the Police in the next fifteen years were deteriorating economic conditions and the isolation of the Department within the public service.

CHAPTER 2

A 'Cinderella Department' (1922–35)

The administrative pattern of policing established by 1922 was to continue largely unchanged during the inter-war years. Other state employees such as teachers also saw themselves as belonging to underfunded and unprogressive 'Cinderella departments' which forced them to work in sub-standard conditions. 'The average large police station is a dingy forbidding and ramshackle building, and the average long established school is badly lighted, ugly and ill planned', a Christchurch primary school headmaster observed in July 1935.[1] But unlike teachers, policemen did not discuss openly how the Force should adapt to changing times; nor did the rank and file have any organisation to represent their views before 1936.

For the Police, the scene was set by the Reform government's response to economic recession in 1921–22. A slump in export prices beginning in 1920 was quickly reflected in pressure from businessmen and farmers for 'considerable economies' in government spending.[2] Early in March 1921, an 'Economies Committee' chaired by the Public Service Commissioner was appointed to suggest ways to curtail departmental expenditure and 'promote efficiency'. Its findings were sent to Massey on 4 October and became the basis of a wide-ranging program of retrenchment. The Police got off lightly – apart from the salary cuts suggested for all state servants. Of the 41 departments closely scrutinised, it was one of only seven where no specific reduction of expenditure was recommended.[3] O'Donovan's advocacy and the degree of economy already practised explained this. Even so, in the next financial year, 1922/23, expenditure on the Force fell by 8.1 per cent, more sharply than total government spending. In part this reflected a second salary cut in July 1922.[4] More significantly, the Police Department underspent the money voted for it by £27,472, or 7.3 per cent. Such restraint stood in sharp contrast with 1920/21, when its spending (largely on salaries) had been just within the appropriation. Underspending was characteristic of other departments such as Health and Education, but it was achieved more rigorously and consistently by the Police, with only two exceptions (1931 and 1936) in the remaining inter-war years. In 1922 travelling expenses and building maintenance (the most costly items after salaries and house allowances) were pared back substantially. Expenditure on buildings increased when prosperity returned between 1923 and 1926, but a tight rein was kept on transport.

1922 to 1925

In the eyes of the government, Arthur H. Wright, who became Commissioner on 1 January 1922, was a man for the times, 'certainly not a man', as his Minister put it, 'who would run the country into unnecessary expense'.[5] He was the second in seniority of the Superintendents from amongst whom the government looked for a successor to John O'Donovan. Besides seniority, length of service yet to run was a consideration. Late in 1921, John Dwyer at Christchurch was on the eve of retirement, while Joseph McGrath at Dunedin had just eighteen months to go. But S.P. Norwood at Wellington was due to retire only two months before Wright.[6] Personal qualities were obviously important.

Wright shared some common features of background and experience with Norwood. Both were English-born, and had joined the New Zealand Constabulary Force in 1882 at the age of 21. Both were Anglicans – a fact unlikely to be ignored by a Cabinet sensitive to sectarian pressure from the Protestant Political Association.[7] More importantly, both had been clerks and so were quickly drafted into the district offices which provided a career path for three of the four Commissioners appointed in the inter-war years. There the parallels ended. Wright's capabilities quickly shone. In 1890 he obtained the only first class certificate issued for a police examination. Eight years later he was promoted to Sergeant, two years ahead of Norwood. On 1 January 1906 he was promoted to Sub-Inspector and appointed Chief Clerk and Accountant on the Commissioner's staff, then a position of some authority and responsibility.[8] There he remained until, following the recommendations of the 1909 Royal Commission, he was in 1911 promoted to Inspector and sent to take charge of his first district at Thames. As Superintendent in Auckland from September 1919, he knew at first hand the pressures on the Force. But above all he was well practised in economy.

One area of retrenchment in 1922 was beyond Wright's control. The Public Expenditure Adjustment Act passed in January 1922 provided for a substantial reduction by three instalments in the salaries of all state servants. Such an expedient had been raised but not clearly recommended by the 'Economies Committee'.[9] When public servants were granted a substantial pay increase from April 1920 to meet the rising cost of living, it had been agreed that the increase would be revised in line with changes in the cost of living. Although the latter continued to move upwards, no further adjustment was made. When, however, living costs began to fall in 1921, the government saw itself justified in cutting salaries – albeit in an arbitrary manner. In 1920 a flat-rate increase had benefited most those at the bottom of the scale; the flat-rate reductions in 1922 worked in the opposite direction. Together, the cuts of 1 January and 1 July brought reductions ranging from 6 per cent in the salaries of Superintendents to 10 per cent in the wages of newly appointed constables. Indeed the application of the statutory salary reductions to police wage scales disadvantaged NCOs and constables. In June an Adjustment Committee was established to deal with anomalies. At its first meeting, Wright secured an exemption for District and Native Constables, and Police Surgeons, on the grounds that as part-time staff they had not received the usual cost of living bonuses. The Commissioner also sought relief from the second cut for the 'wages men' of the Force, since they had given up more than was required in the first reduction. A small concession was given, but this was insufficient to bring the income loss of the rank and file into line with that of public servants on an equivalent salary.[10]

The cuts produced conflict. There had been a growing sense of independence amongst the police representatives on the PSA. In 1921 the PSA conceded that they could deal directly with the Commissioner on purely police matters, 'falling back upon the full Association's power in the event of their not securing satisfaction'.[11] Independence also implied separate treatment. When the Public Expenditure Adjustment Bill was introduced, policemen were disconcerted. They believed Massey had suggested their wages would not be touched. In fact Massey followed the advice of the 'Economies Committee', which had ruled out any exemptions – and this view was shared by the PSA.[12] Policemen had shared in the 1920 pay increase negotiated by the public service unions. Why should they be exempt from cuts? The unpalatable consequences of collaboration were apparent – more especially as the PSA, along with the other organisations of state servants, began to move closer to the 'militant' Alliance of Labour. Fifty police members of the PSA in Wellington met as the bill was about to become law and denounced talk of 'extreme action' by some civil servants. Following the lead of their representatives on the executive, they too decided to resign from the PSA, with the intention of forming a police association.[13] Wellington delegates met Wright, who was known to oppose rank and file links with the PSA, but was also concerned that a police association might weaken his control of the Force.[14] The Commissioner wanted evidence that Wellington men represented the views of their fellows elsewhere. Yet he did not offer another ballot similar to that of 1918. Nor did the Wellington men seek the good offices of the PSA to assist them. Instead their search for proof engendered disunity and revealed confusion. Remembering the fate of the Police Association begun there in 1913, 60 members of the Auckland branch voted on 8 March 1922 to remain in the PSA.[15]

This did not imply militancy on the part of the Aucklanders. Rather they looked for representation free from the Commissioner's influence and uncompromised by political affiliation or the threat of 'unconstitutional action' (strikes). In February, Constable J. Coutts, secretary of the Auckland branch, turned down an invitation to hear Labour MPs and the secretary of the Post and Telegraph Officers' Association attack the government's retrenchment policies. He sent the cyclostyled letter to his superior officer with the comment that the Labour Party 'no doubt think it is an opportune time to gain some influence over members of the Force'.[16] Instead, the Detective Sergeant responsible for political surveillance reported on the meeting. Resentment at the wage cuts coupled with fears that the PSA was becoming 'too militant' now led large numbers of constables to 'defect'. By June less than a third of the Force were represented by the Association. Its executive therefore resolved that 'no good purpose could be gained by proceeding with Police matters'.[17] Policemen could retain membership, but their subscriptions would not be collected for the time being. When the number of police members reached 350, the PSA would again become active on their behalf. Resignations of policemen continued – 500 had left the Association by August. But the hope of many for a police association remained unrealised. Wright gave it no encouragement. Members of the Force remained prohibited from any 'combination' other than the PSA. Attempts to organise their own association could be 'severely dealt with as subversive of discipline'.[18] For this reason, perhaps, the offer of the PSA to assist was not taken up. And so, unlike their counterparts in Australia and Britain, New Zealand policemen from July 1922 lacked 'a mouthpiece'.[19]

Discontented men could write to the Commissioner, but only on their own behalf, 'every man being held to be the best judge of his own grievances'. Complainants had to be both resolute and deferential. Reports 'disrespectful in tone or of a frivolous nature' could bring 'severe punishment'. And the disaffected who dared to complain also courted trouble by having to submit reports through their immediate superiors.[20] Cynics believed that some matters never reached the Commissioner.[21] As a constituent, a constable could turn to his MP – though if discovered using 'influence' on matters of discipline, promotion or transfer, he was 'liable to immediate dismissal'.[22] Matters of pay and conditions were safer ground. They could be raised by backbenchers in general terms, and were from 1922, particularly by Labour MPs.

More covertly, the rank and file could turn to the newspapers, especially the Wellington-based weekly claiming the largest nationwide circulation, *New Zealand Truth*.[23] Its banner, 'The People's Paper', summed up a populist tone and search for scandal. Stories of oppressive or bungling police methods, appearing more frequently in the late 1920s, were seen as red meat for the 'little men'. Getting a 'scoop' often required assistance from the Force, particularly the 'Ds'. And so the paper's critical edge was turned increasingly against the 'bosses' of the Department, the Commissioner and his Minister.[24] For some of their grievances, then, the rank and file could find a voice, albeit one of variable quality and doubtful influence.

Dissatisfaction amongst the Wellington men was picked up by newspapers in January 1923.[25] Leave seemed difficult to get. In the middle of a seamen's strike that had lasted since November had come a general election campaign involving much uncompensated overtime. According to a correspondent writing in February under a nom de plume to *Truth* and then to the *Dominion*, men chafed at other aspects of the Force's regimen.[26] Police boxers were debarred from entering public contests – a claim admitted by Superintendent Norwood at Wellington ('to preserve the dignity of the Force'),[27] but denied by Wright.[28] On the monthly pay day, notionally free afternoons were 'forfeit' for a general 'inspection parade'. And the system of discipline seemed harsh: 'motes', as *Truth* put it, could be 'magnified into beams'.[29]

Working hours were a source of widespread discontent. Different sections in the Force perceived disparities. NCOs in charge of suburban stations often worked twelve-hour days for no extra pay; the 'eight-hour system' made permanent by Wright a year earlier[30] was still not applied to some of the smaller towns; beat men averaging only one Sunday off a month looked with envy at district office staff working a five and a half day week. A six-day week and the ' "leave" question' were later raised in the House by W.J. Jordan (a Labour MP who had been a London 'bobby') and Wilford (now the Leader of the Opposition). In reply, the new Minister, C.J. Parr, supported the Commissioner's postion that leave would be given only when men could be spared. Parr was 'not aware of any complaints in that direction', nor that constables 'would prefer to work only on six days and be paid for six'.[31] In such a manner Minister and Commissioner alike dismissed the unsourced complaints echoed by politicians and newspapers. Without recognised representatives, the rank and file were hobbled in establishing their claims.

For the Commissioner, police wastage was more worrisome than words. In 1922/23 the rate at which men left the Force rose to its highest point between the wars (figure 1.1). Resignations compounded the pressures on the men remaining. In his first annual report, written in July 1922, Wright rehearsed a familiar theme that was soon taken up by *Truth*: there were far fewer police in relation to population in New Zealand than in any of the Australian states, and their cost per head was much lower. There were also, in proportion to population, fewer police than 40 years earlier; but work done then for other departments 'is not to be compared with that done now'. Districts had asked for a total of 70 more men. After 'giving full consideration to the economical aspect', the Commissioner recommended an increase of 'at least fifty'.[32] This fell on deaf ears. The Force's total strength *fell* by six in the year to April 1923. Recruitment had failed to keep pace with wastage. Men were offering, but some recruits had 'only just come up to the standard'.

Disgruntled older constables and NCOs feared the effects of 'undersized and under age' juniors on the streets: 'the habitual criminal sizing [them] up ... carries on' as before.[33] Wright saw higher pay rates in Australian forces siphoning off both potential recruits and men from his Force. In addition, an 'unusually large number' of young constables had left to 'better themselves' as economic conditions improved in New Zealand. For an economy-minded Cabinet, the Commissioner underlined the point in July 1923: since it cost £100 to produce an 'efficient' constable, the recent loss of 50 trained men was 'a serious and expensive matter'.[34]

This comment applied with even greater force to the Detective Branch, weakened by loss of staff during the previous two years. Amongst its members there was lingering resentment at the outcome of the Committee of Inquiry in 1919. The Branch 'should be a separate unit', with its own 'chief inspector of detectives' and higher pay scales, a detective told a *Dominion* reporter in November 1923.[35] Chief Detectives, in charge of the Detective Offices in the four main centres, were equal in rank to Senior Sergeants in the Uniform Branch and had to wait their turn for promotion. Because of his poor pay and lack of prospects in the Force, 45 year old Chief Detective Alfred Ward left to become Chief Inspector for the New Zealand Racing Conference in 1921.[36] In the year to April 1922 seven other detectives also resigned, and the total number of detectives in the four main centres fell from 36 to 29.[37] Commissioner O'Donovan, however, did not regard the common seniority list as sacrosanct. Just before his retirement in December 1921, he promoted Detective Sergeant 'Jimmie' Cummings to Senior Detective over the heads of seven other Detective Sergeants and a large number of uniformed men qualified for promotion and with longer service. Immediately, 'grave dissatisfaction' rumbled from the ranks of the Force to the ears of reporters.[38] Amongst detectives a strong feeling that overwork was inadequately compensated for by allowances deepened discontent. Between 1920 and 1922, the number of files on 'serious crime' went up by 40 per cent, with an increase in the number of burglaries reported from 573 to 872.[39] Detectives' hours of work were not limited to eight per day – the 1919 Committee of Inquiry had considered that this 'would be detrimental to the proper performance' of their duties.[40] Yet the allowances which recognised their long hours and out-of-pocket expenses had not been increased since 1919. And the margins which these gave over the wages of the uniformed men shrank substantially with the 1920 pay rise.

In 1922 Superintendent McGrath urged Wright to seek increased allowances for detectives.[41] But 'strict economy' remained the rule. Instead, Wright sought to appease by promoting three men (in order of seniority) to Senior Detective. The regulation requiring two years experience in uniform before entering the Detective Office was waived; 'preference' was to be given to 'younger and more energetic men'.[42]

Staff numbers at Auckland, where the pressure was greatest, were increased from eight to eleven – at the expense of Wellington and Christchurch. In June the Commissioner also tried to establish regular hours of work in the main Detective Offices, with alternating seven and ten hour days, every second Sunday off, and one half day a week. However, these hours could 'only be followed when the duty in hand is normal'.[43] Such conditions were rare in Auckland. When, early in September 1923, the hours of duty were extended to midnight, *Truth* gave vent to a pent-up frustration: 'It is notorious that the detective staff in Auckland has for long been disgracefully undermanned, making for very long hours and great strain on the few who are available for plain-clothes work, [and] the delaying of investigations'. Longer hours were the 'last straw'. An Auckland detective rarely had a night off, and indeed 'considered himself fairly lucky' if he got home by 10 pm. He was thus 'a comparative stranger to his wife and children'. And from the point of view of 'the public', 'a sweated police force is a distinct menace to society and an encouragement to crime.' To keep 'good men' in the Force, and attract others to join, the 'remedy is simple .... PAY GOOD WAGES and work the police reasonable hours'.[44]

By now the Minister was getting the message. Morale was clearly slipping. A series of parliamentary questions on police grievances (especially from Jordan) coincided in July 1923 with reports which indicated, as one put it, that the Force was 'suffering one of its periodical seasons of depression'.[45] When asked early in August about police pay, Parr replied that he was examining the matter 'carefully'. His attention was further concentrated by an amendment moved to the Police estimates (a rare event) on the grounds that detectives received travelling allowances at a lower rate than other public servants. Massey assured the House that money would be found to put matters right – 25 further men would be employed in response to Wright's repeated request for 50.[46] Meanwhile rumours reached the Commissioner of an attempt to form a police association in Auckland, and uniformed Sergeants in the south added their grievances to those of detectives and beat men in the north.[47] The Police role had been crucial in the employers' victory over striking seamen in January.[48] But would the rank and file remain loyal? After a ballot of its members, the Alliance of Labour threatened a general strike against wage cuts. In July the West Coast miners stopped work. There was unrest amongst railwaymen.[49] In September 1923, as in April 1919, the government decided that 'there were special circumstances' warranting 'a small increase in pay'. From 1 October constables received an extra 6d a day, while margins were increased for NCOs and detectives. Parr saw the latter as 'especially deserving'. Their increased allowances were a 'special recognition of satisfactory work accomplished'.[50]

The government's concession was small but significant. Public servants received no pay rise until April 1924, and railwaymen who struck in that month suffered an extension of hours. Not until 1925 did the Arbitration Court award a general wage increase.[51] For the time being, covert police complaints to the press were stilled. Indeed there was apparently 'no sympathy' amongst the rank and file for the 600 Melbourne police who struck and were quickly sacked between 31 October and 2 November 1923.[52] After visiting Melbourne, Senior Sergeant C.W. Lopdell, who had represented the views of beat constables to the 1919 Inquiry, declared pay and conditions to be better in the New Zealand Force.[53] While prosperity lasted over the next three years, men continued to leave the Force looking for something better, but not at the same rate as hitherto. Until June 1926 at least, the 'abundance of private employment' also reduced the pool of potential recruits. Though 'candidates' to join the Force were more than sufficient to fill the vacancies, some men (Wright grumbled) had to be accepted who 'only just come up to the standard height and chest measurement'.[54] In August 1924 Parr felt that 'the Force was fairly well satisfied' with 'what they got six months ago'. More staff in the cities 'would ease the duties of the men, and would perhaps satisfy them as well as an increase in pay'.[55] Parr reflected the priorities of Wright. For the Commissioner and his senior officers, a mounting concern for morale during 1923 soon gave way to an ongoing preoccupation with the adequacy of the Force and its facilities.

Wright had been forthright in July 1923: police 'strength' had been 'kept down solely in the interest of economy'. It was 'impossible to meet the present requirements of the public without materially increasing the Force.' The 24 men added by March 1924 made little impression on the appetite for staff. By this time the total number of extra men asked for by districts had risen to 83, three-quarters of them needed in the three largest cities. Public works and prosperity in the provinces also brought demands for more police, especially in the settlements adjacent to the North Island main trunk railway line. Bookmaking, made illegal by the Gaming Act of 1920, existed 'in most towns and villages' as well as the cities, and was 'not so easy to suppress'.[56]

The Commissioner did not accept uncritically requests from officers in charge of districts. After all, they had been enjoined not merely to maintain 'an effective Force' but also to build up 'reserves'.[57] Auckland's Superintendent C.W. Hendrey, for one, might be suspected of interpreting this instruction liberally by asking 'urgently' for 35 more men. As a rough and ready yardstick, Wright employed the most favourable ratio of police to population recently achieved, that for 1915. Using this 'standard' in July 1924, he judged the Force to need 'at least 45 more men'. Another 25 were conceded by the government. In 1925, Wright again failed to press fully the claims of his officers when they asked for a further 89 men. (Auckland, which had gained five, now wanted another 37.) If granted, this number would bring the Force's strength to 'considerably more' than the notional 'standard'. With a sense of what was possible rather than desirable, he asked for and was granted yet another 25 men.[58]

Wright fared better with buildings. Perhaps he pressed harder; certainly, the need for maintenance was more visible and less costly than increased manpower. In 1922/23, expenditure on police premises fell to the lowest level (except for 1918/19) since the turn of the century. This was false economy, warned the Commissioner. Buildings in disrepair would soon have to be replaced. The five men at Hawera were still in offices long since condemned by the local Medical Officer of Health.[59] Eketahuna police station was unsafe to lean against because of borer, the local MP was told.[60] At Kawhia the police dwelling had become 'uninhabitable due to leaky roof and borer', and the local constable had retreated to a farm he owned nearby.[61] Married men could not be stationed in settlements such as Leeston near Christchurch and Ohura in the Wanganui District because of a lack of adequate premises. Fortunately loan-based expenditure from the Public Works Fund increased more markedly than did spending from the Consolidated Fund between 1923 and 1925. And so Wright was 'pleased to say' in July 1925 that police premises were 'fast approaching a satisfactory condition'.[62] Yet this represented a backlog of maintenance made up, rather than a substantial refurbishing and investment for future development. With facilities, as with manpower, the chance to make significant improvements before prosperity began to evaporate was missed.

1926 to 1930

The years 1923 to 1925 were the most prosperous of the 1920s. Officers in charge of districts reported (with respect to the summer months at least) that 'work and money appear to be plentiful', with 'practically no unemployment'. Totalisator receipts at race meetings were increasing. Conventional wisdom on the relationship between working-class want and crime seemed confirmed by the changing pattern of police business: there were more arrests for drunkenness and related offences, and fewer reports of 'offences against the rights of property'.[63] However, in June 1926 there was a sharp downturn in the precarious prosperity of the farm-based economy. The usual winter peak of seasonal unemployment was some four and a half times larger than the year before, and the numbers of registered unemployed did not fall away significantly as summer approached. Henceforth there was a permanent pool of jobless which became larger each winter until, in 1929, recession turned into the Great Depression of the early 1930s.[64] Again the changing 'barometer of crime' was seen to be a 'reflex of economic conditions'. Arrests for drunkenness began to fall steeply; so too did reports of common assault. Relatively few incidents of serious violence came to police attention. For Superintendent Wohlmann in Auckland, the rising numbers of property crimes reported, particularly in winter, went 'hand in glove with times of financial stress' amongst the casual labourers congregating in the city.[65] Yet in Christchurch a similar expectation was not realised: 'considering the amount of unemployment there has been', Inspector Allan Cameron observed in August 1927, 'we have got through the winter with very little crime'.[66]

Much of the steady growth of routine police work in the late 1920s did not stem from the changing economic climate. It came rather from the continuing process of population change and the rapidly growing use of motor vehicles. Cities and the largest provincial towns continued to expand, causing marked disparities in the overall workloads of police districts, those of Auckland and Hamilton being roughly one and a half times those of Wellington and Christchurch, and three and a half times that of Dunedin (figure 4.2). Sergeants and constables at the declining Central Otago towns of Lawrence and Clyde, for example, enjoyed quiet lives in comparison to the two constables at busy Frankton Junction near Hamilton or the overworked one at Mt Albert in Auckland. Calls for service and increased surveillance came particularly from the outer suburbs of Auckland, Wellington, and Christchurch. Whether or not there was an increasing sense of insecurity may be debated. 'So far', *Truth* conceded in 1927, 'there has been very little crime in the suburbs, but the real problem is that of the larrikin'; there had been a 'big crop of complaints' following rampant 'orchard-raiding' at St Martins on the fringe of Christchurch.[67] Motorised crime and disorder was also a source of gradually mounting concern about careless 'speeding'; 'joy-riders' who 'converted' cars; the more affluent youths whose access to cars facilitated noisy 'keg parties' in Aranui (Christchurch);[68] or sheep-stealers in the North Island who used lorries.[69] The Motor Vehicles Act of 1924 provided some means of regulation and control; the number of breaches dealt with by the Police rose from 494 in 1925 to 5,035 in 1930. But the Department lacked both the manpower for sustained enforcement and cars for use in patrolling the suburbs and pursuing offenders. How to make the best use of limited resources was the perennial question which faced a new Commissioner in 1926.

In November 1925, Commissioner Wright informed his Minister that he would retire the following January after 43 years in the Force.[70] His recommendation for his successor is not known, but the press quickly saw only two of the Superintendents as contenders: W.B. McIlveney and C.R. Broberg.[71] Both had made their mark as detectives; both (for the first time) were New Zealand-born. At 55, Broberg was three years younger than McIlveney and had joined the Force just over a year later in 1895. However, he had drawn level with McIlveney in seniority when both were appointed Sub-Inspector on the same date in 1915. Indeed both had passed over others on their way to commissioned rank.[72] In 1918 Commissioner O'Donovan brought Sub-Inspector Broberg to assist him at Headquarters, where he remained under

Commissioner Wright, rising to the rank of Superintendent and acting in effect as an assistant Commissioner.[73]

William Bernard McIlveney won the support of the Cabinet, nonetheless. His wider experience caught the eye of the politicians: first as a chief detective employed on special tasks at Headquarters, and later as Inspector in the Wellington District from 1919, then as Superintendent in charge. By 1912 his 'record' was already 'an exceedingly creditable one' in the view of J.A. Hanan, the Minister of Justice. 'For difficult and special work calling for high intelligence and mental alertness, resource, knowledge of the law, and business law, he stands out'.[74] Amongst fellow officers he alone had visited Scotland Yard (in 1907) and studied police methods in Los Angeles and San Francisco (in 1923).[75] Wellington businessmen had praised him for organising the effective protection of strike-breakers during the seamen's strike of 1922–23. His 'vigorous personality' invited vivid pen protraits from *Truth* reporters who were impressed by 'the dominant mental force of the probing eyes', 'shrewd common sense', signs of 'self-assurance', and the 'crisp staccato' speech of a 'man who ... means what he says.'[76] Clearly he was not shy of publicity – as was seen when the 'new broom' set to work.

On the last Friday of February 1926, over 100 city and suburban men paraded at the Wellington Central police station to hear an address from the new Commissioner. A new style of leadership became apparent: more rigorous, visible, and ultimately controversial. Where Wright was a 'very quiet man' known only to the constables who delivered his evening paper, McIlveney was 'flamboyant' and soon recognised by the Wellington beat men who had to salute him in the street to show they had their 'eyes open'.[77] Unlike O'Donovan and Wright, McIlveney visited the districts: Auckland and Christchurch a number of times, while Whangarei had its first visit by a Commissioner in 22 years.[78] At the Central stations men were assembled to hear the Commissioner speak – for two and a half hours at Christchurch.[79] Some young constables saw in his eloquence evidence of great ability and learning; others found him 'extremely arrogant, bumptious, overbearing and officious'.[80] McIlveney gave tacit approval to press reports of his speeches until this became counter-productive. To the Wellington men, McIlveney spelt out the 'qualifications which were necessary for the efficiency of the Force – loyalty, co-operation, strict adherence to duty, duty to the public', and the 'efficient exercise of authority with which they were invested'. He also promised them 'every support'.[81] Indeed, a few days later he introduced, on trial, a changed pattern of shifts to give beat men a full 24 hours off duty three times a week. And he promised to consider 'suitable alterations' in the uniforms of Sergeants and constables to meet the 'extremes of climate'.[82] In August he established an independent board, chaired by W.G. Riddell SM, to conduct the annual police examinations in place of the Commissioner, who had hitherto made the final decision in allotting marks. With a 'square deal' for his men, McIlveney hoped to make 'this fine force of mine one large happy family'.[83]

However the manner in which the Commissioner pursued efficiency and economy unsettled some both inside and outside the Force. By July 1926 the districts had asked for a total of 77 more men. McIlveney thought another 50 would cope with 'the more urgent contingencies'. Cabinet granted an extra 25.[84] Meanwhile, McIlveney tried to relieve the pressure on staffing in other ways. Within days of taking office he revoked O'Donovan's arrangement of four 'Divisions' supervised by Superintendents, a move later criticised as 'centralisation'. He believed that there was duplication of work; Superintendents could do more in their own districts.[85] The closure of the Dunedin Exhibition in May allowed a Sergeant and eighteen constables to be redeployed, particularly to the Hamilton District and Wellington. 'Short-handed' Aucklanders felt neglected.[86]

But above all else, the Commissioner sought increased police efficiency in the 'integrity and strict devotion to duty' of his men,[87] rather than in new methods and technology. The need for economy reinforced his conservative inclinations. Regulations in the 'Black Book' were applied more strictly in an attempt to enhance the authority and standing of the Force by tightening up on 'laxity'. To 'smarten the appearance of the men', McIlveney reverted to distinctive features of the police uniform before 1912 that were redolent of the 'armed constabulary days': a tunic with silver buttons and no pockets, and a military-style shako (with a new badge) for day duty in fine weather; the Commissioner also had a more elaborate uniform made for himself.[88] Uniforms were to be worn at all times, an instruction directed particularly at the country men and constables travelling on escort duty; however, the Commissioner, in his 'bun' hat, 'swallow-tailed' coat, 'ministerial' trousers and walking stick, was exempt.[89] Greater secrecy was to be observed regarding information gathered by the Police – to the frustration of papers such as *Truth* and the Christchurch *Star*.[90] Inspection of stations was restricted to a few public servants, so that (for example) a Christchurch MP had difficulty obtaining access to the local police cells.[91] 'False friends' such as the 'mischief-making slanderer', the 'less you do the better off you are' types, and those who offered gratuities, were to be watched carefully.[92]

Looking to recoup costs and remove 'improper practices', McIlveney cut into 'privileges' enjoyed both within the Force and by some individuals, firms, clubs, and local authorities who sought its services. From April, constables at one-man stations had to pay for office lighting. Nor would the Department supply equipment for horses where an allowance for a private horse or car was given. In future, police rewards would be 'confined strictly' to the suppression of sly-grogging, and to 'meritorious conduct ... clearly exceeding what might be reasonably expected from an efficient member of the Force.' The 'long recognised' practice of giving rewards for convictions in licensing and gaming cases was ruled out. So too were Defence Department rewards when military defaulters were convicted, and the Wellington Acclimatisation Society's payments for zeal in enforcing the game regulations.[93] Instead, with an eye on bookmakers, the Commissioner insisted on 'strict enforcement of the statutory law ... honestly and faithfully, without laying improper traps or having recourse to dishonourable or even doubtful practices.'[94] Nor were the men to receive any 'private reward or gratuity' without the Commissioner's approval.[95] He had in mind payments made by racing clubs to uniformed constables on duty at their meetings, or to detectives who removed 'prohibited' people and escorted cash from the course. Constables with a Saturday afternoon off duty could see a rugby game free (but without payment) if they turned up in uniform prepared to help with crowd control. Citing the recommendations of the 1919 Desborough Committee on the British police, McIlveney now decreed that any 'special services' supplied by the police would be paid for by those asking for them. Payment would be to the Department, not to individual policemen. This arrangement, applying particularly to race meetings and 'gold' (money) escort duty, was either a 'dangerous innovation' ('Taxpayer') or 'long overdue' ('Ex-officer').[96]

The 'infection of police headquarters by the virus of sordid money-making'[97] had its most tangible effects on traffic control. In Auckland the new means of transport was becoming 'a serious problem'. Motor vehicles went ever more frequently and faster along its new concrete roads: in 1924, 19 people were killed and 113 injured there, with 153 collisions reported. Fourteen constables were fully employed (on hourly shifts) directing traffic at seven points in the city. During the Christmas holidays, when very large crowds went to the Ellerslie races and Epsom trots, another sixteen men did point duty.[98] It was testing work. 'Are the worst men put on?', wondered an Automobile Association member. City councillors asked that only experienced men do the duty, and that there be 'uniformity of signals'.[99] In April 1926 McIlveney issued detailed instructions on traffic control, including standard hand signals, and emphasised the need for pointsmen to be 'extremely civil in manner and speech'. Officers were to ensure sufficient 'police supervision at intersections'.[100] Three months later the policy changed abruptly. The Commissioner gave notice that agreements with the Auckland, Wellington and Christchurch city councils to provide police for traffic control would soon end. Unless subsidies for the men on point duty were increased greatly, they would be returned to the beat. The Department now recognised 'no obligation or responsibility' for traffic control – there were simply not enough policemen. All three councils thought it cheaper to appoint their own traffic inspectors, though Auckland was disconcerted at now having to control the 'Race

Traffic'. Newmarket borough, with its busy thoroughfare, renewed its agreement; the Papakura town board protested at being left to control its traffic.[101] The Police retained an important role in enforcing the traffic law.[102] But henceforth the main responsibility lay with local authorities, and ultimately with the Transport Department established in 1929.

By the end of 1926 the fourteen pointsmen had been released for patrol duties in Auckland. The Commissioner felt 'satisfied' that the Force had 'never been more efficient'.[103] Construed in different ways, this claim was probably widely accepted. Peter Fraser, speaking for other Labour MPs, applauded the Commissioner's determination to reduce the time spent on attending to 'private concerns' and to withdraw 'rewards offered for mean actions'.[104] For its part, the Racing Conference (a prime example of an influential 'private concern' in the eyes of some Labour MPs) appreciated the successful prosecution of 'prominent bookmakers'.[105] 'McIlveney's Giants', the 80 hand-picked men who accompanied a royal tour in the early months of 1927, were praised for effectively restraining 'over-enthusiastic crowds' with 'kindness'.[106] And those who accepted 'the fact that we are a law-abiding community' (in the Labour MP John A. Lee's phrase) generally saw this as owing much to the Police. Yet there were 'odd occurrences' which (as Lee put it in 1928) left 'one in doubt as to the efficiency at times' of the Force.[107] He had in mind the police handling of the 'Burwood murder' in Christchurch. This was to be overshadowed in 1929 by the 'Elsie Walker case' and the panic engendered by two Christchurch arsonists. Lee did not, however, share the fears of those who perceived a lack of police protection against an upsurge of burglary and theft.

In April 1927 Superintendent Wohlmann announced that there was an 'epidemic' of burglary in Auckland. New cases were being reported at the rate of one a night. (For a population of over 190,000 this was roughly two and a half times the national rate for 1927, though minuscule in the light of later experience.) To the *New Zealand Herald* it was 'disquieting' that the police seemed 'to have had little success in tracing the criminals', confirming that the city's Detective Office was short-handed and lacked sufficient 'experienced men'. McIlveney soon reacted. Within weeks five detectives were sent north from the other three cities.[108] The Commissioner used the departure of the two Wellington men as the occasion for an extravagant speech, ostensibly of a 'private instructional' nature but pitched at an wider audience. He painted Auckland as 'overrun with criminals' while the 'police there were like telegraph poles, they were so numerous'. McIlveney declared 'war to the death' on Auckland's criminals, telling his detectives to use the vagrancy clauses of the Police Offences Act which he had had strengthened the year before; these gave 'power to keep the place clean and get the criminal out of the way'.[109] But his implicit criticism of Auckland police, particularly its energetic Chief Detective James

Cummings and his men, provoked 'great indignation': it was 'utter rubbish', responded J.W. Poynton, the senior magistrate, echoed by Justice Herdman from the Supreme Court and by the mayor, who pointed to McIlveney's exaggerated and contradictory statements. The local detectives found a speedy answer: 'Criminal Gang Smashed', said headlines two days later. In Parliament, the Minister of Justice claimed that McIlveney had been misreported. 'Undesirable publicity' had redounded on the Commissioner, in whom confidence began to erode.[110]

Auckland's 'crime wave' soon receded, leaving behind it a small increase in staff – 'sufficient for all requirements', according to McIlveney[111] – and some changes in organisation and methods. Complaints that there was no effective surveillance of the suburbs led to a regular night patrol during the winter. Two plain-clothes men on a 'delapidated' motorcycle kept watch on outlying shops, telephone and letter boxes, and other 'property open to mischief and theft'. For Superintendent Wohlmann, this had 'very satisfactory results' and was 'very much more economical' than opening more one-man suburban stations. He asked for two fast machines for the next winter. Meanwhile a mounted constable was stationed at New Lynn, and another joined the 'foot constable' at Mt Albert. In 1928, for the first time, McIlveney urged that commissioned officers and detectives be provided with cars, while arguing that a wireless-equipped car patrol would be 'very costly' and not justified. However, each of the cities would soon need a 'squad of motor-cyclists'.[112]

Given the pressures for economy, administrative changes were easier to achieve. Auckland, Wellington and Christchurch districts each had a Superintendent, Inspector and Sub-Inspector in 1927. The number of men they supervised was similar in the two largest districts, but considerably less in Christchurch. Auckland, however, had 40 per cent more offence files than Wellington, and twice as many as Christchurch. The Commissioner sought to reduce the heavy workload of Auckland's Inspector (his younger brother), while increasing supervision of the detectives. In February 1928 a second Inspector was transferred to Auckland, which was subdivided into three 'co-ordinated' districts. Superintendent Wohlmann had direct control of the 'Head' district: the town and country stations beyond the isthmus and now including those at Huntly, Coromandel and Thames. Wohlmann was also responsible for overall financial management and for hearing the disciplinary cases of the 'Co-ordinated Districts'. In the 'Metropolitan' district, Inspector James McIlveney supervised the suburban stations. Inspector J.W. Hollis (a former detective who had been in charge of Whangarei District) was responsible for 'Central', which encompassed the inner-city and North Shore stations. All detectives were now stationed at Central and supervised by Hollis, who also controlled the few motor vehicles[113] and the local office of the Criminal Registration Branch that was established in June 1928.[114] The three officers were to confer daily on important matters in their districts. In the event of strong disagreement (there was none in practice), the Commissioner was to be telephoned for a decision. Through greater division of labour and more formalised consultation, McIlveney hoped 'to promote efficiency' and 'reduce administrative costs'. The new system, he claimed, was modelled on that of Scotland Yard and the most up-to-date in the world. Six months' trial 'proved a success'. The system was extended to Wellington and Christchurch in February 1929, then to Dunedin in April 1930.[115]

Change seemed to produce results. In Auckland, Wohlmann saw a 'very gratifying decrease in real crime' during 1928. Sceptics, however, saw little improvement in the clear-up rate for property offences.[116] And from June 1927, the 'Burwood murder' shifted the focus of those concerned about police efficiency to a 'steadily-growing list of unsolved mysteries'.[117] On 15 June the body of Miss 'Gwen' Scarff was found in scrub at Burwood on the outskirts of Christchurch; she had suffered extensive head wounds. Next day a blood-stained spanner was found nearby and the main suspect, Charles Boakes, a taxi-driver, was interviewed for eight hours. There were no fingerprints on the spanner, and no definite leads. Inspector Allan Cameron, in charge of the seven detectives working on the case, had 'nothing to say'. So with a zeal that police found 'interfering and obstructive', Christchurch *Star* reporters fed the 'intense interest' by following up those who were questioned. When a week passed with no arrest, the *Star* criticised the secrecy, comparing local police methods unfavourably with those of Scotland Yard. After a fortnight, the disquiet reached Parliament when a local MP asked whether 'outside experts' were needed. Not at all, replied the Minister. Nonetheless a reward was offered for information, and three North Island 'Ds' arrived to relieve local men. Finally, after six weeks, Boakes was arrested. Yet the police failed to sheet home their suspicions. Before packed Supreme Court galleries, the defence counsel, C.S. Thomas, played effectively on weaknesses in the circumstantial evidence, as did Justice Adams in his summing up. Boakes was acquitted of murder.[118] In seeing the result as 'very unsatisfactory', the *Otago Daily Times* caught the prevailing mood: 'Retribution has not over-taken the murderer, and justice has yet to be vindicated .... The smaller the community the more disturbing to the general sense of security, and the more destructive of absolute confidence in the resourcefulness of the police authorities, is the consequence'.[119]

So it proved in the case of Elsie Walker.[120] At 8 am on 2 October 1928, Mrs Constance Bayly of Papamoa rang Constable Jackson in Te Puke to report the disappearance overnight of a car and her seventeen year old niece. Preoccupied with court business and thinking Elsie might have returned to her parents at Raukokore, the constable did not notify other stations until the evening. His message reached Auckland at 9.40 pm. Next morning the car was found abandoned at Papatoetoe; another case of 'joy-riding', it seemed. Early in the evening of 5 October, a woman's body was found under scrub in a disused quarry near Panmure. Since he could see no suspicious circumstances, the local constable was told to take the body to the morgue for a post-mortem in the morning. Letters in the clothes suggested Elsie Walker had been found, and this was confirmed early next day. At the autopsy, the police surgeon, Dr Murray, and hospital pathologist, Dr Gilmour, could find no cause of death. They were as baffled as the police led by the experienced Detective Sergeant Tom Kelly were to be in tracing the young woman's movements before her death. Constable Jackson, alive to rumours that spread rapidly at Papamoa, suspected that Elsie's cousin, Bill Bayly, was involved. On 8 October Kelly interviewed Bayly and became satisfied he had been in Auckland in the critical period. With no evidence of foul play, the investigation was leisurely: police on the routes between Papamoa and Papatoetoe were asked to enquire. When nothing turned up, Kelly left by train on 17 October to cover the ground himself. Meanwhile *Truth* sensed a good story, and reporters were soon busy talking to police, Dr Gilmour, and locals at Papamoa. By 18 October it could confidently cast doubt on the 'fantastic' police theory that Elsie had driven almost 200 miles 'over moonlit mountain roads', then walked eight miles before dying of exhaustion. These doubts were to be decisive.[121]

As *Truth*'s stories unfolded the Commissioner called for urgent reports on the questions raised: 'no effort must be spared to clear the matter up as soon as possible'.[122] Kelly was recalled from Bay of Plenty, and replaced by Detective Sergeant James Bickerdike who (with others) went over the same ground again. By the time the inquest opened on 10 January 1929, a small number of police had interviewed about two thousand people (some, such as the Baylys, a number of times), taken 158 written statements and made 243 reports.[123] Yet detectives still knew little more than they had discovered in the first week of the inquiry. Nothing gave colour to *Truth*'s assertion that there was 'an infamous murderer at large'. Yet the police theory seemed implausible, and two months after their first report the doctors had changed ground: now the 'probable cause of death was concussion following a blow on the head'.[124] Also moved by strong doubts was Vincent Meredith, the Crown Solicitor briefed to appear for the Police at the inquest. He gave little credence to police statements clearing Bill Bayly. Thus Bayly, who did not figure in the police brief, became the focus of Meredith's cross-examination at the inquest. For his part, the Coroner, F.K. Hunt SM, displayed an increasingly critical view of police methods as the inquest proceeded.[125] In his finding, Mr Hunt opined that an unknown man had knocked Elsie Walker unconscious and driven the car. He drew attention to what he saw as 'mistakes that were made and the inefficient way the enquiries were carried out.' A public enquiry should be held at once: the 'public are entitled to a better service from the Police than they received in this case. It is possible that suspicion may rest against a perfectly innocent man for the rest of his life. This might have been avoided had prompt and intelligent enquiries been made.'[126] In fact, Meredith and Hunt ensured that weight was given to 'village tittle-tattle'.[127]

Elsie Walker's inquest caused a sensation, with public interest matching that which was to be engendered by the trials of Arthur Allan Thomas in the 1970s.[128] In December 1928, Thomas Wilford, who was sympathetic to the Police, had again become their Minister. He awaited reports (and pressure from the MP for Tauranga) before appointing Edward Page, a senior Wellington magistrate, as a Commission of Inquiry into the efficiency and conduct of the police in the case.[129] Four days before the inquiry opened in Auckland on 22 February, Superintendent Wohlmann received from the Crown Solicitor a comprehensive list of 'matters appearing to require explanation'.[130] Forewarned, policemen also came forearmed with eminent counsel and copies of the massive file. They almost crowded out the public from the inquiry, which lasted ten days. Page submitted his report on 20 March. He found no fault with police methods in the investigation; existing rules and regulations were adequate. Page concluded that 'the Police steps and enquiries, though they have failed to establish the manner of the girl's journey from Papamoa to Panmure, or the actual cause of her death, were prompt, thorough and exhaustive'.[131] McIlveney sent his 'heartiest congratulations' to the Auckland men. Wilford was euphoric: the inquiry had 'proved, as I have always contended, that there is no finer body of police in the world'. To the *New Zealand Herald*, however, the mystery remained 'a blot on their scutcheon'.[132] And the 'feeling of uneasiness'[133] turned into a nationwide outcry after two women who had said they had not seen Bayly at Papamoa on 1 October 1928 changed their evidence. Again *Truth* broke the story.[134] Hunt publicly recommended reopening the inquest.[135] Wilford resisted mounting pressure to do so, refusing to amend the Coroners Act to provide the necessary authority: the 'new evidence' was not credible,[136] and both Bayly and the Police needed protection from a coronial witch-hunt. As the agitation peaked in late 1929,[137] Wilford escaped to London as High Commissioner.

McIlveney probably rued the departure of such a stout defender of the police. The efficiency, methods, and administration of the Force had all been increasingly questioned. Quite apart from the Elsie Walker case, concern grew with the inability of Christchurch police to track down before December those behind a spate of burglaries and arson in the preceding six months. Wilford's explanation (on McIlveney's 'coaching'), that most of the fires were accidental and the police were being hampered by the press, did little to inspire confidence.[138] Complaints about police methods in taking statements also recurred in 1929; the Law Society Conference asked the Minister of Justice to investigate the matter.[139] Rumours in August that the officer commanding the New Zealand Army, Major-General R. Young, would soon retire to become Commissioner of Police were quashed by the Prime Minister.[140] For his part, McIlveney instructed his officers to keep him abreast of all serious crimes and any 'newspaper criticism'.[141] This was a response not just to editorial pressure to reopen Elsie Walker's inquest and fears about the Christchurch 'incendiaries'. It followed closely on a Christchurch solicitor's call for a Royal Commission to inquire into 'the whole system of the Police Force' which received wide publicity, though little overt support – except from *Truth*.[142] The lawyer (and *Truth*) felt there was 'a good deal of unrest in the lower ranks'. Indeed, the discontent of some city men had surfaced by the end of 1927. During that year recruits barely matched the numbers resigning. *Truth*, with typical hyperbole, spoke of a 'Starved Police Force Seething With Discontent' in which 'Parsimony Strangles Efficiency'.[143] Certainly, since McIlveney had taken the reins, departmental funding had barely increased and spending on police premises had fallen sharply (figure 1.4).

Truth focused on the 'underpaid and overworked' detectives to whom it looked for stories, attributing their lack of success to inadequate numbers, training and transport. However, the burning issues were pay and a desire for earlier retirement on superannuation.[144] A chance for these questions to be more openly pressed by the rank and file came in August 1928, when the Commissioner drafted a bill to amend the Police Force Act. This gave effect to a promise by the Minister, F.J. Rolleston, to appoint women police.[145] McIlveney took the opportunity to introduce other matters, especially the compulsory retirement of officers (other than the Commissioner) who had served 40 years and attained full superannuation rights before the age of 65.[146] With the bill in the offing, Wellington policemen sent a circular letter to all MPs pressing for retirement on superannuation at 55 years of age or after 35 years service, and for 'prompt steps' to bring New Zealand police pay into line with that of their peers across the Tasman. McIlveney supported this initiative, which explicitly disavowed unionism and reiterated 'loyalty to those in authority'.[147] With an election three months away, Opposition members could court votes while debating the Department's annual report. So the Reform goverment moved quickly, giving constables and NCOs an extra 1s a day, and adjusting the detectives' allowances.[148] Action on 'super' was promised. But this was a thorny issue involving questions of cost and parity with other civil servants, and in October 1928 the bill was deferred.[149]

During the next eighteen months discontent deepened within the Force while criticism mounted outside it. Raised hopes for earlier retirement were dashed. In Opposition, Wilford had expressed sympathy; as Minister, he responded positively to renewed pressure from the rank and file, but was unable to make the police a special case in the public service superannuation scheme.[150] Meanwhile, according to the Labour lawyer–MP W.E. Barnard, 'a great deal of unrest and dissatisfaction' arose over issues of discipline.[151] Though apparently solicitous for his men's welfare, McIlveney was also a martinet. Since 1926 the numbers dismissed or forced to resign had been higher than hitherto, and they rose to a peak in 1929/30, outnumbering voluntary resignations for the first time (figure 1.1). Coincidentally, transfers of serving policemen also seemed to increase, and the feeling grew that these were a 'form of punishment'. Constables 'do not feel quite secure in their job', the Labour MP Ted Howard observed of those in his Christchurch constituency.[152] Hanging over them was the 'guillotine' of section 9 of the Police Force Act 1913, by which the Commissioner could dismiss any constable 'unfit to remain in the Force'. In March 1929 the Court of Appeal confirmed that, under this provision, the Commissioner's authority was absolute and unfettered. Now 'Mussolini' McIlveney was 'unstoppable', telling his staff on parade that they could be dismissed 'with one stroke of my pen'.[153] Wilford backed up his Commissioner; but the Feilding businessman, J.G. Cobbe, who succeeded him as Minister on 18 December 1929 with barely a year of parliamentary experience, did not. In June 1930 another storm was raised by *Truth*. A Wellington Sergeant, G.F. Bonisch, was dismissed and refused leave to appeal. 'Numerous representations' flowed in on his behalf. Cobbe followed the Public Service Commissioner's advice and set up an 'informal' Appeal Board. Seeing his 'general control of the Force' to be undermined, McIlveney immediately applied to retire.[154]

Without pause or regret, Cabinet accepted McIlveney's resignation on 30 June. In taking exception to a 'purely administrative direction', the Commissioner had held 'a pistol' at the government, declared Cobbe.[155] Neither the Opposition nor the press disagreed. McIlveney had been energetic but scarcely an effective administrator. During his term public anxieties about police efficiency had increased, and the Force had failed to become a 'large happy family'. True, public expectations of policing were unrealistic, and the political pressures for economy inevitably bred red tape and discontent. But the Commissioner's rhetoric had been incautious, and his actions had often seemed arbitrary. Inconsistencies between rhetoric and behaviour had eroded McIlveney's credibility with police and politicians. By 1930 he had become a liability for the government. To the *New Zealand Herald*, the task was now 'to restore the force to the standard of efficiency expected by the public and demanded by the functions entrusted to it. That can be accomplished only if the commissioner has the qualities that command respect from the rank and file and enable him to enforce discipline without friction'.[156]

The *Herald* was trying to scotch suggestions that McIlveney's successor should come from outside the Force. Following a precedent, the government had appointed R.P. Ward, the Under-Secretary for Justice, to carry out the Commissioner's duties from 1 July while it made up its mind.[157] On 8 July Superintendent Ward George Wohlmann applied for the position. He was (as *Truth* had predicted) the obvious choice, and became Commissioner on 1 August. In both personality and background he was quite different to McIlveney. Aged 57, the 'quiet and unassuming' Wohlmann was both the youngest and the most senior of the four Superintendents. Like Commissioner Wright before him, he had spent much of his career as a District Clerk. His administrative skills had been tested when, as a Sub-Inspector seconded to be Commissioner of Police in Western Samoa between 1920 and 1922, he organised a new civilian force.[158] From 1930 Wohlmann's main challenge was to be maintaining morale while the need for economy intensified and the threat of disorder in the streets mounted.

1930 to 1935

A week before Wohlmann first sat at the Commissioner's desk in Wellington, Prime Minister George Forbes announced that his government faced a massive shift in its Budget, from a surplus in the previous financial year to a deficit in the current one of over £3 million.[159] Sharply falling revenue (especially from customs duties) reflected the onset of depression: export receipts were to fall by 37 per cent between 1929 and 1931; per capita incomes by up to 30 per cent between 1929 and 1933; and unemployment would rise to a peak estimated conservatively to have been 81,000 (or 12 per cent of the workforce) in July 1933. For politicians and economists alike, balancing the Budget was of critical importance, 'an article of faith rather than the product of economic reasoning'.[160] Forbes' view of the crisis was that while additional taxation would be necessary, half the prospective deficit could be removed by pruning expenditure.

On the same day – 24 July – Wohlmann was consulted by Commissioner Ward concerning the Police Force Amendment Bill that had been drafted by McIlveney in 1928 and still awaited ministerial approval. Because of the 'urgent necessity for strict economy', the two men recommended dropping the clauses which provided for an Assistant Commissioner and extended the retirement age beyond 65 where necessary to secure 40 years service for superannuation purposes (a provision that would have benefited McIlveney personally). Similarly, they recommended against the appointment of women police, believing that their ' "police value" ... would not be commensurate with the cost'. In the light of the Bonisch affair, they also proposed new clauses to increase the rights of policemen charged with disciplinary offences.[161] The bill did not proceed. However, Ward had already reinstated Sergeant Bonisch,[162] and Wohlmann was to prove 'softer' than McIlveney in dealing with defaulters. The annual average of fourteen men dismissed or forced to resign between 1926 and 1930 dropped to four during the next five years. The services of solicitors and leave to appeal were now routinely granted in disciplinary cases. Complaints of 'pin-pricking' discipline continued, but Appeal Boards did sometimes overturn charges that had been upheld by commissioned officers.[163] Wohlmann also showed more flexibility in allowing rewards, for example by reversing McIlveney's decision to refuse one for Constable A.T. Gillum, who had arrested the Christchurch 'incendiaries' in December 1929.[164] Accommodating rank and file sentiment, he soon withdrew the unpopular shako.[165] Yet the Commissioner 'sharply discouraged' any idea of a police union. On 7 August *Truth* advocated a 'Police Federation' on the British model. So too did unsigned typed letters posted a week later from Christchurch to the watch-house keepers in all District Headquarters stations. 'Cautious inquiries' revealed no hint of support for such a body.[166] Discipline was strong; economic realities outside the Force helped to keep it so.

From July 1930 the government's pruning knife cut ever more deeply into the public service. For the Police Force, the Training Depot was the first casualty. Recruitment ceased. Cuts were also made in travelling expenses and building maintenance. New buildings and lock-ups were urgently required for a number of smaller stations,[167] but none were begun. There was certainly now no prospect of the new gymnasium long desired by the Christchurch men. Nor was there of new vehicles, especially the motorcycles with sidecars for which Wohlmann had pressed while Superintendent in Auckland. Wohlmann abolished the Co-ordinated Districts in September, arguing that the number of both transfers and promotions needed to fill vacancies in Auckland would thereby be reduced. He had found his role as Superintendent in charge of a large district undercut by McIlveney's sub-divided administration of districts, which now reverted to the 'established principle of relative responsibility through the ranks'.[168] On 3 February 1931 Wohlmann met the 'Economy Committee' appointed by Cabinet to make more cuts. This found little room for further savings, paring only £1,699 from the Department's appropriation of £451,099. Indeed, 'in view of the difficult circumstances now prevailing', the Committee thought it not desirable to reduce Police strength.[169] A year later the same sentiment was expressed by the National Expenditure Commission (composed largely of businessmen instructed to seek further economies), which found the Police to be 'economically administered' and had no recommendation to make.[170] As a proportion of government expenditure, spending on the Force in 1932/33 was at the highest level it was to reach between the wars (figure 1.4).

Indeed the Police fared better than the public service as a whole during the Depression of the early 1930s. Frugally administered even in more prosperous years, the Force had less to lose than the Education or Defence Departments, for example. Between 1930/31 and 1932/33, spending on Police fell by 6.5 per cent, on Education by 19 per cent and on Defence by more than a third. These reductions, and their disparities, resulted largely from salary cuts and changes in staff numbers.

Where Defence costs were pared back by ending compulsory military training and reducing the Permanent and Territorial Forces, 50 more men were given to the Police Force in 1932. Financial straits and social unrest at home preoccupied the government's farmer and business politicians more than mounting tensions abroad. And their concern for police morale, especially in the cities, led them to treat the Force as a special case in another way. On 1 April 1931 all public servants, including police, had their salaries reduced by 10 per cent. A second cut followed a year later – but the Police escaped it by the Coalition government's sleight of hand. In conformity with the National Expenditure Adjustment Act 1932, a second 10 per cent cut in salaries was ostensibly made in the Police vote for 1932/33 and the next two years. However, it was replaced covertly – apparently after strong pressure on the government from meetings of police in Auckland and Wellington early in May 1932 (two weeks after the 'riots' in Auckland);[171] 'allowances to members of the Force for detective, clerical, and special duty' rose from £4,800 in 1931/32 to £43,000 the following year. Opposition Labour MPs soon smelt a rat. Peter Fraser thought it an 'extraordinary thing' that extra money was apparently available for the Police and Mental Hospital Departments: it would be 'far better to give people money to buy food and clothing than to spend money in locking them up.'[172] Not until October 1934 did Cobbe admit unambiguously that the 'special allowance' was in fact equivalent to the second pay reduction.[173] Thus the real income of many if not all police increased by about 10 per cent between 1929 and 1933 – much more than that of most wage and salary earners.[174]

While most wage and salary earners would not have worked overtime in the early 1930s, policemen and Police Matrons did. In theory they were not paid for it. Nonetheless the 'special allowance' was granted explicitly in recognition of the 'additional work and the long hours of duty imposed' by the prevailing conditions.[175] For the country as a whole, the total number of offence files had in fact peaked in 1930 and thereafter declined until 1935. This was the broad trend for reports of arson and robbery. Arrests for drunkenness fell by nearly 50 per cent in this period – by 1932 they were much lower than in any previous year since national police statistics began in 1878. So too with reports of common assault, which fell to their lowest point ever in 1934. While, in this respect at least, beat men might have had a quieter life, detectives and plain-clothes constables were more hard-pressed than ever. Murders rose to an inter-war peak in 1933, and the annual average for 1931–35 was nearly double that of 1926–30.[176] In the early 1930s, thefts and burglaries were also reported much more frequently than hitherto. 'Charge it up to Forbes', an unemployed steward said when refusing to pay for a meal; a maintenance defaulter told F.K. Hunt SM that he had broken a window so as to be gaoled and get work.[177] Typical of those in authority who refused to see unemployment as a context or an excuse was Justice Reed, who informed a Wellington grand jury that it was 'quite exceptional to find that destitution, due to the present economic conditions, has anything to do with the commission of crime'.[178] Even so, Auckland Superintendent Till's maxim – 'less drunkenness, more thieving'[179] – seemed to be borne out in most police districts.

Economic stress and unemployment brought other changes in police business. By the Unemployment Act of 1930, all males aged twenty and older were levied to provide funds for unemployment relief. Policemen were soon chasing up those failing to register or pay the levy as well as checking on applicants for sustenance. They also acted (unofficially) as almoners for some charitable aid boards.[180] Occasionally a discreet word to a Relieving Officer could be a means of persuading 'undesirable' outsiders – especially those who agitated amongst the relief workers – to leave for other districts. Camps of relief workers brought more work, especially for local constables. In Southland, for example, there were fortnightly pay escorts to the remote camps. And the camps themselves needed surveillance. Waihi police found some of the local relief workers 'troublesome'; they were 'heavy drinkers' and not above 'converting' the odd bicycle and car. For Constable Sterritt at Culverden it was often a two-day trip with horse and gig to visit the unsettled Lewis Pass relief camps, looking for maintenance defaulters, investigating thefts, dealing with a 'lunatic' armed with an axe, and bringing arrested men back unaided. Distress warrants increased in number. The local constable at Portobello on Otago Harbour was probably not alone in paying many outstanding fines and debts to clear the warrants, then recovering the money in small amounts later. Local police felt keenly the plight of many of those they dealt with, often assisting with food and clothing. Lord Bledisloe appreciated the police contribution to the Governor-General's Winter Relief Fund.[181] Some, if circumstances warranted, even turned a blind eye to petty thieving. A New Plymouth constable let off with a severe warning a destitute man he discovered going home with a bag of railway coal on his back. City men, to whom the 'special allowance' was particularly directed, spent hours of extra duty keeping order at street meetings, demonstrations and house evictions.[182]

The devastating Hawke's Bay earthquake of 3 February 1931 compounded the police workload, tested Wohlmann's resolve for economy, and raised wider issues of leadership, authority, and organisation in the event of a civil emergency.[183] This disaster was the country's largest civil emergency since the influenza epidemic of 1918. A wide area was affected, from Wairoa in the north to Dannevirke in the south. In both Napier (population about 16,000) and Hastings (11,000) the water supply and lighting, gas and sewer mains were cut; so too were communications with the rest of the country. Much of the towns' central business districts were wrecked; many public buildings collapsed (though not Napier's wooden police station, nor Hastings' new

1. Some of the 'bosses' in August 1919: front row from left, Superintendents A.H. Wright (Dunedin) and N. Kiely (Auckland), Commissioner J. O'Donovan, Superintendents J. Dwyer (Christchurch) and S.P. Norwood (Wellington); back row from left, Sub-Inspector W.B. McIlveney (Wellington), Inspectors J.A. McGrath (Napier) and R. Marsack (Wellington), Sub-Inspector C.R. Broberg (Headquarters). Their dark blue 'lion tamer's' tunics with lines of braided cord were introduced following the creation of the New Zealand Police Force in 1886 and remained unchanged until 1950. *NZ Police Journal, Apr 1939, p.127*

2. 'We keep a baton, but seldom use it; when we do its application should be scrupulously proportioned to the need', was Commissioner O'Donovan's injunction on the use of the detective's stave (left) and general issue police baton in 1920. It was symptomatic of an orderly society that city constables did not routinely carry batons on day shifts during the 1920s, and that when carried they were not visible. *Thomson and Neilson, Sharing the Challenge, p.222*

3. 'A man of gentle manner and fine sensibilities': Commissioner John O'Donovan is wearing the insignia of the Royal Victorian Order awarded for services during the visit of the Prince of Wales in April–May 1920, and the Long Service and Good Conduct Medal awarded in 1893 after fourteen years service. The 'period of exceptional stress and difficulty' between 1916 and 1921 took its toll on his health. *NZ Police*

4. Benign policing – 'The Kind Policeman' in Cathedral Square, Christchurch, 1938: Constable William Gregory befriends a boy with the aid of a bag of lollies before finding his father. *Thomson and Kagei, A Century of Service, p.88*

5. Constable James Dorgan's difficulties in finding decent housing typified those of many married constables in the years immediately after the First World War. His death was also seen to epitomise the dangers faced by beat constables, especially on night duty. He was shot early in the morning of 27 August 1921 while investigating an apparent break-in of a shop in Stafford Street, Timaru. Insufficient evidence was found to charge anyone. *NZ Police*

6. New Zealand Police Headquarters in Johnston Street in the 1920s, with the Wellington Superintendent's offices on the ground floor and the Commissioner and his staff on the first floor. This was one side of a U-shaped building encompassing a courtyard which served as a parade ground, with the Wellington Central police station on the other side, facing Waring Taylor Street, and a cell block forming the connecting arm. *S.C. Smith Collection, ATL, G24870¹/₁*

7. Auckland Central police station in the late 1930s. A two-storey building was opened in 1900 on the corner of O'Rorke and Princes Streets. In 1917 a three-storey building was added alongside, and in 1930 an additional floor was added to the original building. *Donald Scott*

8. During the inter-war years Christchurch Central police station, fronting Hereford Street, comprised a combination of two stone buildings built in 1873, each of two storeys, which were linked in 1906 by a two-storey brick building. Behind this structure were the cell block, sheds and stables which were gradually converted to other uses. *B.G. Thomson*

9. NZP2 was the second police motor vehicle, and one of four prison vans specially built in 1919. The 'Black Maria' was painted dark green and also served as an ambulance. The vans remained in service until the late 1930s. *NZ Police Museum*

TROUBLE IN THE CIVIL CIRCUS

10. When the Massey government imposed pay cuts on public servants in January 1922, police resigned from the Public Service Association, fearing it was becoming too militant and disappointed that they were not exempt from the cuts. For the next fourteen years police rank and file lacked union representation. *NZ Truth, 11 Feb 1922*

11. Arthur Hobbins Wright had acquired considerable administrative experience as Chief Clerk in Headquarters and then in charge of three districts before becoming Commissioner on 1 January 1922. His four years of low-key leadership began a period of stability in police organisation and administration that lasted for 30 years. *NZ Police*

12. With typical flamboyance, Commissioner William Bernard McIlveney embellished his uniform in 1926. His 'vigorous personality' initially impressed the politicians. He was not shy of publicity, and his style of leadership proved to be controversial. *NZ Police*

13. Relaxed policing on the Wellington wharves. The ten-week seamen's strike between November 1922 and January 1923 – the most significant of the 1920s – was peaceful by comparison with the waterfront confrontation in 1913. Barricades rather than Special Constables controlled the pickets; police protection of non-union seamen was not directly challenged by those on strike, but away from the wharves 'scabs' were assaulted. *S.C. Smith Collection, ATL, G48886¹/₂*

14. Point duty at the corner of Manners and Cuba Streets, Wellington, during the mid-1920s. The constable stands on a rubber mat close to the tramlines. The need for 'uniformity of signals' and to be 'extremely civil in manner and speech' made the job demanding. *ATL, F51036¹/₂*

15. A pointsman at the corner of Karangahape Road and Pitt Street, Auckland, uses a mechanical stop/go sign in the mid-1920s. *NZ Police Museum*

16. Tall policemen accompany the Duke and Duchess of York through an orderly crowd in Newtown, Wellington, during the 1927 royal tour. *ATL, F68005¹/₂*

17. A shift of constables march out from the Christchurch police station in mid-1927 wearing recently issued shakos with new silver badges. To 'smarten the appearance of the men', McIlveney reverted to distinctive features of the police uniform before 1912. *Christchurch Police Museum*

18. A Feilding businessman, J.G. Cobbe, became Minister in charge of the Police in December 1929, a year after entering Parliament as a United MP. Though Labour MPs later alleged that he was 'run' by his Department, Cobbe's decision to investigate the dismissal of a Police Sergeant precipitated the early retirement of Commissioner McIlveney in June 1930. *S.P. Andrew Collection, ATL, F43360¹/₂*

19. R.P. Ward, the Under-Secretary for Justice, was appointed to carry out the Commissioner's duties during July 1930 while the United government decided on the successor to Commissioner McIlveney. *NZ Police*

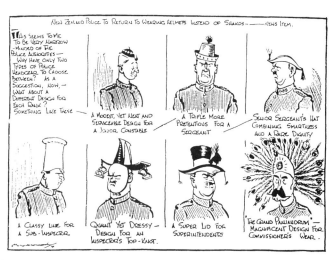

20. 'The Hat Trick': Gordon Minhinnick's response to Commissioner Wohlmann's withdrawal of the unpopular shako in December 1930. While Wohlmann did not adopt the cartoonist's 'magnificent design', he kept McIlveney's additions to the Commissioner's insignia of rank. *New Zealand Herald, 5 Jan 1931*

21. Auckland's dapper Superintendent Ward George Wohlmann became Commissioner on 1 August 1930. With his 'quiet and unassuming' manner and considerable administrative experience in the Police Force, he was more akin to A.H. Wright than to W.B. McIlveney. A keen sportsman, he kept English setter dogs and joined a variety of societies and clubs throughout his career. His frugal and cautious administration was in tune with the conservative governments he served for five years. *G.I. Melville*

22. 'After the "quake" came the fire': a fireman walks through rubble in Hastings Street, Napier, ten minutes after the devastating earthquake at 10.50 am on 3 February 1931. Police led parties to rescue the injured and recover bodies. *P.T.W. Ashcroft Collection, ATL, F139885¹/₂*

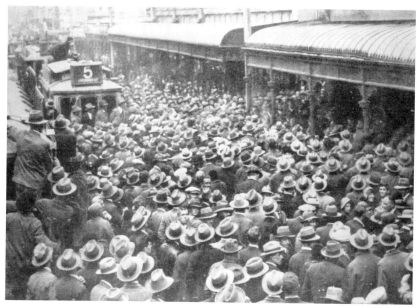

23. The 1932 disturbances began in Dunedin on 9 January, when a crowd of unemployed men sought to rush Wardell's grocery store in George Street. There was a tussle with police protecting the store, and traffic was held up, but no serious violence. *ATL, NP435–36*

24. Aftermath of the Auckland riot: south side of Swanson Street looking east to Queen Street, during the evening of 14 April 1932. Most of the shop windows were smashed and many shops were looted. A dense and often hostile crowd of onlookers made it difficult for police to catch looters. *Auckland Weekly News, 20 Apr 1932, ATL, F31110^1/$_2$*

25. During the first week of a strike by Christchurch tramwaymen which began on 4 May 1932, a uniformed constable travelled on each tram to protect the volunteer motorman. The leaders of the city's unemployed supported the strikers, adding to the threat of disorder. *ATL, NP434–31*

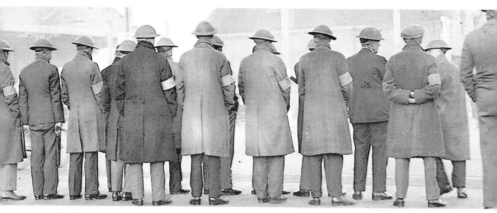

26. 'Temporary Constables' (popularly seen as 'Specials') lined up outside the Christchurch tram sheds with batons, armbands and steel helmets. Some 400 had been recruited on the eve of the strike. They helped police to disperse a crowd of picketers from the tram sheds early on 6 May 1932 – the most violent episode in the city during the inter-war years. *Press, 7 May 1932, p.17*

27. Nearly a riot: a large crowd of tramwaymen, their supporters and onlookers gathered in Cathedral Square, Christchurch, on the afternoon of 6 May 1932. A section of the crowd slowed the trams while police sought to keep the tramlines free. *Press, 7 May 1932, p.17*

brick one); most houses were 'more or less damaged'. Fire quickly followed the violent shock, adding to death and destruction. Three weeks later, police had counted 260 'verified deaths' resulting from the earthquake, including 131 killed at Napier, 92 at Hastings, and 15 who died later in hospital. At least 537 casualties had been admitted to hospital, but the total number injured was unknown. None of the local police were hurt, though some were 'slightly injured' later while rescuing people from burning buildings. A constable's wife and child were killed when the Napier public hospital collapsed.

When the tremors began, only one constable was on beat duty in the Napier business centre. Others soon ran through the streets urging people to make for Marine Parade. Then, as the dust settled and fires began, police in both towns organised parties to extricate people and fight the fires. In Napier they were joined by men from HMS *Veronica*, then in port, and by 14 officers and some 300 men from two further naval vessels which arrived next day. With 19 men at Napier, 12 at Hastings and another 25 scattered through the district, the police led by Inspector D.J. Cummings showed initiative, but were too few to meet the many demands the emergency created. Yet no local organisation existed to cope with it. Certainly ad hoc organisations emerged, but these were community-focused and there was a problem of coordination, both within the region and with the outside world, particularly in the early hours of the emergency. Moreover, in both Napier and Hastings, the local authorities appeared to show a lack of initiative immediately following the event. In Hastings, it was three hours before a relief organisation was established by ex-officers of the Wellington regiment. Nearly 24 hours passed before the Napier Citizens' Control Committee was formed on the initiative of central government officials (including Commissioner Wohlmann) who arrived from Wellington early on the morning of 4 February. For two days Wohlmann chaired the local committee, with the police station at the hub of activities. Meanwhile, assisted by naval parties, police continued to focus on rescuing the injured, recovering and burying bodies, and mounting guards and patrols. Mortuaries were quickly established in the Napier courthouse and the Hastings YMCA. On 11 February, 70 Special Constables (mainly local Territorials) commanded by Captain M.E. Johnson took over from the 60 armed marines who had been patrolling Napier. They were paid 5s a day and rations until their discharge on 18 March. In Hastings, 140 unpaid volunteers recruited by the headmaster of the high school undertook picketing and patrol duties until 12 February. By then local police had been bolstered by 22 from other districts, with Inspector Lander (from Wanganui) in charge until 28 March.

The problem of authority remained. In theory the relief committees acted as committees of the local borough council, which ratified their decisions. It was a moot point, however, whether municipal authority could give legality to every decision made or action taken. 'Is it martial law?', a man concerned about his goods asked the secretary of Napier's committee. 'No law but ours', Mr Girling Butcher replied politely but ambiguously. 'If there is anything we need we take it, but there is no responsibility for the safety of anything.'[184] The armed marines had contributed to the widespread notion that martial law was in force – to the extent that two Cabinet Ministers felt the need to declare that such a belief was 'quite contrary to fact'. Although he had used supposed powers under the Licensing Act to close the hotels on 5 February, Inspector Cummings later emphasised the 'voluntary' compliance of the publicans. His lack of any real authority to deal with those who continued to trade covertly forced Cummings to allow the reopening of bars. In mounting pickets and issuing permits to prevent the unemployed and sightseers from flooding in, police sought the 'co-operation' of the local authorities and the public. But action ostensibly based on 'transport regulations' was only effective against vehicles, and the unemployed continued to filter into Napier hoping for work. In getting about 200 of them to leave – even those who had secured work – police used the sense of emergency and popular acceptance of their authority to obtain compliance. For the most part, the problem of authority was thus more theoretical than real. There was a high degree of social cohesion and cooperation, despite the devastation and shock. Two weeks after the earthquake, Inspector Cummings looked to reduce the number of Special Constables. However, cooperation and cohesion might not obtain in other emergencies, particularly where there was civil strife. Wohlmann saw the need for legislation to enable the police to quickly assume wide powers in an emergency – especially as widespread unrest seemed increasingly likely during 1931.[185]

The 1932 disturbances

During the twelve months from April 1931, measures taken by the Coalition government to deal with deepening economic depression produced the worst crisis of public order since 1913. Wage cuts and the rationing of relief work for unemployed males stimulated threats of strikes and demonstrations which culminated in short-lived outbreaks of violence in the four main centres during April and May 1932.[186] For brief periods, police lost control of the main streets in Auckland and Wellington. With the advantage of hindsight, we can see that the country had not come 'almost to the verge of civil war';[187] the authority of the government was not seriously challenged, nor were communities fundamentally divided. Yet in the 'angry autumn' of 1932,[188] there were considerable tensions and bitter clashes, giving significance to the role of police and the resources mobilised to support them in the production of order or, on occasion, disorder.[189] Though there was a common context for the disturbances in 1932, the catalysts for disorder differed in each of the four cities. The episodes of unrest came in a sequence, with events in one centre shaping the reactions of police in the others.

Disturbances (labelled 'food riots' by the *Otago Daily Times*) began in Dunedin on 9 January when the hospital board's relief depot refused to meet the demands of a crowd of unemployed men and their wives for food. Some 400 then marched to the largest grocery store in the city, Wardell's, and sought to rush the shop to take food. Led by the lame 60 year old Superintendent William Eccles, half a dozen police (later reinforced by night-shift and suburban men) linked arms and held them back. A stalemate ensued as the tussle continued intermittently into the afternoon. As tempers frayed, traffic in busy George Street was held up, a motor van destroyed, and the shop's windows broken by missiles. A sugarbag of batons arrived for the police, yet no batons were drawn. Eventually the tension was defused when the Anglican City Missioner, Bryan King, offered to find food for as many as possible. That a free-for-all had not developed, with more serious violence and the police overwhelmed, owed much to police restraint – a fact acknowledged by the leaders of the demonstration as well as by the press. Superintendent Eccles, however, took no chances. As elsewhere after such disturbances, the perceived firebrands were quickly prosecuted and imprisoned. In turn, the local leadership of the Unemployed Workers' Movement promised there would be no further disorder.[190]

Nor was there until Friday 8 April, when a crowd of unemployed led by women protested against the inadequacy of relief. At the mayor's relief depot, the mayoress refused demands for food to be provided without names and addresses being left. Stones then smashed the depot's window and the taxi taking the mayoress home was attacked. Clearly the mood amongst the organised unemployed had hardened. Next day they marched through the busy main streets carrying banners, stopping at stores and warehouses to canvass for food, and singing the 'Red Flag'. Police kept a watchful eye but did not intervene. To the mayor, Robert Black, however, the demonstrators had been 'allowed too much latitude'; if they were 'not stopped at once I will get the decent men of Dunedin behind me and have the whole business cleaned up'. Superintendent Eccles agreed that the demonstrators 'could not expect to be allowed to make nuisances of themselves indefinitely', and added that he had 500 men 'ready to be sworn in as special constables at a minute's notice'.[191]

By 11 April the tensions were clear in a stormy meeting between the mayor and a crowd of unemployed. Late in the afternoon the crowd tried to rush the hospital board's offices, but were scattered (and some injured) by a vigorous baton charge of a dozen police who had been forewarned. In response, the Unemployed Workers' Movement called for a strike of all relief workers and bigger demonstrations. But the tables had turned. Next morning, when 200 demonstrators arrived in the Octagon, they were confronted by Superintendent Eccles with 30 police drawn up in front of the town hall. After a two-hour stand-off, the unemployed dispersed. Gathering again the following day (13 April), they soon dispersed as a column of 30 police led by Eccles bore down on them. Peacefully, police had reasserted a control of the streets which they reinforced by arresting six of the 'ringleaders' of the demonstrations. Nor did most relief workers want to strike; Eccles promised to prevent 'interference with willing workers'. Even so, to the Labour Party leader, Harry Holland, 'what was happening in the southern city was a faint rumbling of what was likely to happen throughout the Dominion. A most dangerous atmosphere was growing up in this country'.[192]

So it certainly seemed in Auckland, where a new and more volatile phase in local protests against relief conditions began with the calling of a relief workers' strike and the largest demonstration of the unemployed thus far (some 2,000-strong) on Wednesday 13 April. The long procession to the town hall was orderly, apart from a brief clash between some unemployed and half a dozen baton-wielding constables that was calmed by Jim Edwards, a leader of the UWM.[193] Circumstances were different the following evening when an even larger body of unemployed and their supporters followed Post and Telegraph employees who were marching to a meeting in the town hall to protest against wage cuts.[194] Though the demonstration accompanied by some 29 police was generally orderly, stones thrown at shop windows and slogans shouted by Edwards and others indicated that the mood amongst the crowd of several thousand was militant.[195]

Outside the town hall, where there were initially only a dozen police, violence erupted – precipitated by a combination of events, the nature and sequence of which remain a matter for debate. Excluded from the town hall, a section of the crowd sought to force their way in, but were resisted by half a dozen police with batons drawn. Stones and other missiles (including palings with protruding nails wrenched from a nearby church fence) began to be thrown at them. Jim Edwards addressed the crowd through a megaphone from the town hall balustrade, to the effect that 'If the police draw their batons, crowd around them and take their batons off them'. Edwards claimed later that he was seeking to 'avert trouble' as he had done the day before, but to the police his language was inflammatory.[196] When six mounted police and others on foot moved through the dense crowd towards the balustrade, 'pandemonium' broke out, exacerbated by the batoning of Edwards by a Police Sergeant. The small number of police dispersed through the now violent crowd were initially overwhelmed in a bitter and bloody free-for-all. More police arrived and eventually concerted baton charges cleared a space in front of the town hall without subduing the crowd. Casualties mounted: during the evening over 100 (including twelve police, three in a serious condition) were taken to Auckland hospital, mainly with head injuries. Altogether, 21 of the 30 police at the town hall were injured. Shortly before 8 pm, Inspector Hollis arrived at the town hall and quickly sent for assistance from the Navy and the fire brigade.

In the meantime, a second phase of the riot began as a section of the crowd, mainly 'youths' at first, surged down Queen Street smashing about 80 per cent of the shop windows, and soon afterwards looting businesses of tobacco, liquor, clothing and jewellery (fruit and food stores were left untouched). Few police were then visible; fewer made any move to prevent this. Detective S.C. Whitehead, who caught two men breaking a window at the outset of the surge, received severe head injuries when he was 'rushed' by the crowd. Another detective in plain clothes felt himself unable to 'take any effective steps' to prevent the destruction or arrest the culprits.[197] Also passive were the hundreds who poured out of the picture theatres to watch. The uniformed police remained concentrated around the town hall, seeking to gain the upper hand there and prevent the release of eight men already arrested. Window-smashing continued as Commander Berthon marched his armed naval party of two other officers and twenty ratings up Queen Street through a hostile crowd to join the police at 9 pm. Nor was looting quickly stemmed when police with naval detachments subsequently patrolled the footpaths on either side of Queen Street; it continued 'in front and behind them'. After 9 pm, police drawn from the suburban stations were also sent out in pairs to stop the stealing; even so, Constable Charles Bowley found the crowd so threatening that he was forced to release a looter he had arrested.[198] Two detectives, trapped in a shop doorway with a captured looter, kept the crowd back with the threat of a gun.[199]

At 9.23 pm the mayor broadcast an appeal for 'all law-abiding, physically fit men to report at once, armed with batons, to the police station'. The response was immediate. Volunteers appeared at the Central police station in O'Rorke Street (where fire hoses had been rolled out in case there was an attempt to rescue prisoners). They were not sworn in or armed with batons, but quickly sent out with police to arrest looters, or in parties by themselves, with white handkerchiefs as armbands, to stand at intersections or guard shops with broken windows.[200] At 10 pm a detachment of 55 officers and men of the Royal Naval Volunteer Reserve arrived at the town hall to control the dense crowd (now consisting mostly of sightseers), allowing police to 'move off in strong posses and deal with the larrikins'.[201] Together police, naval parties, and 'specials' cleared loiterers from the footpaths and away from shop windows. By 10.30 pm the looting had ended and the crowd in Queen Street had started to disperse. Police and volunteers then set out to catch 'looters going home with their booty', while detectives had a 'roving commission to arrest men known to be leaders of the unemployed movement'.[202] Jim Edwards, however, had been spirited away.[203] By 1 am, 35 arrests had been made, mainly for theft. In its scale, duration, intensity at the outset, and – above all – for what it seemed to portend, the collective violence in Auckland during more than two and a half hours on Thursday 14 April was only rivalled this century by episodes in Wellington between 30 October and 5 November 1913.[204]

Further 'trouble' was anticipated, and the authorities made preparations accordingly. Processions and outdoor meetings were prohibited in Auckland. From early Friday morning over 1,000 Special Constables were sworn in at the Central police station, given batons and armbands, and drafted into eight companies with squads organised for duty. During the morning 98 men of the Waikato Mounted Rifles arrived, encamped at the Epsom Showgrounds and were sworn in as Special Constables, with pick handles replacing their arms. Early in the evening, 201 RNVR men were enrolled as specials. The Army mounted guards at drill halls, magazines, and the Colonial Ammunition Company. Watched by a crowd of nearly a thousand in neighbouring Albert Park and the adjoining streets, an armed naval detachment of 25 men joined police and specials in forming a cordon around the Magistrate's Court during the prosecution of those arrested the night before. Four officers and 84 fully armed and steel-helmeted naval ratings were made ready for the evening.[205]

Also during Friday, Commissioner Wohlmann sent his Minister a bill he had drafted six months earlier for the 'Preservation of Public Safety'. It was designed to remedy 'the present inadequate legislative provision' for dealing with emergencies such as the 'recent serious earthquake' and the 'still more recent exhibition of organised violence and disorder by crowds resulting in extensive damage to property and bodily injury to participants and the Police'. Later that day, Prime Minister Forbes instructed that the draft be made ready for introduction to Parliament in four days time.[206] Like Superintendent Till in Auckland, Wohlmann believed that the disorder was Communist-inspired and would continue. Perhaps echoing rumours that were already spreading through the city, a police agent who had penetrated the local Communist group reported during Friday that Karangahape Road would be the 'scene of an organised outbreak'.[207] In any event, the Friday night crowds concentrated there rather than (as usual) in Queen Street, as did a portion of the 'protective forces' arrayed to control them.

By 7.30 pm a dense crowd of several thousand had gathered at the intersection of Karangahape Road and Pitt Street, and there was a 'general expectation' that 'trouble was brewing'.[208] Police did not seek to clear the intersection immediately, but tried instead to keep the crowd in 'good humour' by talking and cajoling people into moving. Soon, however, window-smashing began in the vicinity, and 'cautious methods' gave way to 'open arrests' and the use of batons. Looting was prevented by squads of police, bluejackets, and specials on foot moving to and fro clearing the footpaths of people and pursuing the window-breakers into the crowd of bystanders. However, intermittent window-smashing continued; controlling it was difficult because of the throngs of sightseers who remained along Karangahape Road after the shops closed at 9 pm. Much hostility was directed at the 150 specials, who were abused as 'scabs' as they moved in tight bands through the crowd.

Brief fracas occurred as they made arrests, with one such developing into an 'ugly fight' when specials used their batons freely and several 'rioters' were injured. That patrolling by specials had the potential to provoke disorder was seen when the Waikato Mounted Rifles appeared on horseback, wearing slouch hats and khaki shirts and waving their long staves. As they cantered past, anger was expressed in a burst of window-breaking. Because their presence was provocative, the mounted specials were withdrawn after only twenty minutes. However five mounted police, assisted by a naval detachment, had cleared a space at the Pitt Street intersection by about 9 pm.

Gradually the crowd was pressed back along Karangahape Road towards Symonds Street by the combined efforts of police, specials, naval ratings and RNVR men. By 11.30 pm the crowds had been dispersed. Thirty-five had been arrested, mainly for inciting violence and 'causing mischief' (vandalism). In the violent skirmishes at least 50 people had been injured (including a few police and specials), with five admitted to hospital, about 50 windows broken and weapons confiscated. Yet while a large crowd with a vocally 'class conscious' section apparently 'spoiling for trouble'[209] had gathered, no looting had occurred, nor had there been a 'general engagement with rioters'.[210] To that extent, the police and the forces assisting them had managed to maintain 'a definite control', according to the *New Zealand Herald*. And yet, the paper feared, specials might have to be 'used in even larger numbers' if the 'riot madness continues'.[211]

Indeed 'grave anxiety' was expressed on Saturday morning, 16 April, at a meeting between the mayor, Superintendent Till and other representatives of the 'protective forces'.[212] The mayor, G.W. Hutchison, had already warned that if there was another disturbance where the unruly intermingled with a crowd of onlookers, he would not hesitate to read the Riot Act. Police expected further trouble over the weekend, with evening attacks on property in the city and suburbs. Accordingly the number of specials enrolled was increased to nearly 2,000. Firms provided buses and lorries to take them where they might be needed. The Waikato mounted specials were kept in readiness, as were naval ratings and RNVR men on the wharf. Bluejackets provided guards for the General Post Office and the town hall, and a patrol for Government House. Commissioner Wohlmann made a hurried visit from Wellington in the evening. Meanwhile, hundreds of shop windows in the city and inner suburbs were barricaded.

In the event, the city had a 'quiet weekend'. On Saturday evening, about 2,000 people gathered at the top of Symonds Street waiting for something to happen. Nothing did, except for one broken window. From a verandah roof, Senior Sergeant M. Flanagan appealed to the crowd through a megaphone to disperse – to little effect until mounted police constables appeared and small parties of uniformed men moved through the throng. 'Specials' had been kept away, as they were on

Sunday afternoon, when police anticipated trouble as hundreds of people gathered at the entrances to the Domain to hear previously advertised speeches, in spite of a ban on public meetings. Given police permission to speak, the MP John A. Lee urged the crowd to go home. Again it was quietly dispersed by parties of police assisted by a detachment of RNVR men. Ostensibly the tensions of the preceding week had dissipated; the city 'returned to normal'.[213]

Superintendent Till took no chances, however. For another week or more, constables on day shifts were brought back to the Central station for evening reserve duty. A local civil emergency organisation incorporating the specials was established (albeit largely on paper) because of rumours (which proved unfounded) of general industrial action, particularly by seamen, against wage cuts.[214] At Till's request, the Mounted Rifles remained in Auckland until 23 April; guards were maintained at the main telephone exchange until 11 May, and at the drill halls and the ammunition factory until 24 May.[215]

Nor was the government prepared to take chances. It sought, Forbes declared, 'to strengthen the hands of the police and local authorities in Auckland and elsewhere to ensure that the outbreaks of lawlessness do not recur'. Forbes signalled that Special Constables would be organised to support the police in the other cities. Moreover, anything that had been 'done outside the law to assist the authorities in the execution of their duty would be validated'.[216] On Saturday 16 April the Cabinet met to consider Wohlmann's draft bill (which followed South Australian legislation) along with an 'Emergency Powers' Bill (modelled on an English Act) that had been prepared for Massey's government in 1921. On Monday revisions were made in line with the Imperial Emergency Powers Act 1920. The Public Safety Conservation Bill was introduced into Parliament the next day and passed on 23 April. It allowed the Governor-General to proclaim a state of emergency 'at any time' it appeared that 'any circumstances exist, or are likely to come into existence, whereby the public safety or public order is or is likely to be imperilled'.[217] Wohlmann had had a clause introduced which empowered the senior police officer in any locality to 'assume responsibility for the issuing of all orders and instructions necessary in his opinion for the preservation of life, the protection of property, and the maintenance of order', pending the Governor-General's proclamation. The Act also gave immunity from any action or claim made against those exercising emergency powers.[218] In a civil emergency, police could now act with greater authority and legality than they had in the past. By 13 May, Wohlmann had drafted for comment by his officers regulations that would come into effect should a state of emergency be declared in any part of the country. But these enhanced police powers remained potential; they were not to be employed in peacetime until a countrywide state of emergency was declared during the confrontation on the waterfront in 1951.

On 16 April, Inspector Cameron in Christchurch did not think that Auckland's disturbances would be repeated in his city with its Labour-dominated council. He shared a local belief that there was 'more done' in providing relief for the Christchurch unemployed than in 'any other city in the Dominion'.[219] To Cameron, the 'city's reputation rests not in its suppression of trouble, but in its avoidance of it.'[220] Nonetheless, as in the other cities, the names were taken of nearly a thousand men who volunteered to be Special Constables. The city's unemployed seemed more responsive than hitherto to the speeches of local Communists, most of whom were soon prosecuted – including H.E. Barnsley for suggesting a hunger march to the Prime Minister's farm at Cheviot.[221] Tensions mounted in Christchurch in the aftermath of an ineffective relief workers' strike, the reverberations of Auckland's disturbances, and as a stand-off developed between the Christchurch Tramway Board and the local Tramways Employees Union over adverse changes to working conditions.[222]

On 1 May Christchurch tramwaymen voted to strike three days later. Superintendent D.J. Cummings (recently promoted and transferred from Napier) arranged for a 'strong posse' of police to be at the tram sheds to protect the 'loyal employees and volunteers' on the first morning of the strike; for two uniformed constables to travel on each tram of a skeleton service during the day; and for others to protect vital points. However, there were 58 miles of track, and Cummings recognised that police could not 'adequately protect the whole line, though 'good supervision' would be possible over 'an extended area'. On the eve of the strike, the Superintendent had 400 'good men' sworn in as 'temporary constables' (without pay) under the Police Force Act to assist in an emergency. A further 300 men had been enlisted.[223] Cummings warned that picketing would not be allowed. A crowd of about 300 who turned up at the tram sheds at 5 am on 4 May were moved on by uniformed police without resistance, and few picketers turned up the next morning. However, in the suburbs there were attempts to interfere with trams, drivers were jeered and abused, and some were threatened after work.

From the outset, leaders of the unemployed had promised support for the strikers. On Thursday evening (5 May) at the Trades Hall, large meetings of a 'United Front Council' and the unemployed agreed to picket the tram sheds the following morning. Forewarned by a police agent,[224] Cummings had 400 specials summoned to the King Edward Barracks at 3 am. They were given batons, armbands and steel helmets, then assembled in companies and sent by bus so as to be concealed in the tram sheds by 5.30 am, while uniformed police patrolled outside. As the first tram left, it was met by a hail of stones from a crowd of well over a hundred, mainly unemployed men. They in turn were charged by police (led by Inspector Cameron) and some two hundred specials. After a short 'running battle' (the most violent episode in Christchurch since the turn of the century, in which Superintendent Cummings took part) the picketers quickly dispersed. For the rest of the day, police and squads of specials patrolled the tram sheds and accompanied trams on the suburban routes, deterring 'trouble'. Frustrated and angry, however, a 'large party' of 'trammies' and their supporters arrived at 3 pm in Cathedral Square, where a crowd of up to 4,000 gathered, mainly onlookers. For the next hour, groups of police sought quietly but firmly to keep the tramlines free as a section of the crowd (in which members of the local UWM were prominent) moved about the Square slowing trams and abusing their drivers. Gradually tempers frayed, and hostility became focused on the police. A number of arrests were followed by skirmishes and a rush on the taxis in which prisoners were being removed. Brandishing their batons, police reasserted control and the 'riotous element' melted away. A force of nearly 300 specials had been kept in reserve.[225] As a local magistrate saw it, police restraint had prevented 'a great disaster'.[226]

Cummings recognised that tensions remained. A group of police were sent to protect the city's power station at Lake Coleridge. The number of specials was also increased to about 1,500, so as to maintain both increased protection for the tramways and night patrols of the city to deter window-breaking and other 'mischief'.[227] Overlooked, however, was the publicised decision of a meeting of the unemployed to declare 'black' three rugby teams for which 'specials' played. The day after the skirmishes in the Square, a 'howling crowd' of about 2,000 outside Lancaster Park smashed windows in waiting trams and besieged the Christchurch club rugby team, who escaped in the 'Black Maria' after uniformed police with batons drawn had cleared the way. While policing had contained the tensions, the advent of a tribunal on 10 May to settle the tramway dispute helped to defuse them. Henceforth, Christchurch was 'quiet' – although 'specials' were kept on duty until the end of the strike came with the tribunal's decision on 17 May. Even then Cummings feared further disturbances. Another relief workers' strike had been called on 12 May, and he had banned all outdoor public meetings after 4 pm.[228] In this action Cummings was mindful of recent events in Wellington.

Even before the disturbances in Auckland, Wellington police had sought to maintain a tight control over public meetings and processions in the capital. But they were caught off guard by the largest demonstration yet in the city. Fears that changes to the urban relief scheme no. 5 would disadvantage them precipitated a decision amongst Wellington's relief workers to strike from 10 May.[229] By 2 pm that day, between three and five thousand relief workers and their supporters had gathered at the Basin Reserve.[230] They set off on a long and orderly procession to Parliament, accompanied by all the police that could be spared from the city and suburban stations – 60 uniformed men as well as detectives under Inspector John Lander (of the Commissioner's staff), who had determined a route that avoided the main shopping streets.[231]

At Parliament a deputation went to see the Minister of Employment, J.G. Coates, while the crowd outside the closed gates grew to some six or seven thousand, becoming very restless while it waited. Traffic was halted, some missiles were thrown at police, and threats made to rush the gates. Leaders of the unemployed appealed for patience but also led the crowd in singing the 'Red Flag'. As a precaution, Inspector Lopdell went back to the Central police station to arrange for the 'prompt calling out' of Special Constables if necessary.

After nearly two hours, the deputation returned to report that the Minister would issue a statement the next day. Clearly this was impolitic and there was intense frustration. On the edge of the crowd someone yelled, 'Up the town!' A group of 30 or 40 men raced along Lambton Quay to Willis and then Manners streets, breaking nearly 200 shop windows as they went. There was little time for looting. However, with most of the police massed inside Parliament's gates as a precaution against the crowd which remained, the window-smashers and the large number who followed to watch were unhindered for some twenty minutes. Hurrying in pairs from Parliament through the straggling crowd, police halted its advance with a baton charge near the end of Lambton Quay. Meanwhile the window-smashers were checked at Manners Street by police from the Taranaki Street station. Soon squads of specials in steel helmets arrived to back up the uniformed police and patrol the main thoroughfares of the city throughout the night. Loiterers were moved on. That evening Commissioner Wohlmann (and later the mayor) appealed for more men to enlist as Special Constables so that 24-hour patrols could be maintained. By contrast with the situation in Auckland, the naval authorities were no longer willing to have their men on patrol.[232] Fortuitously, a wet night helped to thin the crowds.

The man in charge of policing Wellington's demonstrations and outdoor meetings, Inspector Lander, was determined not to be caught out again. Next morning, when relief workers returned to the Basin Reserve for another meeting, the gates were locked and police turned them away. Hundreds of unemployed then gathered in the vicinity of the inner-city Trades Hall where the strikers' delegates held meetings; spectators also thronged the streets. Lander had six mounted constables patrolling there from 10 am to keep traffic moving. Three platoons of specials were also stationed in the area, occasionally making patrols to the Trades Hall, where they were heckled by the unemployed; 'an atmosphere of electric tension existed'.[233] When not all relief workers could be accommodated in the Trades Hall to hear the delegates' decisions, a crowd surged to nearby Cuba Street; some 2,000 men and a few women filled a vacant section, and onlookers lined the footpaths. Inspector Lander and some twenty uniformed police pressed close to the two men wishing to speak, while a similar number mingled with the crowd and the six mounted constables drew up on its edge.

Outside meetings had been prohibited. Wanting to avoid trouble,

Lander permitted the speakers to tell the crowd the result of the Trades Hall meeting; but they were to be brief. The first was; the second, Lander deemed, was not. At this point, as with the similar situation outside the Auckland town hall a month earlier, the nature and sequence of events became controversial. When the 'Communist' Kelly (in Lander's view) did not do as he had been asked, he was told 'That's enough', and pulled down off his chair. The largely 'passive crowd became vociferously hostile', showering the police with stones and bricks. 'Get into them', shouted Lander, and within two minutes the crowd was dispersed by foot and mounted constables 'laying about them with swift, deadly strokes'.[234] Several were injured by batons and others trampled in the stampede; a man had his leg broken by a fence that was pushed over by hundreds seeking to escape. No police were injured. A persistent (but unfounded) rumour soon circulated that an injured boy had died in hospital. Police were taunted that evening as they patrolled in force through the large crowds that again packed the streets near the Trades Hall. Again the specials were kept in reserve, and they became even less visible during the following days. 'The position was very difficult', Lander noted; 'It would have taken very little to have caused serious disturbances'.[235] In Wellington, as in the other cities, police had reasserted control; but it was some time before the authorities relaxed their grip.[236]

There were no further significant disturbances in the cities, or elsewhere, apart from meetings and mounting tensions at Huntly which culminated in a march on a Farmers' Trading Company store by 80 unemployed who helped themselves to groceries on 19 May.[237] Altogether, there were 185 prosecutions for offences arising from the disturbances: in Dunedin 8, Auckland 84 (including Jim Edwards, who was convicted in both the Magistrate's and Supreme Courts), Christchurch 32, Wellington 43, and Huntly 18. Of these, 55 received sentences of between three and six months imprisonment, ten were given one year each, and seven (including Edwards) got two years.[238] Prosecutions for 'seditious offences' continued into 1933. Effectively, many of the leading activists were incapacitated. To the government during the 'angry autumn' of 1932, police had proved again to be (in Sir Francis Bell's words) 'the most valuable servants of the Crown'.

Events had also shown that police could not always contain disorder, and that their misjudgements might help to ignite it. Other 'protective forces' were seen to be required, even though their presence was likely to exacerbate tensions. The *Evening Post* editorialised (somewhat ambiguously) in the aftermath of Wellington's window-smashing that 'the police were set a task which they ought not to be asked to face again'. The government's response at 'a time of public distress and excitement' was also crucial: 'The maintenance of law and order is the fundamental duty of every Government, and we are entitled to ask Mr Forbes and his colleagues, in their discharge of that duty, to look not only to the criminal denouement of yesterday's proceedings, but to the opening which they inevitably provided'.[239] A constable who confronted the crowd in Lambton Quay expressed a widely-held feeling more simply later: 'the situation was poorly handled' by the government.[240]

'The Cinderella of the Public Service'

The disturbances and the precautionary policing that persisted in their aftermath placed a great strain on the city police, who worked long hours in often difficult conditions. The numbers of uniformed police had fallen during 1931, but were quickly increased in May 1932. More police and the remission of the second cut in public service wages in 1932 were the only concessions the Coalition government was prepared to give its 'most valuable servants'. During 1933/34, expenditure on police (and police numbers) barely increased (figures 1.1, 1.4). An ethos of penny-pinching continued.

Now the key issues of policing the cities, and especially the largest city, Auckland, shifted back from the maintenance of public order to the detection of crime. Nationwide, 16 per cent fewer 'serious crimes' (overwhelmingly burglaries) were reported during 1933 than the previous year. Against the trend, recorded burglaries and thefts from dwellings in Auckland continued to increase, and some 650 (a large majority) remained undetected. With typical hyperbole, a *Truth* headline proclaimed in January 1934: 'Organised Looting By Daring Criminals. Crime Wave In Auckland Baffles Police'; 'unless something is done ... women and children in suburban homes will live in a continual state of terror'.[241] Moreover, the number of murders rose to 22 in 1933. Particularly in Auckland and Christchurch (where burglaries had also continued to increase), detectives had a 'very strenuous year'. There was a major triumph of detection with the conviction of Bill Bayly in June 1934 for the murder of Samuel and Christobel Lakey at Ruawaro (near Huntly) seven months earlier.[242] However the unsolved murders of an Auckland taxi-driver (J.H. Blair) and a Christchurch hotelier (D. Fraser), both late in 1933, caused considerable public disquiet.

From early in 1933 there was mounting press criticism of old-fashioned police methods and the lack of up-to-date equipment; in effect, this was criticism of perceived weaknesses in the existing system of 'preventive policing' of suburbs and crime detection.[243] With the Superintendent's Hupmobile and two motorcycles beyond repair by 1932, Auckland police had been 'reduced' to one Ford car and bicycles (or else public transport) to cover an urban population of some 200,000 spread over an extensive area. Superintendent Till had asked unsuccessfully for an additional car to 'deal more promptly with urgent matters' and provide a suburban night patrol to deter house-breakers. Critics were aware of the advent of wireless-controlled motor patrols across the Tasman. To the *New Zealand Herald* (in March 1933), the activities of motorised thieves and 'joy-riders' showed the need for an 'efficient motor corps' of Auckland police. The *Herald* recognised that the government was 'intent on economy', but continued to press for changes. Wohlmann conceded that 'high-powered motor cars and wireless sets' would be 'helpful', but (in tune with his Minister) [244] was not convinced that the system of motor patrols being developed in London, Melbourne and Sydney would be appropriate for New Zealand cities, even Auckland; New Zealand lacked 'organised crime'. [245] In the meantime, an extra car for Auckland would do. Wohlmann deemed the one police car in Christchurch to be adequate – as in all the cities during the 1932 disturbances, 'sufficient' vehicles could be made available from private sources 'to meet any urgent call'. [246]

From late November 1933, as investigations of the murders of the Lakeys, Blair and Fraser dragged on, criticism of the organisation, methods and conditions of detective work grew. Looking to an idealised model of the London Metropolitan Police, critics like the poet and penal reformer Blanche Baughan urged that a criminal investigation department be created, separate from the uniformed police, and that detectives be given specialised training and more up-to-date scientific aids. [247] Wohlmann responded by pointing out that courts had praised the quality of the detective work which had led to arrests for most murders. Nonetheless the broad issue of training persisted, especially as the closing of the Training Depot in July 1930 was now seen to have been a 'false economy' by critics alarmed at the growing of numbers of constables without formal training. Wohlmann admitted that reopening the Depot would be of 'great value', but (since his Minister had said this was improbable in the near future) 'it could not be looked upon as an absolute necessity'. [248] To the critics, the closed Depot symbolised that 'the Police Department has been too long "the Cinderella of the Public Service".' Little change in the Police vote for the next year further underlined the perception that the Force was 'still the "poor sister" of the Government Departments', with inadequate equipment and dilapidated facilities. It needed (according to the *New Zealand Herald*) to 'advance with the times to meet new conditions'. [249]

Criticism intensified when, late in September 1934, the *Auckland Star* published a series of detailed articles pressing for an 'overhaul' of the 'police system' and focusing on the position of detectives – their organisation, recruitment, training, promotion, and conditions of work. Claiming to represent 'strong feeling' both inside and outside the Force (and certainly the opinions of some disgruntled local detectives), the paper called for a commission of inquiry into the administration of the Force. [250] This was echoed in Parliament by A.J. Stallworthy, an independent local MP, after further criticism of police methods when Constable Thomas Heeps of Morrinsville was killed in October by Henry Hona, who had already killed a family of four. An inquiry would be considered, replied Cobbe, if the MP could provide 'reliable evidence that matters are not right in the Police Force.'[251] Meanwhile, Wohlmann, seeking to gauge the extent of unrest, visited Auckland and questioned all the detectives and uniformed Sergeants individually about the issues raised by the *Auckland Star*.[252] In fact, the most widely-held grievance, apparently felt more strongly in Auckland than elsewhere, lay in the reduction of the special allowances to police that would follow a proposed 5 per cent increase in public servants' pay: rank and file police felt they would be short-changed by 2s a month.[253]

From late in 1934 Wohlmann made some relatively inexpensive and piecemeal innovations as a modest response to the criticism of police efficiency.[254] Outside experts lectured detectives and other police in the four main cities on aspects of forensic science and criminal investigation. A number of technical works on these topics were added to the small police libraries in the main centres. Arrangements were made to send two detectives for a course of training at New Scotland Yard in London. New equipment was provided for a newly appointed ballistics expert at Headquarters. Supervision at the main stations in the four cities was increased by appointing Sergeants for night duty in the watch-house. In August 1935, the Training Depot reopened; Wohlmann emphasised the 'improved standard' of recruits. As a sop to the rank and file, he belatedly reversed another of McIlveney's changes by reintroducing patch pockets on the police tunic. Another and much more significant innovation, the formation of a police reserve (or part-time auxiliary police), proved to be very controversial, however.

Between 1932 and 1934, Labour MPs, representing the broader views of the labour movement and the unemployed, became increasingly critical of various aspects of public order policing. Soon after the violent dispersal of the unemployed in Cuba Street in May 1932, Peter Fraser had led a deputation to the Minister, Cobbe, complaining that the police had acted precipitately and excessively, and he asked (to no avail) for a judicial inquiry. To the Wellington MPs, police leadership had been wanting in the handling of the crowds; the disturbances could have been avoided by better judgement.[255] Resentments persisted for a considerable time afterwards. Incidents such as one during the Lyttelton by-election in 1933, when Inspector Cameron snatched the Labour candidate's photograph off the lapel of an unemployed worker; or in Wellington, where hunger marchers advertising a meeting with sandwich boards were ordered off the streets; or the prosecutions of Jim Edwards and others in Auckland in 1934 for holding unauthorised meetings – all suggested what the *New Zealand Worker* termed bluntly a 'dirty form of discrimination'. In Parliament, Peter Fraser called on Cobbe to 'insist that his officers should see that unemployed workers had the same rights as all other citizens and that they were protected in those rights'.[256] Resentment rankled also over the policing of the Christchurch tramway strike, especially when in June 1932 Superintendent Cummings was reported as telling the Napier Rotary Club that it was the specials 'which to a very considerable extent broke the back of the strike. "They [the tramwaymen] are all back at work now, and sorry that the strike ever happened. As far as Canterbury and Christchurch are concerned, there will be no more strikes".'[257] Labour MPs saw this as a partisan comment; police were not supposed to 'take sides'. Cummings claimed he had been misreported, but Christchurch unionists (like their counterparts elsewhere) remained sceptical of Cobbe's reassurance that it was not government policy to use police or specials to break strikes.[258]

Such scepticism fuelled Labour Party opposition to the formation of the police reserve in late 1934. Ostensibly modelled on police reserves in England, the auxiliary police were intended to be a part-time, paid and trained supplement to the Uniform Branch: they would number 150 in Auckland, 100 in Wellington, 60 in Christchurch, and 40 in Dunedin. When in uniform, the auxiliaries would be indistinguishable from other constables – by contrast to the specials. They were intended, Cobbe said, to be called out on 'abnormal occasions', such as processions, demonstrations, or when 'there was a large influx of visitors'. Indeed, the auxiliaries were used during the visit of the Duke of Gloucester between December 1934 and January 1935. They were also a cost-cutting measure at a time when the full-time Force needed to be increased in size. From the outset, the auxiliary police were vigorously opposed by the Labour MPs, who saw them as likely to be recruited from only one section of the community; 'inclined to act as spies and informers' and be regarded as a 'gang of pimps', they were likely to 'destroy the good feeling which now existed between the Police Force and the people generally'. They would undermine the regular police and therefore (it was claimed) were opposed by the rank and file. To Robert Semple, it was obvious that the police reserve 'did not emanate from the Minister's mind – it came from some one behind him', 'a timid, nervy individual in the Department who was unreasonably afraid of what might happen in an emergency.'[259] Wohlmann's leadership was being called into question.

Though the disturbances of 1932 had not been insurrectionary, the outcome of the general election in 1935 was a peaceful political revolution, or so it seemed to many at the time. For four and half years Commissioner Wohlmann had been a cautious administrator befitting the times. He had made do with the resources available, and acted in sympathy with the conservative governments he had served. What would be his fortunes, and those of his Force, under the first Labour government?

CHAPTER 3

Careers and Community

In January 1920, aged 23, Bill Murray arrived in Wellington from England. When his military service ended he had chosen to emigrate rather than return to his pre-war job as a clerk in the post office at Bolton. He considered British Columbia, but New Zealand seemed more like Britain. Arriving with little cash in his pocket, Murray sought work at a West Coast sawmill. Soon dissatisfied with the pay and prospects he moved to Auckland, responded to a newspaper advertisement, and became a farmhand for £3 a week plus bed and board. Still restless, and impatient with his rate of saving, Murray returned to the city in April 1921. British Columbia still beckoned. In the meantime, 'I thought ... now what job with my experience would give me the best chance to accumulate some good money? And I thought of the Police.'[1] Murray waited eight months, while the Police made enquiries about him, before being called up for training at the Depot in Wellington. On 1 March 1922 he was sworn in as a constable. Soon he had met the woman he wanted to marry; only then did the Police become a career. Indeed it became his life. In the 1920s the New Zealand Police Force was a distinctive occupational community, in which 'the worlds of work and non-work [were] closely interdependent, each world permeating and affecting the other'.[2] This convergence of work with 'non-work' was more extreme than in other occupations during the inter-war years, or in the lives of police 50 years later.

Policing in New Zealand was an occupation which generally separated its practitioners from the wider society by both the nature of their duties and their methods of performing them. Potentially, though not necessarily, their coercive authority set them apart. Inevitably, as one retired man recalled, 'if a Policeman did his duty, he was not a very popular person, ... having to administer laws that he knew very well the public did not want or like, for instance the Licensing Act.'[3] Especially to drinkers, gamblers, and working-class youth, police in the inter-war years could expect to have the image of 'bogey-man' – the 'John Hop' or 'Demon' you looked out for. In varying degrees New Zealand police shared characteristics that have been observed amongst police elsewhere: a strongly masculine occupation emphasising the values of physique, hardiness, and comradeship; a pervasive code of conduct shaping their lives; social isolation associated with internal solidarity in the face of danger or criticism; attitudes that were often suspicious of outsiders and secretive; a 'working personality'[4] that was often hard to shake off. 'Once a policeman, always a policeman', was a common aphorism amongst retired men the author interviewed in the 1970s. Those like Bill Murray who made the Police their career soon became imbued with its ethos.

By 1920 the rudiments of professionalisation had appeared in New Zealand policing.[5] Standards for recruitment had been adopted, as well as basic training in law and practice at a Depot, and promotion examinations. With the exception of a few part-time District and Native Constables in isolated rural areas, policing was a full-time occupation which recruits could envisage as a career – with superannuation benefits if they remained until retirement. Most importantly, an ideal of service had been articulated in 1920 by Commissioner O'Donovan in his eloquent 'Address' to the Force. The extent to which the organisation's ethos was realised in the behaviour of individual police depended on the qualities of the recruits as well as on their training, discipline, and ultimately their degree of commitment to policing as a career.

The recruits

In his background Murray was atypical. More than two-thirds of the 78 men who were permanently appointed to the Police in 1922 were New Zealand-born. Of the remainder, more came from Ireland and Scotland together than from England – an attenuated nineteenth-century pattern which was about to disappear. Half the Irish had previous police experience.[6] Not that this was an advantage in the eyes of Peter Fraser, who asked the Minister of Justice whether Irish applicants had been members of the notorious 'Black and Tans' (the reply was negative).[7] Some former members of the Royal Irish Constabulary (disbanded in 1922) did join the New Zealand Police in the mid-1920s – notably John Feely, who was long remembered as a 'hard case' country constable in Southland. More significant in the view of the Protestant Political Association was the number of Catholics in the Force. Figures produced by the Minister of Justice, Wilford, in response to a deputation from the PPA in April 1918, showed that Catholics then comprised a third of the Force, as did adherents of the Church of England; Presbyterians made up another 28 per cent and a variety of Protestant denominations (including twenty who like Murray were Methodists) the remaining fraction. The top ranks of Police were evenly divided between Catholics and non-Catholics.[8] (By 1936 the overall balance had changed, with Presbyterians comprising a third of the Police, while the proportion of Catholics had fallen to 22 per cent – both proportions nearly 10 per cent greater than those in the wider population.)[9] Publicly at least, sectarian feeling had passed its peak by the mid-1920s, but sectarian suspicions were to long endure covertly in the ranks of the Police.

At nearly 26, Murray was slightly older than the median age (24) of those who were permanently appointed in 1922. They ranged from 20 to 38 years, with 22 and 26 being the most common ages; new constables in both 1882 and 1932 were slightly older. Senior officers generally favoured men in their mid-twenties. Superintendent Bartholomew Sheehan told nineteen year old Bill Fell that he did not want men until they were 25; men who joined at that age were likely to stay longer in the Force. Even so, Fell went to the Training Depot at twenty.[10] In theory, candidates for the Police Force had to be males aged between 21 and 30, but Commissioners accepted some outside these ages who were otherwise well qualified.[11] Four of those permanently appointed in 1922 were under 21 (one had been nineteen when first accepted as a temporary constable), while nine were over 30 – mainly former soldiers or members of the Force who were being reappointed.

That a majority of the new constables were in their mid-twenties or older meant that most came to the Police with considerable experience of the routines of hard monotonous work. Unlike Bill Murray (who began work in the post office at sixteen after private secondary schooling), most constables had left school at the age of fourteen (some earlier) and undertaken a range of manual jobs. Indeed, about two-fifths of those recruited in 1922 came directly off farms, and at least another fifth came from other forms of outdoor manual labour; they had been bushmen, teamsters, linemen or labourers. Urban trades and white-collar occupations were sparsely represented amongst recruits in 1922. Ten years later, however, in the depth of the Great Depression, the numbers recruited from farm and bush were more than equalled by those who had been laid off from the building and metal trades, sales jobs and offices.[12] Among the many New Zealand-born recruits during the 1920s, Willis Brown, the musterer and rabbiter who was to become Commissioner in 1958, was typical of South Island seasonal workers: he had a horse and five dogs when he was sixteen, and was his 'own boss', doing 'dirty hard work'.[13] Ken Burnside, Commissioner of Police from 1974 to 1978, left school at fourteen and worked on the small family farm in North Auckland for nearly eight years before joining the Police in 1940; with cows to milk before school, 'I really.started work the same time as I started school'.[14] In the North Island, the small family dairy farm, barely able to provide a decent standard of living, was a major source of recruits.

Why join the Police Force? For some there appeared to be no choice. To Tom Allsopp, like others who had migrated to New Zealand in the early 1920s and found no future in farming, the Police 'seemed to be the only thing open' at the time.[15] Others, such as Reese Hodge, an assistant butter maker in the Raetihi dairy factory, were 'looking for something better'.[16] Both were looking – along with most who sought to join – for better pay and a secure job. In July 1922, the daily pay for a constable with under three years' service (13s 6d) was less than the minimum hourly award rate for unskilled labourers (13s 10d for an eight-hour day).[17] This equation remained largely true until the mid-1950s. However, police were paid for seven days work, whereas in 1922 a majority of workers were working a 44 or 45 hour week, and most not more than 48 hours.[18] Hence, in 1922, a new constable could expect to earn £4 14s 6d a week, whereas an unskilled labourer working 48 hours on the minimum award wage would receive £4 3s. Outside workers on hourly rates could also expect to lose time in wet weather. This was the main consideration for E.J. Gaines, an electrical linesman, who sought a fixed and secure income by applying to join the Police in 1928. For Gaines, as for many others whose work was intermittent, the pursuit of better pay and greater security was made more urgent by marriage and a young family.[19] Because of the hours they worked (as well as the allowances and increments received), the median annual income of constables in 1926 was higher than that of virtually all groups of male manual workers, and rivalled only by that of those in white-collar jobs.[20] This disparity became even greater during the early 1930s as police pay was cut less severely than others', and as intermittent, short-time working and unemployment grew. Before 1936, moreover, farm workers did not have minimum wage rates. Their wages did not grow as fast as those of other workers in the 1920s, and they fell more steeply during the Depression – by more than a third between 1929 and 1933.[21]

Small wonder then that the Police came increasingly to be seen as 'a plum job'. By comparison with the 'small amounts of money' that he had been able to earn as a labourer from the age of fourteen, L.M. Hansen thought he was 'a millionaire' when he received the 'princely sum of 11/- per day' as a temporary constable in 1932.[22] And, so long as he ' "toed the line" there was no worry of unemployment', a policeman told Ray Henry, who at the age of 25 was then in his third insecure white-collar job.[23] The number of applicants on the waiting list grew from the late 1920s to (reputedly) well over a thousand by the mid-1930s. Gordon Diffey, a freezing worker, was not the only man to have waited four years after his application before entering the Training Depot in the late 1930s.[24]

According to conventional wisdom, all branches of government employment offered a secure income; but for many unskilled male workers the Police seemed the only option. For a few in the late 1930s, the Force was a second choice after they were turned down by the Army.[25] The Police requirement of having passed at least the primary school fifth standard was a barrier for some, but less demanding than the Public Service Entrance examination. Determined to join the Police, Reese Hodge (then aged twenty) received evening tuition from a local schoolmaster in order to obtain his fifth standard certificate before applying in 1929. In the early 1930s, as the competition for government jobs increased, the minimum educational qualifications for entrance into the public service rose markedly. Most police recruits had now passed the Proficiency examination taken at the end of the sixth standard.[26]

A few men who were sufficiently qualified for other government jobs nevertheless chose the Police, which offered more than merely a good secure income. The sports-loving Gideon Tait took a position in the Railways until he was old enough to enter the Police. Impressed with the 'upstanding, clear-cut type of manhood' and 'smart blue uniforms' of constables on duty,[27] Tait was not alone in seeking in the Force a respectable occupation that allowed for physical prowess, a chance for self-improvement, and (as another put it) 'the attractions of mixing with better types of persons for workmates' than hard-drinking foul-mouthed freezing workers, bushmen and farm labourers.[28] More generally, those who chose the Police rather than white-collar work sought variety in place of routine, and 'healthy' outside activity instead of being cooped up in a classroom or office.[29] Giving up clerical work at the Fairton freezing works for the Police in 1936, Colin Urquhart (a future Commissioner) thought the job would be 'interesting, challenging, and offered some degree of adventure or excitement'.[30] Such expectations moved others for whom becoming a policeman was a long-held, often boyhood, ambition. Youthful 'hero worship' of the 'man in blue' was professed by Charles Belton, who at 21 gave up 'bright' prospects as a clerk in a 'leading' commercial firm to join the Police.[31]

After 1920 the Police did not need to advertise for recruits. In a variety of ways police themselves shaped the decisions of many who chose the Force as a career. Family traditions of employment in the Police had already appeared, and these developed further over succeeding generations as sons (and from the late 1940s, daughters) followed fathers, brothers their elder brothers, and nephews their uncles. Wally George represented the third generation of his family in the New Zealand Police Force when he joined in 1947.[32] Amongst the Inspectors in the early 1920s, W.G. Wohlmann and Tivy Emerson had emulated the careers of their fathers, while W.B. McIlveney had a younger brother in the Force. By the mid-1920s there were quite a number of sets of brothers amongst constables and NCOs – notably the Cummings and Edwards families with three each, joined during the 1930s by the three Alty brothers. Typically, Frank Brady's youthful ambition to become a policeman (which he realised in 1923, aged twenty) stemmed from the influence of two uncles who were then serving. His brother and two nephews followed him into the Police.[33]

Individual police were a more pervasive influence than family links in encouraging men they felt suitable to join, and persuading those who had doubts. After being laid off by a Wellington car dealer in 1932, E.F. Barry's association with local constables led him to apply. When the starting pay offered a temporary constable gave him second thoughts, Barry was persuaded to accept by Superintendent Emerson, a keen follower of rugby who did not leave the prominent player of the game long on the waiting list.[34] More usually, it was the country constable who proved to be the main recruiting agent, both directly and indirectly. Working for his father as a road contractor, Gordon Howes crossed the path of the local constable, who asked if he had ever thought of joining the Police. 'You're big enough', the constable remarked; Howes went into the Training Depot ten months later, in 1925.[35] Image and personal authority was important: a telling-off that Eric Ward and his schoolmates received from an impressive country constable, with his big bay horse and highly polished leather leggings, planted the seeds of a youthful ambition to become such an officer.[36] Often country constables were friends of families that provided recruits. Sometimes there was no direct suggestion of going into the Police – rather, it was the presence and local standing of the constable that counted.[37]

'Anti-police' attitudes were present amongst the rough-living seasonal labourers and bushmen who sought liquor outside licensing hours, and amongst wharfies and West Coast coal miners whose traditional militancy had brought them into confrontation with the forces of the state. More subtly, amongst urban skilled workers and white-collar families, there was a diffidence about the work and status of ordinary policemen which led some parents to seek to dissuade their sons from joining and encourage them into schoolteaching or a skilled trade such as printing.[38] Small-town respondents to a survey of occupational status in the early 1950s ranked policemen much more highly (just below schoolteachers) than did those in Wellington, who placed them below commercial travellers, clerks, fitters and carpenters, and just above chefs and bricklayers.[39] By the 1920s policing had become a respectable occupation, requiring (according to an MP) 'the brains of a lawyer and the muscles of a navvy'.[40] Yet in popular perception the work was more manual than mental. As a civics textbook for school pupils put it: 'A man who wishes to become a policeman must be of strong physique, for he is often called on to do hard physical work'.[41] Sergeant Flanagan – R.M. Burdon's fictional stereotype of a small-town policeman – perspired at the very sight of pen and paper: he was 'very bad at writing reports and very lax at filling in forms'. His qualities lay elsewhere, in conversation and in methods of keeping the peace that kept locals out of court.[42] Diffidence about the work and status of police was thus weakest amongst farming and small-town families, and self-employed semi-skilled manual workers. Here could be found those most likely to look upon the police as an 'honorable career' at the outset, those who entered it with an 'admiration for the job'.[43]

While most recruits in the inter-war years had made a deliberate choice to improve their lot, many did not initially see policing as a vocation. Indeed, for some who applied to join the Police, the decision was apparently fortuitous. Orme Power, a farm labourer keen on wrestling, was persuaded to apply by a friend who had already done so: 'it was sheer accidental association with this chap'. Only later did Power develop a 'sense of service or belonging' and come to see the Police as a career.[44] When Henry Holmes married in 1927 after nine years at sea, his wife 'wanted him ashore'. The choices were working for the Wellington Harbour Board, the Railways, or the Police; Holmes chose the Police because his sister was going out with a constable.[45] In 1928 George Donnelly found that the Central Otago rabbiting season was short; he was out of a job by August. It was too early to go shearing, so he went to Dunedin to see the rugby match between New South Wales and the All Blacks. While there he put his name down for the Police: 'I did not think I would last long as I had been more or less my own boss since leaving school' at thirteen. He was to spend 35 years in the Force.[46] For D.J. O'Carroll, a stockman at the Moerewa freezing works, it was literally a toss-up: heads he stayed, tails he joined up.[47]

It was a common belief that policemen 'who came off the turnips turned out the best practical men'.[48] Formal education beyond the basic requirement was not a disadvantage. Nonetheless, other qualities were more strongly emphasised in the process of selection. This had three stages: an interview by the local Superintendent or Inspector accompanied by a preliminary examination of physique and medical fitness; a close investigation of character; and finally (at the Training Depot) a test of ability to submit to discipline and acquire the rudiments of law and police practice.

Adequate physique was the first requirement: candidates were to have a chest measurement of at least 38 inches and be 5 feet 9 inches or more in height. The popular image was of a Force of 'six-foot' giants, like Burdon's Sergeant Flanagan, 'a big, well-built, exceedingly powerful man'.[49] This was certainly an image cultivated by Commissioner McIlveney in his selection of the 80 police who accompanied the 1927 royal tour: all were over 6 feet tall.[50] However, at 5 foot 10½ inches Bill Murray was more typical. In both 1922 and 1932 only a third of the recruits were over 6 feet, and a fifth were under 5 feet 10 inches.[51] What some lost in height, they generally made up for in breadth, strength, and manner. Rugby, wrestling and boxing were common pursuits amongst applicants. 'Everybody laughed' when D.J. O'Carroll, 'a little fellow', applied for the Police; but he had been an amateur boxer for six years, and had only been beaten once.[52] Not only did many recruits have well-developed skills (and a readiness to use them) in defending themselves, the rural men were generally well-versed in the mores of those they would be policing. Like many others, George Donnelly found that ten years of seasonal labouring before he joined 'stood to me more than anything when dealing with men on the street .... I understood men and they understood my way of talking to them'.[53]

After a Police Surgeon had certified the candidate to be of 'good physique and medically fit' to join the Force, inquiries were made into his character and conduct. This was no perfunctory exercise. It normally took months for references, family and associates to be checked, and employers interviewed.[54] No candidate would be accepted who was 'nearly related by consanguinity or otherwise' to anyone convicted of crimes or of 'notoriously bad character'. Prospective wives of constables faced the same test.[55] Sobriety, industry, and above all honesty were looked for. School pupils were told that 'it is less harmful to the community that a policeman should be stupid than that he should be dishonest.'[56] Confidence in the honesty of the Police was the bedrock of public support. Once inquiries were completed, the file was sent to Wellington with a recommendation from the local senior officer for the Commissioner's approval. Of the 187 applicants on whom inquiries were completed in the year ending March 1924, 55 per cent were rejected; the proportion fell to 40 per cent in the following year.[57] If accepted, applicants were notified that they had been 'placed on list', to wait generally six months or more for a call-up to the Training Depot. Eventually a local constable would arrive to give the would-be policeman notice – often only a week – to settle his affairs and travel to Wellington.

After a second medical examination, most went straight to the Depot. In the late 1920s, however, Commissioner McIlveney paraded each batch of new recruits in the yard of the Wellington Central station. There he made remarks that 'seemed calculated to impress rather than encourage us', Charles Belton recalled.[58] As another man remembered vividly 50 years later, the Commissioner 'warned us of the evils of wine and women which he said was the chief downfall of policemen. Those that couldn't cope with them would be instantly dismissed. The way he hissed those ss's sounded as though he meant business'.[59]

Depot training

In essence the regime of police training at the Depot during the inter-war years had changed little since it began in 1898.[60] Continuity was ensured by the background of the Sergeant–Instructors who kept almost to the letter of the regulations governing the Depot that had been drafted by Commissioner O'Donovan, himself the first Instructor. Senior Sergeant John McNamara, who had been in charge when the Depot closed in December 1916, resumed his position when it reopened on 17 May 1921. Soon promoted to Sub-Inspector, McNamara (florid, stout, and a 'good talker' who liked his beer)[61] was assisted, and then succeeded in November 1921, by Sergeant Harry Scott. The 'precise, abstemious' Scott, 'one of nature's gentlemen' or a 'dour disciplinarian' according to one's perspective,[62] was the first Instructor to have himself come through the Depot. He typified in other ways his successors in the inter-war years, G.B. Edwards, George Paine and Dan Beard.[63] All had been Uniform Branch men, serving (with the exception of Beard) both at country stations and as sectional Sergeants. They were well-seasoned in the practice of everyday policing, but not (initially at least) in instruction, where they followed their predecessors' methods.

There was little change either in the facilities, with the exception of a period between August 1921 and October 1925 when the old Alexandra Barracks on Mt Cook in Wellington were occupied by larger intakes,[64] and again in 1937 when military facilities at Trentham were used for two 'big batches'. Otherwise, all intakes of recruits until July 1953 went to the two-storied weatherboard Depot which had been purpose-built in 1908 at Rintoul Street, Newtown (popularly called 'Wellington South'). Here, for three months, instruction and most of the social life of an intake (usually numbering between 20 and 23) would be contained within the lecture room, social room, gymnasium, messroom and kitchen. Drill was conducted on vacant ground out the back that was overlooked by neighbouring dwellings. Upstairs, each recruit had a cubicle with an iron bedstead and a wooden box for clothing. He supplied his own bedding. Meals were prepared by a cook and paid for fortnightly. The Sergeant lived with his family next door, and so the 'batches of young men were continually under his surveillance'.[65]

Soon after their arrival, the rules were made clear to many who had hitherto seen themselves as their 'own boss'. Recruits became 'probationers', not yet in uniform but now subject to a strict code of discipline. They were to get up at 6 am each day (7 in winter, and 7.30 on Sundays). Physical training and fatigue duty occupied the time until breakfast at 8 am; woodwork and floors were vigorously polished, and rooms and grounds made tidy for inspection. None were to leave the Depot until after 6 pm; and then only with the permission of the Sergeant–Instructor. They had to be back by 10 pm, meaning that special permission (for a 'late leave' to 11.30 pm) was necessary to go to the pictures. This was generally granted only on Friday and Saturday nights. No liquor or gambling was allowed on the premises. Lights had to be out by 11 pm. Probationers were free from 1 pm on Saturday, with a church parade and inspection at 9.30 am on Sunday the only demand on their time for the rest of the weekend. They were advised to spend their time off doing plenty of walking, which was 'better training for beat duty than sitting in picture theatres or riding in tramcars.'[66] This barracks life would continue for single men who were posted to the main centres. As Charles Belton remarked, it 'proved to be good training for the future as it taught us never to expect to be absolutely free, and always to remember we must ask very nicely if we wanted anything and to explain just exactly what we intended to do .... Freedom as understood by the average New Zealander simply did not exist'.[67]

Seated alphabetically in the classroom by 9 am each day, probationers learned by rote basic law, their duties and powers of arrest. The Instructor dictated extracts from statutes, especially the Crimes Act, Police Offences Act, Justices of the Peace Act, Licensing Act, and Arms Act, as well as the Police Force Act and Regulations. Probationers laboriously inscribed the extracts into black covered exercise books – many developing their writing skills and their spelling in the process. (Indeed, McNamara and Scott endeavoured to 'refresh' the education of their recruits, 'brushing up' their knowledge of arithmetic and geography through essay assignments.)[68] As an aid to memory, succinct definitions of law and police practice were also written, classified alphabetically, in a smaller notebook. Under 'Discipline', for example, a probationer wrote in 1930:

> The fi^st ['r' inserted] duty of a Constable is strict obeidience to all lawful order received from a supior [struck out] s^perior ['u' inserted]. He must receive such order with defference & respect & execute them with alacrity. (Regn. 47) For list of disciplinary breaches see Reg.353.[69]

Apart from the provisions of new statutes (such as the Police Offences Act 1927), the extracts barely changed during the inter-war years. Successive Instructors followed the same pattern. Questions on previous notes accompanied the ongoing dictation, with the probationers 'parroting' their responses: 'Everyone commits an offence who ....'

Instruction in the law relating to the most common offences encountered by beat constables was intermixed with hints as to its application by means of anecdotes drawn from the Sergeant's experience. Discretion and tact might be enjoined, but ultimately 'common sense' had to be the guide. Not only powers of arrest (and, importantly, their limits) had to be learned. Appropriate methods – for walking the beat,[70] writing reports (including the necessary commencing phrase, 'I respectfully report'), taking statements, giving evidence in court, classifying fingerprints, making measurements and plans of motor-car accidents, dealing with 'sudden deaths', identifying suspects and preserving exhibits at the scene of a crime – all had to be acquired, along with other skills. During the 1920s there was some practice in point duty. One evening a week, the Wellington Police Surgeon would lecture on first aid. Other evenings might be spent at 'mock courts' or in Swedish drill, jujitsu, or learning how to handle a brawl. Competence in swimming and life-saving had to be acquired (at the Te Aro baths in summer and the Tepid Baths in winter). There was squad drill on some afternoons to 'smarten up' the fledgling police.

In the course of training there were three written examinations in law and duties. Before the first test, Senior Sergeant Edwards warned that any who failed to achieve 50 per cent would have to resign. In each intake, one or two did not make the grade and left. A few others were dismissed because their 'character' was not as it had seemed on entry, or they were unwilling to accept the discipline. Attributing his success to his 'better academic knowledge' and good writing skills, Bill Murray topped the examination results of his intake. And true to form, he rose to a higher rank (Chief Superintendent) than any others sworn in during 1922.[71] Of course, success in Depot examinations was not necessarily a guide to subsequent advancement in the Force. Otto Anderson, for example, who was ranked fourth of the sixteen sworn in from his 1922 'batch', resigned a year later, while a fellow probationer who was ranked eighth (and eleventh in the law exam) rose to the highest rank to be achieved by that group, retiring as a Superintendent.[72] At the end of training, the Instructor reported on the probationers and commented on their 'general adaptability' before making a recommendation as to their permanent appointment. 'Probationer Sutherland', for example, was 'a steady sensible young man. He has made fairly good progress with his studies but cannot be said to be exceptionally bright. He should, with experience, make a useful Constable'.[73]

Depot training did not of itself produce ready-made, effective, policemen. Then as later, raw ('red bum') constables had much more to learn on the job, particularly from the 'old hands'. This was especially true of those who joined at times when the Depot was closed (between December 1916 and May 1921; July 1930 and August 1935; November 1939 and May 1946). They went straight onto beat duty, usually undertaking night shifts alone, wearing a dark greatcoat, until their uniform was made and they had learned the ropes.[74] Little was apparently gained from the perfunctory 'lectures' (reading of extracts from statutes) given weekly by local NCOs in the main centres. Conscientious and ambitious constables had to further their theoretical knowledge by self-disciplined study in their own time. Thus in the acquisition of skills, as in social background, the New Zealand Police was an 'artisan' force similar to those elsewhere.[75]

Nonetheless, the role of the Depot was crucial. It gave a technical training, supplying the rudiments of a craft. It provided the first test of commitment to the job as well as the first inculcation of discipline and of ideals. Here, some recruits began to see the Force as a career. In the closeted environment of Rintoul Street, the foundations were laid for a sense of occupational community, a developing feeling of comradeship. This emotional identification with one's new mates could endure after they dispersed from the Depot, despite the fact that the new constable might not see his fellow trainees again during his career. In the back of his exercise book, Bert Bevege listed the names of the 61 others in his 1937 'big batch', noting where they had come from and their destinations on leaving training at Trentham. Years later, near the end of his police career, Bevege put a tick, a cross, or left a space beside each name, and summed up: '22 remaining, 7 dead'.[76]

Symbolic of the transition from raw recruit to new constable was a series of rituals of induction. First came the fitting of the uniform near the end of training; the Department supplied the cloth, and the probationers paid to have it tailored. Then, on the day before their departure from the Depot, they were sworn in by the Commissioner, taking the oath of office as constables. Each was then allotted a registered number, often in alphabetical order. Some (like Bill Murray) saw in this sequence an order of seniority that would pattern subsequent careers. In theory the position on the seniority list was the same for each member of the intake, dating from the day of swearing in.[77] A group photograph of the newly uniformed constables was taken. They were fingerprinted, and then told to which of the four main centres they would be posted. The last night was one of celebration – often at a 'social' put on by the Instructor – and anticipation.

Job or career?

A necessary but not sufficient condition of an occupational community is that its members are emotionally involved in their work skills and tasks; they are doing it not just for the money, but also for personal satisfaction.[78] And indeed the self-image of constables came to be bound up with the qualities identified by successive Commissioners and officers as making 'good' policemen. This can be observed in the reflections of retired men who joined in the 1920s and 1930s: they saw being sober, honest, trustworthy, tolerant and understanding, patient, loyal to one's workmates and superiors, fearless, and (above all) dedicated to the job as what made a 'good' policeman (and implicitly, themselves).[79] Amongst the qualities identified, variations on a common theme reflected different personalities and styles of policing. Some emphasised the need for a sense of humour, restraint and 'common sense'. The conventional wisdom of seasoned constables in the inter-war years was 'run to a fire, walk to a fight'. This attitude was rejected by men like Gideon Tait, who relished a scrap and whose credo was 'never back down'.[80]

The reminiscences of retired policemen are those of survivors who have generally felt positive about their work, its comradeship, and the organisation's ethos. Not all did so. What then of those who merely tolerated the job in return for its economic rewards and left when something better turned up; or those who did not survive the rigours of policing, or who were ultimately unwilling to accept the Department's discipline, and have left (in their short police careers) few traces for the historian? Clearly they were not an insignificant number. By 1948, only 42 per cent of those who had joined in 1922 and 44 per cent of those appointed as temporary constables in 1932 remained in the Force.[81]

Not all lived to see retirement. Between 1919 and 1939, 119 members of the Police died.[82] Only three of these deaths were directly the result of criminal acts. All were constables who were shot: Vivian Dudding in 1919 while attending a domestic dispute in Wellington; James Dorgan in 1921 by a burglar (it is surmised) of a Timaru shop;[83] and Thomas Heeps on a farm near Morrinsville in 1934, by a young man suspected of murder.[84] Others died as the result of injuries sustained while on duty: at least two indirectly from violent blows,[85] and some from accidents involving trains or cars.[86] One constable drowned while seeking to save a woman's life;[87] another collapsed after bringing a resisting prisoner to the station.[88] Even more died from accidents while off duty, with motor vehicles prominently involved. Six years after his retirement from a distinguished athletic career, 42 year old Constable E.G. ('Buz') Sutherland fell off his bicycle and broke his neck.[89] Several suicides were directly attributed to the stress of work.[90] Most deaths, however, were ascribed to natural causes. During the early 1890s, the life expectancy of Pakeha males in their early twenties was little more than the age of compulsory retirement from the Force, 65 years. For their counterparts, overall life expectancy had increased by about three years in 1922, and a further year in 1931.[91] In 1948, five of those appointed in 1922 (or 6 per cent) had died, as had six (8 per cent) of those appointed in 1932. Many more who reached retirement age did not enjoy superannuation for long. Living to the age of 94, Bill Murray was an exception.

In fact mortality is a crude measure of occupational stress. Most of those who retired from the Force in the 1920s did not qualify for a full pension from the Public Service Superannuation Fund: they had neither served for 40 years nor reached the age of 65.[92] Clearly many would not achieve 40 years' service because of their age of entry into the Force. But it is striking that only two of 34 men who retired between 1924 and 1928 received a full pension, and that none of the 52 who retired between 1928 and 1931 did so; the average length of service of the latter was 27 years and $8^3/_4$ months.[93] Many left (with the 'Minister's consent') after at least 30 years' service and having reached the age of 55. Others (four or five each year, on average) retired earlier on medical grounds as being unfit for further duty. Because of the loss of income that resulted from 'medical retirements', a transfer to 'sedentary duties' was more common, where this was possible. Constable John Bruton, for example, lost his leg in a motor vehicle accident early in his career and was transferred to the Auckland District Office, where he died seventeen years later at the age of 51. Similarly, Senior Sergeant C.W. Kelly, ailing after 30 years in the Police, was transferred from active duty in Christchurch to take charge of the Police stores in Wellington, where he died a year later, aged 55.[94]

Constables began their service with good health and a high level of fitness, but years of beat duty could break this down. Walking at the regulation pace of two and a half miles per hour, a beat constable could cover sixteen miles in a day on the asphalt of Auckland streets or the stone flag pavements of Wellington. 'Nervous tension' was often engendered by being in the public gaze during the day, and by potentially hazardous situations at night.[95] Over a long period, irregular hours for meals and sleep, and exposure to the elements, impaired health and fitness. Between April 1931 and November 1932, the Christchurch Police Surgeon registered as sick 127 members of the Force in the city and suburbs: 54 cases were of influenza ('due mainly to exposure on outside duty in cold weather'), while 21 were due to accidents, seventeen while on duty – one causing death.[96] Reported serious injuries through assault were less common, but the hazard remained real nonetheless.[97] During the early 1920s, at least three policemen were shot in separate incidents and recovered.[98] Others had close shaves. Police who tackled drunken ships' firemen and stokers rarely came off unscathed. And 'strained muscles, wrenched joints, etc' became more common as youthful constables passed into middle age. Detective work also had its costs: out of eight holding the rank of Senior Detective in February 1922, four had died in the job by August 1928, another had retired early, and a sixth had had a nervous breakdown.[99] Overall, the Auckland Police Surgeon thought that the 'general health' of police could be 'looked upon as having deteriorated from 20 to 25 per cent. at the retiring age, as compared with other Civil Servants.'[100] Not surprisingly then, from 1928 (when the opportunity first appeared), rank and file police sought to modify the conditions of the Public Service Superannuation scheme by pressing for 'early retirement' on a full pension after 35 years' service.[101] They would have to wait another 30 years before the age of compulsory retirement was reduced to 60.

Between 1919 and 1939, 154 policemen were dismissed or compelled to resign, thereby losing any contributions towards a pension. This was the most severe sanction for a breach of Police Regulations; more common were fines, and an entry of conviction on a defaulter's sheet which would (in theory) compromise chances of promotion. Rank, seniority, and pay could also be reduced. Transfers were used as a means of punishment. There was no discretion to merely caution where the charges were trivial.[102] Discipline was perceived to be strict. 'Young ambitious constables on making technical errors through inexperience, are brought before the heads of their Department, much like the ordinary criminal, ... and in many cases fined, to the extent of two or three pounds', declared a correspondent to the *Dominion* in 1923.[103] Police Regulation 353 specified 52 disciplinary offences with which a member of the Force could be charged, including a catch-all: 'Any act, conduct, disorder, or neglect to the prejudice of good order, morality, or discipline, though not specified in these regulations'. In its scope, the disciplinary code contained the potential to 'dampen enthusiasm' and 'shake morale'. For the conscientious, however, it also reinforced norms of behaviour that the Force looked for in its recruits: obedience to orders, loyalty, sobriety, regularity, restraint, independence from outside influence, and above all honesty. Few departmental records remain of the disciplinary process or its outcomes in the inter-war years. Specific cases suggest that its application varied according to circumstances and individuals.

The Commissioner and his senior officers had two avenues open to them in dealing with allegations of serious misconduct: holding an internal inquiry from which the press and public were excluded, or laying a charge under the criminal law in open court. Convenience, the seriousness of the offence, and the appropriate means of protecting the image of the Force determined the choice. Few cases were brought before an open court, and most of these were for dishonesty on the part of constables. Typically they reflected the sources of temptation for police on duty: the monies received as Clerk of Court or for registering firearms;[104] property taken from prisoners in the watch-house;[105] theft from shops while on night duty.[106] Amongst the most serious cases prosecuted (at least in terms of the publicity received) were one in 1928 in which an Auckland constable and a former policeman were convicted of the arson of a grocer's shop for the purposes of insurance fraud,[107] and another in 1930 in which two constables and an accomplice were found guilty of a series of burglaries of a Wellington clothing store.[108]

Police prosecutions in court for complaints of violence on the part of constables were very rare. Given the realities of street policing (and a widespread acceptance of 'summary justice' for insolent behaviour), allegations of police brutality were difficult to sustain. A broad view was taken of the concept of 'reasonable force', not just by senior officers but also by judges and juries, who generally treated unsympathetically the occasional private prosecutions that came before them.[109] Where there was adverse publicity, however, the Commissioner's attitude could harden. When Peter Fraser raised in Parliament a report in the *Dominion* of an apparently brutal assault by a constable, the Minister promised 'a searching inquiry' by the Commissioner. On McIlveney's instructions, Constable Douglas was charged with a breach of police regulations. His conviction and dismissal followed after a three-day internal inquiry. However, Douglas was reinstated after a Board of Inquiry (chaired by a magistrate) upheld his appeal. The Department also reimbursed his legal costs in successfully defending a civil suit for damages.[110] Not so fortunate was Detective William Cooper, who had been found guilty of assault by an internal police inquiry and fined £2. Though this was his second disciplinary fine for assault, Cooper was not forced to resign until after he was successfully sued for damages, amidst considerable publicity. Commissioner McIlveney then declared that the detective 'had proved himself unworthy to remain a moment longer in the Force'.[111]

During the inter-war years, only one constable was charged in the Supreme Court with accepting a bribe (and only a few cases were reported of attempts to bribe police).[112] Commissioners apparently preferred to deal with the very rare allegations (usually from bookmakers or Chinese opium smokers) though internal inquiries, which were speedier, more certain of having a desired outcome, and (hopefully) would avoid damaging publicity. Inconveniently, under neither the Police Force Act nor the Police Regulations was it a disciplinary offence to accept a bribe. So Commissioners had to use other means at their disposal. Suspected of demanding money from a man against whom he had secured a conviction, the long-serving Detective C.A. Lambert was dismissed in 1927 for accepting a 'gratuity' from the complainant without the sanction of the Commissioner.[113] During a wider departmental inquiry into disaffection amongst police in the Timaru District in 1935, Detective L. Studholme was charged with accepting bribes from bookmakers. The charge was not sustained by the senior officer conducting the inquiry, but Studholme was dismissed nonetheless by Commissioner Wohlmann, with no right of appeal. He was only reinstated (as a uniformed constable, and posted to Kumara on the West Coast) when Parliament's Public Petitions Committee recommended a magisterial inquiry.[114] Parliamentarians representing mainstream public opinion believed in the integrity of the Police Force. So too did judges. 'Sensible people knew that there was no such thing as "graft" in the New Zealand Police Force', a Christchurch magistrate declared.[115] Justice Alpers went further: 'I have been twenty years at the Bar and I have been looking for the wicked policeman, but have never found him.'[116]

Most dismissals and forced resignations in the 1920s and 1930s appear to have been not for 'wickedness' but for rather less heinous infractions of the disciplinary code. This was especially the case during the regime of Commissioner McIlveney between 1926 and 1930, when nearly half of those forced to leave in the inter-war years did so. In his quest for discipline, McIlveney was not necessarily more exacting than his fellow officers. The convictions he dealt with generally stemmed from charges laid by others. Amongst officers and NCOs of the 1920s, a legacy of military discipline still remained, inherited from the New Zealand Constabulary Force and (for those like McIlveney and Wohlmann who had joined in the 1890s) from prior service in the Permanent Artillery. Their successors, schooled in hard police discipline and rising to senior ranks during the 1930s and 1940s, were often no less exacting, using what their critics termed 'petty pinpricking tactics'.[117]

As Commissioner, McIlveney differed from his predecessors and successors only in his readiness to apply the most severe sanctions for behaviour that appeared to tarnish the Force's image or threaten its discipline. Thus he compelled to resign (rather than merely transferred) a country constable who was sued for slander,[118] and a Senior Sergeant charged on a private information with perjury in a civil matter;[119] their personal affairs were perceived to impinge adversely on the Police's standing. He ordered that Christchurch constables be charged in court with converting a car (lent to them by a local firm to transport a police cricket team) when they damaged it on a joyride; the charge was dismissed.[120] Constables who might hitherto have been dealt with by internal inquiry and merely fined for (say) entering a hotel without good cause were now charged in open court with breaches of the Licensing Act. Those convicted were dismissed by McIlveney.[121] When a magistrate asked why a constable had been dismissed and *then* prosecuted in court for possessing an unregistered revolver, a Sub-Inspector replied opaquely: 'This is the cause of his dismissal, but not the reason'.[122] 'Dissentients' were quickly removed from the Force, as W.V. Sanvig, a night-duty constable, discovered when he and his Christchurch barracks-mates refused their Sergeant's order to wash up their dishes. They were quickly hauled before the Superintendent and fined £1 each for disobedience. Sanvig claimed the right to appeal, but was told 'to get out' by the Superintendent. Submitting his resignation, Sanvig found himself dismissed by McIlveney under the notorious section 9 of the Police Force Act, as 'unfit to remain in the Force'.[123] Nor were NCOs immune from the Commissioner's heavy hand.[124] However, as we have seen, the dismissal of Sergeant George Bonisch for failing to make the full number of visits to his beat constables and making a false entry in his report was seen as 'harsh' and proved to be McIlveney's undoing.[125]

The seemingly capricious application of discipline in the late 1920s eroded belief in the security of employment which many recruits had sought in the Police.[126] Even so, only in the year to March 1930 were more forced to leave than left voluntarily. Overall, voluntary resignations from the Police averaged 34 a year between 1918 and 1928, or roughly half the annual recruitment of new constables. The rate fluctuated with economic conditions, falling sharply from 1929, averaging less than seven annually between 1931 and 1936, and rising again as the economy improved. Of the 78 constables who were permanently appointed in 1922, 24 had resigned and three had been dismissed by 1929. More left of their own volition between 1935 and 1940, and from 1944. Similarly, by 1948, a third of those who had joined in 1932 had resigned.[127] That so many left voluntarily suggests that many had only an ambivalent identification with police work. Any initial commitment to policing as a career had been eroded by the conditions of beat work, the discipline, and also by a mounting sense of social isolation.

A separate community?

A second major determinant of an occupational community is the degree to which an organisation constrains the non-work life of its members, raising barriers to their interaction with others and shaping perceptions of social isolation. As has already been discussed, the New Zealand Police had many norms and rules that shaped its members' lives beyond work. To a degree, single men were quarantined in barracks. More generally, police had to be mindful of their associates. Many felt inhibited from joining sports clubs by the obvious gap between the liquor licensing law and social practice. Playing a round of golf, for example, might require them to overlook an offence – the so-called 'nineteenth hole' in the clubhouse.[128]

More than this, leisure pursuits were clearly constrained by the hours of work. Until August 1937, police worked seven-day weeks. For every month's service, two days of paid leave were allowed from 1925. But the occasional Sunday off was construed as a 'privilege' rather than a right.[129] In reality, suburban and country constables were never off duty, and especially when social functions were being held. Police could not leave their sub-districts without permission when off duty; they were always on call. In the towns, while eight-hour shifts were the norm for uniformed constables and Sergeants, extra hours were frequently worked because of the need to attend court, sports events and race days. Social life was difficult to plan for in advance. NCOs and detectives could expect to work longer hours and broken shifts. Beat constables in the cities generally worked on night duty two weeks in every four, and alternating shifts on day duty.[130] Regular participation in outside organisations was thus difficult.

Like their predecessors since the 1890s, Commissioners in the 1920s discouraged their men from sporting activities which might reflect adversely on the Force, require leave or cause injuries that interfered with the performance of police duty.[131] Sport was played by police at their own risk: they would receive no sick pay or medical expenses if they were injured. Professional boxing was not seen as respectable by senior officers, though police were not debarred from amateur contests. Indeed some police boxers and wrestlers left their marks in local championships.[132] But perseverance was needed. Bill Tyree, a constable at Palmerston North in the early 1920s, had to circumvent his Senior Sergeant, who did everything possible (such as changing Tyree's shift) to prevent him taking part in boxing contests in the local Opera House. Eventually Tyree left the Police to pursue his boxing (and rugby) career in Wellington.[133]

Since Commissioner McIlveney (in particular) frowned on it, playing the most popular winter sport – rugby – was also difficult.[134] Sympathetic officers arranged shifts to allow E.F. Barry to play rugby on Saturday afternoons in Wellington. After two years on the beat, 'Ned' Barry was appointed to the District Office which, with its five and a half day week, allowed him to play the sport. Barry played representative rugby for many years, as did others in the Force. In 1932 (when he joined the Police), and again in 1934, he toured Australia with the All Blacks.[135] By the early 1930s, some senior officers, often keen sportsmen, had begun to appreciate the public relations value of rugby, and annual 'charity' games were organised by local police against Post and Telegraph and 'Press' teams in Wellington and Christchurch.[136] From this time, police rugby teams and inter-district rivalry began to develop.

Athletics produced the most prominent police sportsmen of the inter-war years, notably Peter Munro, 'Buz' Sutherland, and J.W. ('Jack') McHolm. Between them, these three men won 54 New Zealand titles.[137] E.G. Sutherland found it difficult to maintain his level of performance after he joined the Police in 1926 and began pounding the beat. By contrast, Peter Munro was fortunate to be transferred in 1924 to the Wellington District Office, where he remained until promoted to Sergeant supervising beat constables in 1935. In that year, aged 42, Munro retired from athletics. He eventually took up bowls, which was then the most common sporting activity of police, especially after they had escaped from shift work to office duties or higher rank, and thereby gained more regular leisure time.[138]

Generally speaking, then, the worlds of work and non-work were closely interdependent for many police in the inter-war years. The retrospective comment of one man who joined in 1927 summed up the feelings of some police in the cities at least, and especially detectives: 'In those days the Police were very much a separate section of the community. In the main they stuck solely to Police work and rarely took part in any social or community activity, except with and among other Police.'[139] This sense of separateness was expressed, for example, in the annual Police family picnics in Auckland and Christchurch. However other retired men, often those who had worked in small towns and the country, did not recall a great degree of social isolation: their families made close friends outside the Force. Nonetheless at social functions they would invariably encounter reserve: the word would go round that 'a cop was present' and 'conversation would become guarded.'[140] Still others who joined between the wars 'did not find [that] being in the Police was any social embarrassment.'[141] Thus there was a range of experience and of perceptions of social isolation, varying with personality and career path.

A Pakeha male preserve

A third feature of the New Zealand Police as an occupational community, but one which was not distinctive to the Police, was its undiluted masculinity and its European ethos. With apparently no more than one exception, Maori and women were essentially auxiliaries to the Force and excluded from pursuing a full career within it.

William Carran, dubbed a 'half-caste' when he joined the Force in 1920,[142] seems to have been the first Maori since the 1880s to receive a permanent appointment; he was the first before the 1960s to reach the rank of Sergeant (in 1937). Three years before he retired in 1960, Carran was appointed Assistant Commissioner. He was a stark exception to the rule. The few other Maori who were already in the Police, or who joined in the 1920s and 1930s, were Native or District Constables.[143] The five Native and eight District Constables in 1918 (diminishing to one Native and three District Constables by 1933) were a legacy of the past.[144] Desire for a police presence in an isolated area, together with a lack of resources or sufficient work, had led to the appointment of these part-time police. Native Constables, working under the direction of the nearest Pakeha police, had been seen to have the expertise (especially in the Maori language) needed to assist in policing specific localities. With his competence in the language, 'Bill' Carran spent the last nine years of his seventeen as a constable at three sole-charge stations (Otaki, Ngaruawahia, and Kawhia) where there were sizeable Maori communities.

Well before the 1920s, however, most Maori were policed by Pakeha, where they were not self-policing. In most rural areas where Maori were concentrated, Maori constables came to be seen as unnecessary, as fluency in English became widespread amongst a people viewed as increasingly 'Europeanised'. Where Native Constables might still be desirable, well-qualified men were difficult to recruit: they needed to be of the local tribe and have mana to be effective. Yet such men might well be subject to local influence, which contravened a basic principle of Pakeha policing. Indeed, as policing professionalised, untrained part-time police – especially those focusing on one race – were seen as an anachronism. Moreover, the growing intermingling and intermarriage of the races in some areas made the separate policing of Maori seem impractical as well as increasingly invidious in the eyes of experienced Pakeha police.[145] Thus, by 1936, Rawiri Puhirake ('Dave') Hira (at Te Kaha) and Louis ('Heke') Bidois (at Te Whaiti) were the last of the Maori part-time police. Coinciding with the passage of the Maori Social and Economic Advancement Act in 1945, they were both appointed temporary constables in the 'regular' Police, a status they held until retirement.[146]

Though the inter-war years were the end of an era for Native Constables, there was little compensating recruitment of Maori into the 'regular' Police, before the mid-1950s at least. Certainly, in 1950, some Pakeha officers working in the King Country, on the East Coast, and at Kaitaia saw the value of having the expertise of Maori as 'regular' Police to assist them.[147] But other attitudes and processes apparently militated against the recruitment of Maori. Unlike their rural Pakeha counterparts, Maori were unlikely to have been encouraged to join the Force by local constables, and probably felt other inhibitions from doing so anyway. If they had ventured to apply at a city station, a discouraging response was likely. In 1929, Tau Henare (the MP for Northern Maori) alleged that a Maori youth who had applied to join the Police had been told 'that it was not going to tolerate a member of the Maori race in the Force'. (The Minister promised to look into the matter.)[148] Stimulated by the Maori contribution to the war effort, concern at the lack of Maori in the Police was aired regularly in Parliament from 1941. The acting Minister in charge of the Police,

Paddy Webb, claimed that four Maori constables had recently been appointed. But there were 'places in which it would be difficult for a member of the Native race to act as a constable, and the matter must be left to the discretion of the Department'.[149] In 1950 the Senior Sergeant at Taihape was more explicit:

> The average European would strongly resent being corrected or reprimanded by a Maori, particularly in some districts where the colour line is still observed. On the other hand the average Maori appointee would be inclined to suffer from an inferiority complex when dealing with Europeans, or be imbued with his authority and fail to use discretion when dealing with pakehas.[150]

Old attitudes were dying hard. This applied not just to the acceptance of Maori in positions of authority, but also to belief in a 'Maori temperament' which, with 'certain exceptions', meant that Maori should not be appointed policemen. This was the view of Inspector Peter Munro of Whangarei in 1950; and it seems to have been shared by the Commissioner, J.B. Young.[151]

Physical and temperamental characteristics were also seen by police administrators as disqualifying women from recruitment into the 'regular' Police during the 1920s and 1930s. The Force had long employed a few women, but only on the grounds of necessity.[152] At most stations part-time 'female searchers' (usually policemen's wives) were hired to search and attend to female prisoners. In the four main centres, a full-time Police Matron was permanently appointed for this work. They took charge of all women and 'stray children' brought in custody to the station, keeping the keys of female cells. They provided the escort for female prisoners, especially to court, where they remained with them. The volume of this work was such that during 1917 each of the matrons was given an assistant. Then, in Dunedin at least, the two matrons could also 'devote considerable time to outside matters, such as visiting [the] railway station, picture-theatres, parks, and other places where girls frequent, with the view of their protection' – though (it was noted a year later) 'in no instance have they had occasion to interfere.'[153] This expanded role reflected unremitting and mounting pressure from women's organisations for women police.

Such pressure was resisted effectively by successive Commissioners and their Ministers until 1938. In response to the first wave of lobbying which began in 1914, the Minister of Justice (Herdman) and Commissioner Cullen both sought information from overseas, particularly from the USA, Britain and Australia, where some women police had recently been appointed. For them, overseas experience merely confirmed the status quo, as it was to do for their successors. From his senior officers, Cullen also obtained views that were virtually unanimous and were to change little in the next three decades. For 'ordinary Police duties', Superintendent Wright thought that women 'would be useless; as an adjunct to the Detective branch, they might be occasionally useful, but so seldom that their appointment would be a waste of money.' It was then inconceivable that women had the physical capacity for policing unruly males. Nor was it acceptable that they should be exposed to physical danger. All agreed that female criminals were too few in New Zealand to warrant appointing policewomen. Pointing to the small number of reported offences against women and children, the officers were complacent about the possible extent of sexual molestation. The notion that female victims of sexual offences might be inhibited from complaining to policemen, and prefer to be dealt with by women police (a point made strongly by lobbyists), was barely considered. Most officers deemed women to be temperamentally unsuited to police work. 'From what I have seen of women in other capacities where tact and discretion is required, I am not sure that women police would be a success under any conditions', was Superintendent Dwyer's opinion. Echoing the views of senior officers, Herdman told a deputation of women's groups in 1916 that:

> 'it took two years to train a policeman, and that the most difficult thing to teach him was to hold his tongue. (Laughter.) How long would it take to train women?'
> Voices: 'Half that time.' 'Three months'.[154]

The lobbyists – particularly those from the Women's Christian Temperance Union, the Society for the Protection of Women and Children, and later the National Council of Women – would not go away. Each year deputations waited on the Minister of Justice, and an ongoing stream of letters from women in small towns as well as cities crossed his desk. Occasionally, Ministers and Commissioners professed to be confused about what was wanted: women patrols or policewomen? Both were. In part, the WCTU and the SPWC were reacting to the greater freedom being demonstrated by young women in the cities, especially during the 1914–1918 war and just after it, as well as to persistent fears about sexual assaults and harassment. Patrols were needed by women police who, as the President of the WCTU put it in 1916, 'by their wise counsel, will be able to prevent girls from becoming immoral.'[155] Advocates of social purity and female protection asked that women patrols be vested with the powers of 'ordinary police' *only* in regard to their own sex, to enable them to 'to arrest and detain', 'protect or control as the case might need.'[156] Indeed, asserted one member of a deputation to Herdman in 1916, 'We don't want to have anything to do with the criminal classes.' To which Herdman expostulated, 'But they are the only classes with whom the police have to deal!'[157] Critics feared that the 'ladies of the WCTU' were seeking powers to interfere with 'breaches of conventional morality' outside the sphere of the criminal law.[158] Thus Commissioner O'Donovan argued in 1921:

> If women police are required to do certain things not attended to by the police because of their being outside the scope of police duty and not authorised by law, it will be necessary first to have legislation to enable such things to be done .... It is, therefore, for those who urge the appointment of police women to define exactly the duties they desire them to do, and afterwards for the Legislature to enact the necessary laws to enable such duties to be carried out.[159]

Yet the advocates of women patrols had already made clear what they wanted: preventive surveillance that did not require legislation.[160] And in response the duties of Police Matrons were (in theory) expanded in 1917 to include patrolling public places to protect women and children, and providing assistance (but not the primary role) in the taking of statements from females regarding sexual assaults or molestation.[161] However the numbers of matrons remained at eight during the inter-war years. Nor were they 'sworn in' as constables and given powers of arrest. Indeed they remained invisible, not being in uniform and spending most of their time dealing with women as prisoners. Thus Police Matrons were not women police in the eyes of the lobbyists. Nor was the gap filled by the advent of female 'Health Patrols' (between 1919 and 1921) possessing the powers of constables in their monitoring of women with venereal diseases.[162] The issue of women police remained.

It was not merely a question of insufficient 'women patrols'; there was also a feminist impulse. Seen in a broader context, the agitation for women police was part of a wider movement to remove 'all disabilities' hindering women from being 'appointed to any public office ... which men may hold', in the words of the final resolution of the first convention of the National Council of Women in 1896.[163] This impetus for greater equality included pressure for women jurors and JPs as well as police, especially from 1916. Citing the words of a male judge, Kate Sheppard observed that 'the woman wrong-doer' had 'a grievance' in the fact that she was arrested, represented (if at all), tried, and sentenced by men.[164] Thus for feminists, women employed on patrol work should have appropriate training (preferably from women) and the same powers and status as policemen. This did not imply, as one advocate put it, that women police would be 'mere duplicates of policemen'[165] – rather they would have largely separate spheres of policing, on the basis of equality. To this, successive Commissioners could not agree. Indeed, in this respect, the Police Department proved to be a bastion of anti-feminism. To have women with the same powers and status would clearly threaten the masculinist ethos of the Force which was epitomised by its emphasis on the physical, coercive, aspects of policing, and by the closed inner world of police stations and barracks. New and separate facilities would be required – here Commissioners (and their Ministers) took refuge in the argument that the cost would be unwarranted. As a delaying tactic they also used the ploy that a legislative change was needed. In 1916, John Salmond, the Solicitor-General, had given his opinion that the 'nature and purposes of a police force indicate sufficiently that it was intended by the Legislature to be a force consisting of men.'[166]

During the late 1920s, lobbying for the appointment of policewomen reached an intensity rivalling that of the war years. And for the first time a Minister of Justice, F.J. Rolleston, was sufficiently sympathetic to contemplate making the necessary legislative change. At his instigation, a clause was inserted in a bill drafted in 1928 to amend the Police Force Act allowing the appointment of policewomen with the powers of constables.[167] It was no simple clause. Women police might be given the same 'powers and protection' as policemen, but Commissioner McIlveney was opposed to giving them the same status, because (as he saw it) they could not perform the same duties. Hence the bulk of the Police Force Act was not to apply to the small number of policewomen who were envisaged. The distinction proved academic. The 1928 election saw a new government and a Minister, Thomas Wilford, who preferred to have Police Matrons on patrol where necessary rather than policewomen.[168] The fortunes of the bill were now shaped by an ongoing debate over police superannuation, and Wilford's departure from the Cabinet after a year. His successor as Minister of Justice, Sir Thomas Sidey, told a deputation he would support the appointment of policewomen.[169] But he was not Minister in charge of the Police. Again, the Department stymied the initiative. In July 1930, interim Commissioner Ward and his putative successor Wohlmann recommended to their Minister, the conservative J.G. Cobbe, that the provision for appointing policewomen be dropped from the draft Police Force Amendment Bill. They argued that its purpose was 'largely for carrying out what is more "social uplift" than strictly police work'. If some were appointed, pressure for more would grow, which would be costly at a time when 'strict economy' was needed. Altogether the ' "police value" of women police would not be commensurate with the cost'.[170] The bill lapsed, and there things stood for another decade.

For most matrons, the Police was either a full-time career in place of marriage, or a second career following the death of their husband, usually a constable. Women aged in their forties, with Police 'connections', were favoured as appointees. Mrs Catherine Ledger (nee Cummings) was notable for having three brothers in the Force when she became Assistant Matron at Wellington in 1917. Typically, Mrs Ledger served 21 years until retiring as the senior matron. Her death while on retiring leave merited a police funeral with a detachment of nearly 100 police marching with the cortege.[171]

Even more than policemen's, matrons' lives were shaped by the demands of the job. They lived rent-free in their own 'comfortable quarters' in each central police station in the four cities. Matrons worked alternating 24-hour shifts, being 'on call' for a range of duties while also monitoring the female prisoners. At Wellington, the women's cells were next to the back door of the matrons' flat, and nights could be disturbed by inmates making a 'real royal din – cursing and swearing, fighting and throwing utensils about the cell'.[172] For their 84-hour week, the matrons received an annual salary of between £141 and £172 in July 1922 – from 57 to 70 per cent of the basic annual income of a new constable living in barracks, a ratio that did not change in the inter-war years. Behind the differential lay a basic assumption that the matrons' work was not only different, but less demanding. In fact it could be just as distasteful as any confronted by a male constable (removing property from bodies in the morgue, informing relatives of a sudden death, intervening in domestic disputes, searching drunken and filthy women suspected of venereal disease), and just as physical, as when violent mental patients had to be escorted or drunken prisoners restrained. At first Miss Edna Jeffrey (a matron in Wellington from 1941) hated aspects of the work. Eventually she came to 'take it in my stride', and went on to serve for 28 years in the Police. She enjoyed the 'social part' of the job. Matrons were members of the police occupational community, albeit on its periphery in the inter-war years.[173]

A cohesive community?

When the characteristics of a distinctive occupational community have been discerned, the question remains: how cohesive was it? Clearly the 'organisational embrace'[174] of the Police Force, its rules and routines, provided a common basis of experience. Yet the organisation of police work also inhibited the development of rank and file solidarity, and resulted in rivalries and varying levels of commitment from those in the front line.

Until the late 1930s at least, police had relatively weak institutions of workplace solidarity, in contrast to archetypal occupational communities such as those of coal miners on the West Coast of the South Island.[175] In 1922, the 1,000 full-time police were dispersed in 327 stations. More than 70 per cent of these were one-man stations, while only thirteen had more than ten men, and only six (all in the four main centres) had more than twenty. Most front-line constables worked alone for much of the time, with limited means of summoning back-up quickly. In meeting danger and difficulty they had to rely on their own resources and public support in the first instance, rather than on their workmates. A country constable who spent nearly 30 years working in rural Otago commented that 'he did not get to know many other Police.'[176] Isolation from other police could shape survival skills that were self-interested rather than necessarily reflecting the organisation's ethos – emphasising summary justice rather than prosecution, for example.

Nor, between 1922 and 1936, could individual police seek support from their peers against the consequences of strict discipline, or to press their grievances. They could write to the Commissioner only on their own behalf, thereby courting further trouble by having to submit their reports through their immediate superiors. Before the advent of the New Zealand Police Association, there was no union to shape and give voice to collective sentiments within the Force as a whole.[177]

To the extent that it existed, a strong sense of camaraderie was local and station-based, focused on the barracks and its 'Library' (cum billiards-room) in the main centres, or on the small work groups of the city beat section, detective office, and provincial towns. The officers and men of the Timaru and Hamilton districts erected headstones for colleagues (James Dorgan and Thomas Heeps, respectively) killed on duty.[178] In 1922, Napier police began a relief fund for a constable forced to retire because of failing eyesight which raised £284 from police throughout New Zealand.[179] Camaraderie was expressed conventionally at rites of passage which involved all ranks: street processions at police funerals, and the eulogies at socials accompanying retirements and transfers.

On these occasions – by contrast to those of the miners – 'the bosses' were part of the police occupational community. Even so, they generally appeared aloof from the ranks. As Commissioner, McIlveney was more visible to his men than most in the inter-war years. Yet in his presence, jocularity (as a form of resistance, perhaps) had to be anonymous. When in 1930, 'according to his custom', McIlveney interrogated a large number of Auckland constables and detectives on aspects of their work, 'he fixed his eyes upon an efficient looking constable and asked "What would you do if you found £2?". There was a brief silence and then there came a gleeful voice from the ranks: "Put it on Star Stranger".'[180] This anecdote was long remembered within the occupational community. Also remembered by retired men was a common phrase of the stern Senior Sergeants who were seemingly indifferent to the feelings of new constables: 'If you don't like the job, get out; there's plenty waiting!'[181] At Ashburton, Timaru, and Gisborne during the inter-war years, antagonisms between officers and men precipitated internal inquiries, prosecutions, resignations and transfers.[182]

The degree of cohesiveness within the police occupational community was shaped by levels of satisfaction and commitment, as well as by perceptions of social isolation, which again depended largely on the type of work undertaken. This may be demonstrated by a sketch of the police career path before the 1950s.

All new constables began their careers walking an inner-city beat, and many remained for years on beat work. While there were moments of excitement and interest, walking the beat soon provided little satisfaction for most, and especially for those who wanted something more than merely a secure job. Shift work, monotony, fatigue, isolation at night, the inability to relax in the public gaze during the day, and the pinpricks of discipline for failing to work the beat adequately, all led many men to seek other work during their first years of service. Many recognised that, given their age and/or educational attainments, their chances of promotion were slim. Opportunities to move quickly to alternative work within the Force seemed to be few. Of those who remained, some would eventually enter the small Detective Branch,[183] a station watch-house, or be put on uniform inquiries. A few would perform clerical duties in a district office. More likely was an eventual transfer to a provincial centre where duties were more varied and relaxing than in the city, and the public more friendly. From here would come the chance to be a junior at a two- or three-man station, or to take charge of a suburban or country station. This career path to country constable could take fifteen years or more, as did promotion to Sergeant in charge of a section of city beat men. Opportunities (especially transfer to the Detective Branch) depended largely on perceived aptitude for particular work, and otherwise on seniority and keeping a clean charge sheet. Single men were generally not sent to small towns or country stations. From 1913, those seeking promotion to a higher rank had also to pass a qualifying examination.

Promotions sometimes caused resentment, jealousy, and suspicion within the Force. According to the Police Regulations of 1919, 'due regard shall be paid to seniority of service and good conduct' in deciding on promotions, 'but preference must always be given to those who possess a superior education, and who have displayed superior intelligence, zeal, and integrity in the discharge of their Police duties.'[184] The author of the Regulations, Commissioner O'Donovan, placed 'merit' over 'seniority' in promoting Detective Sergeant James Cummings in 1921. The resentment he created, especially amongst detectives at the time, and amongst uniformed Senior Sergeants in 1927 when Cummings was transferred to the Uniform Branch in readiness for promotion to Sub-Inspector, probably inhibited later Commissioners (apart from Cummings himself) from following suit.[185] Seniority – the promotion of 'qualified' men in their turn – was the rule, and harmony over promotions was generally maintained until 1949. A few had a suspicion (probably unwarranted in the inter-war years) that the annual qualifying examinations were used as a means of reducing the pressure for promotion.[186]

Out of the 78 constables appointed in 1922, seventeen qualified by examination for promotion to Sergeant. Examinations could not be taken until after seven years' service. Four of the 1922 intake passed the Sergeant's exam as soon as they were able. Although they kept an eye on the seniority list, the remainder were in no hurry to sit their exams. For some, the swot was slow and arduous. There was no detailed syllabus (only the precedents of past papers) for the examinations on law and 'Practical Police and Detective Duties'. For those rusty in the English, arithmetic and geography necessary for the 'Literary' examination, there was coaching by correspondence from the examiner,

Robert Darroch of the Terrace School in Wellington.[187] In 1931, fourteen of the 38 candidates failed all their Sergeant's exams; only three passed in all subjects. In the same year, five out of eight failed their Senior Sergeant's exams, and five out of nineteen failed the Sub-Inspector's.[188] Bill Murray passed both his Sergeant's and Sub-Inspector's exams in the two years before his promotion to Sergeant in 1937. After fifteen years of service, Murray was in the first group of the 1922 intake to be promoted. Others, slow in passing their exams, waited up to nineteen years to become Sergeants. Of those appointed in 1922, seven made it to commissioned rank, with the first of them (Bill Murray and J.J. Kearns) becoming Sub-Inspectors in October 1950. Three who had qualified by examination for the rank of Sergeant were never promoted, and two others who had passed their Sub-Inspector's exams before Bill Murray were never appointed to commissioned rank. They were not necessarily seen as 'unfit' for promotion,[189] though one was 'discharged' after 23 years' service.

Like many who chose not to take their exams, preferring instead a long sojourn at a country station, those 'passed over' for promotion had probably refused the inevitable transfer that would accompany it.[190] For men with families, transfers were often costly and inconvenient, wrenching wives and children away from slowly nurtured friendships and local contacts. Only the ambitious or restless readily accepted transfers, which were ordered for the Department's immediate interests rather than those of the men. Some preferred to resign rather than be uprooted. Bill Murray became a detective (constable) in 1924 and remained in this branch of policing until 1953, when he was promoted to Inspector in charge of the Gisborne District. Typically, during his career as a detective, Murray had less than half the number of transfers (four) of his peers appointed in 1922 who rose to high rank after spending their careers in the Uniform Branch.[191]

For police, then, work patterned a variety of careers within a distinctive occupational community. Detectives and uniformed men in the cities had different worlds, and sometimes rivalries, shaped by their work. Most rank and file police were in the Uniform Branch. For them, beat work and work at country stations represented opposite poles of satisfaction, social standing, and styles of policing. Those who eschewed promotion generally aspired to a country station. There, constables were financially better off (even than Sergeants, some complained) and had much more autonomy. They were also the least socially isolated of the police, and the least well integrated into its occupational community.

In May 1936, Bill Murray, strategically placed in the Wellington Detective Office, joined others in moves to form a Police Association. He became the first President of its Management Committee. From the mid-1930s a variety of developments began to reshape the nature of the police occupational community, and the pattern of careers within it.

PART TWO

Patterns of Policing

CHAPTER 4

The Broad
Patterns

According to Charles Belton, many people in the 1920s and 1930s judged 'the work of the Police Force by the apparently aimless ramblings of the beat duty constable seen in the streets of the large towns and cities. From appearances it seem[ed] that there could not possibly be much work for a New Zealand policeman.'[1] The many avid readers of *New Zealand Truth* probably had a different picture: of hard-working police, especially detectives, bringing cases ranging from the mundane to the sensational before the courts.[2] Still, the point remained. New Zealand was 'truly the policeman's paradise', argued a critic of moves in 1928 to lower the age of entitlement to full police superannuation: its public were 'more governable from the police standard', and 'police work and risks' were 'less relatively to other lands.'[3]

Certainly, in the 1920s and 1930s, New Zealand did not have the organised crime of other countries with larger metropolitan centres. The number of murders and manslaughters reported by the Police bore favourable comparison with figures from other English-speaking countries. (Per head of population, however, the rate of homicides appears to have been broadly on a par with those in Australia and England – but people did not usually think in these terms.)[4] By the early 1930s, recorded assaults fell to a level (per head of population) that was lower than at any time before or since in the peacetime statistics of the New Zealand Police. During 1919 and 1920 industrial tensions engendered widespread fears amongst farmers, employers and conservative politicians that a general strike resembling 1913 or worse might break out.[5] But it did not, and the years between 1922 and 1937 were relatively peaceful in industrial relations.[6] Nor did demonstrations of the unemployed, culminating in the disturbances of 1932, really threaten the stability of New Zealand's social order. From the perspective of 50 years later (and in complacent contemporary comparisons with other societies), New Zealand during most of the inter-war years was indeed a 'paradise' for the Police in terms of at least one of its traditional priorities: the maintenance of order.

Yet officers in charge of districts regularly asked for more men during the 1920s, and many of the rank and file in the cities found their work unremitting and often arduous. In fact, as Belton's memoir makes clear, there was a great variety of work and variation of workloads amongst police. Many features of police work are constant, determined by the unchanging mandate of the Police to preserve the peace, prevent crime and detect offenders against the law. Nonetheless, social changes rendered the world of the inter-war years different in many respects from that of 50 years earlier, bringing shifts in the balance between different kinds of police work. Growing pressures were felt by members of an organisation whose leadership lacked the capacity to initiate fundamental changes in the way their work was performed. Thus experiences of policing continued to have much more in common with those of the 1880s and 1890s than with those of the 1970s and 1980s. This chapter serves as an introduction to chapters five to ten, which examine the nature of police work during the 1920s and 1930s: the kinds of work, its organisation and distribution, and varieties of experience.

From its inception as a centralised Force in 1877, the Police provided annual statistics on its law enforcement activity. Contemporaries saw in them an index of the moral health of society. They also viewed them as a yardstick of the efficiency of a 'preventive' police. For either purpose they were misleading measures. Essentially, police statistics were (and remain) an exercise in bureaucratic accounting; an indication of the nature and extent of police business in enforcing the law.[7] And even in this they are an imperfect guide.

Recording as they do the formal processes of law enforcement – the reporting of offences, the detection and prosecution of offenders – police statistics provide only a partial view of the variety and overall quantum of police work. As has been already noted, police performed a range of other tasks besides law enforcement. Time spent on patrolling, surveillance, and order-maintenance (ranging from domestic disputes to wrestling contests) was not quantified, though hints as to priorities are suggested by the pattern of 'public order' offences recorded.[8] More crucially, police had discretion as to whether or not to intervene, and in the degree of formality of intervention, which could range from warning to prosecution. Police statistics in the inter-war years give no evidence as to the extent to which this discretion was exercised. They are essentially an index of the number of files, large or small, resulting from arrests or summonses.

Clearly, however, the degree of police discretion varied with the circumstances. A major influence on the exercise of discretion stemmed from how police work was initiated. Citizens initiated the investigation of most cases of violence and property crime that were dealt with, and most 'maintenance' cases under the Destitute Persons Act, in terms of which police chased up defaulters. Ships' officers called on the Police to assist in punishing deserters and offences against discipline under the Shipping and Seamen Act. Similarly, the Post Office looked to the police to catch those who tampered with the mail. Much work also came from requests for assistance from members of the community or other government agencies. Depending on the nature of the request or complaint, the scope for discretion could be limited. A request from another government department could not usually be turned down. Complaints of assault or theft needed at least a preliminary investigation. A participant in a neighbourhood dispute seeking police intervention might be told by a watch-house keeper that it was a 'civil matter'. However, information that a dead body was lying in grass could not be ignored, even though in one case (in 1928) staff at the Wellington Central station redirected the informant to the suburban constable at Brooklyn (who said it was the Mt Cook station's responsibility) – and in another, the corpse proved to be that of a cat.[9]

Not just false complaints were ignored in the annual return of offences. Officers compiling the returns were instructed that 'petty offences for which proceedings can be taken only by summons should be omitted.' Complainants of theft might expect attention, but no case was to be shown in the statistics 'unless there there are reasonable grounds, after inquiry, for believing that an offence has been committed.'[10] This allowed a lot of latitude. As a retired watch-house keeper commented on practice in Christchurch during the 1930s:

> With so many bicycle thefts in Christchurch, our percentage [of thefts for which offenders were detected] was always low, about 70 per cent when I started doing the returns. After a few years they were up over 80 per cent. However, one day I was called to the Superintendent's office and asked why such a poor return, why these few hundred undetected thefts which was killing the return? I pointed out that about half of them were bicycles listed in the Police Gazette as stolen and they could hardly be left out. I was told they were not stolen but merely mislaid and lost. My attention was drawn to the percentages of some districts the previous year and told to see what I could do as we had had a very good year and our staff was as efficient as any in the country. I checked on a few complaints and made a few alterations, thinking that perhaps in some cases no offence had been committed. I believe District Clerks did likewise with the main return to be sent to Wellington and everyone was happy. Statistics on crime can be very misleading ....[11]

The apparently high detection rate for property crime (in comparison with published clearance rates from the 1960s) was submerged within an even higher overall 'clearance' rate for all offences reported during the inter-war years, which at well over 90 per cent in most years remained at a level similar to that achieved since the turn of the century. Only in 1931 did it fall below 90 per cent (to.89 per cent); in 1936 it reached nearly 99 per cent. Such evidence of police 'efficiency' was

Figure 4.1: Broad Categories of Offences Recorded by the Police 1919–1945 (numbers)

OFFENCES	1919	1922	1925	1929	1932	1935	1939	1942	1945
Seditious offences	2	1	-	-	16	-	-	2	-
Misleading justice	38	29	32	24	43	33	125	16	46
Escape from custody	57	35	25	18	18	12	39	35	67
Offences against religion	9	3	9	6	1	1	-	-	-
Offences against morality	50	90	120	80	73	115	148	171	148
Offences against person	1,165	1,064	1,187	1,016	930	901	1,266	1,118	1,160
Offences against property	5,429	7,051	7,114	8,823	12,188	10,469	11,112	11,867	13,430
Police Offences Act	10,994	9,199	11,367	9,901	7,147	5,591	9,465	6,250	4,904
Gaming Act	324	328	434	280	471	580	491	304	1,001
Post and Telegraph Act	63	52	128	127	259	234	196	232	174
Destitute Persons Act	2,258	2,805	3,621	5,187	4,636	3,769	4,202	2,946	2,872
Shipping and Seamen Act	229	120	1,240	152	49	111	282	171	274
Licensing Act	3,298	3,052	3,888	3,941	3,115	3,222	4,642	4,383	4,147
Arms Act	-	512	313	272	390	434	308	143	289
Motor Vehicles Act	-	-	494	3,965	5,556	7,285	13,724	6,600	4,826
Miscellaneous	362	358	498	458	476	411	378	370	406
Total Recorded Offences	24,278	24,699	30,470	34,250	35,368	33,168	46,378	34,608	33,744
% resulting in prosecution	96%	92.5%	94%	92%	90.5%	92%	93%	89%	83%
Offences per police officer	27.6	24.5	29.7	29.7	30.6	27.2	32.2	26.5	21.6
Person/property offence ratio	1:4.7	1:6.6	1:6	1:8.7	1:13.1	1:11.6	1:8.8	1:10.6	1:11.6

Source: calculated from Annual Reports.

cosmetic, an artifact of the selective process of compiling statistics.[12] It also reflected the other source from which police work stemmed.

Most of the cases recorded in the police statistics were initiated by members of the Force. Offences against provisions of Police Offences Act, Licensing Act, Gaming Act, Arms Act, and other regulatory legislation were largely detected by the Police themselves. Since most of this work arose from police initiative, its overall volume (as recorded in the statistics) was partly determined by the degree of discretion exercised, and by the priorities of policing. This, in turn, was influenced by the capacity of police to meet a variety of demands. Recorded offences grew fairly steadily from a total of 24,278 in 1919 to 46,378 twenty years later (figure 4.1). Broadly speaking, the number of police kept pace with this growth. Here we can see the results of bureaucratic accounting: increased workload justified more police.

Yet the fact that the annual number of recorded offences per policeman remained virtually constant between the wars (at 29 to 30, the figure was about half that in the 1970s) also suggests another interpretation. Apparently there were limits to the number of certain types of cases (or files) that the organisation could (or would) handle formally each year. These limits were not consciously determined, for (as figure 4.2 suggests) the workloads of districts and stations varied greatly, especially because of work initiated by citizens and government agencies. While the timing of individual complaints and requests could not be predicted, a certain volume was anticipated. Overall limits to the various types of cases dealt with formally were shaped by the number of staff, priorities given to particular offences, procedures and technology employed, and ultimately by the zeal of individuals. During the early 1930s, for example, the perceived demands of public order in the main centres saw men diverted from other duties to political surveillance and the monitoring of demonstrations. On the beat, complaints of assault or theft (or arson in the case of Christchurch in 1929) took priority over patrolling to detect drunkenness. Murder inquires drew detectives from the routine investigation of petty offences. However, there was a fairly stable pattern in the broad categories of offences formally recorded – especially those categories relying solely on police initiative.

Between 1919 and 1954 offences were recorded according to the legislation being enforced. From these broad categories, continuities as well as change can be discerned in the distribution of cases dealt with formally by police. Every year a small number of people took up police time when they escaped from prison or police custody, or were prosecuted for offences against the administration of justice (especially for making false statements). More significantly, recorded offences

Figure 4.2: Number of Offences Reported Per Policeman in Each Police District 1922–1939

District	1922	1925	1929	1932	1935	1939
WHANGAREI	29	32	32	49	38	40
AUCKLAND	29	46	32	35	27	37
HAMILTON	27	36	39	34	34	39
GISBORNE	27	32	43	38	34	42
NAPIER	26	30	32	32	25	30
NEW PLYMOUTH	22	26	38	29	34	22
WANGANUI	29	28	26	26	26	29
PALMERSTON NORTH	27	25	31	32	36	42
WELLINGTON	23	26	28	32	30	34
NELSON	-	-	29	30	31	25
GREYMOUTH	31	29	38	24	20	23
CHRISTCHURCH	29	28	30	33	24	30
TIMARU	22	23	30	18	17	21
DUNEDIN	12	15	15	21	27	35
INVERCARGILL	17	23	27	27	23	25
OVERALL	25	30	30	31	27	32

Source: calculated from Annual Reports.

against persons and property (or simply, violence and mainly theft) averaged about 28 per cent of police cases in the 1920s and roughly a third in the 1930s. Police detections of offences against the Gaming, Licensing, and Arms Acts remained relatively stable in number during the inter-war years. There was a similar broad stability in the requests for police assistance under the Post and Telegraph Act and the Shipping and Seamen Act.[13] Arrests under the Police Offences Act fluctuated in number but remained a significant proportion of police business.

Within this broad pattern, however, there was change. Apart from a sharp increase in 1919, the number of assaults reported annually remained fairly stable between 1916 and 1926, and then declined during the late 1920s and early 1930s (figure I.2). By contrast, the level of recorded thefts and burglaries, which had been tending to decline since the mid-1890s, began to rise sharply from the end of the First World War, and especially from 1926, reaching an inter-war peak in the early 1930s (figures I.5, I.6). Despite the selectivity of police recording practices, we may still detect in the trends of much citizen-initiated work (as did police administrators) the impact of economic and social change. Hard times seemed to bring more 'maintenance' cases, more reports of theft and fewer arrests for drunkenness and assault, especially during the Depression.

Other complex social changes were also apparently at work over the longer term. As economic conditions improved, the number of recorded thefts and burglaries at first dipped between 1933 and 1936 before beginning another long-term increase. Conversely, improved prosperity did not mean a speedy return to the pre-1914 levels of street disorder as reflected in police statistics. Indeed, the First World War marked the end of an era in the contribution of arrests for drunkenness to the total number of police prosecutions: averaging 46 per cent annually in the decade up to 1915, these fell to a third of all prosecutions in 1919, a fifth in 1929, and a tenth in 1935, before rising to an eighth in 1939.[14] During this period drunk and disorderly pedestrians came to provide less police business in court than intemperate and other drivers who offended against the Motor Vehicles Act 1924. As a focus for theft and joyriders, as a means to accomplishing other crimes, as a source of death and destruction, or merely by failing to have tail lights, the car marked the beginning of a new era in the evolving pattern of police work – not least because its owners were often amongst the most vociferous complainants about police methods.

The format of the annual police statistics also provides a rough indication of the organisation and distribution of work within the Police. Here again, the patterns in the inter-war years were already long-standing. As befitted the concept of a 'preventive police' discussed in the introduction, a majority of the Force was deployed in uniform ostensibly for surveillance and deterrence: to deal with perceived threats to public or personal safety and detect offenders in the act rather than after the event. Administratively, work was organised and distributed between and within the two Branches of the Police, Uniform and Detective, each with its own hierarchy of NCOs in the main centres. In fact both Branches had both preventive and investigative roles. Though the numerically small Detective Branch was clearly perceived as a specialism, there was (by contrast with 50 years later) relatively little subdivision of work into specialist units within either Branch. Nor was there formal training for detective or any other work, apart from what was imparted to probationers at the Depot. Given specific tasks, men learnt on the job; they needed to be adaptable and resourceful. There was an expectation that police were (or should be) generalists able to perform a variety of basic tasks. Thus there was a unified career structure, and those who sought promotion were expected to be cognizant of the variety of roles within the Force.

In practice, there were four broad spheres of work within the Police. That of the largest element, the rank and file of uniformed men in the cities and largest towns, is partially revealed by the number of regulatory offences prosecuted under the Police Offences Act, Licensing Act, Arms Act, and Motor Vehicles Act, plus the 'maintenance' cases handled. Property offences were grist to the mill of detectives, who focused also on investigating serious crimes of violence, offences 'against morality' (relating to sex) and the gaming law, as well as (for a few of their number) 'seditious offences' as a by-product of political surveillance. Uniformed men at small stations were in effect a third sphere of policing, given the nature of their work. They were generalists *par excellence*, and the statistics are less indicative of their activity. The fourth element of work was that of the NCOs and commissioned officers who were engaged in supervision and control. Their role was not merely to maintain the quality of policing and determine its priorities, but also to do the tasks requiring additional experience, authority, or expertise. The cases recorded in the annual statistics represent part of the growing number of files they monitored. In theory, the Police conformed to the military model in terms of the control and surveillance of front-line staff. In reality, much control over routines remained with the front-line men themselves, the uniformed constables and detectives. This will become apparent when the experience of police work in each of the four spheres is examined more closely.

CHAPTER 5

City Constables

What were the working lives of constables stationed in the cities and largest towns like? All new constables were posted from the Depot to one of the four cites. Those arriving in Auckland and Christchurch were met at the railway station by 'the official taxi of the Force – the Black Maria', which took them to the Central police station. There they were paraded before an officer, assigned their duties, and (if single) allocated a cubicle in the barracks.[1]

Barracks life was integral to the initial work experience of police. Most who joined between the wars without training at the Depot spent a week or more as barrack orderly (cleaning and polishing) before going onto the beat. Regular 'fatigue duty' could be anticipated by all those who lived in barracks. All district headquarters stations had barracks, and men were also housed at Newton station in Auckland, and at Taranaki Street and Mt Cook in Wellington.

In all the city barracks, similar conditions prevailed. There were 'definite levels of accommodation', with 'new chums' receiving the worst. At Auckland Central, the newcomers were given 'dingy' cubicles (labelled the 'Dungeons') on the first floor of the old Princes Street building. These were stuffy (with the aroma of smelly socks after men arrived from night shift at 5 am), most either lacking windows or facing the wall of a neighbouring building. Thin cubicle walls, extending to just over head height, gave little privacy. The 'constant comings and goings' of boots on the linoleum floor were 'not conducive to easy rest.' Nor were the drunken prisoners in the cells below, singing and 'letting us know what kind of bastards they thought all police were.' Also unsettling could be the inspections of the Station Sergeants, who checked that all men were in their rooms by midnight, and often woke sleeping men, due to get up at 4 am for the early shift, by shining torch beams on their faces As men married or were transferred, bachelors with years of service moved to better upstairs rooms 'with a view and fresh air'. Conditions were widely felt to be uncomfortable, and the regulations irksome.[2]

Yet some enjoyed barracks life: there were 'plenty of good mates to associate with'; billiards, yarning and practical jokes; the sharing of a bottle of beer or two smuggled in off the beat (empties found in the Mt Cook barracks were supposedly sent to Wellington Central for fingerprinting); and (in Christchurch) working out with your mates in the YMCA gymnasium next door, or (for a few) joining in a covert game of crown and anchor in a cubicle.[3]

In each batch from the Depot, one or two new constables would be detailed temporarily for 'special duty', mainly to catch bookmakers and sly-groggers. After a period they would don a uniform and join their fellows on beat duty. With only one or two exceptions in the inter-war years, all police experienced beat work.[4]

Constables were expected to appear a quarter of an hour before the beginning of the shift, to write in their notebooks the names of people wanted by the police, details of stolen cars, and the daily instructions posted on the noticeboard near the watch-house. Then the city sections of six to eight constables 'fell in' for inspection by the Senior Sergeant or Sub-Inspector on duty. Names were called, beats allocated, and the constables ordered to produce their 'appointments': notebook, pencil, and handcuffs (as well as baton, whistle and torch when on night duty). Their Sergeant then marched them out to their beats.

New constables generally began work on night duty (9 pm to 5 am), getting used to the routines of walking the beat out of the public gaze.[5] The protection of property was the main objective on this shift, and a larger area was patrolled (requiring more men, if they were available) than during the day. Where, on day shift, beat men walked on the outside of footpaths in the business district, at night they bestrode the inside, observant but less observable, checking alleyways and that shop doors were locked. If an open door aroused suspicion, a man from a neighouring beat might be called to assist in going through the premises, or the owner contacted. Here the probity of constables (and the reputation of the Police) could be tested. When, at supper one night, an 'older hand' on his Christchurch section related how easy it was to purloin goods from shops found open, the new Constable Thyne warned him that he would be locked up if Thyne caught him. (The 'dead silence' which followed suggested Thyne courted ostracism.) Thereafter Thyne was never called on to accompany others through shops found open; he always asked civilians to accompany him.[6] Occasionally a burglar might be caught red-handed, a fire attended to, or loiterers watched; but usually night shifts were uneventful. The only 'occurrences' reported by the six beat constables on night duty at the inner-city Taranaki Street station on 2–3 May 1930 (a Friday night) were two shop doors found open.[7]

Monotony could produce slackness, as police officers well knew. Hence the British tradition of timed beats was followed. Beat men were expected to reach a certain point every quarter or half hour, and 'punctuality was paramount.' Sergeants visited their men generally four times a night; 'if you were not where you should be you had to make a good excuse for it' or be 'matted'. Visits could not be predicted, though some might follow a regular pattern, and indeed be looked forward to as a source of company and advice. Other 'grumpy' Sergeants were, it seemed, 'always trying to catch you out.' (In fact, Sergeants felt their own pressures, as will be shown.) Constable Bill Carran (later a strict Sergeant himself) was, after eighteen months' service at Taranaki Street station, fined 10s for failing to work the Boulcott Street portion of his beat between 1 am and 2.50 am 'in accordance with defined instructions.' Among Auckland city constables in the late 1930s, the story was told of how a sectional Sergeant with the habit of hiding in doorways was spotted and grabbed roughly by a constable with baton raised on the pretext that he was catching a burglar. The Sergeant, it was said, learnt his lesson.[8]

The meticulous timing of beats, with their 'fixed points', might produce regularity in patrolling, and a means of readily finding constables (in the absence of radios or 'police boxes').[9] Yet this was also seen as its disadvantage from the point of view of crime prevention – especially on long 'outer' beats from the margins of business and industrial areas into the residential suburbs. Ray Henry, who plodded along three- or four-mile timed beats from Newmarket station, was convinced they were a 'waste of time'. Occasionally, when he was on night duty at Newmarket by himself, Henry 'bicycled round the beats in the opposite direction to instructions and caught offenders through being irregular.' One such offender 'knew exactly what the night duty police did, and had been stealing from the Railway Workshops regularly for a considerable time'.[10] Standing in a Wellington shop doorway one night, yarning with a workmate, Constable W.S. Hammond caught a thief with his loot. Sub-Inspector Lander (a 'nice chap' who 'never made it hard for a man', in Hammond's view) observed knowingly that his men always seemed to be off their beats when they made their 'good catches.' Hard case 'Wally' Hammond was quite often off his beat, but generally not through zeal.[11]

Night duty could be bleak, especially on the outer beats where there was no shelter. Patrolling Wellington's wharf or the city's back streets during the winter (as Hammond did) was 'a cold and miserable life.'[12] There was no officially recognised break other than suppertime, or when an arrest or some other incident took a beat man back to the station. George Austing's first beat on night duty in Auckland was aptly dubbed 'Siberia' because of its isolation and lack of shelter or passing people. Trams finished running about 11.30 pm and the street lights went out at 1 am. It was 'Nice and dark and spooky'. Austing soon found the Post Office garage where drivers worked the night shift to be a 'good place for a rest and a cup of tea if the Sergeant was not about .... Many a beat constable was driven out of the garage to be dropped on his beat at the right spot.'[13]

Boredom, tiredness and heat or cold thus inevitably produced 'easing behaviour' which made work more congenial.[14] The 'slow walking pace and having to pause to keep on time' tempted George Innes to rest on window ledges – but there was always the 'fear of going to sleep.' In hot summer weather 'sore feet was the greatest bugbear': Innes and his mates would kick off their boots around 3 or 4 am and soak their feet when Christchurch gutters ran with water. On Auckland's Queen Street, where the beats were shorter, Austing and a mate, with batons in hand, chased rats down the kerb late at night. Near hotels, bottles of beer might be found to quench a thirst or be smuggled back into barracks. A few inner-city Christchurch beats were notorious for the beer left out by publicans. Some beat men were tempted inside – Hammond was not alone in being caught in a Wellington pub, just as he was also nabbed having a cup of tea in a Wellington wharf office. Practical jokes played by older hands to 'straighten up' new constables (and a sleepy Dunedin watch-house keeper) sometimes enlivened the early hours. Such was the nature of night duty, Charles Belton commented, 'it is expecting too much of some men to bear the monotonous, fatiguing work without a little diversion.'[15]

Sergeants decided when supper would be taken. Constables from Taranaki Street, for example, were sent to their station in pairs for half an hour between midnight and 2 am. Men from remote beats did not have much time for a cup of tea, however. They were mindful that their Sergeant would probably be waiting to see if they arrived back late, which could cost them a 10s fine.[16] In Christchurch, men on the beats near the station took their supper first, while those on the outer beats moved in 'to be nearer for the dash when their turn came.' It was the task of the constable on the 'station beat' to have the kettles boiling for the supper rush.[17] A more primitive system continued in Auckland until the late 1930s. Men on night duty took their supper in a pocket. Congregating in particular shop doorways to eat it, and using improvised seating such as rubbish baskets, they drank tea brought to them in a billy by the station beat man on a bicycle. Cold tea gave little 'in the way of good cheer'.[18]

Even the fittest found beat duty arduous. 'Many a time after pounding every inch of beat No. 6 in Wellington Central, I could hardly drag myself up the [barracks'] stairs to bed at 5 am,' Ned Barry recalled.[19] At the end of a long night shift, living in barracks was an advantage; married men faced a long walk or bicycle ride back to their homes in the suburbs.

After fourteen consecutive days of night duty, day shifts were welcomed. In Christchurch, the night-duty men were divided to make up the two day shifts. At Taranaki Street station in Wellington, the day-shift sections were not much smaller than those on night duty. Wally Hammond would leave home on foot at 4 am to arrive five minutes before day duty began at Taranaki Street: lateness (as he discovered) could mean a 5s fine. On the early shift (5 am to 1 pm), one or two men would be put on fatigue duty at the city stations. Others would begin patrolling at what was a quiet time. Then the noise of tramcars and vehicles would begin, along with the 'rush of workers.' Now work could become interesting. Breakfast was half an hour (in reality, often no more than ten minutes to gulp down some food and tea) between 8 and 9 am. By this time, some of the men from the central stations would be immersed in traffic control work.[20]

During the 1920s, point duty was a routine part of the work of beat men on the main city thoroughfares between 8 am and 6 pm. Men on adjoining beats would spend alternate hours directing traffic. George Innes remembered well his first few days on point duty in Christchurch. After making two circuits of his beat around Cathedral Square, he took his position at the intersection of Hereford, Colombo and High streets, standing

> amongst whirling traffic ... tram cars, motor cars, trucks, horse drawn vehicles, bicycles for ever more. Tramway motormen often gave me a smile when I signalled a tram to go south along Colombo St. and it went off to the left along High St. The poor fellow had no hope of obeying my signal .... However I never had a collision there and after a few days was able to get all traffic through with very little delay. Everyone gave signals by hand, except perhaps one fellow who drove an express wagon with a speedy horse. He seldom made left or right hand turns but stuck his whip straight out in front and kept going at a very fast pace. He would pass probably half a dozen times during a four hour shift and sooner than risk an accident by trying to stop him I'd give him preference where possible .... he had been using that method for years, apparently with the desired effect.[21]

Other constables were less tolerant. Constable Archibald Moore was charged with using obscene language to a motorist of 'good character' in Auckland's busy Quay Street (the charge was dismissed).[22] After Wally Hammond gave a middle-class motorist a 'blast' for not stopping as required at the intersection of Taranaki Street and Courtenay Place, an irate letter appeared in the *Dominion*.[23] Pointsmen in Wellington had added pressures. The Governor-General required right of way (and an elegant salute) on his passage to and from Government House. Superintendent (then Commissioner) McIlveney was 'a stickler' for the correct hand signals (as well as for the lower ranks saluting senior officers and VIPs), and stalked the main streets to observe constables at work. Invariably, it seemed, criticism followed. 'Genial greetings' from regular travellers gave satisfaction, but point duty was 'tiresome in hot weather'.[24]

Heavy uniforms made the summer heat of Auckland, in particular, 'an ordeal'. The blue serge tunic was buttoned up to the neck, with a white starched collar, worn inside, showing a quarter of an inch above it. Wearing no shirts, and 'with perspiration streaming down their backs for hours on end,' some beat constables grew surly.[25] When he became Commissioner, McIlveney promised a lighter uniform, but that introduced in 1927 was only marginally so.[26] More disconcerting was the removal of pockets from the tunics, and the reintroduction of the shako in place of the helmet for day duty. It was popularly believed that the Commissioner wished to prevent constables standing about with their thumbs hooked in their pockets (which also bulged with their tobacco tins).[27] In fact, as we have seen, with the introduction also of silver buttons and a new silver badge, McIlveney sought to 'smarten up' the appearance of police by recapturing the paramilitary image the Force had presented until 1913. Amongst constables, however, there was resentment at a headdress that was 'most uncomfortable to wear and awful looking.'[28] Soon after McIlveney left in 1930, helmets were reintroduced for day duty.

Marked out by their attire, beat men could not easily relax. By late morning, Belton recalled, 'My legs ached and my arms seemed heavy hanging from my shoulders as one cannot have hands in pockets, even for a short spell on beat duty.' Feeling removed from passers-by (and, in turn, perceived as aloof), one retired man could remember even the day shifts in Dunedin as 'most depressing and uninteresting ... little crime and nothing to do.' In fact, day shifts were not always uneventful – incidents (especially from traffic) did occur in busy streets, and their unpredictability required alertness. Much also depended on personality and initiative. Soon Belton, like many of his mates, sought 'easing' activities. Boredom quickly set in if you did not take an interest in people; watching 'the faces of workers passing up and down .... serious, thoughtful, obtaining an occasional good morning'; getting to know the regulars on your beat, the taxi-drivers, city council 'blokes', newspaper sellers, and shopkeepers. Their confidence secured, they might drop hints on 'suspicious characters' and provide assistance when needed. A cup of tea, and a chance to rest, could well be offered at the back of a shop: 'Blow the Sergeant! Here was a break at last.' Some Wellington beat men became well-known figures. Amongst them, Constable Joseph Quinn was remembered for spending 'many hours talking to his numerous friends on the seat at the Railway Station concourse.' Yet (Quinn excepted) you still had to be a 'clock watcher' and be at the fixed points on time. George Austing found himself accused of gossiping when he claimed his delay came from 'supplying directions to strangers in Queen St.'[29]

The afternoon or 'late' shift (1 to 9 pm) was the busiest. Indeed the potential was such that a few constables at Taranaki Street station (at least) continued to work the broken shift that had prevailed until 1919: 9 am to 1 pm and then 5 to 9 pm. (During the four hours off constables might have both dinner and tea, which was 'inclined to play up with the gastric juices.')[30] As crowds thronged the main streets, city councils expected police to control the pedestrian traffic. In the early 1920s, Constable R.T. Hollis, whose 'great height made him a conspicuous figure', was specially detailed to walk the middle of Wellington footpaths. Seeking to shape habits that other beat men preferred to ignore, he became known as 'the constable who makes you keep to the left'.[31] More commonly, loiterers were told to 'move on'. New constables were most likely to make their first arrests in the early evening, as rowdy men staggered away from hotels which since 1917 had closed at 6 pm. During the three shifts of Taranaki Street constables in the 24 hours from 5 am on Friday 2 May 1930, only three arrests were made, all on the afternoon shift and all for drunkenness; two were pedestrians, while the third was 'intoxicated in charge of a motor car'.[32]

Arrests were a test of your mettle, physique and 'tact'. On his first day on the beat, Charles Belton walked along 'looking to see who I could arrest' – his mate on the neighbouring beat claimed he had arrested three men on his first day. Typically, Belton's opportunity came the next afternoon: a drunken man was patently a nuisance to others and (in falling into the roadway) might come to harm. Fortunately the arrest was easy: no resistance was offered, and a taxi was at hand to get the prisoner to the police station.[33] Lacking their own transport, police relied on cooperative taxi-drivers, occasionally prosecuting those who refused to assist.[34]

But arrests were often not so easy. A small number of drunken women who were regularly picked up could be difficult by creating a 'scene'. At Lyttelton and Port Chalmers, in the port areas of Auckland and Wellington, and around Dunedin's notorious Maclaggan Street (the haunt of prostitutes), 'droves of greasers and stokers' off the steamers issued from pubs 'under the influence' and looked upon police as their 'natural enemies'. Fights were expected. 'One rarely made an arrest in those areas without a struggle', a Dunedin policeman recalled. If a seaman won, a constable 'was always too ashamed to tell his mates as he would only be ragged.'[35] Generally, however, police seen as able to 'handle the rough element' (such as the wrestler and boxer A.T. Cleverley) were posted to the wharf stations (and to public works camps up-country).[36]

'Cheek' and resistance came also from young men of inner-city working-class areas, especially if a constable sought to walk them to the police station (taxis generally being allowed only for drunks). Typically, Wally Hammond brooked no nonsense. Early one Friday evening in May 1932 (two days after police had violently dispersed a crowd in Wellington's Cuba Street), he arrested a young man, loitering in the flow of Cuba Street shoppers, who responded 'Why should I?' when asked to 'move on'. A crowd soon formed, 'showing marked hostility to the police.'[37] Such crowds were not unusual in Auckland and Wellington, especially during the immediate post-war years and the early 1930s. Curious bystanders drawn to a spectacle of resistance were a by-product of street policing. They offered little or no assistance to a beat man, and could easily become hostile. When in November 1918, for example, Constable McMillan arrested a man for drunkenness and began to walk him to Taranaki Street station, his prisoner resisted by kicking violently, which attracted the support of a returned soldier and the attention of a large crowd. As McMillan sought to handcuff his prisoner, he was tripped, his helmet kicked off, someone yelled 'Put it into him', and he was laid out by a kick which fractured two of his ribs; the prisoner escaped.[38] Lack of support for constables in such circumstances was symptomatic of a long-standing ambivalence in working-class attitudes towards city police and their often brusque attempts from the late nineteenth century to enforce greater regularity of public behaviour according to a particular moral code. During the inter-war years, police who served in Auckland or Wellington before moving south to Dunedin, or to provincial towns, found people noticeably friendlier in the smaller, more intimate, urban centres.[39]

As constables grew more experienced, many (but not all) learnt self-control and discretion, and made arrests only if compelled to. 'Even after a few days I was no longer on the lookout for any person I could arrest', Charles Belton recalled.[40] Drunks would be watched to see if they were capable of boarding a tram, and it was 'not uncommon' for them to be shepherded into an adjoining beat.[41] In the United Kingdom, arrests for minor offences (or the recording of cars without tail lights) could provide some interest on a dull shift, and a chance to get back to the station.[42] For most New Zealand beat constables, however, such arrests were not worth the trouble, especially on night shift. Reports had to be written in their own time, at the end of a shift. Those on afternoon and night shifts had to come back in the morning to see their prisoner (or the drivers or cyclists summonsed for lacking lights) through the Magistrate's Court. A ticket for two hours relief from duty would be handed out; but only a small proportion were apparently redeemed, since sectional Sergeants rarely felt they had sufficient men on their shifts. Little wonder then that, when circumstances allowed, 'summary jurisdiction' ('a swift boot up the arse and a smack round the ear')[43] was sometimes preferred. Ultimately, however, some street arrests had to be made (or summonses issued), if only to maintain the authority of the police. In their methods, constables had to be mindful of the class background (and age) of those who challenged them – as Constable Benson Gillard learnt after he marched Harold Brown, an elderly Wellington merchant, to the Taranaki Street station with his arm up his back. Brown had been very uncooperative, but the magistrate, in dismissing a charge of driving while intoxicated, was sympathetic to his complaint of public humiliation and rough handling.[44]

Reflecting on his experience as a beat constable at Taranaki Street in the 1920s, a retired man considered that 'all we were expected to do was to clean up the streets of drunks, prostitutes and dead bodies.'[45] In this respect, the experience of urban beat work in the inter-war years differed little from that of the nineteenth century. Arrests for drunkenness were still the most common 'public order' offence; they were usually made not merely for public intoxication but rather for troublesome behaviour or to remove 'methos' and other vagrant alcoholics, who were often ignored during night duty but a source of complaint during the day. In the cities and some of the provincial towns, those with previous convictions constituted up to half of those arrested for drunkenness. A small number of women, identified as prostitutes, accumulated convictions for drunkenness as well as for being 'idle and disorderly'.

The advent of 'six o'clock closing' marked the beginning of an overall decline in arrests for drunkenness (in tandem with a longer-term decline in alcohol consumption) to a level in 1935 which was little more than a third of that in 1920. Other public order offences that often accompanied drunkenness arrests fell also, such as using indecent or obscene language, assaulting or resisting a constable, and breaching a prohibition order.[46] There were variations amongst regions and cities in the pattern of decline of public order offences in the early 1920s – Whangarei and Wanganui police districts (for example) maintained a relatively high level of arrests, comparable to the city-dominated Auckland and Wellington districts. In general, there were more arrests for drunkenness in the North than in the South Island. The 'dry' areas (electorates without hotel licences)[47] had some influence on the low rates of the Dunedin and Invercargill police districts. Amongst the cities, Wellington maintained the highest rate in the early 1920s, double that of quiet Dunedin. As rowdy street behaviour apparently receded in the early 1930s (or was dealt with in other ways), the activities of alcoholics bulked larger in arrests for drunkenness: males with more than five previous convictions comprised 18 per cent of those arrested in 1935, having been only 4 per cent in 1921. A 'little liked part' of the beat work of those stationed at Mt Cook (adjacent to inner-city Wellington slums) in the early 1930s was to 'hound' the 'down-and-outers' – especially those inebriated by drinking 'meths' and sleeping rough – and prostitutes.[48]

Attending to 'sudden deaths' was another distasteful but long-standing feature of a constable's work. During the inter-war years, motor vehicles greatly increased this as well as other disliked aspects of police work. Between 1926 and 1938, 2,449 people died from motor vehicle accidents.[49] These, and the many more traffic accidents where injuries were not fatal, were 'the great bugbear in a policeman's life.'[50] Paperwork was massively increased; serving summonses and calling witnesses was a lengthy process; well-defended motorists and critical judges required great attention to detail; plans had to be carefully drawn.[51] Thus, in the overall pattern of city beat work (as well as in that of some suburban and country constables), the inter-war years saw a shift from a preoccupation with public order offences to include the delinquencies (and worse) of motorists. In Wally Hammond's book of newspaper clippings relating to offences he dealt with as a beat constable at Taranaki Street in the late 1920s and early 1930s, traffic offences and incidents predominate: incidents on point duty; car conversion; theft from a car; 'hit and run' motorists; and (above all) intoxicated drivers. These last and dangerous drivers caused the most trouble, not merely because they were often uncooperative, but also because of the difficulty in having evidence of reckless behaviour accepted in court.[52] Seemingly more trivial, but much more common, were the many reports by city beat constables of cars and bicycles having insufficient lights. According to George Innes, any Christchurch beat man who

> had not caught an offending cyclist during the fortnight [of night shift] would perhaps be spoken to by a superior, for the offences were easy to see. However they were not so easy to catch by a constable on foot, although by pouncing out on suitable occasions one had an occasional catch. Sometimes a constable would be sent out on a bicycle for a couple of hours in the evening when he might bag a dozen or so .... One often sent out on this duty boasted that he carried with him a short length of dog chain and throwing this in the rear wheel of a cyclist who refused to stop was the most effective way of bringing him to a halt.[53]

Some constables, like Wally Hammond, remained on inner-city beat duty for years. Sooner or later most were selected for other work as the need or opportunity arose. Charles Belton entered the Auckland Detective Office after only a few months on the beat. More commonly, beat men were posted to other Uniform Branch duties, according to their seniority, perceived skills, failing health, or just because they were on the spot. Some duties away from the beat could be short-lived, such as escorting prisoners from Auckland to the Borstal at Invercargill, a return trip which took a week of non-stop travelling by train and boat. Or there could be 'special duties' to detect particular offences. On a quiet Sunday, a beat man might be told to don plain clothes and catch shopkeepers selling cigarettes. Prosecutions for Sunday trading fluctuated between 50 and a hundred annually during the 1920s, then rose sharply in the early 1930s to a peak of 292 in 1934. Few such cases were dismissed, though magistrates refused to convict a man for making blocks to build his house, or Auckland Aero Club officials for 'transacting business' on a Sunday.[54]

Other special duties arose when disorder threatened. A constable did undercover work on the Auckland wharf during the seamen's strike between November 1922 and January 1923. Similarly, others monitored meetings of the Communist Party and allied organisations in the early 1930s.[55] Some industrial disputes involved hours guarding 'free labour'

28. A crowd of Wellington relief workers and their supporters at the gates of Parliament late in the afternoon of 10 May 1932. They became restless while awaiting the return of a deputation to the Minister of Employment. Upon being told that J.G. Coates would make a statement the next day, a group of men from the back of the crowd ran up Lambton Quay breaking shop windows. *Evening Post Collection, ATL, G84210¹/₂*

29. A group of Wellington Special Constables called out after the window-smashing on Lambton Quay on 10 May 1932. As in Auckland and Christchurch, squads of specials patrolled the main shopping area. Because of the hostility they engendered, specials were generally kept in reserve when police were dealing with crowds. *Evening Post Collection, ATL, G84842¹/₂*

30. 'A Police Nursery': J.C. Hill captures the reaction amongst Auckland police to the proposal in 193[ ] a part-time auxiliary police to be trained in the weekends and called out on 'abnormal occasions', acco[ ] to the Minister in charge of the Police, J.G. Cobbe. *Auckland Star, 2 Oct 1934*

31. 'This Age of Speed': A popular image of a behind-the-times Police Force is captured by J.C. H[ ] *Christchurch Times, 3 Nov 1934, p.12*

32. William Robert ('Bill') Murray in 1938, taken when he stood down after two years as the first President of the New Zealand Police Association. After eight months on the beat, he spent most of his career as a detective. His diplomatic manner and dialectical skills marked him out amongst his colleagues, who esteemed his integrity, loyalty and competence. *NZ Police Journal, Jun 1938, p.29*

33. Notable careers – the Cummings brothers: from right to left, Denis joined the Police Force in 1899 and rose through the Uniform Branch to become Commissioner in 1936; Edward, the father, a farmer near Lawrence, Central Otago; James, the youngest, was persuaded by Denis to enter the Permanent Artillery, from which he was appointed a constable in 1906 and gained prominence and rapid promotion as a detective during the 1920s, succeeding Denis as Commissioner in 1944; Timothy, the oldest brother, joined in 1904, eschewed promotion, and became an archetypal small-town constable at Whakatane from 1911 until he retired in 1940. *Cummings family*

34. 'The "Policeman's Holiday" ': J.C. Hill's ambiguous response in 1935 to the sending of two New Zealand detectives to London for training. Here the image of a local Criminal Investigation Department modelled on that of Scotland Yard is one of elitism as well as of effective deterrence. *Auckland Star, 7 Sep 1935*

35. A new intake of recruits at the Police Training Depot, Wellington South (Newtown), in 1928. Living together for three months laid the basis for a close-knit occupational community amongst 'probationers' drawn from a variety of jobs. The English-born seaman W.S. Hammond is in the second row from front, third from right. Senior Sergeant G.B. Edwards, the Instructor, was well seasoned in the practice of everyday policing. *ATL, G5423¹/₁*

36. The first intake of recruits to complete training at the Wellington South Depot after it was reopened in August 1935. Sergeant George Paine was the Instructor. Introduced at the turn of the century, the white helmets were for summer day shifts, with the dark helmets (or shako between 1927 and 1930) for night duty and wet weather. Emblematic of British-style policing, helmets were valued for marking police off from other uniformed officials. *John Robinson*

37. Constable Thomas Heeps had been at the sole-charge station of Morrinsville for seven years when he was shot on 20 October 1934 by Henare Hona using a stolen .32 revolver. Heeps had found that Hona, a new farmhand in his area, fitted the description of the person wanted for killing four members of the Davenport family near Otorohanga eleven days earlier. Hona later shot himself when surrounded by police. *Heeps family*

38. The funeral of Constable Thomas Heeps at Morrinsville, 1934. Funerals for police who died while in the service were public events accompanied by the rituals of an occupational community. They served to underline not only the loss of a comrade but also the special standing of police in their communities. *Heeps family*

39. Tribute to a local identity: the 'impressive' funeral march on 27 April 1929 for Constable R.T. Hollis, who was known as the 'constable who makes you keep to the left' on Wellington footpaths. Led by Senior Sergeant Donald Scott, over a hundred police preceded the hearse through the city's central streets. Two notable athletes led the columns, Constables Peter Munro (right) and Christopher McRae (left). *Donald Scott*

40. The annual charity rugby match between the Police and Post and Telegraph departments in Wellington, 1933. Senior Sergeant Donald Scott (left) led the police pipers. 'Cops' and 'Posties' entertained the crowd with stunts in fancy dress at half-time. Demonstrating commitment to his comrades, Constable W.S. Hammond broke records each year as a ticket seller, foregoing his annual leave to sell over 4,000 in 1938. *Donald Scott*

41. There were very few Maori in the Police Force between 1918 and 1945. Rawiri Puhirake ('Dave') Hira was the last Native Constable. Appointed at Te Kaha on 11 January 1933, he served there until 1 June 1945, when he left to become a full member of the Force as a temporary constable at Ruatoria. This photograph was taken after the introduction of an open-neck tunic with blue shirt and tie in 1950. *NZ Police Museum*

42. Reacting to the proposed appointment of 'health patrols' to advise and warn young people in public places at night, Mack portrays a misogynist view of policewomen then prevailing – that they were likely to be busybodies acting without 'tact and discretion'. *Free Lance, 29 Aug 1918*

THE COMING TERROR—NEW ZEALAND'S POLICE-WOMAN.

43. 'Wanted. "Joan 'Ops" ', 1918: Tom Glover ridicules the idea that women could be 'John Hops' by playing upon popular stereotypes of femininity. During the 1920s and 1930s, physical and temperamental characteristics were seen by police and politicians as disqualifying women from recruitment into the 'regular' Police. *NZ Truth, 31 Aug 1918*

44. Having three brothers in the Police Force led the recently widowed Catherine Ledger to join as an Assistant Police Matron at Wellington in 1917. Seen as having 'remarkable vitality, ability and memory', she was the longest serving matron in the Force on her death in March 1938. Here Catherine (left) stands next to her brother Denis Cummings, his wife Catherine and daughter Mary. *Cummings family*

45. Like other inner-city stations in the four cities, Auckland's Newton police station, with a house for the Senior Sergeant attached, provided a barracks for beat constables. It had a shorter working life than most other inner-city police stations, being opened in 1906 and vacated in 1969. *G. Dunstall*

47. Until 1937, Auckland beat constables on night duty took their supper with them and had tea brought to them in a billy. A Committee of Inquiry in 1919 recommended eight-hour shifts but disapproved of night-duty men leaving their beats for refreshments. Here, in 1934, station beat Constable Ted Hotham delivers tea to Constable Jack Cassill, who is sitting on a rubbish basket in a Queen Street shop doorway. *NZ Police Museum*

46. Walter Sydney ('Wally') Hammond remained a uniformed constable, mainly on beat duty in Wellington, during his fourteen-year police career. Like many constables, he could be selfless when called upon, relished the camaraderie of his mates, and made a difficult job more tolerable by selectively ignoring police rules. *NZ Police Museum*

48. Monitoring the goods for sale rather than the public: two beat constables mingle with orderly sale crowds in Colombo Street, Christchurch, on 21 November 1930. *Canterbury Museum*

49. Most crowds were orderly during the inter-war years. Though a few constables were on the street, this section of a Christchurch crowd observes an invisible boundary without the immediate presence of police while waiting for a procession celebrating the coronation of King George VI in 1937. *Thelma Kent Collection, ATL, F3267¹/₄*

50. Sometime after becoming a beat constable in Wellington in 1922, Chris McRae was posted for duty to the Wellington Wharf. He won the national amateur heavyweight boxing championship in 1924 and was seen as being able to 'handle the rough element'. *John Robinson*

51. A Wellington traffic accident in the late 1920s – 'the great bugbear in a policeman's life'. As the number of accidents increased, so did the paper work, especially for city and suburban constables. *Evening Post Collection, ATL, G799$^1/_2$ –EP*

52. The 'terror of the Hutt Road'. After the main road between Wellington and the Hutt Valley was tarsealed in the mid-1920s, Constable Bert Morrison was appointed as the first Hutt Road motorcycle patrolman (paid for by the city council) to enforce the 30 miles per hour speed limit. In 1932 he was transferred to the Wellingon Arms Office and a city council traffic officer took over the role. *S.C. Smith Collection, ATL, G48917½*

53. Police protection for men working a Blackball mine under the 'tribute' system in 1931. Angry unionists, prosecuted for intimidation and disorderly conduct, believed that police exaggerated the disorder. Constable George Donnelly, sent to Blackball from beat duty in Wellington, remembered his time there as peaceful. *ATL, NP47738*

and facilities against the wrath of unionists. The strike by railwaymen at Easter 1924, for example, led to police recruits being sworn in only halfway through their training at the Depot. Some were assigned to night duty at Wellington's Thorndon station and railway yards. But 'there was nothing very exciting about it', one recalled; 'my mate and I had to dodge a few stones that were thrown and listen to a lot of shouted abuse, largely because we looked after a couple of "loyal" signalmen and a couple of drivers.'[56] A year later, the 'Home Boat' strike by British seamen entailed the guarding of ships and provision of safe passage for seamen who wished to return to them. Some strikers managed to set fire to a cargo of copra, leaving constables on the Wellington wharf with 'some pointed questions to answer.'[57]

In fact the experience of the great strike of 1913 had given lessons to both police and union leadership. 'In dealing with strikers', police were enjoined by successive Commissioners to 'maintain an attitude of perfect impartiality, and refrain from all action of an irritating nature'; to 'avoid hasty arrests, or unduly rough handling of men who may only be boisterous and unruly without a dangerous degree of disorder'; to 'exercise patience and avoid precipitate action'; and to 'not move about in large bodies unless circumstances render such a course necessary.'[58] Indeed the brief clash during the early days of the Christchurch tramway strike in May 1932, between 'strikers' (mainly their supporters) and the police (assisted by Special Constables) was atypical. Yet the police role was to prevent effective picketing, and thus (in effect) to assist in breaking strikes. Much then depended on the restraint of unionists in the face of resolute, albeit 'tactful', police action.

This may be observed in events on the West Coast in mid-1931, when parties of police were sent from Christchurch and Wellington to mines at Charming Creek and Blackball to protect 'cooperative' (or 'tribute') miners from intimidation by unionists. Though unionists were prosecuted for intimidation and disorderly behaviour, and Inspector James Fitzpatrick later spoke of 'practically mob rule on the Coast', there were no violent clashes with police. George Donnelly, sent to Blackball from Wellington, remembered his few months there as peaceful. Police were housed in three local hotels which the unionists promptly declared 'black', thereby depriving themselves of beer – 'things were not too good.' However a 'good snow fight' 'seemed to thaw the strikers feelings towards us.' Police in Donnelly's hotel were approached by a few of the unionists, who said 'they would come back to the pub if we would put a man up against their man to drink beer. We had a real champ, so we set them up [and won – the 'Coasters are slow drinkers and not much good when hurried'] .... I made a lot of good friends in Blackball.'[59]

For his first eighteen years in the Police, Donnelly remained single, lived in barracks, and had 'no family worries about being shifted around.'[60] Experienced and unmarried city constables were the most likely to receive short-term postings to remote places where the facilities might be primitive. Typically, single men were sent to police public works camps. Willis Brown lived in barracks for 29 years, until he became a Sub-Inspector in 1950. During that time he was sent on nine periods of 'special duty'. In October 1936 he went from Wellington to a public works camp at Bartletts (south of Gisborne) for nine months. Then, from May to October 1938, he was Sergeant in charge of 30 police who camped near Taharoa (south of Kawhia Harbour) for five months, probing swamp and acres of sandhills unsuccessfully for the body of Dalu ('Jimmy') Desai, who was believed to have been murdered. Similar duty on murder investigations followed in 1943, 1947, and 1949. November 1939 saw Brown despatched from Auckland for seven months duty at the Centennial Exhibition in Wellington. Following Stanley Graham's shooting of four policemen at Koiterangi on 8 October 1941, he led a party of Auckland police to the West Coast to assist in Graham's capture.[61] Two months later, he was en route to Fiji for six months, with six 'hand picked' constables, to curb summarily a go-slow by 'troublesome' New Zealand workers building an airfield at Nandi. Again, as Senior Sergeant, Brown led a party of twelve police to Rarotonga in March 1948 to end the effective picketing of wharves by members of the Cook Islands Progressive Association.[62]

For similar reasons, unmarried police from New Zealand cities were posted to Western Samoa between 1928 and 1936. By 1928, demonstrations and civil disobedience organised by the Mau had effectively challenged the authority of the New Zealand administration in Apia: Mau police, for example, freely picketed European shops. Six constables were sent from Auckland early in 1928 to supplement the Samoan civil police force; most returned within six months. Meanwhile, police in New Zealand assisted army officers in recruiting and training a new force of 74 Samoan Military Police, under the control of the Defence Department. When a year later this military unit was disbanded, 27 of its members joined the local civil police, which was further strengthened by another sixteen men from Auckland. These new men were specially recruited and trained under the oversight of Superintendent Wohlmann, who had previous Samoan experience. In April 1929 the new recruits were despatched to Apia, accompanied by R.H. Waterson and W.R. Fell (acting detectives who were given the rank of Sergeant in Samoa).[63]

In March 1929, Sub-Inspector Lander was sent from Wellington to supervise the transition from military to civil control of policing. Concerned at the 'military element' that still pervaded the Samoan Constabulary, and the inexperience of its members, Lander recommended that all the European officers and constables should be provided from the New Zealand Police, either on loan to the Administrator, or under the direct control of New Zealand's Commissioner of Police.[64] Unfortunately, perhaps, this suggestion was not taken up. With better police leadership, the disastrous events of 28 December 1929 in Apia might have been avoided: an attempted arrest (by Fell) turned a large Mau demonstration into a violent clash (with Waterson firing a machine-gun over the heads of the crowd). One European constable and ten Samoans died, including the high chief Tupua Tamasese.[65] In the aftermath, further New Zealand police (including George Donnelly) were sent to assist the Samoan Constabulary. Donnelly's time on 'Upolu during 1930 was spent first walking round the island 'on a goodwill tour', and then guarding prisoners who were out working, as well as on night raids into villages seeking to arrest wanted members of the Mau.[66]

City constables with particular skills were taken off regular beat work for other uniformed duties. Some with mechanical expertise and a driver's licence were detailed to drive the few departmental motor vehicles. A future Commissioner, C.L. Spencer, spent much time during his first years as a constable in Wellington driving Commissioner McIlveney's car and the police van. On his Harley–Davidson motorcycle, Constable Bert Morrison became the 'terror of the Hutt Road' in the late 1920s, strictly enforcing the traffic regulations.[67] Thanks to their prior experience with horses, Willis Brown and Fred Banks, after three years on the beat, both became mounted constables stationed at Taranaki Street, a role each retained for twelve years. In 1931 there were about twenty horses used by city and suburban police. Like their counterparts based at the Auckland and Christchurch Central stations, the two Wellington city mounted men (augmented by up to four others at times) were essentially a reserve force for special duty: as ceremonial escorts for the Governor-General at race meetings and state occasions, and for crowd control, especially during demonstrations of the unemployed in 1931–32. As the Queen Street riots demonstrated, however, the efficacy of a small number of mounted police could be limited, and they became an expensive anachronism in a motorised society. Regular mounted patrols of city and suburban streets ended in the late 1930s. Police horses were maintained until the early 1950s only for ceremonial duty at the Ellerslie and Trentham race meetings.[68]

For much of the time, mounted constables like Brown and Banks undertook suburban enquiry work similar to that of other Uniform Branch men detailed for city enquiries, and that of men at suburban and country stations. By the late 1930s each of the main centres had a sizeable Uniform Branch enquiry section, the first members of which had been appointed in June 1915.[69] During the inter-war years, enquiry work initiated by citizens and other government departments seemed to become 'almost unlimited'.[70] On their timed beats, constables could do little of this work. Nor did the Detective Branch have the resources to deal with the mounting volume of requests to trace missing persons, ship deserters, and those who did not turn up for compulsory military training (in the 1920s) or had not paid their unemployment levy (in the early 1930s) – let alone follow up all the complaints of property reported

as lost or stolen. Government departments and local authorities looked
to the Police for reports on the character and circumstances of a wide
variety of people – those (for example) seeking licences as hawkers,
taxi-drivers, publicans, or land agents, or recommended for appointment
as Justices of the Peace. Until the late 1920s, at least, annual inquiries
regarding pensioners were routine. The State Advances Office turned
to the Police for assessments of defaulting borrowers' ability to pay.
Railways Department officials sometimes asked police to collect unpaid
fares. The Registrars of Electors, and of Births and Deaths, wanted
police to look out for (and warn) those slow to comply with their
requirements. In Christchurch, two constables were continually out on
'bicycle inquiries' during the 1930s. Much work stemmed also from
the judicial process itself: sudden deaths required a report for the
Coroner; there were new demands from the Child Welfare Act of 1925;
warrants had to be executed for default of maintenance or non-payment
of fines, and summonses served, not just on offenders and witnesses,
but also for jury service. Compiling jury rolls (including purging them
of people with criminal records and those seen as 'anti-establishment')
was a Uniform Branch responsibility. By the late 1930s, some constables
worked only on motor accident enquiries, and a separate motor accident
enquiry office had been established in Christchurch.[71]

Given the modes of transport used (horse, tram, bicycle or by foot),
city enquiries were conducted at a leisurely pace on matters sometimes
trivial by comparison with work patterns 50 years later. On the morning
of Friday 2 May 1930, Mounted Constable Banks rode from Taranaki
Street station to an outlying Wellington suburb to interview three
pensioners. His colleague (Constable W.T. Paget, in place of Willis
Brown who was on annual leave) rode to Ngaio to serve a summons.
In the early afternoon both worked on the jury list. Paget then served
a jury summons in Oriental Parade, while Banks served another and,
on returning, arrested a man for being drunk in charge of his car. On
the same day, Constable Charles Reardon, the only Uniform Branch
enquiry man on duty at Taranaki Street, spent his morning making
inquiries into a sudden death and then into a complaint of a lost bicycle.
After lunch Reardon turned his attention to the theft of a clock from
a restaurant, reported on the background of a man recommended as a
JP, and looked into the loss of a number plate belonging to a local car
dealer.[72]

Though uniformed mounted constables were conspicuous in making
their enquiries (preventive patrol being also part of their role), most
men placed full-time on Uniform Branch enquiries worked in plain
clothes. This was in deference to respectable opinion, which often
feared that the visible visit of police suggested wrongdoing to neighbours.
Where possible, pensioners were to be visited in plain clothes, for
example,[73] as were schools when children were to be interviewed.
(Though even this was not sufficient for some headmasters and education

boards, there being long-standing objections to police questioning children at school without the presence of parents.)[74] However Commissioner McIlveney, who permitted only a few exceptions to the wearing of uniform,[75] resisted pressure from the Child Welfare Branch for police to appear in the Children's Courts only in plain clothes.[76]

Not surprisingly, beat constables aspired to plain-clothes duty – not just for its relative anonymity, but also for the clothing and typewriter allowances it brought, along with regular 'nine to five' hours and more interesting work. After a short period of beat work and some time in the Wellington Detective Office, Charles Reardon (as a married man) much preferred the patterns of enquiry work at Taranaki Street, where he remained for nine years before being transferred to Masterton for nearly five years on country enquiries. City Uniform Branch enquiry men, like those in the district Arms Offices and at suburban stations, were also a reserve frequently called on for special duties in the evenings and at the weekends, particularly at race meetings, rugby games, and wrestling and boxing matches.[77]

Beat constables destined for one-man stations would usually spend some time in the watch-house at a city station. After about eighteen months on the beat in Christchurch, George Innes was given a trial as a shift watch-house keeper, and told he would soon have sole charge of a country station if he proved suitable. Innes was rightly sceptical. Not until five years later (and after he had bought a car) was he sent periodically to relieve country constables at stations around Canterbury. And it was another five years before Constable Innes became boss of his own station, as Chief Officer in charge of the Cook Islands Police at Rarotonga. Nonetheless, watch-house duties did give Innes 'a new outlook' on police work, and he decided to remain in the Force.[78]

George Innes worked on shifts in the Christchurch station watch-house for two years before being appointed to the senior position of day watch-house keeper. Ostensibly, a watch-house keeper's main responsibility was for the prisoners who were brought in: to receive and search them, recording their possessions; formulate the charges against them (being satisfied that an offence had indeed been committed); bail those charged with minor offences; and ensure the proper care and treatment of those detained. (Then, as later, a few – especially drunks – died in the cells.) The watch-house keeper held the keys and had personally to open and close all cell doors. After ten years, Innes was glad to miss the clanging of the cell door more than ten times a day.[79]

Innes found the work varied and demanding. The period from about midnight to 9 am was 'usually fairly quiet', with time to type the charge sheets for the next day's court sitting. Here too was a chance to complete the considerable work involved in writing up, 'in extenso', the daily diary of duties of each man at the station (there were 62 Uniform Branch constables at Christchurch Central in 1929), copying from the Sergeants' sectional reports, as well as those of the enquiry men. The day watch-house keeper prepared the fortnightly duty rosters as well as special rosters, such as for race meetings, sports and Anzac days. Beat men sometimes suspected favouritism.[80]

From 9 am to 7 pm 'there was no let up' in dealing with a great variety of inquiries and receiving citizens' complaints of perceived breaches of the law, lost and found property, motor accidents and domestic problems. The 'greatest bugbear' for a Christchurch watch-house keeper was inquiries for stolen bicycles – a thousand were reported stolen each year, and a similar number (not always the same ones) were found. On other matters, distressed complainants were sometimes difficult to convince that their problem was not one police could deal with. There was also no privacy. Statements were typed slowly by Innes standing at the office counter, where interviews with callers were frequently cut short by interruptions – the telephone had to be answered, other inquiries needed a quick response, a drunk was brought in to be locked up. Many complainants were 'not impressed.' Often with insufficient assistance, Innes had to deal with all telephone calls, recording messages and passing them on to detectives, the district office or suburban station concerned (where the constable, during the day, might well be out). Circulating information about stolen cars, escaped prisoners and mental patients to seventeen suburban stations 'was a lengthy and tedious business.' At night, when the Sergeants were out visiting their men and the constable on the station beat called in only every half hour, the lone shift watch-house keeper could not have beat men attend quickly to an urgent matter. In theory, men sleeping in the barracks could be called out. Except for unmarried acting detectives, however, this rarely occurred: 'the risk of abuse was great.' By the late 1930s, watch-houses in city stations had become one of the pressure points of police work. After ten years there, George Innes was on the lookout for a change.[81]

Meanwhile, during the 1930s, Wally Hammond remained at Wellington, mainly on the beat but for a period also on uniformed inquiries. One night in 1942, while on station beat duty at Wellington Central, he was caught playing poker with American marines. Once again he was on the mat. It was one delinquency too many, and his police career ended.[82] Yet, as with other 'hard case cops', Wally Hammond's easing behaviour did not imply that courage and zeal would be wanting when required. In fact, there are many instances in the history of the New Zealand police of brave and self-sacrificing behaviour by constables who did not subsequently have distinguished police careers. Some outstanding actions have received public recognition and awards that have been detailed elsewhere.[83] Wally Hammond was one of five New Zealand police awarded the King's Police Medal for gallantry, and one of four to receive the Royal Humane Society's Silver Medal, between 1918 and 1945.[84] 'Delinquents' could also be heroes.

CHAPTER 6

Detectives

On a visit to Auckland in January 1930, Commissioner McIlveney addressed a parade of two hundred police on the quality of their work. 'Who can give me a description of ....?', he asked. 'He's wanted and particulars have been published in the *Police Gazette*.' Dead silence followed until a young constable stepped forward and read from his notebook the official description of the wanted man. Next day the constable was told to report for duty in the Auckland Detective Office. Amongst reporters and members of the public at least, this transfer was perceived as a 'promotion'.[1]

As the findings of the Committee of Inquiry in 1919 (and the regulations which followed) made clear, 'a detective on appointment acquired a status somewhat higher than a constable'. He received a higher rate of pay (with allowances), and was senior to all constables associated with him on an enquiry. However, for the purposes of promotion and transfer, there was a common seniority list and a detective was equal in rank to a constable. Nor (in the Committee's view) could a distinction be made in the value of the work done. Certainly, by comparison with constables at city stations, detectives' duties could be construed as 'special, their hours more irregular, and their responsibility varies according to the work they have in hand.' Yet the 'relative value' of work done by a detective or a uniformed constable could not be fixed. Both branches were 'equally necessary in order to secure an efficient police service.' The Committee's sagacity (reflecting an Antipodean egalitarian ethos) shaped departmental policy, preventing jealousies and elitism developing to the extent that has been observed of the Criminal Investigation Department within the London Metropolitan Police.[2]

Amongst detectives in the largest offices of Auckland, Wellington and Christchurch, a sense of separateness and superiority persisted nonetheless. So too did a belief that detective staff should constitute a distinct department within the Force, in greater numbers, 'freed from the police routine altogether', and with their own commissioned officers, career and salary structures.[3] During the 1920s, New Zealand detectives shared with their counterparts elsewhere a mystique fostered by journalism and fiction. *New Zealand Truth*, in particular, constructed images of detectives as 'sleuths with greater intelligence and skill' than the ordinary 'John Hops'.[4] The small numbers of detectives in each office meant that most became familiar names to avid readers of the daily court reports. Sympathetic pen portraits in *Truth* gave personalities to some 'D' men.[5] Local reputations were gained from apparent feats of investigation. Detectives' status within the Force was also underpinned by selectivity in the recruitment of constables for duty in detective offices.

The small number of vacancies in the Detective Branch were to be filled by 'constables of exemplary conduct' possessing the 'prescribed qualifications' – which were left undefined (until 1930 at least),[6] and must be inferred from the backgrounds and activity of those who were recruited. Preference was explicitly given to 'younger and more energetic men'. Indeed the necessity for constables to have two years service was waived in January 1922,[7] so as to counterbalance the loss of energy and health of aging detectives. (Of the nine detectives and acting detectives in Christchurch in 1919, for example, four were over 50 years old, three were in their forties, and the youngest were aged 34 and 30.)[8] Hence many of those taken into Detective Offices during the 1920s (such as P.J. Nalder, Charles Belton, and Orme Power) were apparently more youthful than their counterparts before the First World War, and they often had less experience of beat work. Signs of zeal and initiative were looked for in candidates. Some (like Nalder, Belton, Ray Henry and Bill Murray) had the opportunity to demonstrate this, by being selected for undercover work in detecting bookmakers or slygroggers. Others (including Power, Dick Waterson, and notably A.V. Gillum, who caught two brothers responsible for a spate of arson in Christchurch) demonstrated their qualities in particular arrests made while on the beat. Frank Brady, E.A. Stevenson and J.W. Hill had prior experience on Uniform Branch enquiries. An ability to handle the paperwork was essential. Here (in the case of H.E. Campin in 1925, and Colin Urquhart in 1937, for example), educational background and performance at the Training Depot were taken as indicating suitability. Size could also be a consideration, especially for those put on special duties: it was better not to look too much like a policeman. (Nalder, Belton, Power, Murray, and Waterson, for example, were all under 5 feet 11 inches in height.) Conversely, detectives placed on the wharves to investigate pillaging (notably, Michael Gourlay, A.G. McHugh, and William Tricklebank) were powerfully built. Bill Fell, who stood well over six feet, began his rise to the top position in the Criminal Investigation Branch by being seconded from the Auckland watch-house to work on briefs of evidence for the Commission of Inquiry into the police handling of the Elsie Walker case. An ability to type and drive a car saw Charlie Reardon made clerk in the Wellington Detective Office. Though this was not spelt out, it is apparent that single men were preferred as recruits to the

Detective Branch: they would be in barracks and on call after 10.30 pm, when married detectives had usually gone home.[9]

After being selected for a trial on detective work in one of the four main centres, new recruits (still designated constables) reported to the Chief Detective. Equivalent in rank to uniformed Senior Sergeants, these senior detectives allocated and supervised the work of the local Detective Office. By the mid-1920s they directed investigations, usually without being involved in field work. Three of the four Chief Detectives in 1919 had been unable to pass the qualifying examinations for commissioned officer rank and were soon to retire.[10] Their positions were taken at three- or four-yearly intervals during the 1920s by a succession of senior detectives destined for higher rank. Notable amongst the 'Chiefs' were 'Tom' Kemp and 'Reg' Ward in Wellington, seemingly dour, blunt-speaking men with reputations as 'thief-takers', and the more affable James Cummings in Auckland, a future Commissioner who had achieved rapid promotion to Senior Detective in 1921 for 'ability, intelligence, and zeal' shown in investigating two murders.[11] To the new recruit Charles Belton in 1927, Chief Detective Cummings (then aged 42) was 'a comparatively young man for his position, very neat, precise, and businesslike'; a 'quick thinker' with 'plenty of initiative'; a non-smoker and total abstainer who 'apparently lived entirely for police work'.[12] Others looking back over their dealings with 'Jimmie' Cummings as a senior officer as well as Chief Detective saw him as kindly towards staff who were sick, but also 'a big bluff', 'full of bull', and sometimes ruthless, especially in interrogating suspected criminals. All three Chief Detectives were perceived by their subordinates as tough men, hard taskmasters and very exacting.[13]

Belton, like other newcomers, was given a brief outline by the 'Chief' of what he was to do, told that a typewriter would be a useful purchase, shown the detectives' work room, and left to discover the routines of the office. By the late 1920s the main room housing Auckland detectives was congested, and it became more so during the 1930s. There were about 26 staff in the Auckland office by the time of the Elsie Walker inquiry, late in 1928: one Senior Detective, four Detective Sergeants, ten detectives, and the remainder acting detectives and constables on trial or assisting with the office work and enquiries. (Wellington and Christchurch had about half, and Dunedin a quarter, of this number.)[14] As in Wellington, the Auckland detectives' room looked 'much like the literary department of a daily newspaper' with its half-dozen large tables, typewriters, 'correspondence' baskets, telephone, and men in shirtsleeves. The new men had to find a clear space and a spare chair. To one side of the Auckland office there was a small interviewing room. When this was in use, complainants had to stand in the main room while detectives typed their statements; there were not enough chairs. Adjacent was a storeroom with a jumble of exhibits and stolen property, and the room of the local fingerprint expert (then

Detective Sergeant R.J. Issell). Along a passageway was the 'Chief's' room, and that of the office clerk. Constable M.L.Vial filled the latter role for most of the inter-war years, taking telephone messages and statements from complainants about small thefts, and distributing the files allocated by the Chief Detective to his staff, noting briefly their contents and outcome in an official Record Book. Handling every file, Constable Vial (and his counterparts in other offices) became a rich source of information on names and modus operandi. As Charles Belton sat at a table wondering what to do, Vial strode into the room with a handful of files and, 'with a mischievous smile', gave one to the newcomer.[15]

Would-be detectives were usually 'thrown in at the deep end' with no training except, perhaps, for a few words of advice at the outset from the 'Chief' or one of the more experienced men. On joining the Wellington office, Colin Urquhart was told to wear a hat (a trilby or homburg), especially in a bar. To their regular clients at least, detectives (in their grey suits and waistcoats) had their own subtly distinctive style of dress. 'While you are in here, you never let your right hand know what your left's doing', Jimmie Cummings told Dick Waterson on his first day. Detectives could be singularly tight-lipped, to the frustration of reporters. Usually, after the newcomer had swept out the office, a file would be 'minuted' to him for enquiries – typically a complaint of theft (in Belton's case, of an alarm clock from a shop) that was unlikely to be detected. Now real learning on the job began: applying the advice of more experienced men in the procedures of enquiry and the methods of reporting on the investigation, or 'writing off' a file when nothing was detected. Incomplete files (such as, in Belton's first case, a file without a formal statement from the complainant) would be returned by the Chief Detective, who also monitored those which were overdue. Junior men often delivered 'stop notices' (lists of stolen property) to pawnbrokers and second-hand dealers, and from such enquiries might come their first arrests. Sometimes Detective Sergeants had a new recruit assist them in their work on more serious crime. Some would be good at explaining things, others more reticent; the junior man would have to pick up, by observation and experience, the techniques of investigation, interviewing suspects, and preparing 'tidy' files with the evidence necessary for prosecution.[16]

After six months' trial, a constable was eligible for appointment as an acting detective with an increased daily allowance. Not all achieved this status. A few chose to return to the Uniform Branch, seeing the hours of work in the main Detective Offices as too long and irregular. In theory, from 1922, the hours of duty were from 9 am to 5.30 pm and 9 am to 10.30 pm on alternate days, with a half-day off each week as well as every second Sunday, and relatively generous meal breaks by comparison with the uniformed men. Indeed, 70- to 80-hour weeks were often worked, especially when there was a 'run of crime' or a major enquiry. It was part of the ethic that a detective was 'always ready to sacrifice his comfort and pleasure to the demands of duty'. Though they grumbled about the hours, those who became and remained detectives found their work more stimulating and satisfying than that undertaken in uniform; and there was more freedom to shape the pace and nature of work.[17]

Some of the constables on trial in detective offices were not perceived to have the necessary attributes: the ability to work without close supervision to get results or satisfactorily 'write off' a file. Results mattered. Clearly there could be an element of luck; or perhaps 'favouritism' (Belton alleged), when some tended to receive 'name and address' files, where the offender was known. For a successful detective, however, patient and meticulous attention to detail, a good memory for faces and names, and skill in 'ferreting out' criminals were more significant. The 'art of observation' had to be well developed. Amongst detectives it was also a truism that the essence of success often lay in effective interrogation to secure confessions from suspects, especially in cases where there was little other incriminating evidence. A detective's ability to 'suit his manner and conversation to those he is dealing with' was often crucial. Personality could shape a career in the detective office. For whatever reason, one constable who worked in three detective offices found that he 'could not progress' under the 'Chiefs' in Auckland and Christchurch, but 'got on well' under the Detective Sergeant at Greymouth.[18]

After two years, acting detectives could apply for appointment to the prized status of detective, with a doubled allowance. Now the accoutrements of the uniformed constable were handed in, and a new warrant card was issued. Acting as well as full detectives carried automatic pistols, but only on special duties or night patrols, when confrontations with armed burglars might occur. Instructions on how to handle pistols were stapled into the 'Black Book' from 1923, but no formal training was given until at least 1936.[19]

Detectives continued to learn on the job. It was common for them to keep newspaper clippings of their cases in scrapbooks. These were not merely a source of satisfaction. Sketchy though the reports might be, they provided a means of recalling names of criminals, modus operandi, legal argument, and court judgements on a wide variety of cases. A few, like James Cummings and J. Bruce Young (who was to succeed Cummings as Commissioner), were very systematic, keeping large volumes alphabetised according to types of case and points of law. Their clippings were accompanied by typed opinions from magistrates and legal counsel.[20] Seasoned Detective Sergeants and Senior Detectives became self-taught prosecutors, pitting their wits in the Magistrates' Courts against defence counsel who also often lacked formal training and were learning their craft on the job.

Where the pipe-smoking Sherlock Holmes (and his fictional

successors) worked alone and untroubled by paperwork, solving murders and mysteries by feats of deduction from a few clues, New Zealand detectives in the 1920s and 1930s (like their counterparts elsewhere) usually 'rolled their own' cigarettes, spent many hours 'pecking away at a typewriter', and used 'rule-of-thumb methods which permit[ted] nothing to be taken for granted'.[21] On the routine cases assigned to them, New Zealand detectives generally worked alone. For the most serious and complex crimes, however – usually murders, and those where detection involved the element of surprise (such as gaming and opium cases) – teamwork was the norm. Frank Brady, who spent much of his time as a detective during the early 1930s working with others on gaming cases, felt that there was 'more of a team spirit amongst the ranks' in the Auckland Detective Office than existed in the Uniform Branch: there was a much more 'marked division' between uniformed constables and their NCOs.[22]

In real life, the work of individual detectives encompassed (as it still does) a variety of tasks and cases, normally mundane. Actual investigative work (including interviews) occupied only part of a detective's time. Depending on the nature of the case, as much if not more time was spent in the office on paperwork relating to files and preparing cases for court.[23] (For example, the case of the Dunedin man prosecuted for indecently assaulting a female required statements, twenty printed forms, and two caption sheets to be typed.)[24] For those with a varied caseload, time at court could be expected fairly regularly, usually amounting to between two and five days a month.[25] Much more time during working hours was spent simply travelling, on foot, or by taxi (if the matter was urgent) or public transport. (An Auckland detective's enquiry in outlying Papakura or Browns Bay could take a whole day, where 50 years later it might be completed in a couple of hours.) By the late 1920s, a car was available for detectives in the three largest centres. In practice it was used only in emergencies. 'When one understands how ill-served is the detective office for transport', a *Dominion* reporter commented in 1934, 'the wonder is that so many fleeing criminals are apprehended'.[26]

Quite apart from making enquiries, detectives were constantly on the lookout for known and suspected criminals (especially pickpockets and spielers) frequenting the streets, and those 'consorting' with them. For similar reasons, vessels from Australia were met, as were (for example) trains arriving in Dunedin during its Exhibition in 1925; sideshows at Agricultural and Pastoral Shows were monitored, and race meetings always meant extra work. (Indeed, some experienced detectives were recruited by the New Zealand Racing Conference as racecourse inspectors to 'warn off' or exclude 'undesirables'.)[27] Junior detectives could also expect to spend nights on patrol or surveillance at a fixed point. Following a spate of safe-blowing in the late 1920s, for example, E.A. Stevenson spent eight nights 'watching' the Mt Albert post office, going out from the Auckland Central station by tram, then walking home in the early hours of the morning. During the same period, Charles Belton and a colleague rode an old motorcycle with sidecar through Auckland's suburbs after nightfall, 'keeping a watch on outlying shops, telephone boxes, letter boxes and such property open to mischief and theft'. On their own volition, other detectives sometimes went out in the evenings 'vag hunting' in the detectives' car: looking for 'vagrants' or people who were 'idle and disorderly' in terms of the Police Offences Act, potential thieves and 'mischief' makers who were on the streets or dossing down in yards or empty buildings. As the ranks of the unemployed swelled in the main centres from the late 1920s, this 'was a way in which you could keep a watch and check on the lower levels.'[28]

A detective in one of the main centres usually had fifteen to twenty current 'jobs' (files) assigned to him, and often many more, particularly if he was relatively junior. Belton saw himself as a 'willing horse' who (with 'at least a few dozen' files in his correspondence basket) received more than his fair share of 'jobs'. Belton's load was not atypical.[29] Most correspondence baskets seemed to fill up faster than they emptied. Even in the largest office, Auckland, there were no permanent squads focusing on particular types of crime during the inter-war years. To most detectives, the work seemed to be randomly allocated. A basic diet of theft and burglary cases was interspersed with a variety of other types; typically, car conversion, false pretenses, forgery, bigamy, indecent assaults or exposure, gaming and opium offences, and the occasional sudden death, manslaughter and murder. The wide range of routine 'jobs' is well illustrated in Charles Belton's memoir. Apart from those detailed for political surveillance, few detectives were conscious of specialising. Some were, however, assigned more of one type of case than others. After about four years in the Auckland Detective Office, H.A. Wilson, for example, worked for the next eleven years mainly on detecting car thefts and crimes associated with cars. He kept out of gaming raids by other detectives so as to maintain his links with informants.[30]

From the time he entered the Wellington Detective Office four months after joining the Force, Bill Murray kept a record of all the cases he dealt with that led to prosecution.[31] Since his files that did not come to court are not recorded, we have only a partial view of Murray's workload as a detective. Some patterns may be observed nonetheless. Between June 1922 and September 1937, when Bill Murray became a Detective Sergeant (still at Wellington), he prepared 360 cases for prosecution. Just over half of these cases occurred between 1925 and 1930. Murray generally was given a month's annual leave each year from 1927 (the year of his marriage), but two months' sick leave early in 1931 reflected the toll of work. By the mid-1930s, Murray briefed only a third as many cases for court annually as he had a decade earlier. There may have been a growing amount of other work; perhaps there were more insoluble cases which were not recorded. Certainly Murray was being given (or taking) his annual leave regularly (and there was a further two months' sick leave in 1935). Moreover, the proportion of these files that led to a prosecution within seven days of his receiving them fell fairly steadily from 84 per cent for his first six months as a constable in the Detective Office to 40 per cent in 1933. Whereas no files that came to court took more than a month to do so in 1922, three (out of ten) did so in 1934 – one taking five and a half months, and involving a month's escort duty to Melbourne and Perth.[32] Perhaps the more experienced detective, now in his late thirties, with a young family, sometimes in indifferent health, and aware that seniority rather than zeal determined promotion, was becoming less assiduous. He applied to transfer to Levin as a constable in 1932. Equally plausibly, Murray (like other colleagues with similar service) may have increasingly been given more complex and difficult cases. Chief Detective Reg Ward and his successors tended to direct files concerning thefts by employees, fraud, false pretenses, and bigamy to their pipe-smoking subordinate.[33]

Ninety-three per cent of Bill Murray's cases that came to court between 1922 and 1939 culminated in conviction. This apparently high success rate was typical for most detectives handling a variety of cases. However it did not include an unknown but probably sizeable number of burglary and theft files that were 'written off'. The high conviction rate reflected the nature of the cases brought to court. Most were dealt with summarily by the small group of magistrates who came to know and respect many of the police who appeared before them as witnesses. Where there was a conflict of evidence, that of the police was usually preferred. Not always, however. Stipendiary Magistrates W.R. McKean and Wyvern Wilson, for example, looked critically at testimony of Auckland detectives who sought during 1933 to have various showmen, labourers and seamen convicted for being 'idle and disorderly persons who habitually consorted with reputed thieves'.[34] Similarly, Murray found that charges of attempted false pretenses and conspiracy to defraud were hard to make stick, as were some allegations of indecent assault, and a charge of fighting laid against the prominent trade unionist, Fintan Patrick Walsh, in 1937. He found also that Supreme Court juries could be reluctant to convict those charged with offences relating to abortions, or motorists on serious charges such as manslaughter.[35]

For Bill Murray and his colleagues, a key element of success lay in securing an admission of guilt from a suspect by interrogation. Such admissions were more easily gained from some types of offenders than others. Seasoned burglars, for example, were not only hard to catch in the act; most would make few concessions under interrogation. Partly for this reason perhaps, files on breaking and entering comprised only 2.5 per cent of Murray's cases that came to court between 1922 and 1939. There were nearly twice as many prosecutions for bigamy and sexual offences, and three times as many gaming cases. Significantly, at least 35 per cent of Murray's court cases related to false pretenses, fraud, forgery, and theft of money while in a position of trust.[36] In most of these cases, Murray obtained a confession. By contrast with most cases of theft and burglary, complainants of breach of trust by employees or of false pretenses could name a suspect – and generally there was damning evidence. Whereas prosecutions followed complaints in only about 55 per cent of burglary cases, they were almost invariable for complaints of false pretenses and thefts by employees in the late 1920s and early 1930s.[37] By the time Murray interviewed those accused in such cases, many were apparently ready to admit the offences. Without such assistance in 'clearing up the defalcations', Murray conceded during one case, 'the police would have been put to very great difficulty and trouble'; and this was evident in the few cases where the evidence was contested.[38] Compliance by defendants may well have been stimulated by a police willingness on occasions not to press the most serious charge possible: in one of Murray's cases, for example, the judge told an accountant who had pleaded guilty to misappropriating a large sum of money that he 'was lucky in the way the charge was framed. But for that, said his Honour, he would have imposed a heavier sentence'.[39]

'Held up on its own, I should say there would be a reasonable chance, in a bad light, of its possibly being mistaken for a bank-note', was Bill Murray's comment in a contested case where a firm was charged with issuing a special discount coupon resembling a banknote. In response, the defence counsel commended to the Bench the 'fair manner' in which the prosecution witness had presented his evidence.[40] A conviction followed, nonetheless. Like other experienced police, Murray managed often to convey an aura of fairness when giving evidence in court. Charles Belton was not alone in maintaining that, in all his cases brought to court, 'I always mentioned everything I knew in favour of the accused.'[41] However, a study of many individual cases reveals that this practice was more likely for first offenders dealt with in the Magistrate's Court than for those with a long list of previous convictions or charged with a serious offence. Moreover, police methods in identifying and interviewing suspects were not immune from criticism during the inter-war years. *Truth* protested at the 'Evil effect of Over-surveillance of Ex-prisoners by Police Officers', alleging that it was 'usual', whenever an 'ex-prisoner appears on the streets, to give the whisper to an employer that the man in question has "done time".'[42] Following criticism in the Christchurch Supreme Court by both judge and jury of the 'unfair' manner in which suspects had been identified by complainants, Commissioner McIlveney felt it necessary to issue a circular specifying the procedure to be observed in conducting identification parades.[43]

More persistent were allegations of threats made, inducements offered, and unfair methods used by some police when interviewing suspects and securing statements.[44] There were some tough, and probably rough, detectives. McIlveney reminded all ranks in 1926 that 'even the greatest delinquents should not be brought to justice by unjustifiable means.'[45] Given the extent to which police learnt their skills on the job, however, varied practices in dealing with suspects were only to be expected; court cases and anecdotes from retired men also suggest this. Certainly the extent to which front-line police in the inter-war years knew of, or felt bound to follow, the English 'Judges Rules', first formulated in 1912 for the conduct of interviews and the taking of statements, is not clear.[46] To critics, section 20 of the Evidence Act 1908 seemed to leave a loophole for what they dubbed 'the third degree'; much depended on the view of judges in particular cases.[47] In 1929, leading defence lawyers managed to have a remit adopted by the annual Law Society conference recommending that the Minister of Justice investigate 'the whole system of taking statements by the police'.[48] Nothing came of this. Criticism of police methods was often seen as a ploy by defence counsel, and was thus discounted by some magistrates and Supreme Court judges (especially Justice Herdman, the former Minister in charge of the Police).[49]

Where offenders were not identified by witnesses, and suspects did not confess, detectives had to seek solutions by other means: through fingerprints (especially in the case of burglary); by building a finely worked chain of circumstantial evidence from a variety of sources (notably in murders); and by undercover work and raids (empowered by search warrants) to secure incriminating evidence of gambling, opium smoking, or sedition. Particular cases might involve a variety of approaches.

Fingerprints had 'revolutionised' the work of detectives in the 'past few years', Chief Detective W.B. McIlveney declared in 1911.[50] This rather extravagant claim reflected the mystique of the seemingly 'infallible' system of identifying criminals begun with the setting up of a Fingerprint Bureau (later renamed Criminal Registration Branch) at Police Headquarters in Wellington eight years earlier.[51] Identification by fingerprints was a specialised craft rather than an exact science. The usefulness of fingerprints rested on skill in identifying, collecting, classifying and matching them. Considerable expertise was demonstrated by E.W. Dinnie, who headed the Criminal Registration Branch from 1904 until his retirement in 1947. He kept abreast of developments in Britain, introducing further refinements into the original 'Henry' system of classification when other work permitted.[52] By 1919, the Branch held 22,332 sets of fingerprints; twenty years later the figure was 55,801. An Auckland branch office was opened in June 1928.[53] From the outset police administrators appreciated that the system's effectiveness depended in part on the number and quality of the prints held. Until 1947, only those sent to prison or a police gaol by the courts were legally required to submit to fingerprinting.[54] While those arrested by police could not be forced to have their prints taken, 'if care and judgement are exercised there should be no difficulty' in getting those needed, Commissioner O'Donovan observed in 1919.[55] Not until the late 1950s did police call publicly for the universal fingerprinting of the population.[56]

The effectiveness of 'criminal registration' also depended on the development of police photography. In the main centres, police fingerprint experts doubled as photographers, developing their skills and often using their own equipment on the job.[57] E.W. Dinnie's work was not made easy by a broken departmental camera purchased second-hand in 1909 and not replaced with modern equipment until 1934.[58] Not only were prisoners photographed (some 700 'mugshots' a year were reproduced in the *Police Gazette* during the 1920s), so too were their fingerprints for enlargement, preservation and circulation. Increasingly during the inter-war years, the part-time police photographers were also detailed to record scenes of crime to strengthen police evidence in murder trials. During the successful investigation of the murder of E.J. Blakeway near Palmerston North in 1931, for example, the Criminal Registration Branch supplied over 600 photographs, including microscopic enlargements.[59]

Though a prominent detective, J.B. Young, echoed the conventional wisdom in seeing fingerprints as 'a most valuable part of detection',[60] a broad view of detective work suggests that their value remained more potential than actual. Lack of expertise amongst police in recovering fingerprints at the scene of a crime, especially outside the main centres, meant that their possibilities were not fully exploited. Certainly there were some dramatic identifications as a result of fingerprints. Most notably, Dennis Gunn was convicted and executed in 1920 for the murder of the Ponsonby (Auckland) postmaster, A.E. Braithwaite, essentially on the basis of prints left on post office cash boxes and on a revolver. (Gunn's fingerprints had been taken when he was imprisoned as a military defaulter in 1918.) In New Zealand courts, this case marked a turning point in the ready acceptance of fingerprints (and the testimony of police fingerprint experts) in the identification of an offender, an acceptance that was underscored by the special publication of a report of the trial at the direction of the Minister of Justice.[61] Even so, very few murder trials hinged on fingerprint identification: the next notable example was the trial of Angelo La Mattina for the murder of Angelo Odorico at the Garibaldi Club, Wellington, in 1957.[62] In the investigation (headed by J.B. Young) of H.W. Brunton's murder at Wairoa in 1948, police took fingerprints from several thousand local residents without finding a match for a bloodstained print.[63]

In accord with the initial conception of the Fingerprint Bureau as focusing on 'habitual criminals', burglars were the most common category of offender identified by fingerprints. Through the inter-war years Police Department annual reports gave examples of successes.

When identified by their prints, burglars generally confessed, saving much time and expense in court work. They would often also admit earlier offences, thus boosting the clear-up rate. Yet the results were meagre, given the considerable labour involved in gathering, classifying, recording, and searching prints. In the best year (1936), when 1,063 burglaries were recorded, 51 offenders were identified and prosecuted on the basis of their prints; the annual average between the wars was 25. More commonly (an average of 234 annually), prisoners were found to have been previous offenders, which had an impact on their sentencing. In reality, fingerprints proved to be only a minor aid in the solution of crime. Their main value lay in helping police keep tabs on professional and persistent criminals (or at least those who were careless). To this end, the Criminal Registration Branch regularly exchanged prints and photographs with their counterparts in British and Australian forces – the Auckland office received some 1,500 prisoners' records from New South Wales annually during the 1930s. In Auckland in 1937, the first steps were taken to establish a 'modus operandi' system of the kind developed by some English provincial police forces nearly 30 years earlier, by indexing reported crime according to its pecularities and the idiosyncracies of known criminals.[64] This had long been recommended by individual detectives like Bill Murray, but it was not to be implemented on a national basis until the late 1940s.[65]

Even if it had existed in the inter-war years, a modus operandi system would have been of little assistance to detectives in clearing up homicides. According to the statistics derived from death certificates and inquests, there were some 254 homicides (criminal and non-criminal) between 1921 and 1939.[66] In the police statistics for this period, 177 people were reported as murdered – an average of nine a year, with numbers ranging from two in 1928 to 22 in 1933.[67] Determining which homicides were criminal was not always a straightforward task. In fact police statistics of murders and manslaughters reported were (and remain) an ambiguous guide to the number and nature of homicides deemed to be criminal: they reflected the initial police assessment, not what the courts finally decided. Moreover they were (and remain) statistics of those killed, not of the number of criminal assailants or of separate events of fatal violence. Each year during the 1920s and 1930s there was usually at least one multiple killing. Each was recorded as a separate murder, distorting popular perceptions of the nature and incidence of criminal homicide.[68]

Though there were multiple killings, there were apparently no serial killers in the inter-war years. Certainly, 'Bill' Bayly, convicted and executed in 1934 for the murder of Samuel and Christobel Lakey, was widely but mistakenly rumoured to have caused a number of unsolved deaths.[69] While some of those accused of murder apparently had a propensity for violence, most had no criminal history in the eyes of the police; they did not kill for gain. Only a handful of homicides were associated with robbery or burglary.[70] Most homicides were eventually 'cleared up' because the circumstances of the event (usually in small communities) pointed to the assailant and whether he (or, much less commonly, she) might be criminally liable. In most homicides there was a prior (usually familial) relationship between assailant and victim; and if there were no witnesses, there was often a confession. 'I've saved you a bit of unsavoury work, old man', Detective Sergeant J.B. Young read in a suicide note from a man who had murdered his wife after being interviewed regarding indecent assaults on schoolboys; 'cease fire; this job is over; pigeonhole the papers, and thank God you don't have to see it through.'[71] Remorse or despair meant that suicide was the final outcome in roughly a fifth of the culpable homicides during the inter-war years.[72]

For detectives, then, difficulties in dealing with homicide or nearly fatal violence did not usually begin with the task of identifying the assailant. More commonly they arose in assessing the assailant's motivation and the degree of culpability, and then (if laying an indictment for murder, manslaughter or attempted murder) in securing a conviction. Of the 106 people indicted for murder between 1920 and 1939, seventeen were acquitted, seven were found not fit to plead, 27 were found not guilty on the ground of insanity, and 25 were convicted of manslaughter; only 30 were convicted of murder and sentenced to death.[73] Vincent Meredith in Auckland and Arthur Donnelly in Christchurch were astute Crown prosecutors, but they found juries susceptible to the arguments of defence counsel regarding the possibility of insanity, provocation, or lack of murderous intent in the accused. No women were convicted of murder during the inter-war years, though they were a fifth of those indicted. Juries often preferred, it seems, the special defence of insanity, or the lesser charge of manslaughter, to the prospect of sending someone to the gallows.[74] In theory, police were not interested in the outcome of a trial; their job was merely to marshal and present the evidence. In practice, however, the adversarial system of justice meant that an acquittal could be perceived as a defeat, a reflection on the quality of their work. Indeed, when the Crown failed to secure a conviction against C.W. Boakes for the murder of Ellen Scarff at Burwood (Christchurch) in 1927, the *Otago Daily Times* observed accurately that the 'public may well regard this as very unsatisfactory'. The verdict carried with it 'the measure of reproach which attaches to failure'.[75]

This reaction was also stimulated by the circumstances of the killing and the length of time taken by detectives to bring their suspect to trial. In the Scarff case, as in a few other homicides, linking a suspect to the event with sufficient evidence to convince a jury was the key problem of detection. Such cases required considerable time and labour in building up a chain of circumstantial evidence. This was not always appreciated by newspapers resentful of police reticence as to details of an investigation, or by readers impatient for results. When they were successfully prosecuted, however, these cases were triumphs for the police, especially given the limitations of forensic science in the inter-war years.

In New Zealand, as in British and Australian police forces, the application of science to the craft of detective work was in its infancy in the early 1920s. A decade later, however, scientific aids and expertise were being increasingly used by police in solving major crimes, though their application to 'more ordinary crimes ... was slow to develop'.[76] While British police had established a number of forensic science laboratories by the late 1930s, New Zealand police continued the long-standing practice of turning to specialists outside the force, especially public hospital pathologists[77] and the Government Analysts[78] in the four main centres. Local gunsmiths and professors of chemistry and physics were also utilised until the Police appointed its own ballistics expert, G.G. Kelly, in 1935.[79]

Such experts came to play a crucial role in determining several issues regarding deaths shrouded initially in mystery. The first issue – especially where firearms were involved – was whether such deaths were accidents, suicides, or homicides. (Of the 1,231 deaths by firearms recorded between 1921 and 1939, 64 per cent were found to be suicides, 31 per cent accidental, and 5 per cent to result from homicide.)[80] In a number of cases an expertise in ballistics proved to be crucial – such as that in 1929 dubbed by reporters the 'Motu Murder Mystery', where the most plausible explanation was demonstrated by Kelly to be accidental death.[81] Expert evidence about spent cartridges could also help determine another issue by linking an accused with the scene of the crime in the eyes of a jury, as in the case of three sensational trials relating to murders in the same rural area of the lower Waikato valley: those of S.J. Thorne in 1920, W.A. Bayly in 1934, and Arthur Allan Thomas in 1971 and 1973. Such evidence was challengeable, albeit not effectively so until the Thomas case. In fact the equipment available to firearms experts in the 1920s and early 1930s was primitive. Kelly recalled the 'poverty of evidence provided by the gun experts' in 1920. Nor would his admission in the Bayly trial that he had not examined the damning rifle shells under a microscope (a pocket lens was adequate!) have met the standards of evidence required four decades later. Not until 1937 did the Police Department acquire a comparison microscope and new equipment for microphotography, which 'revolutionised' (as Kelly put it) 'the science of fire-arms identification'.[82]

Pathologists and Government Analysts also increasingly provided vital assistance in reconstructing the circumstances of a death, and in shaping (or, in the Elsie Walker case, confounding) police theories. Autopsies and laboratory tests could check the validity of statements made. When he was tried for the murder of Phyllis Symons in 1931, George Coats' claim that the girl had fallen and struck her head, supported by the opinions of three respected Wellington doctors, proved unconvincing to the jury in the face of conclusions drawn by Dr Lynch from his post-mortem examination.[83] Similarly, when James Talbot claimed in 1939 that his heavily insured Australian cobber (Gordon McKay) had been burnt alive in a cottage at Piha, it was Kenneth Griffin, the Government Analyst in Auckland, who (indirectly) turned a suspicion of fraud into a certainty. By comparing a hundred samples from newly dug graves around the city with clay taken from a shovel supplied by Detective Sergeant Frank Aplin, Griffin was able to tell Aplin which grave was likely to have been robbed of its body. And so it proved.[84] Much of the work done by Government Analysts for police related to suspected poisonings, from which stemmed some notable enquiries and trials during the 1930s: of A.T. Munn (1930), nurse Elspeth Kerr (1933), and Eric Mareo (two trials in 1936), all in Auckland; and of the West Coast miner, J.S. Page, in 1934 for murder and attempted murder by chocolates laced with strychnine.[85] In such cases (notably those of Kerr and Mareo), the key issues were the link between the suspect and the victim, and whether the poison (and especially veronal, which was then freely available) had been self-administered.[86] Here experts could be of only limited assistance; medical opinion was contested at trials. Much then depended on the craft of detectives.

Albeit often crucial, the results of forensic science were merely a part of an incriminating chain forged by observant and shrewd detectives in successfully bringing murderers to book. Methodical interviewing and searching provided the necessary foundation of information for all such cases. Fingerprints may have been the essence of the case against Dennis Gunn, but by the conclusion of the trial Justice Chapman was impressed with the police work generally, and especially with the 'diligence and intelligence' shown by Detective Sergeant James Cummings in 'the investigation and the preparation of the prosecution', as well as his 'conspicuous' fairness towards the accused. So too was Superintendent Wright, who recommended rewards recognising both individual merit and teamwork.[87] Again, after the case against S.J. Thorne, Justice Chapman pointed publicly to 'the amount of intelligence and industry' shown by police, and especially by Detective Sergeant Cummings, who led the enquiry. And again, this was a team effort by ten police in the course of which 116 dwellings were visited, the hooves of 1,303 horses were examined, and cartridges were collected from 60 farms, in order to establish Thorne's link with the scene of the murder. Once again rewards were given.[88] The conviction of George Coats in 1931 also brought praise (and rewards) for police, especially for 'the marked skill and thoroughness' of Detective Bill Murray, whose close interviewing of Coats, neighbours and fellow relief workers led to his hunch that the body of Phyllis Symons had been recently buried under tons of soil in the making of Wellington's Hataitai Park: a week's shovel-work by a small army of relief workers and police revealed her body where Murray had suspected it to be.[89]

For nearly three weeks, Bill Murray had had a strong suspect but lacked a body. Not until the conviction in 1951 of George Horry for murdering his wife just after their wedding nine years earlier was there to be a prosecution without any evidence found of the victim's body.[90] At his second trial in 1925 (the jury at his first trial having failed to agree on a charge of murder), Frederick Mouat was convicted of manslaughter, essentially on the basis of 31 fragments of burnt human bone found in his Christchurch garden and alleged to be the remains of his wife.[91] Though there were parallels in the significance of burnt bones, the web of circumstantial evidence ensnaring Mouat was not nearly as elaborate, nor as convincing to a jury, as that in which police eventually bound William A. ('Bill') Bayly.

At midday on Monday 16 October 1933, Inspector J. Hollis in Auckland received a request for assistance from Constable David Robertson, ringing from a farmhouse at Ruawaro, near Huntly. The body of Mrs Christobel Lakey had been discovered lying face down in an adjacent duck pond. Her husband Samuel had disappeared, as had two of his guns, suggesting the possibility of a murder/suicide. This was an awkward time: police were preoccupied with the murder of a taxi-driver (J.H. Blair) in Mt Roskill the day before. By 4 pm, nonetheless, Detectives Thomas Sneddon and Thomas Allsopp, together with three constables, had travelled south some 60 miles to the remote settlement in a car borrowed from the Post and Telegraph Department. An early theory (propounded initially by a neighbour, Bill Bayly) was that Mrs Lakey had drowned in the pond after a seizure, and her husband had gone away in distress. Settlers and police led by Allsopp searched the surrounding area intensively while Sneddon focused on interviewing the neighbours. On the evening of 16 October, Sneddon and Allsopp systematically searched the Lakey home (which became the police headquarters), finding an unposted letter from Mrs Lakey to Frank Bayly complaining about the 'spiteful annoyances' of his son Bill, who 'is on the warpath again'. This accorded with information of bad blood between Bayly and the Lakeys. Bayly now became a definite suspect, and the two detectives began to consider the possibility of a double murder. Soon, other evidence pointed in that direction, though there was no sign of Samuel Lakey. Searching and interviewing continued, with a number of items and statements being taken, over succeeding weeks, from a composed and 'coldly polite' Bill Bayly.[92]

The 'Ruawaro murder mystery' (or the 'Bayly case', as it came to be known) was the most notable criminal investigation of the inter-war years. Ostensibly a routine homicide inquiry at the outset, it quickly became an exceptional one in terms of the scale of the police effort, the contribution of forensic science, the popular suspicion that Bayly had been involved in the death of Elsie Walker five years earlier, and the publicity given to the 'mystery' by newspapers, 'creating intense interest throughout the Dominion'.[93]

After four days of enquiry, Allsopp and Sneddon were joined at Ruawaro by their 'Chief', J. Sweeney, and another detective. Soon there were eighteen police living under canvas around the Lakey farmhouse, searching in miserable weather. After two weeks, Commissioner Wohlmann (responding to the clamour for results) visited Ruawaro and plans were made for a much more intensive search over a wider area for the body of Samuel Lakey. For the first time in a police homicide investigation, an aerial search was made and photographs taken. Unprecedented resources were now brought to bear, especially in terms of both the numbers (rising to more than 50) and rank of police involved at Ruawaro: from 7 November, a succession of Inspectors with mana as detectives (first and briefly J. Cummings from Wellington and R. Ward from Wanganui, then J. Hollis, and S. Rawle from New Plymouth) directed the enquiry until its conclusion in January 1934. There were no days off. By late November there was a determination to prosecute, even without a body. On evening of 26 November, at his 'office' in the Lakey house, Inspector Rawle read 'various authorities re murder' and summed up 'all provable points re murder to the number of 29'.[94] This was before the discovery of burnt bones, supposedly those of Sam Lakey, in Bayly's garden provided a solution to the mystery, seven weeks after it had begun.

Ultimately the conviction of Bayly hinged upon the contribution of forensic science. The case (as Dr Lynch observed) 'marked the beginning of detection's scientific age'.[95] The range of exhibits, and the expertise employed, caught the public imagination. Journalists played on the statistics. The Magistrate's Court hearing of the charges of murder against Bayly in January 1934 was one of the longest on record, lasting ten days. Sixty-four Crown witnesses were heard and 251 exhibits produced. In addition to pathologists, general practitioners, and the Government Analyst, a textile designer identified various pieces of material, a dental expert gave an opinion on false teeth presented to him, a clerk was called in as a handwriting expert, and the Professor of Physics at Auckland University College reported his findings on various cartridges and on knife marks on wood from Lakey's implement shed. Even more witnesses were called and exhibits produced at the Supreme Court trial during May and June, which lasted 24 days, much longer than any trial hitherto, except that of Rua Kenana in 1916. 'In building up the case against Bayly tremendous trifles played their part', commented a *New Zealand Herald* reporter: 'There were the minute fragments of bone, the piece of hair, faint drops of blood, wheel and sledge marks in the paddocks ....'[96] For the detectives who found these 'trifles', the direction of the tracks in the paddocks had made Bill Bayly their prime suspect.

Given the charge of inefficiency levelled at police during the Elsie

Walker case, they could not afford to fail this time. That there was a definite suspect was another reason for the degree of effort applied to establishing who had killed the Lakeys. By contrast, the enquiry into the murder of J.H. Blair which began a day earlier required less police resources, for detectives soon drew a blank: there was no witness, no suspect, no motive established or weapon found. The Blair case became one of at least fourteen 'unsolved' homicides during the inter-war years, including five unidentified newborn children, but not including a similar number of disappearances or deaths where foul play was suspected.[97] Though his diligence helped to secure convictions for murder, J.B. Young led more than his fair share of enquiries that were ultimately inconclusive – notably those into the disappearance of E.M. Burr (in 1930) on the West Coast of the South Island, the killings of Ellen Scarff (in 1927) and Donald Fraser (in 1933) at Christchurch, and of Rosamund and Annie Smythe (in 1942) and H.W. Brunton (in 1948) at Wairoa.[98] Failure was not for want of effort, but of enough of the elements necessary for detection – including luck. Murder enquiries that did not lead to a successful prosecution were unsettling. Though the Bayly case represented a triumph of detection, there remained critics who considered that detectives lacked adequate training and technological resources. Between 1936 and 1939 there was to be some attempt to remedy this.[99]

CHAPTER 7

Policing Gambling

Detectives used guile rather then forensic science to fight illicit gambling. Some 15,200 gaming cases were dealt with by detectives between 1918 and 1949, a significant proportion of their work yet only a fraction of the potential offences during the period. Policing gambling entailed peculiar difficulties. The enforcement of laws which were widely flouted required methods which threatened the standing of police in their communities. More than any other sphere of policing, the attempt to control illegal gambling had the potential to compromise the integrity of individual police and the image of the Force as free from corruption. The period was the heyday of the covert bookmaker. This floresence of bookmaking was the unintended result of a sustained attempt to reshape a popular pastime by quarantining it to licit forms while seeking to penalise activity deemed illicit.

Whereas burglars and murderers broke 'fundamental laws', as ex-detective Charles Belton put it, 'the bookmaker is an example of one who breaks experimental laws' (laws designed to control behaviour that was frowned upon by the state but not widely seen as immoral).[1] By 1920, most gaming and betting practices were deemed illegal. Such behaviour was not seen as immoral, however, by probably a substantial majority of New Zealanders in the inter-war years. Many who did not bet on horse races, and saw those who did as foolish, regularly sent for a ticket in 'Tatts' (Tattersalls), the very popular Australian lottery, thereby circumventing the prohibition on such opportunities to gamble in New Zealand.[2] Gambling was well-entrenched as a pastime, especially amongst male wage-earners, for whom betting on horse races and the 'infatuating game' of 'two-up' had become national 'sports' by the first decade of the twentieth century.[3]

The Gaming Amendment Act 1920 represented the high point in statutory constraints which had developed from the first general piece of legislation in 1881 intended to control the use of totalisators, suppress gaming and betting houses and abolish most lotteries.[4] The 1920 Act declared the business of bookmaking to be illegal. Betting with bookmakers was also made an offence. With one exception (L.M. Isitt), politicians supporting the measure did not express a concern to actually suppress the 'gambling evil'. Instead the Act resulted from mixed motives: a desire by racing and trotting clubs to eliminate a strong rival to on-course betting on totalisators from which they gained a commission, and a wider concern (already present in earlier legislation) to control and regulate betting by recognising its inevitability and confining it to racecourses.[5] The government could also benefit through increased revenue from its taxation of totalisator 'investments' and 'dividends'.[6] (Language marked off the distinction between respectable and illicit betting.) By offering off-course 'doubles' and betting on credit, bookmakers were perceived to have a 'malign influence' in fostering the gambling spirit amongst those who could ill afford it, and in 'fixing' races.

Even at their most stringent, the legislative prohibitions against gaming and betting remained partial. This selectivity (as well as the widespread desire for opportunities to gamble) established the preconditions for police ineffectiveness in enforcing the law, and ultimately brought the legislation into widespread contempt. Sweepstakes were banned, except those on racecourses, which were restricted to a maximum contribution of £5. Lotteries were not permitted, although some 'art unions' (small raffles with works of art or other worthy objects as prizes) were allowed. From 1929, governments began to grant licences for larger art unions to raise money for specific goals; but the use of small fund-raising raffles by voluntary organisations was tightly controlled. Conversely, the purchase of overseas lottery tickets through local agents remained unfettered.

The selectivity of constraints on betting proved to be counter-productive. Prohibiting the use of telephones and the telegraph to put money on the totalisator served to promote the business of bookmakers, who provided the only means of off-course betting. Not allowing totalisators to offer 'doubles' left illegal bookmakers with a monopoly of this popular form of betting. Similarly, making the publication of dividends illegal merely reinforced the relationship of bettors with bookmakers, who soon developed telephone networks to provide this information. Since 1894 bookmakers had been prohibited from offering 'totalisator odds'.[7] As well as being ignored, this proscription was often irrelevant: some bettors (especially the 'big punters' amongst horse owners and trainers) preferred the fixed odds and credit accounts offered by many 'bookies'.[8] Whereas 10s was the smallest amount that could be 'invested' on the 'tote', many small bookmakers confined themselves to 2s 6d or 5s bets which met the needs of their working-class clientele. For some would-be 'silver bettors', however, the dubious respectability of small bookmakers and their locales could be the rub: 'Honest working men do not like going into hotels and booze dens to have a bet', complained one in 1945.[9]

The selectivity of the law, especially regarding betting, was perceived by its critics (notably amongst Labour MPs) and off-course bettors to be hypocritical, unjust, and implicitly class-biased. It seemed to serve the interests of the Racing Conference ('a bigger factor in this country than is realised') rather than the small punter who had difficulty getting to the racetrack because of work, lack of means, or isolation.[10] When the Minister introducing the 1920 legislation pointed out that it was not an offence 'for two people who are not bookmakers to have a bet' on a horse race, Thomas Wilford commented from the Opposition benches: 'That is the protection for you and me.'[11] By contrast, the new offence of carrying on the business of a bookmaker carried the heavy penalty of a £500 fine or two years imprisonment. For those so charged, the right to trial by jury was conceded. To the frustration of police, popular sentiment was soon revealed: with only one exception during the 1920s, juries disregarded judges' directions and refused to convict bookmakers of following an unlawful occupation.[12]

For most gaming offences, however, securing a conviction proved to be the least of the difficulties of detectives who had the task of enforcing the law. By the late 1920s, police had apparently moved effectively against street betting: the numbers prosecuted for this offence were relatively few.[13] Henceforth illicit betting was to varying degrees covert, conducted in workplaces, offices, shops, hairdressing and billiard saloons, hotels, suburban dwellings, and (by novices and the audacious) at racecourses. Though bookmakers operated covertly, police felt able to estimate that in 1946 at least 763 people were engaged in bookmaking (about twice the number then belonging to the 'bookies'' front organisation, the Dominion Sportsmen's Association).[14] While many were suspected, only some were prosecuted. Who was caught, and how frequently, depended partly on the methods and resources of both the bookmakers and the police.

By the late 1920s, and probably much earlier, a hierarchy of bookmakers had developed in the main centres, differentiated by their methods, clientele, and scale of operations.[15] At the top were the wealthy 'big men' whose identity, journalist Robin Hyde observed ironically in 1932, 'seems to be well known to almost everyone except the police.'[16] As the principals of large-scale bookmaking businesses, these men used a variety of measures to protect themselves from prosecution. The rapid growth in telephone connections facilitated bookmaking, as did the use of private post office boxes and telegraph codes. Essentially the 'big men' avoided direct contact with bettors, employing salaried clerks and working from city offices or suburban dwellings through unlisted telephones and agents.[17] Stimulated by radio broadcasts of racing (from the late 1920s)[18] and its detailed coverage in newspapers, the growing number of people with access to telephones could bet at their convenience from workplace, home or hotel. Impersonal contact particularly suited those with pretensions to respectability who wished to make their illicit wagers in privacy. A.L. Albertson, one of the largest bookmakers in Christchurch in the decade to 1944, numbered

Members of Parliament, banking officials, horse trainers, jockeys, horse owners, racing officials, lawyers, doctors and businessmen amongst his thousand regular clients.[19] Specially printed 'day cards' and 'double charts' bearing the distinctive symbols of bookmakers, but no names, were posted out to clients, or issued by agents.[20] Unsuccessful bets by telephone would be followed in a few days by a debit note in the mail.[21] Only if he was caught on the premises at the time of a police raid, or if it could be proved that he was technically the 'occupier' of premises deemed to be a common gaming house, was a principal likely to be prosecuted.[22] H.C. Sallery was not in his offices in the Union Building on Auckland's Customs Street when police arrested his three clerks staffing the telephones. Nonetheless, he turned up 'voluntarily' at court to pay their fines, and his own, totalling £310.[23] Almost invariably bookmakers' clerks and agents refused to identify their employer.

In lieu of touts on the street, agents provided crucial access to working-class clients. Typically they were small shopowners, and especially tobacconists, billiard-saloon keepers and barmen with access to a telephone. Despite their vulnerability to detection, the commission of 1s or 1s 6d in the pound (depending on who would pay any fines) was an attractive supplement to often meagre business takings. Equally important was the need to 'oblige' customers if they were to be retained in the face of rival agents.[24] Besides agents working for particular bookmakers, there were also 'commissioners' engaged by punters looking to place large sums with any bookmaker who would take them, as well as on the totalisator.[25]

More numerous than the 'big men' who were rarely if ever caught were city bookmakers, some with a substantial business, operating more openly by styling themselves ambiguously as 'commission agents' or working behind the 'front' of a tobacconist's shop. Notable examples were the tobacconists Thomas Curran and W.T. Osmond in Hobson Street, Auckland. In Osmond's shop in the early 1930s working men read the 'acceptances' published by the *Auckland Star* and listened to broadcasts of the races. Though it was fitted out as a tobacconist's, there was (according to the police prosecutor in 1934) 'absolutely no stock in it, apart from advertising material'.[26] By 1936, Curran had been convicted nine times and Osmond eight, with a total of £585 and £580 respectively in fines, over a period of more than a decade.[27] At the other extreme were the 'small fry', some disparagingly termed 'hotel rats' by police, whose operations were even more visible to those who knew where to look. With their home-made double charts they frequented public bars and billiard saloons, and even ventured on to racecourses. Many were merely part-time 'pencillers' seeking to supplement their wages or pensions with some 'silver betting'.

Underpinning the service provided by many bookmakers in the cities and provincial towns was the role of the Dominion Sportsmen's

Association established in Wellington in 1921, ostensibly to endeavour by 'constitutional methods to have the statutory restrictions on the operation of bookmakers removed.'[28] Lobbying Labour MPs to this end, it succeeded in having a bill introduced in 1931 to license bookmakers.[29] The bill lapsed. Like the Communist Party (against whom similar policing methods were used), the Association was regarded as subversive by the authorities. Perhaps then it was no coincidence that increased activity by detectives against bookmakers accompanied visible lobbying by the Association in the early 1930s and again in 1944/45.[30] Not visible, but much more significant, were the services provided by the Association to its membership through offices in the four main centres. The location of the Wellington office, two blocks from the Central police station, must have been known to police, but (presumably) since there was no evidence of illegal betting occurring there, it was not raided.[31] Instead the Association's offices were nerve centres in the rapid distribution by telephone of vital information from racecourses to bookmakers about scratchings, results and dividends. Results from Trentham (for example) could be telephoned through to Christchurch in five to twenty minutes, depending on how busy the toll lines were. Thus 'professional' bookmakers could accept bets on races throughout the country, and quickly discover their liability.[32] Until the 1930s at least, bookmakers in the smaller towns (such as Nelson) transacted business with other members elsewhere by telegrams using codes supplied by the Association.[33] As was frequently commented on by critics, the services provided by the Post and Telegraph Department frustrated the enforcement of the law against bookmakers and their clients by another arm of the state.[34]

In such circumstances, what was police policy? For governments and police administrators at least, turning a blind eye to illicit gambling was not an option. The law had to be enforced, whatever doubts there may have been about its effectiveness. Critics soon noted that the passage of the Gaming Amendment Act 1920 had apparently made no difference to the operations of bookmakers. In response (a move that underlined the political pressures for strict enforcement) the Minister of Justice, E.P. Lee, announced that he had conferred with the Commissioner and had issued instructions 'to permeate through the whole of the Department, down to the constables', to see that the law was observed: not only were bookmakers to be prosecuted, but also 'every member of the public who infringed the law' by betting with them. The onus was on the Police: if the Commissioner and his officers 'were not able with the law in force now to check betting he would be very disappointed with the work of the Department'.[35] In his last annual report in 1921, Commissioner O'Donovan took the opportunity to reply to censure of the Police 'for permitting the bookmaker to exist'. Though the 1920 Act had made it 'more difficult' for bookmakers, police continued to find it 'very difficult' to convict them. Those who believed that it was possible 'to extinguish' bookmakers

> with legislation backed up by drastic police action are as confiding and
> credulous as those who suppose that the thief and the burglar, the
> unlawful practitioner and murderer, may be extinguished by means of
> the Crimes Act ... put into operation by a Police Force which is generally
> admitted to be reasonably efficient. Drastic legislation followed by
> vigorous police action can keep these evils in check, but the causes are
> deeper-rooted than legislation or police efforts can reach. The same
> applies with at least equal force to the evils the Gaming Acts were
> intended to combat. The police, I am confident, have done, and will
> continue to do, all that is possible to enforce these Acts.[36]

What was possible? To an extent that was perhaps not appreciated
by contemporaries, detectives' pursuit of bookmakers was assisted by
complaints. Typical was the prosecution in November 1932 of Charlie
Matthews for keeping a common gaming house at his fish shop in Mt
Eden Road, Auckland. Bookmaking was apparently a sideline to
supplement his earnings, and Matthews came to police attention only
through complaints. According to Detective Sergeant Thomas Kelly,
who prosecuted, police were 'constantly "on the road" testing the
accuracy of anonymous letters, and quite a number of bookmakers
were located in this way.'[37] Complaints came from a number of sources:
their anonymity suggested dissatisfied bettors and rival bookmakers, as
well as those in the local community who regarded bookmakers as a
nuisance (or worse) and disliked seeing an unpopular law blatantly
broken. But that was the limit of public assistance. Since complainants
never appeared as prosecution witnesses, police had to seek the necessary
evidence. Again typically, in Matthews' case a plain-clothes constable
attached to the Detective Branch placed two 5s bets with him, followed
by another two bets a few days later. Soon after, Detectives F. Brady
and A. Moore, armed with a search warrant, raided Matthews' shop
and seized a small quantity of betting material. While there, Brady
answered the telephone; two callers asked for bets while the others
became suspicious and 'rang off'.[38]

In some districts, and especially in small towns, police rarely acted
against bookmakers except when complaints came in, and then (as one
retired detective put it) 'you had to do something about it ... [and] get
a man from another district' to obtain the evidence.[39] In the cities,
where there were more police resources, detectives did not wait for
complaints. Once under suspicion or convicted, a bookmaker became
subject to periodical surveillance, especially by those new constables
from each batch who spent some weeks on undercover work. Like
others who subsequently became detectives, Charles Belton was selected
for this task because he did not look like a 'typical' policeman.
Apparently less worldly than the usual run of recruits, Belton was

ignorant of the 'intricacies of betting', and needed instruction from a senior detective in the methods of bookmakers before being sent to certain hotels to secure the incriminating betting confirmation slips.[40] Once these were obtained, detectives procured the necessary warrant from a JP and made the arrest, hopefully catching the 'bookie' with his notebook and double charts. Timing was all-important. In Auckland during the early 1930s, Detectives Moore and Brady (who were then mainly, but not exclusively, preoccupied with detecting gaming offences) had 'a habit of dropping in' near midday on Saturday racedays, when 'the pencillers are hard at work' taking bets over the counter or the telephone. Particularly during the popular race meetings of the Christmas and New Year holiday season, simultaneous raids by detectives and constables on a number of shops and offices were usual. Invariably their 'acquaintances' were caught red-handed.[41] Taken to the Central police station, they were bailed (£100 often being readily found) after a couple of hours of paperwork by detectives and formalities before a JP.

Very few bookmakers were committed to trial in the Supreme Court, where the likelihood of acquittal had to be balanced against the prospect of imprisonment if convicted.[42] Both police and accused settled for summary jurisdiction. Between 1925 and 1950, 95 per cent of those prosecuted before magistrates for bookmaking offences were convicted, and virtually all were fined – usually much less than the maximum amount prescribed.[43] That most pleaded guilty[44] and were fined suggests that generally a tacit trade-off developed to secure the semblance of law enforcement without either the obstruction of popular sentiment or the 'unduly severe'[45] penalty of imprisonment. Instead of charging those identified as 'big men' and their agents, as well as the smaller bookies like Charlie Matthews, with the offence of carrying on the business of bookmaker created by the 1920 Act, police prosecutors resorted to the long-established charge (under the Gaming Act 1908) of keeping a common gaming house, which carried a lesser maximum penalty.[46] Matthews, who had no court record, was fined £30 and given fourteen days to pay (or two months' imprisonment in default). 'Big men' who reappeared were generally levied the maximum for the 'gaming house' charge, £100. Magistrates occasionally expressed frustration at this, especially when the accused conceded that bookmaking was his occupation.[47] By contrast it was the part-time 'small fry', especially labourers taking bets in pubs and on racecourses, who pleaded guilty to carrying on the business of bookmaker. Even so, the comments of detectives ('he's only a small better', 'never been in trouble before', a 'decent chap' out of work and betting to 'keep his family', 'not really a bookmaker') usually ensured that such men and the occasional woman were fined relatively small amounts (£5 or less) and given time to pay.[48] Indeed, Detective Sergeant Michael O'Sullivan's words in favour of a one-legged Maori war pensioner caught taking bets at the Avondale races led F.K. Hunt SM to adjourn the charge for two months 'to see how he behaved'.[49] On average, therefore, the fines levied for keeping a common gaming house were heavier than those applied to a charge that in theory carried a more severe penalty.[50]

In effect, the unintended consequence of policies generally adopted by police and magistrates in different localities was a system which licensed rather than suppressed bookmaking. What might seem to be a heavy fine was (as Charles Belton observed) viewed by successful bookmakers 'merely as a license fee'.[51] It was 'not usual' (one former 'big man' noted) that 'when you get 'caught ... they come within a period of a few months and [you] get caught again.'[52] Moreover, these gaming entrepreneurs had their books returned to them after conviction.[53] Removal of their business telephones (which could only follow a conviction) was soon circumvented.[54] Routinely, magistrates professed not to be swayed by defence counsels' arguments that bookmaking was an 'artificial offence'; that their clients were honest, reputable, met the demand of a large section of the public, and paid income tax on their turnover. Their job, the judges replied, was to enforce the law while it remained on the statute books. Nonetheless, some openly acknowledged that fines were not a deterrent. Most magistrates, however, were reluctant to send bookmakers to prison. Fining an Auckland bookmaker, W.T. Osmond, the maximum penalty of £100 a third time for keeping a common gaming house, W.R. McKean SM observed in 1932: 'The only solution is to license bookmakers. But that is not for me to say .... I suppose that some day we will reach the stage of sending one to prison without the option of a fine.'[55] Two years later, his colleague on the Auckland bench, Wyvern Wilson, reached that stage. When the 'big' bookmakers Francis Brewer and Thomas Curran reappeared for the fifth and seventh times respectively, Wilson gave each a month's imprisonment without the option of a fine. It was 'not the law', he declared, that a man had 'to pay £100 every year or so, and keep on keeping common gaming houses.'[56] When Wilson sent Curran to prison for two months in 1936 (he had been fined £100 yet again in 1935), there was an outcry; some 10,000 people signed a petition for his release.[57] Occasionally, then, the de facto licensing system broke down. But not until 1944, when a leading Christchurch bookmaker (A.L. Albertson) was sentenced to twelve months' imprisonment, was the reaction sufficient to provoke a major reassessment that effectively changed the law.[58] However the bookmakers failed to achieve legal recognition and were eventually supplanted during the 1950s by the off-course betting facilities of the Totalisator Agency Board.

Though illegal betting and gaming was not suppressed, officially there was no let-up. In June 1926, a few months after he became Commissioner, W.B. McIlveney enjoined police to 'strictly enforce' the provisions of the Gaming Acts, desiring 'it to be recognized that no relaxation of required effort will meet with approval'. His successors

Figure 7.1: Charges for Gaming Offences 1878–1954

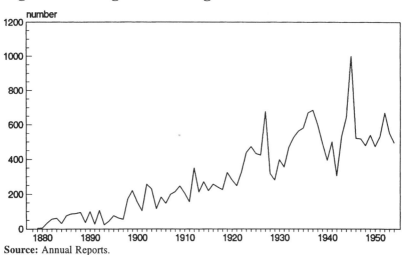

Source: Annual Reports.

reiterated the command.[59] During the inter-war years, growing numbers of gaming offences were identified by detectives, continuing a long-term upward trend apparent since the turn of the century (figure 7.1). There was a wave-like pattern in prosecutions, with ever higher peaks in 1919, 1924, 1927, 1937, and 1945, and troughs in 1921, 1926, 1929, and 1942. A variety of influences shaped this pattern. Possibly significant, but not to be presumed, were political pressures from the Racing Conference and its supporters for increased enforcement. That any such pressure (or suggestions) came directly through the Minister to the Commissioner cannot be documented after 1921. More likely was the influence of a wave-like pattern of critical comment in the press and by some politicians. McIlveney's circular was probably a response to such criticism, and it produced a sharp but short-lived upswing in activity. Early in 1927, Inspector Allan Cameron in Christchurch denied a journalist's suggestion that a 'concerted drive' against bookmakers had begun in various parts of the country: 'We are out to catch these men at all times. Just as quick as they come along we will prosecute them.'[60] Shortly afterwards, however, Sir George Clifford, President of the Racing Conference, wrote to Commissioner McIlveney congratulating him on the recent prosecutions of 'more prominent bookmakers', which were 'especially valuable as an answer to the widespread criticisms' that only the business of 'smaller men' was being 'checked'.[61]

Fluctuations in prosecutions also reflected broad changes in the visibility of gaming and illicit betting activity. Prosecutions of bookmakers and those found betting with them comprised only a minority, albeit a steadily growing proportion, of all those for breaches of the Gaming Acts.[62] During the early 1920s detectives periodically raided 'two-up' schools on the Auckland and Wellington wharves, as well as those that appeared on Sundays in secluded spots around the main towns.[63] Such 'games of hazard' were not suppressed, but they became more covert, often reappearing in billard saloons and in 'clubs' (with controlled entry) established in the main centres by gaming entrepreneurs catering especially for a working-class clientele. These became the focus of large-scale raids by detectives, especially in Auckland from the mid-1930s.[64] New forms of gaming appeared – and were soon prosecuted – such as 'roll-down parlours', first seen in Dunedin during its Exhibition in 1926, and then in Auckland and Wellington.[65] Indeed, as we have seen, the zeal of police in pursuing possible infringements of the Gaming Act, such as euchre tournaments, created a growing wave of indignant comment in the late 1920s. In the early 1930s, Chinese 'pakapoo dens' (especially those in Auckland's Grey Street and Wellington's Haining Street) were subjected to frequent raids as their clientele grew, recruited (it seemed to police) from the burgeoning ranks of the unemployed.[66] Hard times also provided a seemingly inexhaustable supply of recruits to the ranks of small and part-time bookmakers visible to police in the 1930s: 'as soon as one of these men finishes, another springs up to take his place', commented a Detective Sergeant.[67]

The broad contours of police statistics concealed local variations in the policing of illicit gambling.[68] This was to be expected, if only because there were limits to the resources police could apply to detecting breaches of the Gaming Acts. The variety of demands on individual detectives outside the main centres meant that they gave fitful attention to gaming and illicit betting. In small towns, moreover, local police were well known and their movements were often readily monitored by bookmakers (and publicans) with the support of their clients. In some localities, a modus vivendi may well have been reached. Thus in 1913, Inspector Wilson, in charge of the Wanganui District, had called for a special section of detectives to focus on bookmakers throughout the country, as was then utilised in Victoria.[69]

This idea was not taken up. Instead, when the visibility of bookmaking made them necessary, simultaneous raids on a number of small towns would be made by police drawn from outside the locality, such as those carried out with 'military precision' in Taranaki on a Saturday afternoon in March 1934.[70] Enforcement of the gaming laws was unpopular with many in his Force, Commissioner J. Cummings conceded; but it was a matter of 'duty'.[71] Amongst detectives, then, zeal was also a factor in detecting gaming offences, marking off (for example) the pertinacity of J.B. Young in Christchurch (which was rewarded by an accelerated increment in pay in June 1927)[72] from its absence seemingly shown by Michael Gourlay at Wanganui in the mid-1920s.[73] Similarly, when Detective Sergeant Eric Compton took over responsibility for detecting bookmakers in Wellington, the numbers prosecuted increased sharply from sixteen in 1943 to 60 in 1944, and continued to rise until 1947.[74] With some justification, a long-standing Auckland bookmaker could comment in 1947:

> In parts of New Zealand it is notorious that Bookmakers operate freely without interference from the Police while in other parts the Bookmaker is continually and continuously harassed and interfered with and sentenced to terms of imprisonment. Yet in other parts he is always subject to a fine, which goes to show the reluctance of some Police to take action and how some Policemen will administer the law irrespective of the penalty. This applies also to Magistrates.[75]

Though strict enforcement of the Gaming Acts was ordered, police practice was perceived to be selective, apparently focusing on some gaming offences rather than others, upon the bookmakers rather than those who bet with them, and on the 'smaller fry' and the pakapoo dens rather than the 'big men'. A.L. Albertson believed that while he was bookmaking in Christchurch there was 'no rigid control' by the Police. Some of his fellow bookmakers were never prosecuted, 'some were treated with lenience, and some [like himself] were fairly regularly convicted.'[76] To a degree this belief in police selectivity was ill-founded: 'Sometimes we don't get the evidence to prosecute, and the public does not hear about these cases', Inspector Cameron explained in 1927.[77] Those who were regularly 'pinched' could be seen as the least successful in covering their tracks. As the likelihood of prosecution increased, particularly in Wellington during the mid-1940s, some big bookmakers retreated to their telephones behind locked doors, and shifted their offices 'from raceday to raceday'.[78]

Given the difficulties in securing convincing evidence (especially against telephone bettors), prosecutions for betting with bookmakers were rare indeed. Detectives found it easier to secure a conviction (albeit with a lighter fine) if clients found in bookmakers' premises were charged with the offence of being found in a common gaming house.[79] In dealing with apparently new types of gaming activity, and 'borderline' cases concerning raffles and lotteries that came to their attention, police often chose to prosecute and let the courts determine whether an offence had occurred.

Yet detectives clearly did exercise discretion. They might warn bookmakers in the first instance. Sometimes this was bluff, for lack of evidence. Part-time bookies especially might be deterred, saving detectives the trouble of prosecution. Commissioner J. Cummings admitted that, as a detective, he had warned suspected bookmakers himself: 'It may be that where I had a feeling a man might start I'd say, "There's not enough room here for you" '.[80] The danger was, however, that such warnings could be perceived as favouring some bookmakers over others; as regulating rather than effectively suppressing illicit activity.[81]

More broadly, discretion was apparent in police enforcement of the Gaming Act 1908. At least one of its provisions had become a dead letter by the late 1920s, section 30 applying to 'tipping'.[82] Latitude was also sometimes allowed the sideshowmen who followed the circuit of Agricultural and Pastoral shows in the country towns. They might be 'permitted to play a gambling game for small stakes in one town, but not another', Belton observed. Thus showmen made 'a point of finding out' about the local detective or constable: 'if they know him to be a "hard man" they are careful what games they play'.[83] Similarly, a 'growing inclination' during the 1930s, amongst those running local raffles for 'works of art', to ignore the conditions of their permits reflected haphazard monitoring by local police.[84] Again, Senior Sergeant E.J. Carroll was not alone in being remembered for his 'fine tolerance for the spirit of an occasion, even if it was outside the letter of the law.' At Rotorua during the late 1930s he turned a blind eye to illegal sweepstakes at the 'non-tote' meetings of the local trotting club – overruling a Detective Sergeant from Hamilton who wished to suppress them.[85] However, when only the organisers of a big 'Calcutta Sweep' in the Te Aroha Masonic Hall (preceding a popular local raceday in 1935) were prosecuted after a raid by Hamilton detectives, allegations of political influence, and of 'one law for the rich and another for the poor', quickly followed. The names of about 200 people had been taken, including local professional men, racehorse owners and other 'sportsmen of good character'. Normally all those present would have faced prosecution for being found in a common gaming house – and prohibited from attending the next race meeting. In this case, the exercise of discretion (authorised by Commissioner Wohlmann) was remembered by a prominent Hamilton lawyer as a 'most scandalous thing', though he did not blame the local police.[86]

The prevalence of illegal betting, the apparently selective and fitful nature of police activity in attempting to suppress it, and the fact that some bookmakers seemed rarely if ever to be prosecuted, raises the question of whether the de facto licensing system became corrupt: were payments or gifts made to some detectives to prevent prosecutions? Certainly, the official opinion (of judges and parliamentarians) was that the New Zealand Police were not corrupt. And public allegations were extremely rare – inevitably, since bribery is covert consensual behaviour. Thus the issue was not addressed by the Royal Commission on Gaming and Racing during its hearings in 1947. However, in various American, British, and Australian cities during the inter-war years and later, the prevalence of illegal gambling was associated with corruption – seemingly an endemic feature of policing, in the eyes of its critics at least.[87] Why then should this not be the case in New Zealand? There are two aspects to the issue of police corruption as it was defined between the wars: bribery to secure protection from prosecution, and misplaced zeal leading to unethical or illegal methods in securing convictions.[88]

The solitary conviction of a constable for taking a bribe between 1918 and 1945 was unrelated to illegal gambling. In the same period only one bookmaker (in a 'big way' at Hamilton) was prosecuted for offering a bribe: a case of pipes and £10 was mailed blatantly to two detectives who had raided him just before Christmas 1929.[89] According to a *Truth* reporter, such attempts to induce police to accept bribes were 'not uncommon, but it is seldom that the public hears anything about them in court.'[90] This comment could only have been based on hearsay. As some bookmakers were 'pinched' and others not, rumours could be expected amongst them (and sly-groggers) that some police took 'backhanders', 'slings', or 'hush-money' paid under the guise of 'winnings'.[91] The extent to which these rumours circulated or were believed is difficult to determine. When C.S. Lees set up a bookmaking business in Auckland in January 1930, he apparently believed 'immunity' could be bought, being persuaded by his partner P.F. Farnworth, a former policeman, that Detective Sergeants Andrew McHugh and 'Paddy' Doyle should be paid £10 each. Farnworth managed to convince others that he could 'square the police'. Lees provided the money; but Farnworth did not pay it – and was subsequently charged with intent to defraud Lees![92] This episode suggested that certain prominent police officers could not be 'squared', though a few bookmakers and their associates believed it possible. With this belief, generalised rumours continued. Yet they proved impossible to substantiate. A Commission of Inquiry into police conduct in 1953–54 failed to discover any evidence of 'hush money' being paid by bookmakers to detectives during the preceding decade.[93]

Ultimately it is very difficult, if not impossible, to obtain confirmation of bribery unless one of the parties (including witnesses) to an initially consensual arrangement is prepared to testify. In the 'Fitzgerald' inquiry into Queensland police corruption between 1987 and 1989, the granting of immunity from prosecution to serving and former police officers was 'a vital step in cracking the facade which had previously defeated every attempt at penetration.'[94] Such immunity was not granted police and bookmakers called before the New Zealand Commission of Inquiry into police conduct. None of those cross-examined admitted offering, being offered, or receiving bribes, or any knowledge of police corruption. A few admitted to having heard non-specific rumours; that was all.[95] A disgruntled former acting detective, J.B. Ritchie, gave evidence implicating his superiors (E.H. Compton and G.E. Callaghan) who had focused on catching bookmakers in Wellington between 1944 and 1948. He proved not to be a credible witness.[96] Thorough inquiries were made by accountants drawn from other government departments into the financial affairs of all detectives who had been engaged in detecting bookmakers in the four main cities since 1944. In all except three cases the results raised no suspicion that 'hush money' had been received – thereby (in the view of the Commission) affording 'assurance that the integrity of those concerned could not thus be impeached.'[97] The personal finances of Compton, Callaghan, and J. Gibson called for further public examination. Nothing material emerged which suggested that bribes had been received, though suspicions of Compton and Callaghan (engendered by the Inquiry) remained amongst police.[98] Ambiguous relationships with bookmakers revealed in a few instances were perhaps symptomatic of a wider pattern of behaviour. Detectives notable for their zeal in pursuing bookmakers, such as 'Jimmie' Cummings, J.B. Young and Eric Compton, were avowedly non-bettors. Callaghan and Gibson, however, did admit to winning substantial amounts from betting, and not just on-course. Gibson maintained a long-standing friendship with a 'big' bookmaker, R.D. Donaldson, whom he had arrested in Dunedin. Both Gibson and Ritchie borrowed from Donaldson after he had given up bookmaking. Gibson was also generous with letters of introduction, which he provided for Donaldson and another Wellington bookmaker to give to Australian detectives whom he had met.[99] To a degree, then, the New Zealand Commission of Inquiry did penetrate the facade of detectives' relationships with bookmakers. It found (by contrast with Queensland in the same period) no 'common knowledge'[100] of police corruption. Plausibly, few New Zealand police were 'on the take' during the inter-war years.

The obverse of 'bought' leniency was zeal that produced 'dishonourable' or illegal practices in pursuit of a conviction. 'Fair play was bonny play, and every person was entitled to receive it', declared Commissioner McIlveney. He inveighed against 'deliberate misrepresentation for the purpose of obtaining the confidence of suspected offenders and inducing them by deceit to contravene the law.'[101] McIlveney presumably did not have in mind police undercover work in pursuit of bookmakers, gambling dens, brothel-keepers and sly-groggers, which was seen by some (such as the MPs V.H. Potter, Frank Langstone, and Paddy Webb) as offending this principle.[102] It was not merely a question of 'spying'. In laying a bet or buying liquor from an unlicensed seller, plain-clothes police could be (and were) seen as *agents provocateurs* manufacturing evidence of a crime. At the turn of the century some magistrates, echoing popular opinion, criticised such 'entrapment', to which Commissioner Tunbridge replied that such methods were not applied against 'innocent or ignorant' people.[103] By the 1920s any doubts about the legality of undercover work had been removed, though the issues of fairness and of corroborative evidence remained and were occasionally raised by defence counsel, especially at jury trials.[104] Bookmakers who pleaded guilty in the Magistrate's Court rarely challenged the methods of detectives. Indeed, A.G. Williams, an Auckland tobacconist facing his third yearly conviction in 1937, spoke of 'some talk of a riot outside my shop on Saturday when the detectives called, but I want to say nothing against them. They have carried out their duties in a gentlemanly fashion. It is the legislation on the Statute Book that I complain about'. After shaking hands with Detectives Brady and Moore, Williams left the Court 'carrying his betting paraphernalia'.[105] Detectives' guile generally stayed within certain tacit bounds of 'fair play'. They did not, for example, seek to tap telephones – apart from two attempts by Detective Sergeant Compton in Wellington between 1944 and 1946. Compton acted on his own initiative, without the permission of either the Post and Telegraph Department or his superiors, which would not have been given. Compton's methods, then considered improper, became illegal in 1948.[106]

Corruption, defined in terms of contemporary standards, was apparently not endemic amongst detectives, or police more generally, between 1918 and 1945. Its absence was part and parcel of a wider ethic of public administration in New Zealand. More specifically, the possibilities for corrupt practices resulting from the distinctive nature of police work were counteracted by other influences. Detective work, like police work generally, was largely decentralised. It was, nonetheless, closely monitored by Chief Detectives or the officers in charge of the smaller districts. Before 1942, there were no special squads focusing on vice or bookmaking. Detectives were rarely engaged solely for an extended period on detecting one type of offence. Most did not spend their whole careers in one locality. Promotion brought transfers, with many detectives having to don a uniform at some stage of their careers. From the Commissioners and senior officers there was a strong emphasis on integrity.[107] The police leadership showed little compunction in investigating, transferring, or (if their suspicions seemed well-founded) compelling to resign or dismissing those whose integrity was compromised. Even in the main centres, the small number of New Zealand detectives did not become a 'firm within a firm', unlike their counterparts in London during the inter-war years.[108]

CHAPTER 8

Suburban and Country Constables

In December 1932 Bill Murray applied for a transfer to the two-man 'country' station at the small town of Levin. His ten years' service in the Wellington Detective Office was advanced 'as a favourable factor ... as against some other applicant whose period of service may have called for the performance of less exacting and arduous duties'. Then 36 years of age, married with three young children, Murray thought this 'particular transfer' would bring 'considerable benefit to my family and myself.'[1] His ability counted against him. Inspector Lander reported to the Commissioner that the detective was 'a very capable officer' whose 'transfer to uniform duty at the present stage of his career would, I think, be a loss to the service.'[2] Bill Murray remained a detective until becoming Inspector in charge of the Gisborne District twenty years later.

Career paths

It was rare for detectives to be transferred to Uniform Branch duties at rural or small-town stations.[3] Some spent part of their careers as the sole detective (or as one of two or three) attached to a district headquarters station outside the four main centres (as indeed Bill Murray did at Hamilton between 1941 and 1950).[4] A few ended their careers with long stints in small provincial towns.[5]

Other aspects of Bill Murray's application were more typical. Like others who sought transfers, Murray heard about the possible Levin vacancy through the departmental grapevine, and applied 'in anticipation'. During the inter-war years the only vacancies advertised in the *Police Gazette* were those at the Cook and Chatham Islands. Publicly, the justification was that advertising would 'create unnecessary work and expense without the corresponding benefit'.[6] Transfers were central to the Commissioners' exercise of discipline: those out of favour could be sent to remote stations (particularly on the South Island's West Coast).[7] Staff preferences might be taken into account, but generally the needs of the Department came before those of the men. Advertising positions could also raise expectations, as well as promote restlessness and frustration amongst men who believed that, by and large, length of service should determine appointments.

In the early 1920s constables could expect to have served at least ten years at city, larger suburban or town stations before being considered for a one-man country station. A decade later the norm was thirteen to fifteen years, more than double the usual waiting time of those appointed constables at the turn of the century. Thus constables were generally in their mid-thirties when sent to their first sole-charge station, whereas their counterparts before the First World War had typically been in their late twenties. In part this 'aging' stemmed from the long-term decline in the 'wastage' of police during the inter-war years, and the lengthening periods for which constables remained at many sole-charge stations. It also reflected a broader stability within rural and small-town society than had existed half a century earlier; at most country stations the work had gradually become less strenuous. It was probably this aspect which appealed to Bill Murray, as it did to others looking for a country posting offering the prospect of 'a quiet station', of being left to a much greater extent than in city policing to one's own devices, of being better off financially, and (perhaps) having a better family life.

Though this was not spelt out, Commissioners looked for other qualifications besides length of service on the beat. Experience as watch-house keeper (in particular), court orderly, on plain-clothes enquiries or relieving at one-man stations also counted. 'Can you ride a horse?', a Wellington Senior Sergeant asked Creighton Chesnutt before he was posted in 1921 to do country enquiries from the four-man Stratford station.[8] By the 1930s, if not earlier, a privately owned car available for rural police work could weigh in the balance. Certainly, having a wife who could be companion, housekeeper and unpaid helpmate in managing the routines of a 'one-man' station was a key consideration in most cases.

At first sight, the career paths of constables posted to small stations appear to lack any discernible logic, with the number of transfers ranging from two or three to nine or more, and a great variety in the sequence and location of destinations. 'Out of the blue' (typically), W.G. Wood was transferred in 1935 from suburban Takapuna on Auckland's North Shore (where he had spent nearly eleven years) to the small, quiet, Southland town of Winton. Wood did not know where Winton was, but soon found it congenial and remained there until his retirement in 1960. Whereas William Wood had only two transfers in his career, James Skinner, who joined the Police in the same year and place (Auckland in 1921) and also remained a constable, had nine: to Kopua (Gisborne District, sole charge), New Plymouth, Waitotara (Wanganui District, sole charge), Blenheim, Nelson, Richmond (Nelson District, sole charge), Normanby (New Plymouth District, sole charge), Taupo (in charge of a two-man station), and Hamilton (Arms Officer). Where Wood spent only three years at Auckland Central before going to the two-man station at Takapuna, Skinner spent nearly eight years on the beat before being stationed for two years at the Kopua railway construction camp. The two men were of similar ages, had passed their primary school Proficiency examination, and did not aspire to promotion. Wood, however, married soon after he joined, unlike Skinner, who did not marry until he was 43 and stationed at Nelson. Wood spent two years as a shift watch-house keeper, and sought his first transfer to Takapuna. Superior officers discerned different qualities in James Skinner, who spent five years stationed at Auckland Wharf before being despatched to deal with the potential rowdies at Kopua.[9]

Though no careers of constables at small stations were identical, those of Wood and Skinner are suggestive of patterns that can be discerned – patterns that were shaped by the ambitions and attributes of individual constables, the timing of transfers, and the types of station. For those in the Uniform Branch who passed their exams and looked for promotion, time spent at country stations could be short, often merely a year or two before promotion to Sergeant on sectional duty in the cities.[10] Those who failed their exams or eschewed promotion could move through a variety of sole-charge stations, often at three- to six-year intervals, transferring from more physically demanding to 'quiet' ones. Constables were not usually (or at least knowingly) sent to small-town stations where they had close family ties.

By contrast with James Skinner's experience, however, a career in a succession of sole-charge stations was quite commonly spent mainly in one police district, reflecting perhaps the influence of local senior officers on the Commissioners' decisions. After eight years on the beat in Dunedin, for example, 33 year old Irish-born Peter Fallon was posted (in 1920) as the junior to Constable Joseph West at the two-man Roslyn station in the western suburbs of the city. After four years Fallon was transferred to Christchurch, beginning his long career at Canterbury sole-charge stations with four years in suburban Fendalton. Fifteen months at Christchurch Central were followed by a further four years apiece at the rural villages of Little River and Darfield, eighteen months at the coal-mining township of Blackball across the Southern Alps, then back to another small Canterbury township, Lincoln, for three years, before his return to a Christchurch suburban station, Phillipstown, for eight years until his retirement in 1949.[11]

In another respect, the pattern of William Wood's career was as common as Peter Fallon's during the inter-war years: some constables spent lengthy periods at sole-charge stations. This was especially true of Christchurch suburban stations where there were, overall, fewer transfers than in other cities: ten of the thirteen one-man stations had no more than two changes of staff between 1919 and 1939. Except at Linwood, most stints were from ten to sixteen years. When they retired in 1939, the constables at Lower Riccarton and Islington had spent 21 and 30 years respectively at their stations.[12] This stability was reflected in the rural hinterland where, over two decades, seven of the fifteen sole-charge Canterbury country stations had no more than two staff changes. Parallel low staff turnover was found in other areas with well-established farming communities and prosperous small townships that were generally not remote from larger provincial centres, particularly in the New Plymouth, Palmerston North, Napier, Timaru, Dunedin and Invercargill police districts. Here were to be found constables who spent most of their careers at one country station, becoming long-remembered local identities such as Fred Longbottom (Inglewood 1914 to 1942), George Clouston (Opunake 1911 to 1938), John O'Donoghue (Kaponga 1923 to 1952), Lewis Skinner (Woodville 1917 to 1947), James Gartly (Taradale 1919 to 1948), and Andrew Mackintosh (Fairlie 1914 to 1944).

At more isolated stations, where living conditions were more primitive and community institutions less well developed (or at least the constable experienced greater social isolation than elsewhere), a higher turnover of staff could be expected. This was broadly true of sole-charge stations in North Auckland, the inland Wanganui District, the Gisborne District, and on the West Coast of the South Island. Some of the highest rates of staff turnover during the inter-war years were at the West Coast mining settlements of Millerton, Blackball and Waiuta, and at Kaitangata in southern Otago.[13] The unmarried, English-born Jim Clements, posted to Millerton for a year in 1932, found the miners friendly so long as he 'did not interfere with the pubs and the bookmakers'. In this tight community, however, with 'most of the inhabitants ... pro Communist and seemingly anti most things including authority', Clements felt lonely; he erected a flagpole on which flew the Royal Navy's White Ensign 'daily as a token of my anti-ism.'[14] There were, of course, exceptions to the general rule. Constable A.J. Adams remained for ten years at a similar coal-mining village on the cold, bleak Denniston plateau – three times the usual sojourn.[15] Meanwhile, successive Commissioners apparently forgot about Constable Richard Allan, who was posted to the gold-mining ghost town of Charleston in 1909, and left to go opossum-trapping and run a farm until his retirement in 1942.[16]

While there were common features of police work at small stations, differences between stations influenced the choice of constables and the pattern of careers. Amongst the 240 sole-charge and 29 two-man stations in 1932, some were perceived to be 'hard' or 'busy' and many more to be 'quiet' (colloquially, 'old men's homes'), both in the countryside and suburbs. Typically a contrast might be pointed between, for example, the relatively 'quiet' Wanganui suburban stations of Aramoho, St John's, Wanganui East, and Gonville (with their counterparts in the larger cities), and the seasonally busier Canterbury country stations (with their annual influx of harvesters and files received for inquiry) at Rakaia and Methven,[17] or the more isolated, physically more demanding stations of Houhora (the most northerly station), Te Araroa (near East Cape), Matawai (in the Ureweras), or those on the remnants of the bush-working, mining, gumdigging, 'development' frontier at Otira, Waiuta and Murchison (on the South Island's West Coast) or Raurimu, Whangamomona and Tangarakau (on the southern reaches of the King Country), and at various stations in Northland. From another perspective, a clear distinction could also be drawn between busy stations based (say) in the expanding Auckland suburbs of Mt Albert, Point Chevalier and Takapuna, and those in tranquil farming communities such as Little River and Leeston in Canterbury, where there was relatively little work (apart from routine station duty and patrolling) during the inter-war years.[18]

The demands of patrols and enquiries, the need for coercion or merely a symbolic presence, were shaped by the nature of the local population: its rate of growth, degree of concentration, masculinity, transience, youthfulness, anonymity, and access to liquor. With their proximity to a larger station, suburban constables could expect more assistance, but also closer supervision and a greater likelihood of being called for duty outside their district. Suburban stations also recorded more complaints of housebreaking and petty theft. By contrast, country policemen were likely to have a range of other government 'appointments' and a greater variety of work. Depending on the territory to be covered, and the local requirements for liquor control, work could be expected to be physically more strenuous in a country district than a suburb.

As in earlier times, younger unmarried constables were stationed in potentially rowdy public works camps, or where conditions were too primitive for a family. Thus James Skinner was sent to Kopua, and later to Waitotara where the police house had been condemned. Big Thomas Shannon bolstered the strength of Shannon station from 1921 while the Mangahao dam was being built and thirsty men flocked into town on payday. Then in July 1929 he was despatched to open a station at the Waitaki Hydro public works camp.[19] The early career of Michael Conway captures well the transition from 'hard' to 'quiet' stations. Standing six feet tall, the broad-shouldered, unmarried 30 year old, with four and half years' experience in the Royal Irish Constabulary to back up his three years on the beat in Wellington, was sent in 1926 to monitor pub pugilists and two-up schools in the remote gold-mining settlement of Waiuta. Two days after his marriage in 1928, Conway was posted to the then more peaceful coal-mining township of Blackball, where union squabbles were to culminate in a bitter strike in 1931. In its aftermath, early in 1932, Conway was transferred 'over the Hill' to a 'quiet' two-man station in largely self-policing Kaiapoi, where he provided physical back-up when necessary for the aging Constable James Holmes, who was then in the 24th of his 32 years of service in the town.[20]

Sixteen years after joining the Force, Michael Conway became a Sergeant in Dunedin, beginning a second phase of his career in the

Uniform Branch during which he was to be transferred between the larger centres. Conway left behind a pattern of work which in its range, methods, rhythms and conditions differed markedly from that of city constables and their supervisors.

The local 'Pooh-Bah'

Staff at small stations, especially sole-charge country stations, were the real 'generalists' in the ranks of the police, combining patrolling with enquiries, detective, administrative and clerical work. Indeed the country constable remained the 'Pooh-Bah of the Force', often holding many government appointments, as he had since the advent of state policing in New Zealand.[21] Typically, Constable Lewis Skinner (at Woodville) was a bailiff, clerk to both the local Magistrate's Court and the Pahiatua Licensing Committee, probation officer, inspector of factories and of weights and measures, almoner and maintenance officer for the local charitable aid board, agent for the Public Trust Office, and Collector of Agricultural and Pastoral Statistics.[22] Other constables also acted as Census Enumerators, Collectors of Customs, and Registrars of Births and Deaths, while a few attended meetings of local Maori Councils.

Even this catalogue of appointments does not fully describe the range of work that constables at sole-charge stations performed for other government departments, much of which paralleled that of the uniformed 'enquiry' constables in the cities. Nor is the scope of suburban and country policing fully revealed by the extensive record-keeping required of such constables – their station diaries; registers of correspondence; crime, charge, summons, bail, and firearms registration books. The 'probabilities are that his Annual Returns are numerically small', observed one veteran of sole-charge stations, 'but it is what does not go on paper that counts'.[23] Usually less than a dozen arrests, often only one or two, and sometimes none, were recorded each year in the charge books of one-man stations.[24] Most of those taken into custody were either 'outsiders' – transients committing petty offences within the district or arrested on a warrant for offences committed elsewhere – or those 'locals' whose disorderly behaviour could not be dealt with by other means.[25] Until the depth of economic depression in the early 1930s blurred perceptions of those travelling in search of work, long-standing suspicions and practices continued: unemployed transients without lodgings ('suspicious strangers') still risked being charged with vagrancy, though such prosecutions were more common in the cities.

If formal action by local police was required, serving a summons to appear in court was the preferred method. The volume of summonses (civil as well as criminal) served annually by local constables was influenced by the number issued by courts outside the sub-district. Localities with a floating population of manual labourers were likely to attract more summonses and warrants than more stable communities. The number of summonses dealt with by the Roxburgh constable rose from four in 1919 to 27 in 1924 as railway construction intruded into his patch. Coinciding with the completion of the track, summonses fell away to an annual average of twelve in the 1930s. By contrast (and typical of expanding suburbs with their growing number of traffic cases) the constable at Point Chevalier received an average of 61 summonses a year to serve in the early 1930s, and the number soared to 268 in 1939.[26]

While the local constable might be a generalist, his basic work of surveillance had changed little since the nineteenth century. Indeed the growth in work for other government departments merely expanded this fundamental role. Albeit often incidental to 'making enquiries', daily patrols through suburb, township and neighbouring rural district, to see and be seen, were routine. Predictably, surveillance focused on public gatherings where there were opportunities to hear local gossip (race meetings, dances, football matches, Agricultural and Pastoral Shows, stock sales, dog trials); on pay days and at other potential times of trouble (especially the pubs at 6 pm); and on outsiders. 'Enquiries at Coal Creek re strangers in District' occupied the Roxburgh constable in July 1920 – and a 'military defaulter' was soon arrested.[27]

Patterns of surveillance

Systematic surveillance provided vital local knowledge, not merely to assist in detecting fugitives and likely troublemakers, but also in meeting the expanding demands of police and other state agencies for information on individuals and organisations. From this surveillance flowed further constraints on behaviour. Local constables (like the city enquiry constables) provided character references on applicants for a wide range of official permits and licences. During the early 1920s, constables stationed in the mining districts of the West Coast were asked for periodical reports on the likelihood of strikes, the presence of 'revolutionary' organisations and agitators, and people willing to act as temporary constables if need be. Similarly, local constables, like detectives in the main centres, kept an eye out for banned books (especially those on birth control) and indecent film posters, and ensured that the decisions of the Film Censor were followed. (In 1920, for example, *The End of the Road* was to be shown to audiences of men and women separately.) Typically, until the Department of Internal Affairs and the Government Statistician acquired alternative means of gathering the information, local police were asked to provide annual returns on fire brigades and private schools in their districts. Again acting as agents for Internal Affairs, country constables on the West Coast and in the King Country issued licences to opossum trappers, who brought their cured skins to the station to be stamped before they could be sold.[28]

From 1921 the annual collection of agricultural and pastoral statistics was an autumnal 'duty' for both rural police and some in the outer suburbs of cities. In a leisurely fashion, schedules were taken to occupiers of holdings (from the 1930s they were posted), then collected, checked and transcribed by the constable (and often his wife) into 'collection books' which were sent to the Government Statistician. Expenses were not reimbursed. In theory, this time-consuming work was done in conjunction with other police enquiries for which travelling allowances were paid. To stimulate zeal, however, the Government Statistician offered a small amount for each schedule collected. By 1930, the total cost had reached £3,800 and, as an economising measure, the Census and Statistics Office sought to rely on postal returns. After a year the job returned to the local police. Like other bureaucrats during the inter-war years, the Government Statistician was loath to give up the convenience of having police ensure compliance. For their part, country constables both increased their incomes and acquired a more intimate knowledge of their districts.[29]

Also time-consuming for country constables, in the early 1920s at least, was the administration of the Arms Act passed in 1920. In prescribing a much tighter mesh of restraint than hitherto, the Act (and its accompanying regulations) focused on the location of firearms rather than the fitness of a person to possess them.[30] Thus constables in charge of stations became 'authorised' Arms Officers in police sub-districts outside the cities and main provincial centres (where there were Arms Offices with full- or part-time staff). All firearms had to be registered with the 'nearest authorised officer in the district in which the applicant usually resides'. A rural dweller wishing to buy a rifle in town had first to secure a permit from the local constable, and then return to register it with him. Every transfer of a firearm, no matter how temporary, had to be notified. Each purchase of ammunition required a separate permit from the local officer.[31] So too did any purchase of explosives by farmers, miners or quarrymen.[32] Moreover, a person possessing a firearm had to notify the local Arms Officer within six days of any 'change of place of abode'.[33] A certificate of registration applied only to the district in which it was issued – the firearm had to be re-registered in any new district to which its possessor moved.[34] Arms Officers had to keep copies of the registration certificates they issued, send copies and any changes to the Arms Offices at district headquarters (for entry into Arms Registers), and every July forward to district Arms Offices detailed returns on the permits and registrations current in their sub-districts.[35] Given the widespread possession of firearms, a potentially close, albeit cumbersome, system of surveillance was set in place. In reality, accurate knowledge of the location of rifles and shotguns could not be guaranteed. Given the methods of record-keeping, police ability to trace a lost or stolen firearm was in practice limited.

So far as the initial registration of firearms was concerned, widespread compliance was apparently achieved within a year. By 1922 some 200,000 arms had been registered, probably a sizeable majority of them at small-town and country stations.[36] Eight years later the total number of firearms registered, minus the number of cancelled licences, had reached 230,559, including 113,045 rifles, 97,284 shotguns and 19,702 pistols. The annual volume of new and re-registrations ran at a much higher rate: over 19,000 in the 1927/28 year alone.[37] The surveillance of firearms thus continued to entail a 'great deal of work'.[38]

By 1928 senior officers were divided on whether the compulsory registration of shotguns and sporting rifles should be maintained, with those most sensitive to the views of country constables and rural dwellers opposing the existing provisions.[39] From 1921 Senior Sergeant Charles Lopdell had been 'stationed in or near the King Country where most people have Arms, and few – even farmers – have permanent addresses.' Quite apart from the 'lot of trouble to the owners and the Police' in securing the initial registration of firearms, Lopdell reported that, in seeking to comply with the law, some owners faced 'considerable inconvenience and some expense' when they changed their address or disposed of their firearms ('for they are constantly losing their certificates'). Others simply did not bother to meet the requirements. Keeping track of firearms was thus difficult. Many country constables, Lopdell believed, shared his view that the benefit of registering shotguns and rifles was 'not worth the expense and work involved'. Also recognised by police was the 'undue hardship' experienced by farmers and others in the backblocks in travelling considerable distances to the local police station for a permit to buy small quantities of explosives, and then having to wait for hours because the constable was out on enquiries.[40] Moreover, prosecution for non-compliance also entailed 'undue hardship in very many instances' (according to Dunedin's Superintendent J.C. Willis), and 'in the country districts at least, helps to create an antagonism to the Police, from a class of people, who are usually well disposed towards the Force and to whom we look for support.'[41]

Such views coincided with mounting pressure from sportsmen and farmer lobbyists to relax the surveillance. Thomas Wilford, the Minister of Justice, was sympathetic, and in 1929 he introduced a bill to remove the need for permits to purchase, or even to register, shotguns and rifles.[42] This was too much for a majority in the conservative Legislative Council, whose spokesmen continued to fear the use of firearms by revolutionaries. Such views were quickly ridiculed in the press.[43] Nonetheless, the Arms Amendment Act passed in 1930 reflected a compromise. Shotguns used for sporting purposes were now exempt from registration, but not rifles. With over 113,000 rifles then registered, and the 'possibility' of New Zealand being 'affected' by the 'spread of revolutionary organisations' elsewhere, Commissioner Wohlmann considered it 'unsafe to relax the present restrictions'.[44] Permits were no longer required for explosives used in 'lawful work'. Police were given a more definite authority than they had hitherto possessed to seize firearms, ammunition and explosives from individuals seen as a danger to themselves or others.[45] For country constables, the paperwork of registering arms was reduced somewhat, but the perceived need for close surveillance remained.

Together, the administration of the Arms Act and the collection of agricultural and pastoral statistics had 'augmented' the work of constables at country stations 'by quite 20 per cent', reported Inspector Wohlmann from Hamilton in 1922.[46] Besides the increased paperwork arising from these duties, much record-keeping resulted from being prosecutor, clerk and bailiff of the court in small settlements.[47] Here again the nineteenth-century pattern continued, with many local courts. At Darfield in rural Canterbury, for example, a sitting of local JPs would be convened as required (at the police station) to deal with those arrested for the petty offences of disorder or theft. Those summonsed as well as those arrested for more serious offences would be tried before a Stipendiary Magistrate in Christchurch, 30 miles away. In larger or more remote country towns, a magistrate came on circuit for periodical sittings to hear both civil and criminal cases – sometimes in the evenings (as at Roxburgh). While the Waitaki Hydro works were being completed (between 1928 and 1934), the Kurow constable prepared more cases than usual for the three-monthly visits of the Dunedin magistrate, H.W. Bundle.[48] When the workload fell, Mr Bundle resisted Justice Department pressure to end his circuit there and leave minor cases to local JPs: the 'poor persons' amongst the scattered population of the upper Waitaki Valley were 'entitled to apply to and appear before a Magistrates' Court without travelling unreasonable distances.' Moreover, it seemed to the magistrate 'a most invidious and ... improper practice for a defendant, whatever the charge against him, to be dealt with in a Police Station, the Officer in charge of which decides whether the case be a minor one or not and acts as prosecutor before Justices summoned by himself.'[49]

Though the Justice Department construed the court work at Kurow to be light, some MPs for rural electorates echoed their constituents' concern at the amount of office work apparently required of many country constables by the late 1920s. Compiling statistics and filling in forms seemed to make such an officer 'much more of a clerk than a police official' by preventing him from 'taking periodical turns through his area'. 'Uneasiness in country districts' had grown with the belief that some town magistrates had begun to make 'convictions and discharges conditional on the prisoner going into the country.'[50] Surveillance was expected to be the country constable's basic role, and he needed to be seen about his district performing it.

A personal authority

Besides being visible, constables at sole-charge stations had also to become credible by establishing their personal authority in the eyes of the local population.[51] A.C. Strawbridge and R.S. Rusbatch, posted to Te Araroa and Cromwell respectively, both saw themselves as succeeding constables who had been unable 'to control the rough element'.[52] Initiative, firmness, and discretion were all required. Strawbridge made up his mind he 'would enforce the laws'; nor would Rusbatch brook a challenge. At Te Araroa, with 'your nearest police neighbour being thirty miles away' and 'two or three unbridged rivers to cross, a policeman has to be a man of his word', emphasised W.D. Thom; 'his word must be law even if he has to use pick handles to enforce it', as he did during a 'strenuous struggle' there one Saturday night in April 1929.[53] For the more unruly in some small towns and rural districts, a new constable often had to establish his authority with a public fight or show of force. Constable A.J. Maiden's daughter's earliest recollection of Tuakau in about 1924 was of her father fighting a Maori in the main street, with a crowd gathered round; 'finally Dad won, and the Maori got onto his horse ..., Dad calling out to him "get out and stay out" '; 'all the crowd cheered and clapped Dad'. Henceforth local Maori asked for 'the Boss' when they came to the police station.[54]

Being fearless in maintaining one's authority was, of course, a quality expected of all constables. More than city beat men, however, suburban and country constables had to take a longer-term view of the effects of their actions on local lives and opinion. 'Undoubtedly', W.D. Thom believed, a country constable turned a 'Nelson's eye towards a lot' he discovered 'going on' in his district; he 'must perforce be prudent' about much he was told, for he had 'to live with the people of the district'.[55] Effective surveillance required close rapport with a majority of those policed. To establish such a rapport local constables needed to work, as far as possible, within a local consensus of common understandings about disorder and crime. Ideally, according to Charles Reardon, who spent time on country enquiries at Masterton, and later was Senior Sergeant at Ruatoria, a country constable should 'handle the community like a bee farm' and not 'go around putting his stick in the hive and stirring them up.'[56]

Firmness had to be coupled with both initiative in using informal methods to keep order and enforce the law, and responsiveness to requests for assistance and advice. Particularly in country and suburban localities, the law was a resource to be used in the last resort when other methods to resolve disputes and secure compliance had failed. When, for example, 'a dozen young chaps had a bonfire with some old timber' which belonged to a builder in the small Hawke's Bay township of Clive, he complained to Constable George Murray. With twenty years' knowledge of his district, Murray soon 'rounded up the culprits' and sent them to see the complainant, who told them 'it would cost them Twenty Pounds or a charge against them. They paid up, no police court proceedings and the local policeman was happy.'[57] Such methods seem to have been commonplace. Reflecting on his twenty-odd years at Cromwell, R.S. Rusbatch remembered bringing 'only one boy before the Court' – and in that case, the complainant was not a local resident, 'otherwise I would have had it adjusted'.[58] Besides the consent of the complainant, the use of informal methods depended also on the age of culprits, whether they were 'outsiders', and the visibility and seriousness of the offence. At Roxburgh, charges were not pressed against orchard-raiders; but they were against sheep-stealers. For certain troublemakers, summary justice was meted out, as for example when one night Constable Reece Hodge (responding to a complaint) found a man prowling around an isolated house in the King Country, scratching on its windows. The woman living alone there with her children identified the prowler as a neighbour, 'so I did not arrest him, but took him outside and gave him some "Home Rule" on the spot, and let him go at that.'[59] Similarly, breaches of the Arms Act that were prosecuted by city Arms Officers were more likely to occasion warnings from country constables. At Kaitaia, Constable E. Buckley lent his shotgun to a local Maori to go duck shooting, and in return received a brace of duck and a pheasant. Later he enquired if the borrower had a licence and was told: 'License! What the hell do I want a licence for to shoot with the policeman's gun!'[60]

Looking back over his experience during the inter-war years, W.D. Thom thought that local residents both expected and admired a country policeman who could 'control the people in his district without outside help'.[61] Certainly country constables dealt with most local complaints of crime and instances of disorder without other police assistance. Even so, detectives were occasionally called in, especially where alleged offences were deemed serious. At Roxburgh the local constable dealt (apparently not successfully) with reported thefts of rabbit skins. For complaints of sheep-stealing, however, a detective from Dunedin was generally brought in – even though he was dependent on the constable's local knowledge in identifying offenders. Sometimes it was expedient to send for an 'outsider', especially where the questioning of certain locals was concerned. A country constable might strongly suspect an offence, but not wish to pursue the matter himself (as with rumours of incest),[62] nor wish to interrogate someone who had become a firm friend. To local police, 'one of the hardest jobs was to lock up a friend and have to inform his wife and family.'[63] Bringing in outside police could help preserve the personal authority of local constables.

For many country constables, the personal nature of their authority was symbolised by the absence of their uniform – despite repeated injunctions from Commissioners.[64] 'What are you wearing your uniform for today?', a local supposedly asked Constable John O'Donoghue as he strolled up Kaponga's main street to collect his mail; the reply was that the Inspector from New Plymouth was making his annual visit.[65] In fact uniforms were usually donned when a more than personal authority needed to be demonstrated: on public occasions (such as Agricultural and Pastoral Shows), and for policing local dances and making evening patrols of the township – particularly at 6 pm to see that the hotels had closed their public bars, and on Friday and Saturday nights when rural workers were most likely to be in town.

Liquor control

While there were common features of small-town and rural policing, the pattern of liquor control revealed some variation in attitudes and methods. The statutory restrictions on access to liquor provided a potential point of friction between the local constable and a majority of males in his district. While attitudes and behaviour were slowly changing, beer drinking in pubs remained a focal point of masculine culture, and indeed was accentuated by the curbs on sociable drinking of liquor.[66] Depending on the district, the main possibilities of friction lay in policing the six o'clock closing of bars, 'sly-grogging' (the sale of liquor without a licence), and the particular restrictions on supplying liquor to Maori.

As with off-course betting, readiness to observe the law relating to six o'clock closing did not apparently increase with the passage of time. '[L]arge numbers of people in New Zealand have no hesitation in breaking these laws', a majority of the Royal Commission on Licensing reported in 1946. After-hours trading in country districts was seen to be 'widespread', meeting the demands of many rural workers unable to reach a pub before 6 pm on weekdays. Moreover, the relatively small population for the number of pubs in areas like the South Island's West Coast and Central Otago increased the competitive pressures for after-hours trading.[67]

These realities were recognised by local constables, who also subscribed to the dictum: 'if you keep your pubs clean, you'll keep your district clean'.[68] Keeping control of publicans and their patrons was seen as crucial for the orderliness of a locality. Suburban and country constables took different approaches to hotels in their districts. Some were remembered, or (in retirement) saw themselves, as having been 'strict' on pubs by not tolerating after-hours trading.[69] Others were 'easy', with a few going so far as to join the locals for a drink in the evenings.[70] At Hunterville, for example, the degree of supervision oscillated with changes in constable.[71] Most local police enforced at least the semblance of the law. Typically, there would be a 'closing down visit' at 6 pm – at least for hotels near the police station. The few arrests for disorderly behaviour were most likely to be made about this time. Thereafter the pattern varied. Some constables paid routine, albeit merely formal, visits to hotels after hours, usually on Saturdays between

9.30 and 11 pm, at the end of a patrol through the township. After-hours visits were usually infrequent, only following a complaint or when a suspicion of covert trading could not be ignored.[72] Sunday visits were rare. In effect, the prevailing pattern of visits could allow publicans to trade in the evenings with some measure of immunity – providing the curtains were drawn, the clientele did not come in through the front door, and drinking was orderly.

On the West Coast such a pattern of after-hours trading was notorious, with (in places such as Reefton) customary agreements amongst publicans over hours which were in practice enforced by the late-night visits of local police. Even on 'The Coast', however, laxity of supervision was not universal.[73] During the early 1920s, indeed, the Greymouth District recorded significantly more prosecutions of hotel-keepers than any other district – 190 out of a national total of 515 in 1921 – though police zeal declined as the Coasters proved recalcitrant.[74] Though it was the stuff of folklore, the West Coast pattern was not unique. It existed in other isolated, sparsely populated areas such as North Auckland, East Cape, and Central Otago.[75] At Alexandra, for example, visits to the three hotels were never made before 10 pm, and rarely on Saturdays: 'if they'd run them well, we'd give them a bit of a break', recalled a constable.[76] Long-serving staff at one-man stations often 'eased up' on supervision, allowing local practices which their successors could find difficult to reverse. Constable O'Donoghue's last prosecution of a publican for after-hours trading at Kaponga was in 1930 – 22 years before he retired there. Constable Lewis Skinner's successor at Woodville found 'open slather' in after-hours trading and felt the need to continue some latitude.[77] By contrast, Constable W.P. Gilligan's supervision of hotels at Roxburgh in the early 1920s became noticeably more diligent on the eve of his promotion to Sergeant.[78]

Knowledgeable contemporaries saw the local patterns of after-hours trading for what they were: a tacit modus vivendi between local desires and the law. Police were seen as likely to enforce the law if they 'came in contact with after-hour trading'. But generally, they 'did not, by reason of the system of visitation adopted, meet with breaches of the law.'[79] Bribery was not publicly alleged, although uneasiness was occasionally expressed at the substantial presentations from hotel-keepers (and others) that were accepted by some police when they departed on transfer.[80] In fact, for the conscientious country constable, after-hours trading could be difficult to catch, especially at hotels remote from police stations. As in the larger towns, the movements of well-known police could be monitored. Another difficulty was the so-called 'lodger/guest racket'.[81] Occasionally (and particularly when a complaint suggested that the local constable was lax), raids on hotels were mounted by police from outside the locality. On such a raid, the Senior Sergeant from Whangarei found Constable William Butler having a sociable drink in the Hikurangi Hotel.[82] When the Tatapouri Hotel was raided by Gisborne police in 1925, they found the bar open, a gramophone playing, two lodgers and two 'guests'. A sheep-station owner escaped conviction for being unlawfully on licensed premises by claiming he had called to discuss the local football ground with the licensee, and had been invited to have a drink. The licensee was fined £1.[83] He was unlucky; 48 per cent of hotel-keepers prosecuted in 1925 were acquitted. As with bookmaking, the penalties imposed on publicans by magistrates were often 'no more than very moderate licence fees for the continuation of illegal practices.'[84]

'Sly-grog' selling presented different problems of enforcement. As might be expected, it was to be found mainly in areas where access to hotels was not readily available – not merely in 'no-licence' areas.[85] Police activity in detecting sly-grogging was lowest in those districts where pubs were relatively plentiful and accessible to the population, and where after-hours trading was prevalent. Thus sly-grogging was apparently more common in the cities and larger towns, where hotels were concentrated in certain areas and six o'clock closing was more easily enforced, and in 'dry areas' such as Oamaru and Invercargill,[86] than in country districts well-endowed with hotels. It was more likely to be found amongst the scattered population of North Auckland (where Dalmatians sold locally made wine) and in the 'no-licence' areas of Southland (where locals of Scots ancestry made illicit whisky) [87] than on the West Coast or in Central Otago. The unlawful sale of liquor was to be expected also in the rural North Island areas where Maori were concentrated, for only Maori men could be supplied with liquor, and then (in the North Island) only on licensed premises. Where Pakeha could legally import liquor into 'no-licence' areas for their own consumption, Maori were effectively prohibited from legal access to alcohol in 'dry areas' – notably the King Country, which saw the most sustained police activity against sly-groggers.[88] In the early 1920s at least, fines were levied on sly-groggers disproportionately in the Hamilton and Wanganui police districts, which between them had more than half the national total in some years.[89]

In the methods employed, the detection of sly-grogging was similar to that of bookmaking. A local constable might develop well-founded suspicions. Indeed, some King Country sly-groggers were notorious – like Elsie Coffey (or 'Coffee') in Taumarunui, who 'would be on the look out for bushmen arriving in town'. Soon 'broke' (and complaining of having been 'rolled' for their money by the 'chuckers-out'), a few aggrieved workers might seek police help. Others might turn informant 'after some pressure' when they were caught with bottles of dubious liquor in their sugar-sacks. 'Droppers' who brought liquor in by back roads and left bottles and kegs in the bush were sought. Even so, undercover work by new constables from the Training Depot and raids by uniformed police were often needed to collect evidence. (In the case of 'Hokonui', the illicitly distilled Southland whisky, one local constable reckoned he could identify its drinkers by the 'oily appearance' of their skin.) Since the police involved received a proportion of the fines as a reward, there was a stimulus to zeal. However undercover work was potentially dangerous – especially in the King Country, where (it was rumoured) 'a misplaced word could spell almost death to a young constable placed in some outback sawmill and working as a slabby.' Moreover, until they were known, police in the King Country were 'always regarded with suspicion ...; people used to avoid speaking with you, as others thought they might be giving you some information about sly grog'. Constable A.T. Breed (at Raurimu between 1933 and 1939) was remembered by locals mainly for his dealings with sly-groggers. Recognising that he could not suppress the illicit trade, Breed attempted to control it by laying down 'rules'. When this failed, he warned the inhabitants that there would be raids – police arrived from Taumarunui and Wanganui, and 'large scale confiscations and arrests followed'. Henceforth (it was said) the locals followed the 'police rules'. Though police activity against sly-groggers intensified in the late 1930s, sly-grog selling continued to be widespread in the King Country, where there were 'dens by the dozens'.[90]

Policing Maori communities

Enforcement of the liquor laws specifically affecting Maori was no more effective, within the King Country or beyond it. By the first decade of the century, the paternalistic intent of legislation was to confine Maori consumption of liquor to males on licensed premises. Supplying liquor to Maori women was prohibited, as was the introduction of liquor into a Maori 'kainga, village or pa'.[91] Such constraints were widely flouted. Pakeha could be found who would, out of mateship or for a commission, buy liquor on behalf of Maori. Shearing gangs pressed farmers to procure it. In more isolated areas (notably in eastern Bay of Plenty) a few storekeepers or travelling salemen (allegedly 'Hindus') supplied liquor. As private cars and taxi-drivers superseded pack horses, supplies became even more accessible – as the quantities of 'empties' visible in some Maori settlements from the late 1930s showed. By then, both Maori men and women in various parts of the North Island sometimes drank large quantities of liquor at 'parties'. In kainga, liquor was often available at weddings, tangihanga, feasts, and other large gatherings. It was sometimes, according to one East Coast constable, 'well concealed and kept under control', with 'tea' being offered either hot or 'cold'.[92] The continuing inaccessibility of some Maori settlements meant that those along the upper reaches of the Wanganui River, for example, did not get much supervision from the constable at Raetihi.[93]

Penalising only the supply of liquor to Maori, the law was a weak constraint. Between 1911 and 1945, senior police officers pressed in vain to have it made an offence for Maori to procure liquor or have it in their possession off licensed premises.[94] They also wanted powers to search Maori without a warrant and seize any liquor found – a practice employed circumspectly by some local constables where they were not empowered to do so within a kainga on the authority of a local Maori Council.[95] Police also resorted to charging Maori found in possession of liquor with aiding and abetting its supply. Though this charge could be difficult to sustain, the rate of convictions of Maori for illegally supplying liquor to 'Natives' was higher than that of Pakeha on the same charge in the Hamilton, Gisborne and Whangarei police districts between 1935 and 1944. Few Maori were convicted of sly-grogging.[96] Essentially, to prevent drink-related disorder amongst Maori, police at country and small-town stations outside no-licence areas relied on publicans to be strict, and needed the cooperation of local kaumatua.

Shortly after his arrival at Te Kuiti in March 1921 as Sergeant in charge, C.W. Lopdell announced in the local court his opposition to Maori being charged with aiding and abetting the illegal supply of liquor, since the 'King Country law' had been intended to protect Maori rather than make them victims of the law. Instead, the 'principal offenders would be caught'. According to Lopdell's account, local Maori conveyed his views to an 'old chief, Mr. Hetet', who sent for the Sergeant to tell him he was the first policeman who had shown any sympathy for Maori and offered complete cooperation not just with 'liquor matters but also ... with our [the Police's] other difficulties'. To Lopdell it seemed such cooperation was soon forthcoming, allowing the entrapment of some of those supplying liquor to Maori.[97]

How widespread such cooperation was, and whether indeed local Maori shared Lopdell's perspective of the events he described, is impossible to say. Apparently kaumatua in the King Country remained generally opposed to the sale of liquor, but they could not override the wider opinion of their communities and on occasions permitted alcohol at gatherings such as tangi and weddings.[98] Within the King Country and beyond, much depended on the ability of local kaumatua and komiti marae (given authority under the Maori Councils Act 1900 and its amendments) to control drunkenness and the introduction of liquor.[99] To Pakeha officials, 'control' and 'discipline' were apparent in some kainga and on some marae, but less so on others.[100] Apparently also, there remained widespread ambivalence amongst Maori towards Pakeha law and police. Indeed the racially discriminatory nature of the liquor laws until 1948 added a further point of friction in police dealings with Maori. Lopdell himself noted that 'the young fellows, the sons of these old men, who could see their contemporaries, footballers and others drinking their bottles in the street and they were prohibited by law from participating in any way, and after they got a drink or two on the quiet they would get defiant and would go down the street with a bottle in their hand to let the public see they did have it'.[101]

In the broader pattern of policing of Maori in their rural settlements, the inter-war years were part of a longer period of transition between the 1880s and the 1950s during which Pakeha legal sanctions came to take priority over those of kin.[102] For most North Island tribal communities in the late nineteenth century, 'the law' was generally 'an invited guest whose attributes supplemented, but did not replace, those of its host.'[103] The authority of kaumatua and of village runanga or committees was usually accepted, but Pakeha police and courts were a resource for Maori victims and offenders to use if it was to their advantage to do so. From the turn of the century, the 'guest' came to be invited more often, and indeed increasingly arrived uninvited to enforce more strictly a growing range of breaches of 'the law'. The annual number of charges against Maori rose steeply from 529 in 1910 to 2,226 in 1919, before falling in 1921 to 1,984, at which level it broadly remained before again rising steeply in the late 1930s (figure 8.1). As a rate per thousand of the Maori population, the number of charges rose from 11 in 1910 to 40 in 1919, rising briefly above the non-Maori rate and then doing so permanently from the late 1930s (figure 8.2). As with the Pakeha rates, the number of charges against Maori for violence and drunkenness per head of population fell during the 1920s and early 1930s before rising from 1936 (figures 8.3, 8.4). However, the number of theft charges laid against Maori increased markedly during the 1920s, rising from a fifth to two-fifths of all charges, with the rate per thousand Maori more than doubling between the wars (figure 8.5). During the First World War the per capita rate of charges against Maori for offences against people, property, and public order became higher than the corresponding Pakeha rates; and they

Figure 8.1: Charges Against Maori in Magistrates' Courts 1880–1940

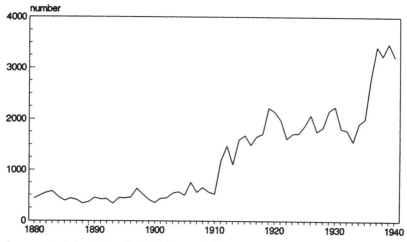

Sources: *Statistics of New Zealand*, 'Law and Crime', 1880–1920; *Justice Statistics*, 1921–1940, table, 'Offences by Maori'.

Figure 8.2: Charges Against Non-Maori and Maori in Magistrates' Courts 1880–1940

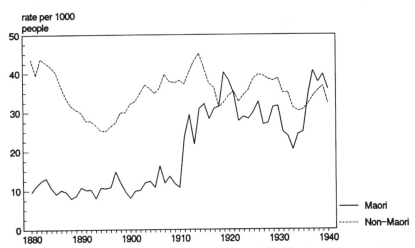

Sources: *Statistics of New Zealand*, 'Law and Crime', 1880–1920; *Justice Statistics*, 1921–1940, tables, 'Total Charges' (excluding Maori), 'Offences by Maori'.

Figure 8.3: Charges of Assault Against Non-Maori and Maori in Magistrates' Courts 1880–1940

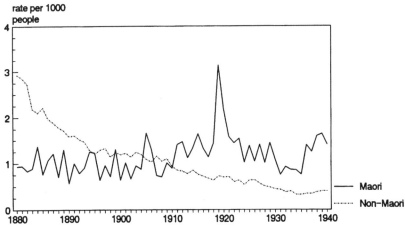

Sources: *Statistics of New Zealand*, 'Law and Crime', 1880–1920; *Justice Statistics*, 1921–1940, tables, 'Total Charges' (excluding Maori), 'Offences by Maori'.

remained so, with the gap increasing.[104]

Such a pattern was reflected at the grass roots of policing. At Te Araroa, where the local population was predominantly Maori, the constable recorded more charges than were laid at most sole-charge

Figure 8.4: Charges for Drunkenness 1880–1940

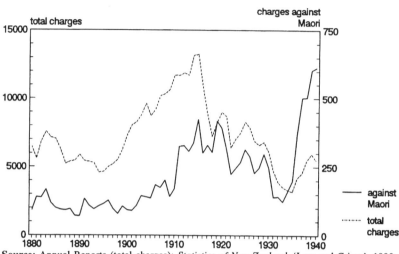

Source: Annual Reports (total charges); *Statistics of New Zealand*, 'Law and Crime', 1880–1920; *Justice Statistics*, 1921–1940, 'Offences by Maori'.

Figure 8.5: Charges of Theft Against Non-Maori and Maori in Magistrate's Courts 1880–1940

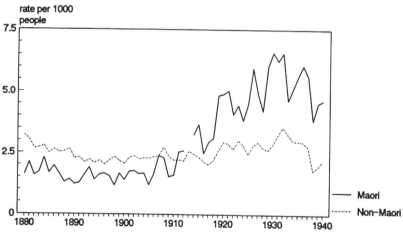

Sources: *Statistics of New Zealand*, 'Law and Crime', 1880–1920; *Justice Statistics*, 1921–1940, tables, 'Total Charges' (excluding Maori), 'Offences by Maori'.

The 1913 data for Maori have been excluded because of an apparent error in the table.

stations between the wars, especially during the 1930s.[105] About 84 per cent of the 335 individuals charged between 1919 and 1939 were Maori. Over a third were arrested for acquisitive crimes, with the highest number of arrests coming between 1933 and 1936. From 1936 drunkenness and other offences 'against good order' became the predominant charges.

Around the country stations in Northland a similar experience could be found. From time to time, Supreme Court judges commented on the lawlessness they perceived to prevail amongst Maori youths in the north, especially in the Hokianga and Kaikohe districts.[106] Statistics for 1935, compiled to test these strictures, provide a glimpse of possible variations in both the social cohesion of Maori settlements and the manner in which they were policed. Though just over a fifth of New Zealand's Maori population then lived in the Whangarei Police District, they accounted for a third of all charges laid against Maori in 1935. Within the District, variations can be observed in the numbers and types of charges faced by Maori. In the Far North, covered by the Magistrates' Courts at Houhora and Mangonui, few charges were laid and then virtually only for regulatory offences such as breaches of the Licensing Act, failing to register a dog, and having no heavy traffic licence. In the Whangaroa/Bay of Islands area there were more charges, including some for assault, theft, disorder, and 'mischief'; but as in the Far North, regulatory offences comprised the largest proportion. Considerably more charges than elsewhere in Northland were prosecuted in the courts at Rawene (on the Hokianga Harbour) and Kaikohe. Here theft comprised by far the largest category of prosecutions, followed by offences against 'good order'. At Rawene, charges of 'unlawful carnal knowledge' and 'mischief' (ten of each) were more common than at any other Northland court. (Both in the numbers and types of charges recorded, the experience of the constable at Te Araroa paralleled that of his counterparts at Rawene in 1935.) At the three largest towns (Whangarei, Dargaville, and Kaitaia) there were fewer charges than at Rawene and Kaikohe; here offences against order were the largest category, followed by theft. In these main centres, relatively few Maori were prosecuted for breaches of regulatory legislation.[107]

How far these local patterns were sustained through the inter-war years cannot be readily gauged. Annual fluctuations in charges could be expected. Nonetheless the statistics seem to accord with (and probably served to reinforce) the perception of Pakeha observers that delinquency amongst Maori youth appeared to be greater in Northland (and amongst Nga Puhi in particular) than elsewhere.[108] At Bluff, and in Taranaki and central Hawke's Bay, by contrast, the smaller Maori communities were seen by local police to be 'well behaved', with offenders coming from other places, usually as seasonal workers.[109] In part the local and regional patterns reflected the rural concentration of a rapidly growing Maori population, and its youthfulness (providing a population with a higher risk of delinquency than the Pakeha), especially in Northland.[110] In part also, the local patterns suggest different degrees of cohesion in Maori communities. Inspector P.J. O'Hara believed that a doubling in the number of charges of mischief in the Whangarei Police District in 1934 was 'largely caused by bands of Maori youths and children wandering at night under no parental or tribal control.'[111]

The extent to which informal controls were maintained within Maori communities during the inter-war years can only be guessed at, and their importance may be too readily discounted. There was a high degree of participation by Maori in tribal hui and other gatherings. In Waiapu county (on the East Coast), for example, 80 per cent of the families were observed in 1933 to be in 'constant' contact with relatives and friends.[112] At Ahipara, in the Far North, misdemeanours of community members were discussed at gatherings on local marae, offenders against community mores were censured by elders, and penalties were imposed if necessary. Such meetings seem to have become rare by the 1940s. Even so, in the mid-1950s the Police still rarely intervened at Ahipara.[113] Similarly, at both Bluff and Raetihi in 1950, police saw elders as continuing to exercise an influence over the behaviour of local Maori youth.[114]

Supplementing the authority of elders, a tradition of Maori policing had developed in the nineteenth century and persisted into the 1920s and 1930s in some communities. In 1921, for example, a local komiti marae near Otorohanga borrowed some handcuffs from Te Kuiti's Sergeant Lopdell, 'appointed their own Police and did good work in controlling and watching their own people.'[115] How long or widely such authority was exercised is unknown. Marae police with distinctive insignia were appointed by elders at large tribal gatherings in Northland, such as the Waitangi celebrations in 1934 and the Catholic centenary celebrations at Totara Point in 1938. On these occasions, contingents of Pakeha police were symbolically present as the ultimate authority, but the actual policing was left to Maori.[116] Similarly, in the tradition of Ringatu communities with their pirihimana (policemen), the Ratana Church appointed its own katipa to carry out surveillance over its members and keep order at its meetings.[117] In 1933, however, when a katipa, Tuhi Karena, sought to act as 'peacemaker' by handcuffing a women in a domestic dispute amongst members of the Church in Tokomaru Bay, he was prosecuted for assault.[118] For Maori 'police', the exercise of coercive authority was tacitly permitted only on the marae; it lacked the sanction of 'the law'.[119] Partly because of their lack of real power, most district Maori Councils and many komiti marae apparently became less willing or able to exercise policing functions from the 1920s.[120]

Nonetheless a local initiative eventually produced an enduring institution of Maori policing, albeit one still circumscribed in authority. Concern at excessive drinking in Rotorua led to a conference between the mayor, publicans, and local Maori in December 1937. The Arawa Trust Board agreed to appoint 'wardens' to help the Police and publicans maintain order in hotels. The wardens' authority amongst Maori rested upon their mana, their powers of persuasion, and their support from the Police. This system of Maori policing beyond marae was extended to other areas after the Maori Social and Economic Advancement Act of 1945 gave it authority.[121] The warden at Raetihi in the late 1940s, Samuel Arahanga, was seen by the local constable to have considerable mana and influence through his birth, education and age. But his work as warden could only be part-time because it was unpaid. In some other districts, wardens were perceived by local police to lack mana and to be reluctant or unable to exercise authority. Some who exercised their influence effectively within their villages were averse 'to operating outside those areas.'[122] Indeed wardens continued to lack the independent coercive authority which some saw as real power.[123] Furthermore, the traditional bases of personal and community authority had eroded to a greater or lesser degree in Maori communities by the 1940s.

From the 1920s at least, a variety of influences had the potential to weaken the authority of kaumatua and wider opinion within Maori communities: the youthfulness of the burgeoning population, and its increasing landlessness; the growing dispersal from close-knit villages and pa in search of work or onto individual holdings; the fragmentation of community leadership, with the authority of elders becoming in effect limited to family affairs; unemployment or irregular employment which led to idleness, boredom and 'mischief' amongst youth; and the pressures of poverty (especially in the early 1930s), which might strengthen customary interdependence but could also lead to the opportunistic theft or 'conversion' of coveted items such as sheep, horses, riding gear, watches, shoes and clothes. Ultimately also, the presence of Pakeha law weakened attachment to tribal sanctions.[124]

At Te Araroa during the 1920s, violence was rarely reported to the local constable, and most of the charges against Maori for theft involved Pakeha victims. By the mid-1930s, the higher number of charges against Maori (mainly for theft, but also for assault) related mostly to Maori victims. Maori charged at Te Araroa seem to have come mainly from a few families who were perhaps less susceptible to the opinion of the wider community.[125] During the 1920s the effects of 'individualised farming' on community relations in the Gisborne Police District could possibly be observed in complaints received by the Port Awanui constable from Maori about other Maori damaging fences, stealing stock, and injuring animals.[126] The Pakeha 'guest' was being invited more often when the customary means of resolving disputes were found wanting. Indeed, police at Dargaville and Kaikohe in 1950 believed that local Maori had 'little faith in the capacity' of those who acted on the tribal committees, preferring 'to have their differences dealt with by Europeans.'[127]

Though informal community controls might be weakening, kin were still likely during the inter-war years to protect offenders, conceal offences from Pakeha authority, and support a family member charged by the police.[128] When a doctor was called to a sick child in a Northland Maori village, he asked in vain for the father (who had telephoned him) until he revealed he was indeed 'The Doctor': 'I thought you were a policeman', was the explanation. 'Protect our Maori people from the policeman', concluded Bishop F.A. Bennett, who retailed the story in 1932.[129]

Variations in the numbers and types of charges laid against Maori suggest subtle differences in the manner in which local communities were policed. On country enquiries in the Kaitaia district from 1929, Constable E. Buckley worked closely with the local komiti marae, leaving them to deal with domestic disputes and complaints of 'young men playing up'.[130] At Te Whaiti in the 1930s, District Constable Hugh Macpherson sought to solve some complaints of theft without pressing charges. In one instance he questioned three Maori at the local pa regarding a stolen coat; next day the coat was found on the road. In another case he visited the pa and outlying Maori settlements and 'told certain Maoris that I expected the stolen articles returned, which was done.'[131] The relatively high number of charges of theft and mischief laid at Rawene and Te Araroa in 1935 indicate that the constables there took a tougher line. That indeed was the intention of Constable Strawbridge at Te Araroa between 1933 and 1938, when the highest number of charges for theft and disorderly conduct during the inter-war years were recorded. Strawbridge had youthful thieves convicted, and persuaded the local Child Welfare Officer to recommend the birch, which he administered. Seven Maori boys (aged seven to fifteen) he caught breaking telegraph insulators in November 1935 were brought before JPs at Ruatoria, where they were ordered to make restitution and placed in the care of the Child Welfare Officer for twelve months.[132] In dealing with youthful theft and mischief amongst Maori, Strawbridge's approach seems to have become more typical than Buckley's. By 1943/ 44, the rate of charges for theft and mischief was almost three times higher for Maori boys aged eight to sixteen than it was for Pakeha boys – causing a contemporary researcher to comment that 'there is likely to be [an] immediate readiness to bring a Maori child before the court on an occasion when a European boy might well get by with a reprimand.'[133]

Despite the firmness of Strawbridge's manner of policing, he could not have achieved results, especially in detecting theft, if he had not received cooperation. It appeared to him that 'the better class of Maori in this district liked the way I was carrying out my duties.' He was told that some saw him as 'a real Tohunga. If you lose anything and tell him, he will find it for you'.[134] Support from influential members of Maori rural communities remained crucial for effective policing well beyond the inter-war years.[135] To achieve this, empathy and fairness needed to be demonstrated, as well as a readiness to consult the elders. A forthright manner could be respected if it was accompanied by an ability to listen.

54. The investiture of Constables F.A.H. Baker and W.S. Hammond with the King's Police Medal for Gallantry at Government House, Wellington on 6 May 1932, a year after they had shown 'conspicuous bravery' in attempting to rescue some of the crew of the steamer *Progress*: from left to right, Inspector C.W. Lopdell, Constable Baker, Lady Bledisloe, Lord Bledisloe, Constable Hammond, Commissioner W.G. Wohlmann and Superintendent A.T. Emerson. *NZ Police Museum*

55. The Auckland Detective Branch outside the Central station at the time of Sub-Inspector Thomas Gibson's promotion and transfer to be Inspector in charge of Invercargill District in January 1933. Gibson recalled his three years supervising the Auckland Detective Office as 'the hardest time I ever had'. From left to right (back row), Acting Detectives E.W. Mahood, S.C. Whitehead, F.J. Brady, M.L. Vial, Detective Sergeant T. Kelly, Detectives C.P. Belton, K.W. Mills, Acting Detective R.J. Hamilton, Detective J. Hunt, Acting Detective W.H. Slater; (middle row) Acting Detectives J. Hayes, A. Moore, Detectives G.A. McWhirter, T. Sneddon, C.L. Packman, P.J. Nalder, T.W. Allsopp, Acting Detectives H.A. Wilson, C.H. Davis, Detective N. Kempt; (front row) Detectives E.A. Stevenson, H.C. Murch, Detective Sergeants R.J. Issell, A.G. McHugh, Inspector T. Gibson, Detective Sergeants P. Doyle, J. Martin, M. O'Sullivan, Acting Detective J. Bowman. *NZ Police Museum*

56. Detective Sergeant James Cummings' reputation was established during 1920 by the separate convictions in Auckland of Dennis Gunn and Samuel John Thorne for murder. Justice F.R. Chapman singled him out for his 'diligence and intelligence' in leading the investigations and preparing the prosecutions, as well as his 'conspicuous' fairness towards the accused. *NZ Police Museum*

57. The fingerprint office in the Criminal Registration Branch, Police Headquarters, Wellington. Seated with his head down at the back is Edmund Dinnie, who headed the Branch from 1904 until his retirement in 1947, when fingerprints on more than 70,000 people were held. *B.G. and D. Thomson*

~Finger Print inside Lid of Cash Box Nº 1.~   ~Photo from Finger Print Form.~

58. A comparison of the fingerprint inside the lid of the Ponsonby post office's cash box no. 1 with Dennis Gunn's left ring fingerprint. Gunn was the first New Zealander to be convicted and hanged mainly on the basis of fingerprint evidence. *NZ Police*

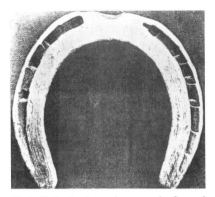

59. A distinctive horseshoe worn by Samuel Thorne's employer's horse Mickey was part of the chain of circumstantial evidence presented in the successful prosecution of Thorne for murder in 1920. Detective A.G. McHugh, a former blacksmith, examined 1,303 horses and found no other matching shoe. *NZ Police Museum*

60. Ballistics expert G.G. (Greg) Kelly assisted detectives with homicide enquiries before he was appointed police firearms advisory officer (with the rank of Senior Sergeant) and set up an Arms Bureau in Headquarters on 1 June 1935. From 1937 a comparison microscope and micro-photographic equipment 'revolutionised' his work. *NZ Police*

61. The police encampment around the Lakey homestead at Ruawaro in November 1933. Unprecedented police resources were mobilised to investigate the death of Christobel and disappearance of Samuel Lakey, culminating in the successful prosecution of W.A. Bayly for their murder. *ATL, C23994¹/₂*

62. Chief Detective J.B. Young in his Dunedin office, February 1936. With no formal training for detectives, he collected newspaper clippings, wrote notes of cases, and initiated regular lectures to his staff. Although methodical and meticulous, he was not always successful in the homicide investigations that he led. *Young family*

63. A male two-up school with a gambler tossing pennies into the air, watched by others in a characteristic circle. Deemed illegal, two-up was played covertly – especially at workplaces, camps and secluded areas around the towns that were free from routine police surveillance. *Historical Branch collection*

64. 'Forty-fives' being played by coal miners at Ngakawau in 1944. This recreational gambling game was widely played on the West Coast of the South Island during the inter-war years, at work, home and the pub. *War Effort Collection, ATL, F1246¹/₄*

65. Legal gambling: an 'Art Union' or lottery to raise money for the Wellington Aero Club in 1930. Some lotteries to raise money for worthy causes were permitted; all others were illegal. *Evening Post Collection, ATL, G32432¹/₄*

66. Bookmakers were banned: the presence of a constable at the Lower Hutt racecourse in 1927 deters illegal betting. *Evening Post Collection, ATL, G544¹/₂–EP*

67. 'You can't touch me. I'm touching wood'. From the early 1920s, 'Ike McToteodds', the bookmaker, flourished away from the racecourses as juries refused to convict him. *Free Lance, Aug 1922*

68. A bookie's odds: away from police surveillance, Alex Brennan, a Southland bookmaker, offers 'doubles' (betting on two horses), a popular form of betting which the totalisator which was not permitted to offer. *Southland Museum*

69. A police raid on a Haining Street, Wellington, 'pakapoo den' in 1934. Gambling entrepreneurs provided a range of illegal 'games of hazard' in the main cities during the 1930s. *Free Lance, 14 Mar 1934, ATL, C19686*

70. Raurimu on the North Island main trunk railway line, about 1920. Sly-grogging was rife as the settlement was within the King Country 'proclaimed' (no-licence) area. Bushmen from the remnants of the 'development' frontier provided the local constable with more physically demanding work than his counterparts experienced in well-established farming areas or 'quiet' suburbs. *J.F. Doherty Collection, ATL, F35451¹/₂*

71. Railway construction camp at Bartletts, Gisborne Police District, about 1936. Typically, an experienced unmarried city constable, Willis Brown, was sent to open a police station there on 10 November 1936, after the construction of the railway between Gisborne and Wairoa began. Constable Brown lived in one of the workers' huts, which was also his office. *Gisborne Museum*

72. Together, the Tolaga Bay courthouse and adjoining police station symbolised the presence of the state in the local community. However, the authority of the highly regarded Constable George Neale at Tolaga Bay between 1927 and 1932 was personal. Only 20 people faced charges in this court during 1930. *Gisborne Museum*

73. Te Araroa in October 1943 differed little from ten years earlier when Constable A.C. Strawbridge was transferred there, determined to 'enforce the laws'. About three-quarters of its hinterland's population were Maori. Rural isolation, the use of horses and occasional disorder gave the settlement a reputation for being a 'wild west' town. Strawbridge recorded more charges in an average year than most other sole-charge constables. *War Effort Collection, ATL, F661¹/₄*

74. By contrast with country constables in well-roaded areas, Constable Martin Campbell, at Port Awanui from December 1921 until October 1926, patrolled his patch by horse. His usual daily round began and ended in the stables or the 'Office'. *John Robinson*

75. The police station at Port Awanui, on the East Coast, was established in 1878, before roads were formed. Little of the settlement remained when Constable Martin Campbell was transferred there in December 1921. Almost daily, Campbell forded the nearby Waiapu River to collect his mail and monitor the hotel, dances, hui and the pictures in the main village of his sub-district, Tikitiki, to which the police station was transferred in 1935. *Gisborne Museum*

76. Constable Martin Campbell with his wife and family at Port Awanui about 1925. Wives – the 'silent unpaid servants' of the Police Department – provided companionship, assistance with police work, and played a significant part in establishing the local standing of the police. They shared with their husbands the pressures of life at sole-charge stations. *John Robinson*

77. Typically, the sole-charge Balmoral police station in suburban Auckland had its office in the residence. In effect, suburban and country constables were never off duty; nor were their wives, who answered the telephone and the door when husbands were out or asleep. *NZ Police*

78. Policing on the margins of an expanding city: not always in uniform, Constable George Rushton became a familiar sight on horseback around Henderson, west of Auckland, from 1927. Here outside the Henderson police station in 1930, Rushton was soon to replace his horse Ben with a 1931 Model A Tourer. *Jack Luckens*

79. Small-town policing: the culmination of the orderly Jubilee procession in Hawera in 1932. Two of the town's four constables symbolise order and add weight to the mayor's status in the carnival. They were probably well known because long service at Hawera was usual, typical of policing in small peaceful communities where there was little significant crime. *J.R. Wall Collection, ATL, G17631$^{1}/_{2}$*

Typically, Constable M. Campbell, stationed at Port Awanui during the 1920s, attended all the (often weekly) tangihanga in his district – paying his respects as well as noting who was there. Similarly, his presence at the weekly rugby matches between local teams was not merely a matter of policing, but also an identification with a local passion. That Maori brought disputes amongst themselves and with Pakeha to him showed they had an expectation that he would deal with them fairly and reasonably. Nor did he seem to meet much resistance in making arrests. He recorded no prisoners seeking to escape as he escorted them on horseback through the rugged and isolated countryside. Like other country constables, he had a relaxed attitude as gaoler to Maori he held in his small lock-up for a month or more for non-payment of civil debts. Prisoners might collect and cut wood, repair fences, and do other odd jobs about the station.[136] At Ruatoria, the 'fabled' Constable George Neale let his prisoners go to the football on Saturdays – and one who went on to the pub rather than returning to the lock-up was (it is said) given a thrashing by the locals, who feared they might lose this privilege when it was their turn.[137]

Pakeha constables were inevitably outsiders in Maori settlements; but some reduced the social distance by force of personality, length of service in an area, and acquiring some ability to speak and understand te reo Maori. Roy Griffith found in making enquiries from Maori at Kaitaia and Ruatoria that 'they would invariably discuss in Maori any questions asked them before giving a reply'. With his control of the situation diminished, the Pakeha policeman felt that the presence of a Maori constable would have been valuable.[138]

By the inter-war years, however, Police administrators had come to see Maori ('Native') constables as unnecessary in most rural areas. In Northland their services were dispensed with at Kaitaia in 1920, Rawene in 1921, Mangonui in 1926, and Whangaroa in 1933. In the Bay of Plenty/East Coast area they were employed until 1928 at Matata and 1945 at Te Kaha. At Te Whaiti, the District Constables had strong Maori connections until 1949.[139]

With their links to local Maori communities and command of te reo, Maori constables were 'insiders' – to a degree. They were also agents of the Pakeha law. 'Dave' (Rawiri Puhirake) Hira at Te Kaha had no compunction, for example, in charging four Maori in August 1934 with the Pakeha offence of vagrancy: having insufficient visible lawful means of support, and consorting with reputed thieves.[140] 'Heke' (Louis) Bidois was so severely assaulted by two Maori youths when he sought to arrest them outside a dance hall at Te Whaiti in 1949 that he had to go on permanent sick leave.[141] To the extent that the Native and District Constables were zealous, they were viewed with the same ambivalence as Pakeha police.

Such ambivalence was apparent when Constable Strawbridge was transferred to Takaka in 1938, after five years at Te Araroa. One of the local elders came to tell him that 'the Maoris would have liked to have organised a farewell to me, but at that time it was not possible because they were then collecting funds for a meeting house.'[142] Farewells, or the lack of them, on the departure of individual Pakeha policemen were a measure of the esteem they were held in by local Maori. Constable Edward Buckley was presented with a korowai by a local elder when he retired at Waiuku in 1959, after 30 years spent in country districts with Maori communities.[143] Similarly, when George Neale left Tolaga Bay in 1932, after five years there and some fourteen years at sole-charge stations on the East Coast, he was presented with a finely carved wakahuia and a korowai was placed around his shoulders.[144] On his departure in 1935, after eight years at Ruatoria, Jack Ryan was farewelled by both Maori and Pakeha at the Mangahanea meeting house. The speeches (in Maori and interpreted) were interspersed with a haka and waiata, and followed by 'handsome presentations'. Pehikura Awatere, the first speaker, established a theme echoed by others: deep regret at Constable Ryan's departure, for 'no one had been better able than he to keep the young people in order'. If the Maori at Ruatoria 'had control of things they would ask that Constable Ryan should be allowed to remain.' Arnold Reedy summed up by emphasising the 'high esteem in which Mr and Mrs Ryan were held throughout the district' and commenting that 'the methods adopted by the Constable were appreciated by all, and from them the younger generation derived much benefit.'[145] In backing up the waning authority of the elders, the 'tough' Jack Ryan was appreciated.

Rhythms of work

In its rhythms, the work of constables policing Maori communities was little different from that of most country constables. Diaries of duty, completed according to convention, reveal a common pattern of a working day that usually covered at least a thirteen-hour period, beginning (as in the case of Constable Campbell at Port Awanui in 1922) in the stables or 'Office' at 8 am and ending there at 9 pm if there were no late patrols or surveillance at dances, the pictures, or other public gatherings. In the same year, Wellsford's constable routinely began his day in the stables between 6 and 7 am, and ended it with 'office duty' between 8 and 10 pm. His counterpart at neighbouring Warkworth officially began at 9 am and often ended at 6 pm, with longer hours on Friday and Saturday nights. At Roxburgh, Constable Gilligan's routine commonly started in the stables at 7 am and ended between 10 and 11 pm after his patrol of the township. Sunday usually saw fewer hours entered in the diary, but it was another working day at sole-charge stations.

These hours were notional. Constables at sole-charge stations were never off duty, and could be called out at any time. On the other hand, 'office' might merely mean being on call while the garden was being dug, firewood cut, or the local courthouse cleaned. Official permission to keep poultry and animals for domestic use was sometimes interpreted liberally. Even so, a significant proportion of time was recorded as being spent in the office: perhaps half or more of the notional hours of country constables; less for suburban constables with more patrolling, increasing numbers of motor accidents to attend, petty thefts and mischief to pursue, and summonses to serve. The time spent in the office reflected the growing amount of paperwork. Each morning, collecting and sorting the mail was usually the first priority: it could shape the rhythm of work for the rest of the day and those following. As enquiries, civil processes, summonses, warrants for commitment and the like were sorted, constables looked to see if they 'could work this job in with that' when they went out on enquiries and patrol.[146]

Other common influences on suburban and small-town work rhythms were meeting passenger trains; the surveillance of hotels, sports meetings, picture theatres and dances; and preparations for local court sittings. For constables in commuter suburbs, a growing amount of enquiry work had to be done in the evening, and there could be 'hectic holiday weekends' at seaside stations such as Sumner (Christchurch) and Portobello (Dunedin). Often evenings were spent in the office laboriously transcribing district notices, circulars and memoranda, at least until cyclostyled copies became available for pasting into the station record books from the late 1920s.

Though the hours were long, the pace of work was leisurely by modern urban standards. This was inevitable while foot patrols and bicycles were the means of suburban policing; and horses remained the main mode of transport for many country constables (and those on the margins of cities) during the 1920s and early 1930s – especially in 'roadless' North Auckland and the East Coast of the North Island. In July 1922 it took Constable Campbell three days (by horse and mail coach) to return the 90 miles to his Port Awanui station from duty at the Gisborne races; by January 1925, the same journey took only a day on the Gisborne Motor Service bus. From Port Awanui during the 1920s, patrols and enquiries were carried out on horseback to settlements across the Waiapu River, which was sometimes too high to cross. To go on 'bailiff duties' to a back-country sheep station or bush camp would take all day.

From the late 1920s, as roads improved and departmental allowances became available, country constables acquired their own cars or motorcycles (marking them off from their suburban counterparts, who were given no such reimbursement). For most, the use of a private car was a matter of convenience rather than profit. This was epitomised by Constable C.L. Spencer who, on his arrival at the Chatham Islands station in 1936, eschewed the departmental horses used by his predecessors and had his own car shipped from Wellington, even though he was limited to the twenty miles of dry-weather roads around the main settlement of Waitangi.[147] To envious outsiders, the use of a private car could suggest that a profit was being made from departmental 'perks'. However the ending in 1927 of the generous allowance for delivering civil summonses saw a significant drop in country constables' incomes.[148] During the 1930s there was mounting dissatisfaction with the meagre annual car allowance – though this could be supplemented considerably by mileage allowances for transporting other police on enquiries and for bailiff's duties. Thus in 1939 Constable Herbert Barrett, at the 'quiet' station of Mangonui, received payments for the use of his car totalling £97 (of which the annual car allowance was £45 12s 6d) out of a gross annual income of £471.[149] Nonetheless at Culverden in north Canterbury, for example, Constable David Sterritt did not claim the car allowance, preferring to draw a travelling allowance for staying in lodgings and to go by horse and gig to Hanmer Springs (a two-day return trip) and the Lewis Pass relief workers' camps (three days).[150] At Te Araroa, Tikitiki, and Matawai on the East Coast, constables continued until the late 1930s to use horses as well as cars in policing isolated Maori settlements. By this time mounted patrols had disappeared from the suburbs, the local constables (as at Ellerslie, for example) finding them an anachronism: too slow for the work to be done, a nuisance to tether in shopping areas, and an unwelcome symbol of a 'Cinderella' department.[151] On his retirement in 1947 after nearly 30 years at country stations on the East Coast, Constable W.H. Bradley regretted the passing of horses: 'a constable cannot keep in contact with the people of his district as well in a car as he could on horseback'.[152]

Knowledge of locals also contributed to the leisurely pace of country policing. There was a lack of urgency in responding to some cases that might have brought a more immediate response in the cities. When a man with a 'deep scalp wound' complained to the Warkworth constable on a Saturday evening in 1922 that he had been assaulted by his brothers, his injuries were attended to; but enquiries were left until Monday morning.[153] Similarly, when the Port Awanui constable received a telephone message in 1926 that a Maori had been assaulted by another (in the context of a long-standing feud), he did not set out to make inquiries until the next day; nor did he make an arrest, but eventually (seven weeks later) served summonses.[154] Like their city counterparts, however, country constables usually responded as quickly as they were able to reports of 'trouble' that, through quarrelling, insanity, or accident, could mean serious injury or loss of life.

While most country and all suburban stations had telephones by the 1920s, the constable could well be out, or sometimes indisposed. Here the role of wives was crucial, though their activities went unrecorded and were rarely acknowledged publicly by police administrators.[155] Instead they are recalled in the appreciative memories of retired policemen and in the companionship suggested by family photographs. In common parlance, wives were the 'silent unpaid servants' of the Police Department. One retired man probably echoed the sentiments of others in declaring his wife to be 'always as good or better than any second Constable on country Station.'[156] Typically, during Constable Sterritt's absences for days from Culverden, his wife Katherine (with three small children) dealt with the callers, offering advice in emergencies. She had a great knowledge of police work, and passed matters requiring immediate attention to the district headquarters in Christchurch. On one occasion, when a sudden death occurred, she consulted her husband by telephone and made all the arrangements for an inquest to be held when he returned.[157] At Charleston, when Constable Allan was 'off relieving' (opossum-trapping in the West Coast bush), his wife 'handled things' including filling out the charge book.[158] As the volume of work mounted at the busy suburban station of Taita in the early 1950s, Mrs Strawbridge deflected many late-night complaints of domestic assault to the larger Lower Hutt station so her husband could rest; since she 'was not paid to answer the phone she could not be disciplined'.[159] Wives at country stations assisted in recording the agricultural and pastoral statistics and fed the prisoners. Indeed they were the (unofficial) gaolers while their husbands were away. Through their personalities and involvement in local activities, wives at sole-charge stations could play a significant part in establishing the local standing of police. At the farewell function on their departure from the Ruatoria station in 1935, Mrs Ryan shared the presentations and the plaudits with her husband.[160]

Although the record is mute, it may be guessed that wives also shared the pressures of life at sole-charge stations with their husbands. Some anxieties were common to most aspects of police work – especially the physical demands and the possibility of injury – but a sense of rural isolation could sharpen concern. Rescues from rivers and mountains, and loosely organised back-country searches (before the late 1930s at least) for missing trampers and pig hunters had the potential for mishaps. (Searching for a suspected murderer near Raetihi, the local Constable Chesnutt lost his way in the bush and himself became the focus of a police search in 1933.)[161] Whether in the city or the country, constables disliked dealing with 'sudden deaths', which were often gruesome and invariably distasteful. Adding to the more varied circumstances experienced by the country men was the rigmarole of organising inquests.

Some pressures on family relationships may well have been weaker at country stations than they were in the cities, where beat constables worked shifts and detectives kept long hours and were frequently absent. Opportunities for companionship between wife and husband were greater at country stations, given the rhythms and conditions of work. Whereas, typically, city policemen rarely discussed their work with their wives, or mentioned it only in general terms, partners at country stations could not avoid a more intimate involvement – with both the satisfactions and the stresses this could bring. Being always on call at sole-charge stations (except when the family escaped on annual leave) could be a further source of tension, especially as wives were more housebound than husbands. Since the station house was the focus of much work, as well as snatches of leisure, its amenities were fundamental to the satisfactions of the job. Dilapidated housing was a source of complaint, especially for wives. So too were unwanted transfers to uncongenial locations. Generally, it seems, wives 'made do', bottling up their frustrations just as their husbands did. Domestic discord which came to the notice of senior officers could (it was believed) lead to pressure on a constable to resign.[162] Ostensibly, then, the marriages of those men who survived in the Force until retirement remained intact – in marked contrast to a later generation of police.

There were casualties nonetheless amongst those at sole-charge stations. Health could deteriorate amongst wives as well as husbands.[163] During a routine inspection of the Port Awanui station in August 1926, Inspector William Eccles noted a change in Constable Martin Campbell's demeanour: 'he appeared to be in a nervous condition & requires a transfer' – which followed, to routine work at Gisborne, two months later.[164] The effect of seeing a man with his head blown off was given by a District Constable as the reason he had turned to drink and deserted his Mangawai station in 1927 with the fees he had collected for the local county council.[165] In an extreme case in 1930, 'worry over the work' led to the suicide after only three weeks at Rakaia of Constable D.O. Brown, who had been ill-prepared for the responsibilities of a country station. A confidant, the local agent for the Public Trustee, commented that 'the job was not so hard'; but the 'very varied' work required 'a man with a considerable amount of common sense' – Brown had been 'over-conscientious'.[166] Others fell into difficulties for being less than conscientious – especially in handling the variety of fines and fees they received.[167]

Defalcations were apparently rare, not merely because an ethic of honesty was reinforced by the annual visits of Audit Office inspectors, but also because pressures to defraud were usually weak. Amongst the rank and file police, country constables were relatively well-off. Certainly 'financial worry' in 1942 led Mangonui's Constable Herbert Barrett to shoot a local kauri gum-digger, Mate Urlich, from whom he had borrowed money, ostensibly to help pay for an expensive new car to replace an old Chevrolet deemed unsuitable on the rough roads of the Far North.[168] At Barrett's trial for attempted murder, the Inspector in charge of the Whangarei District sought to refute any suggestion that the constable's difficulties stemmed from departmental miserliness. In Commissioner D.J. Cummings' view, Barrett's 'domestic worries' ('to live up to my position' and also pay doctor's bills for a sickly wife and child) had 'nothing to do with the Department'.[169]

Over the previous three years Barrett had received in reimbursement
for the use of his new car a sum (£362 2s 6d) that was more than one
and half times what he had paid for it. In 1939, his annual salary as a
constable with nineteen years' service (£336 5s) was supplemented by
income as Clerk of Court (£21), Inspector of Fishing (£10), and Collector
of Statistics (£6 4s 6d). In addition, he received a rent-free house, a
boot and uniform allowance (£5), and an office lighting allowance (£1
10s).[170] Altogether, this country constable earned as much as a newly
appointed city sectional Sergeant without a house allowance, and indeed
more than a long-serving city Sergeant with a house allowance (£50),
if the car allowances were included as income. With other tasks for
government departments, and more schedules to deal with as Collectors
of Statistics, country constables elsewhere earned even more during the
inter-war years. The mid-1920s probably saw the high point of country
constables' incomes relative to other police and other rural incomes.
(Forty-two constables reported annual incomes greater than those of 60
per cent of Sergeants in 1926.)[171] Though their incomes were generally
less in 1935 than they had been in 1926, most country constables still
earned enough to put them amongst the top 5 to 10 per cent of rural
and small-town income-earners in the mid-1930s.[172]

Local standing

Their level of income underpinned but did not determine the local
standing of police. Respect and esteem came from the variety and
methods of work carried out by individual constables and their wives
over lengthy periods at sole-charge stations. Retiring in 1938 after 27
years at Opunake, George and Maude Clouston were farewelled at a
number of functions, including one chaired by the mayor at which the
constable was presented with an illuminated scroll signed by all the
local dignitaries and representatives of community organisations. Two
years later Clouston became mayor of the small town, standing down
in 1947 at the age of 73.[173] Eulogies at public farewells and the rhetoric
of politicians gave local feelings a wider currency. 'Tact' and 'fairness',
'firmness' but restraint in using authority, a readiness to advise rather
than prosecute, 'summary justice' for youths when needed, were some
of the common elements of conventional imagery.[174] Country constables
'were friends in the service of law, and also guides, philosophers, and
friends in all sorts of conditions and difficulties', Prime Minister (and
Minister of Police) Peter Fraser reiterated on a number of occasions
during the 1940s.[175]

By the 1920s the myth of the local constable had been established;
the next 30 years was its heyday. In H.C.D. Somerset's portrayal of the
north Canterbury community of Oxford in *Littledene* (1938), the local
policeman had 'come to be something more than the representative of
law and order .... His advice is frequently sought on problems of law

and he is able to avoid much trouble by meeting it half way.'[176] Similarly, in R.M. Burdon's novel *Outlaw's Progress* (1943), Sergeant Flanagan's

> methods of keeping peace were perhaps unorthodox but they were certainly effective. It was seldom that he ran anyone in for anything but a serious offence. He believed in the prevention rather than the punishment of crime and his system was simplicity itself. He had a wonderful eye for a prospective criminal and if he thought it likely that a certain person was going to do something wrong he would warn him not to do it. If the individual thus warned persisted in breaking the law Flanagan would give him a good hiding. Naturally he did not apply this summary form of punishment to the old and infirm but then most of the minor offences in Rangitira were committed by the young and active members of the community.
>
> He settled many quarrels that might have ended in litigation and here again he had his own way of going to work ....[177]

The myth was captured again by Oliver Duff in his 1940 centennial survey, *New Zealand Now*. At a local policeman's farewell:

> The mayor sat on one side of him, the old doctor on the other side. Half the town was packed in the hall in front of him. It was good-bye. But as one after another rose to praise him his face cried out for mercy. He had arrested them, he had prosecuted them, he had broken up their parties, spied on them, collected evidence against them, warned them, threatened them; once or twice, to save them from something worse, used physical violence against them – and there they all sat smiling and clapping and thumping their feet and shouting the most fervent 'hear-hears' ....
>
> For he was not one of those guardians of the law who think they guard it best by exposing and punishing every breach. If you ended in Court you were incorrigible. You would have been warned. Long before you were warned you would have been advised. Long before that, probably, you would have been made to feel off-side. There must be scores of men, and even a few women, in that district to-day who never read the Court news without realising that they had kept out of the dock by the grace of God and Sergeant C ....[178]

In popular perception, the local policeman personified a sense of security and order; indeed he was seen as maintaining it. And so his absence was a cause for concern. Pressure to acquire a constable might be mounted by residents of a locality. In response, Members of Parliament expressed keen interest in the location of sole-charge stations.[179] More commonly there was resistance when police administrators threatened to remove or downgrade stations where there was insufficient work. The protest of the Lawrence borough council at the prospect of a sole-charge station when its local Sergeant was transferred in early 1927 was sufficient to have the Minister of Police promise two constables for the declining goldfields town of some 600 people. More lightly policed surrounding localities proved unsympathetic to the pretensions of Lawrence, which had its second constable removed within four years.[180]

In the myth of the local constable, his role in preserving order was overplayed. For one thing, the securing of order in a community did not rest mainly with the police – a fact appreciated by insightful local constables. Indeed there was a fundamental stability in most localities during the inter-war years. 'Littledene is a law-abiding community', Somerset observed; 'we are law-abiding', echoed Duff.[181] If Littledene was the archetype, then the pervasive habit of work and a variety of local associations provided mechanisms for a fair degree of self-regulation; social order was locally produced by the residents, sometimes facilitated by the constable, not externally imposed. As a social lubricant, alcohol was still important, but patterns of excess were steadily moderated during the 1920s and early 1930s. Only on the remnants of the bush-working, mining, gum-digging, 'development' frontier did order occasionally need to be imposed.

Even then there were limits to the role of the local constable in producing order. He was as much reactive as preventive – at best intervening to prevent greater disorder or further crime. And here he was generally dependent on local support and cooperation, even more so than police in the cities. (This was explicitly recognised by the government even though it sought to avoid accepting any liability to Mate Urlich for the 'private actions' of its servant, Constable Barrett: after four petitions, and nearly ten years, Urlich was awarded a 'compassionate grant' of £1,000 as compensation for his injuries and loss of earnings.)[182] Widespread acceptance of the local constable's authority was seen as crucial.

Yet the country constable was not merely working within a local consensus, a pattern of locally shared norms, even if such existed. For Somerset, the local policeman was a representative of the 'Great Society' in the community of Littledene: there were laws of the wider society, or at least of its dominant interests, to be applied – and sometimes alternative conceptions of order to be enforced, as, for instance, coal miners at Blackball and Maori at Te Araroa well knew in the early 1930s. More clearly in the country policeman's work than in that of his urban counterpart, we can see a continuing and basic tension between securing the consent of the policed, applying the edicts of government, and the bureaucratic imperatives of the Department itself, made manifest in record-keeping and the priorities of police work. The myth of the local constable concealed the different means of resolving this tension developed by men at sole-charge stations.

CHAPTER 9

Supervision

'In no Department of the Government is the necessity for adherence to orders and regulations so necessary, nor the development and exercise of initiative so important, as in the Police Force'. Thus did Commissioner O'Donovan pose a conundrum to his men in 1920. The solution? 'Strict compliance with orders is the line of safety in normal conditions; a wise discretion is necessary in circumstances where strict adherence to fixed orders and regulations would defeat the object.'[1] Tested against experience, such an answer could seem opaque to individual police. In their day-to-day work, constables and detectives faced both the need to act autonomously and the constraint of rules. Resolution of the conundrum was influenced by another aspect of police work – perhaps its least visible, albeit pervasive – that of supervision and control.

A basic pattern persisted from the nineteenth century in the structure and manner of supervision. It was shaped by an inherently autocratic style of leadership with a military rank structure designed to preserve a line of command from the Commissioner. In 1919, the 20 commissioned officers and 137 non-commissioned officers represented 17.9 per cent of the full-time Force, so that there was a supervisory officer for every five constables and detectives. The proportion of police in supervisory ranks declined to 14 per cent by 1935 (a ratio of 1 to 6 rank and file), before returning to the level of the early 1920s (nearly 16 per cent) during the Second World War. On paper at least, there was a narrow span of control, both of officers over NCOs (1:7 in 1919 and 1939), and of NCOs over rank and file police (1:5 in 1919, increasing to nearly 1:7 in 1939).[2] In reality, the pattern of formal supervision was more complex, with the span of control and the nature of supervision varying among police districts, localities, and stations.

'The bosses': commissioned officers

During the inter-war years, at least half of the commissioned officers commanded districts – 10 out of 20 did so in 1919, and 15 out of 26 in 1939. Despite the proliferation of districts, considerable differences endured in the numbers of staff and types of station within them. In

1939, the provincial police districts under the command of Inspectors ranged from 38 staff in 12 stations (Nelson) to 85 staff in 25 stations (Hamilton). The status, number and location of supervisory positions depended not only on the numbers of rank-and-file police, but also varied according to the distance from district headquarters, the nature of local policing, and the status of the locality. The growing importance of the Rotorua station in policing the eastern part of the Hamilton District meant that the rank of its officer in charge was raised from Senior Sergeant to Sub-Inspector in 1939; Rotorua was the only station outside a district headquarters where a commissioned officer was in charge after 1920.[3] In 1939, the station at Hastings (with sixteen staff) and five in the inner suburbs of Auckland and Wellington had more staff (ranging up to more than 30 at Taranaki Street and Mt Cook), but their proximity to the central station of the district allowed them to be left to the oversight of Senior Sergeants. Similarly, stations at the small provincial towns of Hawera (New Plymouth District), Blenheim (Nelson), and Oamaru (Timaru) were placed under the charge of Senior Sergeants, while others with similar staff numbers (around half a dozen) – Stratford (New Plymouth) and Ashburton (Christchurch), for example – were amongst the 23 provincial police stations at which Sergeants were now in charge.[4] The smaller, isolated police districts, such as Whangarei, Gisborne and Greymouth, maintained a high ratio of sole-charge stations to overall staff.

A hierarchy of provincial police districts was established in the 1920s; so too was one maintained amongst the four largest districts, which were controlled by Superintendents and focused on the cities. Slowly evolving structures of supervision reflected the varied patterns of growth in the main centres and their hinterlands. In Auckland, the number of rank-and-file police increased more substantially than elsewhere, and so too, in rough proportion until 1939 at least, did the number of officers and NCOs. Again, local characteristics of social geography, policing, urban status and the long-standing location of inner-city stations influenced the allocation of supervisory ranks. Auckland and Wellington districts had larger inner-city stations (meriting control by Senior Sergeants) than did Christchurch or Dunedin, which had proportionately more sole-charge stations. In 1939, the inner suburban North and South Dunedin stations, and Sydenham in Christchurch, with Sergeants in charge, had more staff than the five-man Senior Sergeant station at Devonport on Auckland's North Shore, with its growing but relatively dispersed population.[5] Though Dunedin's city status and size of district had long merited a Superintendent to supervise it, the officer in charge probably found his role less demanding than did his counterpart in the Hamilton District during the 1930s. By contrast, Superintendent Stephen Till found his period in charge of Auckland, between 1930 and 1938, to be 'the most strenuous' years of his career.[6]

Of the 53 men promoted to Sub-Inspector between 1918 and 1939, all but three (two of whom died in office) were eventually given charge of a district with the rank of Inspector. Promotion depended on passing the qualifying examinations for Sub-Inspector, and on seniority (length of service in a rank).[7] A quarter of these men had been detectives, though members of the Detective Branch comprised less than 5 per cent of the Force during the 1920s and just over 6 per cent by 1939. In fact, after the common seniority list was established in 1919, being a detective brought no discernible advantage in rising to higher ranks, with the exception of the controversial acceleration in seniority received by James Cummings as a Detective Sergeant in 1921. The disproportionate representation of former detectives amongst the officers reflected their greater willingness or ability to sit the qualifying examinations, as well as length of service.

Longevity – in the sense of maintaining reasonable health and a clean record over an extended period – was crucial. The ages of the eleven men made Sub-Inspectors between 1918 and 1922 ranged from 44 to 54 years, and their length of prior service from 25 to 29 years. The latter increased to over 30 years in the late 1930s, when most of the few new Sub-Inspectors were in their early to mid-fifties. The creation of new districts between 1918 and 1921 meant that some Sub-Inspectors were promoted to Inspector within a year or two. The usual waiting time during the inter-war years was two to three years. The death of five of the eleven officers promoted to Inspector between 1920 and 1922, and the early retirement through illness of another two, increased the opportunities for achieving higher rank. Overall, a fifth of the officers appointed between the wars died or retired early through ill health.[8]

Two-thirds of the officers appointed during the inter-war years eventually became Superintendents – usually in their early sixties, when they had no more than two to four years of service remaining. Such was the strict adherence to seniority that a few became Superintendents (sometimes with a transfer, usually to Dunedin) virtually on the eve of retirement.[9] Only with respect to appointments as Commissioner did length of future service (and possibly other considerations) modify the convention of seniority. A.H. Wright, W.G. Wohlmann, and Denis and James Cummings were all the youngest of their cohorts of Superintendents, with a potential length of service as Commissioner ranging from four to seven years.[10] John O'Donovan and W.B. McIlveney each faced a more youthful contender,[11] but had sufficient length of service remaining (as well as personal qualities) to gain appointment. Thus longevity (or 'grey hairs')[12] rather than merit determined the promotion of officers: the younger the age on joining, the higher the rank likely to be achieved (if the qualifying examinations were passed). Perceived aptitude or the likelihood of future advancement could, however, influence where an officer was posted.

On the evening of 18 August 1919, there was a large gathering of

NCOs and constables at the Taranaki Street station in Wellington. Sergeant Charles Lopdell was presented with a gold Waltham watch, gold chain, and medal for the service he had performed in presenting the case for the uniformed men at the recent Committee of Inquiry: an eight-hour shift, increased pay and a common seniority list had been achieved. Earlier, Commissioner O'Donovan had congratulated Lopdell on the manner in which he had presented the uniformed men's case without leaving ill feeling between the Uniform and Detective Branches of the Force. Amongst the plaudits, Sergeant D.A. MacLean declared, 'Sergeant Lopdell is a man who, if he is spared, will rise to the top of the tree'.[13]

Certainly Lopdell's career path was typical of those of the uniformed men who were potential contenders for the highest office and perceived to have 'zeal, integrity and intelligence'. From Taranaki Street, Lopdell was posted to Te Kuiti in 1921 as Sergeant in charge, and in 1922 to Wanganui, where, as Senior Sergeant, he remained for seven years while advancing up the seniority list. As the likelihood of further promotion approached, Lopdell was transferred to Wellington in 1929 as Chief Detective to give him experience of supervising that Branch. A year later he was promoted to Sub-Inspector. In 1932 he became the Inspector in charge of the Greymouth District and began a typical progression up the hierarchy of districts, with transfers to Hamilton in 1934 and to Wellington as Superintendent in 1940.

Lopdell, the advocate of promotion by seniority, failed to become Commissioner because the seniority system was not entirely sacrosanct. James Cummings, who became Commissioner in 1944, was both seven years younger than Lopdell and more lowly ranked in 1919; but he gained a year in seniority over Lopdell with his promotion to Senior Detective in December 1921. Any chance Lopdell might have had to be considered for the highest rank was removed with the (then) unprecedented deferment of Commissioner D.J. Cummings' retirement by more than two years to November 1944, by when Lopdell was 66.[14]

The six men who became Commissioner between 1916 and 1945 shared at least one common element in their career paths. All had been in charge of either the Wellington or Auckland District. Being Superintendent in Wellington did not imply seniority, though some assumed the incumbent might act as an understudy for the Commissioner, as John O'Donovan had occasionally acted for Commissioner Cullen. The extent to which O'Donovan's successors followed suit is not clear. Commissioners could seek, by their postings, to influence who Cabinet might choose as their successor. Following seniority, W.G. Wohlmann and A.T. Emerson were made Superintendents on the same date in 1926. The newly appointed Commissioner, W.B. McIlveney, transferred his friend, Tivy Emerson, from Whangarei back to Wellington, while Wohlmann went from Hamilton to Auckland. Cabinet subsequently preferred Wohlmann as Commissioner. All four Commissioners who rose from the Uniform Branch had been in charge of at least three districts, including either Hamilton or Napier. As constables, three had been District Clerks, showing an aptitude for record-keeping. The two former detectives, McIlveney and James Cummings, had had fewer postings than their uniformed counterparts, but both had spent time in the Commissioner's office on special duties, and stood out from their peers through their energy and force of personality.

Other officers, who were older on appointment to commissioned rank, or in poor health, or possibly perceived to be less competent, moved through the smaller provincial districts and (if they rose to Superintendent) usually ended up in Dunedin for a short period before retiring. After barely a year in charge of the Whangarei District, Inspector J.W. Hollis was transferred to a supervisory role under the Superintendent in Auckland, where he remained until his retirement. A few other officers followed this path back to the main centres. Overall, nearly two-thirds of the postings of officers in charge of districts were for periods of three years or less – though in most districts, a few officers stayed put for lengthy periods. In large measure, the career paths of commissioned officers were fortuitous, depending on the timing and location of vacancies, and a willingness to fill them. The willingness of D.C. Fraser was exceptional. Between 1925 and 1939, as Inspector and then Superintendent, he took charge of seven districts in succession: Napier, Greymouth, New Plymouth, Hamilton, Dunedin, Wellington, and finally Auckland. On the eve of his departure for Whangarei, Tivy Emerson, newly promoted Inspector, told those (including W.B. McIlveney) who gathered to farewell him in the billiard room of the Wellington Central station that he was 'sorry to leave Wellington, but there was no help for it, if one wished for promotion and advancement.'[15]

Length of service meant that in the experience and outlook of officers, traditions of the nineteenth century persisted well into the twentieth. Amongst the Superintendents and older Inspectors of the early 1920s were nine officers who had served in the New Zealand Constabulary Force during the early 1880s. Most officers appointed in the mid-1920s had joined the Police Force after a period in the Permanent Artillery. Strict adherence to rules and regulations, expectations of firm discipline, habits of command, and aloofness from the rank and file were all part of the norms of supervision and control inculcated in junior officers and NCOs, and passed on by them in turn. A military emphasis on 'discipline and deportment' could be seen in the monthly ritual of pay parades at district headquarters (especially in the main centres), when serried ranks of men were formally inspected, exhorted, and occasionally drilled by the officer in charge.

The appointment of D.J. Cummings as a Sub-Inspector in October 1922 marked the first appearance of officers who had received their initial training as recruits in the Police Depot. (John O'Donovan had been Cummings' Instructor in 1899.) Such officers (including G.B. Edwards and Henry Scott, who had both served as Instructors at the

Depot) began to predominate from the mid-1930s. Possibly as a consequence, there was a shift in the norms of supervision towards a softer and more flexible discipline; but the extent to which such a change occurred before 1945 may be debated. In the late 1940s there remained at least five senior officers (including Commissioner James Cummings) who had learnt their 'discipline and deportment' in the Permanent Artillery at the beginning of the century.[16] In the daily exercise of supervision, much continued to depend on the personality and zeal of individual officers.

Another aspect of a subtle shift in the formative experiences of officers appointed from 1918 was a change in their country of birth and upbringing that paralleled broader patterns amongst politicians and public servants, and in public life more generally. Of the twenty commissioned officers in 1918, the eight who were Irish-born dominated the highest ranks, while six were English and three Scots, and the first three New Zealand-born were amongst the younger officers. During the next decade, only one Irish-born officer was appointed and two-thirds of those promoted were New Zealand-born. Since McIlveney's appointment in 1926, all Commissioners have been born in New Zealand. However the proportion of Catholics amongst the officers (about 40 per cent) did not diminish between the wars (indeed, four of the six Commissioners in this period were Catholics at a time when less than 14 per cent of the population were). This was one reason for the continuing adherence to seniority in promotions: it kept in check potential sectarian jealousy. During the inter-war years, then, the Police Force came to be led by officers who knew at first hand only its local practices and traditions, and saw little need to change them.

This outlook was reinforced by the process of learning on the job which was the only form of training for the supervisory ranks. Officers and NCOs were given formal instructions on their duties in the Police Regulations and Commissioner's Circulars. But competence in supervision, as in front-line policing, was seen as coming from common sense and practical skills acquired through experience rather than formal training. Officers in charge of districts were instructed by Commissioner O'Donovan in 1921 to keep their subordinate officers 'as fully acquainted as possible with the general affairs of the district, and the method of dealing with them, so that each subordinate officer may acquire the greatest degree of experience and training for the higher position that it is possible to attain in the circumstances.'[17] Such guidance as was offered by senior officers was spasmodic, addressed to individuals and framed to meet particular needs. The preparation that was required for the promotion examinations reinforced a narrow conception of supervision. The syllabi for the ranks of Sergeant, Senior Sergeant, and Sub-Inspector prescribed questions of increasing difficulty in English, geography, and arithmetic, as well as in statute law, the Police Force Act and Regulations, and on practical police and detective duties. For

Senior Sergeants and Sub-Inspectors, further questions focused on the keeping of records and the preparation of accounts.[18] Candidates for the examinations had to prepare themselves as best they could with the limited resources available. (Eight of the seventeen who sat the Sub-Inspector's examination in 1933 failed, as did six of fourteen in 1935.)[19] Police 'libraries', where these existed at the district headquarters, did not stock (for example) overseas police journals or modern literature concerned with administration.[20]

No formal meetings of officers or NCOs at which issues of supervision could be discussed were held in the inter-war years.[21] The first conferences of officers in charge of districts in 1940 were narrowly focused on how to deal with wartime aliens and 'subversives', and were dominated by Commissioner D.J. Cummings, who issued instructions and made critical comments rather than encouraging discussion.[22] An opportunity in the mid-1920s for senior officers to undertake short courses at Scotland Yard was not taken up.[23] Annual reports of the Australian state police forces might be read, but no New Zealand Commissioner attended the conferences of his Australian counterparts until 1939, when he did so in the context of preparations for war.[24] Nor, it seems, were innovations suggested by subordinates, including some returning from trips to Australia or England, followed up. 'I got so many knock-backs in suggesting things that I abandoned all interest', Bill Murray recalled.[25] And so the roles and practice of the supervisory ranks remained unchanged, reflecting a fundamental bureaucratic conservatism.

In essence the roles of officers and NCOs had three main aspects: monitoring the performance of subordinates by direct observation and reviewing reports, making the decisions on policing required by their authority or experience, and giving routine attention to files and correspondence. The specific tasks actually performed by individuals depended on their rank and the complexity of the local structure of supervision.

Across the police districts, the responsibilities of the officers in charge were the same, but the range and amount of work varied. With fewer supervisory staff to assist them, Inspectors in the provincial districts were more directly involved in all three aspects of supervision than were Superintendents. In the cities, Inspectors and/or Sub-Inspectors relieved Superintendents of much of the burden of routine correspondence and monitoring staff at the headquarters stations. Superintendents could focus on supervising the suburban and country stations. During periodical (usually annual) visits of inspection, station records were examined, diaries signed, and the state of the buildings observed, as was the morale of local police.

Officers in charge of districts recommended any additions or changes to staff or premises which they saw were needed. When difficulties in prosecuting offences were experienced, changes in legislation might be suggested. They were responsible for scrutinising expenditure, interviewing prospective recruits and dealing with breaches of discipline. They were expected to take the lead in the policing of 'any event of public importance', especially where disorder was anticipated. Strikes, or the threat of strikes, between 1919 and 1922, the growth of an unemployed workers' movement from the late 1920s, and disturbances and their aftermath in the cities during the early 1930s were major preoccupations of the Superintendents in the cities, who kept as close an eye on detectives' political surveillance as they did on the progress of murder inquiries. Similarly, the senior officers took command of police responses to civil emergencies, as did (for example) Commissioner Wohlmann and Inspector D.J. Cummings in the aftermath of the Hawke's Bay earthquake in 1931, and Superintendent Donald Scott during the flooding of the lower Clutha district in 1944.

Officers in charge of provincial districts such as Gisborne and Whangarei spent the equivalent of several months each year inspecting outlying stations. Every two or three months during the early 1920s, for example, Inspector David Hutton of Gisborne made a regular tour of part of his district: either up the East Coast visiting stations at Tolaga Bay, Tokomaru Bay, Waipiro Bay, Tuparoa (later Ruatoria), Port Awanui and Te Araroa, or across the Urewera range to Opotiki, stopping at Te Karaka and Motu (later Matawai) along the way, and then on to Taneatua and Whakatane. From Opotiki he also visited the Native Constable at Te Kaha. These tours were arduous, each taking four or more days to accomplish by car and on horseback, with the possibility of mishap – Hutton had 'some narrow shaves'.[26] In the Timaru District, by contrast, it was claimed that all the outlying stations could be reached by rail.[27]

The extent to which such stations were visited varied with the demands of other work. At Hamilton, and probably in other districts also, the officer in charge became increasingly burdened with supervisory duties at the central station. In 1938, Inspector Lopdell sought a Sub-Inspector to free him for 'closer personal contact' with the constables at country stations, and 'to assist them' particularly with their court work. The 'constant calls from an intensely busy community' and the demands of supervising 30 staff made it 'desirable that an officer of commissioned rank be left in charge' when he was away from the main station.[28] A Sub-Inspector was appointed, but at Rotorua. As in the other provincial police districts, Lopdell continued to have a Senior Sergeant as his second in command to supervise the central station.

Potentially, officers in charge could influence the patterns and priorities of policing in their districts. But the extent to which they did so is difficult to discern. Most circulars and memoranda to stations came from the Commissioner through the district office. 'District orders' from the officers in charge dealt mainly with the performance of duties already prescribed, especially record-keeping and the completion of returns and reports. The behaviour of local police might also be reprimanded – such as the practice among Auckland city and suburban constables of ignoring Transport Board instructions by riding on the driver's platform of buses and trams,[29] or the tendency of some West Coast police to comment on decisions of the magistrate.[30] Stations would also be warned of local threats to order (such as when prohibitionists lectured on the West Coast in 1922) or occasionally told to give 'special attention' to certain minor offences, such as bicycles without lights.[31] During their usually short period in charge of a district, most officers appear to have seen supervision as managing a system of policing that was already in place, and should be altered only in response to perceived changes in local behaviour, local concerns or those of the Commissioner. Overall, the patterns and priorities of beat and detective work, and of suburban and country policing, were left undisturbed.

Enforcement of the liquor licensing laws illustrates well the tendency amongst officers to leave undisturbed established systems of policing. The distinctive example of the West Coast also suggests the influence that a new officer might have in altering policing priorities – at least in the short term. In Greymouth by the mid-1920s, a pattern of policing hotels had become established whereby routine visits and prosecutions did little to diminish widespread after-hours trading. This system was not tolerated by Inspector Charles Lopdell, a teetotaller (and member of the Salvation Army) with a reputation for zeal in enforcing the licensing laws, when he arrived on the West Coast in 1932. Shortly after his advent, 'a slight deviation from the usual routine' of hotel visits caught a number of publicans trading after hours. The Inspector claimed his staff were acting on 'their own initiative'. Nonetheless, this shift to 'surprise' tactics was widely seen to be the result of Lopdell's influence.

At 1.30 am on 5 October 1932, a small home-made 'bomb' exploded on the roof of the Inspector's house, causing some damage. Seen as intended to intimidate, the bomb had the opposite effect: police 'supervision' of Greymouth's 22 hotels intensified, as did the animosity of some publicans – especially the licensee of the Union Hotel, which did most of its business in the evenings when coal miners (with access to explosives) came to town. Two further harmless explosions on the evenings of 28 and 31 October occurred near the routes that the Sergeant and the Senior Sergeant usually took on their way home. As some local residents became increasingly anxious and ready to assist the police, the two main suspects brought to the police station an unexploded bomb which they claimed to have found. The explosions ceased. During the remainder of Lopdell's two years at Greymouth, the number of prosecutions for after-hours trading fell substantially – in consequence of 'closer police supervision', as he saw it. Much later he was to admit that West Coast publicans were 'pretty well all rebels .... Unless a policeman was at the door, I never knew them to be closed'.[32]

In managing the local system of policing, officers in charge of districts relied on their subordinate officers to make their job easier. In Auckland in 1934 the division of responsibility was more elaborate than elsewhere. Under Superintendent Till was the 64 year old Inspector J.W. Hollis, who had since 1928 overseen the city police, both uniformed and detective. The country and small-town stations remained under the direct control of the Superintendent. In practice Hollis served as a conduit for correspondence, monitoring and minuting files passing between the district headquarters and his subordinate officers. He displayed 'enthusiasm for his work', having 'made the police force his hobby.'[33] Before the appointment in 1930 of a Sub-Inspector in charge of the detectives, Hollis estimated that he handled about 200 files daily, and spent about 60 per cent of his time reading those from the Detective Branch.[34]

In 1934, Sub-Inspector James Sweeney, who had spent most of his career in the Uniform Branch, had charge of Auckland's detectives. Ostensibly he was desk-bound, directing their work and observing their performance indirectly through their written reports and briefs of evidence in cases to be prosecuted by the senior detective.[35] Critics who perceived Auckland detectives to be ineffective and the 'police system of administration' generally to be 'antiquated' saw Sweeney as 'considerably out of touch with modern crime detection'.[36] Unrealistic expectations of success in detective work bred impatience. Even so, as a supervisor, Sweeney did not have the prestige that was to be enjoyed by 'Reg' Ward, a well-known detective who became Inspector in charge of that branch in Auckland on Hollis's retirement in 1935.[37]

In 1934 a second Inspector was appointed in Auckland. Inspector G.B. Edwards[38] was given direct responsibility for the uniformed men in the city and suburbs. He inspected station records, visited the night-duty police at intervals, and paid special attention (as did his counterparts in the other main centres) to the enforcement of the licensing legislation by monitoring files and inspecting hotels. The Inspectors had also to organise the policing of major events in the city. Further supervision of the city and suburban uniformed men was provided by Sub-Inspector Donald Scott,[39] whose main role was to conduct (or supervise) most Uniform Branch prosecutions in the Magistrate's Court. Control of the paperwork ensured that files were properly prepared. The Sub-Inspector also dealt with the rapidly growing number of files on breaches of the Motor Vehicles Act, and made regular inspections of beat men and their Sergeants. As Inspector in Auckland from 1936 until 1941, Scott was to focus on sly-grogging, being seen (in the words of one lawyer) as a 'a perfect _____ with licensing cases.'[40] Scott found Auckland 'a very hard place to do duty.' With about 240 uniformed staff in the city and suburbs to supervise by 1939, 'it was no small responsibility'.[41]

'The backbone of the Force': NCOs

Non-commissioned officers shared the burden of responsibility for supervision. When Sergeant George Bonisch of Wellington's Taranaki

Street station failed to make the required number of visits to constables on his night-duty section in May 1930, and then made false entries in his notebook and sectional report, he was reported by Senior Sergeant W.J. Butler for four breaches of Police Regulations. This was seen as a 'serious matter' by Inspector Sidney Rawle at Wellington Central, 'making it impossible for me to further trust him to carry out his duties' – by implication, Bonisch should be dismissed.[42] The Sergeant's conduct seemed to cut at the root of the structure of supervision and discipline. Similarly, Superintendent James Cummings, at Auckland, took the rare step of having Sergeant P. Geraghty removed from the list for promotion to Senior Sergeant in 1940 because in his supervision of two constables at Huntly he had not demonstrated the 'initiative and controlling power that was necessary for a Senior Sergeant at the four centres.' The Sergeant was seen to be 'a decent, honest, loyal man', but he had not ensured that his men patrolled in uniform sufficiently; his correspondence to the District Office appeared to show a lack of 'ability' or 'attention' in directing his men in their inquiries – more files were sent back to him than to other Sergeants; and Geraghty himself admitted that he could not stop a constable drinking or 'associating with hoodlums or Maoris.'[43] Sergeants and Senior Sergeants were the backbone of the structure of supervision and control. They were seen to be crucial in maintaining the discipline and performance of the rank and file.

The backbone of the Police Force was made up of men well seasoned in policing through spending at least fourteen years as a constable or detective before their promotion to Sergeant. Usually those about to be promoted had varied policing experience, including time at a sole-charge station if they were uniformed men. The first step (and only this step) into the supervisory ranks required a certificate from a Police Surgeon of physical fitness – specifically, fitness to perform shift work as a Sergeant in charge of beat constables in the cities.[44] From August 1935, constables near the top of the promotion list were put on probation as acting Sergeants for at least six months in the main centres.[45] By 1946, when George Austing was on probation as a Sergeant in Auckland, he 'had to submit a list each month of "achievements" – such as arrests, hotel prosecutions, breaches of Police Regulations .... We would get a stir up if the list was considered insufficient.'[46]

Those who aspired to commissioned rank between the wars generally spent fourteen years or more as NCOs – about eight years as Sergeants, and a similar period as Senior Sergeants or Senior Detectives. Many would end their careers in these ranks. Of the 30 Senior Sergeants and seven Senior Detectives on the seniority list on 1 July 1922, nineteen would eventually become commissioned officers. Of those who did not reach higher rank, one died on the eve of promotion, one was forced to resign, another was dismissed (though subsequently reinstated with loss of seniority), and the remainder had not passed the qualifying examination.

This pattern was also typical of Sergeants. Of those on the 1932 seniority list, 22 Sergeants had already been passed over for promotion, and a majority of the other 70 would be in future. A few were passed over, temporarily at least, because of misconduct.[47] Some (three out of the nine who sat in 1933) failed the Senior Sergeant's examination. Many more did not bother to sit it. Some who had joined the Force in their late twenties or early thirties took a pessimistic view of their chances of further promotion. Others lacked the motivation to prepare for exams after their shift work as sectional Sergeants or long hours in the Detective Office. Typically, R.H. Waterson 'did not feel up to' further exams, and was content to remain a Detective Sergeant at Gisborne for the last twenty years of his career.[48] Many, it seems, shared the outlook of those constables who eschewed promotion to remain at a country station: they looked for a station where (to a degree) they could be their 'own boss'. Sergeant F.A. Waterman, in charge of the four-man suburban station at Ponsonby, refused promotion in 1919 to avoid a transfer to less congenial Senior Sergeant duties in another city. Waterman was automatically placed at the bottom of the Sergeants' promotion list, and he remained at Ponsonby until his retirement in 1928.[49] In their different ways, Waterson and Waterman resembled many NCOs whose relatively long period at a suburban or small-town station made them local identities.[50]

Amongst the non-commissioned officers there was a diversity of roles and status which was determined by rank, station, and whether they were detectives or uniformed men. Nonetheless, all the uniformed men began their supervisory work as sectional Sergeants in the cities. Looking back on his career, ex-Superintendent D.R. Sugrue, who had joined in 1920, thought that the 'hardest part of my service was as a Sergeant in Dunedin' between 1937 and 1941. Though he was a relatively youthful Sergeant (in his late thirties), he remembered the physical demands of the job: especially on night shift, visiting on foot or bicycle the city constables on their beats three times a night, as well as inspecting those working from the Dunedin North and South stations at least once, in 'rain, hail, or snow', and 'clearing up any happenings on the beats'.[51] Generally the beats would be quiet, but this became less common, especially in wartime Auckland during the early 1940s. Here, as another recalled, 'the Sectional Sergeant was the "mug" – the man who knocked off late after trying to put the arrest files into order for Court and who had to try and answer such questions as "where was the Sergeant?", "who gave that instruction?", and more, when things went wrong on the streets or wharfs, or in the pubs or parks'.[52]

More acutely than the other supervisory ranks, a city sectional Sergeant could feel tension from being subject to surveillance and discipline and in turn having to exercise it. He was to parade his relief of six to eight constables at the beginning of a shift to see that they were 'present and correct'; march them out onto their beats; 'constantly' patrol his section to ensure the beats were properly policed, paying particular attention to hotels; make at least three 'surprise' visits to each constable on night shift (four to those on day shifts), recording the times and places in his notebook (as the constables were to do in theirs); become involved in difficult situations faced by his constables, providing guidance in the craft of policing through often curt instructions and example; take charge when necessary and make decisions which might subsequently be questioned; call in at the watch-house periodically and visit the prisoners in the cells at least once every two hours; bring in his relief at the end of the shift, and complete a sectional report for the Senior Sergeant on his visits, 'occurrences' and any misconduct by his men. Before he went home he had to minute any constables' reports, ensuring they were properly prepared for scrutiny by the Senior Sergeant. In 1928 an Auckland district order held Sergeants responsible, along with their constables, for crimes committed on their beats – in particular, if burglaries or thefts from buildings occurred during the night shift, the police would have to explain where they had been at the time.[53] Altogether, in the Uniform Branch the sectional Sergeants were perceived to be the 'mainstays of practical police work'.[54]

Like the men under them, Sergeants varied in their approach to their work. All constables experienced Sergeants who were conscientious and exacting (they were probably the norm), but others were perceived to be less so. Looking back on his experience as a young constable at Christchurch in the late 1920s, Martin Thyne recalled Sergeant W.T. Kelly as a 'model policeman'; Sergeant W.A. Almond was 'dour' but conscientious (he caught pubs trading after hours); another was 'the best turned out Sergeant who ever wore a police uniform' but had a drinking problem; a fourth also had a problem with alcohol and often left duty without completing his sectional report, 'which had to be sent to his home for completion'; a fifth (F.C. Harrison) was fined for neglect of duty and failing to carry out an instruction. This conviction, which was overturned by an Appeal Board, was seen by Thyne as 'the sort of thing which happens to Police when the department goes on the hunt to pursue men' – a view shared at the time by a local MP, who alleged 'victimization' by a superior officer.[55]

During the inter-war years some seventeen sectional Sergeants (a very small proportion of all Sergeants in the period) were formally disciplined for breaches of regulations. Half were fined, and almost all the remainder were reduced to the rank of constable.[56] The dismissal of George Bonisch by Commissioner McIlveney was thus seen to be harsh, and he was subsequently reinstated as a Sergeant with the loss of two years' seniority. Bonisch was unlucky, nonetheless.[57] Like others, he had been caught by discrepancies between his record-keeping and that of his constables. Lapses in observing the rules might well be concealed by connivance, however, and this was suspected (probably wrongly) in the Bonisch case. Senior Sergeant W.J. Butler thought that

Sergeant W. O'Donnell (who had brought in Bonisch's relief at the end of its shift) had 'allowed his mistaken idea of comradeship to cloud his vision and sense of duty towards the Department, or that he very much lacks the sense of observation' needed to confirm details that would have led to further charges.[58]

Some Sergeants remained on sectional duties into their fifties, when ill health or lack of fitness brought early retirement or (occasionally) a 'sedentary job' in a central station. More commonly, however, they would be posted to take charge of a suburban or small-town station or (if qualified) promoted directly to Senior Sergeant. Most of the commissioned officers between the wars had spent time as NCOs at stations outside the main centres. Superintendent Frank Lewin's varied experience as an NCO was fairly typical of those who rose from the Uniform Branch. After nearly ten years as a constable in Christchurch and Timaru, he spent six years at the sole-charge Amberley station before being posted to Wellington as a sectional Sergeant in March 1913. In November 1916 he took charge of three constables at the Gore station, with the oversight of four others at Clinton, Tapanui, Waikaia and Mataura. Aged 45, he was promoted to Senior Sergeant at Dunedin in January 1921, and transferred a year later to Christchurch, where he remained for four years before being promoted to Sub-Inspector and transferred to Auckland.

As the number of sectional Sergeants grew during the inter-war years, while the number of stations under the control of an NCO barely increased, the waiting time to take charge of a station lengthened, and gradually the prospects of doing so diminished. Typically, William Almond, who became a sectional Sergeant in Christchurch in September 1920, supervised beat constables for nearly nine years before becoming (in his late forties) the Sergeant in charge of two constables at the suburban St Albans station, where he remained until he died in February 1940. After seven years as a sectional Sergeant working from the various Wellington city stations, Donald Scott (aged 43) became the Senior Sergeant in charge of three Sergeants and 27 constables at Taranaki Street in October 1926. There he would have remained, but the need to give Chief Detective Reg Ward some experience as a uniformed 'Senior' at a busy city station before further promotion meant that Scott was transferred in 1929 to take charge of seven constables at Oamaru and four more at Glenavy, Duntroon, Kurow and Hampden. In 1931 he returned to Wellington as 'Senior' controlling three Sergeants and 23 men at Mt Cook station. Three years later he went to Auckland as Sub-Inspector.

Beyond the district headquarters, much of the direct supervision of staff rested with Senior Sergeants, and especially Sergeants. Much depended on their 'zeal, activity, and intelligence'; not just 'the credit of the Police service, but also responsibility for the legality of all Police action' within their control.[59] In 1939, NCOs were in charge at 59 stations (six more than in 1922); fifteen were controlled by Senior Sergeants and 44 by Sergeants. Between the wars the balance between Sergeant and Senior Sergeant stations had fluctuated according to the needs perceived by different Commissioners.[60] Until in the early 1930s improved communications made possible the direct supervision from Gisborne of the stations to its north, a Sergeant was based with the constable at Tokomaru Bay. Similarly, in Central Otago until the late 1920s, country constables were supervised by Sergeants stationed at Clyde and Lawrence. Typically they monitored prosecution files and correspondence, made periodical visits to sign the station records and observe the local constable, and provided assistance when required. Both at Tokomaru Bay and at Lawrence, the eventual removal of Sergeants aroused local concern: in essence, beneath the rhetoric of insecurity, community status rather than order was at risk.[61]

In Auckland during the 1920s, the Senior Sergeant at Newton and the Sergeants in charge of ten other stations acted as channels for all files from the District Office requiring attention by local constables – the NCOs were 'held responsible for their due attention and expeditious return'.[62] The quality of the correspondence rested on them. There were disparities in workloads and responsibility. At Ponsonby station in 1926, Sergeant Waterman supervised only four beat constables; by contrast, Sergeant J. McAlister had to oversee the sole-charge stations at Mt Albert, Mt Roskill, Kingsland, and Mt Eden South as well as six men working from Mt Eden station. Given the growing volume of correspondence, the NCOs at Newton, Mt Eden, and Newmarket became increasingly desk-bound by comparison with their counterparts in other suburbs and in small towns.

The most hard-pressed amongst the NCOs were the Senior Sergeants at the city stations, especially in Auckland and Wellington. Responsible for the discipline and work of the station, they monitored the constables' and sectional Sergeants' reports as well as the activities of the watch-house, observed constables as they paraded for shifts, and organised the duty rosters. The barracks, cells, and stables also came under their purview, but were generally inspected by the sectional Sergeants. Particularly at the busy inner-city stations, the duties were (or became) mainly 'sedentary': most of the time was spent (as Ray Henry, a former Senior Sergeant in charge at Newton station, put it) in the office 'processing, checking, and directing correspondence, briefing files and formulating charges for various offences.'[63]

Henry was not alone in seeing this as the least enjoyable period of his career. The range of responsibilities and the sheer volume of paperwork could require long hours on duty. At the central station in the main centres, 'Seniors' assisted the Sub-Inspector with the Uniform Branch prosecutions in the Magistrate's Court (this had become almost a full-time job in Auckland by 1940). In the provincial centres they conducted all the prosecutions. The workload was such that Auckland,

Wellington and Christchurch had two Senior Sergeants at the central stations by 1926. By 1939, the number of staff directly supervised by the 'Seniors' had risen (over thirteen years) from 81 to 149 in Auckland, and from 50 to 80 in Wellington.[64] Certainly, in this period, the numbers and ranks of commissioned officers at these stations had increased, but the responsibilities of Senior Sergeants remained the same. They remained the 'go-between' between the officers and the front-line police.[65]

As with the other ranks, the 'standard of efficiency in Senior Sergeants' could vary considerably.[66] This was a rank which seemed to have a disproportionate number of men in their fifties who were in ill health. Between 1923 and 1933, six died on the job.[67] It was the practice to send newly promoted Senior Sergeants to wherever a vacancy arose. Even so, fitness, energy, 'initiative and controlling power' were seen to be at a premium in the cities. The older and less active 'Seniors' tended to be transferred to smaller and relatively quiet stations. On the eve of his promotion to Senior Sergeant, for example, Donald Scott was sent as Sergeant to take charge of the Taranaki Street station in place of Senior Sergeant H.H. Butler, who was in poor health. Butler took Scott's position at the quieter Wellington South station, 'an easy station to work'.[68] Some district headquarters, such as Nelson, were seen as less demanding than a city or larger provincial station. The ageing Senior Sergeant W.J. Quinn was transferred from Rotorua to Nelson in 1928 to replace Senior Sergeant T.J. Barrett, who had died. Quinn himself died on the job at Nelson in 1930.[69] Reinstated as a Sergeant at Wellington Central in July 1930, George Bonisch spent the rest of his career as a peripatetic NCO at provincial stations: briefly under a 'Senior' at Hastings, then in charge at Port Ahuriri and Pahiatua, before becoming Senior Sergeant at Greymouth in 1939, followed by yet another transfer to Palmerston North, where he died in 1945, aged 60.[70] It was at provincial stations (Invercargill, Ashburton, and Nelson) that three Senior Sergeants were formally disciplined during the inter-war years, rather than at the main centres, where (by contrast) Sergeants' breaches of regulations were detected.[71]

Shaping patterns of policing

Like the commissioned officers overseeing them, the NCOs in charge of stations could influence the priorities and patterns of policing in their sub-districts. Again, a touchstone of their proclivities was the level of prosecutions for selling liquor without a licence, especially in a no-licence district. Some broad contrasts in policing may be observed – assuming that the actual prevalence of sly-grogging and difficulties in detecting it did not vary greatly amongst the small-town no-licence districts supervised by NCOs. Between 1921 and 1930, there were thirteen convictions of sly-groggers in Masterton and fourteen in Oamaru

– but 79 in smaller Ashburton.[72] At Masterton and Ashburton, fluctuations in prosecutions coincided with changes in control by NCOs. Over half the convictions of sly-groggers in Ashburton during the 1920s were secured between 1922 and 1925, when Senior Sergeant David Jackson was in charge. Conversely, when Sergeant T.H. Dyer took over from Sergeant J. Sweeney at Masterton in 1925, the number of prosecutions fell away. The paucity of convictions at Oamaru during the 1920s suggest an enduring pattern of 'tolerant' policing.[73] Indeed it was believed locally that the transfer of Senior Sergeant Thomas Shanahan from Oamaru in 1929 had been brought about by pressure from a Presbyterian minister who considered the police insufficiently 'vigilant'.[74]

According to his own account, Donald Scott sought to enforce the law diligently when he arrived to take charge at Oamaru in May 1929. He received 'many complaints' concerning sly-groggers, who proved 'difficult to catch'. Prosecutions increased from 1931, but the illicit activity continued seemingly unabated. Scott also took a firm hand with 'excessive drinking' at the annual Kurow races, where hundreds of thirsty men from the nearby Waitaki Hydro works made the most of a race-day liquor booth. Following Scott's objection, this 'conditional license' was withdrawn by the local Licensing Committee. As he did at other stations, Scott sought also to enhance the image of a disciplined Force: 'stiffening up ... in the matter of uniform', and insisting that 'discipline was carried out to the very letter' by the constables who attended the first sitting of the Supreme Court to be held in Oamaru. (In Wellington, he led the uniformed ranks through the streets at police funerals.)[75]

Soon after Senior Sergeant Scott returned to Wellington to take charge of Mt Cook station in May 1931, he began a series of raids on Chinese pakapoo schools and opium dens which provided a dramatic example of the effect zeal could have in influencing local patterns of policing. The Mt Cook sub-district included the congested and dilapidated housing of the inner-city Te Aro Flat, where a small population of Chinese (mainly males) was concentrated, especially around Haining Street. Here (as in Auckland's Grey Street) playing pakapoo was a long-standing and fairly constant activity, and a source of income for some whose other avenues were limited.[76] Chief Detective Tom Kemp claimed in 1923 that 'fully 100 Chinamen' in Wellington were living on the proceeds of pakapoo – 'they toil not, neither do they spin.'[77] Intermittent police raids (often coinciding with the Chinese New Year) had little apparent effect.[78]

From the late 1920s police voiced concern that pakapoo was becoming more popular amongst Europeans, with growing numbers of male manual workers joining the 'schools', and 'agents' and 'runners' selling tickets more widely. *Truth* and the *New Zealand Worker* both alleged that a 'Ring' of wealthy Chinese financed and controlled pakapoo 'banks' run by paid 'agents' in Haining Street and elsewhere, plundering 'the workers' looking for a large and speedy return on a sixpenny ticket. Many workers apparently trusted the Chinese pakapoo 'agents' who were doing a 'roaring business' in the Te Aro area by the early 1930s. By contrast with the growing number of legal lotteries (art unions) from 1929, the pakapoo tickets were cheaper and the 'draws' were made more quickly, sometimes within twenty minutes. 'Victims' (it was said) frequently played until they were 'cleaned out.' From moralists, self-interested organisers of art unions, and indeed from amongst Chinese themselves, there were pressures on police to suppress pakapoo.[79]

Similar and more insidious fears were also aired (mainly in *Truth*) about the morally and racially corrupting influence of Chinese opium use – particularly to lure white women for sex.[80] By the early 1930s, prejudice against Chinese 'opium dens' was both long-standing and deep-seated. Though Europeans were rarely, if ever, actually found amongst Chinese opium smokers, the dens were seen as a potential source of corruption.[81] Since the Opium Prohibition Act of 1901 and its amendment in 1902, the possession and smoking of opium had been prohibited. (Permits could be issued for opium that was not suitable for smoking, but not to Chinese.) Police were empowered to search without a warrant premises occupied by Chinese (but not those of Europeans) where opium smoking was suspected. From 1910, the onus of proof that opium had been obtained legally lay with those charged with illegal possession. Definitions of offences were broadened and penalties increased in the Dangerous Drugs Act 1927. Police shared with customs officers responsibility for enforcing the law.[82] In the first four years of activity recorded by the police (1904 to 1908) nearly 300 charges of possessing or smoking opium were laid against Chinese. This level of activity was not maintained. During the 1920s, the annual number of prosecutions fluctuated but never exceeded 45. Then in 1932 the number charged with opium offences (including those merely found where opium was being smoked) soared to 129. This higher level of police activity, which reached a peak of 132 charges in 1935, was maintained until 1937.[83]

The growth in police prosecutions of Chinese in the early 1930s could be interpreted as a sign of increased xenophobia in straitened times.[84] More plausibly, increased attention to opium dens reflected official concern that the 'menace of opium' continued to exist. Evidence from raids in 1931 and 1932 seemed to contradict official optimism in 1930 that police and customs officers had been effective in curbing the supply of opium from across the Tasman.[85] Yet there was no concerted countrywide campaign against opium dens. Much depended on the zeal and priorities of individual officers. Donald Scott apparently acted on his own initiative.[86] The raids he organised and led in Wellington between December 1931 and May 1934, and the increased number in

Auckland during the next three years – coinciding with his transfer there as Sub-Inspector – contributed disproportionately to the growth in charges against Chinese. In 1932 and 1933 the Senior Sergeant's prosecutions brought £2,662 in fines on those playing pakapoo, and a further £1,819 in fines for opium offences.[87]

With respect to pakapoo, Scott's prosecutions (and the heaviest fines) focused on the Chinese occupiers of the premises, who were charged with keeping a common gaming house. His preparations for the raids were systematic. A shabbily dressed constable was sent to enter the premises, mark a ticket and observe the activity involving both Europeans and Chinese. A day or so later he returned to see if he 'had a win', and bought another ticket. After 27 premises had been visited, Scott received his first report and obtained search warrants, taking 'great care' that the occupiers received no hint of what impended. Constables were assembled at the Taranaki Street station rather than at Mt Cook, and not told what they were wanted for until the last moment. Then they were despatched in vehicles, two being dropped off for each house. And so 'within twenty minutes, all these pakapoo dens were in the hands of the police.' Evidence was noted, and exhibits were taken along with those arrested to the Mt Cook station. Some were bailed by friends, while others remained in the police cells until they were brought before the Magistrate's Court. All Chinese were fingerprinted and had 'their real identity' established before the court hearing.[88] By October 1933, the persistence and frequency of Scott's raids (and those of detectives in Auckland) caused *Truth* to complain that 'whole armies of police' were engaged in 'running modest gamblers to earth while dangerous criminals get away with big jobs'.[89]

Detecting opium smokers did not require guile. Many of the older Chinese were 'heavy smokers', and local police knew their 'smoking houses' in Haining Street (Grey Street in Auckland). When Scott thought the time opportune, he led a raid by uniformed men, usually after midnight. Carrying this out had become a 'rather more difficult matter' by the 1930s. The premises were usually well-barricaded, and police had to force an entrance with picks, axes, crowbars, saws, or even a timber-worker's 'stumping-jack', breaking down doors or cutting holes through a wall or the roof.[90] To prevent evidence being destroyed in the fire that was always burning, the raiding party sometimes poured buckets of water down the chimney. The search for opium could lead to floors and walls being torn apart. After one such raid, the inside of a house was 'a sorry spectacle'.[91] Such reports moved Commissioner Wohlmann to direct that 'no more liberty should be taken' in entering Chinese premises than those occupied by Europeans – though he added ambiguously that this did not apply when entry was made under 'statutory authority' (as the opium and pakapoo raids were).[92] There is little evidence that police practice changed.

For the convictions he secured against those charged with opium offences, Senior Sergeant Scott received about £20 in rewards from the Customs Department (other police received lesser amounts) – but this was not his main stimulus to zeal.[93] For Scott, diligence was the norm, albeit reinforced by the prevailing attitudes towards Chinese. He was persistent, repeatedly raiding the same premises. Addicts were easy targets. After the third raid on a house within six months in 1933, Scott called on the Health Department to have it 'cleaned up' – to little effect.[94] As with the pakapoo raids, *Truth* became critical of the 'endless series of raids on Chinese opium smokers', which seemed 'to continue as if they are to be a permanent fortnightly episode in the history of the city of Wellington'. Such work was 'futile'; there were 'more serious aspects of crime' to be tackled.'[95] Even so, Donald Scott was to be remembered as the man who 'set Wellington's pakapoo and opium den "industries" on the decline.'[96]

Monitoring detective work

Early in April 1935, Sub-Inspector Scott organised and led simultaneous raids by uniformed police on four pakapoo schools in inner-city Auckland.[97] This was unusual. In all the main centres, with the exception of Wellington in the early 1930s, catching opium smokers and pakapoo players was detectives' work. The amount of time spent on such work was usually determined by the Chief Detective, though there was scope for initiative from individual detectives.[98] A Chief Detective (or Senior Detective) was equivalent in rank to a uniformed Senior Sergeant, and his responsibilities were broadly the same: to arrange and supervise the work of his staff, prosecute cases in the Magistrate's Court (where a Sub-Inspector or another NCO did not do so), and report daily to the Inspector.[99] In practice, however, the pattern of supervision differed because of differences in the nature of detective and beat work, and in the role of Sergeants.

Detecting offenders required different and more flexible rhythms of work than those of preventing offences by visible and routine patrolling of a beat. Whereas the absence of crime was taken to be a measure of successful patrolling, securing a conviction was the measure of successful detection. Whereas beats were timed to allow close supervision, a detective's work patterns were shaped by the files to be dealt with and were inherently unpredictable. Strict regulation of detectives' work routines could be inhibiting, and was difficult to achieve in practice.[100] A detective was both allowed more autonomy and expected to show more initiative than the man on the beat. Even the most junior detectives in the main centres could be left largely to work on their own.

Overall, then, the role of a Detective Sergeant in the main centres was different from that of his uniformed counterpart, a fact epitomised by the much higher ratio of detective NCOs to detectives (more than 1 to 3) than of uniformed NCOs to constables (1 to 7 or 8). A Detective

Sergeant did not monitor the work of detectives or acting detectives, unless he was the senior member of a team. Even then his role was not so much supervision as that of senior co-worker and leader – allocating tasks and (perhaps) giving advice, taking the initiative in interviewing (and obtaining confessions), with his junior(s) in support, and providing an example to the less experienced. Attainment of the rank of Detective Sergeant was a mark of experience and seniority, rather than entailing the supervision and control of subordinates.[101] Accordingly it was usual in inter-war years for the sole detective or the senior partner of two in a provincial centre to be a Detective Sergeant, or to have equivalent experience.[102] Since there was no defined span of control for Detective Sergeants, their numbers fluctuated.

Concern was expressed in Auckland newspapers when, between 1932 and 1934, the number of Detective Sergeants in that district fell from seven to one: the death of one, the transfer of three others to become uniformed Sergeants in charge of stations, and of two more to be Detective Sergeants in other centres, was perceived to represent a substantial loss of experience. Detective Sergeant A.H. McHugh, with twenty years' experience in the local Detective Office, was now the only front-line NCO in a staff of twenty detectives, in addition to three acting detectives and a number of constables who were attached to the office. The burden of supervision and control lay with Sub-Inspector Sweeney and Senior Detective S.G. Hall, who had only recently been transferred to Auckland.[103] Critics who saw the Auckland detectives as ineffective pointed to the lack of NCOs. There were other perspectives, however.

Senior officers were well aware of the key problem of supervision inherent in detective work. As the Police Regulations put it: 'it cannot be too deeply impressed upon [detectives] that however anxious the Government may be for the conviction of criminals, even the greatest delinquents are not to be brought to justice by unjustifiable means'.[104] Officers sought to mitigate the difficulties of control by admonition and by recruiting men who demonstrated zeal, initiative and integrity. Even so, the process of learning on the job – the methods, informal practices and codes; the emphasis on success; the milieux of detective work, with its loyalties to workmates, covert contacts with those prepared to offer bribes and seek trade-offs, and limited resources to enforce laws (those relating to gambling and opium use) which were consistently flouted – provided the potential for lax, illegal or corrupt practice.[105] Transfers of long-standing detectives, as in Auckland during the early 1930s, might dilute experience, but they could serve also to infuse new attitudes, break old loyalties, and weaken dubious local practices. Much still depended, nonetheless, on the Senior Detectives and the commissioned officers overseeing the detectives.

Before Sub-Inspectors were appointed in Wellington (from 1924 to 1926, then from 1930), Auckland (from 1930) and Christchurch (from

1940), to take 'immediate charge' of the local Detective Office, Senior Detectives had this role, which was equivalent in 'responsibility' to that of the Sub-Inspectors overseeing the Uniform Branch in the main centres.[106] Ultimately, as the role of the Sub-Inspectors was defined in 1930, 'the efficiency of the detective police largely depends on the force of character, example, and personality' of the supervisors. They were to 'take a keen personal interest in the administration' so as to know what their staff were doing. They had to 'carefully note' the work of their staff in order to detect 'any apparent standing faults in their methods', lack of the 'necessary qualifications', signs of lethargy or apathy, or 'absence of success for a lengthy period tending to show unsuitability.' The 'reversion to uniform' of unsuitable men was to be recommended by the officer in charge – the 'good of the Service', not 'personal consideration', was the key. Emphasis was placed on both effective detective work and the 'proper observance of Police Regulations' – though in practice there could be a tension between these two requirements.[107] The Chief Detective was to be 'particularly careful to so apportion the work as not to give rise to any suspicion of favouritism.' Cooperation amongst staff and with 'the general Police' was to be obtained.[108]

The monitoring of detectives' practice (as with much uniformed police practice) was essentially retrospective and indirect, resting on verbal reports, record-keeping, and comments and complaints from those they dealt with. Record-keeping consisted predominantly of written reports on inquiries, prosecution files 'briefed' with statements taken from witnesses and suspects, and the office diary, which in theory provided a means of observing work patterns. In the Auckland Detective Office during the late 1920s, it was the practice for entries to be made in the diary by each detective at the end of each week, and it thus provided only a general outline of how his time had been spent. (The diary was scanned and initialled each week by the commissioned officer in charge.) Similarly, written reports were generally only presented to the Chief Detective at the end of an inquiry, or perhaps weekly if it was drawn out. For Auckland detectives in the late 1920s there was 'no rule' that they provide regular written reports. For important cases, however, they were likely to report verbally to the Chief Detective each day. The 'Chief' in turn reported each morning to the commissioned officer in charge, and then usually went off to the Magistrate's Court to prosecute cases. Such was the volume of the Auckland Chief Detective's paperwork that close supervision of the conduct of most inquiries was impossible.[109]

The readiness of witnesses and suspects to complain was thus crucial in uncovering possible malpractice. In 1927, Chief Detective James Cummings followed up a complaint from a man on probation for theft that he was being blackmailed by Detective C.A. Lambert. Using a Uniform Branch Sergeant from a suburban station, Cummings set a trap, and Lambert accepted marked notes from the complainant. Instead of being charged in an open court with blackmail, the detective pleaded guilty in a closed departmental disciplinary inquiry to breaching Police Regulations by accepting a gratuity. Though he was on the verge of promotion to Detective Sergeant and had a 'creditable record', his integrity was now suspect and he was dismissed.[110] The publicity given to the Lambert case was exceptional. The detective claimed he had been 'framed' and issued a statement to the press. Whether Lambert was a 'bad apple' cannot be determined. Records no longer exist of disciplinary hearings,[111] or of the extent to which complaints were followed up, or of the numbers of detectives asked to resign, disciplined or 'reverted to uniform' because of suspicions against them. By contrast with the Lambert case, it seems that allegations from those viewed as self-interested suspects about detectives' methods of gaining evidence or confessions were generally not taken seriously. Moreover, as a Crown counsel, A.E. Currie, observed at the inquiry into police conduct in investigating the death of Elsie Walker, 'Exactly how far the police are justified in going, is difficult to say in general terms.' Certainly, in 1929, Chief Detective Alfred Hammond did not 'attach any importance' to, made no inquiries from his staff about, and did not draw the attention of Inspector Hollis to allegations made at the Elsie Walker inquest that detectives had acted improperly in seeking to search William Bayly's property without a warrant and obtain information from him 'under a seal of confidence'.[112]

The public record suggests that the Chief Detectives' and commissioned officers' confidence in most of their staff was not misplaced: few allegations of malpractice for financial gain were aired, nor were detectives publicly disciplined for using 'unjustified means'. The widespread confidence of the law-abiding in the probity of detectives was apparently maintained not so much by the work of supervision as by the integrity of most staff and the covert management of indiscipline when it was detected.

Relationships between ranks

While the nature of detective work bred its own loyalties and sense of fellow feeling, relationships between ranks in the Detective Branch differed only in degree from those elsewhere amongst police. Again the size of station and personalities of supervisors influenced the quality of relationships. At most stations, nonetheless, there were public rituals of farewell, associated with the promotion and transfer or retirement of officers and NCOs.

After three years as Inspector at the Dunedin station, James Cummings was transferred at the end of 1931 to special duties in the Commissioner's office. At his farewell, to which reporters were invited, 'glowing tributes to the worth of Inspector Cummings as a police officer and a comrade were paid by speakers representative of every branch and rank' of the city and suburban police. Typically, Superintendent William Eccles drew lessons for his staff from Cummings' 'swift passage through the ranks': 'every member should bear in mind' that the 'most wonderful thing in the Police Force was service'. The Inspector 'was a model for every young man in the Force': his position 'could be regarded merely as the just and due reward for devotion to duty, sober habits and enthusiasm for his job.' J.C. Willis, who had recently retired as Superintendent at Dunedin, reiterated Cummings' 'exceptional ability' and noted too that he 'was a worker all the time' – 'a policeman for the whole 24 hours', which all members should be if they wished 'to get on'. Willis also voiced another theme common at farewells: that of the ideal supervisor. He had 'heard it said' the Inspector was 'a hard man'. And perhaps he was, 'in the view of slackers', but 'no man who was keen to do his job and anxious to do his best ever found him hard.' Certainly Cummings was a 'disciplinarian' – without discipline the police would 'merely be a rabble' – but he was 'quite sure that the young men would all miss Mr Cummings' kindly help and assistance.'

Then, in order of seniority, others gave their plaudits. Chief Detective A.G. Quartermain, who had been Cummings' superior twenty years earlier, continued Willis's theme: the Inspector had been 'scrupulously fair to his comrades and subordinates'. So too did Senior Sergeant Donald Cameron, who had first met Cummings 'many years ago when they were comrades in the firing squad at the interment of Mr Richard J. Seddon'. Cameron thanked Cummings for his 'ready assistance at all times', and the 'just and fair treatment he had always accorded to everyone under him. Even defaulters found him just and never harsh.' He had won the 'loyalty and confidence of his men.' Three Sergeants, a Detective Sergeant, and three constables then expressed 'the regret of the rank and file' at the Inspector's departure. James Cummings was presented with 'a large easy chair' and a gold pencil, as well as a 'handsome handbag' for his wife. He, in turn, replied with conventional expressions of gratitude, 'advice to the young men', and the usual flattering of the local esprit de corps: 'after long experience in both Wellington and Auckland ... he had yet to find a more efficient body of police than those in Dunedin'.[113] Whatever the degree of warmth and sincerity, the rhetoric and the gifts at the station farewells expressed the camaraderie of an occupational community (or what Charles Lopdell called 'fraternal associations') that transcended the social distance of rank and marked the participants off from 'outsiders'.[114]

Looking back, retired men who had derived satisfaction from their careers saw substance in the rhetoric. Some saw themselves as forthright but respectful, and felt they had 'got on well' with their superiors; 'if one carried out one's duties efficiently, and behaved himself, there was usually no problem with superiors'.[115] While commissioned officers were generally 'a race apart' from constables, NCOs in particular could be held in some regard.[116] Senior Sergeant (later Inspector) E.J. Carroll of Rotorua was remembered as the 'Old Senior' who had 'wonderful thought for the men in the front line' when they were called out at night to an emergency. He 'never forgot to see that these men were looked after and he not only worked himself, but he used to have his wife up making hot scones and these he would take round with hot tea to the different men and keep the men well posted as to what was doing.'[117] Similarly, Senior Sergeant George Bonisch and Sergeant Robert McRobie at Greymouth were 'always more than helpful to a young Police Constable', earning his 'utmost respect'.[118]

By the 1940s, some new recruits, especially 'mature' men in their late twenties, probably found relationships with sectional Sergeants to be friendlier than those two decades earlier. At Dunedin during the war years, some of the Sergeants would 'spend hours' walking the beat with a new constable, 'talking about Police work generally' and teaching the craft 'in a practical manner'.[119] But while relationships with superiors may have been 'very good', a constable who was appointed at Blenheim in 1942 conceded, 'truth to tell, my respect for them was motivated more or less by a certain fear of them and the powers they wielded over a man's destiny, and of course their superior knowledge of what was right and what was wrong.'[120]

Policemen with initiative were often frustrated by the strict adherence to rules and cautious attitudes and actions (or inaction) of their superiors. George Donnelly, an independent spirit, found that 'alot of men were a bit frightened to make a decision in case they were a bit off line .... One night a Commissioner had me on about the regulations and my reply was that the regulations were for people who could not think.' Donnelly respected Senior Sergeant G.B. Edwards, a 'good boss' who had taught Donnelly the skills of beat policing at the Depot, and continued to take an interest in 'his boys'. But, as Superintendent in Wellington, Edwards was (in Donnelly's view) 'a real old time cop and did not want any trouble with the Commissioner'.[121] Even in the 1950s, as one Senior Sergeant saw it, ' "all down the line" ' was 'the attitude': each rank 'wanted to coast along undisturbed and did not have the fortitude to demand from a senior authority what was actually essential.'[122]

Constables who were 'inclined to be a bit wayward', as was D.R. Sugrue in the early years of his service, did not 'take kindly to strict discipline'. Thus Sugrue appeared before his Superintendents 'on a few occasions for minor breaches, such as not working the beat to time ..., and ticking off a Sergeant.' He 'appreciated the fatherly advice only for the minor breaches, but not the £1 fine for ticking off the Sergeant – however it was worth it.' In later years, when young policemen appeared before Superintendent Sugrue on minor breaches, he remembered his own past and 'was lenient where possible'.[123] Also inclined to be wayward, Wally Hammond was 'on the mat' a number of times during his fourteen years as a constable in Wellington. Typically, he developed strong views about his supervisors, distinguishing the 'nice chaps' from the 'nasty buggers': Sub-Inspector John Lander and Sergeant George Paine, for example, were liked because they were seen as understanding, even flexible; but not so Sergeant Peter Munro, Senior Sergeant Donald Scott, or Sub-Inspector Lopdell, amongst others.[124]

Thus the rhetoric of station farewells concealed mixed feelings. A 'strain of bitterness'[125] ran through the recollections of some former policemen. Despite enjoying the camaraderie of the Auckland Detective Office in the early 1930s, Charles Belton came 'to realise that detectives were not trusted to any large extent by the senior officers' – a personal feeling probably stemming from his superiors' reaction to his complaints and suggestions for improvement.[126] W.T. Thom could not accept the way he was treated by his superiors when, a few months after he had led a deputation to the Superintendent at Dunedin in 1934 'to discuss what I considered was a hardship on the Sergeants doing shift work', he was convicted at a departmental inquiry of writing an anonymous letter (of which he claimed to have no knowledge) and reduced in rank to constable for the rest of his career.[127] Policemen who were not 'slackers' might have cause to rue the inflexibility and suspicious nature of supervisors. To some in the rank and file, the rhetoric of a station farewell might seem hollow.

Crises in supervision

At times, crises in supervision meant there were no formal farewells. Such crises rarely came to public attention. Those that did were at the smaller provincial stations and had common characteristics. Those charged with breaches of regulations, or worse, found support amongst other staff and brought counter-charges against the officer in charge, thereby fatally undermining confidence in him. While differing circumstances might produce a crisis (it was not simply a matter of a supervisor's personality or poor judgement), the outcome was the same: the officer in charge of the station was transferred, as were other staff.

At Ashburton, Senior Sergeant I.H. Mathieson's relations with his staff were ostensibly good until early 1927, when he charged several of his constables with breaches of regulations. This was apparently perceived as a breach of loyalty, and the constables then made allegations which turned the tables on their supervisor. They not only alleged that Mathieson had sought to influence their statements, but also revealed informal practices that were probably long-standing, such as 'improper use of Government stores' – using coal in the Senior Sergeant's house – and permitting official stamps to be used to pay for long-distance telephone calls contrary to Police Regulations. Eventually, after an internal disciplinary hearing and an appeal (during which most of the charges were dismissed), Commissioner McIlveney reduced Mathieson to the rank of constable and transferred him to Matamata; three constables were also transferred, one to Port Chalmers and two to Christchurch, where they soon resigned. Though the division amongst the Ashburton staff had made Mathieson's position untenable, and Commissioner McIlveney found the breaches of regulations intolerable, the Senior Sergeant had not lost the confidence of 'influential' people in the country town. A petition against the severity of his punishment led to his eventual reinstatement as Sergeant (at Hamilton), and then as Senior Sergeant (at Timaru).[128]

If the rhetoric at his farewell from Gisborne in July 1934 had substance, Inspector Lott O'Halloran was a popular officer. The 'highest tributes' were paid him by staff he had supervised for six years. Senior Sergeant H.C.D. Wade set the theme that was echoed by others of all ranks: O'Halloran's 'treatment of his staff had been such that every man who had served under him had always been of good behaviour and carried out his duties efficiently'; he had been 'fair and considerate'. In reply, the Inspector commented that his relations with staff had been of 'a most cordial nature' – it 'had always been his belief that one of the first duties of a police inspector was to help and encourage the men.'[129] With such warm feelings, the 62 year old officer looked forward to a final posting in charge of the quiet Timaru District, where his predecessor had just retired. Visiting the out-stations there would be less arduous; and the existence of a Timaru police rugby team seemed evidence of a strong esprit de corps.[130]

Though the details are cloudy, Inspector O'Halloran soon found 'some changes to be necessary for the working' of the Timaru station; these produced 'a very decided improvement'. Two constables were disciplined 'for minor breaches'.[131] About the same time, O'Halloran investigated allegations that some local police were 'making a levy' on bookmakers.[132] Whatever the source of their discontent, some Timaru police made allegations against their Inspector that cast serious doubt on his 'competency', especially on 'grounds of character', to 'exercise his high office in the district.'[133] There was no official admission of a crisis of supervision but, after an internal departmental inquiry in May 1935, Inspector O'Halloran was transferred to a desk job in Dunedin for his last eighteen months of service, while five staff (including two office staff and a detective) were moved to other districts.[134] A new officer had thus unsettled some existing practices to the extent of breaching the loyalty of some staff.

O'Halloran's successor at Gisborne in 1934, Inspector Henry Martin, also 'put the back up' of some constables and NCOs at the town station, though in different circumstances.[135] This crisis of supervision was precipitated when, in August 1935, Martin heard four charges laid against a married constable, R.C. Hendren, for 'scandalous conduct' in associating with a married woman who was portrayed as sexually immoral. Though the degree of 'scandal' was debatable, Martin found

the charges proved and the breach of regulations so serious as to warrant
a recommendation of dismissal. That five constables, some with long
service in Gisborne, were prepared to give evidence for the defence
indicated the developing division of loyalties. In October, an appeal
heard by a board consisting of the local magistrate, a JP, and Hamilton's
Inspector Lopdell upheld two of the charges but recommended, instead
of dismissal, a reduction of five years' seniority and pay. There matters
might have rested, but for a counter-attack on Inspector Martin mounted
by the defence at the appeal hearing: a fellow constable, H. Scandrett,
joined Hendren in claiming to have seen Martin drop a woman off at
a local hotel early one morning. Martin (like O'Halloran at Timaru)
faced allegations of sexual impropriety from his staff. After Lopdell
investigated, Hendren was again charged, along with Scandrett, with
prevarication and/or making a false statement. At another disciplinary
hearing, begun in December and then adjourned until April 1936,
Inspector Lander (from Wanganui) found the charges proved and
recommended the dismissal of both constables.

   In the meantime, at the instigation of Constable Scandrett, a woman
began a private prosecution against Martin for 'wilful indecent exposure'
(while drying himself after swimming) at the local beach. The Inspector
now went on leave and Lopdell returned again to Gisborne, taking
charge while investigating the new allegations, which proved to be
flimsy. The private prosecution was abandoned in February 1936, but
the damage had been done; rumours magnified as police inquiries
dragged on and publicity was given to the private prosecution. At the
second disciplinary hearing in April 1936, Senior Sergeant H.C.D. Wade
and a former officer in charge at Gisborne, D.D. Hutton (now a JP),
were witnesses for the defence. Early in 1936, Wade was transferred to
Napier temporarily before being posted to Petone. In July he returned
to be formally farewelled at the Gisborne station. Martin was absent,
while Hendren and Scandrett were present, along with others who had
sided with them. Further transfers (and the eventual dismissal of Hendren
and Scandrett in September 1936) left 'few of the old familiar faces on
the "beat" '.[136] A new officer in charge (Inspector G.B. Edwards) did
not have to contend with long-standing local loyalties. When Henry
Martin was transferred in September 1936 to become Inspector in charge
of the Uniform Branch in Christchurch, there were no public tributes
from his staff and no eulogy in the local paper.[137]

   In some circumstances, the loyalty of staff to their officers might be
broken. Effective supervision required a balance between the observance
of rules and the need to maintain staff morale. It was not just a matter
of when the rules should be applied, but also of how they were applied.
A conviction for a breach of the Regulations could be accepted so long
as the officers themselves followed the rules, acted fairly, and applied
penalties that were not perceived as Draconian. Effective supervision
thus entailed a cautious approach to the task. Tried and true methods

were preferred to innovation. 'Strict compliance with orders' remained 'the line of safety'. Overall, in fact, a conservative pattern of supervision did much to shape a fundamental stability in the system of policing – as was revealed in the broad patterns of recorded offences that depended on police initiative, which was often exercised with 'a wise discretion'. Discipline and morale, and overall public confidence in the integrity of police, were maintained. Even so, this cautious approach to supervision was increasingly challenged from the mid-1930s by the changing social milieu of policing and by the advent of an organised voice for the rank and file – the Police Association.

CHAPTER 10

Political Surveillance (1919–35)

At the end of January 1919 Commissioner O'Donovan sent a confidential memorandum to his officers in charge of districts:

> In view of the fact that considerable industrial and other unrest is reported from other countries and that such may extend to this Dominion it is necessary that special precautions be taken to keep in touch with the movements and actions of persons of revolutionary tendencies who are already here, or who may arrive, with a view to ascertaining whether they are advocating lawlessness or disorder or anything likely to lead to such.[1]

The meetings of such persons were to be attended. Any information of 'value' was to be immediately reported to Police Headquarters in Wellington; in addition, fortnightly reports were to be sent. In April, O'Donovan ordered that detectives in each district compile an 'alphabetical list' of individuals who had 'extreme revolutionary, socialistic or I.W.W. ideas or tendencies and who as such would be likely to cause disorder or lawlessness.'[2]

Thus began routine peacetime political surveillance by police. It probably did not become systematic until September 1920, when O'Donovan ordered that 'increased attention be given' to the extent to which revolutionary organisations existed and revolutionary propaganda was being disseminated.[3] A detective in each of the four main centres was selected for full-time surveillance work. From this point, the regular monthly reports and special reports from detectives were kept in a separate registry of secret files. Taken together, these new arrangements suggest that post-war surveillance was no mere continuation of the police monitoring of opposition to the war effort between 1914 and 1918.[4] Perceived threats to public order during the transition to peace had brought political surveillance to a new level.

Bureaucratic rivalry

Commissioner O'Donovan's initiatives in January 1919 and September 1920 were shaped by his own bureaucratic concerns. They were independent of political direction and of the interests of the Defence Department, which was also developing, independently, its system of intelligence. Nor, it seems, were O'Donovan's initiatives shaped by demands from London. Early in December 1919, the High Commissioner in London had telegraphed the Prime Minister, Massey, with a request from Basil Thomson, the 'Director of Intelligence' at Scotland House, for periodical reports on 'extreme movements' or local revolutionary organisations, in exchange for any information that Thomson had on 'plans for promoting sedition in New Zealand'.[5] Assistant Commissioner Thomson headed the operations of the Special Branch of the London Metropolitan Police, and was not connected with MI5, the military wing of Britain's security service, which was based at the War Office in London.[6] Massey, then Minister in charge of the Police,[7] was apparently unaware of the distinction between police and military intelligence gathering, and also of O'Donovan's earlier initiative regarding political surveillance. He passed Thomson's request on to the Defence Department. It was symptomatic of the bureaucratic distinctions (and rivalries) in both London and Wellington that General E.W.C. Chaytor promised to send periodical reports to the War Office, not to Thomson.[8]

The Defence Department had already moved to better organise its intelligence. In August 1919, headquarters staff decided to establish a card index covering a number of categories, notably aliens and 'persons using influence to establish Bolshevism'.[9] This information would be the basis of monthly reports to the War Office. However, the small Permanent Staff did not have the resources to undertake systematic surveillance of people whom they considered potentially dangerous.[10] Nor was it wise (as an Australian military intelligence officer advised) for 'the military branch to openly deal with labour & industrial matters'.[11] The Defence planners therefore sought the cooperation of the Police. At the beginning of February 1920, General G.S. Richardson, in charge of administration at Defence Headquarters, asked Commissioner O'Donovan if they could meet 'to arrange a Central Committee for Intelligence with Agents throughout the Dominion'. He proposed that a monthly report be made either 'conjointly by you and I or [by] the Central Committee', and forwarded to the Prime Minister and to the War Office in London.[12] Clearly the local military authorities were thinking in terms of the British security system, with its supposedly close links between MI5 and the Special Branch.

In mid-February, General Chaytor informed the Director of Intelligence at the War Office that a committee comprising Commissioner O'Donovan and General Richardson 'had been appointed' to organise 'an Intelligence system for New Zealand'.[13] This was premature. At that time O'Donovan was taking his own steps to coordinate the surveillance of literature that could be seditious, by seeking the cooperation of the Post Office and the Customs Department.[14] Having ensured that the Police were now at the centre of domestic surveillance activity, O'Donovan met Richardson late in June. Again Richardson proposed the formation of an Intelligence Committee which would decide who and what should be watched.[15]

To this proposal O'Donovan was very cool. He saw political surveillance as a police responsibility which only a shortage of manpower had prevented from being 'developed'. Even so, at this time the Commissioner still felt that there was 'insufficient of such work to engage the sole attention of one detective' in any district outside Auckland and Wellington. At these two ports, detectives (working with Customs officers) were needed to provide constant surveillance of overseas travellers. More significantly, O'Donovan was opposed to the suggestion that a 'Central Committee' should supervise police surveillance and provide regular reports to the government and the War Office. He did not think 'our Government would desire regular reports of a general nature.'[16] Nor, it seems, did the government get such reports during the inter-war years – by contrast with the weekly Special Branch reports received by the British Cabinet from April 1919.[17]

The autonomy of the Police was the nub of the issue. O'Donovan feared that, through a Central Committee, the military authorities would have full access to all police reports. They 'would soon control the whole position & could send everything to the War Office'. The Commissioner wished to trade secrets, but on his own terms. An apparent willingness by the military to supply information did not give them the right to see police reports: 'We must continue to maintain full control over all secret information obtained by our officers; no persons military or otherwise should be entitled to see anything'. O'Donovan did not believe that Scotland Yard was working closely with MI5 in London: the Special Branch 'probably realise that faulty handling of secret information would only reveal the identity of the informants, and that it would be a case of experts obtaining information & handing it over to amateurs'. Nor did he see any 'alliance' between the Police and the military authorities in Sydney. Accordingly, O'Donovan did not wish to provide lists of 'undesirables' who were departing the country for Australia: 'We have all to lose by such an arrangement as Australian undesirables will get into this Dominion whilst some of ours will be sent back'.[18] Thus the Intelligence Committee was stillborn. Bureaucratic suspicion and self-interest limited cooperation,[19] and gave the Police Force the dominant role in political surveillance between 1919 and 1939, by contrast with the situation in Australia and Britain.[20]

Sources of concern

Given Commissioner O'Donovan's definition of the police role in 1920 as that of a preventive force defending constitutional authority,[21] it was logical for the Police to seek any threats to that authority. Increasingly from early 1919, such threats were seen as coming from two overlapping sources: 'industrial unrest' and 'Bolshevism'. By contrast to the concerns of the Defence Department, the Police showed little interest before 1938 in spies or possible threats to the country's military security, but focused instead on potential threats to public order from trade union militancy and those preaching class war. O'Donovan's concerns paralleled those of his counterparts in Britain, Australia, Canada and the USA.[22]

O'Donovan's first directive concerning systematic political surveillance had followed the appearance, in January 1919, of an Alliance of Labour dominated by the national unions of waterfront and transport workers, who were soon joined by the seamen and the miners.[23] Here, it seemed, was a powerful combination whose leaders spoke in militant terms. A concerted use of the strike weapon appeared likely in 1919. Indeed the possibility of a general strike conjured up images of the disorder of 1913, underlining the need for adequate intelligence which would allow precautionary measures to be taken. Though severe legal curbs on picketing had been introduced in 1913, both employers and the Police still expected the militant unions to resist the use of so-called 'free labour'. The Police approach was not merely pragmatic; it was also legalistic. Since 1913 the concept of sedition had been expanded (by wartime regulations made permanent in 1920) to cover strikes in industries deemed 'essential to the public welfare'.[24] Close observation was thus necessary to determine whether an offence was being committed. Above all, in 1919 and 1920, O'Donovan was sensitive to employers' fears that the ultimate purpose of the Alliance of Labour was the establishment of One Big Union and worker control of industry. Potentially then, in the eyes of police, the Alliance of Labour was a revolutionary organisation in the syndicalist tradition represented by the Industrial Workers of the World (IWW), which was then apparently regaining its strength across the Tasman.[25]

Anxieties engendered by union restiveness were magnified by mounting fears of revolutionary socialism, or what was loosely termed 'Bolshevism'. Between 1918 and 1920 an upsurge of unrest and revolutionary movements in Britain and Europe reverberated in New Zealand. In the month preceding O'Donovan's directive at the end of January 1919, signs of instability mounted in Britain: coal miners voted to strike; engineers on 'Red' Clydeside began a general strike; 20,000 troops refused orders at Calais; sailors hauled the red flag up the masthead of a warship at Milford Haven.[26] As the Legislative Councillor J.T. Paul put it in March 1919, the germ of a new disease, 'Bolshevitis', had entered New Zealand 'through the cables' – the afflicted conservatives 'believed that everything opposed to their beliefs was Bolshevism'.[27] At this time, for example, the Te Awamutu borough council, concerned about 'rampant' unrest abroad and the rhetoric of 'Labour Leaders' at home, informed the Minister of Defence of its fears of 'the turbulent faction which is at present in a state of agitation'.[28]

For its part, the Reform government led by Massey (the wartime National government broke up in August 1919) banned literature which it saw as seditious, and in October passed both an amendment to the Police Offences Act containing a section aimed at anyone who 'incites, encourages, or procures disorder, violence, or lawlessness',[29] and the Undesirable Immigrants Exclusion Bill, which enabled the government to prohibit from landing or to deport non-residents who (as Massey put it) were 'disaffected, disloyal, or dangerous', particularly those who 'favour Bolshevism and I.W.W.-ism and who have sympathies with revolutionary socialism'.[30]

The government's actions probably did not stem from the results of police surveillance, given Massey's apparent unawareness of O'Donovan's initiatives. Rather, it seems that the legislation (which made permanent some of the wartime regulations) reflected calculations of administrative convenience and political advantage, as well as a touch of panic. As it turned out, systematic political surveillance eventually bred a greater sense of realism (amongst police at least) about the prospects of revolution in this country.

Even so, Labour rhetoric continued to be militant and disturbing in 1920.[31] Tension mounted, especially when a major strike encompassing a variety of unions was expected. Early in September, the Secretary of Labour (on behalf of his Minister) asked the Commissioner if the movements of Jim Roberts, the leader of the Alliance of Labour, could be watched 'for a few weeks'.[32] The next day a Wellington detective reported presciently that 'Roberts is not regarded as an extremist'.[33] Nonetheless, O'Donovan ordered that unions be watched for any strikes which might develop into 'revolutionary disturbances'. Strikers' plans were to be monitored so as to determine 'what areas, buildings, or property should be especially guarded'.[34] It is in this context that Commissioner O'Donovan's second and more detailed directive was issued, marking the effective beginning of the systematic surveillance of 'Revolutionary Organisations and Propaganda'.

The Defence Department made its own assessment of the current tensions and sent it to O'Donovan on 23 September. This concluded that 'Labour Extremists' imbued with 'Bolshevik' theories were 'organised to employ violence' during strikes 'to enforce their demands'. It was 'reasonable to assume ... that the authorities would be required to deal with outbreaks of Bolshevism, and strikes on a large scale in New Zealand.'[35] This gloomy forecast shaped O'Donovan's thinking in the short term at least, especially as Defence staff warned that (apart from logistical support) military aid would 'not be available in the event of labour troubles', and that 'it is well known that the present strength of the Civil Police is inadequate to cope' with the scale of the 'disturbances' envisaged.[36] Late in September, therefore, the Commissioner asked the military authorities to supply camp equipment for 5,250 'auxiliary police', with an increased provision in December after the Arbitration Court awarded a smaller cost of living bonus than had been expected, and the unions' advocate predicted 'great industrial strife' as a result.[37] Gradually, as the monthly surveillance reports of detectives began to flow in to O'Donovan's office from late October 1920,[38] a more realistic assessment began to develop. By the middle of 1921, the gap between militant rhetoric and actual intention that had already existed in 1920 had patently widened. Growing unemployment, as the Wellington detective on surveillance work noted, kept 'violent talk of a strike from breaking out'.[39]

Close surveillance of trade unions and industrial conflict continued; but from 1921, the main focus of such police activity shifted to other individuals and organisations whose activities were seen as potentially seditious. Here again the approach of the Police was legalistic and primarily concerned with order-maintenance rather than subversion; police looked for the possibility of an offence or an outbreak of disorder, rather than merely monitoring those who sought a revolutionary change in the existing system of government.

The scope of sedition

In fact there was nothing illegal in desiring to change the existing system of government. Rather (as the Crown Solicitor put it in terms of the Crimes Act) the 'boundary of sedition is only crossed by a person who advocates that such a change should be brought about by violent means, or who promotes his object by raising discontent or disaffection, or promoting feelings of ill-will and hostility between the classes.'[40] Such a definition of illegality allowed a broad view of 'revolutionary organisations and propaganda'. For one thing, by the Crimes Act of 1908, an offence of raising discontent or disaffection could (in theory) be committed in New Zealand against the government or constitution of the United Kingdom, not merely that of New Zealand. Thus, for example, those who were active in seeking Irish or Indian independence were subject to surveillance. Indeed, the uproar over Bishop Liston's assertion on St Patrick's Day 1922 that Ireland was 'determined to have the whole' of her 'freedom', and his reference to the 'men and women who in the glorious Easter of 1916 were proud to die for their country – murdered by foreign troops', led Massey's Cabinet to order his prosecution for sedition.[41] 'Revolutionary propaganda' did not need to advocate violence explicitly to be deemed seditious. In dealing with Communist literature during the 1920s and early 1930s, the Solicitor-General (who authorised prosecutions) and magistrates were prepared to accept a broad view of a 'seditious intention', especially of an apparent intention 'to promote ill-will and hostility between different classes of His Majesty's subjects'.[42] Even more broadly, those who challenged the authority of the New Zealand government without threatening violence could be charged with inciting lawlessness under the Police Offences Act.[43] A member of the Unemployed Workers' Movement, for example, was thus successfully prosecuted for distributing to a gathering of unemployed in Wellington in 1931 a pamphlet (entitled *A Swindle*) calling on them not to register under the Unemployment Act 1930 or pay the compulsory levy.[44]

Though the scope of surveillance was potentially broad, the Police concentrated on the possibility of sedition from left-wing groups. This reflected both the ethos of the department and the dominance of conservatism in New Zealand political life before 1935. By contrast with their counterparts across the Tasman, New Zealand police did not have to (or at least feel the need to) monitor radical right-wing groups. There was, for example, no local equivalent to the New Guard, a conservative paramilitary organisation which the New South Wales Police confronted in 1931 and 1932.[45] From early 1934, an Auckland detective monitored the activities of the local German Club, where Nazi sympathisers had taken control.[46] Fundamentally, however, political surveillance remained focused on the proponents of revolutionary socialism. There were a number of phases in the development of this focus during the inter-war years.

Until the development of a local Communist Party steadily sharpened the focus, the Police took a broad view of potential revolutionary organisations that encompassed the Labour Party and groups pressing for Irish independence. While the Wellington detective identified 'various revolutionary Societies and bodies' (including the Labour Party and Sinn Fein) in his first monthly reports,[47] detectives responsible for surveillance in the other districts could find no 'revolutionary organisations', though they noted that individuals within the Labour Party held 'revolutionary principles'.[48] The identification of such 'revolutionaries' reflected the ongoing debate within the labour movement over the best path to socialism: Marxian socialists berated the Labour Party MPs as 'Political Opportunists and reactionaries', while Holland and Fraser maintained that the Labour Party was just as extreme as any Socialist Party.[49] Consequently, the Police paid attention to Labour rhetoric during 1919 and 1920. Despite the fact that Labour Party leaders by then believed in achieving socialism through parliamentary means, their rhetoric seemed sometimes to belie this. In July 1920, for example, Harry Holland 'likened the case of Ireland to that of Russia, fighting for freedom from capitalistic exploitation'.[50] During 1920 and 1921, the Labour Party's campaign in support of Irish economic and political self-determination compounded its potential for sedition in the eyes of the Police.

Refocusing on Communists

Early in April 1921, police observed that the Socialist Hall in Wellington's Manners Street had been renamed the Communist Hall.

Apparently unobserved by police, the Communist Party of New Zealand had just been formed at a conference of revolutionary socialists in the capital city.[51] Soon afterwards, however, increased activity and propaganda by Communists in Wellington and Auckland was noted by police and politicians alike. In September the Minister of Justice asked for a report on the history, strength and membership of the 'Communist Club' in Wellington. (There is no evidence that this rare formal request influenced the pattern of police surveillance, which already had its own momentum.)[52] Experienced detectives were already sensitive to the differences between the Communists and the Labour Party. As the Wellington detective monitoring them noted:

> From the appearance of things there is no doubt that the Labour and Communist Parties are drifting apart somewhat. This applies of course only to matters of routine, and would not apply in the matter of a strike.
> The Labour Party does not aim to sell literature of a dangerous kind. The Communist does. The Labour Party members state definitely that they do not believe in violence or other methods not constitutional to gain their ends. The Communist does not agree with this view, and is inclined to call the Labour members and the Maoriland Worker, YELLOW.[53]

During 1921 surveillance began to be refocused, with the emphasis placed increasingly on the Communist Party. The Labour Party was not ignored, however. Its Sunday night concerts and public meetings were regularly attended, and its publications (such as the *Auckland Labour News*) were purchased for scrutiny. A legacy of suspicion remained. Not until Communist Party adherents among its members were effectively expelled in 1925 did surveillance of the Labour Party gradually become less routine.[54] For their part, the Communists, in their various factions, were watched closely, but were not yet perceived to be a threat. The Wellington detective commented in July 1921, 'The least push now would probably send the Party to the wall, but not much would be gained by that, as the party would not disband, but would adopt hole and corner tactics, and be more difficult than ever to handle'.[55] In fact, the early 1920s were a time of considerable difficulty for Communists in New Zealand as they struggled for organisation and unity in the face of factionalism and police harassment, especially of sales of literature.

In May 1926, Commissioner McIlveney enjoined his officers in charge of districts to give special attention to 'Communistic Propaganda' and the movements of Communist leaders or speakers.[56] Ostensibly this was merely reiterating a well-established policy. From some districts, however, reports of surveillance activity had become irregular. A year earlier the Christchurch Superintendent had asked whether a monthly report needed to be furnished if there was nothing to report.[57] Also concerning the Commissioner was the current tour of the country by Norm Jeffrey, an organiser from the Communist Party of Australia.[58] More urgently, McIlveney was responding to the general strike then continuing in Britain, thinking it 'quite probable' that local Communists and other agitators might consider the time 'opportune for increased activity'. Substance for this fear seemed to be provided by events in Auckland, where (in the view of the local Superintendent) 'communist agitation [was] being intensified' – especially amongst the unemployed, whose numbers had increased noticeably with the onset of winter, and amongst trade unionists to create a militant 'minority movement'.[59] In the event, the very small number of active Communists made little headway amongst the local unions, and 'demonstrations' of the Auckland unemployed in 1926 were short-lived. Nonetheless, police became increasingly sensitive to a new and ever more threatening source of disorder, as the ranks of the unemployed grew in the four main centres, and Communists and non-Communists jockeyed to lead them.[60]

From 1929 police concern at the possibility of disorder increased sharply; so too did the level of their surveillance. In May the Wellington detective on surveillance duties noted that there seemed to be 'more Communists in Wellington than is usual'. In fact, numbers remained very small throughout the country (about 40 active Communists were then known to police),[61] but during the year there was a transition to greater activity, especially in Wellington, Auckland and Christchurch. In January, R.F. Griffin (who had been active in the Irish nationalist cause, and then in the Communist Party in Wellington) had returned from a World Congress of the Communist International in Moscow to become the first full-time General Secretary of the Party. By May, the Central Committee (and the publishers of the Party newspaper) had transferred to Wellington from the West Coast of the South Island, where it had been based since 1926.[62] Two months later (after a probationary constable had attended Communist study classes and bought literature) police raided the Party's headquarters and library. The prosecution and conviction of four leading members for distributing seditious literature soon followed. Failing to pay a £50 fine and costs, two (including Griffin) were imprisoned for three months.[63]

Within weeks of Griffin's release from prison in March 1930, he was once again very active amongst the unemployed, first in Auckland and then in Wellington.[64] On the streets, Communists competed for an audience with the Labour Party, which was supported by the trade union leadership. Now, more than ever, there were men willing to listen at street meetings and join demonstrations and deputations to civic and charitable aid authorities, and to Parliament. First in Auckland, then in Wellington and Christchurch, it became apparent to police that the Communists had launched the nascent organisations for the unemployed that were by 1931 known collectively as the Unemployed Workers'

Movement, which in turn became a target for surveillance. In May 1930, a correspondent to the Labour Party's newspaper was 'satisfied we will have a good riot in Auckland this winter unless Cabinet does something practical to relieve the existing distress'.[65] It was in Wellington and Christchurch, however, that deputations of the unemployed led by Communists proved to be most troublesome in the eyes of the authorities during 1930. The disorder was only minor – police reports tended to play down the seriousness of the threatening language and behaviour by comparison with newspaper accounts.[66] Even so, police wasted no opportunity to prosecute the 'firebrands'.[67]

From early 1931, Communist activity amongst the unemployed was viewed more seriously by police, particularly in Wellington. Some Communist-led demonstrations now culminated in brief clashes between police and the unemployed – such as those outside the Auckland Labour Bureau office in February, and in Parliament's grounds in April and September. In March, Communists in the Unemployed Workers' Movement in Auckland and Wellington were reported to be planning for a general strike of relief workers. They attempted to declare relief works 'black' when pay rates were cut from 1 April. Few relief workers responded to the call. Attempts at picketing were frustrated by a strong police presence – Commissioner Wohlmann thought that 'our policy should be not to acknowledge any right to "picket" or to acquiesce in the practice'.[68] In June, a conference of unemployed organisations called by the Communists met in Wellington. On paper at least, a national organisation was established; police noted that speakers advised the unemployed to refuse to pay the unemployment levy. A second conference was held in Wellington in September. Again police noted the potentially seditious consequences: instructions were issued to organise opposition to work camps for the unemployed, to hold mass meetings and to demonstrate.[69]

In March 1931, the conjunction of growing restiveness amongst the unemployed with the threat of a general strike (led by the Alliance of Labour) against government-inspired wage reductions led Wohlmann to take steps to prepare for the worst – as O'Donovan had done in 1920. The Defence Department was asked whether it could assist in providing camps and men, if need be, for some 4,200 'auxiliary forces'.[70] The need did not arise. As the President of the Alliance of Labour pointed out (just as Wohlmann made his preparations), 'the majority of the New Zealand unions are not in a position to adopt the strike weapon.'[71]

A harder line

In the mind of Commissioner Wohlmann, however, a sense of crisis deepened during 1931. A harder line towards Communists became apparent. In April warrants were secured to search Party premises in

Wellington, along with the homes of R.F. Griffin and two other prominent members of the Central Executive, for evidence of the crime of 'seditious conspiracy'.[72] Books and correspondence were taken away, but 'no arms or ammunition [were] found'.[73] For Wohlmann, the raids merely confirmed what he already suspected. They reinforced his fears of the Communist Party as a semi-secretive organisation, directed from abroad in its efforts 'to carry on a war against constituted authority by every means at [its] disposal, whether legal or illegal'.[74] Enough evidence of seditious literature had been found, it seemed, to incarcerate the leading Wellington-based members of the Party.[75] For once, however, the Solicitor-General failed to authorise the prosecution of some of the key leaders.[76] The succeeding months brought more evidence that the local Communist Party was receiving written instructions from the Executive Committee of the Communist International to carry out 'street demonstrations' and 'revolutionary illegality' which (in Wohlmann's mind) were echoed in the tactics of the Unemployed Workers' Movement and other 'front' organisations of the Party.[77] In October 1932 the Commissioner would submit this material to his Minister in support of proposed legislation to declare the Communist Party illegal.[78]

In the meantime, from November 1931 Wohlmann sought to prevent the re-entry to New Zealand of Communists who had received training at the Lenin School in Moscow. The first such graduate, F.E. Freeman – 'a particularly dangerous type of disloyalist' – was due to return, and it was anticipated that he would take over the Party leadership.[79] To his Minister, the Commissioner noted that Canada and Ireland had already 'legislated against the Communists'. He did not propose to go that far 'at present', but rather to give better effect to the existing legislation designed 'to restrict Communist intercourse' between New Zealand and 'certain other countries'.[80] Eventually, on 17 March 1932, the government issued a regulation (by Order in Council) to restrict the entry of Communists who had recently visited the Soviet Union. To Wohlmann's chagrin, the specific target of the legislation arrived back in New Zealand undetected by Customs or the Police, and could not be deported.[81]

That the Commissioner continued to fear a crisis of public order can be seen by his moves in December 1931 to prepare legislation for 'Public Safety Preservation' which was ready to be rapidly enacted as the Public Safety Conservation Act after Auckland's 'Queen Street riot' on 14 April 1932.[82] The possibility of such a riot, in Auckland or another main centre, had been anticipated by Wohlmann. For more than a year demonstrations of the unemployed had been viewed as having the potential for violence; some had resulted in clashes with police. Where rumours of intended violence reached local police, precautions were usually taken. Information (for example) that demonstrating unemployed workers in Wellington would smash windows and loot the DIC and Kirkcaldie and Stains on 7 May 1932 led police to keep their march from the Basin Reserve well away from the area.[83] Three days later, however, the windows of these and other buildings were smashed. Police surveillance did not reveal specific plans for any of the disturbances that eventuated, as these were spontaneous expressions of frustration,[84] precipitated in part by police actions (especially in the case of the Queen Street riot) and indeed surprising the Communists themselves. Perhaps, given the small numbers of police present at the large demonstration that led to the Queen Street riot, police took insufficient heed of information they had received two days earlier from a committee meeting of the Auckland Unemployed Workers' Movement: on the march up Queen Street, the 'leaders [were] not to try to control [the] mob'.[85]

In reality, the Communists had little power to shape events, yet Commissioner Wohlmann thought otherwise. The appearance of a Friends of the Soviet Union organisation in 1931, and its growing activity in succeeding years, seemed to broaden the scope for subversion.[86] Militant rhetoric flowed unabated from the *Red Worker*. To Wohlmann, the Communist newspaper was

> not published in the interests of the working class, but is the mouth-piece of an anti-British and anti-social organisation inspired from a foreign source. Its object is to take advantage of existing conditions to incite and foment disorder and disregard of the law. Even the most biased must admit that the publication of such documents is the reverse of helpful in the preservation of law and order in these unsettled times.[87]

Raids and prosecutions therefore continued. In June 1932, for example, Griffin and two other members of the Central Executive received sentences of three years' imprisonment (later reduced) for publishing a pamphlet entitled *Strike Strategy and Tactics* and a provocative May Day edition of the *Red Worker*. In August 1933, six other members of the Central Executive were imprisoned for six months for publishing *Karl Marx and the Struggle of the Masses*.[88] Whereas historians have tended to see the 1932 riots as cathartic and leading to quiescence amongst the unemployed, Wohlmann continued to fear the worst, especially with the resurgence of the Unemployed Workers' Movement around the country during 1934. Ominously, it seemed to the Commissioner, a demonstration of the unemployed had taken place on Auckland's Queen Street in May, breaking a two-year-long ban on processions.[89] The 'Charter of Demands' drawn up by the UWM in June 1934 was seen by Wohlmann as a device 'to get the unemployed organised in one body'. That accomplished, the Communist leaders would 'make use of the unemployed to demonstrate in sympathy with the transport workers (seamen, watersiders, and others) as they anticipate trouble in shipping circles before long'.[90] The vision of a national strike had returned. In August Wohlmann made provision for an auxiliary police body for use in an emergency. Two years later it was disbanded. With the advent of a Labour government in December 1935, a new and (until 1940) less obtrusive period of political surveillance began, as peacetime prosecutions for sedition ended.[91]

Organising surveillance

There was no separate political surveillance unit or 'special branch' within the Police during the inter-war years. Instead, individual detectives (usually one in each of the four main centres) were detailed for the work. As they advanced in their careers, others replaced them. In the smaller towns and country districts, detectives and constables reported as necessary on strikes, and on the movements and activities of those with 'revolutionary tendencies'. Two of the first four selected in September 1920 to undertake full-time political surveillance, Detective Sergeants W.E. Lewis (in Wellington) and Thomas Gibson (in Christchurch), were already experienced in the work. Detective Sergeant Reg Ward (in Auckland) was selected by his Superintendent for the opposite reason: having been recently transferred to the city, he would 'approach the matter without any preconceived ideas'.[92] As with other tasks in the Police, knowledge and skills were acquired on the job. Men whose occupation required them to be neutral, if not naive, politically, had to quickly develop some sense of the subtleties of doctrine. Detective F.J. Beer, who took over the task in Dunedin, made his first acquaintance with 'Carl Marks' when a Communist from Wellington spoke on 'Communism and Industrialism' in June 1921.[93] Those who advocated 'Bolshevism' were considered dangerous. Like his colleagues, however, Beer took a legalistic view in seeking the ingredients of an offence in the many speeches he listened to and assessed; did they advocate violence, or were they (as they almost invariably were) 'harmless', 'tame', or 'fairly temperate'?[94]

In Auckland and Wellington in particular, the detectives on surveillance work soon found they needed assistance in attending the variety of meetings where there was potential for seditious utterance, and in gathering information, especially at times of industrial conflict. From the early stages of systematic surveillance, other detectives and men from the Uniform Branch (generally in plain clothes) were drawn in as required to attend public meetings, especially those on the street. Beer soon found it 'almost impossible to get any information regarding the doings of the extreme element' as he was so well known – so he worked at gaining the confidence of an informant.[95] Ward, by contrast, found his lack of local knowledge a handicap. 'If the Department will sanction the expenditure of a few pounds for this work, some useful information might be obtained', he suggested in November 1920.[96] It appears that Police funds were not spent in this way. Instead, from November 1922, a constable performed 'special duty' in 'civvies' as an agent on the Auckland waterfront during the seamen's strike; he also joined the local Communist Party branch and attended its meetings. A probationary constable was employed as an agent amongst Auckland's Communists in 1926, and others joined the Party in Auckland, Wellington and Christchurch in the early 1930s.

A mountain of reports was soon created by the local agents and detectives, minuted by their senior officers, and scrutinised by the NCO in charge of secret correspondence at Headquarters, before (generally) crossing the Commissioner's desk. In contrast to the effort expended in acquiring information, no personnel other than the officers in charge of districts were assigned to its assessment. There were no regular appraisals of surveillance activity as a whole. This task was expected to be embodied (often implicitly) in the detectives' monthly reports, and to be an ongoing process in the minds of the Commissioner and his senior officers. Access to the information collected was cumbersome by modern standards. The core of the surveillance system was a register of secret files which included an index of names and organisations and a synopsis of each file received and dispatched. Most individuals referred to in reports could be traced only through the index in the register. Only in a small number of cases were specific files opened on individuals, with extracts copied from the reports received. Not until 1937 was a card index begun.

At the outset, the main focus of police surveillance was on public meetings. This served a number of ends. Ostensibly, the primary aim was to detect instances of seditious utterance. In fact, few prosecutions for inciting violence or lawlessness came from public meetings. Detectives quickly noted that their presence moderated the language being used; this in turn became a reason for their presence. Even so, they faced difficulties. Words might be indistinct amongst the babble of competing voices (not to speak of the roar of passing buses) at the regular Sunday soapbox meetings in Auckland's Quay Street.[97] More seriously, to Detective Sergeant Ward in December 1920, the speeches at the Auckland Labour Party Sunday night concerts were 'usually carefully worded so as to avoid prosecution, but the spirit of what is said is revolutionary. To be properly handled these meetings should be reported by a short hand reporter.'[98] The latter were expensive, however, and successive Commissioners thought that two experienced police should usually suffice. It is notable that the most politically sensitive prosecution for seditious utterance, that of Bishop Liston, was based on a newspaper report – no police admitted to being present to hear the rhetoric.[99] Swearing was more common than incitement amongst platform speakers of 'revolutionary tendency'. Prosecutions for indecent language were likely to follow. Here police discretion was important. Constable J. Smyth, reporting on an Auckland Labour Party meeting at Quay Street, noted that the speaker attacked the British aristocracy for being descended from 'bastards'; however, 'He did not use the word "bastard" in an indecent manner but in its correct application'.[100] Smyth was given no more of this work.

Attendance at public meetings also enabled police to gauge the appeal of the radicals' message by the numbers present and their responsiveness. Sympathisers could be identified. Public meetings were also where literature was sold; initially openly by Communists and others, until a series of prosecutions in 1921 made them more circumspect about purchasers.[101] Selling seditious literature was the offence most frequently prosecuted. Naturally, this was very much resented by Communists and their sympathisers, especially in the unions. Public meetings could also provide information about future plans, especially for demonstrations. In Wellington, however, Communists were generally refused permits for street meetings by the city council on police advice; prosecutions for speaking without a permit followed.[102] Predictably, this drove the Communists into halls (a more expensive and less effective means of attracting an audience), and then 'into Committee', in an attempt to exclude police. That excessive harassment would be counter-productive to the gathering of information was quickly recognised by detectives. Accordingly, a long-standing desire to ban the Communist Party was not carried through.[103]

Even so, covert surveillance became increasingly important. Where detectives did not seek to be inconspicuous at public meetings, they brought with them constables in plain clothes who did. If the readily identified police were excluded by the meeting going 'into Committee', their less prominent colleagues remained. Where this was not possible, agents were employed. In both Auckland and Christchurch police constables became office-holders in Communist organisations. In Christchurch, the police agent (still thought to be a 'Comrade') was subpoenaed to give evidence for the defence of Communists; he became a delegate to the Party conference in Wellington in 1932, and was asked to see the local police Superintendent to request the return of Party banners seized in demonstrations.[104] The agents' reports gave a clear picture of the strength of the local organisations (which was never great), their policies, and the movements of key individuals. In Christchurch, the detective on surveillance reported in November 1931 that 'Communist Party activities have been so effectively checked they are unable to get a meeting together'.[105] Potentially disruptive activity was effectively neutralised. Police agents did not, it seems, act as *agents provocateurs* during the inter-war years.

The impact of surveillance

Essentially, police surveillance turned the Communist Party into 'a semi legal organisation'.[106] Possessing the ability (and discretion) to prosecute and use coercion, police had significant means of harassment available to them. Where there was insufficient evidence to prosecute party workers for offences related to sedition, those living on a bare subsistence might be prosecuted for vagrancy. Police took a strict view of their powers (where these were conferred by civic authorities) to ban demonstrations – in Christchurch, for example, by stopping a band playing the 'Red Flag'.[107] In the early 1920s, and again in the early 1930s, powers to prevent the entry of 'undesirables' into the country were exercised as far as was possible. In the early 1930s police informed employers (including university authorities) of the Communist leanings of certain employees, some of whom lost their jobs.[108] Similarly, avenues for the dissemination of the message were closed by informal actions such as securing the eviction of Communist meetings from a vacant section in Wellington's Cuba Street, or warning the owner of radio station 1ZR in Auckland that Friends of the Soviet Union were Communists and should not be given access to listeners.[109]

Yet there were constraints on police action against Communists and those perceived as 'sympathisers'. Such constraints were not caused by the possibility of supervision by the Minister, of which there was apparently very little before 1936. Nor were the limits set by the prevailing political mood unduly constraining during the 1920s and early 1930s, rather the reverse. Even so, the climate of opinion had changed by 1935. Symptomatic of this, in 1936, was the instruction from the new Minister in charge of the Police, Peter Fraser, to return to R. Griffin books which had been seized during the raids five years earlier and retained by the Police (despite repeated requests from Griffin) because they were deemed to be seditious. Fraser considered that the books were 'for students, and have little bearing on New Zealand conditions'.[110]

Rather than being political, the constraints were legal and bureaucratic. Police needed the sanction of the Solicitor-General to prosecute for seditious literature; this was usually forthcoming, but not always. A case had to be carefully prepared. Similarly, magistrates were usually sympathetic to the police case, but might throw out charges that were patently oppressive. In November 1931, for example, Christchurch police refrained from prosecuting Communists for distributing pamphlets in breach of local by-laws because the 'Magistrate dislike[d] petty charges being brought against Communists'.[111] The support of civic authorities was needed to ban demonstrations and public speaking in the street. When the Wellington city council relaxed the curbs in 1931, local police were not impressed, but had to tolerate the situation.[112] Wellington Communists also took the opportunity offered by the 1931 general election to mount their soapboxes as political candidates (and therefore immune from police harassment) for the first time. It was no coincidence that in the same month Commissioner Wohlmann began his initiative to have the Party declared illegal. More broadly, a sense of legalism shaped police behaviour: they did not raid houses without search warrants and were generally careful in their use of force. The legal limits were pressed, however. When the head of the New Guard in Sydney received an unsigned threatening letter from Greymouth early in 1932, a local detective suggested a search of the informal ballot papers from the election.[113]

The other main constraint was bureaucratic. Police relied on the cooperation of other state agencies besides the Solicitor-General. Assistance from Customs was necessary in the surveillance of immigrants and imported literature. The Comptroller of Customs did not wish, for example, to have legislation against the entry of Communists as restrictive as that Wohlmann desired.[114] Similarly, police had no powers to open mail – unlike their counterparts in Britain, on whom they relied for the surveillance of mail between New Zealand and the Soviet Union. Accordingly, police relied on the cooperation of the postal authorities in interpreting the postal regulations leniently to monitor who was receiving mail, and the nature of the publications received. This cooperation was forthcoming in the cities, but not necessarily so from country post offices on the West Coast, for example. One local constable commented, 'In a district like this a Postmaster who can be trusted is of great assistance to the police, but as far as Denniston is concerned it is not safe to make inquiries of a confidential nature at the Post Office'.[115] In 1926, the Communist Group at Blackball (the headquarters of the Party between 1926 and 1929) had no doubt that its private mail was being opened, and that the postal authorities were deliberately delaying delivery of overseas Communist newspapers.[116] In the same vein, an Indian resident wrote to the Wanganui Postmaster in 1932 asking that all his newspapers be delivered directly to the police, since they were apparently being informed when they arrived.[117]

Despite some constraints on their surveillance, police had a discernible influence on the political life of the 1920s and early 1930s. They helped to set limits on who could participate effectively in political activity. They protected governments from challenges to their authority. They constrained political rhetoric – the prosecution of the *Grey River Argus* in October 1920 for incitement to lawlessness quickly encouraged moderation of language in Labour Party publications.[118] Overall, police activity helped to weaken the discourse of the extreme left and to reinforce the foundations of conservatism in New Zealand politics.

PART THREE

Transitions

CHAPTER 11

False Dawn
(1936–39)

For the Police, the election of the first Labour government on 6 December 1935 suggested the likelihood of a new beginning; 'a bright light appeared on the horizon', recalled Charles Belton.[1] Before its election, Labour had pledged to improve public servants' conditions of employment.[2] Amongst police there were heightened expectations that the department would no longer be the 'Cinderella' of the public service. Certainly, the first three years of Labour's administration saw the founding of the New Zealand Police Association, improvements in working conditions and police equipment, and a decision to recruit women police. Yet the degree of change for police was limited compared with innovations elsewhere in state policies and administration, and the gains other public servants had made by 1939. In policing, as in the prison system, a long-standing ethos and pattern of administration persisted. Between 1939 and 1945 a nascent impetus for change was stifled by the demands and constraints of wartime. Measured against expectations, the years 1936 to 1939 proved to be a false dawn for the police rank and file, as it was for those critical of existing methods of policing.

A new leadership

A key influence in shaping the nature and degree of change was the new Minister in charge of the Police (and deputy Prime Minister), Peter Fraser – a 'whale for swallowing departments'[3] and a dominant member of the new government. In the allocation of portfolios, Fraser was also given Education, Health and Marine. Since 1896, successive Ministers of Justice had been given charge of the Police, except for seven months under Massey in 1918–19.[4] The allocation in December 1935 marked a new departure. Oversight of the Police was much less important than Education or Health in terms of Labour's goals; Fraser took charge (it is said) because Walter Nash believed the Force would need a 'strong man' to control it.[5]

Such a belief reflected long-standing suspicions and fears amongst the political representatives of the labour movement. Some, like Fraser, had shown an interest in rank and file concerns and come to know and respect individuals within the Force.[6] Even so, police were perceived to have 'partisan' attitudes towards strikers, the distributors of allegedly 'seditious literature' and law-abiding Communists. Officers had appeared inept in handling the demonstrations of workers and unemployed which led to disturbances in Auckland and Wellington during 1932. The auxiliary police recruited from 1934 were believed to be 'pimps and spies'. Instances of harsh discipline suggested that there was a 'vindictive spirit' amongst officers towards subordinates who lacked an 'official channel' to voice collective grievances. Unsolved murders and inadequate equipment indicated 'a want of efficiency.'[7] More broadly, the new Labour government was concerned to secure the cooperation of state servants after a long period of rule by conservative farmer-dominated governments. It intended to 'assert firm ministerial control over departmental functions.'[8] For the Police, Fraser proved to be 'the boss among bosses'.[9]

Four days before Peter Fraser became Minister, Commissioner Wohlmann, a widower, married again in Auckland. He was then 63 and had 40 years' service, with 21 months remaining before his retirement. Wohlmann had been Sergeant at Waihi during the bitter strike in 1912 when 'with the connivance of the police a reign of terror [had] been instituted' – according to Fraser, speaking then for the 'Red' Federation of Labour.[10] Long memories and subsequent events served to reinforce mutual suspicions.[11] If Wohlmann found the new government led by former 'Red Feds' unpalatable, then his remarriage may well have precipitated a decision to retire early. After completing a countrywide tour of inspection in February 1936,[12] Wohlmann informed Fraser of his intention. He agreed to Fraser's request to defer beginning three months' retirement leave until April. During March the Commissioner was relieved of active duties so that he could live in Auckland and prepare a 'comprehensive report' on the Force. The signs were that Fraser was contemplating an overhaul of the Police. By the end of April, however, Wohlmann had not submitted his report; nor is there evidence that he ever did so.[13]

Having recently expressed satisfaction with the efficiency of the Auckland police,[14] the Commissioner was unlikely to have recommended substantial changes. He had been a cautious administrator at a time of severe pressures for economy, making do with the resources available and justifying existing methods. Subordinates saw Wohlmann as 'quiet' by contrast with his flamboyant predecessor.[15] Probably unfairly, critics perceived him as being 'too soft' in pressing the claims of his department, and thus responsible for the stagnation in police facilities and working conditions. Methods and equipment had failed to keep up with the times. Fraser found Wohlmann firm on one issue at least: he was hostile to the idea of police unionism.[16] There were no public eulogies from the politicians for the Commissioner on his retirement.

Fraser did not announce Wohlmann's successor until 1 July 1936, the day after the Commissioner had officially retired. In the meantime, between April and June, the civilian Secretary of Police, R.F. Madden, acted with the government's authority as 'Deputy Commissioner'.[17] Both the title and the background of the person filling the office were novel and based on an extended reading of statutory authority.[18] Hitherto, the Superintendent of the Wellington District had generally acted as the second in command, albeit informally, when necessary.[19] By 1936, 'Dick' Madden had been a public servant attached to the small Police Headquarters staff for 26 years. As Chief Clerk, redesignated Secretary of Police in 1929, he had gained the confidence of successive Commissioners along with considerable knowledge of police administration. In terms of his salary as a state servant, Madden ranked more highly than the police Superintendents in 1936.[20] His appointment was a convenient stopgap measure while the government decided on Wohlmann's successor. It also provided an opportunity for the promoters of a Police Association.

Newspaper speculation assumed that the new Commissioner would be the most senior officer with sufficient length of 'prospective service'. As the government took its time, other possibilities were canvassed. A 'prominently-placed civil servant' was rumoured as 'likely to receive consideration'; the precedent of F.G.B. Waldegrave was noted.[21] Recently transferred by Wohlmann to take charge of Wellington District, and in the running for the Commissionership, Superintendent Denis Cummings (a Catholic) felt sufficiently worried to enlist the support of the capital's Archbishop Thomas O'Shea. The Archbishop promised 'to do what I can' with his friend Peter Fraser, and asked Bishop Liston to 'put in a word with the Auckland Ministers' whom he might know – notably the Prime Minister, Michael Joseph Savage. On this occasion, the prelates' influence was probably 'minimal'.[22] With the controversial appointment of Lord Trenchard as London Metropolitan Police Commissioner five years earlier in mind, O'Shea noted that there had been 'some talk about appointing a military man instead of a police officer – a man with legal knowledge, but I can not imagine a Labour Government agreeing to this.'[23]

His instincts were correct. Whatever misgivings Labour Ministers might have had about senior police officers, they were opposed to 'militarism' and had a broad respect for the interests of the rank and file. They proved reluctant to break with what had become an established pattern of Commissioners rising from the ranks of the Force. In seeking stability rather than innovation, Fraser eschewed the possibility of appointing a progressive outsider to chart a new direction for the Police (by contrast to his recruitment of C.E. Beeby for the Education Department).[24] In fact the possibility was hypothetical. Progressive outsiders who were both knowledgeable and acceptable were hard to find in the world of Australasian policing.[25] Nor, indeed, did Labour ministers wish to change the prevailing patterns of policing.

Denis Cummings had the qualifications to provide stability. True, he had been severely criticised in 1932 by Fraser and other Labour MPs for a 'very partisan speech' praising the contribution of Special Constables to breaking 'the back' of the Christchurch tramway workers' strike. (Cummings claimed he had been misreported.)[26] Yet Fraser had also noted that Cummings had done 'very good work during the earthquake [as the Inspector in charge] at Napier.'[27] More to the point, stability required (as Fraser later put it) an able man who had 'come up right through from the ranks' with experience of 'every phase' of police work, and who had 'a reasonable period of years' to serve as Commissioner.[28] Cummings was 'a man who understood men.'[29]

In fact, Cummings' career had been spent entirely in the Uniform Branch and mainly on clerical work and supervision at district offices, with interludes as an NCO in charge of the Rotorua and, later, Wairarapa police sub-districts. There, and at the Christchurch and Wellington stations, he built up a reputation as a skilled prosecutor well versed in the complexities of the law, and especially of liquor licensing. Considerably taller than previous Commissioners at 6 feet $2^1/_4$ inches, D.J. Cummings cut an imposing figure. Quietly spoken, genial and 'gentlemanly', with some 29 years' experience of supervision, he had gained widespread respect amongst both staff and 'prominent citizens' at stations under his control, and most notably in Napier and Christchurch, where he had encouraged the 'social side' of police life. Appointed Commissioner shortly before he turned 58, Denis Cummings had then seven years of 'prospective service'.[30]

On 1 July 1936 Commissioner Cummings moved from one office to another within Wellington Central station. Although, since 1918, the number of city police based at the station had increased by twenty, or more than a third (in line with the number of police in the country as a whole), the Headquarters staff had grown by only four (to ten police and eight 'civilians'), despite the greatly increased volume of files and correspondence. Only two more public service clerical staff were added before 1941. With the transfer of his younger brother, Inspector James Cummings, to take charge of the Palmerston North District, the Commissioner was the only commissioned officer at Headquarters from February 1936.

The long-standing pattern of administration remained unaltered. Indeed, with the civilians (apart from Madden) being essentially clerks and typists, and the police largely confined to tasks in the Criminal Registration Branch, Arms Bureau, Gazette Office and Police Store, the Headquarters staff were inadequate to undertake the efficient and detailed planning required by any major programme to rapidly improve working conditions and facilities, let alone to reappraise methods of policing. As Keith Sinclair has observed of the early implementation of Labour's economic and social policies, public servants were generally

80. Superintendent W.H. Mackinnon makes his last inspection of men at the Christchurch police station before retiring in February 1926. The Scottish-born 'disciplinarian' Bill Mackinnon had joined the paramilitary Reserve Division of the New Zealand Constabulary Force at the age of eighteen in 1879. There was a military emphasis on 'discipline and deportment' at the monthly pay parades. *Weekly Press, 4 Feb 1926, p.27, Canterbury Public Library*

81. Oamaru police station: when Senior Sergeant Donald Scott took charge in 1929 he supervised seven constables at the station and four more at country stations. *Donald Scott*

82. Breaking into a barricaded opium den in Haining Street, Wellington, 1932. Senior Sergeant Donald Scott (left) led the late-night raid, which used crowbars and a bushman's stumping jack (leaning against the door) to force an entry. *Donald Scott*

83. The transfer into the Black Maria of Chinese arrested in a 2 am raid on opium smokers in Haining and Tory Streets, 1932. Senior Sergeant Scott (left) and a constable climbed onto the roof of the two-storey building in the background and cut a hole in it to gain access. *Donald Scott*

84. Senior Sergeant D. Scott and Constable W.T. Paget survey an opium smoking room with its barricaded windows and pakapoo tickets scattered on sleeping benches in a Haining Street house, 1932. Scott commented that 'There was nothing we did not do about opium and pakapoo'. *Donald Scott*

85. Superintendent Allan Cameron is farewelled on 17 May 1939 after 42 years in the Police Force. In the Christchurch Central police station library, 90 police heard speeches from representatives of different ranks, followed by the Commissioner's presentation of a silver tea service and a tribute from the Minister, Peter Fraser. From left: Inspector H. Martin, Commissioner Cummings, Superintendent Cameron, and Fraser. *NZ Police Journal, Jun 1939, p.288*

86. Camaraderie across ranks: when he retired in 1935, Wellington's Superintendent A.T. Emerson was photographed with staff who had served together in Dunedin between 1906 and 1909. Top row from left: Sergeant J.W. McHolm, Constable F.A.H. Baker, Sub-Inspector (detectives) J. Carroll, Senior Sergeant G. Sivyer, Sergeant C.R. Duke and Constable R. Phillips; bottom row: Senior Sergeant J.A. Dempsey, Inspector G.B. Edwards, Superintendent Emerson, Sub-Inspector C.E. Roach and Senior Sergeant D.J. O'Neill. *Crown Studios, ATL, C24018¹/₂*

87. New Zealand Labour Party MPs in 1922. Police monitored the rhetoric of Labour Party leaders during 1919 and 1920, especially that of H.E. Holland and Peter Fraser (front row, second and third from left respectively). A detective noted in June 1921 that they disclaimed 'violence or other methods not constitutional to gain their ends', whereas the recently formed Communist Party did not. *ATL, F44402¹/₂*

88. James ('Big Jim') Roberts, secretary of the New Zealand Waterside Workers' Federation, and of the New Zealand Alliance of Labour formed in 1919. His rhetoric suggested to Commissioner O'Donovan that the Alliance of Labour was a revolutionary organisation. In September 1920, a detective monitoring Roberts concluded that he was 'not an extremist'. *R. Holland Collection, ATL, C23998$^{1}/_{2}$*

89. A Communist-led demonstration by some of the unemployed in Wellington, circa 1930, the year Communists initiated organisations for the unemployed in the main centres, with demonstrations and deputations to civic and charitable aid authorities. The Unemployed Workers' Movement became a key target for police surveillance. *Evening Post Collection, ATL, G84831¹/₂*

90. A Communist-led demonstration leads to a disturbance near Seddon's statue in front of Parliament, circa 1931. Police sought to prevent such demonstrations from entering Parliament Grounds unless a Minister agreed to meet a deputation. A police officer (front, left) holds the Communist flag. *Evening Post Collection, ATL, G84186¹/₂*

91. 'WAKE UP! New Zealand': Commissioner Wohlmann was not alone in seeing Communist activity among the unemployed as dangerous and following the instructions of the executive committee of the Communist International – represented here by a bearded Bolshevik with a dagger clenched between his teeth. *New Zealand Home Pictorial, 12 Aug 1931, ATL*

92. Communist reaction to police harassment: a Labour Defence League leaflet of 1929. Between 1921 and 1935, police surveillance turned the Communist Party into 'a semi legal organisation'. *Roth Collection, ATL*

Do you know?

Free Speech,
Freedom of the Press,
Freedom for Political
Propaganda

Are FORBIDDEN in N.Z.

Literature is Censored,
Raids are made on
Workers' Organisations,
Meetings are Prohibited,
Liberties are Restricted.

LABOUR DEFENCE LEAGUE,
Room 10,
30 COURTENAY PLACE, WELLINGTON

THE RED WORKER

(Registered as a Newspaper)   TUESDAY, APRIL 26, 1932.   PRICE: ONE PENNY

WORKERS OF THE WORLD UNITE

(Banners depicted: WORKERS OF THE WORLD, UNITE! / LONG LIVE INTERNATIONAL SOLIDARITY! / MAY DAY / FIGHT AGAINST IMPERIALIST WARS! / DEFEND THE SOVIET UNION! / UN-EMPLOYED UNITE! / FREEDOM OF SPEECH AND ASSEMBLY!)

MAY DAY—ITS SIGNIFICANCE.

The workers' day of struggle has never been satisfactorily held in New Zealand. Miners have stopped work, demonstrations have sometimes been held, but in the main the real purpose of the Day as a special day of struggle has not been understood.

The workers of this country have been defeated in almost every direction in the last few years, and this defeat in the main must be laid at the door of the union officials and reformist politicians who were also responsible for destroying the significance of May Day by diverting it into safe Sunday meetings and in making it a kind of picnic day, or, on the other hand, substituting Labour Day (Eight Hour Day) for the First of May. Their acts in this direction are characteristic of their acts in every other direction and consequent betrayal of our class.

May Day this year comes at a time of special importance. The workers have at last become wearied of the attacks of the bosses and the tyranny of the Coalition Government and are almost in revolt.

The unemployed workers have taken the lead and are making a stand, and the employed workers are also being drawn into the struggle. The tide of retreat before the attacks of the bosses has been stemmed and the First of May marks a festival when we renew our youth and vigour, throw down the gauntlet of new demands and prepare for counter-attack.

The tasks before us are enormous, but we have all the workers

We must build the united front of employed and unemployed workers, we must build up a militant movement inside the trade unions and in all factroies and workshops, etc. We must commence an agitation against all restrictions on working class liberty. We must prepare to prevent war against our fellow-workers in any part of the world and especially against the victorious workers of Soviet Russia. When we have built up committees of the workers in all enterprises and when we have linked these togethr in a united front of struggle and when we have built up a virile, strong and disciplined revolutionary party to act as the vanguard in our struggles we shall be able to look forward with certainty to the day when New Zealand will celebrate a victorious May Day, when Capitalism and its evils will only be a memory and when we are after our long winter of struggle shall prepare to enjoy the fruits of the earth.

Altogether then, fellow workers—

Fight for Non-contributory Unemployment Insurance!
No Wage Reductions! No Wage Taxes!
Down with the Slave Camps! Demand Release of Class War Prisoners!
Prepare to Defend the Soviet Union!
Form a United Front of Struggle!

May Day marks the commencement of preparation for the

---

93. A provocative May Day edition of the local Communist Party newspaper, the *Red Worker*, in 1932. Wellington's magistrate, E. Page, found that: 'Veiled in parts though they be, the articles throughout incite and encourage lawlessness, disorder, and violence and express a seditious intention'. *Red Worker, 26 Apr 1932, ATL, NP478*

94. R.F. ('Dick') Madden, the long-serving civilian Secretary of Police, acted as 'Deputy Commissioner' between April and June 1936 while the new Labour government decided who would succeed W.G. Wohlmann as Commissioner. *B.G. Thomson*

95. Denis Cummings became Commissioner of Police on 1 July 1936. He proved to be a cautious administrator who sought to build on well-established practices rather than to innovate. Between Cummings and the equally strong-minded Peter Fraser, Minister in charge of the Police, a mutual respect soon developed. *NZ Police*

96. Delegates to the annual conference of the New Zealand Police Association in Wellington, 7 to 9 September 1937, include NCOs and a disproportionate number of detectives: from left, back row, Detective Sergeant H.E. Knight (Greymouth), Constable W.J. Theyers (Nelson), Constable F.W. Edwards (Wanganui), Senior Sergeant G. Sivyer (Napier), Constable E.C.H. Wigmore (Gisborne), Detective T. Smith (Invercargill), Detective H.C. Murch (Auckland), Constable W.A. Calwell (Palmerston North), Sergeant F.W. Johnsen (Dunedin); front row, Sergeant P. Geraghty (Whangarei), Senior Sergeant D.J.M. Hewitt (Timaru), Detective A. Jenvey (New Plymouth), Sergeant J. Edwards (Wellington), Sergeant T. Kelly (Hamilton), Detective W.R. Murray (President), I.D. Campbell (General Secretary), Detective D. McKenzie (Christchurch). *Police Association*

97. The 26 year old barrister and solicitor I.D. Campbell was appointed full-time General Secretary of the New Zealand Police Association at its first conference in December 1936. His first main task was to produce the inaugural issue of the *New Zealand Police Journal* in February 1937. For three years, Campbell was a pertinacious advocate of the rank and file's concerns. *Police Association*

98. Members of the first 'big batch' of 124 police recruits line up in Army uniform at Trentham Military Camp in mid-1937. Two large intakes were trained at the Camp to enable a 48-hour six-day week to be introduced from August 1937. Gideon Tait, fifth from the right, saw the two instructors, Sergeants George Paine and Dan Beard, as 'big, personable, friendly men but with an unquestionable air of authority'. *M. Colbourne*

99. A *New Zealand Police Journal* cartoon directed at the handful of the rank and file who refused to join the Police Association but benefited from its achievements. By 1939, night-duty men who had attended court in the morning were exempt from the monthly parades and drill. Here a principled night-duty constable turns up for drill because he does not belong to the voluntary organisation. *NZ Police Journal, Apr 1939, p.143*

100. The Petone police station was built in 1909 and used until 1941. By 1938, a Senior Sergeant, Detective Sergeant and eight constables were housed in the small two-roomed building, which had long been seen as 'deplorable'. The dog Jock had adopted the station and accompanied a constable on his nightly beat. *NZ Police Journal, Feb 1939, p.79*

101. A new police station was built at remote Te Whaiti in 1937 for the District Constable, Heke Bidois. Its opening by the Minister, Peter Fraser, accompanied by Commissioner Cummings and Inspector Lopdell, was a major event in the small Maori community. The *New Zealand Police Journal* reported that Mrs Bidois was not to be 'outdone in her welcome in their home, now new and modern, and stoutly built to keep all snug inside' from heavy winter frosts. *NZ Police Journal, Apr 1938, p.55*

not 'experienced in sophisticated administration.'[31]

Commissioner Cummings was no exception, though he came to be seen by Foss Shanahan (a senior public servant in a position to observe him) as a 'good administrator and a wise man too.'[32] Like others seasoned in reactive administration who 'struck a knotty problem', Cummings might file it away for a while to see if it 'solved itself'.[33] Indecision might reflect shrewdness; it also suggested caution when decisions were made. The new Commissioner wished 'to leave the Service better than I found it.' He saw there was 'room for improvement.'[34] Yet fundamentally, like his predecessors, Denis Cummings preferred to manage an existing system rather than to innovate. Such attitudes shaped his responses to the formation of the New Zealand Police Association.

Forming the Police Association

On 2 April 1936, the day after Wohlmann began his retirement leave, Madden asked the Commissioners of the six Australian police forces for information on their associations.[35] Publicly, Fraser had said nothing yet about allowing the rank and file to organise; but clearly the change of government had made a difference. Already the Prime Minister had promised that the Public Service Association would be consulted concerning changes in the public service. Did not the police also need a 'union' to 'cooperate with the Government', asked a correspondent in Wellington's *Evening Post*.[36] Its lack of a police union marked New Zealand off from forces elsewhere in Britain and the Dominions. 'There was no ring fence round the Government', Savage asserted in April; members of the Police Force or of any other government department could lay matters before him or any other Minister. Carefully clipped from the Labour Party's *Standard*,[37] this declaration accompanied a request by Auckland's Detective Sergeant A.B. Meiklejohn on 1 May for permission from the Minister 'to form a Police Union', and for meetings of 'non commissioned officers and men' to be held at each district headquarters to canvass their opinion. Superintendent Till referred the request to Madden without comment.[38]

Common expectations and the isolation of staff at separate stations saw individuals submit similar reports independently and receive differing responses from their superiors. A week after Meiklejohn, Detective Charles Belton at Hamilton wanted the Minister to consider the 'advisability' of a 'Police Association'. Inspector Lopdell sent the report back, asking 'in what way would an Association benefit (1) the Force, and (2) the Public?' Belton responded vaguely and his report was also sent on without further comment.[39] On 12 May, Constable T.F. Smith, assistant District Clerk at the Wellington station, asked permission for a deputation to Fraser on the formation of an Association. He claimed that the Minister had indicated his willingness to meet it, but did not reveal that he had already spoken to him.[40] Superintendent D.J. Cummings (in charge of the Wellington District) asked if a meeting had been held to discuss the matter. When other officers reported no knowledge of a meeting, Cummings referred Smith's request to Madden with the peremptory comment, 'See regulations 170 to 176'. Since 'combinations' were still regarded as being 'subversive of discipline' and no man could 'complain on behalf of another' (Regulations 172 and 176), the promoters of a police union had to proceed carefully.

Madden sent the reports to Fraser on 21 May, recommending that meetings be held at each district headquarters, with the Wellington meeting choosing the members of a deputation. Meanwhile, a few backbench Labour MPs – the most prominent the enthusiastic unionist Archibald Campbell from Port Chalmers[41] – had bypassed 'official channels' to gauge opinion amongst rank-and-file police wherever they found them (such as Constable R. Fletcher on duty at Parliament, and Constable R.M. Walden at the Ashburton railway station, and during informal visits to police stations).[42] Whether it was with Fraser's connivance or to force his hand is unclear, but on 20 May Campbell (along with six other government members) tabled a parliamentary question asking if the government was prepared to 'consider favourably' the formation of an Association and to receive representations from police.[43] A public statement of the Minister's position was seen to be needed.

A week later, Fraser informed Madden that he had 'no objection' to the formation of an Association and approved his recommendations. Madden drafted a similarly tepid reply to Campbell's parliamentary question: the government would 'favourably consider' authorising the formation of an Association 'along the lines of' those in England and Australia, if there was a 'general desire' for it. The tenor of this response (which was not used by Fraser) sought to meet anxieties in the conservative press about a police 'union', especially if it were to be 'very much bent upon getting its own way in certain directions' or 'to become affiliated, or even linked in sympathy with other class-conscious organisations.' The Minister, cautioned the *Otago Daily Times*, would be 'wise if he exercises all due circumspection in his answer.'[44] Not until 11 August did Fraser respond positively in the House to the idea of a Police Association.[45] In the meantime, the Minister could not be accused of actively promoting police unionism.

At the end of May, Madden instructed the officers in charge of districts to arrange meetings at their headquarters stations. Men unable to attend were to have the opportunity to give their views in writing. It was six weeks before Madden received all the reports. The results were conclusive. In all but four of the fifteen districts, three-quarters or more of the NCOs and constables responded to the chance to give an opinion. They were virtually unanimous in supporting the formation of an Association.[46]

Variations, such as they were, in the degree of support within and amongst districts reflected differences in the measures taken to canvass opinion, and the proportion and degree of isolation of country stations. In Auckland, voting papers were sent to all stations, producing the highest rate of response amongst the four largest districts. In Wellington, an ad hoc committee organised both a well-attended meeting and absentee voting. Christchurch and Dunedin districts had proportionately lower levels of response because the rank and file were less well organised and there were higher proportions of country stations at a distance from the cities. Country constables were more likely to express no opinion in their reports to officers, or (like Richard Allan at Charleston) to declare that they were not interested. Long settled in congenial stations, some country men were less preoccupied with issues that exercised city and suburban constables. Indeed, in Wanganui District, only two men at stations outside the city showed any interest. By contrast, those at the less isolated small towns in the neighbouring New Plymouth and Palmerston North districts responded much more readily. On the West Coast of the South Island, the effects of isolation were mitigated through the holding of a series of meetings around the district. Chaired by the local NCOs, these passed unanimous resolutions for an Association. At the Greymouth meeting, however, six of the sixteen present voted against – a much higher proportion than at meetings in other districts.

The officers in charge of districts differed in the roles they adopted and attitudes they expressed. Most remained aloof from the process – especially Superintendents Till in Auckland and D.J. Cummings in Wellington, who made no comments on the merits of an Association.[47] At Christchurch, Inspector Rawle felt it his duty to be present at the district meeting, though he denied wishing to interfere. In opening the meeting he drew attention to the nature of the Police Federation in England.[48] Others merely opened the meeting and withdrew, recognising that this was a matter for the rank and file. NCOs, detectives or constables chaired the meetings – except at Gisborne, where Inspector Martin presided. Only one officer, Inspector O'Hara at Whangarei, told Madden that he thought an Association unnecessary. Inspector Lander, at Wanganui, expressed a more common feeling of ambivalence: he was not against an Association, 'provided its rules did not conflict with the accepted discipline in the Service', and that it did not have 'any connection with any outside association or union.' Inspector James Cummings added that 'no outsiders should hold office in the Association'[49] – an attitude he was to maintain later as Commissioner. Four Inspectors in charge of smaller districts were more positive in seeing an Association, 'formed on proper lines', as likely to be 'beneficial to all concerned', including 'those in authority'.[50]

In fact there was a large measure of consensus amongst the rank and file as to the 'proper lines' for an Association. Its promoters were familiar with the models of police unionism in Britain and Australia. In his report on 1 May, Meiklejohn commented that the 'Police Union', if formed, would be registered as an incorporated society and 'NOT federated or affiliated with any other Union, Society or Association' – words that were echoed later in resolutions from most of the district meetings.

Various sentiments stimulated this strong expression of independence. Detective Sergeant Meiklejohn, like other older staff promoting unionism, remembered the brief and unsatisfactory experience of police membership of the Public Service Association. Ever since the police branches had broken away and then collapsed in 1922, Meiklejohn and others had 'nursed the idea' of having a separate union able to pursue 'Police matters' more effectively.[51] This had its logic, given that the Commissioner of Police and his Minister were the ultimate arbiters of working conditions. Occupational isolation also strengthened separatism. Rather than identifying a common cause with other state servants, advocates of police unionism (typical of craft-based unionists) emphasised distinctive conditions and interests. In this respect, Constable T.F. Smith underlined that 'loyalty to the Government is the first essential, whatever government may be in office'[52] – a sentiment that was reiterated in resolutions from districts. An emphasis on loyalty did not make police unique amongst public servants, but it implied a more conservative attitude towards unionism, and restraint in pressing demands. It was also prudent, since the government had not yet formally authorised an Association. More fundamentally, it reflected the police ethos, with its emphasis on an image of political neutrality and independence from 'outside' sectional interests.[53]

For the promoters of an Association, however, other issues remained to be settled: official recognition, compulsory membership, and whether a General Secretary would be appointed from outside the Force. De facto recognition came when a deputation representing all districts met the Minister on 8 August.[54] Fraser now welcomed moves to form an Association, and promised to 'do everything possible to encourage' this. He saw it as providing a channel through which aggrieved members could make 'representations in an orderly, recognised way'. Above all, it would 'create a feeling of security, a feeling of comfort and well-being' for men and their families, and 'promote a spirit of co-operation and good will inside the Force'.[55] Nonetheless, hesitancy amongst the rank and file made some form of legal recognition necessary. This came once the Minister and the Commissioner were satisfied with the proposed rules of the Association – that its objectives accorded with Fraser's sentiments.[56] Regulations 172 and 176 were then quickly amended to permit membership of a Police Association whose executive could make representations on behalf of any member. (Airing grievances through unofficial channels remained punishable.)[57] This recognition was not statutory, and could just as speedily be withdrawn if the new 'combination' proved aggressive. On 28 October 1936, the New Zealand Police Association was registered as an incorporated society. The astute and eloquent Detective W.R. Murray of Wellington was its first President.[58]

The Wellington-based management committee pressed for compulsory membership. Fraser supported the principle (in fact the government had just introduced it for workers covered by Arbitration Court awards), but saw 'serious difficulties' in its application to police.[59] (Unlike their counterparts in three Australian states, but like other New Zealand public servants, police were denied access to the Arbitration Court – a 'long felt want', according to Meiklejohn.)[60] Here, it seems, Fraser reflected the new Commissioner's fear of a militant union.[61] Far from commanding the support of the rank and file through compulsion, the Association would have to gain it – and it did so quickly, helped by an official message from the Minister urging every eligible man to join.[62] By June 1938 only six of the 1,397 NCOs and constables had not done so.[63] If they had expected voluntarism to produce docility, the Minister and the Commissioner were to be disappointed.

Much rested on the leadership of the fledgling Police Association, and especially on the full-time General Secretary. Cannily, the Minister offered to 'lend' the Association a man from the Force, playing on the conservative instincts of those who felt that 'an inside man will on all occasions be able to act diplomatically whereas an outside man might be inclined to go too far.'[64] But the desire for independence prevailed and I.D. Campbell, a very able young lawyer, was appointed.[65] Unlike his namesake Archibald Campbell, the trade unionist and Labour MP who had earlier offered to organise a police union 'free' (and been reprimanded by Fraser),[66] the new General Secretary had no ostensible political affiliations. Neither was he – nor was his successor from 1940, the lawyer Jack Meltzer – conditioned by years of Force discipline in his dealings with the Commissioner. I.D. Campbell proved to be a pertinacious advocate of the rank and file's claims, and Meltzer even more so.

From December 1936 the rank and file voiced their claims. The Association provided a new impetus for change within the Police, not merely in pressing for better working conditions but also in promoting a stronger sense of occupational community amongst a dispersed Force. Here the Association's *Journal*, which first appeared in January 1937, played a significant role by providing extensive coverage of district news (including the social activities and opinions of members, as well as a Women's Page for their wives), and articles and editorial comment on current union issues. In its district meetings, annual conferences and deputations to both Commissioner and Minister, the Association fostered a trade union consciousness. Yet it served also (as Fraser had hoped) to preserve discipline by allowing the collective expression of grievances while constraining the pressure for redress to an 'official channel'. It was implicitly understood that industrial action was unthinkable; nor henceforth should grievances be aired in the press or taken to Opposition MPs.[67] As Fraser told an Association deputation in April 1938, 'the less that came before Parliament from the police, the better.'[68] And not much did, for a while. During the late 1930s, morale improved as heightened expectations were fuelled by concessions from the government.

Shorter working hours

During 1936, state servants' salaries and wages, including those of police, were restored to the levels existing before 1 April 1931. Public servants other than police began to enjoy reduced working hours. Mental hospital staff, who also had Fraser as their Minister and were seen as a difficult case, had their weekly hours reduced from an average of 53 to 42, with excess hours compensated by time off or extra pay. In the Marine Department, Fraser also conceded a five-day, 40-hour week. The Prime Minister also held out the prospect of earlier retirement for public servants.[69] For his part, Fraser signalled in Parliament that Police Association proposals, 'made in a cooperative spirit, would be sympathetically considered.'[70] In a Christmas message to the Force, he looked forward to a new year in which increased efficiency would be 'acknowledged by considerable improvement in the conditions of the service.'[71] Predictably, then, increased pay, shorter hours and earlier retirement were the most prominent claims to be pressed by the Association from the outset.

The first remit passed at the Association's conference in December 1936 asked for a 40-hour week, to be worked on not more than five days in any one week. A principle was being asserted. Its implementation for detectives and at suburban and country stations was another matter. Pending the necessary increase in staff (estimated at 350, or 27 per cent of the existing strength), who 'could not be trained offhand',[72] a more limited concession was sought as a 'temporary solution': a 48-hour week, entailing one day's leave a week, and an increase of 3s per day in lieu of overtime.[73] Commissioner Cummings dismissed the idea of a 40-hour week as 'impracticable': detectives' inquiries, for example, 'often had to be pursued irrespective of hours.' After the Association presented examples of rosters, he conceded in principle a 48-hour week 'in those classes of the service where it could be worked.' He would ask the Minister for an extra 100 men (Association delegates thought 175 were needed). When it was argued that other departments paid overtime rates, Cummings agreed to a flat-rate pay increase. Though very concerned about costs, the Commissioner was being pushed to shake off the 'policy' of his predecessors, whose success, as W.R. Murray put it very effectively to a sympathetic Minister, 'appeared to have been ... gauged by their ability to run the Police Force at less cost' than those before them. The result was that an understaffed force worked long hours in poor conditions.[74]

Fraser announced in April 1937 that a 48-hour/six-day week would be introduced as soon as sufficient new men could be trained. One hundred and twenty-five applicants from the waiting list would be called up for a course lasting three months which would begin in May. Another 50 were to be recruited to increase the effective strength of the Force. In lieu of a 40-hour week, the government's 'general standard' for the rest of the public service, police were given a pay increase of 10s a week, backdated to January. (Henceforth, in response to an Association request, constables and NCOs were to be paid an annual salary rather than a daily rate.) A further reduction of hours would be considered when a 48-hour week had been 'established successfully.'[75] The substantial growth in salaries and allowances meant that Police Department expenditure rose by 21 per cent in the 1937/38 financial year. While this was the largest increase since 1920/21 (see figure 1.4), the overall rate of growth in spending on Police since Labour had come to power was less than that on Fraser's two main portfolios, Education and Health.[76] Cost, and the practicalities of implementing shorter working hours for police with an unsophisticated administration, meant that there were constraints on concessions.

Nonetheless, Fraser's announcement was warmly welcomed by I.D. Campbell, who anticipated the 'general satisfaction' that was soon reported from most districts. Mixed feelings were voiced, however, by Auckland's rank and file, the most restless of the Association's members from the outset: 'any concessions' brought some pleasure, but many had hoped for 'considerably more, particularly shorter hours.'[77] Their expectations consistently outran those of their advocates. 'Remember the path of progress is, as a rule, steep and difficult to negotiate, and oft-times very slow', Murray warned those who were dissatisfied; 'loyalty and some sense of discipline' was necessary from Association members, and unauthorised statements embarrassed the executive – 'let there be no discordant note.'[78] For the time being the disappointed were silent, as they waited for the government's concession on working hours to materialise.

The ad hoc nature of the arrangements that were made to train the numbers required for a 48-hour/six-day week suggests that there was no long-term plan to move beyond this goal. The Training Depot at Wellington South (reopened only in August 1935) was too small for such a project. Commissioner Cummings hired facilities at Trentham Army camp for two 'big batches': 124 were trained between May and August, and 62 between August and November 1937.[79] There were only two Instructors, Sergeants George Paine from the Depot and Daniel Beard from the Wellington District Office. Both were remembered as 'big, personable, friendly men but with an unquestionable air of authority.'[80] Taking turns, they lectured the 'big batches' en masse, or had individual trainees read sections of statutes to the rest. In its essentials, this training differed little from that at the Depot during the inter-war years, especially in the emphasis on rote learning of law and Police Regulations embroidered with the Instructor's practical experience. Conditions at Trentham were primitive. A military atmosphere prevailed; the recruits wore Army-issue uniforms, and were drilled by Army instructors. In tune with changing attitudes towards the place of sport in the Force, however, the first 'big batch' had 'a mighty good rugby team and beat the New Zealand army 30-nil.'[81]

A 48-hour/six-day week formally began on Monday 23 August 1937, following the arrival of new constables from Trentham in each of the main centres, the subsequent transfer of additional experienced constables from the cities to smaller stations and detective offices, and the creation of more NCOs. Organising these transfers and promotions was a major logistical exercise for the Commissioner, and the extra men compounded the problem of inadequate accommodation, especially in the city barracks. For some city constables, the shorter working week did not become effective until those from the second 'big batch' arrived in mid-November.[82] Even then, city staff found that their weekly day off was not inviolate when attendance at drill, lectures, pay parades, court or extra duty was required. For country and suburban constables at sole-charge stations, the weekly 'day off' remained notional in most cases, just as shorter hours were for many detectives and some uniformed NCOs at city stations. In the detection of 'serious crime', the 'hours of duty are not considered – they cannot be', Cummings insisted. Any 'overtime' worked would not be paid for, but recompensed when 'slack times' permitted.[83]

Nonetheless, most delegates to the Association's annual conference in 1938 believed that the significant improvement in working conditions that had been gained by many needed to be consolidated for all before they pressed for what remained the ultimate goal of a 40-hour week, a goal not yet achieved by forces elsewhere.[84] Indeed, this objective was now eschewed until delegates could be certain that it would not mean a reduction in pay or annual leave. This had been suggested by Fraser to Murray; realistically in terms of the government's more difficult fiscal position by 1938, but somewhat mischievously in the light of its earlier rhetoric and the gains made by other public servants.[85] Furthermore, delegates did not want continuing pressure for shorter hours to compromise what had now become their main objective: earlier retirement.

The Association's 'main aim'

Retirement on a full pension at 60 or after 35 years' service was an aspiration which had been voiced by police since at least 1928.[86] This quickly became Association policy. At its first conference, the 'retiring age' was the next issue considered after the 40-hour week. There was unanimity that the Public Service Superannuation Act should be amended so that seven years' service in the Police Force would count as eight for superannuation purposes. When interviewed by delegates a month later, Commissioner Cummings opposed the Association's request because of its potentially 'drastic effect on officers', who had 'not been invited into the Association', nor asked for their views on the matter. However, he would have 'no objection' if the commissioned officers were excluded. Delegates pondered a compromise, then thought it expedient to wait until further discussion at the next conference. In the meantime, the General Secretary sought to strengthen the case by gathering statistics from the Public Service Superannuation Board and information on the policies of other Forces, and seeking the views of commissioned officers – at least three of whom referred his circular letter to the Commissioner as the 'official channel'.[87] The annual conference in September 1937 reaffirmed the goal with minor concessions: that retirement at 35 years' service be optional for those under 60, and that the Commissioner be exempt from compulsory retirement at 60. As an interim measure, the Association sought compulsory retirement after 40 years' service for all except the Commissioner.[88]

Long-standing arguments were elaborated in the case put to the Commissioner and then the Minister. Emphasis was placed upon the 'burden' of active duty being unsuitable for 'men of advancing years or declining physique'; and on the distinctive features of police work which placed it 'apart from other public service.' Here the Association drew on the 'authoritative' Desborough Committee's report on the British police presented in 1920.[89] Moreover, police were at a 'serious disadvantage' as members of the Public Service Superannuation Fund: none were recruited under the age of 21, and the average age on joining had been over 25 in the five years to March 1937. Of the 200 recruits in this period, 104 would not acquire the 40 years' service needed for a full pension even if they stayed in the Force until their compulsory retirement at 65. Some would die and more would retire medically unfit before that age.[90] The case was buttressed by pointing to the 'advanced conditions' prevailing in forces in Britain, Canada and across the Tasman, where compulsory retirement at 60 and a full pension after 30 years' service was the norm.[91] By producing a more youthful Force, earlier retirement would increase its efficiency. Indirectly, it would also lead to 'earlier promotion and provide a valuable incentive' to those who were 'at present discouraged by the seriously retarded rate of promotion.'[92]

Not until three months after the second Association conference were the President and General Secretary able to put their case to a hitherto peripatetic Commissioner, and a further four months passed before they saw an overworked Minister. A generally cool reception for the

Association's remits compounded mounting frustration at the delay.[93] By December 1937, Cummings' stance had hardened: while earlier retirement was a policy matter for the government, the Commissioner was also concerned. Compulsory retirement at 60 would do a 'great injustice to many men', he believed. Men at country stations had told Cummings that 'it would be an extreme hardship', and he saw them as a 'better asset to the Department at 60' than a recruit. Nor was a full pension after 35 years sustainable at the current rate of contributions: the superannuation fund was already 'bankrupt or nearly so.'[94]

Murray and Campbell finally met Fraser on 2 April 1938 – the day the Prime Minister announced the government's proposals for social security, including a means-tested pension at age 60.[95] During the preceding seven months, Fraser had been involved with the Minister of Finance, Walter Nash, in finalising a national health and superannuation scheme.[96] Though health was Fraser's main concern, he was well aware of the complex issues surrounding superannuation (especially its cost), and immediately placed the Police Association's proposals within a larger context. With the birth rate then in long-term decline, he saw a 'grave danger' of New Zealand 'becoming a nation of old people being kept by the young people.' Was then retirement after 35 years' service 'an economic limit' for the country? 'People now lived longer and one view was that it would be futile and foolish to rob the country of people who were at their best' – a point reiterated by Fraser, then aged 53. He professed to have an 'open mind' on 'making retirement optional', but wanted the Association to consider the problem 'from the country's point of view.' Sceptical of some Association arguments, Fraser thought that earlier retirement of the 'lower ranks would make way for recruits but not for promotion.' Cummings responded to claims that police were disadvantaged by joining the Superannuation Fund at a comparatively 'high' age by pointing out that prison warders and mental hospital attendants did too; likewise meat and traffic inspectors, Fraser added. There was also the 'question of finance', since the Public Service Superannuation Fund depended on state subsidies. While Fraser conceded that there was 'room for improvement', the Association's proposals would have to be considered as part of the wider question of public service superannuation, which he promised would be dealt with in the next Parliament, 'if the Government is returned to office.'[97]

In October 1938, Labour was re-elected with increased popular support, but in a changed economic climate. The increased prosperity of the last three years was threatened by a crisis in the country's balance of payments.[98] Where total departmental spending had grown by 36 per cent between 1935/36 and 1937/38, it increased by a mere 1.4 per cent in the next financial year (figure 1.4). Speaking for the first time to a conference of the Association a month before the election, Fraser had sounded a warning note: 'it is possible for employees in Government departments to ask for more than it is possible for the resources of the

Government to provide.' Working conditions and wages could not be improved 'unless the production of the country is increased. That is the economic position.'[99] The Minister did not refer to early retirement, apart from suggesting that there would be 'no overwhelming desire' amongst Association members for his in a few weeks' time.

Such confidence was not yet misplaced. Delegates spoke of not 'embarrassing' the government by pressing for a 40-hour week. Nonetheless, they reaffirmed their policy on early retirement, which was now their 'main aim'. When Murray[100] and Campbell met Fraser again on 8 May 1939, the Minister gave little ground, repeating his earlier warning with greater urgency: 'the Government is up against it, especially in regard to finance .... we want to stabilise otherwise we simply cannot carry on.' Perhaps in three years time, with industry 'built up' and overseas funds improved, the government could once again consider 'a fair distribution of the country's wealth.' In the meantime, police, along with other public servants, would have to 'make up their minds that the progress made so far has to be stabilised.' More specifically, the Minister repeated his earlier doubts about the Association's policy on earlier retirement: 'I would not like to see it applied to Parliament. We would have most of the able men eliminated.' Murray was not fazed. Fraser conceded that he put the case 'very well', and promised again to 'go into the whole question.'[101]

In October, after consulting the Public Service Superannuation Board[102] and in the shadow of a new emergency, war, Fraser responded more decisively. To grant the 'concession' asked for by the Association would mean 'remodelling the whole' of the Public Service Superannuation Fund, which would 'lose five years' contributions' from those who retired on a full pension after only 35 years' service; 'could any Fund stand it? I think not.' Granting such a 'privilege' to police would also cause a 'great deal of dissatisfaction throughout the Public Service.' Members of other government departments 'equally exposed to risks' as were police would expect to receive a similar concession. Earlier retirement could not be considered 'in view of the present outlook.' Fraser (like Cummings) remained opposed to the compulsory retirement of men before the age of 65 merely on the grounds of age or length of service.[103] Not only was the argument that police were a special case dismissed by both Cummings and Fraser, so too was compulsory retirement after 40 years' service, which had become the policy in other major departments such as Railways and the Post Office.[104]

Faced with a stalemate, the delegates to the Association's conference in October 1939 proved to be anything but deferential. Instead a strong sense of injustice prevailed; war was 'not a reason for refusing to consider our demands.' Once again the policy of retirement at 60 was reaffirmed, now with neither exemptions nor an interim policy of compulsory retirement after 40 years' service. Believing that the Minister reflected the views of an intransigent Commissioner, and unhappy about the delays, the delegates decided to canvass MPs if no satisfactory reply was received within three months.[105] Confidence in the Minister was dissipating rapidly.

A building programme

Commissioner Cummings did not refer to the issue of early retirement when he addressed the Association conference in 1939. His 'main object' was now to 'push on' with his building programme as a significant means of improving police working conditions, as well as their morale, public image and efficiency.[106] Here he sought to overcome a legacy of neglect. All the district headquarters buildings had been built before or during the First World War, as had most of the suburban and country stations. From the mid-1920s a diminishing amount had been spent on maintaining facilities, let alone improving them. Wohlmann's warning in 1935 that 'a fairly heavy building programme' would have to be faced 'within the next two or three years' was echoed by Cummings a year later when he secured increased funds for urgent repairs.[107]

During his first year as Commissioner, Cummings visited all the district headquarters stations and as many country and suburban stations as he could (mainly in the North Island and sometimes with Fraser). He heard the views of staff and saw for himself the condition of the buildings. Many were in a 'bad state' – 'out of date, and tumbling down with dry-rot and old age.' Obsolete and inconvenient, they would have to be replaced; it would be 'a waste of money to attempt to repair many of them.' Others, mainly country and suburban stations, were basically 'sound' but needed to be renovated for the 'convenience and comfort' of their occupants. In the four main centres, the central stations were congested, with insufficient office space and primitive quarters for single men. Here, as elsewhere, there were competing priorities. (Auckland police thought the 'complete overhaul and reconstruction' of their Central station to be a matter of urgency, while those in Dunedin felt Aucklanders had a 'palace' by comparison with their former prison, with its 'perspiring walls'.) Inner suburban stations at Newmarket (Auckland) and Mt Cook (Wellington) had become obsolete. New buildings were also urgently needed to replace those at Whangarei, Wanganui, Nelson, Greymouth, Timaru and especially Palmerston North, which had the 'worst' headquarters station. The Hutt Valley, where the suburban population was growing by 'leaps and bounds', needed three new stations (at Moera, Petone, and Lower Hutt). Only the premises in Invercargill were not on Cummings' four- to five-year building programme which, 'running into six figures', began to crystallise in 1937.[108] Fraser supported Cummings' initiative, acknowledging publicly that conditions at Auckland Central (which he visited in September

1937) were appalling and that those of many police houses were a 'disgrace to the country.'[109]

Thus Cummings secured what was, for the Police Department, a huge increase in funding for renovations and new building, which was to rise from the £8,000 authorised in 1936/37 to £55,000 in 1937/38, and £160,000 in 1938/39. Total expenditure of nearly £600,000 had been agreed to.[110] Of this sum, £150,000 was to be spent over a period of years on the reconstruction and expansion of the Auckland Central station: more land would be acquired, and new offices, a barracks, a garage for cars, a new lock-up and a parade ground would be constructed. At least that was the plan. In fact only £32 was spent of the £12,000 allocated for the Auckland station in 1938/39. Modernising the Dunedin Central station was seen as a 'more difficult problem'. None of the £28,400 earmarked for its reconstruction had been spent by March 1939. Neither had any of the £20,000 for remodelling the Christchurch Central station and building a new wing; nor the similar amounts which were to be spent on replacing the dilapidated district headquarters at Wanganui, Nelson, Greymouth, and Timaru. On the other hand, by June 1938 land had been acquired for new buildings in Whangarei and Hamilton, and at Mt Cook in Wellington; a new 'thoroughly modern' station had been completed at Newmarket; three country stations and one in the Hutt Valley (Moera) had been built; 'good dwellings' had been bought for five other country or small-town stations; the staff accommodation at Wellington Central had been remodelled; and the foundation stone of the new district headquarters at Palmerston North was soon to be laid with much ceremony.[111]

Cummings sought to make 'big advances on the old obsolete system of patch, patch, patch all the time'. Usually attending to the wishes of country constables and more particularly of their wives in the process of renovation, he became remembered by them as a 'good boss'. Cummings instructed the builder of the new station at Kaeo to 'Erect as planned by Mrs Buckley.' Sleeping porches were added to new police houses, along with electric stoves (where there was electricity) and other 'modern conveniences about the kitchenette and scullery.' Recognising that there were a 'variety of tastes' – some wanted open fires, others electric heaters – he did not 'hope to please everybody.'[112]

Completed in November 1939 at a cost of nearly £29,000, the two-storey Palmerston North station was also intended as a model for others in its layout, provision of central heating and other modern facilities, and use of reinforced concrete construction with textured plaster finishing incorporating Maori motifs. Cummings thought it superior to the latest police stations in Victoria which he had recently observed. But the Palmerston North model was to be followed only for the Rotorua station which opened in August 1940; it had become obsolete by the time other districts acquired new headquarters stations from the early 1960s.[113]

Progress on the building programme was much slower than

Cummings and Fraser had anticipated; perhaps inevitably, given its scope and complexity.[114] The time it took to acquire additional land held up work on the Auckland Central and Nelson stations in particular. The preparation of plans by the Government Architect involved consultation with local staff as well as the sanction of the Commissioner. By 1939, two sets of plans for the Dunedin station had been rejected. There was also a cumbersome process in carrying through renovations of country and suburban stations, involving inspection and supervision by the Public Works Department.[115] Here, as elsewhere, the limited administrative resources available to the Commissioner constrained the implementation of policy. Even more so did the priorities of other Ministers and departments. Expenditure on the police building programme was but a tiny fraction of a massive increase in the government's programme of public works and house construction between 1935/36 and 1938/39. At its peak in the latter year, the actual amount spent on police buildings (£77,745) comprised only 3.6 per cent of that on public buildings, which in turn averaged little more than a fifth of all expenditure from the Public Works Fund in this period.[116] Schools and post offices had a higher priority; the Ellerslie police station was not completed in 1938 because the Public Works Department took men away to complete the local post office by Christmas. Similarly, the booming state housing programme meant that private contractors and tradesmen were hard to find by mid-1938. Such difficulties were compounded as the anticipation of war saw the Defence Department given priority in public building during 1939. Thus Commissioner Cummings spent less than half the amount that had been authorised for his building programme between 1937/38 and 1939/40. Conditions in the Auckland and Dunedin barracks remained primitive, and city station offices were still 'out-of-date, inconvenient and ill-equipped.'[117]

Concessions and discipline

Taken together, the implementation of shorter hours, increased pay and allowances and the projected building programme meant a substantial increase in spending on the Police. With these 'concessions', it was 'no use coming along to me with any wild-cat schemes and no good suggesting schemes which will involve heavy expenditure', Cummings told the 1937 Association conference – a heavy 'hint' which he repeated the following year.[118] Delegates were not deterred. By December 1939, a number of small, piecemeal gains in working conditions had been won by their persistent advocacy. Some changes Cummings made readily: ending the consumption of meals in shop doors by Auckland beat constables on night duty; allowing single constables on transfer to travel first class on the inter-island ferries; giving a day's leave after extended escort duty and one day home a month for those away on relieving or special duty.[119] More slowly and grudgingly conceded were exemptions from lectures for staff on their days off, and from drill for those night-duty men who had attended court in the morning. (Cummings refused, however, to extend late leave beyond 11 pm for those in barracks.)[120] More significant to the ambitious was making the appointment of Sergeants retrospective to the beginning of their probationary period, and the concession of a partial pass as part of other changes in promotion examinations instituted in 1938. To I.D. Campbell, a more liberal interpretation of the sick leave regulation was 'one of the biggest improvements' gained by 1939.[121] However, continuing pressure for extending a variety of allowances[122] was resisted by the Commissioner. A widespread sense of disadvantage persisted amongst country constables despite a 34 per cent increase in spending on car allowances between 1936 and 1939, and the issue remained a 'hardy annual'. The allowances did not match the actual costs of running and maintaining vehicles, especially if interest payments and depreciation were included. But the Commissioner did not agree that the Department should pay for the 'whole car', whose owner 'gets a good deal of enjoyment and benefit from [it] apart from using it on our business. He does not keep the car for our convenience.'[123]

While Cummings was receptive to some suggestions for improving working conditions which did not cost money, he was much less so to any Association remits that might diminish his authority, especially in matters of discipline, transfer and promotion. Such issues, as I.D. Campbell observed, were 'probably more vital to members of the Force than any other question affecting them as individuals.'[124] Here a touchstone was the notorious section 9 of the Police Force Act 1913, which gave the Commissioner unfettered power to dismiss constables without right of appeal. Older police with long memories, notably of Commissioner McIlveney, had cause for unease at the potential for abuse, especially in forcing resignations.[125] 'Abolition of Section 9' followed a shorter working week and early retirement in priority among the requests made to Fraser after the Association's first conference. Cummings had not made use of section 9 by 1939; but neither did he wish to lose it (or be constrained by a right of appeal), seeing it as 'a good deterrent.'[126] Similarly, he opposed Police Association remits requesting that officers in charge of districts not hear disciplinary cases where they had ordered the prosecution or had prior knowledge of the case, and that the Appeal Board be reconstituted to include a member of the Association.[127] Cummings challenged Association delegates to show that any injustice had arisen from 'present methods'. In reply, Campbell asserted the principle of procedural fairness. Nor would the Commissioner accept that those charged at disciplinary hearings could be represented or assisted by another member of the Force rather than a solicitor; this 'was not in the interests of discipline.'[128]

Promotions and transfers also provided ongoing issues with respect to which Cummings was generally inflexible. Against a feeling that prospects for promotion were stagnating, he maintained that between 1936 and 1938 more men had been promoted than 'ever before in a similar period of time.'[129] Association remits urging the ending of the probationary system for promoting Sergeants, the raising of the status of stations to increase the number of promotions, limitations on the period of service that constables were 'compelled' to spend at remote stations, and the advertising of vacancies (as in four Australian police forces) were all rejected by Cummings as being policy matters for him alone, and not to be 'dictated' by the Association.[130] He had a similar attitude towards Association advocacy in individual cases upon which he had already made a decision. In particular, the case of Sergeant G. Holt and four others, who saw themselves as being displaced on the seniority list when the Commissioner made the appointments of Sergeants retrospective, produced tensions – both between the Management Committee and the Commissioner, and amongst Association members. For the Management Committee (now under Chief Detective J.B. Young's leadership), Holt's case represented an issue of principle, even if redress for him would disadvantage other members. When Cummings refused to reconsider his decision, a Committee of Inquiry 'to go fully into the matter' was requested. This, too, Cummings rejected in the strongest terms: 'I am not going to allow the Association to question discipline or seniority .... I am going to have discipline at all costs.'[131]

Ultimately, Fraser backed Cummings. He proved reluctant to arbitrate on such matters, assuring Murray and Campbell in 1938 that 'Ministers were very grateful when problems were adjusted outside their offices.' Fraser recognised the general principles raised by Association delegates,[132] but was more concerned with the practicalities of police administration. Changes were obviously unnecessary if no injustice could be demonstrated.[133] The Minister exuded confidence in his Commissioner: 'I do not think anybody in the Force at the present time need have any fear of injustice.'[134] The sentiment was genuine, and it was to be reiterated. By 1937 a mutual respect had developed between two strong-minded men. Cummings had followed Fraser's wishes on politically sensitive matters of policing, such as by abolishing the small Police Reserve within eight days of becoming Commissioner.[135] In turn, Fraser did nothing to undercut Cummings' role in administering the Force: 'we do not want the power of the Commissioner lessened in any way', he asserted in rejecting remits regarding section 9 and the advertising of vacancies. Fraser shared Cummings' concern to maintain the long-standing structure of authority within the Force. 'If I joined the Police Force', he told Association delegates in September 1940 (echoing the views he had expressed to their first deputation four years earlier), 'I would join up to go anywhere and to do anything, to be at command and to obey and to do the job.' That 'may not represent the main body of opinion in the Force', rejoined Jack Meltzer, the new

General Secretary. While he would always consider 'the opinion of the Force', Fraser responded, 'what I consider most is the discipline of the Force and the spirit of it.'[136]

For Fraser, as for Cummings, discipline was essential to the pursuit of greater efficiency. 'The Force required mobility, and promptitude, and "springing to it"', he told the August 1936 deputation. This implied a need for greater zeal in law enforcement. Yet Fraser had already developed a broader conception of the police role which was underscored by his closer and more sympathetic observation as Minister, especially on visits to country and small-town stations between 1936 and 1938. Retailing police self-perceptions to some extent, Fraser believed that their work had 'expanded beyond what was formerly recognised as being its accepted scope'; it was 'now more intricate', requiring 'as good a type of man as any kind of profession in the Dominion.'[137] Besides detecting and preventing crime, police were 'called upon to perform a great social service' to the 'ordinary citizen'. This Fraser saw most clearly with respect to the country constable, who was 'generally the guide, philosopher, and friend of the whole community and is so regarded.'[138] While such rhetoric was in part a eulogy to a receptive audience of Association delegates by an adroit politician, it also expressed a genuine belief and showed a touch of idealism regarding the existence of a wider police role. For Fraser (and even more so for his colleague, the Minister of Labour, Paddy Webb, who stood in for him at the 1939 Association conference), police 'efficiency' should be looked for not merely in 'repressing people or safeguarding life and property', but also in their provision of 'social services.'[139] Fraser did not suggest, however, that the prevailing pattern of policing needed changing. Maintaining law and order, not social work, remained the *raison d'être* of the Police Force.

The pursuit of efficiency

Like the building programme, the pursuit of efficiency was left to the Commissioner's initiative. Here he sought no fundamental changes but rather to supplement and enhance long-established practices. Cummings' thinking did not proceed much beyond that of his predecessor, even though his opportunity for pursuing innovation was greater. His modest horizons stemmed partly from isolation. By contrast, newly appointed Commissioners in Victoria, New South Wales and Queensland had all experienced or directly observed recent overseas developments in policing which, in turn, they sought to press forward more vigorously.[140] To Cummings, the existing pattern of rural and small-town policing seemed reasonably effective. It was in the main centres, with their expanding but sparsely patrolled suburbs, that policing was increasingly perceived to be 'old fashioned' and 'inefficient', and to require greater mobility and better equipment, as *Truth* kept reminding its readers.[141]

Yet New Zealand lacked cities on the scale of the largest in Australia, North America or Britain, where new models of centralised, radio-controlled policing by car had gradually begun to supplement if not supplant decentralised systems of foot patrols during the 1920s and 1930s. Since New Zealand police were much less concentrated in one metropolitan area than their counterparts in Australian states, such innovations would be more costly here. Nonetheless, Cummings' initiatives paralleled those then occurring across the Tasman, albeit more modestly. To 'brighten up the efficiency of the Service', the Commissioner focused on in-service training, improved transport, experiments with 'the efficiency and value of wireless communication', and 'acquiring adequate technical equipment for our experts to work with.'[142]

Late in 1936, Commissioner Cummings selected Inspectors James Cummings and Reg Ward to give a series of lectures in all the police districts on practical police and detective duties, thus extending the quarterly lectures in the main centres Commissioner Wohlmann had initiated eighteen months earlier. Instruction was to be given by experienced and 'practical' police officers rather than outside experts. This coincided with a renewed emphasis on training by most Australian Police Commissioners. Where they focused (in post-recruit training) on the formal instruction of detectives through special courses in the capital cities (notably in Victoria and Queensland), Cummings attempted to reach at 'convenient places' all his staff, including country constables, whom he perceived as being 'to some extent out of touch with the general run of police work.'[143] He could not afford to transfer men to the Wellington Depot for further training. Nor did he see any advantage in more detectives going to the London Metropolitan Police College, following observations made by the two sent in 1935 by Wohlmann.[144]

In 1937, Cummings set in place a modest system, first in Auckland and later in the other main centres: a compulsory course of fortnightly lectures at district headquarters by local officers in 'practical duties' for three separate classes of detectives, uniformed Sergeants and constables (probationary constables attended weekly). Smaller districts were to have lectures at least monthly. Also during 1937, the firearms expert recruited by Wohlmann, Senior Sergeant G.G. Kelly, visited stations to train a large number of men in the correct handling of firearms.[145] In addition, constables and Sergeants were to undergo twenty minutes of drill at each monthly pay parade, so that they would 'march well and look the part', with uniforms neater and tidier than hitherto.[146] The men were not only to *be* more efficient, but had to *appear* so.

While the Commissioner detected a 'marked improvement' in the men's marching, the lectures were of 'varying merit', W.R. Murray told him. Typically, while some were well-presented and informative, more were 'dry' and taught experienced men little. 'The majority can always learn', Cummings responded, seeing lectures as 'most essential and necessary' for efficiency.[147] Potentially, the advent of formal in-service training benefited those who (as Cummings observed) 'wanted to get on'; but because of its meagreness it merely supplemented for most constables their more formative experiences on the job.

Better knowledge of the law, Police Regulations and procedures was nonetheless required by the Commissioner when he recast the qualifying examinations for promotion. He saw new examination regulations issued in June 1938 as 'raising the standard' and thereby increasing efficiency. Instead of being able to short-circuit the system of qualifying by passing only the Sub-Inspector's examination (as the best men had done hitherto), candidates had now to take the examinations for each rank in turn, and obtain a higher percentage of marks for each subject within both the Literary and the Law examinations. As a quid pro quo for the greater demands now placed on largely self-directed preparation, passes in only two law subjects were required in any one sitting.[148] This encouragement to ambition more than counterbalanced the potential deterrent of higher standards. Examinees apparently did better with 'Prescribed Acts' and 'Evidence' than they did with the more practically-oriented 'Police and Detective Duties', where (according to Chief Detective J.B. Young) 'you get a variety of opinion as to the correct answers.'[149] From the rank and file came requests for a 'Law Coach', an up-to-date Police 'Handbook' or 'Code', and 'refresher courses' at the Training Depot.[150]

Since Police Regulations and the Commissioner's General Instructions comprised one of the four subjects in the Law examinations for each rank, they needed to both reflect current practice and be accessible. Many were obsolete. While the regulations were conveniently indexed in the 'Black Book' issued to all constables since 1920, the Commissioner's circulars and memoranda were published in the weekly *New Zealand Police Gazette* and then copied into local station books. It was becoming 'impossible to keep track' of those that remained operative. Single-handedly, Cummings began their revision in 1937, hoping to complete the process within a year; it took more than a decade.[151] In the meantime, the 'Black Book' was not reprinted. Thus few were available for the influx of new constables, who had to borrow them from 'old hands' where they could. Preoccupied with the building programme and other issues, the Commissioner found little time to work on consolidating regulations and circulars. Association delegates first expressed concern in December 1938; but by 1940 Cummings could no longer say when the task would be completed, 'with so much war work to attend to.' By now Association delegates saw an up-to-date police Handbook or Code as 'fundamental' to the efficiency of the Force, and suggested that the Commissioner delegate the task to other officers. Unwilling to do so, Cummings responded tangentially and defensively: 'I do not run the Force on circulars. We do it with equipment in a practical way. We have the finest fleet of motor cars now that one could wish to have. Four years ago we had nothing'.[152]

By 1940 the Commissioner believed that he had established an efficient system of transport for police, one sufficient to meet the needs of a largely unchanged pattern of rural and urban policing. Again he built on inherited practices. Constables' own cars at country stations and the bicycles of suburban men (where they did not walk or take trams) had largely superseded horses by 1936. Cummings encouraged the process, dispensing with horses where possible, building garages at country stations, and increasing the annual and mileage-based allowances for the use of 'efficient' privately-owned cars on police work. Only constables possessing cars were to be sent on relieving duty to country stations (they would receive the appropriate proportion of the incumbent's annual allowance).[153] In practice, then, country constables both provided the Department with modern transport and bore some of the expense of doing so. With the shift from horses to cars, their readiness to patrol over long distances (when not making enquiries or delivering summonses) may well have been influenced by perceptions of the personal expense this entailed.

This system was not transposed to the towns and cities, where patrolling on foot (or bicycle) was still seen as basic to preventive policing. Suburban men and city constables on routine enquiries generally continued to be ineligible for car or mileage allowances. Even so, more rapid and flexible night patrolling of suburbs, especially Auckland's, had come to be seen as necessary by the early 1930s. Similarly, detectives in the main centres were perceived to need greater mobility in pursuing inquiries and motorised criminals. More generally, city and small-town police now required cars to respond to emergencies: anything less was viewed as inadequate.[154]

Again Cummings' approach was modest. In the provincial centres and smaller towns, commissioned officers, detectives and uniformed men on country enquiries were paid mileage for using their own cars. Should 'necessity arise,' Cummings declared optimistically, 'cars can be hired from motor garages or taxi-proprietors at a moment's notice' – a system which 'has met every emergency that has arisen.'[155] Departmental vehicles were provided only in the four main centres, where, by 1936, there was a total of eight cars, three prison vans and a motorcycle, for a combined population of 574,000. (Melbourne, with a population less than twice this size, had more than 60 vehicles.)[156] Most of these vehicles were obsolete or worn out, and commissioned officers had first call on the cars. Only in Auckland (with three cars and the motorcycle) had a night patrol begun. Within four years, the fleet in the four cities had doubled in size and been modernised with 'fast cars' – mainly Chevrolets, black and without police markings or emergency lights, but with sirens and spotlights added to some from 1937.[157] In Auckland at least, motorised night patrols by a detective and two constables became routine. Even so, Wellington constables still pursued converted cars by taxi, and Christchurch detectives, like their counterparts elsewhere, resorted to bikes, public transport, or (when permitted) their own cars on mileage allowances.[158]

Efficient patrolling by car required effective communication with the central station. Familiarity with the location of suburban telephone boxes became a necessity for police drivers. Without 'wireless', however, car patrols were not readily directed. In 1937, Cummings gained Fraser's approval to 'experiment' with wireless communication, and called on experts from the Post and Telegraph Department. Here, too, the Commissioner proceeded 'with caution' because of the expense and technical problems. In fact, there was already considerable experience in using wireless telegraphy and Morse code (in one-way and then two-way communication) with patrol cars in Melbourne, Sydney and London. Locally, businessmen like former Detective N.W. Laugeson were well versed in such systems.[159] During the late 1930s, the Australian police forces and others began changing to radio telephony – first in Sydney, where fourteen cars were brought into operation in May 1937. Cummings looked to develop such a system with police-controlled transmitters, though his Force lacked the substantial incremental investment in radio communications that had already been made by the New South Wales Police. Urban topography (especially in Wellington, where Cummings chose to make the first experiments), the limitations of medium-frequency transmission (high-frequency not then being available), and the application of insufficient energy and expertise to developing local solutions produced meagre results which compounded the Commissioner's caution. In a changing economic climate, Fraser also saw the facilities required as being 'very expensive'. During both the 1938/39 and 1939/40 financial years, money authorised was not spent; the purchase of radio equipment was deferred for 'further investigation'. Not until 1946 were the first radio-controlled patrol cars introduced in Auckland and Wellington, using a system that had potentially been available since 1938.[160]

While the New Zealand Police lagged behind the larger Australian forces in making use of modern communications (teleprinters as well as radios), the gap was not so apparent in the adoption of the latest scientific aids for crime detection. By the late 1930s, a growing emphasis on 'the scientific approach to criminal investigation' in some United States police departments (symbolised by the much-vaunted 'professionalism' of the Federal Bureau of Investigation) influenced developments in Britain and Australia, where there was more formal training of detectives, more systematic methods of collating information on crime and criminals, and the development of police forensic science 'sections' or laboratories. Such trends were mirrored in New Zealand, though more weakly. Following the recommendations of the two detectives sent to study developments at Scotland Yard, the Battley single fingerprint system was adopted in Wellington during 1936 and a 'modus operandi' system was initiated at Auckland the following year. At Headquarters, expertise in aspects of forensic science developed within both the Criminal Registration Branch (which was responsible for photography as well as fingerprints) and the Arms Bureau, where G.G. Kelly spent a 'fair amount of time' on 'experimental and research' work as well as testing firearms. New equipment was acquired for forensic ballistics and microphotography, and the Headquarters' library was 'brought up to date' during 1937 and 1938, coinciding with similar developments at the New South Wales Police headquarters. Like their counterparts in Sydney, New Zealand detectives also looked increasingly to experts outside the Force, and especially to chemists in the Dominion Laboratory's branches in the main centres. Implicitly claiming that this led to increased efficiency, Cummings pointed to the 'excellent work' of police in solving the Piha arson case during 1939 'with the aid of scientists'.[161]

Prosperity and order

By contrast to the early 1930s, detectives' performance in solving murders was not a significant policing issue between 1936 and 1939.[162] In part, this reflected a period when the number of murders recorded fell to the lowest level between the wars. Between 1936 and 1938, reported thefts and burglaries also fell from the high point reached in the early 1930s, though they continued to be of concern to suburban and small-town shopkeepers and householders (see figures I.5, I.6). Instead, more police work was created by an upswing in prosperity (with more employment, higher wages, and shorter hours) which saw a sharp increase in alcohol consumption and arrests for public drunkenness and related offences (figure I.4). Similarly, the number of prosecutions for being found intoxicated while in charge of a motor vehicle rose from 272 in 1934 to 806 in 1938, and total breaches of the Motor Vehicles Act virtually doubled in this period to become the largest single element in the broad categories of offences dealt with by police (figure 4.1). The rapid growth in this aspect of police work reflected a substantial increase in car ownership (there were some 64,000 new registrations between 1936 and 1939) resulting from a more widely diffused prosperity. More cars also meant that more were 'converted' (at least 30 in Auckland during March 1938, for example), mainly by youthful 'joy-riders'.[163] Indeed, the increase in the number of young offenders being prosecuted, which had levelled off during the early 1930s, accelerated markedly, especially for property offences, with Children's Court cases increasing by nearly half between 1935 and 1940. Though these were countrywide trends, they were more pronounced in Auckland (where an upswing in drunkenness arrests was first noticed in 1935) and in the northern provincial police districts, notably Whangarei, Hamilton, Gisborne and Palmerston North (figure 4.2). In North Auckland, Bay of Plenty and the East Coast there was a sharp increase in arrests of Maori, especially for drunkenness. To the parliamentary Opposition, the overall growth in offences seemed a paradoxical accompaniment to prosperity. Not so, replied Fraser: 'the police are more vigilant now.'[164]

Overall, then, issues of order rather than of 'serious crime' influenced the management of policing in the late 1930s. Breaches of the Licensing Act were prosecuted more vigorously, especially those relating to Maori.[165] Concern about rowdy country dances, and drunken driving after them, led to strict enforcement of a ban on liquor in the vicinity of dance halls enacted in 1939.[166] Accidents, whether involving firearms or on the road, were the focus of increased bureaucratic attention. In June 1935, G.G. Kelly, a civilian expert on firearms, had established an Arms Bureau at Police Headquarters. His main tasks were to investigate shooting accidents and fatalities (mainly amongst males in their twenties), and to prevent them by having unsafe shotguns and rifles excluded from sale or removed from their owners. Though educational work in schools on the handling of firearms was planned, lectures and demonstrations at district headquarters and the Training Depot were the most Kelly could manage, along with his investigative, 'experimental and research' work.[167] Similarly, from March 1937, police had to furnish detailed reports to the Transport Department on every motor vehicle accident involving death or injury: the 4,062 reports in the first year involved 5,334 casualties.[168] As the growth in recorded traffic offences and accidents created much extra work, the Police Association urged (in the hope of increasing both resources and efficiency) that the Police take over full responsibility for traffic control from local authorities and the Main Highways Board. 'You do not want me to have civil war inside the Cabinet do you?', responded Fraser in dismissing the suggestion.[169] Altogether, the upswing in the volume of disorderly and reckless male behaviour dealt with by police, along with growth in their other work, brought an increased workload. As a crude measure, the number of offences 'reported' per police officer (albeit unevenly distributed in reality) rose from 27 in 1935 to 32 in 1939 – the highest rate of the inter-war years. Though the Training Depot was 'kept at top speed' during 1938 and 1939, insufficient men were trained to meet the demand for more police.[170]

Heightened perceptions of drink-related disorder added impetus to the long-standing campaign for women police. According to one prominent Auckland proponent in 1937, parents 'were becoming alarmed' at drinking amongst young people; 'spotting' had become 'commmplace' and women police were 'necessary for protective work'.[171] Though Elizabeth McCombs, the first woman MP, had pressed for women police from the Labour benches between 1933 and early 1935,[172] Peter Fraser was cautious when questioned by his predecessor as Minister in charge of the Police, J.G. Cobbe, in August 1936. 'Representations' had already been made to him – including no doubt by his wife, Janet

– in favour of women police.[173] However, D.J. Cummings had been Commissioner for barely a month and was, initially at least, as conservative on the issue as his predecessor, Wohlmann. Thus Fraser waited (as he did with respect to the formation of the Police Association) for renewed lobbying: 'If some conclusions could be arrived at as to the nature of the work to be undertaken, and suitable women were available, he would go into the question in a sympathetic spirit.'[174] To the women's organisations who had long argued for policewomen, the 'conclusions' remained clear and unchanged: 'preventive work' should be undertaken among women and children by trained, mature women who had the power of arrest and would take over many of the enquiries involving females currently undertaken by male police; suitable candidates were available. By early in the election year of 1938, the time was ripe. Fraser told a deputation from a women's branch of the Labour Party that he had been 'forced by the facts to the conclusion I had long ago reached in my own mind, that women police can be a great help to the Police Force and to society in this country.' They would be appointed 'as soon as possible'.[175] In September a clause in a Statutes Amendment Bill enabled women to be appointed to the Police Force on the same terms as men.[176] It was to be three years before the first group of policewomen were trained and posted for duties shaped largely by the special circumstances of war.

To the extent that the expectations of women's organisations were frustrated by the slow and limited implementation of an innovation, the advent of women police epitomises the ambiguities of change in the Police Force during the late 1930s. Amongst older police – those whose experience stretched back to before the 1920s – there was a sense that working conditions had improved by 1939. Shorter hours allowed a consciousness of occupational community encompassing all ranks to flourish in station-based leisure activity which was encouraged by Commissioner Cummings and publicised by the *Police Journal*. Especially in the main centres from 1936, social committees and sports clubs were formed to organise annual balls and picnics, regular 'card and dance' evenings (involving wives); debating (in Christchurch), and a male-only district 'smoke concert' (in Auckland); police orchestras, and a Highland pipe band (at Wellington); police rugby and cricket teams (with annual inter-district contests between Auckland and Wellington, and between Christchurch and Dunedin), as well as miniature rifle matches, tennis and lawn bowls (the most popular sport). With the support of the Commissioner, an eleven-member team (drawn mainly from Auckland and Wellington) was sent to the New South Wales Police sports carnival in February 1938. The 'En Zedders', who wore black blazers with a Silver Fern monogram headed with 'N.Z.P.', were the first representative police team to go overseas. 'Great strides have been made in the Police Force recently', commented an Association correspondent to the *Police Journal* in April 1938, 'but none so great' as when the Commissioner 'competed in the chain-stepping event' at the first New Plymouth District picnic a month earlier. [177]

Yet a florescence of police social life was not a salve for the impatient. By 1939, improvements in working conditions had been piecemeal and limited, and neither of the two major objectives of the Police Association in 1936 – a 40-hour week and earlier retirement – had been achieved. Optimistic in 1936, Detective Charles Belton had become disillusioned two years later at the lack of a 40-hour week and the 'many difficulties' in working conditions which persisted. 'Rome was not built in a day' was I.D. Campbell's response (echoing the predominant view among the Association's membership) when Belton made his disappointment public in November 1938. The ambitious detective left the Police Force three months later.[178] Amongst a growing number of the rank and file who remained, and especially amongst the younger uniformed men in Auckland, seeds of frustration were to sprout with the pressures of wartime.

CHAPTER 12

Policing the
Home Front (1939–45)

From the outbreak of the Second World War on 3 September 1939, the scope of police work grew rapidly. As in the Australian states, the New Zealand Police Force was the lynch-pin of internal security.[1] Its traditional responsibilities for political surveillance, maintenance of order, and the prosecution of illegalities were extended, while other roles were added – including the control of aliens, supervision of watchmen at 'vital points', and training of auxiliary police for the Emergency Precautions Scheme. In particular, the control of 'subversives' and aliens, and the prevention of sabotaging of the country's war effort, soon took priority over routine policing. In October 1940, Commissioner D.J. Cummings emphasised to his South Island commissioned officers that 'the war-work side of the Police work has got to have preference. As the Minister says, if we lose the war, what's the devil's the use of anything?' Sub-Inspector W.H. Dunlop, in charge of the Detective Branch at Christchurch, agreed; 'but it is a job to get the public to believe it, if their houses are burning or their cars are being pinched.'[2] Such competing pressures characterised policing on the home front.

From early 1938, committees of the Organisation for National Security had begun considering Police responsibilities in the event of war.[3] This planning was rudimentary, but it laid the basis for the rapid introduction of emergency regulations. Once the war began, Cummings played a pivotal role in adapting policies and seeking new powers. Though police were allocated new tasks before the war, there was no planning for extra staff. Unlike their counterparts in Australia and England, no police reserves were created, nor were retired police called back or wartime auxiliaries used to free the regular police from routine tasks.[4] A shortage of staff remained a persistent problem. Nor was there any pre-war training for the wartime duties that might result from, for example, air raids or an invasion. The editor of the *New Zealand Police Journal* commented in October 1939 that

> Many members have in fact wondered why the individual members of the Police Force have not been made more fully acquainted with the

probable nature of their work if such an emergency arose. At all events, it is a tribute to the men themselves if it is officially considered that they can adequately carry out emergency orders immediately the occasion requires.[5]

That indeed was the expectation, and police met it. Though there were no air raids, nor an invasion, the many new tasks of the wartime emergency required initiative, commitment, often a sense of urgency, and long hours of work.

Organising 'security work'

Increased wartime responsibilities for internal security required effective surveillance and the sharing of information with the various state agencies which needed it. Until September 1939, the Police had virtually the sole responsibility for internal political surveillance, and the pattern of organisation had not changed since 1919. (The Customs Department did have a significant role in curbing imports of 'subversive' literature between 1916 and 1936.) More men were committed exclusively to this work as security surveillance became a priority from September 1939. At Auckland, Detective Sergeant Jim Nalder headed a team of five detectives between 1939 and 1941. All reports went to the Commissioner, who directed the work. Between 1937 and 1944, the information was collated in the Commissioner's office by Detective Sergeant A.M. Harding[6] (assisted by two or three constables), who liaised with the intelligence sections of the armed forces and the various security agencies in Britain and its empire.[7]

Since 1919, political surveillance had developed largely through police initiatives rather than any specific instructions from the government. A relaxation in the censorship of 'seditious' literature in 1936 reflected the change of government.[8] But political surveillance continued, and was not confined to the Communist Party. The Police focus continued to be shaped by its basic mandate – to prevent or suppress illegality and disorder that might challenge 'constituted authority'. Ministers might offer hints; but equally, local events and overseas security agencies (especially MI5 in London) suggested new targets for surveillance. Periodically, when circumstances required it, Commissioners told Ministers what they considered it necessary they know. However, it appears that, before the outbreak of war at least, Ministers did not generally seek to know the results of police surveillance. Indeed, they seem to have been unaware of its scope. So too were other government agencies, with regard to which police could be circumspect in passing on information. To the armed forces in particular, police surveillance appeared to have its limitations in wartime. By April 1938, it had 'become apparent' to Lieutenant-Colonel W.G. Stevens, Secretary of the Organisation for National Security, that an

'Intelligence Bureau' would need to be established in the event of war, 'to deal with all matters of furnishing information to the enemy, violation of censorship, subversive activities, etc.'[9] Harding joined intelligence officers from the Army, Navy, and Air Force in meetings at Army Headquarters from April 1938 to consider what action should be taken. The Police peacetime role was soon agreed on: to record arrivals and departures of aliens (a new task, requiring assistance from the Customs and Statistics departments), and to monitor those perceived to be likely to 'instigate sabotage or anti-war agitation' – a function which was seen as being 'already adequately carried out'. A procedure for circulating information 'of common interest' was established. With the Police's peacetime responsibility for internal intelligence and security reaffirmed, and now deemed to be 'satisfactory', the wartime organisation of intelligence was left for further discussion. In September the Chiefs of Staff of the Army, Navy and Air Force agreed to set up wartime combined intelligence centres in Auckland and Christchurch to sift and test information before it was sent to an intelligence centre at Defence Headquarters in Wellington. Cummings agreed that Harding would liaise with the Wellington centre, as would the detectives involved in security work at the other centres.[10]

Practicalities as well as separate departmental interests were thus reflected in this limited attempt to *coordinate* intelligence gathering and appraisal, rather than to establish a single national organisation for internal security surveillance. Indeed, the outbreak of war saw the range of agencies involved in security surveillance multiply, with the advent of Post and Telegraph censorship, a new Director of Publicity who censored the press, and an expansion of the Customs Department's role in monitoring the arrival of shipping, people and goods.[11] Formally and informally, departments sought each other's assistance – Police supplied lists of aliens to the postal censor, and Customs worked closely with the Navy in gaining information on shipping and seamen, for example.[12] But by 1940, police liaison with the armed forces' combined intelligence centres was seen as inadequate.

As in Australia, the Navy became increasingly concerned at the absence of a 'central security service' to coordinate the gathering of security intelligence and act as a 'clearing house' for the information 'pooled'. Information would thus be centrally appraised and appropriate action taken where necessary. In August 1940, the Naval Secretary sought a discussion of the matter by the Chiefs of Staff. Central to Navy concerns was the absence of a security service which met the British Admiralty requirements of Naval Intelligence, namely: to protect armed forces from injury by spying, sabotage, or any other activities; to provide a 'standing liaison between the fighting services and all civil and police activities on security matters', as well as 'general supervision of all foreigners and disaffected persons on British soil'; and to maintain a record of all those classified as 'dangerous or unsuitable for "security" reasons' for employment in the armed forces or government departments.[13]

While it was 'axiomatic' that such a security service would use the services of the Police, the Navy felt that some investigations could be more effectively handled by men outside the Force. Police inquiries were perceived to be 'conducted on lines which are too stereotyped to meet present war conditions'. In essence, police methods were seen as constrained and too legalistic in 'usually' seeking to identify a 'person responsible for a crime already committed'. To the military mind, concerned with the 'very real' possibility that there were in New Zealand 'active enemy agents' professing to support the British cause, an 'entirely different' approach was needed: to 'visualise the position of the enemy agent' aiming to inflict maximum damage to the country's war effort. The 'sudden collapse' of Holland, Belgium, and France during May and June 1940 appeared to indicate the effectiveness of 'insidious and devious' methods in sapping the 'moral fibre and the "will to resist" ' of their inhabitants. Naval authorities thought the 'tactful but firm suppression' of any 'fifth column' movement in New Zealand to be 'outside the scope of normal police activities.'[14] Naval ignorance of both the scope of police surveillance and its methods was thus revealed, as well as heightened fears of subversion which reflected the wider sense of crisis that had developed from May.

In November 1940 the Navy's initiative was strengthened by the arrival from London, en route to Australia, of Lieutenant-Colonel J.C. Mawhood of the British Army General Staff. He had been sent by MI5, backed by the War Office, with a proposal that New Zealand establish a security intelligence service on the British model. This would be (like MI5) under Army control, but separate from existing military and police surveillance, which would continue and 'act in the closest co-operation'. Just as he later impressed senior Australian federal government ministers,[15] Mawhood secured agreement from the New Zealand War Cabinet before approaching the Chiefs of Staff who, in turn, recommended that his scheme be implemented without delay. They also strongly supported Mawhood's view that a British officer should be obtained, on loan, to control the new organisation, as there was 'no person in New Zealand with sufficient training in Security Intelligence duties'. Thus Kenneth Folkes, a junior officer from MI5 with very limited experience who proved to be temperamentally unsuited for his role, was appointed Director of the Security Intelligence Bureau.[16] It began its work in February 1941, after a short period of staff training. Its 44 staff were 'youngish, well educated' Army officers and NCOs distributed between three district bureaus (in Auckland, Palmerston North, and Christchurch) and the central bureau in Wellington. Folkes was responsible to both the Chiefs of Staff and the Prime Minister, to whom he had access – a division of control which the Chiefs of Staff were to find embarrassing.[17]

To the Chiefs of Staff, the primary responsibility of the SIB was to ensure the security of the armed forces. Folkes (like Mawhood) had a broader conception of its role as 'a link in the chain of Security Service[s] throughout the Empire, which is "fed" by M.I.5.' Thus he replaced the Commissioner of Police as the New Zealand correspondent of MI5. And he took a comprehensive view of the SIB's interests in civil security, which he saw as encompassing the detection of bribery and corruption within government; the activities of aliens, pacifists, and any organisation 'likely to cause disaffection' or the 'impairment of morale'; subversion; illicit photography or signalling; evasions of censorship; and rumours and their sources. Other concerns included preventing sabotage in wartime production and administration by vetting, selecting and culling staff, and ensuring the security of wharves, shipping information, and government communications.[18]

Though Folkes took the view that, henceforth, police would only do 'security work' when asked by the SIB, he sought no such demarcation of roles from the Commissioner. Nor is it likely that Cummings would have acquiesced. Police security surveillance continued. Indeed it had intensified in the detection of subversion, monitoring of aliens, protection of wharves and 'important places' from sabotage, and investigation of the many complaints from nervous or imaginative individuals alleging spying, signalling (flashing lights), disloyal statements, or enemy submarines at sea.[19] Inevitably, there was much duplication of effort and organisational jealousy. With a sense of superiority, the SIB did not recruit detectives, who were apparently viewed 'as the policeman of the English comic paper.' Detectives, in turn, saw the SIB officers (of Army background) as amateurs who were privileged in their access to Army cars and secret funds. Cooperation did not come easily. Information received by the SIB was passed on only if it was perceived to be a 'police matter'. Similarly, police were cagey in supplying information from their 'secret' sources. SIB officers were not permitted to copy Police files. In September 1941, Fraser indicated to the Chiefs of Staff that the 'whole question' of the functions of the SIB needed to be discussed; but the degree to which it was responsible for 'civil security' remained cloudy.[20]

By mid-July 1942, the SIB under Folkes had been discredited by an elaborate hoax. Over a period of three months (when there were heightened fears of a Japanese invasion), SIB officers, including Folkes, came firmly to believe in stories concerning plots of sabotage, invasion, and other matters told to them by a convicted conman, Sidney Gordon Ross.[21] That Ross should be believed (indeed, be funded to assist in uncovering alleged conspirators while masquerading as 'Captain Calder') reflected on the Bureau's methods, on Folkes' credulity and on his unwillingness to seek police assistance. More than this, Folkes' exaggerated conception of his role led to his undoing. In asking the Chiefs of Staff for soldiers to arrest alleged fifth columnists involved in the plots, he lost their confidence – not so much because the plots seemed far-fetched or his approach was extra-legal, but for failing to inform them earlier of an alleged invasion plot. When Folkes urged Fraser to give him special powers to arrest the alleged conspirators without proof of any illegality, the Prime Minister (who had sent Ross to Folkes in the first place) turned to the Police. Superintendent James Cummings responded with alacrity. Local police at New Plymouth and Rotorua had already spotted Ross. In a couple of days a small team of detective NCOs experienced in security work[22] had interrogated Ross at Rotorua and exposed the hoax – a success trumpeted soon afterwards, on 29 July, by *Truth.*[23]

At Fraser's request, the Attorney-General reported on the 'Ross case'. From his scrutiny of police files, particularly regarding the internment of aliens, Mason had some insight into the police approach. He noted that the SIB was 'very conscious of the difference between its methods and those of the Police'. He drew a stereotypical distinction: the SIB did not take statements 'as the Police do.' Rather it 'observes, tabulates, accumulates reports, and slowly builds up a picture. It does not check, test, and verify (as far as it can) as it goes along.' To Mason, the SIB approach displayed a concern for secrecy 'appropriate to a secret service in a hostile country.' Its method could 'accumulate, and in this case did accumulate, much rubbish.'[24] In fact the distinction Mason drew was too sharp. Police were also concerned with secrecy in their surveillance; they too accumulated and tabulated reports of observations. But the broader experience of detectives and their more legalistic approach perhaps (but not necessarily) made for more realistic assessments of the information they gathered.

Though the SIB had been brought into disrepute, the issue of what should take its place remained. On 18 September Mason recommended that civil security (as well as the port security work that the SIB had begun earlier in the year) be handed over entirely to the Police. Each of the armed forces should be responsible for its 'internal' security matters. Yet there was still the issue of co-ordination. Mason felt that a 'small Security Bureau' should continue as a 'clearing house' and 'a point of contact' between the armed forces and the Police. And so he proposed a hybrid: the Bureau would be controlled by the Chief of General Staff and headed by a military officer, but be housed at Police Headquarters so as to 'keep the work of the Bureau in proper perspective.' To ensure the smooth working of this arrangement, the creation of an advisory security committee was suggested. Fraser took his time. On 22 December the Chiefs of Staff urged the immediate dismissal of Folkes, but were undecided on whether the SIB should be disbanded, observing that it had been valuable in enhancing port security, and that duplication of work could be removed by 'proper organisation'. They wanted further discussion with the Commissioner of Police.[25] Eventually, with no agreement yet reached between the Chiefs of Staff and the Commissioner, Fraser directed that Folkes be replaced by Superintendent James Cummings as Director of Security Intelligence on 19 February 1943.[26]

Ostensibly, little changed. The Director of Security Intelligence remained in offices attached to Army Headquarters and retained direct access to the Prime Minister. Police security surveillance and SIB work (including port security) continued separately as before, with the division of responsibility still unclear. In July 1943, the Commissioner felt the need to direct his staff to co-operate with Security Bureau officers, while exercising 'a careful discretion.'[27] Duplication of work continued despite greater co-ordination. Until 1944, the Director continued to offer separate and occasionally different security assessments from those of the Commissioner.[28] James Cummings replaced some of the SIB's Army personnel with civilians from legal or business backgrounds, but apparently maintained a low opinion of the 'amateurs' in his Bureau.[29] After James Cummings succeeded his brother as Commissioner on 1 November 1944, the SIB became more clearly an adjunct of the Police Force. Though Cummings retained the title of Director of Security, Senior Detective P.J. Nalder took charge of the SIB.[30] From this point the records of the Bureau were merged with those of the Police, and detectives came to take sole responsibility for security investigation. Virtually all the Bureau's non-police staff left, and Nalder moved to an office in Police Headquarters and took control of the Force's security work. The SIB was closed down at the end of September 1945.[31]

Controlling dissent

Fundamental to the maintenance of internal security was the nature and degree of dissent from the country's participation in the war. An overwhelming majority in the small, homogeneous Pakeha society supported a wholehearted contribution; so too did most Maori. Social tensions arising from the war effort were to be far less acute than during the First World War. Overt opposition to the war was largely confined to its first two years and to very small numbers of committed pacifists (members of the Christian Pacifist Society and the Peace Pledge Union), members of the Communist Party (until Germany's invasion of the Soviet Union in June 1941), and Jehovah's Witnesses – probably little more than 2,000 in total.[32] In addition there were those (fewer than 2,000) who kept quiet, but whose nationality or ancestry made their loyalty widely suspect in the early years of the war. At the outset of the war, the Police had identified a tiny number (mainly Germans with Nazi sympathies) who were likely to be disloyal; otherwise they perceived little risk of sabotage.[33] Nonetheless, the issue of 'subversive activity' (broadly conceived as anything undermining the war effort) remained.

Here the police responses were shaped by a number of influences, chief among which was the attitude of Peter Fraser to the prospect of social divisions in wartime. For Fraser, the importance of the war effort quickly became overwhelming, and unity of purpose had to be pursued, at the expense of freedom to agitate against participation in the war, or even to criticise government policy.[34] This tendency to 'authoritarianism' intensified with the stresses of wartime administration. Indeed, in the suppression of 'subversive activity', the relative autonomy of police from ministerial direction diminished (though it did not completely disappear).[35] Police perceptions of subversion or 'disorder', or its possibility, could lead them to take their own initiatives.[36] Where, however, J.T. Paul, the Director of Publicity who was in frequent contact with Fraser, was seemingly unconstrained in deciding what could be published,[37] police were generally imbued with an ethos of legalism that led them to consciously look for the ingredients of an offence. They needed specific powers to deal effectively with dissent. In tune with Fraser's hardening attitude, Commissioner Cummings played an important role in developing and refining the necessary emergency regulations.

Two days before New Zealand entered the war, the long-prepared Censorship and Publicity Emergency Regulations were issued, making it an offence to communicate a 'subversive report', orally or otherwise. To speak against the recruitment of soldiers, or the war effort more broadly, could be deemed subversive. To police, however, the regulations were 'administratively deficient', providing no means of quick action if an offence was detected; they had neither power of arrest nor any means of 'preventing an offender continuing to make subversive statements.' The Attorney-General's consent was needed for prosecution. Surveillance of pacifist organisations and the Communist Party increased, with police sending full reports of their public meetings to the Solicitor-General.[38]

In the first months of the war (until January 1940 at least), the government seemed reluctant to suppress outspoken dissent, or at least to test the nature of a 'subversive statement' in the courts. Nonetheless, police acted against pacifists, ostensibly to prevent disorder. On the day war was declared, three (including the charismatic Methodist minister and war veteran, Ormond Burton) refused to stop speaking outside Parliament Buildings. They were arrested for obstructing the police – to the embarrassment of Peter Fraser, who respected Burton and wanted to avoid incidents which could prove divisive.[39] A pattern was soon established, especially in Wellington, where Burton was arrested several times. A few pacifists continued to speak in the streets at places and times when they could be sure of an audience. Some, but not all, were ordered to stop and, when they invariably refused, arrested for 'obstructing a constable'. Magistrates (and ultimately the Chief Justice in the case *Burton v. Power*, in April 1940) endorsed such a method of forestalling disorder – even though the speakers were not inciting it and the meetings were quiet, at least until late November 1939 when soldiers began to turn up, sometimes in organised demonstrations. Burton thought that only one of his meetings (at the Wellington Trades' Hall in January 1940) was in serious danger of breaking up into violence.[40] In effect, unpopular views could now be quashed by the hecklers' veto. From January 1940, government attitudes hardened in line with signs of increasing public hostility towards pacifists as well as Communists who, in Auckland, spoke at some rowdy meetings against the 'imperialist war'.[41]

While the Christian pacifists on soapboxes were a nuisance in the eyes of the police, Communists were perceived as the main threat to the war effort from 1940. There was a 'fundamental difference of motive' in their opposition to the war, and police found no alliance between the two groups. Where pacifists were generally frank with police about what they intended to do or had done, and were in turn treated courteously, the Communist Party went underground following the outbreak of the war, meeting covertly in small groups in anticipation of being declared an illegal organisation. The party supported the USSR after it signed a non-aggression pact with Germany in August 1939 by calling on the New Zealand working class to oppose the war. Through the *People's Voice,* leaflets, and at street meetings it alleged from December that Labour leaders had sided with imperialist warmongers. Strongest in Auckland, where party membership was estimated by police to be some 300 just before the war, its influence appeared to be growing at various workplaces by early 1940.[42] As yet, however, no one had been prosecuted for making a 'subversive statement'.

Late in January 1940, the Attorney-General, Rex Mason, signalled that the government would no longer tolerate utterances 'designed to distract, divide or disturb' people advancing the war effort. The Public Safety Emergency Regulations were now drafted at a series of meetings involving Mason, the Solicitor-General and Commissioner Cummings, and issued on 21 February. The definition of 'subversive reports' was revised to include statements likely to interfere with wartime production or cause resistance to military service. A Superintendent or Inspector could prohibit a meeting or procession he considered likely to injure public safety, and authorise premises to be searched. Those breaching the regulations could be arrested without warrant, but prosecutions for making a subversive statement still required the Attorney-General's consent.[43]

Though police were armed with increased powers, they did not at first use them fully against the pacifists, but continued to stop their street meetings (and by June, their poster parades in Wellington) on the grounds that disorder was likely. Speakers refusing to comply were prosecuted for obstruction. Magistrates showed their increasing impatience with longer sentences of imprisonment. The number of activists prepared to make a public stand fell away. However, pacifists were not prosecuted for making subversive statements. Their leaflets and pamphlets seized by the police were deemed only 'mildly' subversive by the Attorney-General, who directed, nonetheless, that they be retained along with the machine that had produced them.[44]

To a deputation of Wellington citizens (including churchmen, lawyers and university staff) concerned at the threat to civil liberties, Fraser made it clear that Communists, more than pacifists, were the focus of the new regulations. This was underlined by the creation of the new offence of receiving money for a purpose contrary to the regulations, and the exceptional powers given police to examine bank records. One Auckland party member had been immediately investigated in February, but the regular remittances he received from the USSR were found to be interest on personal investments. Further examination of Communist Party bank accounts found no evidence of money received from overseas or for subversive purposes. Communists, unlike active pacifists, were prosecuted in April for publishing subversive statements (in the *People's Voice* and in pamphlets between October and February), and from May for distributing leaflets and for statements made at street meetings. Though public meetings held by Communists were not totally prohibited by police, they became infrequent and 'of little moment' once the 'able speakers' were imprisoned.[45]

Nonetheless the covert activities of the party, and its persistent opposition to the war effort through leaflets and the *People's Voice,* led to further measures as a sense of crisis deepened. Early in May 1940, Commissioner Cummings directed that a second temporary constable be recruited for 'secret duties' in Auckland. On 29 May, three days after the Prime Minister had broadcast plans for conscription 'as required', new regulations[46] empowered the Attorney-General to suppress publications. Immediately, H.G.R. Mason ordered the seizure by police of the records and press of the *People's Voice* in Auckland. On 4 June further publication was banned, two weeks after similar action against Australian Communist Party newspapers by the federal government. Simultaneously, the left-wing Christchurch-based journal *Tomorrow* ceased publication after local police warned the printer that his press would be seized if he published anything subversive. Illegal cyclostyled issues of the *People's Voice*, along with leaflets, continued to be produced and distributed in Auckland, Wellington and Christchurch. The persistence of such activities opposing the war effort led to a further amendment of the Public Safety Emergency Regulations. On 18 June, three days after the Australian Communist Party was banned, the government gave itself the power to declare an organisation 'subversive' – at which point its activities would become illegal. The Communist Party was not alone in being considered for banning, however.[47]

With the advent of conscription, foreshadowed in May and implemented from July 1940, police took a firmer line. Pacifist meetings were effectively forced indoors; police required newspapers to refuse to advertise them, and a projected Wellington meeting was prohibited in September by Superintendent Lopdell.[48] Such was the concern for social cohesion that the government moved also against the small but (in police perception) 'increasingly troublesome' sect of Jehovah's Witnesses. Continuing complaints about their widespread canvassing, their sectarianism, and their pacifism and defeatist statements about the war, led to discussions in August between officials and Ministers about the best means of curbing the nuisance. With Customs and the postal authorities already cutting off imports of the sect's literature, police seized the remaining material at its Wellington headquarters after a request from the Solicitor-General on 19 August. The desired effect was not achieved: canvassers still had literature and remained active. On 13 October, 'a serious act of violence' (a resentful returned soldier with a rifle sought entry to a Witnesses' meeting at Oamaru) provided the catalyst for firmer action. The local RSA called on the government to ban the sect. Fraser agreed with Cummings' assessment that its activities were a disturbing influence and that it could be declared a subversive organisation – which the Attorney-General duly did on 21 October. Prosecutions of individual members for pamphleting or canvassing followed, although the prohibition on members meeting simply for worship was soon relaxed, informally from December, then formally in May 1941.[49]

In October 1940, the suppression of anti-war publicity became a priority following the distribution of a leaflet to men in Christchurch, Ashburton and Timaru called up in the first ballot for territorial service. The Minister of National Service, Bob Semple, termed this a 'foul and treacherous document'.[50] A week later Commissioner Cummings called an unprecedented conference of North Island officers in charge of districts, followed by one in Christchurch. A 'very perturbed' Fraser made his priorities clear to the Wellington conference, and Cummings underlined it: catching the distributors of subversive literature had 'to take precedence over everything, short of murder. That is definite.' All available staff were to prevent the leaflet against military service from reaching the next group of balloted men; the usual beats would 'have to go short for a while until this thing is cleaned up.'[51] Whether pacifists or Communists had produced the leaflet was not known. However, 'personal history' sheets on Communists and suspected Communists were to be compiled by districts – copies would go to the Minister [Fraser], who could 'give a valuable hint'.[52] At Cummings' request, police were given clearer powers (by a new regulation on 5 November) to arrest and detain those found distributing subversive literature. These powers were used against those handing out leaflets at railway stations.[53] Typically, Constable Jim Beaton of Raetihi was instructed that he 'MUST USE EVERY MEANS TO PREVENT THE CONTINUANCE OF SUBVERSIVE ACTIVITY ON THE PART OF ANY PERSON', and sent the names of men in his sub-district who had recently been called up.[54] Heightened surveillance did not prevent a leaflet against military service being more widely distributed following the second territorial ballot in early November.[55]

It was in this context that both Fraser and Cummings rejected an appeal on 18 November 1940 by Ormond Burton and other Christian Pacifists to be allowed to hold public meetings. These were now totally prohibited, and so when they resumed in Wellington's Pigeon Park every Friday night between 7 March and 6 June 1941, a succession of speakers was charged not only with obstructing police, but also with attempting to address prohibited meetings. They were sent to the Supreme Court for trial and longer terms of imprisonment. An 'unfortunate aspect', from the police point of view, was the publicity given by the trials, which only attracted large crowds to the park. Similar meetings in Auckland during November and December 1941 were also suppressed. Public witness on the streets had effectively ended.[56]

While pacifist organisations dwindled to a few committed individuals, the Communist Party appeared to flourish. From late 1940, it seemed to Cummings that the 'disloyal and obstructive policy' of the party meant that he would eventually have to recommend that it be declared a subversive organisation. Here, it seems, the politicians were more cautious than the Commissioner. Cummings had ongoing discussions with both Fraser and Mason on the subject. He made no definite recommendation until 5 February 1941, when he sent Fraser a Communist Party circular which called on its members to make 'even greater efforts, sacrifices and struggles', without being specific. Not until 26 March did Mason request a report for Cabinet on the wisdom of banning the party. Attempting to make a strong case, Cummings emphasised the party's growth in membership, which was thought to be 690 in April 1941. He noted also its 'strenuous resistance' to the war effort, which included subversive publicity, the threat of sabotage from party members in the armed forces, and the fact that Communists had been (in police eyes) 'at the root' of almost every industrial disturbance since the war began. Again the Attorney-General took his time, drafting the necessary banning orders but not bringing them into effect. On 3 July Mason informed Cummings that, because Germany's attack on the USSR eleven days earlier would probably 'modify profoundly' the local Communists' activities, a banning order would be deferred for the time being.[57] Overnight, an 'Imperialist war' did indeed become a 'People's War'. Nevertheless, police surveillance of Communists continued. From mid-1941, however, far greater police resources were devoted to monitoring aliens and protecting (or supervising the protection of) vital points.

Monitoring aliens

In July 1938, the Aliens Committee of the Organisation for National Security decided that the Police should be responsible for registering and controlling individuals of alien (non-British) nationality in wartime (a responsibility it had shared with other departments during the 1914–18 war). The committee, comprising government departments interested in the control of aliens,[58] maintained an advisory role, helping to formulate government policy and draft regulations. It did not believe that a peacetime system of control was required. The registration of aliens, begun in 1917, had been suspended in 1923. From late 1938, lists of aliens who entered and left the country became available to the Police, whose political surveillance gathered information on individuals with Nazi or Fascist sympathies. Before the outbreak of war, however, police had no systematic information on the number, background, and location of aliens, 'much less their political loyalties'.[59]

Even so, machinery had been set in place to quickly acquire such information. Having been approved by Cabinet in September 1938,[60] draft regulations were sent to the officers in charge of districts the following February as part of a series of secret instructions on steps to be taken in the event of war. Issued on 4 September 1939, within 24 hours of New Zealand's declaration of war on Germany, the Alien Control Emergency Regulations required aliens aged sixteen years or more to register at the nearest police station within fourteen days. Two days later, some 25,000 sets of application forms and certificates of registration were sent to police stations. Uniformed staff who handled the licensing of firearms became the local aliens registration officers, issuing certificates and permits, and later impounding prohibited articles.[61] Country constables and their city counterparts set about locating aliens 'by the blinking thousand. Didn't know there were so many in New Zealand' was a comment from the Wellington District.[62] The need to register was widely publicised. Nearly 8,000 did so, including some 2,600 Chinese and 1,000 Yugoslavs.[63]

Though it was not made explicit in the initial regulations, a distinction was soon drawn between 'enemy aliens' and 'aliens' in general. All aliens were required to notify their local registration officer of a change of name or address. From October, aliens who had *at any time* been nationals of a state then at war with New Zealand required a permit from local police if they wished to leave their residence for more than 24 hours. This created the conundrum for police administrators of deciding who was an 'alien', let alone an 'enemy alien'. German nationals and, from 11 June 1940, Italians were defined as enemy aliens; so too were local Japanese from 8 December 1941, though their numbers were infinitesimal.[64] In November 1939 long-standing British subjects by naturalisation were granted a general exemption from registration – though this did not prevent subsequent investigation of allegiance and internment in a few cases. The question remained of how to categorise the recent influx of refugees from Germany, Austria and Czechoslovakia (some 800 between 1937 and 1939).[65] Police policy was to register as Germans all who were deemed to be so by German law – to the disquiet of refugees anxious to prove their loyalty.[66]

In the early months of the war, being an alien, or even an enemy alien, entailed little more than registration. Police were empowered to arrest any alien perceived to be disaffected or a source of public danger – but this initiative was taken only once.[67] In all other cases, the detention of aliens came only after the Attorney-General ordered their internment following a recommendation from the Commissioner of Police. Here, a predetermined policy of keeping the numbers interned to a minimum was followed; only nine Germans had been interned by January 1940, rising to 31 by June (including fifteen from Western Samoa and Tonga), with another 30 after Italy entered the war. Only 221 people in total were interned during the war.[68] The first internments of Germans were based on police pre-war surveillance, especially of the Deutscher Verein (German Club) in Auckland from February 1934, which identified the small number of Nazi Party members and sympathisers.[69] Evidence for the later police recommendations came from direct inquiries into accusations of openly expressed Nazi sympathies in the immediate pre-war period, and from postal censors following the outbreak of war. The Attorney-General did not automatically accept all police recommendations, directing that further inquiries be made in some cases. But he had no means of independently assessing the police evidence. Nor did aliens have any way to clear themselves of suspicion, or have an internment order reviewed – as critics pointed out to the Prime Minister and the Minister of Justice in June 1940.[70]

The invisibility of police surveillance and control of aliens was a source of anxiety amongst growing numbers in the wider community who were unable to judge its effectiveness. Though most of the recent migrants from Europe were refugees, and 'enemy aliens' comprised only a tiny fraction of the New Zealand population, concern at their presence was increasingly voiced after the 'phony' war ended in April 1940. Fears of a 'fifth column' like that which was perceived to be aiding Germany's rapid advance in Europe led to calls for closer surveillance and the general internment of enemy aliens. Late in May, officials on the Aliens Committee decided that further restrictions, such as controlling aliens' employment, were unnecessary in the meantime. Within two weeks official opinion had changed, as politicians responded to public anxieties, refugees' advocates, and reverses on the battlefields.[71]

On 10 June, hours before Italy entered the war, the Prime Minister chaired a meeting of the Aliens Committee. A sense of urgency was underlined by the presence of the Attorney-General, the Chiefs of Staff, and heads of departments concerned with the control of aliens. Fraser proposed that tribunals modelled on those in Britain be set up to examine systematically enemy aliens, refugees, and other groups of aliens, should the need arise. Most of the committee agreed – public anxieties would thereby be allayed. The tribunals would advise the Attorney-General of their assessment of information supplied by the Police. Commissioner Cummings' objection to secret police information being supplied to the tribunals was overruled, though Fraser directed that details necessary to safeguard police sources could be withheld. The Commissioner chaired the next meeting of the Aliens Committee on 14 June which agreed that greater restrictions on enemy aliens were needed immediately. Four days later a new regulation was issued establishing the tribunals, prohibiting enemy aliens from possessing a range of articles without a permit, and providing that the Attorney-General could impose any other restrictions that he deemed necessary.[72]

Not until early in August, however, did a tribunal of three, sitting in Wellington and chaired by Mr Justice Callan, begin its examination of all enemy aliens. At this time 2,341 enemy aliens were registered – 1,241 Germans, 817 Italians, 179 Austrians and 104 Czechoslovaks.[73] From the outset, the sequence of cases reflected the degree of urgency as judged by Detective Sergeant Arthur Harding, who monitored the surveillance of aliens at Headquarters. Enemy aliens already suspected by police were given priority, and the tribunal recommended further internments which the Attorney-General approved. Within two weeks of the tribunal beginning its work, Justice Callan recognised (as he later put it) that 'the present method ... is dangerously slow and therefore ineffective'.[74] After consulting with Harding, he recommended that a separate aliens authority (a magistrate or barrister) be appointed in each police district, with the original tribunal as an appellate body to review cases. These new tribunals were authorised, and a wider definition of alien encompassing anyone of 'alien/enemy origin or association' was included in new regulations issued on 24 October.[75]

From August 1940, police work in investigating and supervising aliens expanded greatly, claiming all the time of some staff and, for others, taking priority over their usual jobs – especially in the main centres, and particularly in Wellington, where more than a third of the country's enemy aliens were then registered.[76] Hitherto, police investigation of aliens had been selective and largely reactive – responses to public complaints or the following up of information suggesting illegal or subversive activities. But the role of the first tribunal, and of the Aliens Authorities which succeeded it, was to classify enemy aliens (and eventually other aliens) into five categories in terms of their level of threat to public safety (which sometimes simply meant allaying public fears). This required systematic police investigation of all enemy aliens, beginning with an interview by a detective who followed a set of detailed questions and then added his own impressions and the results of other inquiries: personal histories from the entry permit files of the Customs Department; information from the postal censors; statements from those acquainted with the alien; even a house search if there were suspicions of subversion.[77]

While police were no longer responsible for recommending

internment (or the degree of classification), their evidence was the basis for recommendations by the Aliens Authorities. Indeed, the Attorney-General still wished to see relevant police files before he made his decision. If a police file created a favourable impression, the individual was interviewed informally by the local Aliens Authority. If this confirmed the police view, the alien was given an 'E' (exempt from the aliens regulations) or, more likely, a 'D' (subject to the regulations but without any special restrictions) classification. An unfavourable police report precipitated a formal hearing at which the Authority cross-examined the alien with a detective present, but without revealing the sources of police information.[78] Here the usual presumption of innocence was reversed. The Minister of Justice instructed the Aliens Authorities to 'regard it as imperative that under no circumstances should a dangerous alien be left at large.' Justice Callan added his gloss, expanding the grounds for recommending internment: 'If his sympathies are divided or undecided, he must be interned.'[79] Hitherto, the police approach had apparently been more cautious and legalistic. In Commissioner Cummings' view, 'we had concrete evidence of the man's disloyalty before we moved in the matter.'[80] While the practice of individual tribunals varied, the Wellington Aliens Authority was clear that the evidence of police was to be preferred to that of an alien's friends.[81] Much rested then on the quality of police work. In one of the cases dealt with by Justice Callan's tribunal before October 1940, poor investigation by a Napier detective had resulted in the internment of a man who was subsequently released. There were other cases where insufficient care had been taken, through inexperience or pressure of other work. Consequently, the Commissioner directed that an experienced detective in each district be detailed to present cases to the local Aliens Authority so that he would 'have [the] hang of the whole thing' and quickly gain the Authority's confidence.[82]

Thus Orme Power, then one of the four detectives at Palmerston North, was assigned to handle 'aliens enquiries' for the district, leaving his 'normal police work load' to be carried by his already pressed colleagues. Power appreciated (in retrospect) that the local tribunal relied 'greatly' on his recommendations and that, in 'the emotion and patriotism of war involvement, it is hard to reach objective opinions regarding people who are nationals of a country with which one is at war and who happen to be living here at the outbreak of hostilities.' All the more so, when (for example) one German woman whom Power investigated declared that she 'hated the British' (because of what had happened to her husband during the First World War), yet would do nothing to harm New Zealand security. Attempting to present 'a balanced picture', Power recommended that the woman should not be interned.[83]

By the end of March 1941, police had brought most enemy aliens before the Authorities for classification. They then turned to investigating non-enemy aliens who had been nationals of countries under German rule or influence, or who came within the wider definition of alien, including British nationals who had 'alien' parents. Of these, some 900 had been classified by December 1941. With Japan's swift advance southwards during January 1942, both Commissioner Cummings and the Aliens Appeal Tribunal pressed for the immediate internment of 366 aliens who had been classified 'B' (to be interned if invasion threatened). Instead, it was decided to subdivide the Class 'B' aliens into groups for whom the timing of internment would depend on the proximity of Japanese forces (26 were interned immediately). The numbers interned reached a peak of 207 (including Germans and Japanese from the Pacific islands) in November 1942, and then gradually declined.[84] Meanwhile, on 30 March 1942, Cummings had recommended to Fraser that the government take the power to intern disloyal citizens not covered by the aliens regulations who might attempt to assist the enemy in the event of an invasion. He had a very small number of 'totally disloyal' people in mind. Here, after discussions with Cummings, Fraser drew the line against further pre-emptive controls; as the fortunes of war changed, the idea was dropped.[85]

Time-consuming police work in providing evidence for further classification and reclassification continued as the perceived threat of invasion waxed and then waned. 'A lot of wild rumours and stupid reports' had to be 'investigated and probed. Nothing', Cummings declared, 'is left to chance'.[86] By September 1943, 3,781 aliens had been classified, 47 per cent of those registered. Chinese, Yugoslavs, and Americans comprised the majority of registered aliens who remained unclassified. Of those classified, less than 3 per cent were put in Class 'A' (for immediate internment). About 10 per cent were in Class 'B', 3 per cent in Class 'C' (to be subject to special restrictions), and the overwhelming majority (some 71 per cent in 1943) in Class 'D' (exempt from special restrictions, but subject to controls). A smaller but growing proportion from 1943 (12 to 16 per cent) were in Class 'E' and thereby free from controls.[87] Thus the fruits of systematic police work broadly confirmed an earlier official view formed from selective surveillance before May 1940: that the number of aliens judged to be actually or potentially disloyal was small – there were between five and six hundred at most in Classes A, B, and C.

Those not interned but subject to controls (Classes B, C, and D) numbered 3,223 by September 1943. They were subject to ongoing, if spasmodic, surveillance that was recorded in quarterly reports to Police Headquarters.[88] All needed to notify the police of any change of residence and obtain a permit from local police to possess explosives, more than three gallons of petrol, a motor vehicle, boat, or aircraft, a camera or a large-scale map. Enemy aliens in Classes B and C needed special permits to travel more than twenty miles from their residence and to possess firearms, radios capable of short-wave reception or transmission, or (from April 1943) homing pigeons. Seeking uniformity in local police administration, Cummings applied restrictions on the issuing of permits to enemy aliens. As a general rule, permits were not to be issued for motor vehicles, only fishermen would be permitted boats, firearms, cameras and binoculars were to be impounded, travel permits (from December 1941) were restricted to cases of necessity and some areas were declared out of bounds, and addresses and radio sets were to be periodically checked. Though he sought to limit discretion, the Commissioner also warned against prejudice: 'if you are going to say: "He's a damn German, he'll get nothing from me" – well, you're gone'.[89] The Commissioner sought unsuccessfully to have enemy aliens required to notify any change of employment. But the government preferred to leave it to the Aliens Authorities to direct, if need be, those they classified away from sensitive wartime occupations. Cummings then instructed that the quarterly reports on Class B and C aliens note any change of employment. Though the monitoring continued until the end of the war, it was 'tapering off considerably' by 1944, especially as other concerns (such as the presence of American servicemen) took priority in police work.[90]

While the Army took charge of the male aliens interned on Somes Island and then at Pahiatua, the Police were made responsible for the welfare and control of the families of the German and Japanese men who were brought from Tonga for internment in December 1941. Though the government did not want to create family internment camps, the status of these families remained ambiguous. The women were given a B classification and lived under close police supervision, or what the Prime Minister termed 'close parole'.[91] From June 1942 until August 1944, when the restrictions on them were removed, the four German women and their seven children lived, chafing at their constraints, in a bungalow at Pukekohe with a constable and his wife who shared their supervision. Seven Japanese women and their nine children were accommodated less satisfactorily at Pokeno until they were moved to Pukekohe in February 1943, where they remained until leaving for Sydney in November. From their arrival in New Zealand until their landing in Sydney, the Japanese families were supervised by Constable Edna Pearce, who censored their correspondence and saw to their many needs, including by procuring an adequate supply of rice (then tightly rationed), overseeing the birth of two children and the education of others, teaching English and learning some Japanese in turn, and comforting and caring for the survivors of a disastrous attempt at repatriation in August 1943, when some were killed and others injured when their aircraft crashed on take-off at Whenuapai. Eventually, Detective Sergeant Harding and Constable Pearce escorted the survivors to Sydney by ship.[92]

Altogether, the wartime policing of aliens represented a new and considerable development of 'preventive policing', and it was not a role that Commissioners wished to continue in peacetime.[93] Costly in terms of resources, the close monitoring of aliens was also socially divisive and created suspicions of police amongst law-abiding citizens. Any assessment of its efficacy depends on how serious the threat posed by 'enemy aliens' is judged to have been. Police could deem their surveillance to have been successful; so too could the government with its policy of internment: 'No sabotage occurred and no leakage of vital information through aliens was reported.'[94] Could a similar assessment be made of the policing of 'vital points'?

Protecting 'vital points'

In August 1938, the Vital Points Committee of the Organisation for National Security agreed that the Police would be responsible for protecting public utilities from sabotage by civilians in wartime. It drew up a schedule of places where guards should be posted or other forms of supervision would be required. Beyond these 'vital points', local authorities, such as harbour boards, were seen to be responsible for looking after their facilities. 'Mischief making', should it occur, was expected to be confined to individuals supporting the enemy or with anti-war views, rather than concerted or on any large scale. This comparatively relaxed view continued into the early part of the war.[95]

Following the outbreak of war, the Army provided guards for those 'vital points' hitherto scheduled for police protection. At this stage it had better manpower resources, having already established a national military reserve. Requests soon flowed in from various local authorities for further protection of their facilities, particularly water supplies and wharves. Until March 1940, the Vital Points Committee considered the existing measures of surveillance and control to be sufficient. Indeed Army guards were withdrawn from a number of places earlier deemed significant.[96] Police assessed the risk of sabotage to have diminished following the initial controls on aliens (none of whom could work on a wharf or a ship without a permit), and 'organised sabotage' by the 'noisy minority' opposed to the war was seen as unlikely.[97]

Even so, the anxieties of shipping companies, harbour boards, and the Navy led to the control of wharves and the safety of overseas shipping becoming an important responsibility for the Police – and ultimately more demanding of its resources than the protection of other vital points, though not part of the pre-war planning. Around the New Zealand coast, many wharves were vulnerable pivots in the economy, and some were even more important in the transfer of men and materials of war. Few had physical barriers to prevent access. On the outbreak of war, no special measures were taken beyond increasing pre-war patterns of surveillance: police patrolled wharves and supervised ships' guards at gangways, while harbour boards had charge of access to their wharves. Nor, at the outset, were there any moves to re-establish the water patrols which had been absent from the policing of the main ports since at least 1919.[98] After lengthy discussions by members of the Vital Points Committee[99] with harbour board, shipping and waterfront industry representatives, it was agreed on 15 April 1940 that increased protection for overseas shipping at wharves would be provided by the Police.[100]

The Shipping Safety Emergency Regulations were promulgated on 11 June 1940. Police and shipping companies now shared control of access to ships. The latter provided gangway guards and issued passes to their employees, while police issued permits to all others and monitored (by patrols) the waterside workers, carters, shipping clerks and others who worked on the wharves. Initially this pattern was applied only to ships which traded beyond Australia, and the Police assumed control of access to only those wharves, or portions of wharves, at which these ships were berthed. With suitable fencing already in place, the Auckland wharves were totally closed to the general public from June; constables and harbour board officials stationed at the gates admitted only those with permits. The Commissioner was permitted to recruit an additional 65 men exclusively for the land-based protection of shipping – the first increment of extra staff for wartime duties to be authorised. No matter how effectively the wharves were policed, however, the Vital Points Committee recognised in June that police water patrols would be needed to ensure the security of shipping. No decision was taken at that time to establish them.[101]

As losses of merchant shipping in the British trade grew from June 1940, concerns about the security of wharves and shipping increased.[102] Early in 1941, Commissioner Cummings considered the total enclosure of wharves and introduction of entry by permit at the other main ports, where overseas shipping was increasingly concentrated. This was found to be impracticable, except at Wellington. Elsewhere there was some degree of open access, with a constable stationed at the approach to any wharf where an overseas ship was berthed. Meanwhile, naval officers at the main ports expressed concern about the suitability of ships' crew as gangway guards and the adequacy of police wharf patrols. From June 1941, a sub-committee of the Vital Points Committee considered how to improve security. Eventually, by new regulations issued in December, the Police assumed responsibility for guarding ships' gangways and became the sole authority issuing passes for wharves and overseas ships. Fifty-two more police were authorised for gangway duties. Fears of attack on harbours and shipping by two-man submarines and other small Japanese craft launched at sea led to a further extension of controls. From July 1942, ships trading with Australian ports required police gangway guards and entry permits, as did the inter-island passenger vessels sailing between Wellington and Lyttelton, and those in the coastal trade carrying food supplies destined for overseas. Another 47 constables were needed (on paper at least) – making a total of 164 extra police deployed on wharf duties (nearly 10 per cent of the Force's authorised strength) by March 1943.[103]

In April 1941, Cummings sought launches to undertake water patrols at Auckland, Wellington and Lyttelton. Eventually three pleasure craft were requisitioned: the *Tiromoana* at Auckland, the *Antipodes* at Wellington, and the *Lady Elizabeth*, which replaced the *Antipodes* in November when it was sent to Lyttelton.[104] They were provided with rifles, identification and searchlights, but no radio transmitters – communication was maintained by Morse code (using an Aldis lamp) with harbour boards' signals towers. Six extra constables were authorised for each of the launches and patrols began at Wellington in September, and at the other two ports a few months later. On 30 December regulations were issued allowing police to control the movements of small craft, and restrictions which included a night curfew came into effect in February 1942.[105]

When the total number of constables reached its wartime peak early in 1943, the Police Force remained below its authorised strength, and the gap widened considerably during the next two years as staff continued to be lost. Ostensibly, the guarding of ships' gangways was a priority duty, but there were seldom sufficient men to fulfil it, particularly at Auckland and Wellington, where the volume of shipping increased and officers wanted staff for other work that was deemed essential. Delegates to the Police Association conference in October 1942 claimed that insufficient police were guarding wharves and gangways to do the task 'efficiently'. Cummings disagreed, as he did with the suggestion that the military should do the work if more police could not be obtained. Here, *esprit de corps* was at stake: 'saying we could not do the job ... would please some people immensely'.[106] At the ports of Auckland and Wellington during January 1944, some 30 constables were fully occupied in guarding a daily average of nine ships. Only the most important had police guards; ships' crews continued to guard the rest. At these two ports, security was also potentially undermined by a growth in the use of non-union labour to meet the frequent demands for urgent cargo handling. The police who issued passes were often faced with several hundred applications at a time. Finding it impracticable to check the bona fides of each applicant, they relied on the scrutiny of an experienced local detective. Similarly, in Auckland, where more than 4,000 men worked on the waterfront on many days by 1943, the regular checking of passes of all those leaving the wharves had to be abandoned.[107] Hence the Navy's concerns about the security of wharves and ships continued. From mid-1942 the Security Intelligence Bureau established its own organisation for port security: this covertly tested the police measures (to the resentment of constables and Commissioner alike), and went further in monitoring the comings and goings of merchant seamen.[108]

Lack of staff meant that in only a few instances did the Police provide guards for those 'vital points' envisaged in pre-war planning. Indeed, from 1940, there was ongoing discussion over the amount and type of protection (guards or patrols?) that should be given to public utilities, and who should provide it (Army, Police, local authorities or private industry?). Against Commissioner Cummings' judgement, for example, the Vital Points Committee (at the request of the National Broadcasting Service) required a constable to be stationed at the Wellington studio of 2YA following the outbreak of war. Later a watchman took over. Following a Post and Telegraph Department request, a constable was stationed at the Auckland cable office from May 1940. In June, as part of the increased port security, police guards were placed on the Wellington floating dock and the graving docks at Port Chalmers.[109] At the same time, extra police were sent to guard certain West Coast coal mines until restraints on Italians working there were in place. But these were isolated instances. The Vital Points Committee generally rejected requests for Army or Police guards from local authorities or private companies. Every locally 'important' place was not necessarily 'vital' to the national interest; owners or occupiers should take their own protective measures. Otherwise, as the Minister of Defence observed to a weighty deputation pressing for more government protection in August 1940, half the population would be on duty guarding the other half.[110]

Meanwhile, from early 1940, the Army sought to have police replace its guards at 'civilian' facilities (notably the bulk oil installations). Here, as in other spheres of wartime administration, there were conflicting interests. The suggestion that Special Constables be recruited for the purpose was rejected by Commissioner Cummings on the grounds of cost and their unsuitability for retention in the Force at the end of the war. Police would, however, ensure that companies provided watchmen for those 'important' but not 'vital' oil installations which lacked Army guards. (When the oil companies later protested at the expense and unsuitability of their watchmen, the War Cabinet authorised an extra fifteen constables in April 1941 to guard installations in five provincial cities.)[111] With the issue of overall responsibility unresolved, the War Cabinet decided in November 1940 that the Army should continue to guard all vital points. As the number of Army guards grew (to 285 by September 1941) and pressures on military resources increased, the issue resurfaced in June 1941. Again the Vital Points Committee agreed that the Police should protect 'civilian' vital points. The Army was willing to release any of its guards who were prepared to transfer to the Police for similar duty and become the nucleus of a Police War Auxiliary that could expand as the need arose. However, only 29 volunteered, there would be little saving in cost, and an Auxiliary acceptable to the Police would be difficult to recruit. In December 1941, the War Cabinet reaffirmed its earlier decision. The Army continued to protect most vital points for the duration of the war.[112]

The focus of police attention was on supervising the protection of the many places which were seen as important to the war effort but not guarded by the Army. From the outbreak of war the surveillance of 'important' places intensified; particular attention was paid to 'essential industries'. Local police were instructed to visit the management of all freezing and fertilizer works, power stations, woollen mills, dairy factories, wool stores and export cool stores to discuss protective measures and see if any employees were 'disaffected or members of subversive organisations'. To ensure that there was some protection for such industries and public utilities, the Protected Places Emergency Regulations were issued on 16 October 1940. Officers in charge of districts could now require the occupiers of premises declared 'protected places' to provide watchmen and any other 'aids to security' thought necessary. Such watchmen were given the power to detain and search intruders, but were not to be armed (as had been suggested by some freezing companies), except with batons and whistles. Uneventful nightly visits to check on watchmen became part of the routine of many suburban and small-town constables.[113]

As with other aspects of internal security, the degree of protection fluctuated with perceptions of risk. In February 1942, officers in charge of districts were authorised in the event of an invasion to treat particular 'protected places' as 'vital points' and place armed guards. A year later, with fears of invasion evaporating, protective measures began to be relaxed. Police guards were withdrawn from oil installations and from the repeater station at Seddon, to which three constables had been appointed in December 1941. Army guards were replaced at some vital points by watchmen supervised by police. In March 1943, Commissioner Cummings secured the agreement of the naval officer in charge at Lyttelton to the ending of the launch patrol. From September 1943, police gradually relaxed the requirement to maintain watchmen at 'protected places'. In January 1944, the Commissioner urged that police no longer be required to guard ships' gangways. Because of the 'vital importance' of shipping in the view of other members of the Vital Points Committee, however, the Police had to maintain their practice of providing guards within the limits of staff available. A general relaxation of the controls on access to wharves and ships did not come until 10 September 1945, by which time there were very few 'protected places' subject to close police surveillance.[114]

Ostensibly, the various facets of police security surveillance had proved effective. More clearly, the initial police assessment that there was limited risk to vital points had been borne out. No cases of sabotage had been detected, despite fears and suspicions. Neither was there an undue incidence of fires at 'important' places (despite public alarm in 1940), nor evidence that any had been started by saboteurs.[115]

Emergency precautions

War added a new dimension to the police role in meeting emergencies affecting civilians. To the potential hazards of earthquakes and floods were added the threat of air raids and invasion. Though the Hawke's Bay earthquake had shown the need for local preparations for disaster, only rudimentary steps towards a national emergency precautions (or civil defence) scheme had been taken by 1939.[116] In July 1938, the Commissioner sent police stations an emergency precautions booklet prepared by the Internal Affairs Department for local authorities. This focused on preparations for an earthquake; precautions against enemy action were 'deliberately not stressed'.[117] From August 1940, local emergency precautions schemes became compulsory and a recruiting drive began for volunteers to staff the various EPS sections, especially in the four main centres. Law and Order committees of the local EPS organisations were to collaborate with local police in establishing an EPS auxiliary police (or 'wardens'). Now the concern was to protect 'local and civilian' vital points from sabotage and maintain order in the event of an enemy attack.[118] In February 1941, Wellington's mayor publicised the government's appeal for the ranks of EPS police to be filled as soon as possible – 600 'fit and reliable' men were needed in Wellington, more in Auckland, and 400 in Christchurch, to prevent pillage or panic and control traffic. These targets were not reached. Auckland's mayor made a further appeal for 650 men in December, after the attack on Pearl Harbor (he mooted arming some police to prevent looting). Now there was a readier response. By July 1942 the Auckland Law and Order Unit had 830 men.[119]

In the cities, business and professional men, in particular, were selected from both EPS volunteers and the Home Guard and deployed in two branches of the 'Law and Order Unit'. Stemming partly from the experience at Napier and Hastings in 1931 was an Identification Branch which would deal with the dead. The main branch of EPS wardens were distributed amongst the central city and suburban stations for training and direction by local police. In an emergency, they would have the powers of Special Constables and be under the control of the senior police officer in the locality. Clearly the degree of commitment from the volunteers varied, as did the quality of their training. In Auckland, Superintendent James Cummings spoke of issuing 'instructions from time to time'. In Christchurch, Superintendent Rawle planned a series of eight lectures for 200 volunteers at the Central station, beginning with how people had reacted during the Hawke's Bay earthquake. By July 1941, after they had received instruction on dealing with the effects of gas, the city's auxiliary police, parading in their 'civvies' with EPS armbands, were declared by Rawle to be ready to deal with an emergency.[120] Not until May 1943, however, was there an attempt to bring greater uniformity into training, with fifteen NCOs responsible for organising the EPS police in the districts brought to Wellington for a week's course at a newly established Civil Defence School.[121] At Islington on the outskirts of Christchurch, Constable W.T. Thom, without a syllabus, moulded his unit of 48 men into an 'efficient team' who put their weekly parade night before anything else, displayed a keen interest in lectures, marched 'like Guardsmen', made their own first aid kits, and (Thom claimed) raised more money for patriotic purposes than any other Canterbury unit. Though never called out for an emergency, such units (as Constable 'Shorty' Brydon, then at Invercargill, recalled) spent 'many happy hours' in 'close companionship' until they were disbanded at the end of the war.[122]

War and order

Besides creating new concerns for internal security, wartime conditions also added new dimensions to the routine police work of keeping order in the streets, detecting acquisitive crimes and prosecuting illegalities. Yet the impact of war should not be overstated. To the extent that the diversity of pre-war social activities continued during wartime, so too did the policing of enduring modes of disorder and lawbreaking.[123] Investigating thefts remained the bread and butter of detective work, as did the routines of beat patrol for most city constables. By comparison with the years 1914 to 1918, however, police statistics for the years 1939 to 1945 recorded significantly lower rates per capita of prosecutions for assault, drunkenness and associated public order offences, and much higher rates of reported theft and burglary. Overall, the annual rate of recorded homicide (murder and manslaughter) during the First World War was double that of the Second World War. The recorded rates of disorder and theft during both wars can be broadly seen as an extension of the preceding peacetime trends (see figures I.2 to I.6). New Zealand society was thus ostensibly both more orderly and more prone to acquisitive crimes during the Second World War than during the First.

Nevertheless, wartime social conditions and official policies did influence the policing of illegality and disorder in a variety of ways. For one thing, the growth in new offences created by emergency regulations added considerably to police work on behalf of other departments. Here, more was involved than looking for subversive statements, or prosecuting breaches of the censorship or aliens control regulations (such illegalities accounted for 206 charges in 1940 and 106 in 1941).[124] Many more prosecutions stemmed from attempts to circumvent petrol rationing (707 in these two years), the non-observance of lighting restrictions (215 in 1941), and the chasing up of national service 'defaulters' and military 'deserters' (1,162 in 1941). Such enquiries took up a 'great deal' of police time, even though they comprised only a fraction of all police prosecutions.[125] Rationing, especially of petrol from February 1940, and of key food items from 1942–43, made black marketing likely. This was difficult to detect. Since both buyers and sellers in a black market were equally liable to prosecution, secrecy was fundamental to its operation. Police initiative or activity in catching black marketeers seems to have been a by-product of other work. Only by 'the merest chance', for example, did they detect illicit sales of drapery from an isolated farmhouse on the Hauraki Plains in 1943; two policewomen made the purchases necessary for a prosecution.[126]

The application of new restrictions could also lead to much less work for the police in other directions. In particular, the effects of petrol rationing meant that, in each year from 1942 to 1944, the number of motorists charged with causing death or bodily injury was about half that in 1940, paralleling the decline in the total number of traffic offences prosecuted. The numbers charged with drunken or reckless driving fell by two-thirds.[127] Similarly, the surveillance by EPS firewatchers (which was monitored by constables) probably accounted for the annual rate of arson offences from 1942 to 1944 being the lowest ever recorded by the Police. The rate of reported 'mischief' (vandalism) did not diminish, however. Neither did reported theft or car conversion. After a dip in 1941, these rose steeply in 1942 and 1943. Growing numbers of youths appeared in both the Children's and Magistrates' Courts on theft and mischief charges, compounding pre-war concerns about juvenile delinquency.[128]

If unsettled wartime conditions affected some youths, especially in the cities, they also provided opportunities or temptations for adults, servicemen and civilians alike: the theft of patriotic subscriptions, Air Force stores, soldiers' parcels, scarce tyres, and money from a sailor, and the forgery of a pay book, were amongst the many acquisitive crimes prosecuted by Detective Sergeant W.R. Murray at Hamilton between 1942 and 1944.[129] Though the annual number of prosecutions for theft was greater than before the war, the clear-up rate for such offences slumped from 80 per cent in 1941 to 65 per cent in 1944; this was probably a result of the increased pressures on detectives, especially in the cities.[130] During the war, Commissioner Cummings urged his officers not to prosecute 'trivial' or 'paltry cases', especially on behalf other departments; they continued to do so, nonetheless.[131]

Despite the growth in property offences reported, the total number of prosecutions for all offences declined consistently during the war years, falling by 23 per cent between 1940 and 1944. This reflected a steep decline in various (but not all) categories of police-initiated charges (see figure 4.1). In particular, the number of arrests for drunkenness declined by 61 per cent (from 5,470 to 2,132), total prosecutions for breaches of the Licensing Act by 34 per cent (5,286 to 3,466), and traffic offences by 55 per cent (12,136 to 5,409) in this period. Thus police court work declined noticeably, especially in some North Island provincial towns (such as New Plymouth and Napier) and those in the South Island.[132] Ostensibly, the mobilisation of men for war and work produced greater order. Police statistics also reflected increased discretion in prosecuting petty disorder and greater difficulties in enforcing the liquor laws. In Christchurch between 1940 and 1944, for example, servicemen were more likely to be prosecuted for minor acquisitive crimes (133) than for disorderly behaviour (59); only one was charged with being on licensed premises after hours, and none with drunkenness after 1942.[133] Against the trend, prosecutions for gaming offences grew from a low point of 304 in 1942 to a peak of 1,001 in 1945 (figure 7.1). Except in 1942, totalisator investments at racecourses increased substantially each year during the war, as they had done since 1936, rising from £7,224,203 in 1942 to £12,030,432 in 1945. This reflected the increased disposable income of workers who were being paid more for putting in longer hours yet found there was less to buy. The reduction in race days from 319 in 1940 to 163 in 1943, and greater constraints on travel, only aided bookmakers.[134] Some of the resulting growth in gaming prosecutions came from large 'catches' at gambling schools, such as when a party of 23 uniformed police and detectives from Hamilton raided the Horotiu freezing works on a Wednesday evening in 1943, and arrested 32 men who were drinking sly grog and playing two-up and crown-and-anchor.[135]

Some of the changing patterns of policing were related only indirectly, if at all, to wartime conditions. Though reported common assaults fell steadily each year from 781 in 1940 to a low point of 513 in 1944, cases of serious assault rose steeply from 27 in 1941 to 89 in 1944, when the number of murders (23) matched, and of reported rapes (37) considerably exceeded, the pre-war peaks.[136] This upswing in serious violence coincided with, but was not necessarily linked to, the increasing presence of American servicemen from mid-1942 and the return of some New Zealand troops from the Middle East in July 1943. It also paralleled a similar trend in 1917, suggesting a heightened dimension of social stress as war dragged on. In fact, the extent to which patterns of violence reflected the broader social changes of wartime is not easy to dissect. Many wartime homicides, it seems, conformed to pre-war patterns in terms of the methods, motives and relationships involved, though some could be linked to wartime stresses.[137] 'The remarkable thing' about the shooting of two United States Marines in an inner-city Wellington flat by a ship's cook from South Africa was that, as G.G. Kelly (the police ballistics expert) observed, it 'stood practically alone, instead of being, as expected, typical' of the two-year period during which large numbers of American servicemen were stationed in New Zealand.[138]

In its origins, the homicide case which made the largest demands on police resources – the unprecedented manhunt for a West Coast farmer, Eric Stanley ('Stan') Graham, in the rugged bush-clad neighourhood of Kowhitirangi[139] in October 1941 – owed little, if anything, to the circumstances of wartime.[140] At odds with his neighbours and mentally disturbed, Stan Graham shot four local police who sought to remove his firearms, and an agricultural instructor who came to their aid. (Sergeant W. Cooper and Constables F.W. Jordan and P.C. Tulloch from Hokitika died at Graham's farmhouse on 8 October, while Constable E.M. Best from Kaniere and G.S. Ridley died later.) An expert marksman and bushman, Graham then fled to the nearby bush, well armed, before returning to kill two home guardsmen in a shoot-out the following night. Commissioner Cummings, then in Christchurch, went immediately to take charge of the manhunt. He mobilised resources to bolster the small number of police on the West Coast, and asserted police control over local home guardsmen who had taken their own initiatives at the scene. Police were brought in from various North and South Island stations, as were territorial signallers and regular soldiers from Burnham camp, armed with Bren and tommy-guns. Soon a 'small army' comprising some 90 police (including three Inspectors, nine Sergeants, and four detectives – equivalent to the entire staff of the largest provincial police district, Hamilton), 50 troops and 50 home guardsmen was deployed to guard houses by night and make arduous searches through rough country by day.[141] An Air Force bomber flew a number of reconnaissance flights. (A contemporary witticism attributed to the Nazi propagandist, 'Lord Haw Haw', claimed that Hitler had sent Graham a telegram: 'Hold the South Island. Sending another man to take the North Island.')[142] On the thirteenth day, Graham was shot by a young constable from Auckland (following an order to shoot on sight if he was 'found approaching with firearms'),[143] to the considerable relief of locals and his colleagues. But the aftermath proved to be more enduring than the manhunt itself. Preparations for the inquest took three months.[144] Though the Coroner echoed the prevailing view in vindicating police actions, some doubters remained.[145] Constable J.D. Quirke (who had only thirteen months' service) was widely (but mistakenly) believed to have resigned within a year because of the effects of being identified as the man who shot Graham.[146] (As a consequence, the names of police who later had to shoot to kill were not released.) This prolonged manhunt in the context of war served to create a folk legend amongst those who saw Graham as a tough, superb bushman, a 'Man Alone' whose tenacious defiance of authority could be admired, as in Jim Case's ballad sung in his local pub at Kumara in 1943:

> *Now the job of catching Stan*
> *Was too great for the law,*
> *They had to get the Home Guard*
> *And the Army Corps.*
>
> *They even got Bob Semple's*
> *Modern army tanks,*
> *Machine guns and bombers*
> *And formed in four-like ranks.*

Before my story's finished
There's something I'd like to say,
I wish we had a million
Like dear old Stan today.

The Japs would not be game
To come within our shores,
And we would live in quietness
For now and evermore.[147]

Clearly the wartime influences on the state of order were complex. The number of New Zealand men in the armed forces peaked at nearly 154,000 – about 30 per cent of the male labour force – in September 1942; the highest number overseas was 70,000 in November 1943.[148] Though it might be expected to do so, mobilisation did not necessarily lessen the likelihood of disorder or theft in those provincial towns (such as Blenheim)[149] and cities (particularly Auckland and Wellington) to which servicemen came on leave. Indeed the potential for disorder in Auckland and Wellington was increased when American troops arrived to be based for varying periods in adjacent military camps from June 1942, their numbers reaching a maximum of over 48,000 in July 1943.[150] To police, Auckland became virtually a 'garrison city' until about July 1944.[151] That the increasing presence of servicemen in the two largest cities coincided with a continuing country-wide decline in the number of prosecutions for drunkenness and related offences between 1940 and 1945 reflected changes in policing rather than a diminished potential for disorder.

New Zealand servicemen breaching the civil law were liable to prosecution by police.[152] Accordingly, constables were stationed at the main military camps: Rolleston in 1939 (it was renamed Burnham in 1941), and Trentham and Waiouru in 1940.[153] During his first two years at Waiouru, Constable George Donnelly kept 'very busy' catching up 'on a lot we had been looking for before the call up.'[154] However, as their policy towards anti-war meetings suggested, police were reluctant to prosecute or even arrest disruptive soldiers in uniform. In October 1939, Commissioner Cummings had accepted the Army Secretary's suggestion and directed that, where police found it necessary to intervene, soldiers arrested for drunkenness or 'minor disorders' should be handed over to the military authorities to be dealt with, rather than brought before the civil courts.[155] Cummings' thinking was made clear in April 1940 when he deemed it 'inadvisable' to prosecute soldiers for being found in pubs after hours, or for breaching emergency regulations by having liquor while in uniform away from pubs: 'These offences are petty as far as soldiers are concerned and as they are leaving New Zealand to fight for King and Country a prosecution is likely to have an irritating effect and would not do any good – in fact it would have the opposite effect to what was intended.'[156] A similar official attitude shaped policies towards the US forces stationed in New Zealand.

The arrival of large numbers of American servicemen raised the issue of their liability to New Zealand laws. In June 1942, the Commissioner was advised that emergency regulations would be issued consistent with the British government's policy of allowing the American armed forces to deal with all criminal offences committed by their servicemen. From the outset, it seems, this policy was adopted by the Police, albeit informally until the regulations were issued in April 1943 and formal procedures were established.[157] At Auckland and Wellington, and at other places where large numbers of US servicemen were on 'liberty', the US forces' provost corps were available to control their servicemen. In the main centres, the provost had rooms in the central police stations, patrolled the streets, and generally maintained a mobile squad to respond quickly to incidents. Indeed, with their jeeps, American military police could arrive more rapidly in numbers than city police. If police had to arrest US servicemen (which was seldom), they were handed over to the provost. Offences by American servicemen did not therefore enter police statistics, though complaints of serious offences committed by them might do so.[158] Accordingly, police statistics (and, also it seems, the censored newspapers) captured little of the disruption to order created by New Zealand and US servicemen.[159]

The extent to which the behaviour of servicemen created work for police depended on both the efficiency of New Zealand and American military policing, and the effectiveness of constraints on the supply of liquor. Anecdotal evidence suggests that controls on New Zealand servicemen could be lax. Patrolling the Marton railway station in 1940 when troop trains arrived, for example, Constable Charles Bowley saw 'many incidents' involving soldiers who were 'in many cases badly controlled and allowed considerable liquor'; the Railway Hotel was eventually declared out of bounds.[160] Similarly, at Auckland in November 1941, a magistrate, F.H. Levien, warned that more military police were needed after hearing a number of charges of street fighting and assaults involving New Zealand soldiers during weekend leave: 'It is by no means an uncommon sight to see drunken soldiers in town.'[161] By comparison with their New Zealand counterparts, the US provost, with their long batons, seemed to be more visible and effective – and certainly much more heavy-handed, indeed brutal, in controlling their servicemen. At Auckland, the 'never failing cooperation' of the American military police and naval shore patrols 'simplified police work', according to a detective. When a 'stoush' between American servicemen and New Zealand troops back from overseas erupted one night and spilled out on to Karangahape Road, the US shore patrol arrived and 'waded in with their batons. There were no beg pardons, and the Americans were heaved into the paddy wagons but not the New Zealanders.' At Pukekohe – staffed by a Sergeant and four constables – which had thousands of marines encamped nearby during 1943, one of the constables remembered the US military police as being so 'business-like' in dealing with fights and skirmishes that 'many of the offenders ended up in hospital'. At Wellington, a waiter at the Green Parrot late-night restaurant recalled that 'You only had to dial the MPs' number and they would be on the spot in a minute.'[162]

Probably because of effective policing, both civil and military, there were apparently very few instances of large-scale disorder in either Auckland or Wellington – despite the ongoing frictions that could lead to fracas, especially between US and New Zealand servicemen.[163] In Wellington, only two 'disturbances' involving American servicemen became sufficiently large or persistent to cause reports by New Zealand military authorities. The first, on Saturday 3 April 1943, entered local folklore as the 'Battle of Manners Street' when rumours led to exaggerated accounts of violence and injuries.[164] Typically, it began soon after the pubs closed at 6 pm with a street fight between a few drunken merchant seamen, bent on 'cleaning up' visiting servicemen, and US Marines from the nearby Allied Services ('Waldorf') Club – a rendezvous at which New Zealand troops apparently received 'a very "thin hearing" from those in charge'. A general melee developed as other American servicemen, seamen, and New Zealand soldiers and Air Force personnel joined in. No sooner was one 'skirmish' ended by police and provosts than another began elsewhere in the inner city. Not until after 10 pm, when the last leave train departed for Trentham military camp, was 'some semblance of quiet' restored. Police blamed a 'rough (civilian) element' for inciting intoxicated troops to fight, and noted that the provost was absent at the crucial time (6 pm). That night, there were only ten New Zealand military police on duty. Similarly, military and civil police were unable to prevent or quickly quell a brawl between US naval personnel and Maori soldiers which began outside an inner-city dance hall late in the evening of Saturday 12 May 1945. Indeed, an unofficial Maori picquet joined in as combatants. From both disturbances, the product of simmering antagonisms, there were apparently no serious injuries and only two arrests.[165] But they demonstrated the fragility of wartime order in the two largest cities. Indeed in August 1943, the Police Association expressed concern at the 'growing number of unwarranted attacks and interference' with police by groups of American servicemen who were 'becoming a menace' with their 'methods of violence'. Cummings had already urged the American authorities to take action, but conceded that with 'the many thousands of men on leave it is difficult to control the unruly ones'.[166]

Much petty disorder stemmed from ineffective liquor controls, the weaknesses of which were already apparent by 1939 when the Justice Department recommended an overhaul of the licensing laws.[167] As with the gaming laws, a review of the liquor laws was postponed following the outbreak of war, though the increasing numbers of servicemen on leave in the port cities and some provincial towns compounded the pressures for change. In Wellington, and especially in Auckland, public bars were concentrated in the inner city, with the surrounding suburbs being virtually no-licence areas. Inevitably, American troops rubbed shoulders with the New Zealand servicemen and civilians drinking hurriedly in congested bars between 5 and 6 pm, and emptying out onto the streets soon afterwards. Six o'clock closing did not, in fact, reduce the potential for disorder amongst servicemen determined to find liquor which publicans and others were willing to provide. Early in the war, after-hours trading became prevalent. The law was circumvented, particularly in Auckland, by hotels which charged servicemen a nominal amount for lodgings, enabling them and their 'guests' to continue drinking into the evening, and to buy liquor to take elsewhere.[168] Sly-grog selling, already subject to increased police surveillance from 1936, increased markedly at shops and houses near military camps, and at city dances and 'clubs'. In 1940, Commissioner Cummings put off seeking wider powers to suppress it in view of the proposed general overhaul of the liquor laws. He was against any relaxation of controls to meet the needs of servicemen, declaring in 1940 that the 'early closing of hotels was one of the best pieces of legislation on the Statute Book'.[169] Thus, a prohibition on the possession of liquor in the vicinity of dance halls enacted in 1939 was enforced vigorously during the war.[170] Similarly, the stricter enforcement of restrictions on supplying liquor to Maori that had been noticeable since 1938 continued during wartime, though it was perceived to be ineffective by 1944.[171]

Civic and church leaders, along with a variety of pressure groups, became increasingly impatient with tipsy and rowdy soldiers on city streets, trams, and trains; concerned at sexual immorality; and fearful that unrestrained access to liquor would undermine the war effort. In response, Peter Fraser (a tea-drinker), reiterated in April 1942 that the war effort outweighed everything else; if the sale of liquor was detrimental to this, he would not hesitate to prohibit it.[172] In lieu of such drastic action, the Justice Department drafted emergency regulations which were issued in June. These included increased powers that, Cummings had already secured in February to tackle sly-grogging,[173] but not his recommendation to suppress after-hours trading by ending the supply of liquor to lodgers and their guests.[174] Instead, lodgers were merely required to sign an order for liquor. While the Commissioner supported the later opening of hotels (at 10 am), he saw the closing of them between 2 pm and 4 pm on Saturday afternoons as likely to promote sly-grogging, which it did.[175]

Soon after the first American troops arrived, sly-grogging became rife, especially in Auckland. This resulted from a lack of entertainment facilities, the fact that hotels were closed by the time several thousand servicemen arrived each night in the inner city from their camps with the means and willingness to pay exorbitant prices for dubious sly grog (especially when it was labelled as whisky or wine), a variety of sources of supply, and a nightly blackout which made street transactions more difficult to detect. The distribution of sly grog soon became highly organised, often being undertaken by car in Wellington and Auckland. Black marketeers acquired spirits from other parts of the country to supply the sly-groggers in shops, houses, dance halls, nightclubs, boarding houses, and in the vicinity of camps and on the streets, working through touts and droppers. When the supply of spirits dried up late in 1943, local distillation of illicit spirits developed, as did the production of home-made 'plonk' wine. 'Under sly grog conditions', the Sergeant in charge of detecting the trade in Auckland observed, 'the streets were littered with broken bottles and smeared with offensive matter'. Another Auckland sectional Sergeant recalled that 'Servicemen – largely not ours – consumed sly-grog wine in considerable quantity, with more or less expected results': 'all sorts of bother for us, also for Shore Patrols, and Military Police in general.'[176]

During 1942 police action against sly-grogging intensified, with Sergeants and constables specially detailed for the task in the two port cities. The number of prosecutions for sly-grogging peaked in 1943, when there were 142 convictions in Auckland District alone. Initially, some US commanders allowed the Police to use their servicemen from the provost to make purchases from sly-groggers, who 'were given a very lively time'. In mid-1943, however, this cooperation was withdrawn; the American commanders had come to see the liquor laws as unreasonable. They wanted facilities (such as 'wet canteens') for their servicemen on liberty to obtain liquor lawfully.[177] Meanwhile, mounting dissatisfaction with the stringency of the liquor laws was expressed by some magistrates, editors, and politicians.[178] But Cummings looked to tighten up, not to liberalise. In July 1943 he secured increased powers of search and arrest and further controls on the supply of liquor through new emergency regulations. As the trade in 'Hokonui' grew, Auckland police discovered a whisky still north of the city, and convictions for illicit distillation were secured in both major port cities during 1944.[179]

In October 1942, a Uniform Branch 'Special Duty' section (soon known as the 'Vice' squad) had been formed in Wellington. A similar section, including women police, was formed in Auckland a year later to focus not merely on sly-grogging, but also on the 'bad conduct' by women in 'houses of ill fame', nightclubs and hotel lounge bars where there was 'mixed drinking' with servicemen. Sergeant G.E. Callaghan's prosecution of the occupants of apartment rooms at 40 Abel Smith Street, Wellington, for sly-grogging, and of the female proprietor for permitting her premises to be used as a house of ill fame, symbolised the connection that was drawn between illicit liquor and 'dens of immorality'.[180] Public fears of increasing prostitution (especially by teenage girls) and the spread of venereal disease led the Commissioner to seek increased powers (enacted in December 1942) to deal with one-women brothels and the proprietors of boarding houses who let rooms for sex, particularly to servicemen and their generally youthful female companions.[181] Sensitive to criticism, Cummings enjoined police – now empowered to search premises without a warrant – to exercise the 'utmost care'; in no case was 'hasty action to be taken'. Accordingly, searches followed surveillance and women police were present – not merely for the sake of decorum, but also to give young women 'timely advice' in lieu of prosecution. Such advice was also given to 'women of questionable character' frequenting hotel lounge bars, where the role of the women police on their daily patrols was to 'comb out the undesirables'. Police perceived soliciting on the streets to be 'practically non-existent' (only one woman was prosecuted for it during the war – according to police statistics). As was frequently the case in peacetime, the women who were arrested were charged with vagrancy; most were not seen by police as 'professional' prostitutes, but rather as having formed an 'undesirable association' with 'mostly visiting servicemen who possessed more than average means.'[182] Such 'undesirable associations' were also perceived amongst many patrons of the nightclubs which flourished in Auckland during 1943 and early 1944, and which evoked much alarmist public comment from local clergy. However, police had difficulty gaining access to these clubs (women police were used to gain evidence of sly-grogging), and prosecutions under the liquor laws had little effect as great profits were being made. To Sergeant J.L. Adams of the Auckland 'Anti-Vice' squad, the nightclubs were 'completely out of control': dancing was 'only incidental to drinking', and 'young girls' were found intoxicated. Again Cummings sought and was given (in May 1944) increased powers; in this case, to close down places of entertainment which breached the liquor laws, or where conduct was disorderly or 'demoralising'. To Adams, this had 'a steadying effect', even though the new powers were not invoked. In fact, the impact of American troops on local patterns of order had already begun to diminish greatly as their numbers in New Zealand fell from some 24,000 in May to 3,000 by August 1944.[183] Pressures on police resources did not diminish significantly, however.

Resources and working conditions

In its many facets, the growth of wartime work taxed police staff and facilities to an extent not envisaged in pre-war planning. Though such planning gave the Police the responsibility for protecting vital points, Commissioner Cummings did not implement a recommendation to create an auxiliary force for wartime duties, since with war imminent the Army was prepared, initially at least, to provide guards at key installations. He believed then that the 'normal' police strength would be able to cope with any other additional wartime work.[184] In the event, although the number of male police increased from 1,457 to 1,640 in the three years from March 1940, this remained below the authorised strength, and was insufficient to provide the degree of surveillance deemed necessary at wharves, let alone meet the increased demands of other wartime duties and routine policing. During the two years from March 1943, the number of male police fell by 75.[185] The advent of women police, whose numbers increased from nine in 1942 to 33 in 1944, did not offset the increasing pressures of work which remained almost exclusively confined to male police. Insufficient staff meant increased hours of work and restrictions on leave, with many (especially those on enquiries) being called on to complete tasks 'in their own time'. The shortage of staff remained an acute problem for the Commissioner throughout the war.

Until July 1940, when military conscription was implemented, Cummings was able to secure sufficient new recruits not merely to replace those who retired or left to join the armed forces, but also to increase the number of police doing duty on the wharves. He drew on a substantial waiting list of suitable applicants which had grown in the immediate pre-war years.[186] Amongst them was a future Commissioner, Ken Burnside, who joined in 1940, having applied four years earlier when he was eighteen.[187] From July 1940, recruiting became 'increasingly difficult', especially as (until 1942 at least) Cummings would no longer accept any applicant who was single and eligible for military service. However, too few of the married applicants met the long-established minimum standards for recruits. Accordingly some requirements were progressively relaxed, and a 'large number' of new recruits were told that they would not be kept on after the war.[188] In a sample of a third of the 129 new constables recruited in 1942, some 60 per cent were over 30 years of age; almost all were married. As with the pre-war intakes, only a few had some secondary education. About half did not have the Proficiency examination (which Burnside had passed) entitling them to go on to secondary school; some had reached only the fifth standard at primary school, if that. Limited formal education was counterbalanced in many cases by imposing physique (nearly a third were six feet tall or more), or by prior work experience, especially with motor vehicles. Several who did not meet the physical requirements became drivers, and one a police carpenter, thereby releasing those 'capable of performing more active duties'. Three of the 1942 intake were deployed on police launches, joining six recruited for that purpose in 1941. By September 1942, the degree of mobilisation was such that all Grade I (or fit) men of military age, married as well as single, were in either the armed forces or essential industries. Only Grade II or III men were now available as police recruits; even so, the number of applicants fell away. Cummings became increasingly concerned at the lack of fit single men available to be on call at barracks for the arduous work of street policing in the main centres. In November 1942, he gained Cabinet approval to have released to the Police some of the Grade I men in the Army who had been on the pre-war waiting list. Altogether, 90 constables were appointed in 1943, but only 25 in 1944, including a few under twenty years of age who were seen as a liability by senior officers. Some who had resigned to join the armed forces prior to April 1941 were permitted to rejoin; they were the only 'trained' recruits.[189]

The Training Depot was closed in November 1939 to provide accommodation for the 30 police who would be on duty at the Centennial Exhibition until May 1940.[190] It was not to reopen to train regular batches of male recruits until May 1946. Wartime applicants were sworn in as temporary constables as soon as they were accepted. Though their experiences varied, almost all those recruited during the war received no formal training beyond weekly lectures (consisting mainly of readings from the 'Black Book', statutes, and Luxford's *Police Law in New Zealand*) from their NCOs – and these were not common outside the main centres.[191] Typically, Ken Burnside listened with little understanding to a day and a half of lectures by Senior Sergeant Dan Beard before being sent out on night duty from Mt Cook station with a police coat, helmet and baton, and wearing his own navy trousers. Like others who survived to have a career in the Police, he used his initiative, learning from experience and the advice of those senior constables and Sergeants who were not intolerant of a new recruit.[192] Between 1936 and 1939, 90 per cent of the temporary constables had been appointed permanently after a year. From 1 October 1940, no more permanent appointments were made, as the temporary constables had not received a 'special course of training', and growing numbers from 1941 did not conform to the pre-war standards for recruits. Nonetheless, as the Commissioner acknowledged, some were 'outstanding in their work'. By 1945, nearly a third of the 1,250 constables were wartime recruits. After the war, those deemed to be 'fit and eligible' – some 59 per cent of the 463 who had joined between 1940 and 1944 – were given permanent appointments.[193]

Resignations and retirements of experienced men compounded the problem of a lack of staff.[194] From the outbreak of the war, a growing number of police applied for leave without pay to join the armed forces. Anticipating a badly depleted Police Force, Cummings soon decided to release only those men whose applications were supported by the Army or the Navy on account of their previous service and expertise, or who were required by the Air Force (thirteen in total by April 1941).[195] After the introduction of conscription, the Commissioner had the Director of National Service lodge appeals on behalf of police called up for military service; their cases were adjourned indefinitely. 'It is a policeman's duty to stick to his job in New Zealand', the chairman of the Armed Forces Appeal Board told a constable who stated that he did not want an appeal to be made on his behalf.[196] (Similarly, to stem the loss of experienced staff, the Commissioner secured a regulation in December 1940 prohibiting any staff retiring without Cabinet approval – individuals would be released only if they were unable to carry out their work.) Nor would Cummings permit police to resign in order to enlist, or for other personal reasons. Though he recognised the patriotism of those wishing to serve overseas, he remained adamant that experienced police could not be spared; they 'can give equal service where they are at present'.

Even so, an increasing number resigned without permission, thereby forfeiting any entitlements, such as leave due to them. By April 1941, 34 men had resigned specifically to join the armed forces. During the preceding year the total number of resignations had reached a new peak of 52. To strengthen the Commissioner's hand, a regulation was issued in March 1941 prohibiting any police from resigning without the consent of the Minister. However, this move was nullified by the outcome of the first prosecution in August. Constable D.G.M. Kilgour had refused to report for duty at Auckland after being refused permission to resign to join the Air Force. Convicted (with a suspended sentence) in the Auckland Magistrate's Court, Kilgour was then summonsed to face a departmental charge in front of the local Superintendent. In the Supreme Court, Kilgour sought a writ restraining the Police from further proceedings on the grounds that he was no longer a member of the Force (having given the necessary one month's notice in writing); this was granted by Justice Fair, and not appealed.[197] Resignations continued (albeit at a slower rate) and further prosecutions were taken. Magistrates generally imposed nominal penalties on constables who had 'walked out' to enlist.[198] Faced with both a continuing loss of men and much greater difficulty in replacing them, Cummings in June 1942 obtained new regulations which, in effect, required all police to remain in the Force until released by the Minister. The penalties for disobeying were increased.[199] Few, if any, now attempted to 'walk out'. Only one constable was subsequently prosecuted for desertion; he had tried unsuccessfully to resign, then left to go sharemilking after the war ended.[200] Resignations and dismissals continued, as the Commissioner found a growing proportion of the new recruits unsuitable and released older men on compassionate grounds. Despite attempts to stem the flow, the 'wastage' rate of male staff was higher in wartime than it had been during the 1930s (see figure 1.1).

Only to a very limited degree was this loss offset at city stations by the arrival of 'women police'.[201] Though authority to appoint women to the Police Force on the same terms as men had been enacted in 1938, Commissioner Cummings was slow to utilize it – to the growing impatience of lobbyists.[202] Cummings' caution reflected both his conservatism and his uncertainty as to the appropriate status, numbers and role of women police, which varied amongst the Australian police forces he visited in August 1939. There were then only two policewomen at Brisbane, and eight each at Sydney and Melbourne; South Australia, which Cummings did not visit, had eighteen – the largest number – and deployed them more widely than did the other forces.[203] '[M]uch would depend on the type of candidate offering', Cummings observed while awaiting Peter Fraser's report on his discussions at Scotland Yard about its policewomen during a visit to London in November.[204] For Cummings, the first year of the war was the 'most strenuous' he had experienced in his career; appointing policewomen was not a priority.[205] Eventually, in July 1940, £1,400 was set aside for women police in the supplementary estimates. In September, advertisements appeared for unmarried or widowed applicants aged between 25 and 40, who were in good health and had a 'superior' (some secondary) education that had included shorthand and typing.[206] Looking for 'personality, sound common sense, [and] a sympathetic outlook', Cummings took his time to personally select and interview ten recruits from some 150 candidates. They were sworn in as temporary constables after entering the Training Depot on 3 June 1941.[207] Indicative of their ambiguously 'equal' but separate status, they were enrolled on a separate register (with the prefix 'W' to the numbering) and not on a common seniority list. Their ages ranged from 26 to 39, with seven in their thirties. Of the 39 women recruited during the war years, nearly half had been office workers, while most of the remainder were nurses, teachers or shop assistants.[208] Quite a number, it seems, had acquaintances, friends or relatives in the Force.[209] By contrast with male recruits, the women in the first intake came from the cities, rather than from country towns and farms. This was less true of the second and third intakes.

Again by contrast with the male recruits, all but two of the women recruited during the war years received at least three months of formal training. They were housed in the refurbished barracks (now euphemistically called 'flats') adjacent to the Depot. Senior Sergeant Beard provided the same instruction hitherto given to males in the law and the Police Regulations, but with a special emphasis on the duties then expected of the women police: mainly patrols and enquiries dealing with women and children, and the detection of shoplifters. They were taught their powers of arrest, but (according to one recollection) given little tuition in the laws of evidence. Even so, they practised procedure in mock trials. While Beard expected that they would not be called on to deal with traffic control or violent males, they needed to be able to handle 'obstreperous' women – to know 'when to act and when not to act', as Cummings put it. 'Girls, if you have no sense of humour, you might as well resign now', Beard told the first intake; none needed to. Yet force might need to be applied, so they were expected to be fit, with daily exercises and a course in ju-jitsu. A first aid examination had also to be passed, as well as four others, which all did with high marks. Because separate office accommodation for women in the four main centres was not ready, the training of the first intake stretched to

102. The new Palmerston North police station was completed in November 1939. Apart from a two-storey building at Invercargill, it was the only major police station built during the inter-war years, and was intended to be a model for others in its layout. ATL, C23997$^{1}/_{2}$

103. Modern transport: by early 1939 the mounted constable who patrolled and carried out enquiries in the outer suburbs of Christchurch, principally Halswell and Marshlands, had been given a new car in place of his horse. The stables behind the Central station remained. *NZ Police Journal, Feb 1939, p.93*

104. 'Wife: "I don't want you to arrest him, Constable – just give him a fright"': an English cartoon reprinted in the *New Zealand Police Journal* in 1939 captures a growing dimension of police work from the late 1930s as the upswing in prosperity brought an increase in alcohol-related disorder, including 'domestic disputes'. *NZ Police Journal, Apr 1939, p.197*

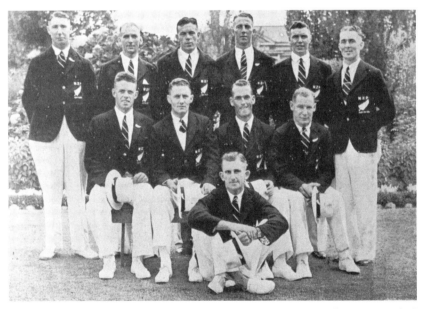

105. The New Zealand Police team en route to the New South Wales Police sports carnival (also called the Australasian Police Games) in February 1938. The 'En-Zedders' were the first representative police team to go overseas. From left, back row, F.T. Furney (Oamaru), H.F. Miller (Auckland), L.D. Ryan (Auckland), A.T. Kofoed (Wellington), W.A. Duncan (Auckland), J.J.N. McCarthy (Wellington); middle row, G. Tait (Hamilton), D.M. Whillans (Auckland), J.S. Callanan (Manager, Whangarei), J. Gillespie (Wellington); front, W.J. Fulton (Wellington). *NZ Police Journal, Apr 1938, p.10*

106. The Auckland Police Orchestra in 1938. Its appearance was part of the florescence of police social clubs in Auckland and elsewhere during the late 1930s. Social and sporting activity amongst police – encouraged by Commissioner Cummings – represented a new phase in the development of an occupational community that was fostered by the district activities of the Police Association. *NZ Police Journal, Dec 1938, p.57*

107. A constable towers above the crowd at the New Zealand Centennial Exhibition, which opened at Rongotai, Wellington, on 8 November 1939. Twenty-four uniformed and seven detective staff under the control of Sub-Inspector D.J. O'Neill were posted to a temporary police station at the entrance of the Exhibition to look out for thieves, lost children and accidents, answer a myriad of questions, and deal with 'dud files' sent by enquiry men from other districts. *ATL, F36224¹/₂*

108. A crowd of 100,000 gave the crew of HMNZS *Achilles* a heroes' welcome as they marched up Queen Street to a civic reception outside the Auckland town hall on 23 February 1940. White-helmeted police lined the route. Two days earlier, new regulations had been issued giving police increased powers to curb overt opposition to the war effort. *ATL, F66944¹/₂*

109. Ormond Burton (carrying a poster) leads a Christian Pacifist Society parade through Wellington streets in April 1940. Police intervened to prevent pacifists speaking at street meetings, but did not stop their poster parades until June. *ATL, F152943¹/₂*

110. A police guard examines a pass at the entrance to Queen's Wharf, Wellington, in June 1940. Wharves for overseas ships were now closed to sightseers; only those with a pass were allowed access. *Evening Post Collection, ATL, C23996$^1/_2$*

111. *Antipodes*, the first police launch at Wellington, began patrolling the wharf area in September 1941; three months later it was sent to Lyttelton and replaced by the *Lady Elizabeth*. Trained launchmen and engineers were sworn in as temporary constables, with experienced police being used as observers. A driver and an observer comprised the usual crew on night patrol. *NZ Police Museum*

112. Swearing in recruits for the various sections of the Emergency Precautions Scheme at the Wellington City Council bus yard on 16 December 1940. Recruiting for the 'Law and Order Units' of the EPS continued during 1941. *Evening Post Collection, ATL, C23995¹/₂*

113. Monitoring the blackout: a constable notes a light in an Auckland shop window, October 1941. Wartime conditions added new dimensions to routine police work. *ATL, C13564¹/₂*

114. A warden during an Emergency Precautions Scheme trial in Auckland in March 1942. EPS wardens in the Law and Order Units had the powers of Special Constables in an emergency and were under the control of local police. *ATL, C24023¹/₂*

115. In October 1941 Eric Stanley Graham shot dead four local police officers and an agricultural instructor who came to their aid. This led to an unprecedented manhunt in the rugged bush-clad neighbourhood of Kowhitirangi on the South Island's West Coast. Graham's passion for firearms is reflected in the cache of weapons that police retrieved from his property. *NZ Police Museum*

116. American servicemen at the Hotel Cecil, Wellington. Here they could buy an ice-cream soda or sundae, milk shake, Coca-Cola, doughnuts or coffee – but not liquor. The lack of a 'wet canteen' or any other legal access to liquor after 6 pm meant that sly-grogging became rife in Auckland and Wellington after the American troops arrived in 1942. *Gordon Burt Collection, ATL, F15935¹/₁*

117. US marines playing blackjack at Whangarei. Both licit and illicit gambling flourished amongst troops and civilians during wartime. *John Pascoe Collection, ATL, F388¹/₄*

118. The first intake of women police (shown with their Instructor, Senior Sergeant Dan Beard) are sworn in as temporary constables after entering the Training Depot on 3 June 1941: by their familiar names, from left, back row, Lyn Brocket, Nan Aitchison, Vera McConchie, Lina Smith, May Berridge, Margaret Holder; front row, Edna Pearce, Eileen O'Connor, Molly Speakman, May Callaghan. *J.A. Beard collection*

119. Edna Pearce, in her policewoman's outfit, with officials on the Wellington wharf in November 1943. Behind them a Union Jack is painted on the 'protected' ship *Wanganella*, which took interned enemy aliens and their families to Sydney. Miss Pearce escorted the Japanese women and children, accompanied by Detective Sergeant A.M. Harding, who oversaw the police surveillance of aliens. *Edna Pearce*

120. Prime Minister Peter Fraser found time to talk to American war correspondents over a cup of tea in June 1942. With many preoccupations at home and lengthy absences abroad, he was slow to respond to Police Association remits. Giving priority to the war effort, he was unsympathetic to the Association's demands and in December 1942 contemplated either dissolving the organisation or seeking to replace its General Secretary. *War Effort Collection, ATL, F5068¹/₂*

121. The 'boss among bosses': Peter Fraser at the first annual conference of commissioned officers in March 1944: from left, back row: Inspectors E.T.C. Turner, L.R. Capp, W. Pender, W.H. Dunlop, D.J. O'Neill, D.L. Calwell, S.G. Hall, W.E. Packer; middle row, Inspectors J. Carroll, E.J. Carroll, D.A. MacLean, D. Scott and H. Scott; R.F. Madden, Secretary of Police; Inspectors J.A. Dempsey and G.H. Lambert; front row, Superintendents D. Cameron, R.R.J. Ward and J. Cummings; Peter Fraser, Commissioner D.J. Cummings, P.C. (Paddy) Webb ('deputy' Minister in charge of the Police); Superintendents C.W. Lopdell and T. Shanahan. *Donald Scott*

122. Jacob (Jack) Meltzer, the General Secretary of the Police Association from early 1940. Responsive to restiveness amongst the rank and file, especially in Auckland, he was persistent in pressing their concerns. Commissioner Cummings came to resent Meltzer's assertiveness and refused to see him during 1943 and 1944. *Police Association*

four months. As 'pioneer policewomen ... a great responsibility rested on their shoulders', Peter Fraser told them at their final parade on 2 October; the 'Government was particularly anxious that the experiment should be an unqualified success'.[210]

Three were posted to both Auckland and Wellington, and two each to Christchurch and Dunedin.[211] They would work in plain clothes (like their Australian counterparts, but unlike London's policewomen), for Cummings felt that a uniform would both 'impair their usefulness' on enquiries and 'subject them to undue attention'.[212] Thus they were attached to the detective staffs at the central stations, working on 'general duties' under the direction of the Chief Detective.[213] After their arrival in Auckland, the first policewomen were given 'a little pistol practice' – scarcely necessary for the generally routine and often office-bound duties they were given. During her first two months in Auckland (before she was seconded for two years to take charge of the interned Japanese women and children), Constable Edna Pearce found that, while she was 'received with courtesy and respect', a 'current of discrimination was present'. Indeed, the unease of some male colleagues at the presence of female constables was expressed (as others put it) in 'sarcastic and belittling remarks', such as, 'the women only joined to get a husband'. Constable Molly Sim 'proved to them that that wasn't my idea', as did Edna Pearce and others.[214] With their capabilities as yet unproven, and supervisors uncertain of what duties to assign, policewomen were often given menial work from the outset – such as dealing with 'dead end' files on thefts reported from offices, schools or hospitals, where there was little prospect of identifying an offender or recovering property. For Edna Pearce, nonetheless, 'each day brought new and varied duties and experiences'. Often she accompanied detectives on their enquiries, 'mostly for their own protection' from accusations when interviewing 'immoral' women. Like those in the other centres, she also patrolled the streets, making the first arrests by a policewoman (two women charged with theft in November 1941).[215] However, fifteen months later in Auckland, Molly Sim (from the second intake) was told roundly by the Chief Detective, after a drunken woman she had taken back to the station was locked up, that it was 'not her job to arrest anyone'. Rather, the main role of women police, as it was conceived at the outset, was one of monitoring the moral welfare of females; or, as Cummings put it in 1941, 'to take a kindly interest in the welfare of all women and girls coming under their notice' as they patrolled bus and railway stations, parks, shops and hotels. As Molly Sim observed, 'we very seldom reported under age drinkers', but 'sent them on their way with a warning.'[216]

The 'invasion' by American troops from June 1942 reinforced the gendered focus of women police on moral welfare, as growing numbers of young women were seen on city streets late at night with servicemen, both local and American. Auckland's mayor, responding to deputations, asked Fraser for more women police, and for them to work in uniform – a call quickly echoed in Parliament by three women MPs, who sought to better 'guard their youth, both male and female'.[217] In August, Cummings instructed women police to focus as much as possible on 'the conduct of young women suspected of leading an immoral life in their association with servicemen'. An increase in their numbers was also agreed to by the government, although not until July 1943 were women police officially declared to be 'beyond the experimental stage'. Even so, their permanent appointment after twelve months' service (promised to the first intake) was deferred indefinitely. Acting Police Minister Webb supported the Commissioner's view that they worked best in civilian clothes, and that attending to drinking among servicemen and young women on the streets and in parks late at night was 'not a woman's job', but one for uniformed male constables. Lobbying for uniformed policewomen continued, nonetheless.[218] Twelve female recruits entered the Training Depot on 29 October 1942 and were posted to the four main centres in February 1943, bringing the total numbers to six in Auckland and Wellington, and four in Christchurch and Dunedin. Further pressure from Auckland in August 1943 for more women police led in November to the formation of the Special Duty section there, and a third intake of fifteen recruits which included a 'half caste' Maori who (it was hoped) would be valuable in dealing with Maori women. By March 1944 there were 33 policewomen, seventeen of them in Auckland.[219]

Though the policewomen's role was ostensibly preventive policing by patrols in pairs, in reality their work became more diverse (and more valuable to their male colleagues) during the last three years of the war. Escort duty – taking women to court, prison, Arohata Borstal or mental hospital – became routine. Women police gained more responsibility in interviewing female suspects and complainants, and in enquiry work. Focusing on young women, especially on the streets and in hotels, they worked with Child Welfare staff to locate girls 'not under proper control'; with manpower officials in detecting defaulters and absentees from work; and with public health nurses in locating venereal disease contacts. Such enquiries could be time-consuming, as were the menial 'maintenance' cases that were passed to them. Women police were soon deployed on undercover work to gain evidence of offences. In Christchurch, for example, visits to eleven tea shops by Constables Nancy Aitchison and Mollie Speakman led to nineteen women and two men being prosecuted in January 1942 for offering to tell fortunes by cup-reading. More common was the use of policewomen in catching sly-groggers and bookmakers, and in searching ships and opium dens for women. The older 'regulars' amongst the prostitutes became used to the early policewomen; using 'the most filthy language one day', and then the next day 'hail[ing] us as old friends'; providing useful information for other enquiries, and sometimes sending Christmas cards or ringing up for a chat. Constable Molly Sim found that work with Auckland's 'Vice Squad' involved long hours but was 'always full of excitement'. There were elements of both risk and enjoyment in being ostensibly picked up by American servicemen for an evening in a night club. Less pleasant was ensnaring abortionists and dealing with sexual offences against children and teenage girls below the age of consent, following up complaints of 'peeping toms' or indecent exposure, and spending hours 'just watching places' to detect brothels. Another task that became more frequent towards the end of the war and after it was the 'more distasteful' one of catching shopkeepers at Sunday trading.[220]

When, early in 1944, Edna Pearce returned to duty at Auckland from her demanding stint in charge of interned Japanese women, she was given 'indoor' work in the district headquarters: typing, dealing with files, and answering telephones. So too were other policewomen as the war ended, reflecting a continuing conservatism amongst some supervisors who had 'difficulty' finding 'something for them to do'.[221] Though there were more policewomen in New Zealand by 1945 than in any of the Australian states, the future of what was by then called the 'Women's Division' remained unclear.[222] There was neither a separate women's branch with its own officers (like the 'Principal' in South Australia's Women Police Office), nor a career structure (as in the London Metropolitan Police). After a year, Edna Pearce returned to the outdoor duties she had missed, 'working with people, not paper'. In practice, however, the wartime dimensions of policewomen's work narrowed in the transition to peace. Aged 39, Edna passed the literary examination for commissioned rank in 1945, but soon realised that she had insufficient time to pass the Sergeant's examination and be promoted before the maximum age of 40.[223] None of the others in the first four intakes of policewomen sat any promotion examinations: some would have, but thought they were not permitted to do so; for the majority, who were in their thirties, the prospects of promotion were small anyway, and for some, marriage generally led to a different career. (Nine of the wartime policewomen married, with four resigning within a few months.)[224]

Even so, from 1944, policewomen at Auckland had meetings with Jack Meltzer each time he visited, seeking Police Association support to clarify their status in terms of pay and conditions. Despite Cummings' initial opposition (on the grounds that women police were an 'experiment'), all 33 joined the Association in 1944, and Constable Mae Kelly was a member of its Management Committee between 1945 and 1948.[225] By 1947, Association pressure had secured the permanent appointment of the 23 female constables remaining from those who had joined during the war.[226] Ostensibly an equality of status had been achieved, yet such pressure stopped short of securing equality of pay or conditions – on the grounds (effectively challenged later, but then accepted by some policewomen themselves) that there was not, nor could there be, a full equality of work. Consequently, in 1945, women police with less than three years service received only 87 per cent of the salary of male constables with similar service (see figure 1.2). The disparity increased with length of service and was to persist until 1965.

During wartime, however, a sense of relative deprivation was felt more acutely amongst the male rank and file than amongst the policewomen.[227] Initially at least, the first policewomen tended to compare their job – its status, satisfactions and conditions – with those of other women in the paid workforce, and could feel better off. By contrast, amongst their male colleagues, and especially the uniformed constables in the largest cities, there was a broadening sense that they were, or were becoming, less well off than others with whom they compared their working conditions: public servants, and manual workers more generally. This sense of deprivation came not simply from a perception that police pay and conditions had improved more slowly than those of others during the first years of the Labour government. (Here, the failure to achieve a five-day, 40-hour week symbolised the disparity by 1939.) There was also a more pervasive sense that police had not received from successive governments the special consideration – especially in relation to pay and pensions – that could be expected because of their distinctive 'obligations and responsibilities'. Wartime stresses caused by work, housing conditions and the cost of living strengthened such feelings, which were to persist long after 1945.

In common with public servants, and manual workers more generally, police worked increasing hours of 'overtime' during the war – on enquiries, on the wharves, clerical work, visiting vital points, and patrolling and surveillance generally. Though there was no precise measure, by 1942 the average working day of police 'far' exceeded eight hours.[228] Police norms regarding working long hours in emergencies, and a strong sense of duty in wartime, shaped a general acceptance of longer working days, at least until 1941. As the pressure of work increased, extra hours became routine, annual leave was curtailed, and growing numbers of men were called back to work on their recently-conceded weekly day off (especially those on the short-staffed wharves). There was no payment for the hours worked in excess of 48 a week, though time off in lieu for overtime was granted – if they could be spared. Time-in-lieu slips accumulated with little prospect of being redeemed. Also unsettling to increasingly disgruntled constables, especially in Auckland, were the disparities in rewards for overtime; in most industries, penal rates became payable after 40 hours. Police on gangway duty at the wharves, working throughout the night and during the weekends for no extra pay, observed the wharfies earning time and a half·or double time, and special rates of pay.[229] By October 1942, overtime was a key issue for the Police Association, as it had become for other public service organisations. Hitherto Fraser, sharing

Cummings' belief that the payment of hourly overtime rates was not practicable, had held the long-standing view that police pay provided for irregular hours. Now he recognised that the war had thrown an extra burden on police, and in January 1943 accepted Cummings' recommendation that a special wartime allowance be paid. From February 1943, an 'overtime allowance' gave NCOs and constables the equivalent of two hours overtime at time and a half for a 48-hour week. This was less generous than the overtime rates for other public servants.[230]

Pressure for overtime payments was part of a wider demand for increased pay, especially as the cost of living increased. A cost-of-living allowance granted to public servants from August 1940 was aimed at the lowest-paid; constables with more than fourteen years' service, and NCOs, received nothing. A second cost-of-living 'bonus' from April 1942 was similarly abated, but did give some benefit to NCOs and commissioned officers, albeit thereby eroding margins for seniority. (The Commissioner's salary remained at £1,000 throughout the war.) Taking into account the police overtime allowance, which was given (retrospectively) from 1 October 1942, only the pay of junior constables (those with less than three years' service) had kept pace with the 14 per cent rise in retail prices between the outbreak of war and December 1942. Overall, the proportional increases in police pay fell with length of service and seniority, from 12 per cent for constables with six to nine years' service to less than 10 per cent for NCOs – well below the average increase in wages outside the public service.[231]

Naturally enough, constables compared their situation with the significantly increased wartime earnings of labourers, wharfies, carpenters and other tradesmen they observed. 'We do not seek to better our position, but only to hold our relative position', declared one who caught the mood of Police Association conference delegates in October 1941 by pressing for a pay increase of 10 per cent.[232] Fraser had already told the conference 'frankly' that there would be no general pay increase and, in mid-1942, turned down the Association's remits, considering the 'present rate of police pay very reasonable'. To this, Meltzer reiterated 'the principle of "EQUALITY OF SACRIFICE BY ALL" '.[233] On 7 December 1942 (with no decision yet on payment for overtime), Meltzer informed Cummings that he had 'never known a more widespread feeling' amongst police for some increase in pay; there were 'many cases' of men 'finding it extremely difficult to make ends meet'.[234] Police Association meetings were held in a number of centres, notably Auckland, to press for government action. With signs of growing restiveness amongst the rank and file, Fraser met a deputation from the Association in January, and a decision on the overtime allowance soon followed.[235] Even had he wished to give the Police Force a general pay increase (which he did not), Fraser asserted that he was bound by the economic stabilisation scheme introduced in December

1942, which took 'precedence over everything' by pegging pay rates –
to the disadvantage of police and other public servants in comparison
with both outside rates and living costs. A further increase in Police
pay did not come until March 1945, in line with a general increase in
public service wages and backdated to June 1944.[236]

In the meantime, police sought other means to maintain their standard
of living. Increases in both the range and amount of allowances were
consistently urged and generally refused.[237] Country constables continued
to be relatively better off than their city colleagues. Even so, the increased
costs of using their cars to visit vital points and for more extensive
wartime enquiries were a continuing source of complaint, despite an
increase in car allowances.[238] Though junior constables' incomes were
the least eroded by the rising cost of living, their right to permanent
appointment, increments, and superannuation were persistent issues until
1943 at least.[239] Older constables with families who lived in the cities,
especially Wellington and Auckland, faced the greatest decline in real
income, as rents as well as prices rose despite the wartime controls.

By 1942, the annual housing allowance of £39 (in lieu of 'free
quarters') represented less than half the annual rentals being paid by
some constables in Auckland.[240] A year later the Stabilisation
Commission knocked back Cummings' attempt to increase housing
allowances.[241] For those on transfer, the shortage of housing in the
cities had become an acute problem by 1942, with men often separated
from their families for lengthy periods and requiring assistance in
meeting the cost of temporary accommodation.[242] Cummings could do
little about the housing shortage; his many approaches to the State
Housing Department had 'little success'. Much had been done by 1940
to improve country constables' houses, and during the early war years
to upgrade barracks accommodation in Auckland and Christchurch; but
Cummings' major pre-war building programme was deferred, and there
was no scope to provide police housing in the cities, as most of the
country's building resources were diverted to defence work by 1942. Married
city constables (like other workers) had to take their chances in securing
state houses, or whatever dwelling they could both find and afford.[243]

As financial pressures mounted and opportunities presented
themselves, some policemen turned to 'outside' employment, and their
wives to paid work, in apparent breach of the Police Regulations.[244] By
1943, a considerable number of the Auckland men – uniformed as well
as detectives – had second jobs, especially on the wharves at night.
Police formed a large proportion of the casual workers who unloaded
and stacked stores at American depots, receiving pay for night shifts
that was double a constable's basic rate. When he became aware of
such work, the Commissioner (like other employers) was immediately
concerned about the efficiency of staff who turned up tired for duty,
especially after one broke a leg while 'moonlighting'. When some
Auckland police were found to be working under a man convicted of

serious crimes, the long-standing rationale for prohibiting police involvement 'in trade of any kind' was confirmed for Cummings. In Auckland and elsewhere there was some public resentment at men in so-called 'sheltered positions' competing with returned servicemen for lucrative jobs. An ambiguity in the Police Regulations meant, however, that casual work without the permission of the Commissioner was not effectively prohibited until their amendment in October 1943.[245]

These new Regulations also regularised Cummings' practice, from 1940, of allowing the wives of policemen to take paid work, especially if they had been 'manpowered' into the public service or essential industries. His permission had to be sought, and was not granted automatically: any work that 'might embarrass their husbands' in their police duties was unacceptable.[246] Indeed, Cummings shared the view expressed by one Association delegate, and prevalent amongst the male rank and file, that 'a constable's wife had a full time job at home.'[247]

Though remuneration became the pre-eminent wartime issue for the Police Association, earlier retirement remained the 'primary object' of its members.[248] Both the Minister and the Commissioner continued to be unsympathetic, with Fraser making it clear to Association delegates in September 1940 that there could be no 'great advancement in wages and conditions' during the war. Moreover, the police case would have to be considered as part of a wider 'overhauling' of public service superannuation. There seemed little prospect of this occurring until after the war. Nonetheless, remits on earlier retirement and superannuation remained 'hardy annuals' at Association conferences – a reminder that the rank and file had not become apathetic with the lack of progress. Meltzer reminded the government of Walter Nash's rhetoric in 1941: 'The war must not be used as an excuse to put the clock back'.[249] Given the wider dissatisfaction amongst public servants over aspects of superannuation, the government established a committee in 1944 to consider changes. Jack Meltzer argued his members' case for retirement at 60 or after 35 years' service, but to no avail.

From 1940, added emphasis was given to the issue by the government's decision to retain police who had reached retiring age (a policy which affected public servants in general). This was seen as retarding promotion. While it was felt strongly, the 'injustice' was more symbolic than real. The number of 'over-service' police is unknown but was probably insignificant: retirements continued, especially on medical grounds; the wartime annual average of police dying on the job was almost twice that of the inter-war years (with those in the supervisory ranks comprising nearly 40 per cent of the deaths); the numbers in the supervisory ranks increased by 34 (16 per cent), a higher rate of increase than that in the number of constables. Amongst the officers, only Commissioner Cummings, Superintendent C.W. Lopdell (at Wellington), and Inspector John Carroll (at Invercargill) were retained beyond the age of 65.[250]

Fraser, Webb and Cummings responded in a variety of ways to pressures from the Police Association.[251] Opening addresses by all three at the annual Association conferences were used to restrain expectations and to justify policies with a mixture of praise, exhortation, and appeals to loyalty. Busy though he was, Fraser appeared at some Police social and ceremonial occasions in Wellington,[252] while Paddy Webb, the acting Minister in charge of the Police for much of the war, visited city stations and played an 'active part' in improving barracks accommodation. Cummings periodically did the rounds of stations, monitoring morale. Though they were generally solicitous in their rhetoric, both Fraser and Cummings were often slow in responding to Association remits, especially during the hectic period between 1940 and 1942, to the increasing frustration of the rank and file.[253] Part of the problem lay in Fraser's lengthy absences overseas, and his many preoccupations when at home. As acting Minister, Webb refused to make decisions on policy, especially where they might contradict Fraser's views. For his part, Cummings was also preoccupied by minutiae and cautious in recommending any changes which would cost money. He followed Fraser in emphasising that the war effort had the highest priority. The Commissioner preferred to deal humanely, albeit firmly, with individual circumstances (by ignoring Police Regulations on occasion), rather than accept remits for general improvements.[254]

Above all, Cummings was concerned to maintain discipline and prevent any erosion of his administrative authority. Here the symbolic issue was the Association's annual remit for the repeal of section 9 of the Police Force Act. Dismissal without right of appeal had become a matter of principle rather than of current practice. Cummings wished to keep such a power in reserve; Fraser backed him in case any police proved 'over-lenient or indulgent' towards subversives.[255] Though the Minister was regularly appealed to when the Commissioner proved obdurate, Fraser rarely (and never publicly) overruled Cummings. A notable exception was the concession of rank and file membership on the disciplinary appeal board in 1941. Cummings resisted any Association 'interference' in his prerogative of administration, as when he was challenged in 1941 on the use of a newly-appointed temporary constable for clerical work. Following this tussle, the Association accepted that complaints on such matters should be made initially through superior officers, though they could be taken up by the Management Committee if 'general principles' were involved.[256] Here, the right to reinstatement of those who had resigned to go to war was an issue pursued persistently by the Association for eighteen months until Cummings and Fraser relented in 1943.[257] Senior officers generally shared Cummings' view that there had been an erosion of discipline since the formation of the Police Association, and told Fraser so in March 1944, when they urged that NCOs form a separate branch of the Association 'in the interests of discipline', and that the Secretary of the

Association be a member of the Police Force.[258]

Cummings perceived the greatest threat to his authority to come from the General Secretary of the Police Association, Jack Meltzer, an 'outsider' who was not easily subject to browbeating. After a cautious beginning as acting Secretary until September 1940, Meltzer became increasingly assertive and stubborn in advancing the Association's concerns.[259] From June 1941 strains began to appear in the relationship between the Commissioner and the General Secretary. Cummings accused Meltzer of seeking to have Webb 'veto Mr Fraser's ruling' on section 9; he refused permission for Meltzer to address the first intake of policewomen at the Depot; and he shared the sentiments of Superintendent Lopdell, minuted in August (after Meltzer was reported in the press urging that early retirement be implemented despite the war): 'If malcontents within the ranks think they can air their views before the Public through a civilian Secretary and that Secretary is willing to be used by them, there will be an end of discipline.'[260] Meltzer had already informed Webb that he was going to acquaint MPs with the Association's 'main problems' and 'major policy matters' by 'occasional conversation' and by sending each of them a copy of the *New Zealand Police Journal*. Soon afterwards, in a patent assertion of authority against a Management Committee which he perceived as 'getting dictatorial', Cummings had the Association's annual conference postponed for nearly two months, and insisted that the President (and not Meltzer) present the remits in the subsequent deputation to him.[261] At the delayed conference, Peter Fraser reminded delegates of the 'vital difference between the members of the police force and workers engaged in trade and industry generally'. He would not let the 'morale, discipline and loyalty of the force' be 'imperilled' by the activities of the Association.[262]

In December 1942, Fraser's stance hardened. After receiving telegrams from Meltzer which reflected the impatience of Auckland branch members, Fraser telephoned him with the threat that if 'this nonsense was repeated he would either take steps to dissolve the Association or see that the Association obtained another Secretary'. He held Meltzer 'personally responsible for the present attitude of the men'.[263] Shortly afterwards, when newspapers reported rank-and-file restiveness over pay, Fraser had J.T. Paul, the Director of Publicity, instruct editors not to publish 'resolutions passed by any branch of the Police Association' or by any police officers without the Director's approval. On 5 January 1943 this order was amended to include 'any discussion of or reference to the subject of police pay.' The Prime Minister was unapologetic: neither newspapers nor the *Police Journal* might 'be used to stir up a spirit of indiscipline and insubordination'.[264] Indeed he continued to contemplate dissolving the Police Association, particularly when, in November 1943, newspapers reported Meltzer questioning the validity of the new regulations controlling the spare-

time employment of police and the paid work of their wives.[265]
Cummings had the Director of Publicity extend censorship to these
matters.[266] By 1944 the relationship between the Commissioner and the
Association's Secretary had deteriorated further, with Cummings refusing
to see Meltzer at all, and securing the virtually unanimous agreement
of his senior officers in March 1944 that the 'present Secretary should
be removed from Office'. This was beyond Fraser's power or inclination,
though he reiterated that if he had to choose between a lack of police
discipline and doing away with the Association, he would choose the
latter.[267] Meanwhile, Meltzer badgered Paul to have the censorship
lifted; but it was convenient for Fraser and Cummings that it remain
while there could be no movement in police pay. Not until 27 March
1945, on the eve of the general pay increase, was the curb on discussing
the subject lifted.[268]

In effect, censorship concealed the widening gap between Fraser's
soothing rhetoric and the mounting dissatisfaction amongst the rank
and file. The increasing difficulties in recruiting and retaining staff
from 1943 revealed the effects of wartime restraints and the deteriorating
position of police within the wider workforce. The pre-war aspirations
of the rank and file for earlier retirement and a 40-hour week remained
remote prospects. In February 1945 Fraser turned down a Police
Association request for a royal commission of inquiry into police pay
and conditions.[269] Wartime inertia continued into peacetime,
accompanied by a deepening malaise within the Police Force.

Conclusion:
A Policeman's Paradise?

Was New Zealand between the wars a 'paradise' for policemen, with a population that was easily 'governed' and better working conditions than those prevailing outside the Force? This question has been implicit in much of the preceding discussion and was partially addressed in chapter four. Essentially the answer must be a comparative one, taking account of other times and places, and other occupations. It will be open to debate, since it will depend on the criteria used for assessment and also on information beyond that given in this account. Even so, a brief discussion of the issue provides an opportunity to take stock of the context and nature of policing in New Zealand between 1918 and 1945.

According to the case made in 1928 by a 'critic' of arguments to reduce the qualifying period for a police pension, the 'New Zealand public' was seen as being 'more governable from the police standard' than populations elsewhere.[1] Between the 1920s and the 1940s, New Zealand was a fundamentally peaceful society, the disturbances of 1932 notwithstanding. And it seemed to be more peaceful than 'America or some of the Continental countries' with which contemporary comparisons were drawn. That New Zealanders were apparently even 'more governable' than similar communities in Australia seemed to be underscored by the relatively small number of police per head of population – a comparison that was frequently made by politicians, newspaper editors and other commentators for varying purposes.

Such a ratio was in fact a crude measure, being influenced by the degree of urbanisation (since police were thicker on the ground in the larger overseas cities) and the conditions of police work (including the hours of work and how police were deployed). The relatively fewer police in New Zealand reflected the high proportion of the Force serving in the Uniform Branch, and deployed in country and small-town stations where police were (in theory) always on duty. The comparatively late advent of the six-day working week for most (but not all) New Zealand police in 1937 brought a sharp increase in their number per head of population, but did not increase the number on duty at any one time.

Nonetheless, with police dispersed as they were in New Zealand, they symbolised the maintenance of order in the inter-war years rather than imposed it.

To Pakeha contemporaries, the 'governability' of New Zealand society stemmed in part from its particular 'social and economic conditions': its standard of living, its homogeneity (or 'purity of race'), the 'temperament' and 'social customs' of the people ('phlegmatic British stock'), the smallness of its cities, and the lack of industrialisation on a scale which 'tends to intensify class consciousness, and troubles arising therefrom'. Thus, as it was perceived by those making the case for a 'paradise', there was a generally 'law-abiding' population with little 'serious crime' or threat to order. A routinely unarmed police in a society with plenty of firearms had experienced four episodes in which a total of seven police were killed between 1919 and 1941. Yet arms control had reinforced customary practice in virtually eliminating the danger of handguns, by contrast to the threat of 'the cosmopolitan gunman of the American cities'. From this perspective, 'police work and risks' were 'less relatively to other lands'.

Moreover, there was a 'healthy public sentiment' which 'condemned faulty practices in the administration of justice'. Such a sentiment also assisted in 'the bringing to book of offenders', thereby aiding the work of the police. In such a context, especially outside the four main centres, policemen could develop a local standing, a personal authority, which reinforced the authority of the uniform. By the 1930s the myth of the country constable had been established: he was the man (who might not routinely wear his uniform) 'to whom all turn in most of their troubles'.[2] The healthy public sentiment could be eroded by the strict enforcement of laws which were not popular or for which support was at best ambivalent. 'Consistency and firmness without harshness should be the guiding principle', Commissioner O'Donovan had enjoined;[3] in practice, the liquor licensing and gaming laws were policed with a 'wise discretion' away from the cities. Overall, there had been a decline in resistance to police authority by the 1920s, and this continued, with a concomitant decline in police use of force; batons were (it seems) not routinely taken on day shifts. That the disturbances in 1932 were short-lived and (apart from the riot in Queen Street) limited in violence was testimony in part to the authority of police, as well as to the mobilisation of resources in their support.

More fundamentally, New Zealand's 'governability' was shaped by the degree to which conservative governments were responsive to the views of all sections of the essentially farm-based small-town society. Only when sharply changing economic fortunes, and the policies with which the government responded to them, failed to meet the expectations of many wage-earners and those thrown out of work in the early 1930s was governability eroded; but not seriously so. With economic conditions making industrial militancy an inappropriate tactic, the labour movement channelled most of the sense of grievance into parliamentary and 'constitutional' protest. The 'revolutionaries' were very few, if they existed at all.

In the 1930s, contemporaries with long memories could recall more disorderly times when some social groups had been less 'governable'. In 1935, 76 year old James Siddells, the deputy mayor of Wanganui, looked back to when he had joined New Zealand Constabulary Force in Waikato in 1877, before becoming a police constable on the East Coast of the North Island four years later. Then there had still been sizeable remnants of a frontier where Maori were not fully subject to Pakeha law and disorderly Pakeha males required the imposition of firm controls. Then there had also been many constables who 'carried on their work in a very rough and ready style'. Siddells remembered 'some who had a very hazy idea of what police duty was'. During the intervening 58 years there had been 'great changes for the better'. The Police had become a 'much improved body of men, both in physique and intellect'. Their training, discipline and conditions of work had improved, with pensions and pay that (given the hours worked) placed them above the median income of all wage and salary earners. Moreover, New Zealand had become a much more orderly society. The 'thousands' who had paraded in the streets of Wanganui on the last New Year's Eve had all been 'well behaved' and out for enjoyment. He also believed they 'knew that the law was on the alert, in the shape of a few (very few) police officials who were prepared to put down any disorder with a strong hand'.[4] Especially in the countryside and the provincial towns, actual order imposition was not required, simply its symbol.

Yet, in the cities and especially Auckland during the inter-war years, the relatively small number of police was not necessarily perceived as a sign of an effective 'preventive force'. New Zealand might be orderly and have little 'serious crime' in comparative terms, but local definitions of order and anxieties about crime shaped assessments of the adequacy of policing. 'Epidemics of burglaries' led to mounting concerns being voiced by residents of more affluent suburbs, and echoed by both local newspapers and *Truth*. Policing methods, and especially police transport and communications, seemed to be falling increasingly behind the times – and little had changed by 1945. For their part, the officers in charge of urban districts seemed always to be hard-pressed for staff as the volume of files grew incessantly, 'extraneous duties' for other government departments continued, and the availability of the telephone in the ever-expanding suburbs brought family disputes and other matters more quickly into the realm of public policing.

Police workloads varied. As earlier chapters have suggested, the 'policeman's paradise' was experienced differently by city beat constables, their suburban, country and small-town counterparts, detectives, and their supervisors. There were different patterns of satisfactions, risks, and frustrations. Society's 'governability' was also experienced differently by police, varying with their circumstances, personalities and clientele. Though police were seen as necessary, a negative or at least ambivalent attitude towards them could be found within most communities. Police in smaller, more stable areas experienced greater friendliness and readier cooperation than those in the cities. The isolated, close-knit coal-mining communities on the West Coast of the South Island, with their socialist beliefs, were more suspicious and stand-offish than the conservative rural communities 'over the Hill' in Canterbury. Again, the attitudes to police of some groups in Auckland were more ambiguous, divided, and even overtly hostile than those in Dunedin, for example. Auckland's size, its role as a port, and the nature of its concentrated inner-city working-class population made policing there periodically more strenuous than in the quieter cities of the South Island. Perhaps, then, the violence that erupted outside the Auckland town hall in April 1932 reflected not just the intense frustrations of the unemployed, but also a greater degree of hostility towards police than was felt elsewhere.

The rate of 'wastage' – of deaths on duty, retirements through injury or sickness, dismissals because of delinquency, and voluntary resignations – was also evidence of the risks of work as well as the varied patterns of expectations, satisfactions, and comparisons made with conditions outside the Police Force. During the inter-war years the Force became increasingly a career service. At the end of 1928, 45.5 per cent of New Zealand police had more than a decade's service; yet fewer than 12 per cent had served more than 25 years (the proportions were almost exactly the same as those in New South Wales).[5] The continuing and fluctuating loss of personnel before retirement age suggests that for New Zealand police, the main yardstick of comparison was not the working conditions of overseas forces (though such comparisons were made when they could strengthen a case for improvement), but rather the conditions of employment in other occupations at home. While a growing proportion of police stayed until they could retire with a pension, there was a growing sense of relative deprivation, especially from the late 1930s, as outside the Force working hours decreased and pay rates increased; retirement at 65 seemed inappropriate for a job as rigorous as policing.

The advent of a Police Association able to press the aspirations of the rank and file more openly and persistently heightened both expectations and frustrations when conditions did not improve as rapidly as was hoped for. More positively, the activities of the Police Association, and particularly its *Journal*, strengthened an already developed sense of occupational community and esprit de corps. It was a strongly masculine Pakeha community, one generally resistant to the idea of women police and which confined them to gendered roles, with inferior pay and conditions, when they were eventually appointed well after their advent in forces overseas. While in retrospect it was not necessarily seen as a 'paradise' for policewomen, the Force nonetheless offered them from the outset status, satisfactions and conditions which compared favourably with most paid work then available for women outside it. It was the expectations and frustrations of male police which determined the morale of the Force after 1945.

Materially conditions for police, both men and women, did improve after the war, but not before the malaise of 1945 had become a crisis ten years later, leading to the appointment of another Secretary of Justice, Sam Barnett, to head the Police for three years. From the late 1950s there were major changes in both working conditions and policing methods.[6] With the introduction in 1959 of retirement at the age of 60 (which he had pressed for 22 years earlier), Bill Murray (then 63) began a long and active retirement. By the time he died in 1990, 'police work and risks' seemed to have increased dramatically since the 1950s, in line with similar changes overseas. From this perspective, the inter-war years did indeed appear to be a 'policeman's paradise'.

Appendix

Ministers in Charge of the Police Department (1918–1949)

	Ministry	Period	Cabinet Ranking	Other Portfolios
T.M. Wilford	National (Massey)	4 Feb 1918 4 Sep 1919	10	Justice, Stamp Duties, Marine
W.F. Massey	Reform (Massey)	4 Sep 1919 3 Apr 1920	1	Prime Minister, Railways, Labour, Industries and Commerce (and other portfolios)
E.P. Lee	Reform (Massey)	3 Apr 1920 13 Jan 1923	9	Justice, External Affairs, Industries and Commerce, Prisons
Sir Francis H.D. Bell	Reform (Massey)	13 Jan 1923 27 Jun 1923	3	Attorney-General, Justice, Prisons, Leader of the Legislative Council
C.J. Parr	Reform (Massey/ Bell/Coates)	27 Jun 1923 18 Jan 1926	6	Education, Justice, Prisons, Postmaster-General
F.J. Rolleston	Reform (Coates)	18 Jan 1926 26 Nov 1928	12	Attorney-General, Justice, Defence, Prisons, War Pensions
W.D. Stewart	Reform (Coates)	28 Nov 1928 10 Dec 1928	3	nine other portfolios in an interim ministry
T.M. Wilford	United (Ward)	10 Dec 1928 10 Dec 1929	3	Justice, Defence, Prisons, War Pensions
J.G. Cobbe	United (Ward, Forbes) and then	18 Dec 1929 22 Sep 1931	9	Defence, Justice, Pensions, Prisons
	Coalition (Forbes)	22 Sep 1931 6 Dec 1935	9	Defence, Justice, Marine, Pensions, Prisons
P. Fraser	Labour (Savage) and then	6 Dec 1935 1 Apr 1940	2	Education, Health, Marine
	Labour (Fraser)	1 Apr 1940 13 Dec 1949	1	Prime Minister, External Affairs and Island Territories (from 1943), Maori Affairs (from 1946)

Source: J.O. Wilson (ed.), *New Zealand Parliamentary Record,* Wellington, 1985.

Notes

Abbreviations used in Notes

AJHR	*Appendix to the Journals of the House of Representatives*
Annual Report	
	Annual Report on the Police Force of the Dominion (*AJHR*, H-16)
AS	*Auckland Star*
ATL	Alexander Turnbull Library
AWN	*Auckland Weekly News*
CS	*Christchurch Star*
CSS	*Christchurch Star–Sun*
CT	*Christchurch Times*
DNZB	*Dictionary of New Zealand Biography*
EP	*Evening Post*
ES	*Evening Star*
GRA	*Grey River Argus*
LT	*Lyttelton Times*
MDT	*Manawatu Daily Times*
NZFL	*New Zealand Free Lance*
NZG	*New Zealand Gazette*
NZH	*New Zealand Herald*
NZJH	*New Zealand Journal of History*
NZLR	*New Zealand Law Review*
NZOYB	*New Zealand Official Yearbook*
NZPD	*New Zealand Parliamentary Debates*
NZPG	*New Zealand Police Gazette*
NZPJ	*New Zealand Police Journal*
NZT	*New Zealand Times*
ODT	*Otago Daily Times*
OPR	Old Police Records
PBH	*Poverty Bay Herald*
PFDB	Police Force Description Book
PSA	Public Service Association
PSJ	*Public Service Journal*
RP	*Rotorua Post*
SM	Stipendiary Magistrate
ST	*Southland Times*
TH	*Timaru Herald*
TP	*Timaru Post*
WN	*Weekly News*
WT	*Waikato Times*

Introduction: Patterns Set

1. The staff at Headquarters totalled 12 in 1919 (7 sworn police and 5 clerical) and 19 in 1945 (10 police and 9 clerical). The total number of police had grown from 878 in 1919 to 1,598 in 1945.
2. This idea is developed in detail by Richard S. Hill in the first three volumes of the *History of Policing in New Zealand*, namely *Policing the Colonial Frontier: The Theory and Practice of Coercive Social and Racial Control in New Zealand, 1767–1867*, Wellington, 1986, esp. part 1, ch.1; *The Colonial Frontier Tamed: New Zealand Policing in Transition, 1867–1886*, Wellington, 1989, esp. the Postscript; and *The Iron Hand in the Velvet Glove: The Modernisation of Policing in New Zealand, 1886–1917*, Wellington, 1995.
3. The number of murders, manslaughters, and attempted murders, as recorded in police statistics, per 100,000 people.
4. H. Zehr, *Crime and the Development of Modern Society: Patterns of Criminality in Nineteenth Century Germany and France*, London, 1976, esp. pp.125–37.
5. *NZPD*, vol.193, 1921–22, p.744. Cf. the form of words reported in *NZT*, 28 Jan 1922: 'the most valuable men in the Public Service were the Police'. Bell was then Attorney-General in the Massey ministry, and Leader of the Legislative Council. He was strongly opposed to what he perceived as individuals and organisations challenging the authority of the state by violence. See W.D. Stewart, *Sir Francis H.D. Bell: His Life and Times*, Wellington, 1937, pp.177–87. For the sense of threat to public order between 1919 and 1922, see ch.10.
6. *NZPD*, vol.257, 1940, pp.769–70. For Fraser's concern to curb dissent against the war effort, see ch.12.
7. *NZPD*, vol.257, 1940, pp.769–70.
8. See, in particular, Mark Finnane, *Police and Government: Histories of Policing in Australia*, Melbourne, 1994. This work was published after this chapter was drafted and has been found useful in revising it.
9. Hill, *Iron Hand*, pp.47, 424.
10. I.e. the 'civil' police as distinct from the Reserve Division or field force of the New Zealand Constabulary Force between 1878 and 1886. Hill, *Colonial Frontier Tamed*, pp.301, 355; *Iron Hand*, pp.7, 27.
11. Apart from Tasmania, which did not centralise its police until 1898. The forces in the other colonies had all been centralised by 1863. See Finnane, *Police and Government*, pp.9, 14–19.
12. See, for example, Sir Robert Mark, *In the Office of Constable: An Autobiography*, London, 1978, pp.149–50, 242–4, 282–4; and *Policing a Perplexed Society*, London, 1977, esp. pp.13–16, 21–5, 32. Mark expresses a long-standing fear, but one not shared by, for example, the British Royal Commission on the Police which reported in 1962. See T.A. Critchley, *A History of Police in England and Wales*, 2nd edn, London, 1978, esp. pp.75, 282–6; and B. Whitaker, *The Police in Society*, London, 1979, ch.5.
13. See [New Zealand Police Inspector] Sidney Rawle, 'Discuss the Advantages and Disadvantages of placing the various Police Forces in the United Kingdom under a Common Administration', essay for the King's Police Medal Essay Competition [in London], 1935 (unpub., copy held by author); S.T. Barnett, 'The Limits of Decentralisation', in J.L. Roberts (ed.), *Decentralisation in New Zealand Government Administration*, Wellington, 1961, pp.20–4; R.C. Savage (Solicitor-General), 'Address to Cadet Wing Graduation [at New Zealand Police College]', typed speech notes, 14 Dec 1977; J. Coatman, *Police*, London, 1959, pp.65–7.
14. A point also made by Mark Finnane (*Police and Government*, p.14) regarding the shape of policing organisation in Australia.
15. The general comments on the development of the public service, in this and succeeding paragraphs, are based largely on: R.J. Polaschek, *Government Administration in New*

Zealand, Wellington, 1958, esp. chs 1, 2, 5, 6; L. Webb, *Government in New Zealand*, Wellington, 1940, chs 5, 6; L. Lipson, *The Politics of Equality*, Chicago, 1948, chs 7, 13, 14; I.S. Ewing, 'Public Service Reform in New Zealand, 1866–1912', MA thesis, University of Auckland, 1979; I.S. Thynne, 'An Analysis of the Social Backgrounds, Educational Qualifications and Career Patterns of Permanent Heads in the New Zealand Public Service, 1913–73', PhD thesis, Victoria University of Wellington, 1978; *State Services in New Zealand: Report of the Royal Commission of Inquiry*, Wellington, 1962; and A. Henderson, *The Quest for Efficiency: The Origins of the State Services Commission*, Wellington, 1990, chs 1–7.

16. Ewing, 'Public Service Reform in New Zealand', p.12, table 1. For different figures, see also Henderson, *Quest for Efficiency*, pp.31–2, and M. Bassett, *The State in New Zealand 1840–1984: Socialism Without Doctrines?*, Auckland, 1998, p.81.

17. Commissions of Inquiry were held in 1898, 1905 and 1909; the two Commissioners to resign were J.B. Tunbridge in 1903 and W. Dinnie in 1909. See Hill, *Iron Hand*, parts 2, 3. For political control of the public service, see also Henderson, *Quest for Efficiency*, pp.20–33.

18. In 1910 the Police Provident Fund (established in 1899) was transferred to the Public Service Superannuation Fund begun in 1908. Hill, *Iron Hand*, pp.103–7, 261–5.

19. Richard Hill, 'Cullen, John', *DNZB*, vol.3, Wellington, 1996, pp.125–7.

20. Calculated from Ewing, 'Public Service Reform', p.12, table 1.

21. For some comparisons between Police, Education and Health, see ch.11; for the Labour Department's rapid expansion from 1936, see J. Martin, *Holding the Balance: A History of New Zealand's Department of Labour 1891–1995*, Christchurch, 1996, pp.204–10. See also, more generally, Henderson, *Quest for Efficiency*, pp.150–3.

22. See ch.3.

23. Webb, *Government in New Zealand*, p.89. See also Henderson, *Quest for Efficiency*, pp.154–60.

24. See, for example, *NZH*, 19 Apr 1937 (editorial); and *NZPD*, vol.248, 1937, p.198 (Barrell).

25. K.J. Scott, *The New Zealand Constitution*, Oxford, 1962, p.137.

26. Spencer to Secretary, Advisory Committee on Higher Salaries in the State Services, 12 Dec 1963, P 3/2/25.

27. Section 14 of the Finance Act 1919 provided that the widow of any police officer killed in the 'exercise of his duties' would receive a pension according to his rank as though he had been killed on active service with the Expeditionary Force. The relative ranks were established (*NZPG*, 1922, p.153) as:

Police:	Expeditionary Force:
Constable	Private
Constable (9 years service)	Corporal
Sergeant	Regimental Sergeant-Major
Senior Sergeant	Lieutenant
Sub-Inspector	Captain
Inspector	Major
Superintendent	Colonel
Commissioner	General

In 1928 Thomas Wilford, a former of Minister of Justice who was soon to resume this office, drew attention in Parliament to the disparity between the annual salaries of the 'Commandant of the Forces' [Chief of General Staff] (£1,200) and the Commissioner of Police (£925), suggesting that the Commissioner 'has just as difficult and hard a job – much more so, in fact, in peace times – and much more responsible'. *NZPD*, vol.219, 1928, p.12. This was also Spencer's argument to the Advisory Committee on Higher Salaries in the State Services in 1963, P 3/2/25.

28. The Naval Board was established in 1921, and Air and Army Boards in 1937. W.D.

McIntyre, *New Zealand Prepares for War*, Christchurch, 1988, pp.45, 172–80. When the Ministry of Defence was established as a unitary department in 1964, it was headed by both a civilian Secretary of Defence and a Chief of Defence Staff.

29.   See *Commemorating Traffic Safety: 55 Years 1937–1992*, Land Transport Division, Ministry of Transport, Wellington, 1992; A. Woolston, *Equal to the Task: The City of Auckland Traffic Department, 1894–1994*, Auckland, 1996.

30.   Regulation 9 of the *Regulations under the Police Force Act 1913*, Wellington, 1919. These regulations are to found in *The Police Force Act 1913, Police Force Amendment Act 1919, and Regulations made thereunder for the guidance of the Police Force of New Zealand*, Wellington, 1920, commonly known in the Police Force as the 'Black Book' because of its cover and the consequences of violating its strictures.

31.   For control of primary education see L. Webb, *The Control of Education in New Zealand*, Wellington, 1937; A.E. Campbell, 'The Control of Primary Schools', in G.W. Parkyn (ed.), *The Administration of Education in New Zealand*, Wellington, 1954; L.J. McCarthy, 'Decentralisation in Educational Administration', in Roberts (ed.), *Decentralisation in New Zealand Government Administration*. For hospital boards see *A Health Service for New Zealand*, Wellington, 1974.

32.   Finnane, *Police and Government*, p.17.

33.   Hill, *Colonial Frontier Tamed*, ch.8.

34.   *Statistics of New Zealand*, 1921, vol.3, p.238.

35.   Annual Report, 1919, p.10.

36.   *Ibid.*, p.10. Twenty years earlier, Commissioner J.B. Tunbridge had listed the 'outside appointments held by police' and commented that 'Frequent complaints are received from the public to the effect that, owing to the numerous other duties the police are called upon to perform, the legitimate police duties are neglected'. Annual Report, 1899, p.5. This complaint was a recurring one: see Commissioners Wright in Annual Report, 1922, pp.7–9; McIlveney in Annual Report, 1926, p.6; and Cummings in Annual Report, 1945, p.3.

37.   H. Robinson, *A History of the Post Office in New Zealand*, Wellington, 1964, p.204.

38.   See ch.2. From 1926 police, whether in uniform or in plain clothes, were prohibited from taking payment for attending functions in their own time. All 'special services' asked for by individuals, firms, clubs or other voluntary associations were to be charged for by the Police Department where the interests of the individual, firm or club were seen to be predominant. All payments received for such special services were to be paid into the Consolidated Fund. Such duties were to be performed during the constable's period of duty, with the charge to be between 10s and £1 plus meals and travel expenses. Commissioner's Circular, 1926, no.457.

39.   Henderson, *Quest for Efficiency*, pp.52–3, 94–5.

40.   Scott, *New Zealand Constitution*, p.137. See also, for example, E.K. Mulgan and A.E. Mulgan, *The New Zealand Citizen: An Elementary Account of the Citizen's Rights and Duties and the Work of Government*, Christchurch, 1914, p.63, which included police in the executive.

41.   *NZPD*, vol.160, 1912, p.45.

42.   *Ibid.*, p.614.

43.   *Ibid.*, p.49.

44.   Ewing, 'Public Service Reform', p.137.

45.   When asked for his opinion as to whether the terms of reference of the Commission covered the Defence Department and the Police Department, apart from the clerical branches in both departments, the Solicitor-General, John Salmond, replied that the Railways Department and Post and Telegraph Department were the only two departments classified by statute and that 'every other Department is included in the order of reference'. The Police Department was therefore included in the list of departments examined. Although the Commissioners made no specific comments concerning the Police Department (other than that it was one of a number that 'work out a separate existence of their own'), this was because (along with other departments

to which they had made no specific reference) 'we have nothing to add to our general remarks dealing with the whole Service.' Report of the Commission of Inquiry into the Unclassified Departments of the Public Service of New Zealand, *AJHR*, 1912, H-34, pp.6, 10–11, 30, 34.

46. Henderson, *Quest for Efficiency*, pp.38–45.
47. *NZPD*, vol.160, 1912, p.49. By contrast, Alan Henderson judges that 'the Hunt Report seems to have had little impact on the provisions of the Public Service Act 1912'; *Quest for Efficiency*, p.49.
48. *NZPD*, vol.160, 1912, p.103 (Herdman), p.615 (Bell). See also Lipson, *Politics of Equality*, pp.473–4; and Hill, *Iron Hand*, p.279.
49. *NZPD*, vol.162, 1913, p.690.
50. See Richard Hill, 'Dinnie, Walter', *DNZB*, vol.3, pp.134–5; and *Iron Hand*, chs 14, 16.
51. Hill, *Iron Hand*, ch.19.
52. *State Services in New Zealand*, p.26. See also J.K. Hunn, *Not Only Affairs of State*, Palmerston North, 1982, pp.61–2.
53. In 1946 the Public Service Commissioner was succeeded by a three-person Public Service Commission.
54. *NZPD*, vol.160, 1912, p.614.
55. The ambiguous nature of the Police Department's constitutional position is clearly revealed by the sometimes conflicting views of the following sources on which this discussion is partly based: G.P. Barton, 'Police Powers: Criminal Procedure', in K.J. Keith (ed.), *Essays on Human Rights*, Wellington, 1968, pp.30–44; Sir Thaddeus McCarthy, 'The Role of the Police in the Administration of Justice', in R.S. Clark (ed.), *Essays on Criminal Law in New Zealand*, Wellington, 1971, pp.170–88; H.A. Cull, 'The Enigma of a Police Constable's Status', *Victoria University of Wellington Law Review*, vol.8, 1975–77, pp.148–69; B.J. Barton, 'Control of the New Zealand Police', LlB (hons) thesis, University of Auckland, 1978; W.C. Hodge (ed.), *Doyle Criminal Procedure in New Zealand*, Sydney, 2nd edn, 1984, pp.137–41; and G. Orr, 'Police Accountability to the Executive and Parliament', in N. Cameron and W. Young (eds), *Policing at the Crossroads*, Wellington, 1986, pp.46–66.
56. Cull, 'Enigma', p.154.
57. The terms of his appointment as Commissioner in 1897, and the findings of a Royal Commission of Inquiry in 1898, which accorded with his own views, gave Tunbridge a 'mandate for sweeping changes'. By 1902, Tunbridge had apparently established his autonomy from political interference. However the Cabinet intervened in his administration by overturning his decisions regarding Nelson police. Ill and disillusioned, Tunbridge applied to retire in 1903. Though the Liberal government had reasserted the principle of political control, public criticism of this government intervention in internal police matters can be seen as having helped to establish the convention of managerial autonomy. See Richard Hill, 'Tunbridge, John Bennett', *DNZB*, vol.2, Wellington, 1993, pp.551–2; and *Iron Hand*, ch.10.
58. Notably in: *Enever v. The King* (1906); *Fisher v. Oldham Corporation* (1930); *Attorney-General for New South Wales v. Perpetual Trustee Company* (1955); and *R v. Metropolitan Police Commissioner Ex parte Blackburn* (1968). In *Osgood v. Attorney-General* (1972), a New Zealand magistrate looked to these Australian and English cases for guidance. He found Lord Denning's judgement in the Blackburn case to be authoritative. The implications of these and other cases are examined in the sources cited in note 55.
59. D.B. Kerr, Legal Section, to Deputy Commissioner [Walton], 'Powers of Executive to Direct Police', 16 Nov 1977, p.1. This memorandum refers to the cases cited in note 58. It was the first clear statement of the Department's view of its constitutional position since O'Donovan's enunciation of his relationship with his Minister in Annual Report, 1921.
60. *Ibid.*, pp.5, 8–10.

61. Police Force Act 1913, sec.11(1); repeated by Police Act 1958, sec.37(1).
62. 'Powers of Executive to Direct Police', p.6. See also Hodge, *Doyle,* pp.139–40.
63. Regulation 47; see also Police Act 1958, sec.30(1); and Police Regulations 1959, no.28. For the implications of these provisions see Cull, 'Enigma', pp.152–3; and Barton, 'Control', pp.14–17.
64. This point was recognised during the debate on the Police Force Act 1913; see *NZPD*, vol.162, 1913, pp.692, 697.
65. Police Force Act 1913, sec.3; repeated in Police Act 1958, sec.3(1).
66. For the 'limited authority' of the Commissioner in the 1890s, see the Report of the Royal Commission on the Police Force, *AJHR*, 1898, H-2, pp.iv, vii–x. Cf., however, Hill, *Iron Hand,* pp.279–80.
67. Education Act 1964, sec.4; Health Act 1956, sec.4; and also Department of Social Welfare Act 1971, sec.5; Electricity Act 1968, sec.6; Customs Act 1966, sec.5. These examples were cited in 'Powers of Executive to Direct Police', p.6, to illustrate the relative freedom of the Police from 'executive control'.
68. Secs 6, 8(1), 16(1).
69. Regulation 7.
70. The Police Force Act 1913, sec.8(1), provided that the Governor could at any time discharge or dismiss the Commissioner, or any Superintendent, Inspector, or Sub-Inspector who had been guilty of conduct 'rendering it unfitting that he should remain in the Force, or who is for any reason unfit to remain in the Force.' However, the case *R v. Power* (1929), *NZLR*, 267, established that 'In New Zealand all police officers are servants of the Crown' and so hold office 'during the pleasure of the Crown' with no right of action against the Crown for wrongful dismissal. In 1929, the Minister of Justice, T. Wilford, commented that 'I can dismiss the Commissioner, and he has no right of appeal'; he added, 'naturally no Minister would recommend the dismissal of such an officer unless he was thoroughly satisfied that his conduct had merited such a course'. *NZPD*, vol.222, 1929, pp.956–7.
71. *NZPD*, vol.277, 1947, p.415.
72. W. Dinnie in 1909 and E.H. Compton in 1955.
73. McIlveney to Minister of Justice, 8 Jun 1920; W.B. McIlveney, personal file.
74. Report of the Commission on Native Affairs, *AJHR*, 1934, G-11, p.48.
75. Webb, *Government in New Zealand*, pp.68–9,152; Lipson, *Politics of Equality*, pp.282–4, 384–9; J.R. Marshall, 'Political Controls', in R.S. Milne (ed.), *Bureaucracy in New Zealand*, Wellington, 1957, pp.56–7, 65.
76. Spencer to the Secretary, Advisory Committee on Higher Salaries in the State Services, 12 Dec 1963, P 3/2/25.
77. Lipson, *Politics of Equality*, p.441; F. Baker, 'Public Servants as Ministerial Advisers', in Milne (ed.), *Bureaucracy in New Zealand*, pp.30, 40–2.
78. Hill, *Iron Hand*, p.280.
79. For example: increased powers requested in 1900 to deal with people allegedly 'habitually consorting with other thieves and prostitutes' were given in the Police Offences Amendment Act 1901; the licensing of second-hand dealers was introduced in 1903 after repeated requests; Commissioner Dinnie's fears that the Habitual Criminals Act passed in New South Wales in 1905 would drive 'the worst class of criminals to this colony' was an important influence in the passage of a similar Act in New Zealand in 1906; the growing police concern expressed from 1909 at their lack of powers to deal with 'one-woman brothels' led eventually to extended powers given by War Regulations in 1916; similarly, the creation of the new offence of 'car conversion' in the Police Offences Amendment Act 1919 reflected police initiative, as did the passage of the Arms Act 1920, which established a new level of control. For recommended amendments to the law from officers in charge of districts, and the comments of Commissioners, see Annual Reports, 1900–1939. The influence of New Zealand Police Commissioners on law-making parallels that observed in Australia; see Finnane, *Police and Government*, pp.34–6; and 'Police and Politics in Australia:

The Case for Historical Revision', *Australian and New Zealand Journal of Criminology*, vol.23, no.4, Dec 1990, pp.218–28. For a perspective on the Police role in the legislative process in the 1970s and 1980s, see G. Palmer, 'The Legislative Process and the Police', in Cameron and Young (eds), *Policing at the Crossroads*, pp.86–106.

80.   Annual Report, 1921, p.8. Cf. the complaint by the Labour MP W.E. Parry that the relationship between Commissioner W.G. Wohlmann and his Minister, J.G. Cobbe, was 'an exhibition of departmental running of the Minister'. *NZPD*, vol.239, 1934, pp.595–6.

81.   See Rory Sweetman, *Bishop in the Dock: The Sedition Trial of James Liston*, Auckland, 1997, esp. pp.130–9.

82.   Second Interim Report of the Commission of Inquiry ... into ... the Conduct of Members of the Police Force, *AJHR*, 1954, H-16B, pp.16–20.

83.   *Truth*, 17 Apr, 5 Jun 1935. For a participant's perspective on the outcome of the 'Biggest Calcutta Sweep Raid in N.Z.', see Charles Belton, *Outside the Law in New Zealand*, Gisborne, 1939, pp.168–71.

84.   Barton, 'Control', pp.70–1.

85.   Lipson, *Politics of Equality*, pp.451–74.

86.   See the Report and Resolutions of the Economies Committee, 1921, SSC 66/10/49; Annual Report of the Public Service Commissioner, *AJHR*, H-14, 1927, p.6; 1937, p.11; 1947, p.14; and Henderson, *Quest for Efficiency*, pp.100–1, 113–16, 131–2, 146–9, 164–8, 176–82.

87.   See ch.11 for the formation of the second New Zealand Police Association. Cf. the New Zealand Education Institute (1883); railway servants' organisations; the Post and Telegraph Employees' Association and Officers' Guild; the first Public Service Association (1890–1898), followed by the Civil Service Association (1907–13), followed by the second Public Service Association from 1913. See Bert Roth, *Remedy For Present Evils: A History of the New Zealand Public Service Association from 1890*, Wellington, 1987.

88.   In 1930, R.P. Ward, the Under-Secretary for Justice, headed the Department for a month, following the retirement of Commissioner McIlveney and pending the appointment of Commissioner Wohlmann. The appointment of the Secretary for Justice, S.T. Barnett, as Controller-General of the Police Force between 1955 and 1958 paralleled the earlier appointment of the Under-Secretary for Justice, F. Waldegrave, as Commissioner between 1910 and 1912.

89.   Hunn, *Not Only Affairs of State*, p.54. For this and other points in this paragraph see also Webb, *Government in New Zealand*, pp.86–91, 160–1; Lipson, *Politics of Equality*, pp.453–60; Thynne, 'Analysis', pp.257–75; and W.H. Hickson (Chairman of the Review Team), N.P. Saunders-Francis and I.N. Bird to Chairman, State Services Commission, 'New Zealand Police: Functional Review', 26 Aug 1982, paras 5.16–5.17, 6.1.12–6.1.13.

90.   Lipson, *Politics of Equality*, p.471. Lipson was Professor of Political Science at Victoria University College, Wellington, from 1939 to 1947.

91.   *State Services in New Zealand*, pp.33–4, 46–8; Lipson, *Politics of Equality*, pp.435–48; Henderson, *Quest for Efficiency*, pp.6–7, 132, 141; Hunn, *Not Only Affairs of State*, ch.5.

92.   McCarthy, 'Role of the Police', p.178. McCarthy was a barrister in Wellington from 1931 to 1957, when he became a Supreme Court judge. In 1962 he was made a judge of the Court of Appeal, and he was its President from 1973 until his retirement in 1976. Instances can be found throughout the period covered by this book of criticism of police actions by both magistrates and Supreme Court judges, especially in relation to the questioning of witnesses.

93.   Commission of Inquiry into the efficiency and conduct of police in the Elsie Walker case (Feb/Mar 1929), discussed in ch.2; Commission of Inquiry into the circumstances surrounding the prosecution of a young women for unlawfully permitting an illegal

operation to be performed on her (Dec 1940), see *EP*, 10, 11, 14, 23 Dec 1940; and *NZPJ*, vol.5, 1941, pp.39–41.

94.   In the second half of the nineteenth century, the percentage of convictions for common assault remained fairly constant at 50 to 53% of charges; it thereafter rose steadily to 80% in 1936–40. Between 1916–20 and 1936–40, the percentage of convictions for serious assault fluctuated while falling overall from 47% to 33%. In the same period the percentage of convictions for homicide fluctuated between 20% and 32.5%. In the Magistrates' Courts the percentage of convictions for theft rose steadily from 70% to 82%, and in the Supreme Courts from 55% to 63.5%, between 1916–20 and 1936–40. The percentage of convictions for assaulting, obstructing and resisting the police rose from 90% at the turn of the century to 95.3% in 1911–15, settling at 92% during the 1920s and falling to 85.4% in 1926–30 and 87.9% in 1936–40. The percentages of convictions for theft have been calculated by the author from the *Judicial Statistics*. The remaining data has been drawn from Miles Fairburn and Stephen Haslett, 'Violent Crime in Old and New Societies: A Case Study Based on New Zealand 1853–1940', *Journal of Social History*, Fall 1986, pp.90–2, tables 1a–1d.

95.   T. Arnold, 'Legal Accountability and the Police: The Role of the Courts', in Cameron and Young (eds), *Policing at the Crossroads*, pp.67–85. For further discussion see also Graeme Dunstall, 'Police in New Zealand', in D.K. Das (ed.), *Police Practices: An International Review*, Metuchen, New Jersey, 1994, pp.385–93.

96.   Hill, *Iron Hand*, pp.285–6, 291–2, 295.

97.   J. Binney, G. Chaplin, and C. Wallace, *Mihaia: The Prophet Rua Kenana and His Community at Maungapohatu*, Wellington, 1979, p.80; Hill, *Iron Hand*, pp.382–90.

98.   Police Force Act 1913, sec.8(1). The ostensible 'purpose and function' of some contemporary European police forces were also defined in these terms. See R.B. Fosdick, *European Police Systems*, New York, 1916, p.4.

99.   Annual Report, 1919, p.10. In 1927 Commissioner McIlveney issued instructions that henceforth the Police would not provide such a service 'gratuitously' unless the patient was charged with an offence. *NZPG*, 4 Dec 1929, p.797.

100.   *NZPJ*, vol.2, 1938, 'Official Report' of the third annual conference [of the Police Association], p.4.

101.   See B. Dalley, *Family Matters: Child Welfare in Twentieth-Century New Zealand*, Auckland, 1998, part 2.

102.   *Dominion*, 10 Oct 1919.

103.   *ODT*, 19 Dec 1923. See also *NZH*, 19 Apr 1937.

104.   R.V.G. Clarke and J.M. Hough (eds), *The Effectiveness of Policing*, Farnborough, England, 1980, p.9.

105.   S. Walker, *A Critical History of Police Reform*, Lexington, Massachusetts, 1977, p.116, makes this point regarding the Boston strike. See also: T.A. Critchley, *A History of Police in England and Wales*, 2nd edn, London, 1978, pp.186–9; A.V. Sellwood, *Police Strike, 1919*, London, 1978, chs 7 to 13; J. McCahon, 'The Victorian Police Strike', BA(hons) thesis, University of Melbourne, 1962, pp.7–13, 60–1; J. Templeton, 'Rebel Guardians', in J. Iremonger, J. Merritt, and G. Osborne (eds), *Strikes*, Sydney, 1973, pp.104–5.

106.   Hill, *Iron Hand*, pp.411, 426–7, 430. Hill's emphasis on 'fundamental factors' other than policing accords with the argument of Miles Fairburn in *The Ideal Society and its Enemies: The Foundations of Modern New Zealand Society, 1850–1900*, Auckland, 1989, part 3. See also V.A.C. Gatrell, 'The Decline of Theft and Violence in Victorian and Edwardian England', in Gatrell, B. Lenman, and G. Parker (eds), *Crime and the Law*, London, 1980, pp.136–7, 275–9, 331–3.

107.   The phrase 'fire-brigade policing' was used both by an ex-Commissioner of London Metropolitan Police, Sir Robert Mark, and by more radical critics of developments in British policing. See *NZH*, 12 Jul 1979; *State Research Pamphlet No.2, Policing the Eighties: The Iron Fist*, London, 1981.

108. Annual Report, 1898, p.2.
109. Lord Brampton, 'An Address to Police Constables on their Duties', in *Vincent's Police Code and General Manual of the Criminal Law*, 17th edn, London, 1931, p.ix. It is clear that this 'Address' was presented to New Zealand police because Commissioner O'Donovan 'strongly recommended to the closest attention of all' Lord Brampton's 'impressive observations' on 'the conduct and actions of the police at the trials in the Courts'. More generally, O'Donovan saw *Vincent's Police Code* as 'a most valuable complement' to the 1919 Regulations. J. O'Donovan, 'Address to the New Zealand Police Force', in *The Police Force Act 1913, Police Force Amendment Act 1919, and Regulations made thereunder for the guidance of the Police Force of New Zealand*, Wellington, 1920, pp.xi–xii.
110. W.R. Miller, *Cops and Bobbies: Police Authority in New York and London, 1830–1870*, Chicago, 1977, p.ix. This paragraph and the next draw upon the argument of this book.
111. *Ibid.*, pp.ix–x.
112. See ch.12.
113. *CS*, 29 Sep 1921; repeated verbatim in *NZH* and *ODT*, 30 Sep 1921.
114. This was the view, for example, of Inspector Cassells of the Christchurch police, who advocated immigration restrictions and an exchange of detectives with Australia. *Dominion*, 12 Jan 1923.
115. Rawle, 'Advantages and Disadvantages', p.9.
116. *CS*, 29 Sep 1921.
117. Calculated from *NZ Census*, 1921, part 8, 'Industries, Occupations and Unemployment', pp.140, 141, 160.
118. Annual Reports, 1922, p.13; 1923, p.13.
119. D.G. Pearson and D.C. Thorns, *Eclipse of Equality*, Sydney, 1983, pp.46–7, present statistics which show a 'quite marked decline in unskilled workers from over half the workforce in 1891 to about a third by 1936'.
120. Annual Report, 1921, p.8. Twenty years earlier Commissioner Tunbridge had 'classed as unpreventible offences' those 'against the person or against public order and decency'. Annual Report, 1900, p.1.
121. *NZH*, 30 Dec 1921.
122. Police Offences Amendment Act 1919, sec.3; *NZPD*, vol.185, 1919, pp.673, 747–8, 834.
123. This may be deduced from the *Justice Statistics* published annually from 1921; and from the weekly returns of those convicted in Magistrates' Courts which were printed in the *NZPG*.
124. See the discussion in ch.8.
125. Arguing for a classification of prisoners, Sir John Findlay, the Minister of Justice, asserted in 1910: 'What is the use of applying the same kind of treatment to some miserable sexual pervert – who has no more chance of being reformed than the greatest lunatic has of being cured of his aberration'. P.M. Webb, *A History of Custodial and Related Penalties in New Zealand*, Wellington, 1982, pp.27–8.
126. See John Pratt, *Punishment in a Perfect Society*, Wellington, 1992, pp.197–8.
127. The Controller-General of Prisons drew attention to the growing numbers sentenced in the Supreme Court for sexual offences: in 1920, 48; 1921, 67; 1922, 73; 1923, 81. Annual Report on the Prisons Department, *AJHR*, 1924, H-20, p.2. The category 'sexual offences' included 'unnatural offences', incest, rape, 'unlawful carnal knowledge', indecent assaults and 'acts'. The total number of offences reported were in 1920, 75; 1921, 127; 1922, 147; 1923, 147; 1924, 189; 1925, 204. The highest number of rapes and attempted rapes reported was 22 in 1925. Annual Reports on the Police Force, 1921–6. For further discussion of the 1920s see New Zealand Department of Justice, *Crime in New Zealand*, Wellington, 1968, pp.190–7.
128. Report of the Committee of Inquiry into Mental Defectives and Sexual Offenders, *AJHR*, 1925, H-31A, p.27.

129. Annual Report, 1922, p.3.
130. The discussion in this paragraph draws upon: A. Somerville, 'Moominpappa Got Away: The State and Child Welfare in New Zealand, 1925–30', BA(hons) long essay, University of Otago, 1982, especially pp.8–22; Dalley, *Family Matters*, esp. pp.94–129, 142–54; and E. Philipp, *Juvenile Delinquency in New Zealand*, Christchurch, 1946, esp. ch.1.
131. 'E.S.' asked, as the theme of his article 'The Policeman', 'how frequently do we hear mothers threatening mischievous children by promising "to call the policeman"?' *ODT*, 7 Oct 1930. Inspector G.B. Edwards condemned 'those parents who endeavour to frighten their children into obedience by threatening to send for the police', for they were 'instilling in the children's mind a fear and dislike of the force which could persist through their whole life'. *Ibid.*, 15 Nov 1940. Cf. comments of Walter Nash, *NZH*, 21 Jan 1935.
132. This was perceived by the Labour MP for the Bay of Islands, C.W. Boswell: 'It was absurd to call minor piccadillos of the youngsters crimes. In the old days a policeman would give those urchins a box on the ears and tell them to go home; today he arrests them and brings them before the Juvenile Court'. *NZPD*, vol.260, 1941, p.60.
133. See, for example, the 'South Auckland Community Services Survey', in *South Auckland Police Development Plan*, Wellington, 1984, esp. pp.39–42.
134. Pearson and Thorns, *Eclipse of Equality*, pp.115–18, 125–6.
135. Minutes of Evidence of the Committee of Inquiry into the Police Force, 1919, typescript, p.389; *NZ Census*, 1921, 'General Report', p.23.
136. From the Hurunui River in the south to north of Hanmer Springs, and from Maruia Springs in the west to halfway between Cheviot and Kaikoura in the east. Rosalie Sterritt, 'Constable David Sterritt, DCM', typescript lent to the author, 1979, p.3.
137. The constable at Fairlie made a similar complaint. Annual Report, 1921, pp.11, 14.
138. S. Lewis to 'Chief Commissioner of Police', 5 Sep 1921, P 1, 1921/1274. The quotation was of 'the words of Lord Fisher speaking on the Navy'.
139. *CS*, 29 Sep 1921; Annual Report, 1922, pp.8–14. See also Annual Report, 1921, pp.9–15; Minutes of Evidence of the Committee of Inquiry into the Police Force, 1919, pp.89–92, 222, 476, 482, 485; and M.B. Boyd, *City of the Plains: A History of Hastings*, Wellington, 1984, p.246.
140. Gatrell, 'Decline of Theft and Violence', p.275, table 2.
141. J.P. Martin and G. Wilson, *The Police: A Study in Manpower*, London, 1969, p.47, table III.4.
142. *Press*, 11 Apr 1934.
143. *Ibid.*
144. *CS*, 29 Sep 1921.
145. It is impossible to test this precisely, since ratios for cities, small towns, and rural areas were not published, if indeed they were ever calculated. Moreover, police districts and sub-districts do not coincide exactly with statistical areas. Nonetheless for larger towns at least, the ratios calculated by the author from published census and police statistics for 1921 may be regarded as an approximate guide.
146. See figure I.8.
147. E. Chadwick, 'On the Consolidation of Police Force, and the Prevention of Crime', *Fraser's Magazine*, vol.77, 1868, p.12. See also Miller, *Cops and Bobbies*, p.138; and Gatrell, 'Decline of Theft and Violence', p.278.
148. *LT*, 7 May 1918.
149. *Dominion*, 25 Oct 1921.
150. *TH*, 29 Aug 1921. For the Dorgan case, see P 1, 1921/1274.
151. *Truth*, 23 May 1925.
152. Chadwick, 'Consolidation of Police Force', p.16.
153. This phrase of Henry Cleary, Catholic Bishop of Auckland, is cited by P.S. O'Connor, 'Sectarian Conflict in New Zealand, 1911–1920', *Political Science*, vol.19, no.1, 1967, p.3. For a longer-term perspective on sectarian conflict in New Zealand see

H.S. Moores, 'The Origins of the Protestant Political Association', MA thesis, University of Auckland, 1966.

154.   O'Donovan, 'Address', pp.iii–xvii.
155.   Miller, *Cops and Bobbies*, pp.14–15.
156.   O'Donovan, 'Address', pp.xiv, xvi.
157.   *NZH*, 9 Jul 1920; *NZPG*, 28 Jul 1920, p.458.
158.   R.T. Lange, 'The Tohunga and the Government in the Twentieth Century', *University of Auckland Historical Society Annual, 1968*, pp.29–32. The Act was repealed by the Maori Welfare Act 1962.
159.   O'Donovan, 'Address', pp.xiii–xiv.
160.   See Hill, *Iron Hand*, chs 18, 20.
161.   Miller, *Cops and Bobbies*, p.13.
162.   O'Donovan, 'Address', p.v.
163.   *Ibid.*, p.xv.
164.   *Press*, 23, 30 Jul 1925; 16 Jul 1927; 29 Feb, 2, 9, 21, 23 Mar, 18 Apr, 20, 21, 30 Jun, 19 Jul, 18, 30 Aug, 7 Sep 1928; 12 Mar 1929; J 1934/42/1.
165.   See ch.8.
166.   O'Donovan, 'Address', p.viii.
167.   *Ibid.*, p.vii.
168.   Police Force Act 1913, sec.24; essentially repeated in Police Act 1958, sec.31. Police Force Regulations 1919, nos 42 and 353(28), the latter being repeated in the Police Regulations 1959, no.46(56).
169.   *NZPD*, vol.277, 1947, p.264; see also pp.265, 267–8, 416–17, 558. See also Belton, *Outside the Law*, pp.254–5.
170.   Police Force Regulations 1919, nos 353(8, 9, 20–7, 33, 47), 354; essentially repeated in the Police Regulations 1959, no.46(11–18, 21, 24–6).
171.   O'Donovan, 'Address', p.xiii.
172.   *Ibid.*, p.viii.
173.   A. Kennaway [Henderson], 'On Safer Ground', *Tomorrow*, vol.1, no.4, 1 Aug 1934, p.8.
174.   *NZH*, 15 Aug 1924. Obituary of Walter Baskiville, who was in the Force for 50 years, joining the Armed Constabulary in Taranaki and retiring from the Devonport police station.
175.   *NZH*, 18 Nov 1939.
176.   Gatrell, 'Decline of Theft and Violence', p.276; R. Walker, 'The New South Wales Police Force, 1862–1900', *Journal of Australian Studies*, no.15, 1984, p.37.
177.   Data from Annual Reports.
178.   R.B. Fosdick, *American Police Systems*, 1st edn 1920, reprinted 1969, Montclair, New Jersey, p.355. Fosdick was in fact criticising the 'conventional methods of policing', and believed that a smaller number of men using different methods might more effectively prevent crime by focusing on its '*causes*' (pp.355–6).
179.   J.Q. Wilson, *Varieties of Police Behaviour: The Management of Law and Order in Eight Communities*, New York, 1971, p.58; see also p.185. In later writings Wilson has been less pessimistic; see J.Q. Wilson and B. Boland, 'The Effect of the Police on Crime', *Law and Society Review*, vol.12, 1978, pp.367–90, who find that aggressive patrol strategies can have an effect on the rate at which robberies are committed. However, research during the 1970s on the effectiveness of patrol strategies was fraught with methodological problems and the findings were contradictory. This was recognised by Wilson in *Thinking About Crime*, revised edn, New York, 1983, ch.4; he then argued that more important than crime control was the 'maintenance of orderly neighbourhoods' (*ibid.*, ch.5). See also Clarke and Hough, *Effectiveness of Policing*, esp. pp.ix–x, 2–12, 17–20, 57–60; K. Heal, 'The Police, Research and Crime Control', *Research Bulletin*, Home Office Research and Planning Unit, London, no.13, 1982, pp.16–19; and Walker, *Critical History*, p.156.

Chapter 1: A Time of 'Stress and Difficulty' (1918–21)

1.   Annual Report, 1921, p.8.
2.   *NZPD*, vol.192, 1921, p.997; vol.196, 1922, pp.108-9 (Wilford). See also *EP*, 22 Jun 1939 (obituary); and 'Fragments from the Official Career of John Dwyer, Superintendent of Police 1878–1921', typescript, [1 Nov 1934], Police College Library, pp.31–3.
3.   *ODT*, 25 Jun 1918.
4.   *Dominion*, 9 Apr 1927 (obituary). See also *EP*, 8 Apr 1927. For further discussion of O'Donovan's career see Graeme Dunstall, 'O'Donovan, John', *DNZB*, vol.3, Wellington, 1996, pp.370–1.
5.   The speech was widely reported verbatim, and was the subject of favourable editorial comment. On the suggestion of R. McCallum, the MP for Wairau, Prime Minister Massey ordered the speech to be printed and circulated to all members of the Force. See *ODT*, 9 Oct 1919; *Dominion*, 10 Oct 1919; *EP*, 11 Oct 1919; *NZPD*, vol.185, 1919, p.280; Massey to Commissioner of Police, 14 Oct 1919, P 1, 1919/1885.
6.   *NZPD*, vol.188, 1920, p.144 (Veitch).
7.   For example Constable Dorgan, regarding his housing difficulties at Timaru (discussed below); Detective J.B. Young regarding the allocation of rewards in the Gunn murder case, P 1, 1920/444; and ex-Constable T.F. Smith, who sought to rejoin the Police in Mar 1918 after war service but was rebuffed.
8.   R. Hill, 'An Uneasy Relationship: The Police and the PSA', *NZ Police Association Newsletter*, vol.17, no.1, Jan 1985, pp.4, 7; and Hill, *Iron Hand*, pp.375–81.
9.   'Report of Committee of Inquiry', *NZPG*, 1919, p.427.
10. M.F. Lloyd Pritchard, *An Economic History of New Zealand to 1939*, Auckland, 1970, p.264.
11. Annual Report, 1918, p.7.
12. Critchley, *Police in England and Wales*, pp.184–7.
13. *Dominion*, 12 Sep 1918.
14. Regulation 172 of the 1919 Regulations.
15. *NZPD*, vol.183, 1918, p.567; *ODT*, 9 Jan 1919; Annual Report, 1919, p.7; *NZPG*, 1921, p.288.
16. *ODT*, 29 Jan 1919; *Dominion*, 31 Jan 1919.
17. *ODT*, 15, 17 Apr 1919; *NZH*, 2 May 1919; *NZPG*, 1919, p.150.
18. *ODT*, 12 Feb 1919.
19. Annual Report, 1919, p.9; *ODT*, 18, 20, 21, 29 Nov 1918. The fourteen constables who died were: J.S. Doak, G.A. Gardine, J. Garvey, D. Hasselberg, H.E. Hicks, W.D. Luke, J.L. McKenzie, W.G. McRoberts, J. Nash, J.J. O'Gorman, R.W. Pettit, J.W.S. Robinson, J. Smyth, and R.F. Thomas. Their names were supplied by Chief Inspector Sherwood Young.
20. *NZH*, 1 Aug 1919; Annual Report, 1919, pp.9–10.
21. Erik Olssen examines the processes and effects of unsettling social change between 1890 and 1940 in his chapter, 'Towards a New Society', in G.W. Rice (ed.), *The Oxford History of New Zealand*, 2nd edn, Auckland, 1992. Miles Fairburn sees a shift from social conflict to consensus between 1912 and 1930 in his chapter, 'The Farmers Take Over', in K. Sinclair (ed.), *The Oxford Illustrated History of New Zealand*, Auckland, 1990.
22. For the other 'Urban Areas', the increase in population in the period 1921–36 was (rounded to the nearest hundred): Hamilton, 5,600; Gisborne, 1,100; Napier, 1,300; Hastings, 4,700; New Plymouth, 5,500; Wanganui, 1,800; Palmerston North, 7,000; Nelson, 2,900; Timaru, 3,300; and Invercargill, 6,500. Calculated from *NZOYB*, 1946, p.28.
23. See figure I.8.
24. For the general context see R.M. Burdon, *The New Dominion*, London, 1965, chs 1, 2.

25.   *TP*, 5 Nov 1920, argued however that the 'wave of crime that is sweeping over the land' should not be blamed on the returned soldiers.
26.   For Dudding's death see P 1, 1919/1885. Four days earlier O'Donovan had received the first draft of an Arms Bill which made no reference to pistols of any type; on 17 Oct he received the second draft in which clause 3 declared 'automatic pistols' to be 'unlawful weapons', and clause 4 declared it to be unlawful for any person to carry a pistol of any other type beyond his dwelling without a licence; P 2/4/-, part 1.
27.   J.W. Poynton, SM, to Under-Secretary, Justice Department, 31 May 1920, P 26/1/-, part 1.
28.   Annual Report, 1919, p.9.
29.   See ch.10.
30.   *ODT*, 5 Apr 1919. The committee comprised the Attorney-General, the acting Minister of Finance, and the Minister of Justice. Wilford later claimed that before the pay increase police numbers were 'about three hundred below normal'; *NZPD*, vol.184, 1919, p.981. From Apr 1919, the hourly rate of 1s 6d for a newly appointed constable was 3d more than the minimum unskilled rate fixed by the Arbitration Court; A.E.C. Hare, *Report on Industrial Relations in New Zealand*, Wellington, 1946, p.119. Altogether the two pay increases received by the Police represented a 33% increase in the new constable's rate since Apr 1914, about 5% greater than the increase received by a public servant on a 'standard salary'; T. Mark, Secretary of the Economies Committee, to W.F. Massey, 4 Oct 1921, SSC 66/10/49.
31.   'Report of Committee of Inquiry', *NZPG*, 1919, pp.417–28.
32.   *Dominion*, 23 Jun 1919.
33.   *ODT*, 12 Apr 1920.
34.   Those subsequently reappointed under the 1919 Act were: C.C. Dunsford (first appointed in 1907), M. Ryan (1910), E.F. O'Brien (1911), J. Thompson (1911), W.C. Brown (1912), E.C. Jarrold (1914), F. Gribben (1914), H. Robert (1914), O.I. Tocher (1914), C. Chestnut (1914), E.W. Straffon (1914), W.D. Thom (1914), A.H. Barnes (1915), H. Sargent (1915), R. Thompson (1915), D.A. McKinlay (1915). Those reappointed under the Police Force Amendment Act 1924, sec.6 (which extended the 1919 Act), were: J.J. Sparks (1910), T.F. Smith (1912), and D. Sterritt (1915). *NZPG*, 1920, p.207; 1924, p.674.
35.   Annual Report, 1920, p.8.
36.   *NZPD*, 1919, vol.184, pp.980–7; vol.185, pp.1256–9; *ODT*, 3 Oct 1919.
37.   *NZPD*, vol.184, 1919, p.983.
38.   *ODT*, 14 Jun 1919; Annual Report, 1919, p.9. See also Hill, 'An Uneasy Relationship'.
39.   Regulations 314, 364, 454–61; *Dominion*, 19 Sep 1919; *ODT*, 15 Oct 1919.
40.   See the correspondence in P 1, 1921/1274. For the insufficiency of the house allowances in 1919, see the 'Minutes of Evidence' to the Committee of Inquiry, 1919, typescript, pp.6, 67.
41.   *Dominion*, 4 Mar 1920; *ODT*, 8, 23, 30 Mar, 12 Apr 1920; *LT*, 6 Jul 1920; Annual Report, 1920, pp.7, 9, 12, 14; Report of the 'Economies Committee', 4 Oct 1921, p.6, SSC 66/10/49.
42.   Though decided upon in Jul and backdated to Apr, the increase had not still not been paid by Sep 1920; *NZPD*, 1920, vol.187, p.777; vol.188, pp.141, 143.
43.   Annual Report, 1920, pp.12, 14; 1921, p.7.
44.   *NZH*, 12 Apr 1920.
45.   No.353(43) of the 1919 Regulations.
46.   Burdon, *New Dominion*, pp.104, 107.
47.   J. Watson, 'Crisis and Change: Economic Crisis and Technological Change Between the World Wars, with Special Reference to Christchurch, 1926–36', PhD thesis, University of Canterbury, 1984, p.614, Appendix C.
48.   Burdon, *New Dominion*, p.108.
49.   *NZPD*, vol.183, 1918, p.567; Annual Report, 1922, p.8.
50.   From 'Examples of Unlawful Use of Firearms', P 2/4/-, part 1. See also *NZPD*,

vol.186, 1920, p.634 (Massey).

51.   See ch.6.

52.   'Return showing Deaths and Injuries caused by Firearms during the two years ended 30th June 1920', and 'Automatic Pistols sold to Retail Customers by Dealers during the two years ending 30th June 1920, and Number they have in Stock', P 2/4/–, part 1. Note that these returns were called for by Massey between the first and second readings of the bill; NZPD, vol.186, 1920, p.643. For the number of firearms imported into New Zealand see *Review of Firearms Control in New Zealand: Report of an Independent Inquiry Commissioned by the Minister of Police*, Wellington, 1997, Appendix 2.

53.   *NZPD*, vol.186, 1920, p.754.

54.   *Ibid.*, p.645 (Massey).

55.   Annual Report, 1921, p.8.

56.   See P 2/4/–, part 1.

57.   As an example of a smaller district: 8,850 arms were registered, 76 automatics surrendered, and a further 210 applications to retain such pistols lodged in the Napier District by Apr 1921. For the country as a whole, some 2,500 applications to retain automatics had been 'favorably reported on' by Nov 1921. Annual Report, 1921, pp.10, 11; Commissioner of Police to Minister of Justice, 16 Nov 1921, P 2/4/–, part 1. For further discussion of the administration of the Arms Act, see ch.8.

58.   Annual Report, 1919, pp.6–7; 1920, p.7; 1921, p.7.

59.   Districts already existing in 1918 were: Auckland, Hamilton, Napier, Wanganui, Wellington, Greymouth, Christchurch, Dunedin, Invercargill. The new districts were: Palmerston North (established 1 Aug 1918), Timaru (1 Dec 1919), Whangarei (1 May 1920), Gisborne (1 Jan 1921), New Plymouth (1 Jan 1921). Compare the maps of North Island and South Island police districts in 1918 and 1939.

60.   See figure I.7.

61.   Evidence of Constable E.J. Whitehouse and Senior Sergeant M. Gaffney to the Committee of Inquiry, 1919; 'Minutes of Evidence', typescript, pp.492–3, 501–4.

62.   T.F. Smith, 'Reminiscences', typescript, 1978, p.10.

63.   Belton, *Outside the Law*, p.135. He describes the routine of the Auckland District Office during the late 1920s in ch.27.

64.   Assisting the Superintendents in 1922 were an Inspector and Sub-Inspector in Auckland, Wellington and Christchurch, and a Sub-Inspector in Dunedin. Annual Report, 1922, Appendix B.

65.   Nos 9 to 33 of the 1919 Police Regulations detailed the responsibilities of officers in charge of districts. For further discussion of the pattern of administration see ch.9.

66.   *Dominion,* 30 Nov 1920; *NZPG,* 1921, pp.309–10; Annual Report, 1921, p.7. The Auckland 'Division' comprised the districts of Auckland, Whangarei, Hamilton, and Gisborne; the Wellington 'Division', Wellington, Wanganui, New Plymouth, Palmerston North, and Napier; the Canterbury 'Division', Christchurch, Timaru, and Greymouth; and Otago was made up of Dunedin and Invercargill.

67.   See Hill, *Iron Hand,* pp.165–6, 210, 229–33, 239, 254–5, 257–8, 265, 281, 364.

68.   Clerical Division, Class IV. By 1921 Madden had been regraded to Class II, then equivalent to a Superintendent in terms of salary; Annual Reports of the Public Service Commissioner, *AJHR,* 1919 and 1921, H-14; *EP,* 1 Jun 1949.

69.   Minutes of Evidence to the Royal Commission on the Police Force of the Dominion, *AJHR,* 1909, H-16B, p.471. In 1909 Wright was Chief Clerk and Accountant on the Headquarters staff.

70.   He remained at this rank until his retirement in Jan 1947. For E.W. Dinnie's early career see Hill, *Iron Hand*, especially pp.170–3, 370–2.

71.   Charles Broberg was transferred to Headquarters in 1918 and remained there until his retirement in 1928. He was promoted to Inspector in Sep 1919 and Superintendent in Jan 1924. For further details of Broberg's career, especially as a detective, see Sherwood Young, 'Broberg, Charles Robert', *DNZB,* vol.3, pp.67–8.

72. Annual Public Works Statement, *AJHR*, 1900–38, D-1; Annual Report, 1918, pp.6–7; John Wilson, *Lost Christchurch*, Lincoln, 1984, p.16. See also figure 1.4.
73. Annual Report, 1919, p.8; 1920, p.7; 1921, p.7; *NZPD*, vol.189, 1920, p.731 (Lee); Annual Public Works Statement, *AJHR*, 1919–22, D-1.
74. Annual Report, 1921, p.7.
75. 'Fragments from the Official Career of John Dwyer', p.33.
76. Annual Report, 1919, p.8.
77. Watson, 'Crisis and Change', pp.259, 261, provides figures for the occupational background of car and motorcycle owners in 1933 which support this impression.
78. Annual Report, 1919, p.8; 1921, p.12; 1922, p.8.
79. *NZPG*, 1921, p.757.
80. Robinson, *History of the Post Office*, pp.210–11.
81. Report of the 'Economies Committee', 4 Oct 1921, Appendix K, p.2, SSC 66/10/49.
82. *NZH*, 4 Apr, 2 May 1923.
83. *NZPD*, vol.188, 1920, p.143 (Hunter). This was a recurring complaint; see vol.202, 1923, p.254; vol.204, 1924, p.541.
84. Annual Report, 1919, p.15; 1920, p.13.
85. Some American police departments, however, were already making extensive use of cars. In Apr 1918 Detroit replaced foot-patrolmen with men driving in over 150 Ford automobiles. Fosdick, *American Police Systems*, pp.310–12.
86. Robinson, *History of the Post Office*, pp.210–11.
87. District Orders 1/24 (dated 1 May 1924), 3/24 (dated 20 Jun 1924), in Culverden Police Station, Christchurch District Order Book, 1877–1949.
88. *NZPG*, 1929, pp.130–1.
89. *Dominion*, 12 Oct 1921.
90. Annual Report, 1921, p.8.
91. *NZPD*, vol.192, 1921, pp.996–7; vol.196, 1922, p.108 (Lee and Wilford).

Chapter 2: A 'Cinderella Department' (1922–35)

1. *Press*, 24 Jul 1935.
2. See, for example, the resolution passed at the Conference of Associated Chambers of Commerce and delivered by a deputation to the Prime Minister (Massey) and Minister of Industries and Commerce (Lee) in Nov 1920, SSC 60/1/1.
3. See the Report and Resolutions of the Economies Committee, 4 Oct 1921, pp.38, 103–4 and Appendix D, pp.1–3, 15, SSC 66/10/49. Under the provisions of the Public Expenditure Adjustment Act 1922, Police Department expenditure in the last three months of the financial year 1921/22 was cut by £4,705. However, this saving was offset by an increase in the strength of the Force which had already been authorised. *NZPD*, vol.193, 1922, pp.481–2; vol.196, 1922, p.323.
4. The first salary cut of 1 Jan 1922 largely accounts for the Police underspending its budget by £24,854 in 1921/22. For this and other statistics on expenditure see *AJHR*, B-1, B-6, and B-7, for the years 1921–39. See also figure 1.4.
5. *NZPD*, vol.196, 1922, p.109 (Lee); also *Dominion*, 9 Nov 1921.
6. Details of service and background are drawn from the 'Police Force Description Book' [henceforth PFDB], vol.1; and *NZH*, 8 Apr 1925 (Norwood).
7. See O'Connor, 'Sectarian Conflict', pp.15–16; Sweetman, *Bishop in the Dock*, pp.112–18, 135–6.
8. Minutes of Evidence to the Royal Commission on the Police Force of the Dominion, *AJHR*, 1909, H-16B, pp.470–6; *Dominion*, 28 Jan 1938 (obituary). See also Sherwood Young, 'Wright, Arthur Hobbins', *DNZB*, vol.4, p.574.
9. Report and Resolutions of the Economies Committee, 4 Oct 1921, pp.6–7, SSC 66/10/49.
10. See the memoranda in SSC 60/3/32, and general comment in the Report of the Public

Service Commissioner, *AJHR*, 1922, H-14, pp.4–5.

11.   Editorial in *Public Service Journal*, 20 Mar 1922, cited by K.J. Holland, 'Police Unionism in New Zealand', long essay for Diploma of Industrial Relations, Victoria University of Wellington, 1977, p.19. This paragraph and the next draw on material in Holland's essay, Hill, 'An Uneasy Relationship', and Roth, *Remedy for Present Evils*, pp.57–60. D. McGill, *No Right to Strike*, Wellington, 1992, pp.20–1 draws upon a draft of this chapter.

12.   Report and Resolutions of the Economies Committee, 4 Oct 1921, pp.6–7, SSC 66/10/49. *NZPD*, vol.193, 1922, p.558; *Dominion*, 1 Apr 1922.

13.   *LT*, 31 Jan, 2, 3 Feb 1922.

14.   On 23 Feb 1922, Commissioner Wright sought the views of Australian Police Commissioners as to whether their police associations had 'adversely affected the discipline of the Force'; replies suggested that they had not done so in New South Wales, Queensland, South Australia or Western Australia. A. Nicholson, Acting Chief Commissioner of the Victoria Police, where there was an association, concluded however: 'On the whole, I am opposed to the formation of an Association, if it be possible to prevent it.' On the file copy of the English Police Act 1919, which authorised the formation of a Police Federation, Commissioner Wright pencilled in the margin against secs 1(2), which maintained that the Police Federation would be 'independent of and unassociated with any body or person outside the police service', and 2(1), which made it unlawful for a member of a police force to become a member of any trade union or any association (other than the Police Federation), 'having for its objects .... to control and influence the pay, pensions, or conditions of service of any police force'. P 13/1-.

15.   *NZH*, 9 Mar 1922; *Dominion*, 1 Apr 1922.

16.   Constable J. Coutts to Sub-Inspector of Police, Auckland, 11 Feb 1922, OPR 21/2/33, vol.1.

17.   *Public Service Journal*, Jul 1922, cited by Holland, 'Police Unionism', p.22; and by Hill, 'An Uneasy Relationship', p.7.

18.   No.172 of the 1919 Regulations.

19.   T.F. Smith, 'Early Days of the New Zealand Police Association', *NZPJ*, vol.4, 1940, p.258.

20.   Police Regulations 171, 173–6.

21.   Smith, 'Early Days', p.258.

22.   Police Regulation 300.

23.   In Oct 1926 *Truth's* average weekly sales were 70,429; in Dec 1933, 74,258; *Truth*, 2 Dec 1926, 31 Jan 1934.

24.   See, for example, the juxtaposition of two editorials in *Truth*, 3 Mar 1923: the first, entitled 'The Third Degree: Mistakes of Overzealousness', criticised the methods of some detectives; the second deplored the Police disciplinary procedures as being too harsh on the rank and file, and commented on the 'splendid detective staff'.

25.   *NZH*, 12 Jan 1923; *Truth*, 13 Jan 1923; *ODT*, 16 Jan 1923.

26.   *Truth*, 3 Feb 1923; *Dominion*, 27 Feb 1923. Similar complaints were reported in the South Island later in the year; see *LT*, 6 Sep 1923.

27.   *Truth*, 3 Feb 1923.

28.   *Dominion*, 27 Feb 1923; *ODT*, 2 Mar 1923; *LT*, 6 Sep 1923.

29.   *Truth*, 3 Mar 1923.

30.   The eight-hour shift 'may now be adopted at all stations where the officer in charge of the district considers it can be satisfactorily applied.' *NZPG*, 1922, p.8.

31.   *NZPD*, vol.201, 1923, pp.12–13. Parr had taken over as Minister when E.P. Lee was unseated in Jan 1923 as a result of an election petition.

32.   Annual Report, 1922, p.8; *Truth*, 19 Jul, 9 Sep 1922.

33.   *Dominion*, 27 Feb 1923.

34.   Annual Report, 1923, p.8.

35.   *Dominion*, 16 Nov 1923.

36. G.H. Scholefield (ed.), *Who's Who in New Zealand*, 5th edn, Wellington, 1951, p.242.
37. *CS*, 4 Jan 1922.
38. *Ibid.*, 4 Jan 1922, also *AS* and *LT*, 5 Jan 1922.
39. Annual Reports, 1922, p.2; 1923, p.2.
40. 'Report of Committee of Inquiry', *NZPG*, 1919, p.425.
41. Annual Report, 1922, p.14.
42. Police Regulation 233 was replaced by a new regulation issued on 16 Jan 1922; *NZPG*, 1922, p.62.
43. At stations where there was more than one detective, the following hours were to be worked: 9 am to 12.30, 2 to 5.30 pm, 7.30 to 10.30 pm. Half the staff were to be 'relieved of duty at 5.30 pm every alternate night'; *NZPG*, 1922, pp.374–5.
44. *Truth*, 8 Sep 1923; see also 3 Mar 1923.
45. *ODT*, 31 Jul 1923. W.J. Jordan, the Labour MP for Manukau, asked questions on allowances, hours, uniforms, and resignations; *NZPD*, vol.201, 1923, pp.11–12, 82.
46. *NZPD*, 1923, vol.201, p.720; vol.202, pp.254–5; Annual Report, p.8.
47. Senior Detective R. Ward to Commissioner, 2 Oct 1923, OPR 21/2/33, vol.1; *LT*, 6 Sep 1923.
48. For the strike generally, see J. Walsh, 'The Seamen on Strike, 1922–1923', in P. Walsh (ed.), *Trade Unions, Work and Society*, Palmerston North, 1994, ch.4.
49. Burdon, *New Dominion*, pp.56–7; H. Roth, *Trade Unions in New Zealand*, Wellington, 1973, pp.46–7; and reports in OPR 40/18/10 and 21/2/33.
50. *ODT*, 2 Oct 1923.
51. Report of the Public Service Commissioner, *AJHR*, 1924, H-14, p.3; Burdon, *New Dominion*, p.57; Hare, *Industrial Relations*, p.119, table 7.
52. *ODT*, 19 Dec 1923.
53. *LT*, 19 Nov 1923.
54. Annual Reports, 1924, p.7; 1925, p.7.
55. *NZPD*, vol.204, 1924, p.541.
56. See Annual Reports, 1923, pp.7–14; 1924, pp.7–12, for details.
57. For the responsibilities of officers in charge of districts, see ch.9.
58. Annual Reports, 1924, p.7; 1925, pp.1, 7; *NZPD*, vol.204, 1924, p.541.
59. Similar complaints were made of the rented police house at Devonport and the station at Wanganui. See *NZPD*, 1922, vol.193, pp.789–91; vol.197, pp.76, 363.
60. *NZH*, 7 Apr 1924.
61. Inspector Wohlmann to Superintendent Hendrey, 29 May 1922, P 1, 1923/707.
62. Annual Report, 1925, p.7. For expenditure from the Public Works Fund on police premises, see figure 1.4.
63. Annual Reports, 1924, pp.8–12; 1925, pp.8–12. Cf. Fosdick, *American Police Systems*, p.374, for the conventional wisdom on the relationship between want and crime.
64. First Report of Committee on Unemployment in New Zealand, *AJHR*, 1929, H-11B, p.19; *NZOYB*, 1931, pp.845–7.
65. *LT*, 7 Apr 1927; *NZH*, 5 Jan 1928.
66. *LT*, 27 Aug 1927. As the Depression deepened, unemployment probably became more severe in Christchurch than in Auckland, Wellington, or Dunedin. Yet, except for 1931, a significant rise in reported offences against property in Christchurch is not apparent from the annual reports of the Police Force. For unemployment in Christchurch see Watson, 'Crisis and Change', esp. pp.100–1, 194–5.
67. *Truth*, 13 Jan 1927.
68. Watson, 'Crisis and Change', p.257.
69. *NZPD*, vol.222, 1929, pp.1138, 1140, 1142–3, 1146.
70. *NZH*, 17 Nov 1925.
71. *LT*, 19 Nov 1925. The other three Superintendents were C.W. Hendrey (Auckland), who had joined in 1879 and was due to retire in Jul 1926; W.H. Mackinnon (Christchurch), 1881 and Sep 1926; and W. Mathieson (Dunedin), 1885 and 1930.

In the event Mathieson died in office on 26 Nov 1926. PFDB, vol.1.

72.   Notably (ranks in 1925): Superintendent W. Mathieson; Inspector A.T. Emerson (joined 1892); Inspector E. Eales (joined 1893); and Inspector J.C.S. Willis (joined 1893). PFDB, vol.1. See also 'Minutes of Evidence' to the Committee of Inquiry, 1919, typescript, esp. pp.81–2.

73.   *LT,* 19 Nov 1925; *NZH,* 1 Oct 1927; *Dominion,* 22 Nov 1937.

74.   Newspaper obituary (unsourced), dated 24 Jul 1956 (held by author). For different accounts of his career focusing particularly on his role as a detective in noteworthy cases see: *NZH,* 2 Dec 1925; *PBH,* 2 Dec 1925; *ODT,* 9 Dec 1925; and also W.B. McIlveney's 'Scrapbook' of newspaper cuttings (1895–1903) in the New Zealand Police Museum. For his career generally see Graeme Dunstall, 'McIlveney, William Bernard', *DNZB,* vol.4, pp.311–12.

75.   *Truth,* 15 Sep 1923. McIlveney was impressed with the 'high efficiency' of the Los Angeles and San Francisco police, and especially with the use of cars in detective work. He seems not to have visited Berkeley, the most 'progressive' of the Police Departments in California. Note the contemporary comments on organisation and methods in Fosdick, *American Police Systems,* esp. pp.194–6, 277–81, 309–12, 327–43, 386.

76.   *Truth,* 28 Nov 1925, 28 Oct 1926.

77.   W.S. Brown, interview, 5 Feb 1977. Willis Brown joined in 1921 and was a constable at Wellington city stations until 1936. Other retired men shared similar recollections: e.g. P. Kearney, interview, 5 Nov 1976; H.E. Campin, interview, 11 Jan 1977, and H. Holmes, interview, 5 Jan 1977.

78.   *NZH,* 14 Feb 1928.

79.   *LT,* 2 May 1927.

80.   P. Kearney, interview, 5 Nov 1976; H.E. Campin, interview, 11 Jan 1977; F.R. Henry, letter to author, 6 Dec 1977. A reporter also commented on McIlveney's 'considerable learning', *Truth,* 28 Oct 1926.

81.   *LT,* 1 Mar 1926.

82.   *Dominion,* 5 Mar 1926. The new pattern of shifts was made permanent at the beginning of Oct 1926; *NZPG,* 1926, pp.131, 653.

83.   *Dominion,* 27 Aug 1926; *NZH,* 27 Aug 1926.

84.   Annual Report, 1926, p.6; *NZPD,* vol.209, 1926, p.1091 (Rolleston).

85.   *NZPG,* 1926, p.106; *EP,* 19 Nov 1926; *Dominion,* 7 Jul 1927.

86.   In fact during the year the Auckland strength was increased by four constables and one detective, new stations were opened at St Heliers Bay and Papatoetoe, and a permanent constable replaced a District Constable at Panmure; Annual Report, 1927, pp.6–7; *NZH,* 5 May, 31 Jul, 15 Oct 1926; *Truth,* 5 Aug 1926.

87.   This was the theme of the Commissioner's Christmas 'Address' to members of the Force. *NZPG,* 1926, p.826.

88.   McIlveney offered a number of different justifications for the uniform changes. The 'patch' or 'side' pockets introduced in 1912 were said to 'afford refractory prisoners a grip which they are not slow to use when resisting arrest.' Similarly, the capes used in wet weather were discontinued because these also could be 'a hindrance to the police in a tussle'. The shako and the other alterations (including a different fabric) were also intended to reduce the weight of the uniform. The blue helmet with bronze badges introduced in 1912 would continue to be used at night and on wet days. McIlveney also asserted that the current police buttons and badges were not distinctive enough. A new badge for the shako, made of silver, was to consist of the royal coat of arms supported by two fernleaves with the words 'New Zealand Police' on a scroll at the bottom. With silver buttons, a policeman would no longer be mistaken for 'a railway porter or tram guard'. However, the appearance of police on the streets in shakos from May 1927 'aroused a good deal of comment', with 'much good-humoured chaff being directed' at constables. A popular explanation amongst police for the tunic without pockets was that it came after the Commissioner saw a constable

standing on point duty with his thumbs stuck in his pockets. Accompanying the uniform changes came increased concern by the Commissioner, expressed in a series of instructions, that there be no 'unwarrantable expenditure' in applications for uniform clothing. Nevertheless, the changes were criticised for their costliness. *NZH*, 3 May, 6 Nov 1926; 19 Jan, 21 Apr 1927; 3 Oct 1930; *LT*, 25 Mar, 2 and 30 May 1927; *AWN*, 2 Jun 1927; *NZPG*, 1926, p.779; 1927, pp.42, 274, 322, 361–2, 867.

89.   *NZPG*, 1926, p.330. The description of McIlveney's dress from interviews with P. Kearney and W.S. Brown, and letter from F.R. Henry.

90.   *NZPG*, 1926, p.222. For examples of press frustration, see *NZH*, 10 Sep 1927 (editorial); *Truth*, 15 Sep, 6 Oct 1927; and the poor relationship between the Christchurch police and the *Star* during the 'Burwood murder' case cited below.

91.   *NZPG*, 1926, p.242; 1928, p.420; 1929, p.550; *LT*, 27 Aug, 1 Sep 1927; *NZPD*, vol.214, 1927, pp.171–2; vol.219, 1928, p.17.

92.   McIlveney's Christmas Address to the Force, *NZPG*, 1926, p.826.

93.   *NZPG*, 1926, pp.222, 427; *ODT*, 19 Apr 1926; *AWN*, 2 Jun 1927.

94.   *LT*, 29 Mar 1927; *NZPG*, 1926, pp.275, 391; 1927, pp.287–8.

95.   *NZPG*, 1926, p.391.

96.   *NZPG*, 1926, p.714; *NZPD*, vol.209, 1926, p.469; vol.214, 1927, pp.172–3; *EP*, 19 and 23 Nov 1926; *AWN*, 2 Jun 1927; *Truth*, 5 Jan 1928.

97.   *NZH*, 18 Dec 1926.

98.   Annual Report, 1925, p.9. See also G.W.A. Bush, *Decently and in Order*, Auckland, 1971, pp.259, 263–72; and Woolston, *Equal To The Task*, pp.39–50.

99.   Town Clerk to Chairman, Finance and Legal Committee, 19 Aug 1925; Chief Traffic Inspector to Town Clerk, 11 Sep 1925; Auckland City Council, Town Clerk's Office, file 123/1926, part 1. Similar complaints were heard in Wellington and Christchurch: *NZH*, 13 Mar 1924; *LT*, 24 Nov 1925; *PBH*, 2 Mar 1926.

100.   *NZPG*, 1926, p.242.

101.   By Sep 1929, only Wellington, Dunedin, and Newmarket had policemen on point duty. Auckland City Council, Town Clerk's Office, file 123/1926; *ODT*, 30 Jul 1926; *NZH*, 7 Aug, 21 Oct, 18 Dec 1926; 1 Mar, 19 Aug 1927; *LT*, 12 Jul 1926; 22 Feb, 29 Mar 1927; *NZPD*, vol.222, 1929, pp.957, 1146; Woolston, *Equal To The Task*, pp.51–8.

102.   For further discussion, see chs 4, 5.

103.   *NZH*, 17 Jan 1927.

104.   *NZPD*, vol.209, 1926, p.469. See also vol.214, 1927, p.171; vol.219, 1928, pp.445–6.

105.   *NZPG*, 1927, p.287; *NZPD*, vol.209, 1926, p.1148.

106.   *ODT*, 22, 23 Feb 1927; *Dominion*, 23 Feb 1927; *NZH*, 14, 25 Mar 1927; *NZPG*, 1927, p.287.

107.   *NZPD*, vol.219, 1928, p.15.

108.   *LT*, 7 Apr 1926; *NZH*, 12 Apr, 18 May 1926.

109.   *Dominion*, 24 May 1927 (an apparently verbatim report). Cf. slightly different accounts of the speech in *NZH* and *ODT*, 24 May 1927.

110.   *Dominion*, 25 and 26 May, 3 Jun 1927; *NZH*, 25 and 27 May, 21 and 27 Jul 1927, 5 Jan 1928; *AS*, 26 May 1927; *Truth*, 2 Jun 1927; *NZPD*, vol.212, 1927, pp.723, 731.

111.   *NZH*, 27 Sep 1927.

112.   *NZH*, 27 May, 27 Jul, 27 Sep, 29 Nov 1927; Belton, *Outside the Law*, pp.74–6; Annual Reports, 1928 and 1929, pp.6–7.

113.   In 1928 there appear to have been (for the Auckland 'Co-ordinated Districts'): a Hupmobile touring car, a Ford car, two prison vans and one motorcycle.

114.   For the work of the Criminal Registration Branch, see ch.6.

115.   The Nelson Police District was also established on 1 Dec 1928. *NZH*, 10 Dec 1927, 13 Feb 1928; *ODT*, 13 Feb 1928; *NZPG*, 1927, p.875; 1928, p.805; 1929, pp.9–10, 43–4; 1930, p.242; Annual Reports, 1928 and 1929, pp.6–7. The working of the

Auckland system was described by Wohlmann, J. McIlveney, and Hollis in the 'Record of Proceedings and Depositions of Witnesses' to the Commission of Inquiry 'into the conduct of members of the Police Force in relation to the disappearance and death of Elsie Walker', typescript, 1929, pp.29–62, P 1, 1928/1724, part 5.

116.   Annual Report, 1929, p.6; *NZPD*, vol.222, 1929, p.953.

117.   *CS*, 29 Jun 1927, P 1, 1927/873. The discussion of the 'Burwood murder' draws on the cuttings and reports on this file, and also on *NZPG*, 1927, pp.457, 553, 572; *NZPD*, vol.212, 1927, pp.201, 667–8; *Truth*, 23, 30 Jun, 7, 14 Jul, 4, 11 Aug, 1, 8 Sep, 17, 24 Nov, 1 Dec 1927.

118.   A second charge, of supplying an abortifacient (ergot) to Miss Scarff, was not pressed. Between the depositions and Supreme Court hearings, the key witness had changed his evidence, claiming that he had been bullied into making a false statement by Detective Sergeant J. Bickerdike, who had been brought in from Auckland to work on the case.

119.   *ODT*, 25 Nov 1927. Miss Scarff's parents felt that the detectives had 'left no stone unturned' and blamed the judge for the result. The Crown Solicitor, A.T. Donnelly, thought that the police had done 'everything that was humanly possible', but that the evidence was 'too weak to establish the case'. W. and E. Scarff to Superintendent, Christchurch, 24 Nov 1927; A.T. Donnelly to Superintendent, Christchurch, 25 Nov 1927; P 1, 1927/873.

120.   There are several accounts of this case: V.R. Meredith, *A Long Brief: Recollections of a Crown Solicitor*, Auckland, 1966; L.P. Leary, *Not Entirely Legal*, Christchurch, 1977, pp.76–84; G.G. Kelly, *The Gun in the Case*, Christchurch, 1963, pp.55–9; G. Joseph, *By a Person or Persons Unknown: Unsolved Murders in New Zealand*, Sydney, 1982, pp.151–68. The following three paragraphs are based on the police reports and newspaper cuttings in P 1, 1928/1724. Details of the police investigation up to Jan 1929 are drawn mainly from the Report of and the 'Record of Proceedings and Depositions of Witnesses' to the Commission of Enquiry 'into the conduct of members of the Police Force in relation to the disappearance and death of Elsie Walker', typescript, 1929, in P 1, 1928/1724, part 5.

121.   *Truth*, 18 Oct 1928; see also *ibid.*, 11 Oct, 1 Nov 1928; *NZH*, 13, 19 Oct 1928. The theory was propounded by Inspector Hollis and Chief Detective Alfred Hammond.

122.   Commissioner to Superintendent, Auckland, 5 Nov 1928. See also file asking for 'special report' dated 25 Oct 1928, in P 1, 1928/1724.

123.   'Record of Proceedings and Depositions of Witnesses', pp.83, 97, 107, 154–5, 159, 185, P 1, 1928/1724, part 4.

124.   Report of Detective Sergeant Bickerdike, 7 Dec 1928; P 1, 1928/1724, part 8.

125.   Specifically, Mr Hunt criticised: (i) the removal of the body before it was inspected by the Coroner and doctors; (ii) the removal of the clothing from the body at the morgue before inspection by the Police Surgeon; (iii) slowness in beginning inquiries; (iv) failure to test Bayly's alibi adequately; (v) delay in forwarding clothing to the Bacteriologist; Superintendent Wohlmann to Commissioner, 1 Feb 1929, P 1, 1928/1724, part 1.

126.   Coroner's Finding, delivered 25 Jan 1929, P 1, 1928/1724, part 1.

127.   *Sun*, 22 Jan 1929. The phrase is that of E.H. Northcroft, counsel for the Bayly family at the inquest. For 'Bill' Bayly see also David Green, 'Bayly, William Alfred', *DNZB*, vol. 4, Wellington, 1998, pp.41–2.

128.   For the Thomas see, for example, T. Bell, *Bitter Hill. Arthur Allan Thomas: The Case for a Retrial*, 1972; Pat Booth, *The Fate of Arthur Allan Thomas: Trial by Ambush*, 1975; D.A. Yallop, *Beyond Reasonable Doubt*, Penguin edn, 1980; *Report of the Royal Commission to Inquire into the Circumstances of the Convictions of Arthur Allan Thomas for the Murders of David Harvey Crewe and Jeanette Lenore Crewe*, 1980.

129.   *EP*, 28 Jan, 7 Feb 1929; *NZPD*, vol.223, 1929, p.748 (C.E. Macmillan, MP for Tauranga); and telegrams and police reports in P 1, 1928/1724, parts 1 and 6.

130. A.E. Currie, Crown Solicitor, to Superintendent, Auckland, 18 Feb 1929, P 1, 1928/ 1724, part 9.

131. Report of the Commission of Enquiry 'into the conduct of members of the Police Force in relation to the disappearance and death of Elsie Walker', typescript, 20 Mar 1929, p.24, P 1, 1928/1724, part 5.

132. McIlveney to Wohlmann (telegram), 5 Apr 1929, P 1, 1928/1724, part 6; *EP*, 4 Apr 1929; *NZH*, 5 Apr 1929. See also *Dominion*, 5 Apr 1929; *LT,* 6 Apr 1929; *Truth*, 11 Apr 1929.

133. *NZPD*, vol.223, 1929, p.748 (Macmillan).

134. *Truth*, 8 Aug 1929. Newspaper cuttings showing the reaction in North Island small towns as well as in the cities can be found in P 1, 1928/1724, part 5.

135. *NZH*, 17 Aug 1929.

136. Statement by the Minister of Justice regarding the Elsie Walker Case [7 Nov 1929], *AJHR*, 1929, H-28. For the preparation of this statement see Wilford to Commissioner, 30 Oct and 5 Nov 1929; and for the reaction it provoked see cuttings in P 1, 1928/ 1724, parts 5 and 6.

137. For the parliamentary pressure see especially *NZPD*, 1929, vol.222, p.485; vol.223, pp.548, 748–53, 1312–13, 1323, 1365. Coinciding with Wilford's ministerial statement on 7 Nov, the Public Petitions Committee reported favourably to the House on petitions (totalling 15,809 signatures) asking for legislation to authorise the reopening of inquests and the inquiry into Elsie Walker's death. The Committee thought that amending legislation should be passed 'as soon as possible'; *AJHR*, 1929, I-1, p.8.

138. *NZPD*, vol.222, 1929, pp.953, 1138–40, 1142–4, 1147, 1149; *NZPG*, 1929, pp.547, 623; *NZH*, 5 Aug 1929; *Press*, 7 Aug 1929; *CS*, 20 Jan 1930. The relevant file, P 1, 1929/1719, contains little on the investigation.

139. *NZH*, 6 Apr 1929; *Truth*, 28 Mar, 15 Aug, 7 Nov 1929; *ODT*, 1 Nov 1929.

140. *NZH*, 6 Aug 1929. Note that Brigadier-General T.A. Blamey had become Chief Commissioner of the Victoria Police in Sep 1925; R. Haldane, *The People's Force*, Melbourne, 1986, p.194.

141. *NZPG*, 1929, pp.550, 567.

142. E.g. *PBH*, 10 Aug 1929; *Truth*, 19 Sep, 24 Oct, 12 Dec 1929.

143. *Truth*, 5 Jan 1928.

144. *Truth*, 14 Jul 1927, 5 Jan, 5 Jul 1928.

145. For further discussion regarding women police, see chs 3, 12.

146. Draft bill on file with notes dated 24 Sep 1928, P 2/1/2, part 1. The other clauses reflecting McIlveney's concerns related to the appointment of an Assistant Commissioner, the short-term exchange of police with Australian forces, increasing powers to dispose of property taken by police and of police entry to 'public places', and making the *NZPG* a 'privileged document'.

147. Circular letter to MPs from 'The members of the Police Force in Wellington', 21 Aug 1928, P 2/1/2, part 1; *LT,* 24 Aug 1928.

148. *NZH*, 29 Aug 1928; *NZPG*, 1928, pp.420, 718. See figure 1.2 for pay rates from 1 Apr 1928.

149. *NZPD*, 1928, vol.218, p.594; vol.219, pp.14–20, 366–7, 442–6, 657, 880–2; *Dominion*, 1 Sep 1928; *NZH*, 19 Sep 1928; *EP*, 25 Sep 1928. For further discussion on superannuation, see chs 3, 11.

150. Senior Sergeant H. Scott and 5 others to Commissioner, 26 May 1929; Commissioner to Minister of Justice, 16 Aug 1929, P 2/1/2, part 1. *NZPD*, 1929, vol.222, p.957; vol.223, pp.309, 1027, 1335. Cf. accounts of Wilford's comments in *NZH*, 12 Sep, 8 Nov 1929.

151. *NZPD*, vol.222, 1929, p.952.

152. *NZPD*, vol.219, 1928, p.16; see also pp.10–11, 20; and *Truth*, 1 May 1930.

153. The Court of Appeal judgement in *Rex v. Power* was reprinted for 'general information' in *NZPG*, 1929, pp.279–81; *Truth*, 2 Jun 1927, 19 Jun 1930; interviews with A.G. Quinn, 4 Jan 1977, H. Holmes, 5 Jan 1977; letter from F.R. Henry, 6 Dec 1977.

154.   The reports concerning the Bonisch affair are on W.B. McIlveney's personal file; see also *Truth*, 5, 12, 19, 26 Jun 1930. The 'informal' Committee was chaired by E. Page, and also comprised the retired Superintendent J.A. McGrath, and the Director-General of Mental Hospitals, Dr T.G. Gray. In Jun 1930, McIlveney was aged 63 with 36 and a half years service. His compulsory retirement was nearly two years away.

155.   *NZPD*, vol.224, 1930, p.249.

156.   *NZH*, 4 Jul 1930.

157.   F.G.B. Waldegrave, the Under-Secretary for Justice, had had control of the Force from Dec 1909 to Mar 1912.

158.   *NZPG*, 1930, pp.583, 868; W.G. Wohlmann to Minister of Justice, 8 Jul 1930, Wohlmann personal file; *Dominion*, 2, 3, 4, 5, 22 Jul 1930; *Truth*, 3 Jul 1930; *NZH*, 22 Jul 1930; *NZPD*, vol.224, 1930, p.611. See also Graeme Dunstall, 'Wohlmann, Ward George', *DNZB*, vol.4, pp.570–1.

159.   *Round Table*, vol.21, 1930–31, pp.217–18.

160.   G.R. Hawke, *The Making of New Zealand*, Cambridge, 1985, p.150, also pp.123, 127. The estimate of unemployment is from J. Macrae and K. Sinclair, 'Unemployment in New Zealand During the Depression of the Late 1920s and Early 1930s', *Australian Economic History Review*, vol.15, no.1, 1975, p.44.

161.   R.P. Ward to Minister of Justice, 24 Jul 1930, P 2/1/2, part 1; *NZPD*, vol.224, 1930, p.117.

162.   *NZPG*, 1930, pp.373, 520; *Dominion*, 9, 11 Jul 1930. Bonisch was reduced in seniority for two years for breaches of the Police Regulations. The government was not prepared to review other cases dealt with by Commissioner McIlveney. *NZPD*, vol.224, 1930, p.601.

163.   See, for example, the cases cited in *NZPD*, 1931, vol.228, pp.36–7; vol.230, pp.612–23.

164.   McIlveney had refused to allow policemen to claim the £250 reward offered by the State Insurance Office and the Council of Fire and Accident Underwriters' Associations. See *NZPD*, vol.224, 1930, p.602; P 1, 1929/1719.

165.   *NZH*, 3, 11 Oct, 31 Dec 1930.

166.   Reports on file P 13/1/–.

167.   E.g. at Roslyn, Little River, Millerton, Opotiki, Waitotara, and Westport. Submission of Commissioner Wohlmann to the Economy Committee, 6 Feb 1931, SSC 60/10/39. Cf. Annual Report, 1931, p.6; the new stations listed had been completed by Feb 1931.

168.   Annual Reports, 1930 and 1931, p.6; *CT*, 6 Aug 1930; *NZH*, 3 Sep 1930.

169.   Report of the Economy Committee, 1931, SSC 60/10/39.

170.   Final Report of the National Expenditure Commission, *AJHR*, 1932, B-4A, p.52. See also SSC 60/10/40.

171.   On 4 May 1932, an official of the Post and Telegraph Officers Association reported to another that 'a large meeting' of Wellington police held the day before had sent a deputation to the Prime Minister, George Forbes, and 'delivered an ultimatum that unless the police force were exempted from the cut, they would down tools. Evidently Mr Forbes recognised the key position the police held at the present time, because he agreed to the request made by the deputation, and promised to see that they received a bonus equivalent to the amount of the cut inflicted. Pretty hot isn't it? It appears that if one has the might it is quite easy to obtain the right.' A day later an Auckland PTOA official reported that 'the AK Police has also revolted last pay day'. Information from the Archives of the Post Office Union kindly supplied by the late Bert Roth. By late Apr 1932, uniformed police in both Auckland and Wellington were working hours of evening reserve duty in addition to their day shifts. According to E.R. Trask, then a constable in Wellington, the extra hours of work caused 'such an undercurrent of unrest' that the government restored the second pay cut. E.R. Trask to author, 3 Jul 1977.

172.   *NZPD*, vol.234, 1932, pp.309–10. Comments on departmental budgets in this

paragraph are based on the annual Financial Statement and the annual Appropriations for Consolidated Fund Services in *AJHR*, 1930 to 1934–35, B-6 and B-7.

173. *NZPD,* vol.240, 1934, pp.273–4. Cf. *ibid.,* vol.234, 1932, p.309; vol.237, 1933, p.560.

174. Police pay fell 10% while the Retail Prices Index fell 20.8% in the period. Money wage rates fell by about 18% between 1930 and 1933. See Hare, *Report on Industrial Relations*; also Hawke, *Making of New Zealand,* pp.125–6. Some retired men, many years later, remembered the second 'cut' but not its reversal by the 'allowance'.

175. *NZPD,* vol.240, 1934, p.274 (Cobbe).

176. Note that, of the 22 murders in 1933, one man killed his family of four; another murdered two adults. They are shown as six murders by six offenders in the police statistics. Annual Report, 1934, p.3.

177. *NZH,* 1 Jul 1931, 24 Jan 1932.

178. *Dominion,* 25 Jul 1933.

179. Annual Report, 1931, p.7.

180. *NZPG,* 1931, pp.80, 513; 1933, p.440.

181. *NZPG,* 1933, p.630.

182. This paragraph has been based mainly on the following sources: letters from C.W. Bowley, 18 Apr 1977; R.E.J. Brydon, 4 Jul 1977; E.J. Gaines, 28 Mar 1977; F.R. Henry, 29 May 1977; J.B. McLean, 28 Oct 1980; R.K. Marley, 13 Dec 1976; A.J. Mills, 12 Dec 1976; M.E. Parker, 4 Mar 1977; R.S. Rusbatch, 28 Nov 1980; J.A. du Temple, 12 Mar 1977; also jottings made by R. Sterritt from the station diaries of Constable D. Sterritt; and C.R. O'Hara, *Northland Made to Order,* Whangarei, 1986, p.93.

183. This and the next two paragraphs on the police role in the aftermath of the Hawke's Bay earthquake are based on the following sources: the Police Department file on the earthquake, P 1, 1931/301; Annual Report, 1931, pp.8–9; Lord Bledisloe to ,J.H. Thomas, Secretary of State for Dominion Affairs, 17, 19 Feb 1931, G 48/E/2; *Dominion,* 4, 5 Feb 1931; G. Conly, *The Shock of '31: The Hawke's Bay Earthquake,* Wellington, 1980; *Hawke's Bay 'Before' and 'After' the Great Earthquake of 1931: An Historical Record,* Napier, 1931, facsimile edn with additional chapters by D.G. Conly, 1981; M.D.N. Campbell, *Story of Napier, 1874–1974,* Napier, 1975, pp.129–39; M.B. Boyd, *City of the Plains: A History of Hastings,* Wellington, 1984, pp.255–64; interview with A.G. Quinn, 4 Jan 1977.

184. *Hawke's Bay 'Before' and 'After' the Great Earthquake of 1931,* p.69.

185. See ch.10 for further discussion of Wohlmann's concerns during 1931.

186. For the most detailed comparative discussion of events in three cities see R.J. Noonan, 'The Riots of 1932: A Study of Social Unrest in Auckland, Wellington, and Dunedin', MA thesis, University of Auckland, 1969.

187. A negative construction of the phrase from W.B. Sutch, *The Quest for Security in New Zealand,* Wellington, 1966, p.130. Sutch also commented (p.138) that the 'riots also seemed to have a cathartic effect – to have acted as an escape valve for pent-up feelings of frustration. Thereafter, unemployed workers could meet in hundreds and there was no breach of the peace.' This interpretation has been adopted by later historians.

188. The phase is taken from R.T. Robertson, 'Isolation, Ideology and Impotence: Organisations for the Unemployed during the Great Depression, 1930–1935', *NZJH,* vol.13, no.2, 1979, and is also used by Leo Clayton, 'The Angry Autumn of 1932: A Micro Study of the Collective Protest in Wellington on May 10 and 11, 1932', Hist 316 research essay, Victoria University of Wellington, 1998.

189. See also the assessments by Burdon, *New Dominion,* pp.142–4; L. Richardson, 'Parties and Political Change', in Rice (ed.), *Oxford History,* 2nd edn, pp.227–8; E. Olssen, 'Depression and War', in Sinclair (ed.), *Oxford Illustrated History,* pp.213–15. Accessible police reports on the disturbances in 1932 are scanty. Files held by the Security Intelligence Service and consulted by the author before they were transferred

to National Archives consist largely of newspaper reports, along with police reports relating mainly to the police dispersal of a crowd from a vacant section on Cuba Street in Wellington on 11 May 1932. Other police reports on the events and on the activities of individuals involved in the disturbances may well be scattered through the political surveillance files still held by the SIS which the author was unable to consult fully. Accordingly the following discussion of the disturbances relies on newspaper reports supplemented by other sources as indicated below. The relevant files held by National Archives are: P 1, 1932/521; P 1, 1932/616; P 1, 1932/628; P 1, 1932/654.

190.   *ODT*, 11, 12, 19, 20, 21 Jan 1932; *Truth*, 14, 21 Jan 1932; Orme Power to author, 24 Feb 1977.
191.   *ODT*, 12 Apr 1932.
192.   *ODT*, 11–21 Apr 1932; *NZPD*, vol.232, 1932, p.13; O. Power to author, 24 Feb 1977; E. Olssen, *A History of Otago*, Dunedin, 1984, pp.180–3.
193.   *NZH*, 14 Apr 1932; *Dominion*, 14 Apr 1932; F.R. Henry to author, 29 May 1977; J. Edwards, *Break Down These Bars*, Auckland, 1987, pp.36–9. See also Tony Simpson, 'Edwards, James Henry', *DNZB*, vol.4, pp.154–5.
194.   Unless otherwise acknowledged, the following account of the disturbances in Auckland is based on reports of the events and subsequent trials in *NZH*, 15, 16, 18, 22, 23, 28, 29, 30 Apr; 3, 4, 24, 25, 26, 27, 28, 30 May; 10, 14 Jun; 29, 30 Jul; 2, 3, 4, 5, 6 Aug 1932; *AS*, 16 Apr 1932; Report of Commander E.L. Berthon, 'Civil Disturbances in Auckland During 14th and 15th April 1932', and Commander F.A. Hull to Admiral Blake, 19 Apr 1932, N 8/15/7; Edwards, *Break Down These Bars*, pp.41–3; and the recollections gained by the author from retired policemen who were on duty at the time: C.W. Bowley, F.J. Brady, E.J. Gaines, F.R. Henry, A.J. Johnston, N. Kempt, R.K. Marley, A. du Temple, and H. Wilson. See also Noonan, 'The Riots of 1932', pp.107–28.
195.   Estimates ranged from '5000 rioters' (Minister of Justice) to '14,000 or 15,000' people (J.A. Lee. This was his first figure in the aftermath of the disturbance outside the town hall. Later, in Parliament, he spoke of 20,000).
196.   The report in *NZH*, 15 Apr 1932, included the added phrase: 'But do not use violence', which Edwards later claimed to have said. This interpretation was contested by police witnesses in Edwards' subsequent trial.
197.   N. Kempt to author, 4 May 1977.
198.   Bowley recaptured the man away from Queen Street at 12.15 am. C.W. Bowley to author, 18 Apr 1977; *NZH*, 25 May 1932.
199.   The pair, Detective Sergeant A.G. McHugh and Acting Detective F.J. Brady, were said to have made 18 arrests between them that evening. *NZH*, 16 Apr 1932; *AS*, 22 Apr 1932. This episode was (like others) incorporated in a modified form into the novel by John Mulgan, *Man Alone*, first published 1939, Longman Paul edn 1972, Auckland, pp.58–60.
200.   For example, Clarence Hirst, a member of the Junior Chamber of Commerce, and a Captain Fitzpatrick took a taxi to the police station, from where they went out with Detective Frank Brady to catch looters. C. Hirst to author, 8 Dec 1980.
201.   Hull to Admiral Blake, 19 Apr 1932, N 8/15/7.
202.   *NZH*, 15, 16 Apr 1932.
203.   Edwards gave himself up on 31 May. Edwards, *Break Down These Bars*, ch.5.
204.   See Hill, *Iron Hand*, pp.308–13.
205.   For further details on military assistance to the civil authorities see McIntyre, *New Zealand Prepares for War*, pp.126–7.
206.   Commissioner Wohlmann to Minister of Justice, 15 Apr 1932, P 2/1/9.
207.   P.J. Nalder to author, 27 Feb 1977. At this time, Detective Jim Nalder was responsible for political surveillance in Auckland. The words cited are from *NZH*, 16 Apr 1932. Commander Berthon was informed by Superintendent Till that 'serious disturbances and riots were expected in the Karangahape Road district'. 'Civil Disturbances in

Auckland During 14th and 15th April 1932'.

208. *NZH* and *AS,* 16 Apr 1932; Berthon, 'Civil Disturbances in Auckland During 14th and 15th April 1932'. This paragraph is based mainly on these sources and telegrams in N 8/15/7.

209. *NZH,* 16 Apr 1932.

210. Admiral Blake to Minister of Defence, 16 Apr 1932, N 8/15/7.

211. *NZH,* 16 Apr 1932.

212. Telegram from HMS Philomel to Navy Office, Wellington, 16 Apr 1932, N 8/15/7; *AS,* 16 Apr 1932. This paragraph is also based on Berthon, 'Civil Disturbances in Auckland During 14th and 15th April 1932'; Commander Hull to Admiral Blake, 19 Apr 1932, N 8/15/7; *NZH,* 16, 18, 20, 21, 23 Apr 1932; Colonel J.E. Duigan to Major-General Sinclair Burgess, 20, 23, 26 Apr, 7, 23 May 1932, AD 11, 2/1.

213. Although according to a naval report, Takapuna food shops were entered and goods obtained without payment after a meeting of local unemployed on the afternoon of Monday 18 Apr. N 8/15/7.

214. Elements of the civil emergency organisation were in place by 18 Apr, with an elaborate scheme on paper by 25 Apr 1932. See AD 11, 2/1. However various union leaders in Wellington denied any knowledge of general industrial action. *EP,* 19 Apr 1932.

215. McIntyre, *New Zealand Prepares for War,* p.127.

216. *EP,* 16 Apr 1932. This paragraph is also based on *EP,* 18, 19, Apr 1932; *Dominion,* 16 Apr 1939; *NZH,* 18, 19 Apr 1932; and memoranda on P 2/1/9.

217. Public Safety Conservation Act 1932, sec.2(1).

218. Secs 4, 5. The Act did allow for 'reasonable compensation for any property used or taken for or on behalf of the Crown'.

219. *CT,* 16 Apr 1932. This was also the view of mayor (and Labour MP) D.G. Sullivan. *EP,* 16 Apr 1932.

220. *CS,* 18 Apr 1932.

221. *CS,* 29 Apr 1932, and police reports in OPR 21/7/5.

222. Unless otherwise acknowledged, the following account of the Christchurch tramway strike is drawn from the Dave Welch, *The Lucifer,* Palmerston North, 1988; and from the *Press,* 4–19 May 1932.

223. Cummings to Commissioner, 3 May 1932, OPR 40/74/1. In contrast to the 'temporary constables', Special Constables were sworn in under the Justices of the Peace Act. However, in organisation, appearance and public perception, the temporary constables were to all intents and purposes 'specials'.

224. Minute dated 5 May 1932, OPR 40/74/1.

225. They had been stationed at the Worcester Street bridge. Lieutenant-Colonel, Southern Command to Headquarters, Wellington, 7 May 1932, AD 11, 2/1.

226. E.D. Mosley, SM, cited *Press,* 9 May 1932.

227. With trouble anticipated on Friday evening, 6 May, 800 specials were mustered for the evening, including 100 at the tramway sheds, 25 at the Addington sub-station, and 50 at the Central police station. A further 350 men were used on patrols the next day. Lieutenant-Colonel, Southern Command to Headquarters, Wellington, 7 May 1932, AD 11, 2/1. The total of 1500 was reported later by Cummings; *Press,* 9 Jun 1932.

228. *Press,* 16 May 1932; *CT,* 17 May 1932.

229. The following account is drawn mainly from *Dominion,* 9–16 May; *EP,* 11–14 May; and police reports in P 1, 1932/521. Also useful was the discussion in Noonan, 'The Riots of 1932'; and Clayton, 'The Angry Autumn of 1932'.

230. Estimates varied: *Dominion,* 11 May 1932 reported 2,500 to 3,000; *EP,* 11 May 1932, 3,000 to 4,000; Inspector Lander to Superintendent, Wellington, 11 May 1932, 'fully 5000 men, women and children'. Some hundreds joined the procession en route to Parliament Buildings.

231. From his appointment as Inspector in Apr 1930 until he took charge of the Wanganui

District in 1934, Inspector Lander was attached to Headquarters' staff for relieving duty throughout the country. He was seen as an able officer, having supervised the transition of Western Samoa from military to civil policing early in 1929. The procession went via Cambridge Terrace, Wakefield Street, Jervois Quay, Featherston and Bunny Streets.

232. Naval Secretary to Commissioner of Police, 11 May 1932, N 8/15/7. See also McIntyre, *New Zealand Prepares for War*, pp.127–8.

233. *Dominion*, 12 May 1932.

234. Quotations from *Dominion*, 12 May 1932; there is a similar account in *EP*, 12 May 1932.

235. Inspector Lander to Superintendent, Wellington, 12 May 1932, P 1, 1932/521.

236. For further comment, see ch.10.

237. *Dominion*, 20, 21 May 1932.

238. Data derived from returns of 'Persons convicted for offences in connection with recent industrial disturbances', P 1, 1932/654.

239. *EP*, 11 May 1932.

240. G.C. Donnelly to author, 19 Jan 1977.

241. *Truth*, 10 Jan 1934; Annual Report, 1933, pp.2, 8.

242. For further discussion of the Lakey murders, see ch.6.

243. In addition to references given below, the following paragraphs are also based on: Annual Reports, 1931 to 1935; *Truth*, 10 Aug 1932; 11 Jan, 5 Apr, 27 Sep, 6 Dec 1933; 10 Jan, 18 Apr, 3 Oct, 7, 21 Nov 1934; 16 Jan, 19 Jun 1935; *NZH*, 25 Mar, 21 Sep, 19 Oct, 1 Nov 1933; 27 Feb, 7 Apr, 14 Aug, 10 Sep, 24 Oct 1934; *Dominion*, 10 Jul, 16 Aug 1933; 27 Jan, 11, 12 Apr, 4 May, 15 Aug, 6, 10 Sep, 24 Oct, 1 Nov 1934; *CT*, 1, 6, 25, 28 Nov, 20 Dec 1933; 9 Nov 1934.

244. *NZH*, 28 Nov 1933. On the same day, J.G. Cobbe stated that 'The supply to all police stations of fast motor-cars would entail a large expenditure which the Government could not face just then, but the matter would be kept in view for consideration when better times arrived'. *NZPD*, vol.237, 1933, p.560. Note that critics focused on motor patrols in the cities rather than the countryside. By the mid-1930s, most constables at sole-charge stations provided their own cars and were paid an allowance for using them.

245. *Dominion*, 11 Apr 1934.

246. *NZH*, 20 Dec 1934.

247. The criticism was given impetus by the publicity given to a 'strong attack' on police methods by Baughan in a speech to the Christchurch branch of the Howard League for Penal Reform. *Dominion*, 27 Nov 1933. Miss Baughan was in part replying to comments by Justice Herdman (at Auckland) that the increase in the number of murders was related to the 'probability' that 'capital punishment will not follow the sheeting home of the prisoner's misdeed'. *NZH*, 25 Oct 1933. Baughan argued that 'crime detection was the first line of defence for the public from criminals'. D.G. Sullivan, a Christchurch Labour MP, followed up by asking the Minister whether there could be an interchange of New Zealand detectives with British officers. *NZPD*, vol.237, 1933, p.559. *Truth*, 6 Dec 1933, criticised 'the antiquated system under which the Criminal Investigation Branch is expected to function.' The *Dominion*, 12 Apr 1934, pressed for overseas training for New Zealand detectives, suggesting that two be selected each year to get a 'thorough grip of English methods of crime detection.'

248. *Dominion*, 4 May, 15 Aug 1934.

249. *NZH*, 14, 30 Aug 1934.

250. *AS*, 17, 18, 19, 20, 21, 22, 29 Sep 1934.

251. *NZPD*, vol.241, 1934, pp.239–40; *Dominion* 1, 3 Nov 1934. For criticism of the 'manhunt blunder' see *Truth*, 31 Oct , 7 Nov 1934. On 2 Oct, Stallworthy had commented that he had recently brought to Cobbe's attention 'serious misgivings amongst a section of the Force regarding the conduct of police examinations, with

particular reference to one branch'. Cobbe had assured him there was 'no room for misgivings' regarding the examinations. *NZPD*, vol.240, 1934, p.275.

252. *AS*, 2 Oct 1934; Belton, *Outside the Law*, pp.154–6.
253. *Dominion*, 4 Oct 1934; *NZPD*, vol.240, 1934, pp.242, 272–5.
254. Annual Report, 1935, p.6.
255. 'Notes of a Deputation from Representatives of Unemployed Workers which waited upon the Minister of Justice ... at Wellington on the 13th May, 1932; together with affidavits in support of the deputation', P 1, 1932/521; *EP*, 14 May 1932; *NZPD*, vol. 234, 1932, pp.310–12, 721–5.
256. *NZPD*, vol.237, 1933, p.560; *NZ Worker*, 14 Feb 1934.
257. *Press*, 9 Jun 1932.
258. *NZPD*, vol.234, 1933, pp.721–5; *Sun*, 10 Jun 1932; *Press*, 9 Jun 1932; *CT*, 9 Jul 1932.
259. *NZPD*, vol.240, 1934, pp.241–4, 841–7; *NZH*, 31 Aug, 1, 29 Sep, 27 Oct 1934.

Chapter 3: Careers and Community

1.   Interview with W.R. Murray, 16 Feb 1978. See also Graeme Dunstall, 'Murray, William Robert', *DNZB*, vol.4, pp.367–8.
2.   Graeme Salaman, *Community and Occupation*, London, 1974, p.45. His theoretical discussion is based on studies of British policing in the 1960s and shapes that of Robert Reiner, *The Blue-Coated Worker*, Cambridge, 1978. pp.208–13. It can be argued that the determinants of the New Zealand police occupational community had changed by the 1980s. See G. Dunstall, 'New Zealand Police, 1920–1980: An Isolated Occupational Community?', in S. Corcoran (ed.), *Law and History in Australia*, Adelaide, 1991, pp.77–87.
3.   A.J. Austin to author, 17 Feb 1977.
4.   The phrase is from Jerome H. Skolnick, *Justice Without Trial*, New York, 1966, ch.3. See also Reiner, *The Blue-Coated Worker*, pp.226–7.
5.   For an application of the concept of professionalisation to the development of policing, see also Samuel Walker, *A Critical History of Police Reform*, Lexington, Massachusetts, 1977.
6.   This and subsequent data on the backgrounds of constables who received permanent appointment in the calendar years 1882, 1922, and 1932 is based on an analysis of biographical entries in the PFDB carried out by Constable Isla Jones. Note that the Annual Reports between 1920 and 1926 give statistics of the birthplaces, religion, and prior occupations of those receiving permanent appointments.
7.   *NZPD*, vol.196, 1922, p.931.
8.   *ODT*, 24, 27 Apr 1918. These were proportions of 825 of the 901 members of the Force.
9.   *New Zealand Census*, 1921, part 7, 'Religions', pp.36–40; *Population Census*, 1936, vol.6, 'Religious Professions', pp.26–7.
10. W.R. Fell, interview with author, 4 Jan 1977.
11. Police Force Regulations 1919, no.142. Sec.2 of the Police Force Amendment Act 1919 provided for the appointment of temporary constables outside the prescribed age limits. The following discussion of the requirements for candidates and the procedures to be followed in making appointments is based on Police Force Regulations 1919, nos 143–160.
12. Note that the occupation listed in the PFDB was not necessarily the occupation immediately before entering, but that in which the recruit had been trained or spent the most time since leaving school.
13. W.S. Brown, interview with author, 5 Feb 1977.
14. K.B. Burnside, interview with author, 29 Jan 1980.
15. T.W. Allsopp, interview with author, 18 Nov 1976.
16. R.D. Hodge to author, 1 Mar 1977.

17.   The daily rate for an unskilled labourer has been calculated from the hourly award rate given in Hare, *Report on Industrial Relations*, p.119, table 7.

18.   *Ibid.*, p.125.

19.   E.J. Gaines to author, 14 Mar 1977.

20.   *New Zealand Census*, 1926, vol.9, 'Incomes'.

21.   Hare, *Report on Industrial Relations*, p.115.

22.   L.M. Hansen to author, 15 May 1977.

23.   F.R. Henry to author, 29 May 1977. Henry had been a law clerk, and then a salesman (on wages and commission) for a hardware company. He was working for the financially precarious Auckland *Sun* newspaper when he joined the Police in 1927.

24.   G. Diffey to author, 27 Apr and 17 Sep 1981.

25.   C.D. Taylor to Sherwood Young, 25 Nov 1989; H. McLean, interview with author, 17 Nov 1976.

26.   By 1950, the minimum qualification for the Police was the primary school sixth standard examination. During the 1930s a growing (but still small) proportion of police recruits had attended secondary school, some had passed the University Matriculation and/or the Public Service Entrance examinations, and a few (the Commissioner claimed) had completed courses at university. H.E. Campin, who joined in 1925, had spent three years at Victoria University College (1918–20) and passed five subjects towards a BSc. Henderson, *Quest for Efficiency*, pp.106, 131, 150, 175; Police Force Regulations 1950, no.32(2); *NZH*, 8 Jun 1935; *Dominion*, 13 Nov 1935; H.E. Campin, interview with author, 11 Jan 1977.

27.   Gideon Tait, *Never Back Down*, Christchurch, 1978, p.30; and more generally pp.24–9.

28.   C.J. Bell to author, 26 Apr 1977.

29.   These were the views of James Skinner, a former pupil teacher who joined in 1921, A.S. Chiles, who had passed both the Public Service Entrance examination and Matriculation and who joined in 1937, and D. Ross, an office worker who joined in 1933. Skinner, interview with author, 20 Jan 1981; A.S. Chiles to author, 5 Mar 1977; D. Ross to author, 2 Feb 1981.

30.   G.C. Urquhart to author, 30 Nov 1976.

31.   Belton, *Outside the Law*, p.14.

32.   W. George to author, 30 Mar 1977. By the 1970s there was a fourth generation of this family in the Police.

33.   F.J. Brady to author, 20 Feb 1977.

34.   E.F. Barry to author, 26 May 1977. He was the first (and until 1976 the only) serving policeman selected for the All Blacks, touring Australia in 1932.

35.   G.A. Howes, interview with author, 17 Aug 1978.

36.   E.G. Ward, interview with author, 3 Nov 1976.

37.   Burnside interview.

38.   M.E. Parker to author, 4 Mar 1977; A. Stapleton, interview with author, 24 Nov 1976; J.D. Walker to author, 20 Dec 1976.

39.   A.A. Congalton, 'Social Grading of Occupations in New Zealand', *British Journal of Sociology*, vol.4, no.1, 1953, p.55.

40.   *NZPD*, vol.188, 1920, p.144 (Veitch).

41.   Mulgan and Mulgan, *The New Zealand Citizen*, p.63.

42.   R.M. Burdon, *Outlaw's Progress*, Wellington, 1943, p.39.

43.   A.E.K. Keown to author, 7 Dec 1976; G. Diffey to author, 27 Apr 1981.

44.   O. Power to author, 24 Feb 1977, and interview with author, 19 Jan 1981.

45.   Holmes, interview with author, 5 Jan 1977.

46.   G.C. Donnelly to author, 19 Jan 1977.

47.   D.J. O'Carroll, interviewed by Constable Pullen, Jan 1982.

48.   R.V. Petrowski, interview with author, 20 Dec 1980.

49.   Burdon, *Outlaw's Progress*, p.38.

50.   *ODT*, 15 Jan 1927; *NZH*, 14 Mar 1927. McIlveney himself was 5 feet 10 inches tall.

51. Analysis of PFDBs by Constable Isla Jones.

52. O'Carroll interview.

53. Donnelly, letter to author. Seemingly naive applicants might be bluntly told to 'go away and grow up', as was a 21 year old apprentice baker at Oamaru. W. Stock, interview with author, 5 Dec 1976.

54. See, for example, the personal file of Archie Sutherland, a casein factory worker who applied (aged 20) at Auckland on 23 Oct 1924. Investigation of his employment history and associates in the North Island was not completed until 8 Dec, when the Inspector sent the file to the Commissioner with a recommendation that the applicant was 'a good type of man .... fit for the service'. (By then Sutherland had turned 21.) The Commissioner agreed; Sutherland was placed on the waiting list and notified accordingly on 18 Dec. He was not called up to enter the Training Depot until Jul 1925. P 38 (Acc 2857).

55. Police Regulations 149, 150, 324; *NZPG*, 1 Sep 1920, p.529; 9 Jan 1935, p.6 (which defined the prohibition of 'consanguinity to persons of definite criminal history, instincts, or conduct, or who are moral degenerates or defectives').

56. Mulgan and Mulgan, *The New Zealand Citizen*, p.63.

57. Annual Report, 1924, p.7, 1925, p.7. The total number of applicants in 1923/24 was 215 and in 1924/25, 229. These are the only years for which such statistics are available.

58. Belton, *Outside the Law*, p.15.

59. G. Innes to author, 31 Jan 1977.

60. For police training before 1921 (when the Depot reopened) see Hill, *Iron Hand*, esp. pp.113–16, 215–17, 258–9. See also L.B. Mason and M.F. Gordon (eds), *Trentham in Retrospect*, Featherston, 1982; and M.F. Gordon, 'Police Training 1869–1992', in S. Young (ed.), *With Confidence and Pride: Policing the Wellington Region, 1840–1992*, Wellington, 1994, ch.4, which also provide an outline of developments from 1921.

61. Willis Brown interview. Mr Brown remembered McNamara as 'Irish', but he was in fact born in Canterbury in 1872. McNamara served at both country and city stations before being promoted to Sergeant and becoming Instructor at the Training Depot in 1911. In Dec 1924, a year after becoming Inspector in charge of the Southland Police District, he retired early because of ill-health.

62. Willis Brown interview; A.J. Austin to author, 17 Feb 1977; N. Kempt to author, 4 May 1977. Scott became a Senior Sergeant in 1926, a year before he was transferred from the Depot to Headquarters in Wellington. He retired in 1950 at the rank of Superintendent.

63. Senior Sergeant George B. Edwards was at the Depot from Oct 1927 until it closed in Jul 1930.
    George Paine reopened the Depot at Rintoul Street as a Sergeant in Aug 1935. He remained Instructor until his promotion to Senior Sergeant on 1 Dec 1938 and transfer to Wellington Central three months later.
    Daniel C.B. Beard was sent to help George Paine instruct the two 'big batches' at Trentham in 1937. Beard succeeded Paine as Instructor at the Rintoul Street Depot in Mar 1939. The Depot closed in Nov 1939, reopening in 1941 (with Beard as Instructor) only for small intakes of women recruits. Dan Beard returned to the Wellington District Office in May 1946 when the Rintoul Street Depot was reopened for male recruits with Sergeant R.A. Prater as Instructor.

64. Standing on the site of the present Dominion Museum bulding, the Alexandra Barracks had also been used (and were known to recruits) as the Mt Cook gaol. With accommodation for 56 men, the Barracks were used to train bigger intakes than could be housed at the Rintoul Street Depot. The date of final use of the Barracks as a Training Depot has been derived from the recollections of retired men, and differs from that of 1921 given in Mason and Gordon (eds), *Trentham in Retrospect*, p.8.

65. Belton, *Outside the Law*, p.16. Except where otherwise indicated, this and the following

paragraphs on training at the Depot are based on Belton, pp.15–19; *ODT*, 25 Oct 1926; *Dominion*, 13 Nov 1935; and information from A.J. Austin, C.W. Bowley, F.J. Brady, H.E. Campin, G. Innes, N. Kempt, A.J. Mills, P.J. Nalder, D.J. O'Carroll, C. Reardon and E.R. Trask. The pattern of instruction at the Alexandra Barracks seems to have been virtually the same as that which both preceded and followed it at the Rintoul Street Depot.

66.   G. Innes to author, 31 Jan 1977.

67.   Belton, *Outside the Law*, p.18.

68.   Patrick Kearney (who was in the Depot between Aug and Oct 1923) remembered Scott saying: 'one thing I advise you to do is to get up in the morning and read the paper ... so that as a beat constable you will be ... able to discuss things with members of the business community passsing by. If you can't discuss things you'll just look a fool'. Interview with author, 5 Nov 1976.

69.   Notebook of H.A. Wilson (sworn in 1 May 1930) in the possession of the author. See also L.D. Monk, '[Notebook for Training School], Police Depot: Mt Cook Station', dated 3 Apr 1925, New Zealand Police Library.

70.   Defined in Police Regulations 124 to 139, with 'gossiping or loitering without lawful excuse' and 'failing or neglecting' to follow the 'defined directions' being disciplinary offences liable to punishment under Regulations 353(40) and 353(41). Harry Holmes remembered Senior Sergeant Edwards instructing his probationers: 'When you go out on the beat, walk as if this side of the street belongs to you and you are contemplating buying the other side'. H. Holmes, interview.

71.   W.R. Murray interview.

72.   Data on the examination results of Otto Anderson's intake (sworn in on 1 Oct 1922) are recorded on endcovers of Anderson's pocket dictionary, which was kindly supplied to the author by Peter Goodyear. Information on the subsequent careers of this intake is from PFDB, vol.2.

73.   Personal file of A. Sutherland, P 38 (Acc 2857).

74.   The common experience of those who did not receive Depot training is reflected in information from G.S. Austing, E.F. Barry, K. Burnside, M.J. Elliot, L.M. Hansen, C. Holmes, E.J.G. Hotham, R.S. Rusbatch, A.H. Stapleton, A.C. Strawbridge, and D.R. Sugrue. See also the experience of Ted Kingsbeer cited in Ray Carter, *'Beyond the Call of Duty'*, Palmerston North, 1988, p.59.

75.   Sir Robert Mark, *Policing a Perplexed Society*, London, 1977, pp.47, 117, sees the British police before the 1970s in these terms.

76.   'Personnel of 2nd Police Contingent, Trentham. 18 Aug – 18 Sep 1937', in B. Bevege, notebook in possession of author.

77.   P.J. Nalder to author, 30 Jan 1977; Willis Brown (interview) commented that at some point in this period the position on the seniority list within intakes was seen as determined by the date of application.

78.   Salaman, *Community and Occupation*, pp.27–30.

79.   The comments in this paragraph are based on letters to the author from and/or interviews by the author with 93 men who joined the New Zealand Police before 1945.

80.   Tait, *Never Back Down*, p.37.

81.   This calculation is based on data drawn from the PFDB, vol.2, by Constable Isla Jones. 1948 was chosen because the entries in vol.2 ended in that year.

82.   At an average of 4.8 annually in the 1920s and 6.6 annually in the 1930s. This calculation is based on data (for calendar years) extracted from the *NZPG* by Lois Baumfield.

83.   The murder was not solved. See a brief account in David A. Thomson and Hendrik Kagei, *A Century of Service*, Timaru, 1987, pp.30–1.

84.   The assailant was Henare Hona, who was suspected of murdering four members of the Davenport family eleven days earlier. Hona shot himself when about to be captured by police. There is a racy account in D.G. Dyne, *Famous New Zealand Murders*,

Auckland, 1974 edn, pp.166–73. Following closely the account in the *Dominion*, 22 Oct 1934, Dyne misspells the name of Heeps. See also the New Zealand Police Association *Newsletter*, Dec 1986, p.288.

85.   Sergeant W.R. Miller died (aged 55) in Feb 1924 following a period of failing health which was attributed to a 'severe blow' received during a street disturbance. Similarly, Detective Sergeant Michael O'Sullivan, who died in Mar 1934 'after a long illness', had been injured in the Auckland 'riots' in Apr 1932. Constable James Butler (aged 33) died of blood clots eight days after an assault by a drunken prisoner in Dunedin police station cells on Christmas Day 1937. A jury found the prisoner guilty of an assault causing actual bodily harm, but not guilty of manslaughter. *NZH*, 25 Feb 1924, 17 Mar 1934; *Dominion*, 10 Feb 1938; *NZPJ*, vol.5, no.4, Aug 1941, p.273.

86.   For example, Constable A.G. Begg (aged 26) was struck and killed by a train while looking for an escaped prisoner in the Parnell railway tunnel. Constable James Shields was killed, and Constable D. Robertson injured, when their car was struck by a train at Huntly. Constable P.S. O'Gorman died as a result of injuries received when he was struck by a taxicab while on duty in Great North Road, Auckland. Constable W.J. Watt was killed and Constable F.J. Black severely injured when their car plunged off a bridge during country inquiries in South Canterbury; *NZH*, 24 Feb 1926, 30 Oct 1933, 24 May 1935; *Press*, 11 Aug 1939.

87.   Constable C.H. Williams received a eulogy in the *Dominion* (14 Aug 1935) and posthumously a silver medal from the Royal Humane Society of New Zealand. J.D. Wills, *To Guard My People: Honours and Awards to the Police in New Zealand, 1861–1995*, Auckland, 1995, p.216.

88.   Constable H. Spence, aged 25, died of heart failure. He had been in the Police at Auckland for only ten weeks, after two and a half years in the NZEF. *NZH*, 18 Jul 1919.

89.   It seems that the fall resulted from the bag he was carrying becoming entangled in the handlebars of the bicycle. *MDT*, 9, 13 Jul 1936.

90.   Constable D.O. Brown shot himself a month after his transfer from Wellington (where he had been editor of the *Police Gazette*) to the Rakaia country station, leaving a note saying that 'worry over the work' was getting him down; *NZH*, 19, 26 Feb, 7 Mar 1930; *Truth*, 6 Mar 1930. Constable J.F.P. Simpson (aged 28) shot himself in the Dunedin police barracks; *Press*, 5 Oct 1932. Constable R.A. Dougherty, with twelve years' service, shot himself behind the Wanganui police station; *AWN*, 26 Jul 1933. Detective Sergeant E.F. O'Brien (aged 44), who had been showing signs of 'nervous tension' associated with his work, took his own life with a razor; *Truth*, 20 Sep 1933. The District Constable at Te Whaiti, H.M. Macpherson (aged 54), apparently concerned about chronic throat trouble and other personal problems, shot himself. *NZH*, 17 Jan 1936.

91.   *NZOYB*, 1946, p.62.

92.   In the first Police Provident Fund established in 1899, the qualification for a full pension had been (as defined by Police Force Act 1908, sec.27) 25 years' service or reaching 60 years of age. The Police Provident Fund was merged into the Public Service Superannuation Fund on 1 Apr 1910, when the conditions for the Police became the same as those for other state servants. See R. Hill, 'The Rise and Fall of the First New Zealand Police Superannuation Scheme', *International Police Association (NZ Section) Journal*, vol.19, 1985, no.3, pp.79–83, no.4, pp.73–5.

93.   Figures from 'Members of the Police Force in Wellington' to Commissioner, 21 Aug 1928, P 2/1/2; and Evidence of Commissioner Wohlmann to the Government Superannuation Funds Bill Committee, *AJHR*, 1932–33, I–15, p.178.

94.   *NZH*, 28 Oct 1938; *Truth*, 17 Feb 1923. Pensions for those retiring as 'medically unfit for further duty' were normally calculated on the basis of length of service. However, an officer retiring as a result of injuries received on duty could be granted a full pension (i.e. three-fifths of pay) irrespective of his length of service. Public Service Classification and Superannuation Act 1908, sec.36; Public Service

Classification and Superannuation Amendment Act 1909, sec.29; *Dominion*, 27 Feb 1923.

95.   Evidence of Sergeant A.E. Rowell to the Police Commission of Inquiry, 1919, typescript, p.442.

96.   Copy of Report to Commissioner of Police by Dr F.L. Scott, presented by Commissioner Wohlmann in evidence to the Government Superannuation Funds Bill Committee, *AJHR*, 1932–33, I–15, p.181. On 31 Mar 1932 there were 109 police stationed in Christchurch city and suburbs. The other police surgeons provided similar though less specific evidence; see *ibid.*, pp.179–81. Bouts of influenza amongst the Auckland police were sufficiently severe to be noted in the press in 1934 and 1939, as was measles in 1937. *NZH*, 10 Nov 1934, 12 Oct 1937, 21 Apr 1939.

97.   Examples from those reported in the press: Constable William Monson of Te Aroha had his ankle broken in a scuffle with a 'violent mental patient'; Constable G.W. Kilgour was rendered semi-conscious by a prowler in the grounds of Auckland's St Helen's Hospital; the injuries Constable J.C. Stewart received while attempting to arrest a car thief placed him permanently on 'sedentary duties'. *NZH*, 24 Jul 1923; *Truth*, 24 Sep 1933, *Press*, 27 Oct 1933, 8 May 1934, 24 Jul, 20 Sep 1935, 18 Apr 1939.

98.   On 1 Nov 1920, Constable Lindsay Templeton was shot in the knee while trying to capture a murder suspect; B. Thomson and R. Neilson, *Sharing the Challenge*, Christchurch, 1989, pp.91–2. Detective C.A. Lambert was shot in the stomach while arresting a burglar; *Dominion*, 10 Jun 1922. Constable H.J. Olsen of Waihi was shot while attempting to arrest a man who had just killed two schoolchildren at Waikino; Annual Report, 1924, p.9.

99.   'Members of the Police Force in Wellington' to the Commissioner, 21 Aug 1928, P 2/1/2.

100.   Copy of Report to Commissioner of Police by Dr C.H. Tewsley, presented by Commissioner Wohlmann in evidence to the Government Superannuation Funds Bill Committee, *AJHR*, 1932–33, I–15, p.179.

101.   An amendment to the Police Force Act 1913 to this effect was sought (unsuccessfully) in 1928 and again in 1929. See P 2/1/2; also *EP*, 25, 26, 27 Sep, 1 Oct 1928. In 1932, Commissioner Wohlmann also urged that police contributors who had reached the age of 60 have the right to retire on full pension after completing 35 years' service in his evidence to the Government Superannuation Funds Bill Committee, *AJHR*, 1932–33, I–15, p.178.

102.   Police Force Amendment Act 1924, sec.4, which amended and clarified the Police Force Act 1913, sec.13. In 1935 Commissioner Wohlmann proposed to amend the 1924 Act to give discretionary authority to senior officers in dealing with 'junior members' of the Force convicted of disciplinary breaches. With the change of government this legislative proposal lapsed, along with others. Commissioner Wohlmann to Minister in charge of the Police, 2 Aug 1935, P 2/1/2.

103.   *Dominion*, 27 Feb 1923.

104.   For example: Constable H.T. Smith of Kawhia, resigned Oct 1922, sentenced to three years' reformative detention Dec 1922; *NZH*, 9 Nov, 15 Dec 1922; P 1, 1923/707. Constable J. Blakely of Tolaga Bay, resigned May 1927, sentenced to three months' hard labour in Mar 1928; *PBH*, 5 Dec 1927, 7 Mar 1928. Constable A. McJennett of the Arms Office, Wellington Central, dismissed when charged in Nov 1923; *Dominion*, 15 Nov 1923.

105.   For example: Constable G.D. Fisher of Timaru, joined 1920, resigned when charged in Sep 1925; *Truth*, 26 Sep 1925.

106.   For example: Constable R.T.B. White of Dunedin, sentenced in Jul 1926 to a month's hard labour; *Dominion*, 22 Jul 1926. Constable J. Baxter of Hastings, charged, along with a nightwatchman, with breaking and entering, and theft since 1934; sentenced to four years' imprisonment in May 1936. Other police were implicated; one had to resign, and several were transferred. *Truth*, 6 May 1936; M.B. Boyd, *City of the*

Plains, Wellington, 1984, pp.246–7.

107. Constable S.F. Waters was dismissed when charged in Sep 1928. T.F. Carroll was attached to the Auckland Detective Office when he resigned in Sep 1927. Waters was injured in the explosion preceding a destructive fire at Carroll's grocery shop. Both men were sentenced to three years' imprisonment followed by two years' reformative detention in Nov 1928. *NZH*, 3, 10, 13 Nov 1928.

108. Constable W.L. Ramm resigned in Dec 1929, two weeks before being charged. Constable H.L. Stevenson was dismissed when charged in Dec 1929. Both were sentenced to two years' imprisonment. *NZH*, 20 Dec 1929, 30 Jan, 8 Feb 1930.

109. For example: at Auckland, Constable F. Hargreaves was acquitted by a jury of a private prosecution for assault causing bodily harm (a broken jaw). In a later case, a magistrate rejected a defence counsel's claim that his client had been assaulted by a constable who had a 'systematic way of annoying people'. Justice Herdman overturned a jury's award of damages against a constable for assaulting an elderly Maori at Mercer on the grounds that it was 'not ... a satisfactory one'. In Ashburton, a magistrate dismissed a charge of assault on the grounds that it was only 'technical'. In Greymouth, a constable was given a 'nominal' fine of £1, while the plaintiff was accused by the magistrate of 'bad blood' and had to pay his costs. In Timaru, the magistrate refused to convict an acting detective on the grounds that the assault had occurred in a moment of excitement. *Dominion*, 13 May 1923; *Press*, 23 Dec 1922, 1 May 1925; *ODT*, 6 Oct 1923, 25 Mar 1927; *NZH*, 6 Aug 1927.

110. *NZPD*, vol.209, 1926, p.1087; vol.216, 1927, p.652; *NZH*, 6, 20, 23 Aug, 7 Sep 1926.

111. *Press*, 10, 14 Sep 1927; *ODT*, 15 Sep 1927.

112. In 1930 a constable was charged and convicted of accepting a bribe of £3 to quash a charge of breaking and entering; *NZH*, 26 Feb 1930. The annual reports list only four charges of attempting to bribe a constable in the inter-war years. Two charges in 1929 related to a bookmaker who posted a pipe and £10 to two Hamilton detectives. He was sentenced to nine months' hard labour. Besides those listed in the annual reports, two other cases have been noted in newspaper reports, both involving money being offered to constables by people 'prohibited' from buying alcohol under the liquor licensing legislation. *Dominion*, 11 May 1926, 29 Sep 1927.

113. Lambert claimed that he had been entrapped into taking marked notes. *Truth*, 14 Apr, 9 Jun 1927; *NZH*, 18, 21 May 1927.

114. *Press*, 2, 5, 24 Oct 1935; *NZPD*, vol.243, 1935, pp.148, 507–9. In Aug 1935 Wohlmann sought an amendment to the Police Force Act making the acceptance of a bribe a disciplinary offence, thereby hoping to 'prevent any repetition' of such 'incidents'. Commissioner Wohlmann to Minister in charge of the Police, 2 Aug 1935, P 2/1/2.

115. *ODT*, 5 Nov 1924.

116. *NZH*, 30 May 1925.

117. *NZPD*, vol.230, 1931, p.613: E.J. Howard echoing the views of local Christchurch constables. See also *ibid.*, vol.228, 1931, pp.36–7: H.S. Kyle doing the same. Complaints of similar tactics were made of Inspector Donald Scott at New Plymouth between 1941 and 1944; Margaret Carr, *Policing in the Mountain Shadow*, New Plymouth, 1989, p.12.

118. Constable J. Carroll, of Reefton; *Truth*, 21 Oct 1926.

119. Senior Sergeant G. Scandrett, of Invercargill; *Truth*, 28 Jul 1927.

120. *Press*, 5 Mar 1929.

121. For example: the cases of Constables A.S. Wade (acquitted but resigned); A.C. Shilton of Hamilton; Garlick (Port Chalmers); and Shanley (Methven), who was given fifteen minutes to resign and was dismissed when he refused to do so; *NZH*, 15, 29 Mar 1928; *Press*, 29 Aug 1929, 10 Oct 1930. Commissioner McIlveney instructed that any entry into licensed premises by constables on duty or in uniform must be reported by the constables concerned; *NZPG*, 1928, p.298.

122. To this comment the magistrate remarked: 'It was the last straw that broke the

camel's back'. Constable Hannah was fined £1. *NZH*, 22 Dec 1928.

123. Sanvig had apparently pleaded guilty and thus was not entitled to an appeal. Since he had sought to resign, Sanvig sued the Commissioner for defamation on account of his dismissal and the grounds upon which it was initially made. On the direction of the Minister, the Commissioner had changed the grounds of dismissal to not having given the required notice of resignation. The judge decided that there was no case to go before the jury. *Dominion*, 27 May 1927.

124. Notably in the 1927 case of Senior Sergeant I.H. Mathieson of Ashburton, who had laid charges against some of his constables and in turn faced charges of offences under Police Regulations. He was found guilty, reduced to the rank of constable and transferred to Matamata. He was reinstated as Sergeant in 1928 and Senior Sergeant in 1930. His treatment was unpopular with Ashburton businessmen. *Press*, 27 Sep 1927; Thomson and Neilson, *Sharing the Challenge*, p.194.

125. Since Bonisch had pleaded guilty to the charges he was not entitled to an appeal under the Police Force Act. However the informal Appeal Board established by the Minister reinstated Bonisch as Sergeant from the date of his dismissal, 23 May 1930. C. Carr (Labour MP for Timaru) then asked the Minister (Cobbe) to set up an appeal court to investigate recent dismissals and disratings. Cobbe replied that such a court would be rendered unnecessary by likely amendments to the Police Force Act. Commissioner R.P. Ward and his successor Wohlmann recommended changes in Jul 1930. Five years later, Wohlmann asked again, while claiming that since 1930 'no member of the Force has been deprived of his right of appeal'. The changes were needed merely to give this policy statutory effect. W.B. McIlveney, personal file; *NZPD*, vol.225, 1930, p.555; Commissioner to Minister, 21 and 24 Jul 1930, 2 Aug 1935, P 2/1/2.

126. This was claimed by W.E. Barnard, the Labour MP for Napier; *NZPD*, 1929, vol.222, pp.951–3; vol.223, p.677.

127. Of the 75 who joined in 1932, one resigned in 1934, twelve between 1935 and 1941, and a further twelve between 1944 and 1947. In addition, eleven were dismissed between 1934 and 1942.

128. I.e. the unlicensed bar. C.E.W. Black to author, 22 Mar 1977.

129. Police Regulations 1919, nos 314 and 316. Regulation 310, which allowed $1^1/_4$ days paid leave for every month's service (this could accumulate for three years so that 45 days could be taken at a time) was superseded in 1925 by the allowance of two days paid leave per month (which could accumulate for two years). Commissioner McIlveney asserted his discretion publicly in rejecting ex-Detective W. Cooper's claim for payment for 46 days' accumulated leave: 'in the New Zealand Police Force leave is a privilege and not a right'. *ODT*, 15 Sep 1927.

130. From 1877 until 1919, beat constables on day duty worked broken shifts: either 5 am to 9 am and 1 pm to 5 pm, or 9 am to 1 pm and 5 pm to 9 pm, alternating between early and late shifts on successive days. In 1919, eight-hour shifts were introduced for beat duty: constables and sectional Sergeants working from 5 am to 1 pm one week, and 1 pm to 9 pm the next, and then two weeks on night duty. From 1926 day-duty shifts alternated from early (5 am to 1 pm) one day to late (1 pm to 9 pm) the next, allowing the possibility of a 'free' evening every second night. Night duty was from 9 pm to 5 am. *NZH*, 5 Feb 1919; evidence of Superintendent S.P. Norwood to the Police Commission of Inquiry, 1919, pp.10–12; *NZPG*, 1922, p.8; 1926, pp.131, 653.

131. In 1895 the Commissioner announced that henceforth no leave would be granted to play football or to travel with football and athletic teams; cited by Carr, *Policing in the Mountain Shadow*, p.153.

132. For example: Chris McRae (boxing); Ambrose Rush and H.R. (Dick) Godfrey (wrestling); and a father and son, A.T. Cleverley (wrestling and boxing) and 'Alf' Cleverley (boxing), amongst others recalled by Wallie Ingram, 'Policemen in Sport', *NZ Listener*, 16 Sep 1966. For wrestling, see also Carter, *'Beyond the Call of Duty'*, pp.290–1.

133. Tyree became the Wellington heavyweight boxing champion in the late 1920s. While at Palmerston North he also played rugby for a local club, representing Manawatu, Bush, and then Wellington in 1927 and 1928. Carter, *'Beyond the Call of Duty'*, pp.281, 283. Commissioner Wright objected to police involvement in professional boxing; *Dominion*, 27 Feb 1923.

134. *AWN*, 2 Jun 1927; *NZPD*, vol.222, 1929, p.955 (Coates), p.957 (Wilford).

135. Barry was the first serving member of the Police to be selected as an All Black; E.F. Barry to author, 26 May, 20 Jun 1977. Amongst other prominent rugby players (and athletes) in the 1920s and 1930s were A.S. Ward (Manawatu) and D.G.McK. ('Dufty') Simpson, who represented both Waikato and Canterbury in rugby, and the New Zealand Police in wrestling and field events at the New South Wales Police Carnival in 1934. Carter, *'Beyond the Call of Duty'*, p.284; Thomson and Neilson, *Sharing the Challenge*, pp.301–2.

136. *Press*, 28 Sep, 3 Oct 1932; *Dominion*, 10 Aug 1933, 23 Aug 1934.

137. Ingram, 'Policemen in Sport'; and *Legends In Their Lifetime*, Wellington, 1962, pp.185–200. See also Max Smith, *Champion Blokes*, Christchurch, 1964, pp.108–11. Sutherland was a track and field all-rounder, winning titles in the high jump; hop, step, and jump; long jump; pole vault; shot put; and javelin. He also competed in hurdles and discus. Munro dominated the national championships in discus, shot put, and javelin; McHolm dominated in hammer-throwing.

138. A good example is C.C. Dunsford, who joined in 1907. After four years on the beat he entered the watch-house and then the district office at Dunedin, to which he returned after war service. A keen bowler, he represented the Police in the annual Government Services bowls tournament during the 1920s. *Truth*, 17 Jan 1925.

139. F.R. Henry to author, 29 May 1977; also G.C. Urquhart to author, 30 Nov 1976.

140. R.E.J. Brydon to author, 4 Jul 1977; G. Diffey to author, 24 Apr 1981; W. George to author, 30 May 1977; E.B.V. Horne to author, 1 Mar 1977; D.R. Sugrue to author, 22 Nov 1976; J.A. du Temple to author, 3 Mar 1977; A.W. Wilson to author, 25 Nov 1976.

141. L. Harrowfield to author, 26 Nov 1976; R.D. Hodge to author, 1 Mar 1977; J.A. Feely to author, 31 Mar 1977; N. Kempt to author, 4 May 1977; A.E.K. Keown to author, 7 Dec 1976; J. Matheson to author, 30 Apr 1977; O. Power to author, 24 Feb 1977; R.S. Rusbatch to author, 30 Nov 1980.

142. Willam Carran was born on the family property at Bell Block, Taranaki on 3 Aug 1898. Both his parents were of the Puketapu hapu of Te Ati Awa. See Sherwood Young, 'Carran, William', in *DNZB*, vol.5, forthcoming. As an NCO in Wellington from 1937, Carran became known as a disciplinarian and a stickler for enforcing the licensing laws, a reputation which he maintained as a commissioned officer. With a racist resonance, some critics within the Force dubbed him 'the black-tracker'.

143. John Beazley, appointed a Native Constable at Rawene in 1897, became a temporary constable in 1921 (at the age of 59) when his station changed its status to one requiring a full-time policeman. He resigned two years later.

144. See Richard Hill, 'Maori Policing in Nineteenth Century New Zealand', *Archifacts*, 1985, no.2, pp.54–60; *Colonial Frontier Tamed*, pp.83–5, 332–3; *Iron Hand*, pp.59–60, 64–7, 127–30, 135–6, 244–7.

145. This paragraph is based on views expressed in 1936 by Inspector H. Martin (Gisborne) and Superintendent D.C. Fraser (Christchurch), and on responses of police to a memorandum in Sep 1950 from Commissioner J.B. Young seeking opinions on the 'employment of members of the Maori Race as Policemen to deal with matters concerning members of their own Race only'; and in particular the views of Senior Sergeants F. Taylor (Taumarunui), R. Griffith (Taihape), C. McRae (Wairoa), G.S. Norris (Gisborne), L.E.G. Wilson (Ruatoria), E.E. Strawbridge (Kaitaia), and J. Greenlees (Dargaville); and Constable F.A.H. Skerritt (Raetihi). *Press*, 15 Jul 1936; *PBH*, 20 Jul 1936; P 25/4/–.

146. With the appointment of a 'regular' constable at Te Kaha in 1945, Hira was transferred

(as a temporary constable) to Ruatoria, where he retired in Jul 1960. The Senior Sergeants in charge of the Ruatoria station received 'valuable assistance from Constable Hira ... in many ways when dealing with matters concerning Maoris in this district.' Reports of Senior Sergeants Taylor and Wilson, 29 Sep, 17 Oct 1950, P 25/4/–. See also J. Rorke, *Policing Two Peoples: A History of Police in the Bay of Plenty 1867– 1992*, Tauranga, 1993, p.258; J. Robinson, *Policing the Tairawhiti: The Gisborne Police District 1769–1995*, Gisborne, 1995, p.135.

In 1950 Bidois left Te Whaiti for Rotorua, where he retired in 1953. He died in 1955. See Jinty Rorke, 'Bidois, Louis Hekenui', *DNZB*, vol.4, p.60.

147.   Reports in P 25/4/–.

148.   *NZPD*, vol.222, 1929, pp.1141, 1143; *EP*, 20 Sep 1929.

149.   *NZPD*, vol.260, 1941, pp.137–8. (Webb was acting Minister in the absence of Peter Fraser. The four appointees have not been identified by the author.) See also *ibid.*, vol.261, 1942, pp.413–14; vol.266, 1944, pp.370, 372; vol.272, 1945, pp.144–5; vol.275, 1946, pp.11–12.

150.   Report of Senior Sergeant R. Griffith, 29 Sep 1950, P 25/4/–.

151.   Young reported to the Minister, W.H. Fortune, that he 'was very surprised to learn that the Officers are almost unanimously opposed to the suggestion' that Maori be appointed 'to deal with matters concerning members of their own Race'. In directing the Minister's attention to Inspector Peter Munro's report, the Commissioner supported Munro's view that 'under the provisions of the Maori Social and Economic Advancement Act, 1945, the Maori has been given all the powers that he should have and which he is capable of carrying out.' Inspector Munro also commented that: 'The Maori temperament appears to direct him to do one of two things: he is either indolent and care free or extreme in how he conducts himself, he does not seem to be capable of contriving a middle course of conduct. With certain exceptions the Maori does not possess the efficiency, confidence, and initiative which should endow one entrusted with the enforcement of the criminal law among his own people.' Munro to Commissioner, 4 Oct 1950; Commissioner to Minister, 2 Nov 1950, P 25/4/–.

152.   Hill, *Colonial Frontier Tamed*, p.354; *Iron Hand*, pp.138–40, ch.25.

153.   Annual Report, 1918, p.11; 1919, p.15. Comments on the role and work of Police Matrons in 1916–17 can also be found in P 22/21/–.

154.   *Dominion*, 19 Oct 1916; Memoranda to the Commissioner from Superintendent Wright (Dunedin), 28 Aug 1916; Superintendent Dwyer (Christchurch), 28 Aug 1916; Inspector Hendrey (Wellington), 2 Sep 1916; Superintendent Kiely (Auckland), 4 Sep 1916; Commissioner Cullen to Minister in charge of the Police, 29 Aug 1916; Commissioner O'Donovan to Minister in charge of the Police, 11 Apr 1921. Unless otherwise acknowledged, this and the next three paragraphs are based on police memoranda and newspaper cuttings on file P 22/21/–. Commissioners were also aware of the development of British official thinking as represented in *Report of the Committee on the Employment of Women on Police Duties*, London, 1920; and *Report of the Departmental Committee on Employment of Policewomen*, London, 1924. See also the account in Hill, *Iron Hand*, ch.25.

155.   Rachel Don, letter to editor, Dunedin *Evening Star*, 4 Nov 1916; the same point was made by Dr E.H. Siedeberg and the President and Secretary of the SPWC in letters of same date to the *Evening Star*, as well as many others subsequently; P 22/21/–.

156.   Report of a deputation from the WCTU, Salvation Army, Civic League, Political League, and YWCA, *AS*, 23 Jun 1917. See also the reported comment of the National Secretary of the WCTU, Miss Henderson, that 'there was no need for the patrol officer to call a policeman. The patrol officer should be given power to take a refractory girl to the police station. That would not humiliate her so much as if it were done by a policeman'; Christchurch *Sun*, 16 Jul 1917.

157.   *Dominion*, 19 Oct 1916.

158.   *CS*, 17 Jul 1917.

159. Commissioner to Minister of Justice, 14 Apr 1921, P 22/21/–.
160. Miss C. Henderson, Secretary, WCTU, to Prime Minister, 31 Jul 1917, listed the 'main duties required of women police in countries where they are now employed' in order to clear up 'some misapprehension regarding the nature of the duties these women would be required to perform'. The list ended with the comment that 'the work of the women police should be largely of a "preventive nature" '.
161. Police Regulations 1919, no.326.
162. The Health Patrols consisted of two women in each of the four main centres, appointed under the Social Hygiene Act 1917, sec.12. They were controlled by the Public Heath Department, and the Police were expected to cooperate with them. The Health Patrols ended after budgetary cuts in 1921/22. *NZPG*, 1919, p.636; J. Green, 'The Society for the Protection of Women and Children: Dunedin Branch 1914–1945', BA (hons) long essay, University of Otago, 1982, pp.14, 24–5.
163. Betty Holt, *Women in Council*, Wellington, 1980, p.18.
164. Christchurch *Sun*, 14 Dec 1916. Sheppard cited Judge Parry, *The Law and the Woman*, published in 1916.
165. Miss Jean Begg, Secretary of the Auckland YWCA, who had served as a policewoman for four months in New York while studying criminology at Columbia University; *NZH*, 29 Dec 1929.
166. Salmond to Commissioner of Police, 16 Oct 1916, P 22/21/–.
167. *Dominion*, 28 May 1927, 17 Feb 1928; *NZH*, 18, 22 Feb 1928; *ODT*, 2, 6 Mar, 28 Apr 1928; *PBH*, 20 Apr 1928; *Press*, 30 Aug 1928; *NZPD*, 1928, vol.218, p.594; vol.219, pp.446–7; draft Police Force Amendment Act 1928, typescript, P 2/1/2.
168. *NZH*, 15 Mar, 7 Jun, 21 Sep 1929; *PBH*, 28 Mar, 15 May 1929; *Dominion*, 12 Sep 1929; *NZPD*, vol.222, 1929, pp.1141–2, 1147, 1149–50. Wilford had long opposed the appointment of policewomen. As Minister of Justice in 1918 he had commented: 'The only women, in my opinion, who would be fit to be women police are women who would not take such positions'. *NZH*, 25 Oct 1918.
169. *Dominion*, 10 Feb 1930.
170. The 1928 bill was redrafted by the Law Drafting Office early in 1930 in the name of Sir Thomas Sidey and retaining provision for the appointment of policewomen. On 26 Jun, the new Minister of Justice, Cobbe, asked McIlveney for his 'notes' on the bill. Shortly before he resigned, McIlveney responded that the bill had been initially prepared to give effect to Rolleston's undertaking that women police would be appointed. While noting that this had been 'strongly urged' for 'many years past' and that there were precedents overseas, McIlveney commented that 'it will not be necessary to increase the present staff of women employees in the Force for some time yet.' McIlveney to Minister of Justice, 27 Jun 1930; R.P. Ward to Minister of Justice, 24 Jul 1930, P 2/1/2. Commissioner Wohlmann did not include provision for the appointment of policewomen in his 1935 draft bill amending the Police Force Act.
171. One of her brothers, D.J. Cummings, was then Commissioner. *NZPJ*, vol.2, no.2, Apr 1938, p.67.
172. Miss E.L. Jeffery to author, 14 Mar, 11 Apr 1978.
173. *Ibid.*; also newspaper cuttings supplied by Miss Jeffery: *WN*, 9 May 1945; *Truth*, 6 Mar 1946; two unsourced cuttings dated 1946 and 1968.
174. Salaman, *Community and Occupation*, p.34.
175. See Len Richardson, *Coal, Class and Community: The United Mineworkers of New Zealand, 1880–1960*, Auckland, 1995.
176. R.S. Rusbatch to author, 30 Nov 1980.
177. For the formation of the Association see ch.11.
178. *NZPG*, 1935, p.142; Thomson and Kagei, *Century of Service*, p.31.
179. *NZPG*, 1922, p.540; *ODT*, 1 Sep 1922. £79 was also collected in Napier for H.I. Montgomery from police and public.
180. This incident (like others) was given currency by the New Zealand Press Association and reported, for example, in the *PBH*, 13 Feb 1930. It was remembered by T.W.

Allsopp and H.A. Wilson, who were present at the parade, and recounted to the author by Mr Allsopp on 18 Nov 1976 and Mr Wilson on 10 Jan 1977. The story was also recalled by other retired men who joined after the event, such as G.C. Urquhart, who joined in 1936 and was never stationed in Auckland. Urquhart to author, 8 Dec 1976.

181. G.S. Austing, 'From Farm Hand to Assistant Commissioner', typescript, 1976, p.10. Mr Austing retired as Assistant Commissioner (in charge of the Auckland District) in 1972.

182. For Ashburton and Timaru, see above for the sources cited regarding the cases of Senior Sergeant I.H. Mathieson (1927) and Detective L. Studholme (1935) respectively. At Gisborne in 1935, Constable R.C. Hendren, convicted of 'scandalous behaviour' at an internal inquiry held by Inspector H. Martin, brought a private prosecution of Martin for 'obscene exposure' on a local beach. The prosecution was eventually withdrawn; Constable Hendren was convicted at another internal inquiry of making a false statement, and then dismissed. So too (after an internal inquiry) was Constable H. Scandrett, who had given evidence in support of Hendren's allegation. Inspector Martin was transferred to Christchurch. *Dominion*, 1 Feb, 30 May 1936; *Truth*, 5 Feb 1936; *PBH*, 10, 24 Feb 1936. See also ch.9.

183. See, for example, Belton, *Outside the Law*, pp.52–4. The recruitment and work of detectives is discussed further in ch.6.

184. Police Regulations 1919, no.400.

185. In 1927 some uniformed Senior Sergeants protested that Cummings was junior to them in service. However, Commissioner McIlveney maintained Cummings' position on the seniority list that O'Donovan had established in 1921. McIlveney asserted in 1926 that 'promotion comes by merit, and ability and seniority, in that order'. Even so, he did not depart from seniority in promoting men who were 'qualified' by examinations. *NZPG*, 1922, p.8; *NZH*, 27 Aug 1926; P 2/1/2, part 2. As Commissioner, James Cummings created a furore in 1949 by attempting to promote Senior Detective W.R. Fell to Sub-Inspector over the heads of 50 others. This accelerated promotion 'on merit' (shown especially in a murder case) was prevented by an injunction obtained by members of the New Zealand Police Association who had been passed over. McGill, *No Right to Strike*, p.51.

186. In 1926 McIlveney established an 'independent' Examination Board, comprising a magistrate (W.G. Riddell) as chairman, and Inspector Rawle representing the Detective Branch and Superintendent Wohlmann the Uniform Branch. The Board would award the marks, whereas hitherto the Commissioner had both set and overseen the marking of the papers. Henceforth the Commissioner would set only the papers on police duties, while the magistrate set the papers on law; Robert Darroch set the examination on 'Literary subjects'. *NZPG*, 1919, p.536, 1926, p.152; *Dominion*, 27 Aug 1926.

187. Police Regulations 1919, nos 409–414, set out the broad prescriptions for the qualifying examinations for the ranks of Sergeant, Senior Sergeant, and Sub-Inspector. These did not change until 1938. Darroch also indicated the textbooks to be studied. *NZPG*, 1932, p.152.

188. In the 1931 Sergeant's examinations, nineteen passed only the 'Literary' paper, and two only the law and police duties papers. In the Sub-Inspector's examinations, six passed only the 'Literary' paper, and seven only the law and police duties papers. *NZPG*, 1931, pp.662–3.

189. Officers were not to recommend for promotion anyone who 'is not of strictly sober habits, and who is not an efficient, energetic, and trustworthy member of the Force'. Nor would anyone be promoted who had been fined for 'any serious misconduct against discipline, or neglect of duty' within the two preceding years, or who had been fined for intoxication within the preceding four years. No constable or detective could be promoted unless he was certified as physically fit to perform the duties of a Sergeant in charge of constables on day and night duties in the main cities. Police Regulations 1919, nos 421, 422, 425. It is not clear how closely these requirements were adhered to.

190.   For example, Sergeant F.A. Waterman took charge of the Ponsonby station in Auckland in 1917 and two years later refused promotion to Senior Sergeant in order to avoid a transfer south. Waterman remained as Sergeant at Ponsonby until his retirement in 1928. A refusal to be transferred (if required) on promotion meant that one's name would be 'placed at the bottom of the promotion list' for the rank. *NZH*, 2 May 1928; Police Regulations 1919, no.424.

191.   Of four others of the 1922 intake who rose to the rank of Chief Inspector, two had nine transfers, one had ten, and one had thirteen. In 1929, Commissioner McIlveney ordered that men under 'orders to transfer' must cease delaying their departures 'to suit their own convenience regardless of departmental interests'; *NZPG*, 1929, p.263. At this time MPs expressed concern at the numbers and methods of transfers; *NZPD*, vol.222, 1929, p.194; vol.224, 1930, pp.601–2.

Chapter 4: The Broad Patterns

1.   Belton, *Outside the Law*, p.14.

2.   This comment is based on my own reading of *Truth*, and also Richard S.L. Joblin, 'The Breath of Scandal: *New Zealand Truth* and Interwar Society, 1918–1939', MA thesis, University of Canterbury, 1990, pp.29–33, 214–16, 221–2.

3.   *EP*, 27 Sep 1928. The unnamed 'critic' was answered by 'Half-century, Not Out', who pointed to the killings on duty of Constables Dudding and Dorgan in 1919 and 1921 respectively (and could have included those of Constable N. McLeod in 1890, Sergeant J.P.H. McGuire in 1910, and Constable John Doyle in 1913) and the injuries suffered by police. The nature and extent of serious offences was also emphasised. *Ibid.*, 1 Oct 1928. For further discussion see the conclusion.

4.   This assessment is based on a broad comparison of the New Zealand conviction rate for homicide with that of Australia in the inter-war years, and of New Zealand rates for reported murders and manslaughter with those of England and Wales. It can only be a tentative judgement, since criminal jurisdictions (and criminologists) have operated differently in defining the offences constituting 'homicide' for statistical purposes. Moreover, the number of murders and manslaughters initially recorded by police may bear little relation to the numbers of such offences prosecuted or for which offenders are convicted: 'murders' may become 'manslaughters', and in both Australia and New Zealand there were high rates of acquittal in the inter-war years. It can be argued then that criminal homicides are probably best defined by conviction rates rather than by the initial definitions given by police. The sources for the comparison were: Miles Fairburn and Stephen Haslett, 'Violent Crime in Old and New Societies', *Journal of Social History*, vol.20, Fall 1986, p.92, table 1d (from which conviction rates were calculated for New Zealand); Satyanshu K. Mukherjee, *Crime Trends in Twentieth-Century Australia*, Sydney, 1981, pp.177–8 (for conviction rates); and Dane Archer and Rosemary Gartner, *Violence and Crime in Cross-National Perspective*, New Haven, Connecticut, 1984 (for rates of reported murders and manslaughters in England and Wales, which were compared with New Zealand rates calculated by the author). For the New Zealand homicide rate per 100,000 people, which includes manslaughters and attempted murders as well as murders recorded by the Police, see figure I.3.

5.   See ch.10.

6.   H. Roth, *Trade Unions in New Zealand*, Wellington, 1973, pp.46–53 and table 5, which gives the numbers of strikes and workers involved.

7.   Keith Bottomley and Clive Coleman, *Understanding Crime Rates*, Farnborough, England, 1981, especially pp.145–53, see criminal statistics as 'indices of organisational processes', but also as more than this. The arguments of this book have influenced the following discussion of police statistics.

8.   For example, arrests (under the Police Offences Act) for breach of the peace;

drunkenness, and being drunk and disorderly; using 'profane, indecent, or obscene language'; inciting violence, disorder or lawlessness'; assaulting or resisting constables; 'soliciting prostitution'; and vagrancy. See figure 4.1 for totals of 'Police Offences' in the inter-war years.

9.   G. Innes to author, 23 Mar 1977; *ODT*, 15 Jun 1928; Belton, *Outside the Law*, p.119.

10.   Police Regulations 1919, no.350; and instructions attached to the Annual Offence Return sent to stations.

11.   G. Innes to author, 23 Mar 1977. The problem of bicycles was of long standing. For Christchurch, Superintendent Dwyer reported that there were 'only 130 undetected offences' during 1919, 'and these chiefly consisted of thefts of bicycles.' In 1932 the Inspector in charge of the Invercargill District saw the increase of recorded offences in his district during the preceding year as being partly 'due to a better system of recording crime reported during the year'. Annual Report, 1920, p.13.

12.   During parliamentary question time in Nov 1945, R. Algie commented that when he mentioned to a detective that the Police Department claimed a detection rate of 90 to 95% 'and congratulated him on the achievement, ... the detective had laughed ironically.' *NZPD*, vol.272, 1945, p.143.

13.   The large number of arrests in 1925 under the Shipping and Seamen Act reflects the effect of an unofficial strike by British seamen, who walked off their ships at the first port of call. See B. Roth and J. Hammond, *Toil and Trouble*, Auckland, 1981, pp.110–11.

14.   The percentages cited here are calculated from arrests and summonses for 'drunkenness' (undefined) in the annual reports, Appendix A, 'Police Offences Act' section. This category represents 'drunk and incapable', which constituted the great majority of arrests for public drunkenness. Compare this data with those in figure I.4, which are calculated from the total of all offences involving public drunkenness, including the categories in Appendix A of 'drunk and disorderly' and 'drunk while in charge of horses etc., or loaded firearms', but not being drunk in charge of motor vehicles.

Chapter 5: City Constables

1.   Belton, *Outside the Law*, p.21; G. Innes and C. Bowley to author. These sources are drawn on extensively for the following discussion of the experience of beat work.

2.   A.T. Kelk, O. Power, F.J. Brady, P.J. Nalder, N. Kempt and E.J.G. Hotham to author, and G.S. Austing's 'From Farm Hand to Assistant Commissioner', detailed conditions in Auckland barracks. Similar conditions in Wellington barracks were described in letters from G.C. Donnelly, L.M. Hansen, E.R. Trask and G.C. Urquhart. A letter from E.B.V. Horne and a memoir of M. Thyne supplied to the author by Mrs Thyne in Nov 1980 commented on conditions in Christchurch.

3.   M.E. Parker, L.M. Hansen, and J.P. Clements to author; interview with D.J. O'Carroll; memoir of M. Thyne, p.19.

4.   The only exception known to the author is that of H.E. Campin, who in 1925 went straight from the Depot into the Wellington Detective Office, where he remained until 1937. Campin did not don a uniform until he became a Sub-Inspector. H.E. Campin, interview, 11 Jan 1977.

5.   And indeed learning the route itself: John Feely, like other new constables in unfamiliar cities, became lost during his first night on the beat in Dunedin and needed directions from a railwayman to get back to the police station for his supper. Feely to author. See also Belton, *Outside the Law*, pp.21–2.

6.   M. Thyne, memoir, pp.5–6, 9–10.

7.   City Sectional Reports, Taranaki Street Police Station, P-Wellington 31/1. These are the only city sectional reports for the inter-war years that the author has found; hence the reliance on them in the discussion of beat work. They seem to relate to the investigation of charges against Sergeant G. Bonisch.

8.   Comments to author by E.R. Trask (letter), G.C. Donnelly (letter), J. Skinner

(interview), A.D. Knight (interview), and A.T. Kelk (letter); Belton, *Outside the Law*, pp.30, 39; William Carran, personal file. M.E. Parker commented in a letter to the author that he found the three Sergeants at Taranaki Street in the late 1920s to be 'unreasonable, pinpricking, tyrannical' by contrast with those at Wellington Central. See also Michael R. Chatterton, 'The Supervision of Patrol Work under the Fixed Points System', in Simon Holdaway (ed.), *The British Police*, London, 1979, pp.83–101.

9.   Police boxes containing a telephone for beat men to report to the station were introduced in British cities between the wars. The system was considered by Commissioner McIlveney and his Ministers, but not adopted, ostensibly because reports on its 'efficiency ... are somewhat contradictory'. Cost was probably also a factor. *NZPD*, vol.221, 1929, pp.425, 601; vol.224, 1930, p.611.

10.   Letter from R. Henry.

11.   W.S. Hammond, interview, 16 Dec 1980. See also Graeme Dunstall, 'Hammond, Walter Sydney', *DNZB*, vol.4, pp.221–2.

12.   Similar comments were made by R.D. Hodge, M.E. Parker, and E.R. Trask in letters to author, and by P. Kearney (interview). H. Holmes dubbed the back streets of inner-city Wellington the 'desert beat', but said nonetheless that he 'loved it' on the beat. (Interview, 5 Jan 1977.)

13.   Austing, 'From Farm Hand to Assistant Commissioner', p.6. The 'Siberia' beat encompassed Beach Road, Stanley Street, and the railway station.

14.   This term was coined by Maureen Cain in her discussion of such behaviour observed in the British police in the 1960s. Maureen Cain, 'On the Beat: Interactions and Relations in Rural and Urban Police Forces', in Stanley Cohen (ed.), *Images of Deviance*, London, 1971, pp.71–3; and Maureen E. Cain, *Society and the Policeman's Role*, London, 1973, especially pp.37, 59–60.

15.   G. Innes (letter); Austing, 'From Farm Hand to Assistant Commissioner', p.7; Thyne, memoir, pp.5, 10–11; L. Harrowfield (letter); Hammond interview; C.E.W. Black (letter); Belton, *Outside the Law*, p.48.

16.   A.J. Austin and A.J. Mills to author.

17.   G. Innes to author.

18.   O. Power, A.T. Kelk, and C. Bowley to author; and Austing, 'From Farm Hand to Assistant Commissioner', p.6. The Committee of Inquiry of 1919 (which recommended the adoption of eight-hour shifts) did not approve of men on night duty leaving their beats for refreshments; 'hot tea or coffee (should be) supplied to them on their beats.' Report of Committee of Inquiry, *NZPG*, 1919, p.428.

19.   E.F. Barry to author.

20.   G. Innes (letter); W.S. Hammond (letter); P. Kearney (interview); Austing, 'From Farm Hand to Assistant Commissioner', p.6; Belton, *Outside the Law*, p.31; City Sectional Reports, Taranaki Street Police Station, P-Wellington 31/1.

21.   G. Innes to author.

22.   *NZH*, 14 Aug 1926.

23.   Undated (c. late 1920s) newspaper item in a clipping book of W.S. Hammond which he kindly lent to the author.

24.   A.J. Austin, M.E. Parker, and A.J. Mills to author; H. Holmes, interview.

25.   F.J. Brady and A.T. Kelk to author; interview with A.D. Knight.

26.   From 1927, the uniforms were to be made of 'a blue worsted weighing 16 oz. to the yard, in place of the 24 oz. blue tweed' issued hitherto. *NZPG*, 1927, p.274.

27.   G. Innes and M.E. Parker to author.

28.   E.B.V. Horne, J.P. Clements, and M.E. Parker to author.

29.   Belton, *Outside the Law*, pp.37, 40; C.E.W. Black (letter); E.F. Barry (letter); Austing, 'From Farm Hand to Assistant Commissioner', pp.6, 8; E.J. Gaines (interview); *EP*, 15 May 1962 (obituary of J. Quinn). Another well-known Wellington beat man was Constable H. Cattanach; see R.T. Hermans, *Capital Coppers*, Wellington, 1985, pp.1–2.

30.   W.T. Thom, 'Looking Backwards. A few personal observations of Forty Years Service with the New Zealand Police Force', unpub. memoir, 1953, p.2.

31.   *Dominion*, 29 Apr 1929 (obituary). Hollis was 'specially detailed' to see that the 'left hand rule' was enforced. When the Police relinquished responsibility for controlling road traffic in Auckland, the city council was concerned that they would nonetheless continue to control pedestrian traffic. The *Herald* commented: 'It is quite certain that the police are paying little regard to the keep-to-the-left by-law'. *NZH*, 18 Dec 1926.

32.   City Sectional Reports, Taranaki Street Police Station, P-Wellington 31/1. Sergeant A.E. Rowell, stationed at Mt Eden in 1919, reckoned that in the main centres 80% of arrests were made between midday and midnight. Minutes of Evidence taken at the Police Commission of Enquiry, 1919, unpub. typescript, p.465.

33.   Belton, *Outside the Law*, p.32. In Christchurch, also in 1926, George Innes made his first arrest in similar circumstances: 'in Cashel St. about opposite the D.I.C. – a drunk man – a very convenient place to do so, for right there on the spot was a stand for three or so Hansom cabs.' Letter to author.

34.   See, for example, in Wellington, *Truth*, 5 Sep 1925; and in Auckland, *AWN*, 22 Mar 1933. Gordon Diffey recalled that the Christchurch taxi-drivers were marvellous to the police: 'they would quietly pull their cab over to the edge of the footpath and open the rear door, and if you had any trouble getting the offender in the car they would promptly assist.' Letter to author.

35.   Comments of T.W. Allsopp (a constable in Dunedin), M.E. Parker (Wellington) and C.E.W. Black (Dunedin); also, in letters or interviews, from police who worked on or near the wharves: W.S. Hammond, E.J.G. Hotham, A.D. Knight, J. Matheson, and H.Wilson. Some battles at Lyttelton were newsworthy; see for example *ODT*, 12 Jan 1921, 9 Jun 1928; *Press*, 19 Nov 1928. A.J. ('Bruiser') Johnston, a beat constable at Auckland between 1929 and 1935, commented in a letter to the author that police often had 'difficulties with the public' when they 'failed to use tact in circumstances that required this'. However, he had his 'own rules with those who wished to knock me or my police mates about. If the Marquis of Queensbury rules were not followed by the criminals I was dealing with, they were also forgotten by myself .... All this brought a lot of respect to myself and others with me.'

36.   Cleverley served at the Wellington Wharf station for 12 years from its inception in 1916, and had an 'unbeaten record for detection of theft' there. *Dominion*, 27 Jun 1928. In 1921, 29% of the arrests for drunkenness in Wellington, and 21% of those in Auckland, were of crew members of vessels in port; calculated from the Annual Report, 1922.

37.   *EP*, 14 May 1932. The defence counsel argued that the fact that the offence occurred 'in a week when the atmosphere had been electrical' should not be allowed to 'disadvantage' his client. The 21 year old clerk (who had a previous conviction) was sentenced to one month's imprisonment.

38.   McMillan was taken to the station in a taxi. The assailant was subsequently caught and prosecuted. *Dominion*, 5 Nov 1918. Other reports of hostile or unhelpful crowds in Auckland, Wellington, and Christchurch include: *LT*, 7 May 1918; 23 Jul 1919; 17 Apr 1928; 16 Feb 1929; 28 Oct 1930; *Dominion*, 3 Aug, 13 Sep 1920; *NZH*, 19 Jan, 20 Oct 1926; 22 Feb 1927; 28 Oct 1930; 30 Jan 1933. In letters to the author, P.J. Nalder commented on 'the usual crowd' which formed when arrests were made in Auckland during the 1920s and early 1930s: much depended on the manner of the arrest; 'unnecessary force' was 'likely to arouse some the crowd to action against the Police'. For Nalder (most of whose career was spent as a detective on political surveillance), the 'most convenient' way of arresting members of the Communist Party (for distributing pamphlets, for example) was from a car. Sometimes Nalder was assisted by members of a crowd who called on the bystanders to keep back and give the police a 'fair go', or who rang the watch-house to report that the police were in trouble.

39.   Comments in letters from F.R. Henry, E.J.G. Hotham, and N. Kempt; and D.J. O'Carroll, interview.

40. Belton, *Outside the Law*, p.35. A similar comment was made by P. Kearney in an interview.
41. C.W. Bowley to author.
42. Cain, 'On the Beat', p.73.
43. D.J. O'Carroll, interview.
44. *Dominion*, 13 May 1926.
45. A.J. Austin to author.
46. Under the Licensing Act 1908, 'prohibition orders' could be issued by magistrates prohibiting a person from entering licensed premises. It was an offence to knowingly sell liquor to a prohibited person. Reported breaches of prohibition orders fell from an inter-war peak of 1,384 in 1919 to 335 in 1934 and 357 in 1935 before rising to 603 in 1939, paralleling arrests for drunkenness. Annual Reports.
47. In the South Island, the following electorates were 'dry': Invercargill, Mataura, Clutha, Bruce (until its abolition in 1922, when part of its territory went to Clutha), Oamaru, and Ashburton (until its abolition in 1927).
48. L.M. Hansen to author. The average annual arrests of women for vagrancy were: 1919–1921, 97; 1922–1925, 62; 1926–1928, 84; 1929–1932, 117; 1933–1934, 82; 1935–1939, 39.
49. Calculated from *New Zealand Statistics – Vital*, 1926–1938.
50. Belton, *Outside the Law*, p.40.
51. See *NZPG*, 1926, p.242; 1928, pp.188 et seq.; 1937, p.200.
52. Between 1931 and 1939 (the period for which figures are available from police statistics): (i) 42% of those prosecuted for causing death or bodily injury through reckless driving were convicted, as were (ii) 94% of those charged with being intoxicated in charge of a motor vehicle and (iii) 90% of those charged with reckless or negligent driving. Note that (i) was prosecuted mainly before a judge and jury, whereas (ii) and (iii) were dealt with summarily by magistrates. Though the conviction rate for (ii) was high, newspapers reported many individual cases where charges were strongly contested and adverse comment was passed on police methods or evidence. See, e.g.: *Dominion*, 20 Feb, 13 May 1926; 10 May 1928; 20 Jul 1930; *Truth*, 21 Oct, 4 Nov 1926; 3 Feb, 3 Nov 1927; 5 Jan, 23 Jun 1928; *NZH*, 7 Mar, 15 Apr 1928; *Press*, 7 Aug, 21 Dec 1929; 8 Sep 1932; and also *NZPG*, 1935, p.236; and the Police file on intoxicated motorists, P 4/1/9.
53. Innes to author. Two retired men who had been on beat duty in Auckland (J. Skinner during the 1920s and G. Austing in the late 1930s) commented to the author on the pressure from Sergeants to catch cars and bicycles without tail lights. Commissioner Wright instructed that 'the police systematically devote a short time each week to the detection of delinquents' having no tail lights on their vehicles, along with other breaches of the Motor Vehicles Act. Commissioner McIlveney reiterated the instructions; *NZPG*, 1924, p.492; 1925, p.270; 1927, p.216; 1928, p.298.
54. *Press*, 26 Jul 1922; *Truth*, 21 Sep 1932. The Police Offences Act excluded 'work of necessity'. In 1927, the Solicitor-General advised the Commissioner of Police that the precise meaning and application of these words 'is one of some doubt and difficulty'. Nonetheless, Chinese market gardeners were convicted for working on a Sunday in their gardens in view from a public road. *NZPG*, 1927, p.288 (reprinting the Solicitor-General's opinion); Auckland District Law Society, Public Issues Committee paper, 'Never on Sunday', issued 16 Jul 1975. See also Belton, *Outside the Law*, pp.40, 45–6. Annual prosecutions for Sunday trading averaged 70 between 1922 (when the first statistics were recorded) and 1930, and 225 between 1931 and 1938; in 1939 the number prosecuted fell to 85. Of the 2,518 people prosecuted between 1922 and 1939, only 6.6% were acquitted; calculated from Annual Reports.
55. See ch.10 for further discussion of this.
56. M.E. Parker to author; also P. Kearney, interview.
57. Parker, letter. During the Home Boat strike there was a fight between strikers and 'volunteer seamen' on the Auckland wharf. But generally the police guarded the

wharves without major incident. *NZH*, 8, 9, 10, 13, 16, 20 Oct 1925; *Dominion*, 12, 14 Oct 1925; *ODT*, 24 Oct 1925.

58.   Commissioner McIlveney reiterated this message in a detailed memorandum on 11 Oct 1929; *NZPG*, 1929, p.695.

59.   G.C. Donnelly to author; J. Quartley interview; also Len Richardson, 'Class, Community, and Conflict: The Blackball Miners' Union, 1920–31', in Len Richardson and W. David McIntyre (eds), *Provincial Perspectives*, Christchurch, 1980, pp.120–3, regarding Blackball; and OPR 40/18/10 for Charming Creek. The tactics of union leadership in the seamen's strikes of 1922–23 and 1925 suggest that they also wished to avoid confrontation. So too did the leadership of the Amalgamated Society of Railway Servants which, at the outset of the 1924 strike, enjoined its members to refrain from any violence, and from congregating around railway premises. It promised to send a 'responsible official' to assist in 'putting down' any threatened violence'. *Press*, 24 Apr 1924.

60.   Donnelly to author.

61.   See ch.12.

62.   Brown married in 1952, shortly after he became an Inspector, at the age of 50. W.S. Brown, interview; A.T. Kelk, interview; *AWN*, 8 Jun 1939; *NZH*, 12, 27 Aug 1938; *Press*, 4, 6 Mar, 9 Nov 1948; Annual Reports of the Department of Island Territories: Cook Islands, *AJHR*, 1948, A-3, pp.7–8, 13; 1949, pp.8–9, 17–18. The three other murder investigations in which Willis Brown led police search parties were: Feb–Sep 1943, searching in Helensville and the Waitakeres for Mary Eileen Turner, who was missing and believed murdered; Jun 1947, looking for the weapon with which Gladys Ruth Rusden had been murdered; Feb 1949, at Whakatane searching for Richard Angus McGill, who was wanted for murdering John Kehoe.

63.   *LT*, 29 Jan, 5, 7, 13 Apr 1928; 9 Mar, 4 May 1929; *NZH*, 20 Feb 1928; 15 Apr 1929; *Press*, 12 Jun 1928; 9, 25 Mar, 11 Apr, 3 May 1929; W.R. Fell, interview, 4 Jan 1977; R.H. Waterson, interview, 26 Jan 1981.

64.   Report of Sub-Inspector Lander to Minister of Justice, 13 Jun 1929. The author's copy of this report is from the newspaper clipping book of ex-Superintendent John Lander.

65.   A detailed account, which is unsympathetic in its appraisal of the New Zealand administration and the police, is Michael J. Field, *Mau: Samoa's Struggle for Freedom*, Auckland, revised edn, 1991, ch.14.

66.   Donnelly, letter. The actual numbers of New Zealand Police sent to Samoa are not known. Waterson and Fell returned to duty as acting detectives in Wellington during May and Jun 1930 respectively. Fell returned to Samoa in Sep 1932 (holding the rank of Sub-Inspector while there) and arrived back on duty in Wellington as a detective in Mar 1936.

67.   Hermans, *Capital Coppers*, p.39; Roly T. Hermans, 'Wellington 1886–1992', in Young (ed.), *With Confidence and Pride*, pp.59–60; *Truth*, 24 Dec 1925.

68.   W.S. Brown, interview; *EP*, 30 Oct 1963 (for career of F.A. Banks); *Press*, 15 Aug 1964 (for career of F.G. Heywood, a Christchurch mounted constable); *NZPD*, vol.230, 1931, p.614; *Dominion*, 6 Dec 1932 (then a squad of six mounted police in Wellington); *NZPJ*, May 1937, p.45; Annual Report, 1937, p.9; *Press*, 5 Dec 1952, and *Dominion*, 7 Dec 1955 (re the phasing out of police horses).

69.   By 1919 there were about 21 Uniform Branch 'plain clothes constables' in the main centres not attached to the Detective Offices and under the control of a Senior Sergeant. The Committee of Inquiry in 1919 recommended that, since the work of plain-clothes constables overlapped with that of detectives, they should be placed under the control of Chief Detectives. This occurred for a short period from 1919. By the mid-1920s, however, plain-clothes constables had reappeared under the control of Uniform Branch Senior Sergeants. Police Committee of Inquiry, Minutes of Evidence, 1919, typescript, pp.7–8, 26, 49–50, 149, 225, 390, 410–13; *NZPG*, 1919, p.425; *ODT*, 4 Oct 1919.

70. *AWN*, 24 Aug 1938 (comment of Superintendent S. Till, Auckland).
71. *Ibid.*; also: W.S. Brown (interview); F. Brady (letter); D. Ross (letter); C. Reardon (interview); G. Innes (letter); H. Holmes (interview); *NZPG*, 1921, pp.370–1 (re enforcement of contributions to support children in industrial schools); 1923, pp.539–40 (re maintenance orders); 1924, p.508 (re warning Maoris to register births and deaths); 1926, p.359 (re looking out for those not registered as electors); 1927, p.703 (prohibiting expenditure on pension inquiries); 1929, p.814 (re reports to Coroner); 1931, p.199 (re procedures for pension inquiries); 1935, p.563 (re police inquiries for the Mortgage Corporation of New Zealand); *NZPD*, vol.221, 1929, p.763 (re police inquiries for the State Advances Office).
72. City Sectional Reports, Taranaki Street Police Station, P-Wellington 31/1. Note that the working day of the mounted constables began at 6.30 am (two and a half hours before that of the uniform enquiry men) with work in the stables, which they also undertook at the end of their duty, between 4 and 5 pm.
73. *NZPG*, 1924, p.229; *Press*, 25 Aug 1927.
74. Such objections came particularly from the Auckland Education Board and were made for 40 years from the early 1920s; see file P 1/1/149. Police insisted on their right to interview children at school where they deemed it necessary to do so. However they were instructed to have the headmaster present where possible, and to communicate the result of the interview to the parents 'without delay'. *NZPG*, 1925, p.658; 1930, p.631.
75. Only members of the Commissioner's staff, the Detective Branch, those designated plain-clothes constables, and police escorting 'insane patients' were exempt from the instruction that uniform 'must be consistently worn'. Until 1936, police escorting prisoners had to wear uniform. *NZPG*, 1926, p.330; 1936, p.720.
76. In the procedures established after the Child Welfare Act of 1925, the practice of wearing uniforms in the Children's Court depended on the discretion of magistrates, who (for example) did not permit it in Dunedin but allowed it in Auckland and Christchurch. Alan Somerville, 'Moominpappa Got Away: The State and Child Welfare in New Zealand, 1925–1930', BA (hons) long essay, University of Otago, 1982, pp.17–19; *Truth*, 21 Jul 1927, 20 Feb 1930.
77. C. Reardon, G. Austing, and W.S. Brown, interviews.
78. Innes to author.
79. *Ibid.*; and Police Regulations 1919, nos 516–574.
80. Innes (letter); A.S. Chiles (letter); J. Quartley (interview); memoir of M. Thyne, p.5.
81. Innes (letter).
82. Hammond was dismissed on 13 Dec 1942; he had been sworn in on 28 Sep 1928. Hammond (interview); PFDB, vol.2.
83. See J.D. Wills, *To Guard My People: Honours and Awards to the Police in New Zealand, 1861–1995*, Wellington, 1995, esp. pp.102–3, 213–14, 216, 219, 234–7 (for the period 1918–45); O.J. Cherrett, *Without Fear or Favour: 150 Years Policing Auckland 1840–1990*, Auckland, 1989, pp.340–1; Thomson and Neilson, *Sharing the Challenge*, pp.322–5; C.E. Spicer, *Policing the River District, 1886 to 1986*, Wanganui, 1988, pp.293–5.
84. Constables W.S. Hammond and F.A.H. Baker were awarded both the KPM and the Royal Humane Society's Silver Medal for their bravery in attempting to rescue the crew of the coastal steamer *Progress*, which was wrecked in Ohiro Bay on 1 May 1931. The first awards in New Zealand of the KPM for gallantry were to Constables R.J. Wilson and F.J. O'Donoghue for arresting two armed burglars who fired shots at them in Wanganui on 8 May 1921. The fifth (and last) award of the KPM for bravery was in 1940 to Sergeant D. Austin, who was also awarded a Royal Humane Society's Framed Certificate of Merit for rescuing a woman from the Waikato River. Between 1918 and 1945, a Bronze Medal and ten Framed Certificates of Merit were awarded by the Royal Humane Society to New Zealand Police constables. The data on Royal Humane Society awards to police comes

from an analysis by Miss Elizabeth Loffhagen of the Society's records, and Wills, *To Guard My People.*

Chapter 6: Detectives

1. *Press* and *ODT*, 29 Jan 1930. This incident was remembered nearly 50 years later by a former detective, T.W. Allsopp, who was present at the parade. Mr Allsopp interviewed by author, 18 Nov 1976.
2. Report of the Committee of Inquiry, *NZPG*, 1919, pp.418, 422–3; Police Regulations 1919, nos 217–237. For views on the position of the CID within the London Metropolitan Police see, for example, Sir Harold Scott, *Scotland Yard*, London, 1954; D. Ascoli, *The Queen's Peace*, London, 1979; B. Cox, J. Shirley, and Martin Short, *The Fall of Scotland Yard*, London, 1977; Sir Robert Mark, *In the Office of Constable*, London, 1978.
3. See, for example, *Dominion*, 16 Nov 1923. G.C. Urquhart, who rose to become Commissioner after spending most of his career as a detective, felt that the Auckland detectives in particular thought they were the 'bee's knees', the 'hub of the universe'. Urquhart interview.
4. Joblin, 'The Breath of Scandal', pp.214–16.
5. Such as William Tricklebank ('the man who cleaned up the Wellington wharf of its one-time rampant cargo pillaging and two-up tossers'); the stocky 'Big Jim Cummings', a 'kindly affable chap'; Tom Gibson, who radiated 'an easy philosophy and good cheer'; Reg Ward, a man of 'few words'; and Tom Kemp, 'a plain blunt man who speaks his mind'. *Truth*, 15 Sep 1923; 22 Mar, 2 Aug 1924; 28 Oct 1926.
6. In a circular giving instructions to 'Sub-Inspectors assigned to Charge of Detective Offices' dated 28 Mar 1930, Commissioner McIlveney reminded his officers that 'the following qualities are essential for a good detective or plain-clothes offical:
    (a) He should be absolutely honest, straightforward, truthful, just and loyal;
    (b) He should be cool and level-headed, as well as sober and steady;
    (c) He should be physically and mentally fearless in the execution of duty, active, energetic, and always ready to sacrifice his comfort and pleasure to the demands of duty;
    (d) He should have a thorough working knowledge of his duties and how to perform them, especially as to arrests, entry, search, questioning suspects or witnesses, and the evidence required to support prosecutions for criminal offences;
    (e) He should have a wide knowledge of men and affairs, and a good address. He should be able to conceal his identity and profession when necessary, and suit his manner and conversation to those he is dealing with, thereby inviting their confidence;
    (f) He should have a good memory for faces, names, places, dates, and facts of every sort;
    (g) He should be able to keep his own counsel, hear everything others have to say, but draw his own conclusions; follow out every channel which may possibly lead to the discovery of truth, and be slow to accept positive theories;
    (h) He should be able to efficiently handle the collection of all necessary evidence in support of a conviction, and present same at Court.' *NZPG*, 1930, p.241.
7. *NZPG*, 1922, p.62 (amending Police Regulation no.233).
8. Minutes of Evidence, Committee of Inquiry, 1919, pp.197, 206, 214–15. Chief Detective James McIlveney, at Christchurch, sought 'younger men to do the work'.
9. Letters from and/or interviews with T.W. Allsopp, F.J. Brady, C.P. Burns, H.E. Campin, W.R. Fell, F.A. Gordon, F.R. Henry, J.W. Hill, N. Kempt, J.B. McLean, W.R. Murray, P.J. Nalder, O.S.W. Power, C.H. Reardon, E.A. Stevenson, E.R. Trask, E.G. Ward, R.H. Waterson, and G.C. Urquhart; Belton, *Outside the Law*, pp.23–4, 52–3; PFDB, vol.2 (for details of prior occupation, height, length of service before being appointed detective, and where stationed).
10. The three were: P.T. McMahon (at Auckland), who retired in 1921; T.W.B. Boddam

(at Wellington), who was posted to Western Samoa in 1919, and when he returned in 1920 became the Police Storekeeper at Taranaki Street (he died in the job in 1926); and F.J. Bishop (at Dunedin), who retired in 1923. James McIlveney (younger brother of William Bernard McIlveney) was Chief Detective at Christchurch in 1919, became Chief Detective at Auckland from 1921 until 1923, when he was promoted to Sub-Inspector; as an Inspector the following year he became officer in charge of the Wanganui District.

11. See *Truth*'s assessments cited in note 5, and *NZPG*, 1921, p.8, for the notification of Cummings' promotion in 1921.

12. Belton, *Outside the Law*, p.53. See also Graeme Dunstall, 'Cummings, James', in *DNZB*, vol.4, pp.121–2.

13. Campin, Fell, H. Wilson, Stevenson (interviews); Nalder (letter).

14. Despite having fewer detectives, the Christchurch and Dunedin offices were similar to that of Auckland in having 'cramped quarters, and very little room for privacy or for interviewing prisoners'. Macdonald Brown (interview).

15. Belton, *Outside the Law*, pp.55, 152; *Dominion*, 6 Oct 1934; O.S.W. Power (interview); F.R. Henry (letter).

16. Urquhart, Power, Waterson (interviews); Belton, *Outside the Law*, pp.55–7; Brady, Macdonald Brown, Nalder (letters); F.A. Gordon (letter and interview).

17. In 1930, after assigning Sub-Inspectors to take charge of the Detective Offices in Auckland and Wellington, Commissioner McIlveney instructed that detectives' hours of duty would 'be regulated by the Officer in Charge according to circumstances'. The broad patterns of duty already established seem to have continued. *NZPG*, 1922, pp.374–5; 1930, p.328; *NZPD*, 1930, vol.224, p.602; vol.226, pp.821–2; Nalder, Power, Stevenson, Kearney, Murray, Burns (interviews); Kempt (letter); Belton, *Outside the Law*, pp.54, 60, 73, 78–80, 89, 94, 151.

18. Power (interview); Gordon (letter and interviews); Hill (letter); J. Bruce Young (comp.), 'Notes on Criminal Investigation', 1937, bound typescript lent to the author by S.I. Young, esp. pp.4–5, 78–80, 89; Belton, *Outside the Law*, pp.58–9, 150–2; Clements (letter). In 1930, Commissioner McIlveney listed the 'qualities ... essential for a good detective or plain-clothes official' which have been incorporated in the preceding discussion. *NZPG*, 1930, p.241. The former Chief Detective, J.B. Young, commented in 1945 that a 'good detective' required 'common sense, energy and a good deal of luck'; *Press*, 27 Jul 1945.

19. Belton, *Outside the Law*, pp.60, 99–100.

20. Comments based on surveying scrapbooks from a number of detectives, in particular those of J.B. Young kindly lent to the author by Chief Inspector S.I. Young. It seems probable that Charles Belton's detailed account of cases was based on scrapbooks. See Graeme Dunstall, 'Young, John Bruce', in *DNZB*, vol.5 (forthcoming).

21. The contrast was drawn by a *Dominion* reporter, 6 Oct 1934; and also by A.E. Currie (barrister representing the Police Department), Record of Proceedings and Depositions of Witnesses, Commission of Inquiry into the conduct of members of the Police Force regarding the death of Elsie Walker, typescript, 1929, p.7; W.R. Murray, reflecting on his career as a detective, *NZFL*, 6 Jan 1960; J.B. Young, *Press*, 27 Jul 1945. See also Basil Thomson, *Queer People*, London, 1922, p.1.

22. F.J. Brady, letter to author, 20 Feb 1977.

23. This conclusion is based on anecdotal evidence from interviews with retired detectives, assessed in the light of the findings of a survey of workloads in the CIB carried out in 1984; see F. Jackson et al., 'CIB Activity Survey', New Zealand Police, Wellington, Apr 1985.

24. An example from Detective William Roycroft, Collected Papers re Indictable Offences, 1920–1942, P 40/2. See also Belton, *Outside the Law*, pp.90–1.

25. The survey of CIB workloads carried out in 1984 revealed that only 3.3% of the activity of detectives nationally during the observation period was spent in court; this was lower than anticipated. 'CIB Activity Survey', p.54. The estimate of detectives'

court time during the 1920s and 1930s has been based largely on a survey of the scrapbooks of W.R. Murray and F. Brady, in the author's possession, which probably understate this element of detectives' activity.

26. *Dominion*, 6 Oct 1934; Power, H. Wilson (interviews); Belton, *Outside the Law*, pp.85, 87, 147–8. Note that the morning after the discovery of Elsie Walker's body, Detective Sergeant Tom Kelly (who could not drive) went with other detectives to the scene in a private car owned by a policeman. Later, because the Detective Office car was not available, Kelly delayed interviewing Bill Bayly for a day; Evidence of Chief Detective Alfred Hammond, Record of Proceedings and Depositions of Witnesses, Commission of Inquiry into the conduct of members of the Police Force regarding the death of Elsie Walker, typescript, 1929, pp.100, 102.

27. From 1902 racing clubs employed men on racedays to deal with people whom they did not want on their premises. These men were employed on a casual basis which proved unsatisfactory. In Jul 1921 the Racing Conference took over 'the whole control of undesirables on the course' and appointed four racecourse inspectors who were all former members of the police. Between Nov 1921 and Feb 1947, 4,937 people were warned off or excluded from racecourses by these inspectors, assisted by detectives. A.H. McLintock (ed.), *An Encyclopaedia of New Zealand*, Wellington, 1966, vol.3, p.15; *NZPJ*, Aug 1951, p.255; Allsopp (interview); Evidence of A.E.S. Ward to Royal Commission on Gaming and Racing, pp.112–23, IA 118/1.

28. Allsopp, Power, Stevenson (interviews); Belton, *Outside the Law*, pp.73–6, 78–9, 123.

29. *Dominion*, 6 Oct 1934; Belton, *Outside the Law*, pp.104–5, 150–2. W.R. Murray (in the Wellington Detective Office) and P.J. Nalder (in Auckland) thought it 'quite common' to have 40 to 50 or 70 to 80 files respectively awaiting attention. Murray, Nalder (interviews).

30. H. Wilson interviewed by author, 10 Jan 1977. As a junior in the Auckland Detective Office in the late 1920s, Belton saw himself as dealing with most of the inquiries for stolen bicycles; *Outside the Law*, p.57.

31. Typed lists of cases as well as scrapbooks of clippings and other material relating to his career were kindly lent to the author by the late Mr Murray. The author has a photocopy of the material in his possession. Mr Murray's record of cases runs from Jun 1922, when he entered the Detective Office, until Oct 1950, when he was appointed a Sub-Inspector.

32. W.R. Murray, Record of Cases.

33. In his first six months during 1922 as a constable in the Detective Office, Murray's files which culminated in court cases comprised: six charges of false pretenses, three each of theft and gaming offences, and one each of obscene exposure, assault with intent to rob, indecent assault, absconding from an industrial school, defaulting on the payment of maintenance, being an incorrigible rogue, as well as a warrant of commitment for non-payment of fines.

Ten years later his prosecution files comprised: thirteen cases of theft; three of false pretenses; two of bookmaking; and one each of trespass on a racecourse; breach of probation; inciting lawlessness; wounding with intent; and a warrant of commitment for non-payment of a fine.

For the period 1922 to 1930, a third of his cases comprised offences of false pretenses, fraud, and theft by those in positions of trust; for the period 1931 to 1937, these offences comprised 41% of Murray's cases. *Ibid.*; also Copy of Report 19 Dec 1932, W.R. Murray, Scrapbooks.

34. *AS*, 17 Jan, 18, 19 Apr 1933; *NZH*, 29 Nov 1933. But cf. convictions secured in other cases where theft could be proved: 20 Jan, 6 Jul 1933. F.A. Brady, Scrapbooks.

35. In cases Murray was involved in: Mrs Elizabeth Neville was convicted of abortion in Dec 1926 (a charge of murder was withdrawn); however, Dr Oscar Jacobsen, who was charged with inciting to commit a crime (abortion), had the information dismissed, while Lily Wilson was found not guilty of aiding in abortion; Clara Nicholson was

convicted in 1934 of manslaughter of a young woman as a result of performing an illegal operation; but in 1939 Mary Wearne was acquitted of performing an abortion. Murray, Scrapbooks.

36. Murray, Scrapbooks.
37. Calculated from Magistrates' Courts data in *Justice Statistics*, 1928 and 1931.
38. *Truth*, 12 May 1937; Murray, Scrapbooks.
39. *EP*, 18 Jul 1932; Murray, Scrapbooks.
40. *EP*, 19 May 1939; Murray, Scrapbooks.
41. Belton, *Outside the Law*, p.58; also pp.122–3. F.J. Brady's Scrapbook contains two letters he received (in 1932 and 1941 while a detective in Auckland) from the fathers of boys whom he prosecuted in different cases. Using almost identical language, the parents thanked Brady for his 'courteous and gentlemanly manner in handling the case against our boy'; his 'very gentlemanly manner' in presenting 'details affecting my son's case'. The issue of police 'fairness' was raised in 1920 by Detective Sergeant Michael Mason, who alleged that his superior officers had pursued the prosecution of two men charged with theft when he (the investigating officer) had doubts as to their guilt, and gave evidence in court accordingly. The accused were acquitted in the Supreme Court. Mason resigned after being charged with disrespectful conduct towards his superior officers and for 'commenting on the orders and official conduct of his two superior officers'. A Commission of Inquiry concluded that Mason's superiors had acted in 'a fair, honourable, and straightforward manner' in directing the prosecution of persons suspected of breaches of the criminal law; that the facts of the case justified proceedings taking place; and that 'there was not the slightest attempt on the part of any of the police officers concerned with the prosecution at suppressing evidence or facts, relevant to the inquiry, which might legitimately have given an innocent complexion to the unquestionably suspicious conduct of the accused'. *EP*, 17, 21 Feb 1920.
42. *Truth*, 17 Mar 1927. The paper detailed only one case where an ex-prisoner who had found difficulty in getting work believed that a 'sinister influence' had been at work.
43. *Truth*, 25 Nov 1926; *NZPG*, 1 Dec 1926. Occasional criticism of police methods in Auckland continued. See *NZH*, 5, 8 Feb 1927.
44. Such allegations were most likely to be made in cases relating to indecent assault, abortion, and burglary and theft, especially where the defendant pleaded not guilty and other prosecution evidence was not strong. Concerns seem to have focused on the manner in which some statements were induced, rather than on the possibility of fabrication. Criticisms of police methods (whether founded or unfounded) have been noted in the following instances (not an exhaustive survey): *NZPD*, vol.193, 1922, pp.650–5 (debate over alleged attempts to extort a confession); *ODT*, 18 Mar 1919 (detention by detectives for questioning); *ODT*, 24 Nov 1919 (leaving arrested men alone in police cells and recording their conversation as evidence for prosecution); *NZH*, 2 Apr 1920 (detention by a detective for questioning); *NZH*, 14 Oct 1921 (criticism of police methods in obtaining statements); *Truth*, 17 Feb 1923 (allegation of threats by a detective); *NZH*, 9 Feb 1923 (allegation that information obtained by 'subterfuge and falsehood'); *NZH*, 24 Feb 1923, *Truth*, 3 Mar 1923 (detention for long periods without food to obtain a confession); *LT*, 25 Feb 1926 (police prosecutor attacked a witness who had previously given evidence for the Crown); *NZH*, 13 May 1927 (police practice in taking statements questioned); *CS*, 18 Jun 1927 (murder suspect detained for questioning for 8 hours); *ODT*, 25 Aug 1927 (charges dismissed because of over-long detention for questioning); *Press*, 22 Nov 1927 (murder trial witness says that he was 'bullied' by a detective); *Truth*, 24 May 1928 (police indemnify accomplices who give evidence against the accused in abortion cases); *Truth*, 28 Mar 1929 (allegations of police violence in an investigation); *LT*, 9 May 1929 ('frame-up' by the police); *Truth*, 15 Aug 1929 (accused induced into making a false statement); *ODT*, 1 Nov 1929 (statements taken from accused after the arrest); *Truth*, 20 Mar 1930 (five hours continual questioning by a detective); *NZH*, 12, 17

Mar 1931 (voluntary admission obtained before formal charge made); *Dominion*, 6
May 1932 ('practice', becoming 'a habit', of detaining suspects for lengthy
questioning); *Truth*, 7 Sep 1932 ('excited' youth 'induced' at midnight 'to sign a
statement in which he admitted something he had never done'); *Truth*, 9 Nov 1932
('feeble-minded' Maori youth who was afraid of the dark taken handcuffed to the
Whangarei police station at midnight for four hours' questioning); *Truth*, 10 May
1933 (accused handled roughly and struck while being questioned); *Dominion*, 30
Aug 1934 (all-night interrogation of wife of accused, denial of access to counsel,
confiscation by detectives of money and a car belonging to accuseds' wives); *Press*,
13 Feb 1936 (requirement that policemen verify on oath written reports that they
submitted on accused persons); *Dominion*, 18 Nov, 12, 14, 23 Dec 1940, *NZPJ*,
vol.4, no.6, Dec 1940 (police conduct in obtaining a statement from a young
woman later arrested for permitting the unlawful use of an instrument and attempting
to conceal a birth criticised); *Press*, 7 Nov 1945 (people accused of a crime should
not be questioned without being warned first; questioning should be done by
senior officers). See also ch.7 for discussion of police methods in prosecuting
bookmakers.

45. *NZPG*, 1926, p.275. The phrasing repeated that of Regulation 219 relating to the
Detective Branch. A year later Superintendent Emerson reminded his Wellington
staff that the 'Commissioner directs that "no methods savouring of oppression or
excessive zeal are to be resorted to by the police in the execution of their duties ....
justice, impartiality and fair play must characterise all our actions" '. Memorandum,
29 Jul 1927, P-Wellington 14, p.5.

46. The English Judges' Rules of 1912 were subsequently modified and amplified at the
request of the Home Secretary; and the varying extent of their application by English
police was considered by the Royal Commission on Police Powers and Procedures
which reported in 1929. This report, and the further instructions of the Home Office
regarding the Judges' Rules, received publicity in New Zealand. However the notebooks
of constables who passed through the Training Depot between the wars that were
consulted by the author refer only to the Evidence Act 1908. J.B. Young, 'Notes on
Criminal Investigation', 1937, gives the rules only as an afterthought in an extract
from the Report of the Royal Commission on Police Powers and Procedure. Though
some of the cases cited above in note 44 indicate that New Zealand judges referred
to elements of the English Judges' Rules in considering the admissibility of statements
taken by the police, these rules did not have the force of law. For the original Rules
and comments on their application in New Zealand, see Hodge, *Doyle*, pp.78–83,
191–4.

47. As Justice Smith put it, sec.20 provided that 'even though a confession is induced
by a promise or threat, it is admissible unless the judge is of opinion that the
inducement offered or made was in fact likely to cause an untrue admission of guilt
to be made.' The essential test was whether a confession was 'free and voluntary'.
Truth, 9 Nov 1933. Criticism of this section of the Evidence Act, and the fact that
it could override the Judges' Rules, was made, for example, by W.J. Hunter, a
Christchurch lawyer; *Press*, 30 Aug 1930.

48. *NZH*, 6 Apr 1929.

49. For example, in dismissing an allegation, Herdman declared: 'You must not make
observations like that about a member of the police force. To say that subterfuge and
falsehood were employed ... is contrary to my thinking, is not to be allowed, and I
will not permit it.' *NZH*, 9 Feb 1923; also *NZH*, 18 May 1927. Similarly, E.M. Page,
SM in Wellington, commented: 'The work of the detectives and police is responsible,
arduous, difficult and sometimes dangerous. My experience of their methods which
extends over a decade, is that they carry out their duties with conspicuous fairness,
and I have no reason to believe that they have departed from that in this case'; *NZH*,
3 Dec 1924.

50. McIlveney was then in charge of the Criminal Registration Branch at Police

Headquarters. Along with E.W. Dinnie, the Fingerprint Expert, he was speaking to the Wellington Philosophical Society. *EP*, 2 Nov 1911. A more satirical account of the meeting appeared in *Truth*, 11 Nov 1911.

51. See Hill, *Iron Hand*, pp.166–74, 370–2.

52. The 'Henry' system of classification of fingerprints was formulated by Sir Edward Henry and adopted by United Kingdom police forces in 1901. In 1936 Dinnie began the 'long and tedious task' of applying the 'Battley' system of classifying single fingerprints to New Zealand's collection of prints. *Dominion*, 3 Sep 1930; Annual Report, 1937, p.5.

53. Annual Reports.

54. The Police Force Act 1947, sec.40, extended the scope of fingerprinting by empowering police to take the fingerprints and photographs of 'any person in lawful custody at a police station on a charge of having committed any offence'. The fingerprints and photographs were to be destroyed should the person be acquitted of the charge. This clause proved controversial during the debate on the Bill. See *NZPD*, vol.277, 1947, esp. pp.266, 274, 276, 555–60; *Press*, 20 Aug 1947.

55. *NZPG*, 1919, pp.679–80. O'Donovan's comment echoed that of Commissioner Tunbridge in Apr 1903. See Hill, *Iron Hand*, p.168.

56. Perhaps echoing the views of detectives, *Truth* advocated universal fingerprinting to assist the police in the 'war against crime' on 17 Jan 1934. Reflecting public sentiment, politicians rejected this call.

57. See Thomson and Neilson, *Sharing the Challenge*, pp.224–5.

58. Annual Report, 1935, p.6; *Press*, 16 Apr 1985.

59. Annual Report, 1932, p.4.

60. *Press*, 28 Jul 1945.

61. *Report of the Trial of Dennis Gunn for the Murder of Mr Augustus Edward Braithwaite, Postmaster at Ponsonby, Auckland, on Saturday 13th March 1920: Held Before the Honourable Mr Justice Chapman at Auckland on 24th, 25th, 26th, 27th, and 28th May 1920*, Wellington, 1921. See also C.A.L. Treadwell, *Notable New Zealand Trials*, New Plymouth, 1936, pp.233–46; Dyne, *Famous New Zealand Murders*, pp.148–55; S. Young, *Guilty on the Gallows*, Wellington, 1998, pp.122–37. Inspector Fowler, a fingerprint expert in the New South Wales Police, was brought from Sydney to corroborate the evidence of E.W. Dinnie.

62. See P.P. Lynch, *No Remedy for Death*, London, 1970, ch.13.

63. G. Joseph, *By a Person or Persons Unknown*, Sydney, 1982, p.38.

64. Annual Report, 1938, p.6; 1939, p.6. The information in this paragraph has been drawn from the reports of the Criminal Registration Branch in the Annual Reports.

65. The MO system was used by various county and borough police forces in the north of England before the First World War. When Bill Murray went to England on special leave to visit his sick mother in 1924, he visited Scotland Yard and was shown an 'elaborate system of indexing, putting a finger on the criminal', which 'impressed me very much'. Sometime after his return Murray submitted a report recommending the introduction of such a system. Commissioner McIlveney thought the idea sound, but that New Zealand was still too small a place to warrant it. The implementation of the first modus operandi system in Auckland followed its recommendation by the two detectives sent to England for training between Dec 1935 and Mar 1936. Critchley, *A History of Police in England and Wales*, p.209; Fosdick, *European Police Systems*, pp.344–8; Murray interview; Report of Detectives W. McLennan and H. Murch, 22 Apr 1936, pp.15–16, P 36/1.

66. Calculated from *New Zealand Vital Statistics*, 1921–1939.

67. Murder statistics compiled for presentation to the Joint Parliamentary Select Committee on Capital Punishment on 2 Oct 1950, P 1, 1947/1594. These figures were derived from Annual Reports.

68. Statistics on recorded murders were provided in Annual Reports from 1934 to 1937. Of the 22 cases of murder (i.e. individual deaths deemed by the police to be criminal

homicide) reported in 1933, for example:
(a) in 12 cases the accused was tried, resulting in 5 convictions, 2 acquittals and discharges, and 5 acquittals on the grounds of insanity.
(b) in 6 cases the offender committed suicide.
(c) in one case the inmate was committed to a mental hospital as not fit to plead.
(d) in 3 cases no offender was detected. Annual Report, 1934, p.3.

69. Namely Elsie Walker (1928), A. Blomfield (1931), and J.H. Blair (1933), all in the Auckland area. Some also believed Bayly to have caused the deaths of a family who died in a mysterious fire at Himatangi in 1929. These rumours developed because of the outcome of the inquest into Elsie Walker in 1929, and the sensational nature of the death of Mrs Lakey and the disappearance of her husband. *Truth*, 4 Jul 1934.

70. Half a dozen between 1917 and 1939. For the cases of F.W. Eggers, D. Gunn, and E. Tarrant, see Young, *Guilty on the Gallows*, pp.108–37, 152–8.

71. Transcript of a letter dated 9 Dec 1927 in J.B. Young, Scrapbook no.3, in the possession of S.I. Young.

72. Between 1920 and 1939, 33 people were killed by offenders who subsequently committed suicide. Murder statistics compiled for presentation to the Joint Parliamentary Select Committee on Capital Punishment on 2 Oct 1950, P 1, 1947/1594. The comments on the circumstances of criminal homicide are also based on an analysis of cases described in Annual Reports, newspaper and secondary accounts of cases, and a selection of police murder files. The author has found useful the comments in Mike Bungay and Brian Edwards, *Bungay on Murder*, Christchurch, 1983, ch.2.

73. Half of the 26 sentenced to death between 1920 and 1935 were reprieved. Between 1936 and the abolition of capital punishment in 1941, all six males convicted of murder were reprieved. Amended Table One, Summary of indictments for murder since 1920, Appendix to Memorandum submitted by Department of Justice to Joint Parliamentary Select Committee on Capital Punishment, P 1, 1947/1594.

74. *Ibid.*; and Young, *Guilty on the Gallows*, pp.9, 281.

75. *ODT*, 15 Nov 1927.

76. This judgement of English policing has been applied to Australian detective work, and seems true of that in New Zealand until the late 1930s at least. Critchley, *A History of Police in England and Wales*, p.212; R. Haldane, *The People's Force: A History of the Victoria Police*, Melbourne, 1986, p.216.

77. Notably Dr Walter Gilmour, head of the Pathology Department at Auckland Hospital, and Dr P.P. Lynch, Wellington Public Hospital's pathologist from 1924 to 1932, then a consulting pathologist until his retirement in the late 1960s. See Lynch, *No Remedy for Death*.

78. Notably the chemists at the head office of the Dominion Laboratory in Wellington, and K. Griffin, who headed its busiest branch in Auckland. From the late 1920s, the Christchurch branch also did much work for police; a Dunedin branch was established in 1928. The Dominion Laboratory became part of the Department of Scientific and Industrial Research in 1926. During the 1920s the number of samples (mainly relating to suspected poisoning, illicit liquor and counterfeiting) received by Government Analysts from police fluctuated between 12 in 1920/21 and 120 in 1926/27. Between 1931/32 and 1933/34, the number of samples rose steeply to 651, with 'diverse materials' being analysed in cases of suspected murder and suicide. From 1934 it was noted that police were increasingly consulting laboratory staff to see if their specialised knowledge could be of assistance. Laboratory analysis and 'non-chemical' scientific work began to be used in a wider range (but relatively small number) of cases relating to intoxication, safe-blowing, breaking and entering, arson, and 'hit-and-run' accidents. Dominion Laboratory Reports in the Annual Reports of the Department of Internal Affairs, *AJHR*, 1920–1926, H-22; Annual Reports of the Department of Scientific and Industrial Research, *AJHR*, 1927–1939, H-34.

79. For example, Colonel W.H. Hazard, an Auckland gunmaker and firearms dealer, gave

evidence on firearms and ammunition in the trials of Dennis Gunn and S.J. Thorne in 1920. From the mid-1920s, the local police began consulting G.G. Kelly on cases involving shooting. Kelly had had a long practical experience with firearms before joining the Colonial Ammunition Company (Auckland) in 1922. Commissioner Wohlmann 'persuaded' Kelly to become the arms advisory officer in the Police Department. G.G. Kelly, *The Gun in the Case*, Christchurch, 1963, p.151 and *passim*.

80. Deaths by firearms comprised 23% of suicides and 25% of all homicides recorded from death certificates and inquests in the period 1921 to 1939. Calculated from *New Zealand Vital Statistics*, 1921 to 1939.

81. Kelly, *The Gun in the Case*, pp.45–8; see also pp.89–91 and 136–8 for similar cases. Conversely, Kelly's evidence at the trial of Charles Colston in 1931 undermined the defence argument that a fatal shooting was the result of a struggle rather than a deliberate act. *Ibid.*, pp.49–51.

82. *Ibid.*, pp.43, 66–7, 151. Annual Reports, 1937, p.9; 1938, p.7.

83. Lynch, *No Remedy for Death*, pp.83–90; Treadwell, *Notable New Zealand Trials*, pp.286–97.

84. Meredith, *A Long Brief*, pp.172–8; Rex Monigatti, *New Zealand Sensations*, Auckland, 1975, pp.151–6; Cherrett, *Without Fear or Favour*, pp.120–1.

85. For brief accounts of these poisoning cases see David Gee, *Poison: The Coward's Weapon*, Christchurch, 1985, pp.60–83. See also Meredith, *A Long Brief*, pp.96–127, for the trials of Munn and Kerr; Lynch, *No Remedy for Death*, pp.115–26, for the trials of Mareo; Carson and Davison, *The Longest Beat*, p.74, for the investigation of the poisoning by chocolates. Munn's wife was poisoned by strychnine, Betty Kerr and Thelma Mareo by veronal. At his Supreme Court trial, J.S. Page was declared unfit to plead and sent to Seaview Mental Hospital.

86. Vincent Meredith cites a number of poisoning cases in which it was 'obvious to the police that murder has been committed, [but] nothing can be done about it' because of the difficulty of proving who administered the poison. Meredith, *A Long Brief*, p.123. Concern about the 'veronal menace' and 'drug tragedies' more generally is echoed in an article written in 1932 by Robin Hyde and reprinted in G. Boddy and J. Matthew (eds), *Disputed Ground: Robin Hyde, Journalist*, Wellington, 1991, pp.256–60.

87. F.R. Chapman to Minister of Justice, 1 Jun 1920; Superintendent A.H. Wright to Commissioner of Police, 3 Jun 1920; Commissioner O'Donovan to Superintendent Wright, 2 Sep 1920; P 1, 1920/444. Thirteen police received rewards, the largest going to Detective Sergeant Cummings (£50), and Detective J.B. Young (£15). Detective Young, who had assisted Cummings in each phase of the enquiry and been instrumental in finding the incriminating revolvers, keys, and money, protested at the 'very unfair distinction made' between Cummings and himself.

88. F.R. Chapman to Minister of Justice, 10 Dec 1920; Superintendent A.H. Wright to Commissioner of Police, 22 Dec 1920, P 1, 1920/1282; and *Report of the Trial of Samuel John Thorne for the Murder of Mr Sydney Seymour Eyre a Farmer at Pukekawa in the Auckland District on 25th August 1920. Held Before the Honourable Mr Justice F.R. Chapman at Auckland on the 29th and 30th November, and the 1st, 2nd, and 3rd December, 1920*, Wellington, 1925. See also Treadwell, *Notable New Zealand Trials*, pp.247–61; Dyne, *Famous New Zealand Murders*, pp.156–64; and Young, *Guilty on the Gallows*, pp.138–51.

89. Lynch, *No Remedy for Death*, pp.83–7; Murray interview; Memoranda from Justice A.E. Blair, 13 Nov 1931, and from P.S.K. Macassey, Crown Prosecutor, 16 Nov 1931, to Commissioner Wohlmann; Commissioner Wohlmann to Superintendent, Wellington, 8 Dec 1931, 22 Jun 1933; W.R. Murray, Scrapbooks. In this case the rewards to the ten police were not monetary, but in terms of special leave on full pay.

90. Lynch, *No Remedy for Death*, pp.62–8; Cherrett, *Without Fear or Favour*, pp.125–6.

91. *NZPG*, 1925, p.133; Thomson and Neilson, *Sharing the Challenge*, p.223.

92. The discussion of the Bayly case has been based on the following sources: Allsopp, interview; H.J. Wilson (ed.), *The Bayly Case*, Wellington, 1934; Meredith, *A Long Brief*, pp.133–71; Leary, *Not Entirely Legal*, pp.85–116; Lynch, *No Remedy for Death*, pp.21–46; Kelly, *The Gun in the Case*, pp.60–8; newspaper reports in the scrapbooks of J.B. Young and J.B. McLean; 'Ruawaro Murder Inquiry: Oct. 1933 – Jan. 1934: Diary of Inspector Hollis and Inspector Rawle' (typescript, in the possession of the author). See also Young, *Guilty on the Gallows*, pp.159–76.
93. Annual Report, 1934, p.8.
94. 'Ruawaro Murder Inquiry: Oct. 1933 – Jan. 1934: Diary of Inspectors Hollis and Rawle', p.9. According to Rawle, the theory of Cummings and Ward was that Lakey's body had been taken away by car and buried in a coalmine dump, or put into one of the many lakes or rivers in the district. This theory was superseded by that of the 'two older inspectors', Rawle and Hollis, that Lakey's body was on or in the vicinity of Bayly's farm. Rawle saw this ability to bring a fresh perspective to a murder inquiry as an advantage of New Zealand's centralised system of policing. 'Maori' [S. Rawle], 'Discuss the Advantages and Disadvantages of placing the various Police Forces in the United Kingdom under a Common Administration', essay submitted for the King's Police Medal Essay Competition, 1935, p.13.
95. Lynch, *No Remedy for Death*, p.19. This comment echoes those made at the time: see, e.g., *NZH*, 25 Jun 1934; and the Dominion Laboratory Report in the Annual Report of the Department of Scientific and Industrial Research, *AJHR*, 1935, H-34, p.70.
96. *NZH*, 25 Jun 1934, also published in *Dominion*, 25 Jun 1934.
97. Murders were classified as 'unsolved' if there was no prosecution. The official police list of such murders between 1919 and 1939 comprises those of Eliza J. Hebbend, whose body was found in Wellington Harbour in 1920; Frank E. Jew at Grey Lynn and Constable J. Dorgan at Timaru in 1921; Mrs Oates at Wanganui in 1923; Allan Cornall at Karamu (near Hastings), who drank liquor containing strychnine; J.H. Blair at Mt Roskill (Auckland) and Donald Fraser at the Riccarton Racecourse Hotel (Christchurch) in 1933; Joan Rose Rattray at Karamu in 1935; and E.N. Nelson, who was shot at Waihou Valley, North Auckland, in 1936. In at least the Jew, Cornall, and Fraser cases, police had a definite suspect, but insufficient evidence to prosecute. In addition, police listed as murders five cases 'where newly born child found and offender not traced'. P 1, 1947/1594. Two cases that the Police regarded as 'cleared' were not seen as satisfactorily solved by members of the public: the deaths of Elsie Walker (1928) and A. Blomfield (1931) in Auckland.
98. For Burr, see Carson and Davison, *The Longest Beat*, pp.71–2; for Scarff, see ch.3; for Fraser, see Evan Swain, *Unsolved Murders in New Zealand*, Auckland, 1972, pp.17–19; for the Smythe sisters and Brunton, see *ibid.*, pp.20–4; Joseph, *By Person or Persons Unknown*, pp.21–42; and Lynch, *No Remedy for Death*, pp.127–33.
99. See ch.11.

Chapter 7: Policing Gambling

1. Belton, *Outside the Law*, p.111.
2. *Ibid.*, pp.113–14. Soon after Tattersalls sweepstakes began in Hobart in 1897, with the sanction of the Tasmanian government, growing numbers of New Zealanders began to purchase tickets from agents in New Zealand; Annual Report, 1902, p.2. For Tattersalls 'consultations' see J. O'Hara, *A Mugs's Game: A History of Gaming and Betting in Australia,* Kensington, NSW, 1988, ch.4.
3. See, for example, the comments in Annual Reports, 1898, p.3; 1899, p.3; 1901, p.2; 1905, p.5; 1906, pp.6, 11; 1908, pp.9, 10; 1921, p.15. 'Two-up' was played by a person tossing a penny using a piece of wood known as a 'kip', with other players forming a characteristic circle or 'school' and betting upon whether it would come up 'heads' or 'tails'. John A. Lee commented that 'two-up' was played 'a good deal'

by New Zealand and Australian troops in France; it was their 'national game'; *NZPD*, vol.205, 1924, p.235.

4. In this and succeeding paragraphs, general comments on the development and nature of New Zealand gaming legislation are based on the Reports of the Royal Commission on Gaming and Racing, *AJHR*, 1948, H-23, esp. parts 2, 4, 7, 9, 10; and of the Royal Commission of Inquiry into *Horse Racing, Trotting and Dog Racing in New Zealand*, Wellington, 1970, esp. ch.3. See also David Grant, *On a Roll: A History of Gambling and Lotteries in New Zealand*, Wellington, 1994, esp. chs 2, 3.

5. *NZPD*, 1920, vol.186, pp.514-38, 744-54; vol.187, pp.182-96.

6. In introducing the 1920 legislation, the Minister of Internal Affairs rejected any suggestion that the government was seeking to increase the amount invested on the totalisator, and hence government revenue; *NZPD*, vol.186, 1920, p.515. It should be noted however that in 1891, ten years after the first statutory regulation of the totalisator, 'the State began to exploit the machine as a source of revenue'. By 1920 both totalisator investments and dividends were taxed, the government taxation representing nearly 5% of the totalisator turnover. In Dec 1921 the dividend duty was doubled, bringing taxation to 7% of turnover. Between 1930 and 1932 the taxation of investments was doubled, and taxation of totalisator turnover reached nearly 9½%. Report of the Royal Commission on Gaming and Racing, p.83; *NZOYB*, 1939, p.492.

7. That is, betting based on the dividends to be paid by the totalisator. The prohibition was based on the well-founded fear that bookmakers and those who bet with them would seek to produce a desirable result by also betting on the totalisator. A notable example was the so-called 'Malacca case' at Napier, where a big punter won from bookmakers in 1945 'a much greater sum than the normal odds would have secured for him'. Report of the Royal Commission on Gaming and Racing, pp.28-9.

8. According to H.H. Clegg, Secretary of the Dominion Sportsmen's Association, in 1947, the 'great majority' of punters bet at totalisator odds, but other odds could be obtained if required. He denied that bookmakers were a source of corruption in racing: he did not know of a single instance of a member of his Association getting a jockey to have a horse subject to heavy betting 'pulled' during a race. But he agreed that bookmakers 'protected' themselves by betting on the totalisator. Evidence to the Royal Commission on Gaming and Racing, pp.143, 149-50, IA 118/1.

9. L.R. Sanders (Christchurch) to Minister of Internal Affairs, 5 Oct 1946, IA 118/9.

10. For the critical views of Labour MPs see, for example, *NZPD*, vol.186, 1920, pp.517-20 (Parry), 522 (Savage), 534-6 (Holland); vol.209, 1926, pp.1136 (Parry), 1148 (Jordan). For the views of those who found betting with bookmakers convenient, see Evidence to the Royal Commission on Gaming and Racing, pp.260-2, 630-6, 865, 867, 1014-19, IA 118/1; Copies of Statements made, IA 118/7.

11. *NZPD*, vol.186, 1920, p.516.

12. Annual Reports, 1922, 1923, 1924, p.7; Report of the Royal Commission on Gaming and Racing, p.136. Juries became more willing to convict in the 1930s.

13. Between 1925 and 1941 (the years for which distinct statistics are available for this offence), 118 were prosecuted for street betting, with 102 convicted and fined a total of £4,436. Annual Reports, 1926 to 1941. In 1947 Commissioner J. Cummings thought that there was 'not as much [street betting] as there used to be. There is a fair number of double charts in the street, but they are making mostly for the hotels now.' Between 1910 and 1920 any bookmaker operating in licensed premises could be arrested without a warrant for 'street betting'. From 1920 those taking bets in hotels had to be charged with either keeping a common gaming house or carrying on business as a bookmaker, and a warrant was required for arrest. Police regarded this, and the penalties for licensees permitting gambling, as unsatisfactory. Evidence to the Royal Commission on Gaming and Racing, pp.1124-5, IA 118/2; Notes of Proceedings, Royal Commission on Licensing, vol.4, pp.544-5, P 1, 1944/901.

14. Report of the Royal Commission on Gaming and Racing, p.25. Senior Detective E.H. Compton, then responsible for detecting bookmakers in Wellington, submitted a list

of 'known' bookmakers; i.e. those with convictions. It was apparently not the practice of Wellington detectives to keep an 'official record' of suspected bookmakers. Notes of Evidence, Commission of Inquiry into Police Conduct, vol.6, pp.1294, 1312. By early 1947 the number of bookmakers belonging to the Dominion Sportsmen's Association had fallen from a peak of 400 to 338, with 107 in the Wellington area, 147 in the Auckland area, 54 in the Christchurch area, and 30 in the Dunedin area. Evidence of H.H. Clegg to the Royal Commission on Gaming and Racing, p.142, IA 118/1; Statement by the Dominion Sportsmen's Association, p.45, IA 118/4/51.

15. The following discussion of bookmakers and police methods has been drawn mainly from an analysis of newspaper reports of court cases involving bookmakers, and especially from those in the scrapbooks of F. Brady and J.B. Young lent to the author.

16. Hyde claimed, for example, that Wellington had its 'big four' who were not prosecuted, two of whom occupied 'an elaborate suite of offices, in the heart of Wellington, cheek by jowl with the offices of a well-known racing club.' *New Zealand Observer*, 29 Sep 1932, cited by Gillian Boddy and Jacqueline Matthews (eds), *Disputed Ground: Robyn Hyde, Journalist*, Wellington, 1991, p.104. The accuracy of Hyde's claims is difficult to verify. Detective Sergeant Thomas Kelly, the police prosecutor in Auckland, referred (without mentioning names) in 1932 to 'the five leading bookmakers in the city', presumably those who had already been prosecuted by the police. *AS*, 31 Dec 1932; Brady, Scrapbooks. When it was suggested that 'if a man had been carrying on for several years, you would have got to hear of it from some source or other', Commissioner Compton replied in 1954: 'You would think so, and there were some that we did, but there were others I have been surprised about – really surprised about.' Notes of Evidence, Commission of Inquiry into Police Conduct, vol.6, p.1295.

17. For Auckland examples, see *AS*, 6 Jul, 12 Dec, 27 Dec, 31 Dec 1932; 3 Jan 1933; 27 Jan, 2 Feb, 11, 18 Jul 1934, Brady Scrapbooks. In Wellington, H. ('Gus') Martindale was a 'big' man who was caught offering 'tote' odds in the New Commercial Hotel in Mar 1927 and fined a total of £110 on 11 charges. Martindale was still operating in the mid-1940s, using telephones and moving from office to office so that he was difficult to catch. *LT*, 28 Mar 1927; *Truth*, 7 Apr 1927; Notes of Evidence, Commission of Inquiry into Police Conduct, vol.1, pp.139, 164, 182; First Report, Commission of Inquiry into Police Conduct, *AJHR*, 1954, H-16A, p.5. In Christchurch, William Whitta admitted to earning £3,000 to £4,000 a year working through his son, a tobacconist, and other agents including a billiard saloon. By 1926 A.V. Whitta had succeeded his father as a 'big man' in Christchurch bookmaking. *LT*, 29 Jan, 4 Feb 1921; *Truth*, 7 Apr 1927; see also Grant, *On a Roll*, p.102. In Dunedin during the mid-1930s, R.D. and J.R. Donaldson operated an 'extensive and lucrative' business as bookmakers by telephone from a house at 24 Calder St, St Kilda. They were assisted by two clerks and the occupier of the house, from whom the Donaldson brothers rented rooms for telephones and for an electric duplicating machine on which they printed their own doubles charts. On 20 Jan 1937 (the first day of the Wellington Racing Club's summer meeting), 489 bets totalling £511 17s 6d had been recorded in the few hours before the premises were raided. During the preceding six months, sums totalling £8,504 4s 2d had been paid into the Donaldsons' bank account. *ES*, 27 Jan 1937; J.B. Young, Scrapbook no.4.

18. Stations of the Radio Broadcasting Company began broadcasting in Auckland, Wellington and Christchurch during 1926 and 1927. The broadcasting of races at city meetings seems to have begun shortly afterwards. By 1928 there were 39,315 radio licences; ten years later there were 305,175. In the same period the number of subscribers to the main telephone exchanges grew from 114,079 to 145,370. Burdon, *New Dominion*, pp.92–4; *NZOYB*, 1939, pp.279, 785.

19. His bets 'ranged from 2/6 to £400–£500'. Police evidence at Albertson's trial in Nov 1944 showed that he had been doing business with at least 570 bettors through three telephones, two post office boxes and a telegraph code address. Between 8 Jan and 29 Jul 1944 he had paid out £19,976 to successful gamblers. Submission to Royal

Commission on Gaming and Racing, IA 118/7, cited by W. Brown, 'Origins of the New Zealand Totalisator Agency Board', MA (hons) research essay, University of Canterbury, 1986; and Rex v Albertson, Notes of address by Justice Northcroft in imposing sentence, 6 Nov 1944, in J.B. Young, Scrapbook no.7. See also Grant, *On a Roll*, pp.124–5.

20. Belton, *Outside the Law*, p.24. Evidence that betting materials found during a raid bore the distinctive trade name and identification sign used by a bookmaker for many years was sufficient to secure Francis Brewer's conviction as the proprietor of premises used as a common gaming house. *AS*, 11 May 1937, Brady Scrapbooks.

21. Justice G.P. Finlay, Chairman of the Royal Commission on Gaming and Racing, commented while hearing the evidence of H.H. Clegg, Secretary of the Dominion Sportsmen's Association, in 1947: 'I have heard friends of mine in the past ring up and give a funny name and make a bet, and I have also seen them a few days later open their mail and find a debit note.' Evidence to the Royal Commission on Gaming and Racing, p.159, IA 118/1.

22. Notably in the cases of H.C. Sallery and C.W. Russell, who had already been convicted for keeping common gaming houses and whose subsequent convictions as 'occupiers', in 1934 and 1935 respectively, followed those of their clerks who were found on the premises. *AS*, 27 Jan 1934; *NZH*, 30 Mar 1935; Brady Scrapbooks.

23. *AS*, 28 Jan 1933, Brady Scrapbooks.

24. When asked at a meeting of creditors whether it was 'quite an established practice for shopkeepers in Wellington to accept bets on behalf of reputable bookmakers', a bankrupt replied: 'Half the shopkeepers could not live if they didn't'. *Press*, 12 Mar 1929. Similar evidence was given in various Auckland cases concerning small shopkeepers in the early 1930s, e.g: G.W. Tucker, butcher; C. Smith, dairy and confectionery shop; G.H. Wilkinson, confectioner; J. Johnson, tobacconist; George Ashe, suburban grocer; A. Forman, tobacconist; W.J. Bird, law clerk; *AS*, 11 Nov 1932, 24 Apr, 9 Aug 1933, 10 Jan 1934, 15 Oct 1935, 3, 10 Jan 1936, Brady Scrapbooks.

25. Evidence of H.H. Clegg, G.L. Edwards and Commissioner J. Cummings to the Royal Commission on Gaming and Racing, pp.146–8, 919–23, 1124, 1128, 1133, 1150, IA 118/1, 118/2; and of Commissioner Compton, Notes of Evidence, Commission of Inquiry into Police Conduct, vol.1, p.180. The notorious 'Malacca case' in 1945 (cited above in note 7) was one where (in the view of the Police) a commission agent had placed bets for a big punter.

26. *AS*, 26 Apr 1934, Brady Scrapbooks.

27. Calculated from newspaper cuttings on file J 1, 1936/35/266.

28. Evidence of H.H. Clegg to the Royal Commission on Gaming and Racing, p.145, IA 118/1; Statement by Dominion Sportsmen's Association, p.1, IA 118/4/51.

29. Early in 1922 the Dominion Sportsmen's Association circulated copies of a petition seeking the licensing of bookmakers. During the 1920s, the Reform MP for Mt Roskill, V.H. Potter, also supported this. H.T. Armstrong (Labour, Christchurch East) introduced a bill in 1931 for the registration and control of bookmakers, and was its chief protagonist for the next two years. *LT*, 13 Mar, 6 Apr 1922; *Truth*, 1 Apr 1922; *Press*, 30 Jun 1922; *NZPD*, vol.205, 1924, p.221; vol.222, 1929, pp.485–501; vol.230, 1931, p.173; vol.233, 1932, pp.21–3; vol.234, 1932, p.65; vol.235, 1933, pp.376–86. Statement by Dominion Sportsmen's Association, pp.7–10, IA 118/4/51.

30. H.H. Clegg commented that when a deputation from the Dominion Sportsmen's Association went to see the Prime Minister, Peter Fraser, to ask for a Commission of Inquiry with a view to legalising bookmakers: 'We asked him, seeing he made a promise to give us a Commission, could he not possibly ask the Police Force to be a little less energetic in their prosecutions against the bookmaker. He said he had nothing to do with the Police, and personally I am rather sorry we asked that question, because they seemed to double their energies after that.' Commissioner J. Cummings replied enigmatically: 'there are equal rights for all and privileges for none.' Evidence to

the Royal Commission on Gaming and Racing, p.163, IA 118/1, p.1147, IA 118/2.
31.   Printed letterhead paper carrying the monogram of the Dominion Sportsmen's
       Association ('Unity is Strength'), together with the address of its Wellington office
       (25 Panama St), telegraphic address, phone number and Post Office box number, was
       used by its secretary H.H. Clegg in 1947. An example may be seen in IA 118/9.
       Clegg maintained that the Association's offices did not accept bets. In Apr 1945,
       Auckland detectives raided a house in Vincent St, near the Ellerslie racecourse,
       where two men were using telephones on a raceday to relay information to the
       Association and individual bookmakers. The men were convicted by J.H. Luxford of
       aiding and abetting a named convicted bookmaker 'and persons unknown' in the
       offence of assisting in the conducting of a common gaming house. *ST*, 29 May 1945,
       in J.B. Young, Scrapbook no.7. Robin Hyde commented that 'Nobody has ... passed
       unpleasant strictures concerning the fact that New Zealand bookmakers have their
       own club headquarters – quite sumptuous ones – in a central position in Auckland.'
       Cited by Boddy and Matthews (eds), *Disputed Ground*, p.287.
32.   By the 1940s, if not earlier, the Association supplied race results to some government-
       controlled broadcasting stations. During the war years the Association also supplied
       information to the Prime Minister's Department for despatch to overseas troops. H.
       Clegg's evidence to the Royal Commission on Gaming and Racing, pp.162, 183–8,
       IA 118/1; Statement by Dominion Sportsmen's Association, pp.1–2, IA 118/4/51.
33.   *Truth*, 24 Jan 1925, citing the case of a Nelson member of the Association.
34.   See, for example, *Press*, 10 Aug 1922, 13 Sep 1923; *Truth*, 20 Feb, 27 Mar 1930;
       NZPD, vol.226, 1930, p.199 (Wright); Belton, *Outside the Law*, p.112. In 1901
       Commissioner Tunbridge had commented that the 'telephone is largely resorted to by
       betting-men in carrying on their illegal calling'. Annual Report, 1901, p.2.
35.   *NZPD*, vol.189, 1920, p.357; *Dominion*, 4, 30 Nov 1920. Lee also made it clear that
       any policeman caught betting with bookmakers would be dismissed, regardless of
       rank. The Gaming Amendment Act 1920 came into force on 28 Aug.
36.   Annual Report, 1921, p.8. These sentiments were reiterated by O'Donovan's successor,
       Commissioner A.H. Wright, *ibid.*, 1924, p.4.
37.   *NZH*, 10 Nov 1932, Brady Scrapbooks. Giving evidence in court cases, especially
       those dealing with the 'smaller fry' in the early 1930s, Detective Brady and his
       Auckland colleagues frequently referred to complaints as the basis for their action.
       G.E. Callaghan usually started his pursuit of Wellington bookmakers after receiving
       'confidential [i.e. anonymous] information' from 'probably a disgruntled punter'. His
       colleague E.H. Compton commented that 'we found on many occasions' people
       reported to be bookmakers 'not to be so.' Notes of Evidence, Commission of Inquiry
       into Police Conduct, vol.1, p.97; vol.6. p.1295.
38.   *NZH*, 10 Nov 1932, Brady Scrapbooks.
39.   P. Kearney, interview, 5 Nov 1976, referring to his experience in the New Plymouth
       District during the 1930s: 'somebody would give you a ring, or a "wheeze", and say
       "I don't want to be drawn into this at all but so and so's ....", and you would go from
       there. You had to get your own evidence.'
40.   Belton, *Outside the Law*, pp.23–8.
41.   Comments by journalists in *AS*, 10 Jan 1933, 2, 13 Jan 1934, 10 Jan 1936, Brady
       Scrapbooks. Simultaneous raids were also a usual procedure in the other main centres.
       They were often widely reported through the Press Association. One example is the
       raids on seven premises by Auckland detectives on the afternoon of 10 Nov 1938;
       Dominion, 11 Nov 1938.
42.   According to statistics in the Annual Reports, 52 people were committed for trial in
       the Supreme Court for bookmaking offences, and 6 for unlawfully establishing lotteries,
       between 1920 and 1940. Of the 34 committed for bookmaking offences in the 1920s,
       only 7 were convicted: 6 for unlawful betting and one (in 1929) for following the
       occupation of a bookmaker. By contrast, between 1930 and 1940, 13 of the 18
       committed for trial for bookmaking offences were convicted by juries: 4 for unlawful

betting, 8 for following the occupation of a bookmaker, and one for keeping a common gaming house.

Supreme Court judges showed themselves more ready to imprison bookmakers than did magistrates. For example, Stan Findlay, caught bookmaking in an extensive way at the Te Aro Hotel, Wellington, in Apr 1930 (beside a telephone there was list of acceptances and betting slips for horses racing at five different meetings outside Wellington), was convicted after only 40 minutes by a jury and sentenced by the Chief Justice, Sir Michael Myers, to 9 months' hard labour. However, the likelihood of acquittal by juries was such that, as Commissioner J. Cummings put it: 'we prefer to charge them on a summary offence'. *Dominion*, 30 Jul 1930, W.R. Murray Scrapbook and Record of Cases; Evidence of Commissioner Cummings to the Royal Commission on Gaming and Racing, p.1126, IA 118/2.

43.   Calculated from statistics in the Annual Reports. Unless otherwise identified, all statistics relating to the enforcement of the gaming laws are derived from this source. The numbers prosecuted before magistrates and conviction rates both increased markedly during the 1930s, while the average fines for the two most common charges concerning illegal betting fell from £50 in the 1920s to £38 for keeping a common gaming house and £25 for carrying on the business of bookmaker in the late 1930s.

The maximum fine for carrying on the business of a bookmaker was £500, and for keeping a common gaming house, £100. Only in five years between 1926 and 1941 was the average fine for the former offence higher than that for the latter.

44.   Notes of Evidence, Commission of Inquiry into Police Conduct, vol.5, p.1050.

45.   This was the description used by a prominent Auckland businessman, F. Myers, in a telegram to the Labour MP, W. Parry, regarding the month's imprisonment imposed on the bookmakers Francis Brewer and Thomas Curran on 17 Jul 1934. Copy on file J 1, 1936/35/266.

46.   Commissioner Wright commented in 1922 that, given the failure of juries to convict bookmakers under the 1920 Act, police 'had to fall back on the 1908 Act'. Annual Report, 1922, p.7. Police prosecutors sometimes made following the occupation of a bookmaker and keeping a common gaming house alternative charges on the same facts before a magistrate. In 1921 an Auckland fruiterer admitted to being a bookmaker (the first charge) because 'If they miss you on the swings they catch you on the roundabouts'. He probably rued the choice, being subsequently fined £200, or 6 months' imprisonment in default. In 1933, Douglas Hipkins pleaded guilty to being a bookmaker rather than to the first charge of keeping a common gaming house (which was then withdrawn by police), probably to protect his principal, H.C. Sallery. Hipkins was also fined £200. *Dominion*, 2 Mar 1921; *AS*, 10 Nov 1933; Brady Scrapbooks.

47.   For example, L. Andrews (who gave his occupation as 'agent', and had an office in the Mining Chambers in central Auckland) pleaded guilty to keeping a common gaming house. When his counsel acknowledged that Andrews had had a long career as a bookmaker in both Australia and New Zealand, W.K. McKean SM commented: 'He admits being a bookmaker and yet he is only charged with keeping a common gaming house .... If he were charged with bookmaking he would be liable to a fine of £500 .... I can only fine him £100 on the present charge.' The magistrate made a similar comment when Thomas Curran appeared for the fourth time in Jan 1933 on a charge of keeping a common gaming house. *AS*, 14 Nov 1932, 3 Jan 1933, Brady Scrapbooks.

48.   Seen, for example, in the cases of S.W. Gedy, labourer, fined £5; Mrs Lavinia Baker, whose husband was on relief work, a total of £3 and £2 18s costs on two charges; Jack Baker, relief worker, £4; G.H. McIver, labourer, £4; A.C. Tait, on sustenance, £10; J.F. Howe, bricklayer, £20; E. Pitman, freezing worker, £15; T. Roach, relief worker, £4; W. Flynn, relief worker, £5; A. Berry, on miner's pension, £5. *AS*, 7 Jun, 4, 22 Nov 1932; 29 Apr, 30 Nov, 19 Dec 1933; 17 Jul 1935; 10 Jan 1936; 18 Feb 1937; Brady Scrapbooks.

49.   The accused, Joseph Hortene, had no defense counsel. Detective Sergeant O'Sullivan
       (prosecuting) commented that Hortene was a disabled war pensioner, 'a married man
       with a large family and ... very honest. I'm afraid if he is convicted of this charge
       he may lose his military pension.' Similarly, a 'young woman' waitressing in an
       Auckland city hotel over the Christmas–New Year racing season 'tearfully admitted'
       taking bets from other staff who could not go to the races. Acting on a complaint,
       Detective Brady interviewed her, and his account in court reinforced the defence
       counsel's plea in mitigation. The accused, whose name was suppressed, was admitted
       to probation for 12 months by W. Wilson, SM. During this period she was not 'to
       frequent racecourses'. *AS*, 30 Nov 1933, 13 Jan 1934, Brady Scrapbooks.
50.   See note 43 above.
51.   Belton, *Outside the Law*, p.111.
52.   Being prosecuted again soon after a conviction 'has never seemed to be the usual
       practice.' R.D. Donaldson, Notes of Evidence to the Commission of Inquiry into
       Police Conduct, vol.5, p.1084. This was also observed from the conviction patterns
       of bookmakers studied by the author.
53.   Belton, *Outside the Law*, p.111. This practice was apparently based on a judicial
       decision at the turn of the century. While cards, dice and other instruments of gaming
       were confiscated, books and documents used in evidence had to be returned (if asked
       for) after conviction. J.B. Young, Scrapbook no.7, p.216, had a note to this effect
       typed from Coleridge, *The Law of Gambling*, 2nd edn, pp.328–9. Some bookmakers
       professed to want the return of their books in order to settle their accounts.
54.   During the inter-war years it became the practice, especially in Auckland and
       Wellington, for the officer in charge to supply the local postmaster with the names
       of those convicted of bookmaking. However, the withdrawal of telephones 'used for
       ordinary social and domestic purposes' usually only followed a second conviction.
       The Post and Telegraph Department would not remove telephones merely on the
       grounds of suspected bookmaking; 'secrecy of communications' was 'fundamental'.
       Of the 71 telephones used by people convicted of bookmaking that were disconnected
       in 1946, 46 were business connections and 25 residential; 32 were leased by someone
       other than the convicted person, including 8 leased by the bookmaker's wife. Of the
       46 business connections, 6 were billiard rooms, 5 hairdressers and tobacconists, 2
       carriers, 2 confectioners, a carpenter and paperhanger, book exchange, dressmaker,
       stationer, blacksmith, and 'land agents, manufacturing agents, indent agents, importers,
       etc .... [giving] a very good idea of the difficulty we have in determining at application
       time or any other time just who the people are.' Evidence of P.N. Cryer to the Royal
       Commission on Gaming and Racing, pp.498–508, IA 118/1; Submission by the Post
       and Telegraph Department, IA 118/5. Bookmakers soon circumvented the removal of
       telephones by using those of others, or leasing them in the names of others. A.L.
       Albertson, a leading Christchurch bookmaker, had his telephones disconnected each
       time he was fined, yet 'was never without a telephone'. Evidence to the Royal
       Commission on Gaming and Racing, p.905, IA 118/2. Withdrawal of the telephones
       of Palmerston North bookmakers in 1939 caused no more than 'a trifle of
       inconvenience'. *Truth*,18 Feb 1939. However, H. Clegg admitted in 1947 that the
       Dominion Sportsmen's Association had had 'much difficulty' in getting telephones
       in Palmerston North, which was a 'distributing centre' for racing information. Evidence
       to the Royal Commission on Gaming and Racing, p.189, IA 118/1.
55.   *AS*, 11 Nov 1932, Brady Scrapbooks. McKean's predecessor on the Auckland bench,
       J. Poynton, threatened to imprison, and occasionally did so; e.g. a billiard-saloon
       keeper, *NZH*, 17 May 1923. However, *Justice Statistics* show that very few were
       imprisoned 'peremptorily' by magistrates for bookmaking offences during the inter-
       war years. A Wellington magistrate, J.H. Luxton, admitted in 1938: 'Probably the
       Courts have not done their duty, and fines have been imposed year after year which
       have been nothing more than licence fees to the bookmakers. I do not propose
       suddenly to change what has been almost an established practice in inflicting fines

in these cases.' Accordingly, he fined R.E. Thompson, a barman operating in a 'small way', £20 for carrying on the business of a bookmaker. *EP*, 3 Jun 1938, W.R. Murray, Scrapbooks.

56. *AS*, 17 Jul 1934. Wilson and McKean had very different attitudes towards bookmakers. Wilson (like Poynton before him) saw bookmakers as 'really parasites, living by an unlawful occupation .... on the earnings of others.' The law 'prohibits the common gaming-house because it is economically a disaster; it prohibits the bookmaker because everything unclean in the sporting world has been caused by the bookmaker.' By contrast, McKean observed: 'Looking at it morally, there is no more harm in investing a half-crown or more with a bookmaker than there is in buying an art union ticket, as one can do any day in the streets'. *AS*, 11 Nov 1932, 10 Jan 1934, 15 Jan 1935, Brady Scrapbooks.

57. File J 1, 1936/35/266 documents the protest. After obtaining a report from the magistrate, the Minister of Justice, H.G.R. Mason, declined to intervene.

58. Between 1933 and 1944, Albertson had been fined on four separate occasions £50, £50, £75, and £100. In sentencing him to imprisonment, Justice Northcroft told Albertson: 'Having regard to the extent and the profitable nature of your business it is not hard to understand why the fines imposed upon you have proved no deterrent. To fine a bookmaker even the maximum amount of £500 is to do no more than take a small proportion of his illicit earnings by way of tribute. Punishment must prevent, or at least it should deter. Fines for bookmakers are inept and futile. One might as well fire a child's pop-gun at a pack of wolves. To those disposed to engage in this unlawful but highly profitable business imprisonment is the only deterrent.' *Rex v. Albertson*, Notes of address by Justice Northcroft in imposing sentence, 6 Nov 1944, J.B. Young, Scrapbook no.7. Petitions provoked by the imprisonment of Albertson led to the recommendation of the Petitions Committee that a Royal Commission be established to consider the gaming law. This was appointed on 22 Mar 1946 and reported in 1948. Given authority by the Gaming Amendment Act 1949, the TAB commenced business on 28 Mar 1951. I owe the point concerning the significance of Albertson's conviction to Brown, 'Origins of the Totalisator Agency Board'.

59. *NZPG*, 1926, p.391 (Memorandum dated 15 Jun 1926). Commissioner J. Cummings cited McIlveney's circular in 1947; Evidence to the Royal Commission on Gaming and Racing, p.1130, IA 118/2. See also the Third and Final Report of the Commission of Inquiry appointed to Inquire into Certain Matters Relating to the Conduct of Members of the Police Force, *AJHR*, 1955, H-16C, p.4.

60. Cameron agreed that it was 'just a coincidence' that there had been increased prosecutions in different parts of the country during the preceding weeks. Similarly, McIlveney insisted in an interview that the Police Force 'stood for strict enforcement of the statutory law .... irrespective of the offenders' position or occupation'. *LT*, 29 Mar 1927; *ODT*, 9 Apr 1927; *Truth*, 7 Apr 1927.

61. In his reply McIlveney assured Sir George that, 'notwithstanding criticism', he insisted upon 'the use by the police at all times of every honourable effort to strictly and impartially enforce the statute laws of the Dominion'. *NZPG*, 1927, p.287.

62. This is an estimate based on comparing different sets of police statistics presented in Annual Reports between 1926 and 1941: those specifically designated 'prosecutions of bookmakers' and offences against the 'Gaming Act', the categories of which included bookmaking as well as other gaming offences. Overall it seems that bookmaking offences comprised some 40% of all gaming offences in the inter-war years.

63. Annual Report, 1921, p.15; *Dominion*, 25 Jan, 29 May 1922; *PBH*, 5 Sep 1924, 30 Jan 1932; *LT*, 8 Apr 1927; *Press*, 22 Feb 1937.

64. A range of gambling activities were revealed by the cards, dice, wooden marbles, and other instruments for 'playing hazards' seized in the raids on 'gambling schools'. Belton, *Outside the Law*, pp.28, 80–3; *AS*, 15 Oct 1935, 14 Nov, 23 Dec 1936, 14 Jan, 19 Jun 1937; *NZH*, 31 Jan 1925, 8 Apr 1932, 29 Aug 1936, 10 Jun 1938; *ODT*,

11 Sep 1933; *LT*, 26 Nov 1934, 30 Mar 1935; *EP*, 30 May 1938.

65.   *Truth*, 10 Jun 1926; *Dominion*, 11 Jun 1926; *EP*, 30 Aug 1926.

66.   See *Truth*, 25 Mar 1922, 15 Apr 1926, 11 Oct 1933; *Dominion*, 28 Mar 1919, 29 Nov 1922, 13, 16 Feb 1926; *NZH*, 2 Jun 1923, 16 Feb 1925, 12 Feb, 28 Jun 1927, 21 Dec 1936, 27 Jan, 1 Sep 1937. Between Oct 1931 and the end of 1932 Detective Brady participated in at least twelve raids on 'pakapoo dens' in Grey Street. When W.K. McKean SM asked relief workers found in a pakapoo den during a police raid in Jan 1933, 'why do you men waste your money in pakapoo?', one replied: 'It's the only chance we have got of getting any money by having a 6d ticket'. All those found in the den on this raid were fined £1 but given time to pay. *AS*, 28 Jan 1933, Brady Scrapbooks. See also Boddy and Matthews (eds), *Disputed Ground*, pp.235, 282–3.

67.   *AS*, 8 Nov 1932, Brady Scrapbooks.

68.   This is revealed mainly by anecdotal evidence and the references to increases or decreases in offences by officers in charge of districts in the Annual Reports.

69.   Annual Report, 1913, p.10.

70.   Similarly, in Jul 1929 (on the final day of the Wellington races) there were raids on bookmakers in Taranaki towns; and there were similtaneous raids in various Waikato towns at the beginning of its racing season in Dec 1929. *LT*, 15, 19 Jul, 19 Nov, 2, 20 Dec 1929; *AWN*, 7 Mar 1934.

71.   This comment was made in response to questioning by W.E. Leicester, counsel for the Dominion Sportsmen's Association. Cummings would not agree to Leicester's suggestion that 'your men do not take any steps [against bookmakers] because that is unpopular'. F.O. Scott, who had assisted in detecting gaming offences in Wellington, described this as 'one of those more or less distasteful jobs where one has to on occasions secret themselves perhaps in places to obtain the evidence .... The gaming squad in particular is not sought after by the general police ... they would very much do other work than work on the gaming squad.' A former Detective Sergeant, N.J.S. McPhee, distinguished between 'criminal investigation' and detecting gaming offences. Evidence to Royal Commission on Gaming and Racing, p.1130, IA 118/2. Notes of Evidence, Commission of Inquiry into Police Conduct, vol.1, pp.103–4, 216.

72.   Commissioner McIlveney to Superintendent, Christchurch, 6 Jun 1927, copy in J.B. Young, Scrapbook no.3. Charges which followed a police raid led by Detective Sergeant Young on the premises of A.V. Whitta, a leading Christchurch bookmaker, were dismissed in Aug 1926. By Apr 1927, however, Young had had Whitta convicted and fined £400 for carrying on the business of bookmaking. Whitta's two employees were fined £75 and £25 respectively. Evidence at the trial showed that Whitta had taken 15,000 bets over the preceding two months. A prosecution by Young in Feb 1927 had the unusual result that a hairdresser's premises at 171–174 Madras Street was declared a common gaming house and effectively closed; anyone found there would be liable to a fine of up to £100 or three months' imprisonment. *Truth*, 2 Sep 1926; 3 Feb, 10 Mar, 7 Apr 1927.

73.   In a submission to the Royal Commission on Gaming and Racing, ex-Detective Gourlay stated that while 'in charge at Wanganui' he made the required quarterly reports on the principal bookmakers in the district. He did not receive any instructions to prosecute, and 'never did so'. Gourlay denied ever receiving a bribe from a bookmaker, or 'any suggestion of a bribe'. Nor had he received 'any complaint of a bookmaker failing to discharge his obligations.' To this Commissioner J. Cummings responded that Gourlay, who was 'not very brilliant' as an officer, had 'apparently overlooked the circulars and his oath and different other duties connected with enforcing the law'. He 'was never very active in the detection of bookmaking'. M. Gourlay, Statement, IA 118/7; Evidence to the Royal Commission on Gaming and Racing, pp.608–10, 1138, 1150, IA 118/2.

74.   Notes of Evidence to the Commission of Inquiry into Police Conduct, vol.5, pp.999, 1170, 1215–16. When Compton became Chief Detective in Wellington in 1949, and then transferred to administrative duties at Headquarters in May 1950, prosecutions

of bookmakers fell away substantially.

75. Submission of H.C. Sallery, IA 118/4/29; see also evidence of H.C. Sallery and Commissioner J. Cummings to Royal Commission on Gaming and Racing, pp.518, 1127, 1149. By the time he made his submission in 1947, Sallery had been a bookmaker in Auckland for at least 25 years; had been fined a number of times and sent to gaol for two months, but had not yet 'retired'.

76. Submission to Royal Commission on Gaming and Racing, IA 118/7, cited by Brown, 'Origins of the Totalisator Agency Board'; Evidence of A.L. Albertson to Royal Commission on Gaming and Racing, pp.902–3, IA 118/2. Though he was imprisoned in 1944, Albertson had hitherto been fined more leniently than most of his Auckland counterparts during the 1930s. H. Clegg, Secretary of the Dominion Sportsmen's Association, agreed that police had not been able to put his members out of business, but 'They have dealt with them and pretty severely'. Commissioner J. Cummings denied all allegations of leniency: 'wherever there is sufficient evidence a prosecution follows'. Evidence to the Royal Commission on Gaming and Racing, pp.153, 162, 1148–9.

77. *LT*, 29 Mar 1927.

78. Commissioner J. Cummings, Evidence to the Royal Commission on Gaming and Racing, p.1138; former bookmaker R.D. Donaldson, Notes of Evidence to Commission of Inquiry into Police Conduct, vol.5, pp.1081–4; vol.6, pp.1190–1, 1194; Commissioner Compton, *ibid.*, vol.6, pp.1295, 1298–1301; Sub-Inspector G.E. Callaghan, *ibid.*, pp.1316–17. Donaldson was between 1935 and 1939 a bookmaker in Dunedin, where he was convicted three times. He then moved to Wellington, where he operated on quite an extensive scale, shifting his premises three times before he was caught by Detective Sergeant Compton and again fined in 1943. Donaldson again moved to new premises (acquiring new telephones under a different name). Between 1943 and 1945 he moved between three city offices (two of them in Woodward Street behind the fronts of a 'wholesale carpet company' and a carrying business, and a third in Willis Street) and his home, particularly on Saturday racedays at Trentham. Donaldson was finally caught at his home by Compton and Callaghan early in 1945. He gave up bookmaking in Dec 1945.

79. Bettors found on premises raided by police often claimed to be merely 'curious' and were generally fined £1. When W.R. Reynolds, a 35 year old carpenter, pleaded guilty to betting with a bookmaker in Dec 1932, Detective Sergeant Kelly commented that this was the 'first time for many years that such a charge had been brought in Auckland'. A charge of being found in a common gaming house brought against Reynolds three days earlier had been dismissed. However, Reynolds had then admitted in evidence that he had made bets with bookmakers and jotted them down in his notebook. Thus police laid a new charge. The magistrate, W.K. McKean, commented that the maximum penalty was £100 or 6 months' imprisonment, but fined Reynolds £5 (or 14 days in default) as a warning. Names were rarely given by bettors over the telephone. Attempting to lay a bet was not an offence, according to a judicial decision. *AS*, 27, 30 Dec 1932, Brady Scrapbooks; Judgement of H.P. Lawry in the case of *Police* v. *W.S. Ingram*, 10 Mar 1941, J.B. Young, Scrapbook no. 7.

80. Evidence to the Royal Commission on Gaming and Racing, p.1151, IA 118/2.

81. See, for example, letter from Paul McQuarrie, tally clerk, Bluff, IA 118/4/49; and Evidence to the Royal Commission on Gaming and Racing, pp.1150–1, IA 118/2.

82. That is, the 'giving of advice as to the probable result of any horse race', which was prohibited. In Mar 1923 the Commissioner issued a circular noting that 'sports writers for different newspapers are getting into the habit of practically tipping the winners of races.' Police were to warn 'every manager of a newspaper' that they would be prosecuted for any contraventions of sec.30. Two months later, when the editor of the *MDT* was prosecuted, the magistrate dismissed the charge, saying that 'the language falls short of giving advice as to the probable result of the races.' From the mid-1920s, racing news occupied three pages of *Truth* every week, and its 'tipping

practice' was more extensive than that of other papers. *NZPG*, 21 Mar 1923; *LT*, 29 May, 26 Jun 1923; Joblin, 'The Breath of Scandal', pp.174–5; Report of the Royal Commission on Gaming and Racing, p.117.

83.   This comment was based on Belton's experience as a detective based at Hamilton and Gisborne between 1934 and 1939. Belton, *Outside the Law*, pp.203–4. In 1927, Wellington's magistrate, E. Page, dismissed a charge against Jessie McCorkindale, showman (and six others who worked for him) for keeping a common gaming house in two booths at Wellington's Winter Show. Page held that McCorkindale's 'rabbit game' was lawful and not a game of chance. Page admitted that 'objectionable features' (such as increasing the amounts of stakes and prizes) would have served to 'make it a gamble rather than a game.' This was one of Detective Bill Murray's cases. *Dominion*, 24 Aug 1927; W.R. Murray, Scrapbooks.

84.   This was the view of the Under-Secretary for Internal Affairs, who asked for stricter supervision by police. *NZPG*, 1934, p.382.

85.   *RP*, 3 Sep 1955. The illegality was that the trotting club was retaining 10% of the sweepstake pools to cover its costs. It seems that many non-totalisator clubs conducted sweepstakes or ran a betting equalisator system in breach of sec.45 of the Gaming Act 1908. Report of the Royal Commission on Gaming and Racing, pp.112–15.

86.   *Truth*, 17 Apr, 5 Jun 1935; Belton, *Outside the Law*, pp.168–71; F.A. de la Mare, Evidence to the Royal Commission on Gaming and Racing, p.590, IA 118/1; de la Mare to Senior Detective Murray, 1 May 1947, IA 118/9. De la Mare made it clear that weaknesses in the enforcement of the law against off-course betting (he cited the Te Aroha case as an example) were not the fault of local police, but of the 'political heads – the people who administer the Departments'.

87.   For further discussion, see especially: D. Dixon, *From Prohibition to Regulation: Bookmaking, Anti-gambling and the Law*, Oxford, 1991, ch.7; A.W. McCoy, *Drug Traffic: Narcotics and Organized Crime in Australia*, Sydney, 1980, pp.29–37, 142–53, 164–7, 176–82, 251–3; McCoy, 'Sport as Modern Mythology: SP Bookmaking in New South Wales 1920–1979', in R. Cashman and M. McKernan (eds), *Sport: Money, Morality and the Media*, Kensington, NSW, n.d., pp.34–67; O'Hara, *A Mug's Game*, pp.188–94, 230–40; *Report of Commission of Inquiry into Possible Illegal Activities and Associated Police Misconduct* (Fitzgerald Inquiry), Brisbane, 1989, ch.2; M. Punch, *Conduct Unbecoming*, London, 1985, chs 1, 7; M. Finnane, 'Police Corruption and Police Reform: The Fitzgerald Inquiry in Queensland, Australia', *Policing and Society*, vol.1, 1990, pp.159–71.

88.   Punch, *Conduct Unbecoming*, pp.13–14, identifies four main types of corruption: (1) 'straightforward corruption' – something that is done or not done for some form of reward; (2) 'predatory (strategic) corruption' – police stimulate crime, extort money and actively organise graft; (3) 'combative (strategic) corruption' – planting or adding to evidence to strengthen cases, 'verballing' (words attributed to suspects in statements taken by police are invented to help incriminate), buying and selling drugs, taking money or goods from suspects or prisoners, revealing the identity of informants; (4) 'corruption as perversion of justice'– lying under oath, intimidating witnesses, planting evidence, etc. Where the purpose of (3) is to make the law work more 'effectively', the actions of (4) are taken to protect police themselves. The following discussion is essentially concerned with aspects of categories (1) and (3). Allegations of possible 'verballing' have also been given in ch.6.

89.   Annual Report, 1930, p.8; *Truth*, 9, 23 Jan, 6 Mar 1930. Accompanying the 'gift' was a card bearing a picture of a racehorse and the signature of A.H. Samuels. Behind the front of a tailoring business in Hamilton, Samuels was bookmaking, probably with agents in other Waikato towns; he banked some £10,000 during 1929. In the Magistrate's Court he was fined £100 for keeping a common gaming house and £200 for bookmaking. For offering bribes he was convicted in the Supreme Court and sentenced to nine months' imprisonment.

90.   *Truth*, 9 Jan 1930.

91. These phrases were used in the hearings of the Commission of Inquiry appointed 'to inquire into certain matters relating to the conduct of members of the Police Force' (hereafter, Commission of Inquiry into Police Conduct) on 23 Oct 1953 which submitted its final report on 30 Nov 1954. See especially, Notes of Evidence, vol.1, pp.207–22, vol.5, pp.985–1081, 1085.

92. *Truth*, 10 Mar 1932. In *Journalese*, published in 1934, Robin Hyde commented: 'So far, the Auckland police have not had the painful duty of pulling in their gallant comrade who, on retiring from the detective force of the Queen City (he was given a presentation and a nice speech when he departed), promptly went into the bookmaking business.' Cited in Boddy and Matthews (eds), *Disputed Ground*, p.287. This comment may apply to Farnworth, though he was not a detective during his short career in the Police.

93. The origins and scope of this Commission of Inquiry will be considered in more detail in vol.5 of the *History of Policing in New Zealand.*

94. *Report of Commission of Inquiry into Possible Illegal Activities and Associated Police Misconduct*, p.12.

95. Third and Final Report of the Commission of Inquiry into Police Conduct, *AJHR*, 1955, H-16C, pp.5–9; and Notes of Evidence, particularly vol.1, pp.207–22, vol.5, pp.985–1081, 1085–90.

96. Third Report, pp.11–14; Notes of Evidence, vol.5, pp.1013–69; vol.6. pp.1345, 1329, 1331, 1334–5. Ritchie admitted to dubious practices (obtaining butter without rationing coupons from a man he knew to be a bookmaker; borrowing money from a former bookmaker; obtaining from a woman the reward she received for giving information regarding sly-grogging, and receiving a present from her husband, who was a sly-grogger); and almost all his evidence was contradicted by other witnesses.

97. Third Report, p.7.

98. *Ibid.*, pp.9–10; Notes of Evidence, vol.5, pp.1106–88; vol.6, pp.1223–74.

99. Third Report, p.10; Notes of Evidence, vol.1, p.223; vol.5, pp.1022–3, 1085–6, 1170; vol.6, pp.1191–9, 1200–14, 1224, 1237, 1240, 1251–7, 1273–5.

100. This is Fitzgerald's phrase in his *Report of Commission of Inquiry into Possible Illegal Activities and Associated Police Misconduct*, p.30.

101. *LT*, 29 Mar 1927; *ODT*, 9 Apr 1927; *NZPG*, 1926, p.275.

102. Potter declared in 1927 that 'If it is all right for a policeman to gain the confidence of an alleged bookmaker in order to make a bet to trap him ... it is equally logical to argue that members of the Force should be provided with jemmies and be told to encourage a man to commit a burglary so that he may walk into the arms of a detective.' Potter was making critical reference to a case in which Charles Belton was involved. *NZH*, 18 Aug 1927; Belton, *Outside the Law*, pp.25–6. Frank Langstone, with an eye on police methods of detecting sly-groggers in his constituency, commented in 1934: 'To get recruit policemen to disguise themselves as fellow-workers of people who were breaking the law was making sneaks of the police and undermining their character.' Similarly, Webb objected to 'a fine policeman' being sent to the West Coast 'in order to try to catch a "bookie". That was not the right thing to do. Policemen should be respected and honoured, and they should not be asked to do unmanly things.' *NZPD*, vol.240, 1934, pp.274, 276–7.

103. Annual Report, 1899, pp.4–5.

104. See, for example: Belton, *Outside the Law*, p.26, concerning a case in 1927; *Dominion*, 19 Aug 1933 – a New Plymouth jury acquitted a bookmaker whose defence counsel attacked the 'vicious method of crime detection' employed by two plain-clothes constables in laying bets.

105. *AS*, 4 Jan 1937, Brady Scrapbooks.

106. First Report, Commission of Inquiry into Police Conduct, *AJHR*, 1954, H-16A, pp.3–6; Notes of Evidence, vol.1, particularly pp.177–81, 195–8.

107. See O'Donovan's Address cited in the introduction, and Police Force Regulations 1919, especially 353(16) and 353(17), re the disciplinary offences of soliciting and

accepting gratuities. Commissioner McIlveney issued circulars and made statements which reemphasised the need for integrity in the Force. On the same day as he ordered the strict enforcement of the gaming laws, McIlveney also issued a comprehensive circular tightening up the policy on 'private rewards' or gratuities: henceforth these could only be accepted with the approval of the Commissioner; *NZPG*, 1926, p.391, 15 Jun 1926.

108.   'Firm' is London police and criminal slang for a criminal gang. A 'little firm in a firm' was the phrase of a London detective publicised by reporters of *The Times* (in Nov 1969) who exposed corruption within the CID, which, in one view, had become a 'thoroughly venal private army' by the early 1920s. This latter view may reflect the perspective of the Uniform Branch leadership of the London Metropolitan Police. B. Cox, J. Shirley, and M. Short, *The Fall of Scotland Yard*, London, 1977, pp.9–16; D. Ascoli, *The Queen's Peace*, London, 1979, p.210; D. Hobbs, *Doing The Business: Entrepreneurship, the Working Class, and Detectives in the East End of London*, Oxford, 1989, p.43.

Chapter 8: Suburban and Country Constables

1.   Report of Detective W.R. Murray re application for transfer to Levin, 19 Dec 1932, copy in W.R. Murray Papers.
2.   Minute on *ibid.*
3.   The most notable of the few examples discovered by the author is Bennet Farquharson, who after seven years as the sole detective at Hastings was in 1937 transferred to the nearby sole-charge station in the small town of Havelock North. In his sixteen years before retiring from this station he made only 43 arrests, by comparison with the 337 he recorded in his previous 22 years of service. C.H. MacDonald (comp.), 'Police Staff: Napier Police District', mimeograph, 1986; C.H. MacDonald, *The Story of the Napier Police District*, Napier, 1986, p.71.

Unless otherwise specified, general comments on the careers and types of stations of suburban and country constables are based on an analysis of (i) details in the following district histories: Margaret Carr, *Policing in the Mountain Shadow: A History of the Taranaki Police*, New Plymouth, 1989; Kit Carson and Yvonne Davison, *The Longest Beat: A Social and Pictorial History of Policing on the West Coast*, Greymouth, 1990; Ray Carter, *'Beyond the Call of Duty': A History of the Palmerston North Police District*, Palmerston North, 1988; MacDonald, *The Story of the Napier District*; June E. Neale, *The Nelson Police: The Story of the Nelson Police District, 1841–1986*, Nelson, 1986; C.R. O'Hara, *Northland Made To Order*, Whangarei, 1986; Miles Singe and David Thomson, *Authority to Protect*, Dunedin, 1992; Jinty Rorke, *Policing Two Peoples: A History of Police in the Bay of Plenty, 1867–1992*, Tauranga, 1993; Charles E. Spicer, *Policing the River District, 1886 to 1896: The First 100 Years of the Wanganui Police*, Wanganui, 1988; B. Thomson and R. Neilson, *Sharing the Challenge: A Social and Pictorial History of the Christchurch Police District*, Christchurch, 1989; David A. Thomson and Hendrik Kagei, *A Century of Service: A History of the South Canterbury and North Otago Police*, Timaru, 1987; Sherwood Young (ed.), *With Confidence and Pride: Policing the Wellington Region, 1840–1992*, Wellington, 1994; (ii) letters from, and interviews with, some 90 retired men, many of whom have been cited in ch.3; (iii) details from the PFDBs, vols 1 and 2 (1877–1948).

4.   In 1932 only one detective was stationed in the Whangarei, Gisborne, Nelson, and Timaru districts, and two in Hamilton, Napier, New Plymouth, Wanganui, Palmerston North, Greymouth, and Invercargill, by contrast with the twenty at Auckland, ten in Wellington, nine in Christchurch, and five in Dunedin. Annual Report, 1932, pp.15–17.

5.   Thomas Quirke was appointed a detective shortly after he was posted in 1906 to Palmerston North, where he remained until retirement in 1935, rising to the rank of

Senior Detective. Detective Sergeant A.B. Meiklejohn had spent ten years as detective in New Plymouth and then two in Auckland before being transferred in 1937 to Palmerston North, where he became a Senior Detective in 1942 and resigned in 1945 to go into business. Detective T.W. Allsopp was in 1940 posted from Auckland to Hawera, where he resigned in 1947 to become a racecourse inspector. Detective Sergeant R.H. Waterson was in 1939 transferred from Auckland to Gisborne, where he retired in 1959. Detective Thomas Sneddon joined Waterson from Auckland in 1941 and retired at Gisborne in 1953.

6. Minister of Justice, T. Wilford, echoing Commissioner McIlveney's views, *NZPD*, vol.222, 1929, p.194.

7. See, for example, ch.3 for the case of Detective L. Studholme, who in 1937 was posted to Kumara, where he remained until retiring nineteen years later. Similarly, for a breach of discipline in 1935, W.D. Thom was stripped of his Sergeant's stripes and transferred from Dunedin to the one-man station at Ross, where he remained until 1939. W.D. Thom to Editor, *NZPJ*, 25 Apr 1953.

8. Chesnutt had about five years' Police service before being sent to Stratford. In 1928 (aged 38) he was posted to the one-man station at Raetihi, where he remained for ten years. Carr, *Policing in the Mountain Shadow*, p.87; Spicer, *Policing the River District*, pp.213–16.

9. W.G. Wood to author, 14 Mar 1977; J. Skinner, interviewed by author, 20 Jan 1981. Despite his later start, Skinner had ten children to Wood's two.

10. Of the 28 commissioned officers in 1956 (all had been appointed constables between 1919 and 1925), eight had been detectives and eleven had served at sole-charge stations (nine of them 'country' stations), all but two of them having waited thirteen to fifteen years for this posting on the eve of their promotion to Sergeant. Nine were between 34 and 38 years of age when first posted to a sole-charge station. In addition to these eleven officers, one had at the age of 35 become the chief officer at Rarotonga, and another had served at two-man stations before being promoted to Sergeant.

11. PFDB, vol.1.

12. Gilbert Roberts and William Worsley respectively. Constable W.J. Hampton had been 29 years at Sumner when he retired in 1931. Thomson and Neilson, *Sharing the Challenge*, pp.139–40, 150–1.

13. In the inter-war period Millerton had ten changes of constable, Waiuta eight, Blackball and Kaitangata seven, and Granity six.

14. Clements had spent only two years on the beat in Christchurch before bring transferred to Millerton at the unusually young age of 25. It appears that because the police house had fallen into a bad state of repair only single men were sent to the peaceful mining village. J.P. Clements to author, 10 Aug 1977.

15. Carson and Davison, *The Longest Beat*, p.149. There were five changes of constable at Denniston between the wars.

16. *Ibid.*, pp.127, 153.

17. G. Innes to author.

18. *Ibid.*

19. Carter, *'Beyond the Call of Duty'*, pp.130–1; Thomson and Kagei, *A Century of Service*, p.131. Soon after construction of the Arapuni power station began a temporary police station was opened in Apr 1925 by Constable Jock Fleming, a 51 year old, 6ft 6in Irish bachelor who had previously been stationed at remote Matiere in the King Country. Rorke, *Policing Two Peoples*, pp.334–5; Spicer, *Policing the River District*, pp.266–8.

20. Details on Conway's career from PFDB, vol.2. For 'pugilists' at Waiuta see E.C. Chandler, *Waiuta Ghosts*, Christchurch, 1962, esp. chs 6, 7, 21; and G. Morris (ed.), *Waiuta*, Reefton, 1986, p.71. For Blackball, see L. Richardson, 'Class, Community, and Conflict: The Blackball Miners' Union, 1920–31', in Richardson and McIntyre (eds), *Provincial Perspectives*, pp.106–27. For Constable Holmes at Kaiapoi, see Thomson and Neilson, *Sharing the Challenge*, pp.160–1.

21. This description was used by Belton, *Outside the Law*, p.159. It is also used by W.J.
     Gardner to describe the range of appointments held by constables at Waiau (North
     Canterbury) from the 1860s. W.J. Gardner, *The Amuri: A County History*, Culverden,
     2nd edn, 1983, p.214.
22. See Jinty Rorke, 'Skinner, Lewis', *DNZB*, vol.3, pp.477–8.
23. W.D. Thom, 'Looking Backwards: A few personal observations of Forty Years Service
     with the New Zealand Police Force', typescript, 1953, p.9.
24. This generalisation is based on anecdotal evidence and an analysis of the charge
     books of a small sample of sole-charge stations. As might be expected, the statistics
     reveal variations amongst stations and over time.
25. At Darfield in rural Canterbury the local constable made 84 arrests between 1919 and
     1939. More than half were 'outsiders' arrested on warrant as absconders or for
     offences committed elsewhere; over a quarter of the charges were for disorder in
     some form – mainly drunkenness – while another fifth were for petty acquisitive
     crimes committed locally. Very broadly, this pattern was observed for other stations.
     R.S. Rusbatch believed that those he locked up during his twenty years at Cromwell
     from 1938 were 'mostly strangers'. Rusbatch to author, 30 Nov 1980. A study of the
     attitudes of a rural policeman in the early 1970s found that 'outsiders' were 'more
     likely to be treated in a strictly formal manner (and therefore more severely)' than
     members of the local community. B.B. Waters, 'The Role of a Rural Policeman',
     Auckland University Law Review, vol.2, no.3, 1974, pp.75–86.
26. Summons Books.
27. Roxburgh Diary of Duty Book, 23, 30 Jul 1920.
28. Memoranda dated 24 Sep, 20 Oct, 11 Dec 1920; 11, 25 Jan, 18 Feb, 11, 24 Mar, 17
     Jun, 19 Oct, 6 Dec 1921; 14, 31 Mar 1922; 24 Nov 1923; 24 Apr, 26 Aug, 26 Nov
     1924; 10 Feb 1925; 11 May, 22 Sep 1926; 27 Jan 1927; Murchison Station, Circulars
     and Memoranda Book.
29. In the late 1920s not all country constables collected agricultural and pastoral statistics,
     and not all who did so were conscientious. In 1930, the Government Statistician
     reported that in the previous year 'civilians' had had to be employed as sub-enumerators
     in 47 police sub-districts. Particularly in the Te Kuiti and Hamilton sub-districts, they
     found that the lists of occupiers had not been kept up to date. From 1932 the
     payment to constables was 3d per schedule collected. *NZPG*, 1921, p.14; 1930,
     p.850; 1932, p.76. Proceedings of the Economy Committee, 3 Feb 1931, on Vote 18,
     Police Department, p.3, SSC 60/10/39. Letter from R.D. Hodge to author, 30 Mar
     1977.
30. Regulations issued under the Arms Act, 1920, *NZPG*, 1920, pp.707–10. The discussion
     in this paragraph is based on these Regulations. Only in the case of licences to carry
     pistols was the requirement that they be issued only to 'fit and proper persons' made
     explicit. It seems that few applications for permits to procure rifles were refused, in
     the 1920s at least.
31. From 1922, members of Defence Rifle Clubs could obtain ammunition for practice
     through their club. In Jun 1923 there were 151 Defence Rifle Clubs approved under
     the Arms Act. Commissioner of Police to GOC New Zealand Military Forces, 20 Jun
     1923, P 2/4/-, part 1. With special permission of the Commissioner, ammunition for
     .22 calibre rifles 'ordinarily used for sporting purposes' could also be purchased by
     individuals without a permit from 1922. The purchase of .22 calibre ammunition
     without a permit seems to have become the norm.
32. In practice, miners could readily obtain explosives from the magazines of the local
     mining company without applying for the necessary permit themselves. This practice
     was accepted in 1922 by an amendment to the regulations which sought to formalise
     the record-keeping of the explosives disbursed to miners. Police conceded that it was
     'impossible to prevent a workman carrying away a portion of the explosive issued to
     him.' Commissioner O'Donovan to Minister of Justice, 15 Aug 1921, P 2/4/-, part
     1.

33. Within 48 hours if the firearm was an 'unlawful weapon' (an automatic pistol).

34. An Arms Officer could endorse a certificate of registration to give a local resident permission to take a firearm into another district for up to a month.

35. Returns contained the names, places of abode, and occupations of every person with permits or registrations, and their numbers.

36. There are no comprehensive statistics on firearm registrations in the early 1920s. However the countrywide pattern was probably broadly similar to that for Wellington for the year ending 30 Jun 1928. This is the only district and year for which statistics of individual stations have been found by the author. Note that these statistics contain an unknown mumber of re-registrations as well as new registrations and licences to carry pistols.

     Of the 3,081 firearms registered, there were 2,085 rifles, 859 shotguns and 137 pistols. The centres recording the most registrations were Wellington (1,026), Masterton (277), Petone (224), Blenheim (213), and Nelson (174). 714 firearms were registered at the 3 stations headed by NCOs, 210 at the 3 two-constable stations, and 957 at the 11 sole-charge stations. Return of Fees collected under the Arms Act 1920 for the year ending 30 Jun 1928, Memorandum from Constable T. Coward, o/c Arms Office, Wellington, 13 Jul 1928, P 2/4/-, part 2.

37. P 2/4/-, part 2.

38. Inspector S. Till (Wanganui) to Commissioner McIlveney, 19 Jun 1928, P 2/4/-, part 2. According to George Innes, who relieved at the Culverden station during the early 1930s, everyone in the district 'seemed to own a firearm, and the buying and selling of these meant a never-ending job of checking registration papers and numbers on firearms. On days when I went to Hanmer I took Arms Registers and Arms Permit books with me, often Saturdays, and I could get quite a number of transactions at the car parked on the street, a minature police station.' Innes to author.

39. Commissioned officers of the Auckland, Wellington, Christchurch, Hamilton, Napier and Timaru districts supported compulsory registration, with those in Whangarei, Gisborne, New Plymouth, Wanganui, Palmerston North, Greymouth, Dunedin, and Invercargill districts opposed. Those in favour of retaining the existing provisions with respect to sporting rifles took 'account of the danger of such weapons getting into the hands of youths or irresponsible persons', reported Senior Sergeant H. Scott to Commissioner McIlveney, 16 Jul 1928, P 2/4/-, part 2.

40. Forthright views typical of officers supervising isolated country stations were also expressed by Inspector Peter Harvey, in charge of the Whangarei District. Report of Senior Sergeant C.W. Lopdell, 16 Jun 1928; Superintendent Wohlmann to Commissioner McIlveney, 11 Jul 1928 (re permits for explosives); Inspector P. Harvey to Commissioner McIlveney, 20 Jun 1928, P 2/4/-, part 2.

41. Superintendent J.C. Willis to Commissioner McIlveney, 15 Jun 1928, P 2/4/-, part 2.

42. The bill followed the recommendations of an unsigned, undated paper on the Police file. It appears that these recommendations were framed in line with Wilford's thinking rather than the Commissioner's. McIlveney's suggested amendments (including one which would authorise the Governor-General by Order in Council to suspend or relax the provisions of the Arms Act where these prevented or interfered with 'any useful or harmless purpose') were not acceptable to Wilford. Apparently McIlveney wished to preserve the broad pattern of surveillance. When a delegate to the Farmers' Union conference in May 1929 claimed that he 'had it from policemen that the [Arms] Act was an infliction on the community', and stated that he believed that 'the police report was overwhelmingly against the Act', McIlveney asked Superintendent Wohlmann in Auckland to ascertain who was the delegate's informant. McIlveney minuted: 'It is surprising how very few police officials appear to be able to hold their tongues. The N.Z. Act is very much less restrictive than those of many other British countries. The N.Z. Police have not reported against it.' *Sun*, 24 May 1929; Commissioner McIlveney minute, 30 May 1929; also Commissioner McIlveney to Minister of Justice (J.G. Cobbe), 12 May 1930, P 2/4/-, part 2.

43. For example: *Press*, 6, 7 Nov 1929; *Thames Star*, 9 Nov 1929; *ES*, 6 Nov 1929; *Sun*, 7 Nov 1929; *AS*, 6 Nov 1929; *Marlborough Express*, 7 Nov 1929; on file P 2/4/-, part 2.

44. However, the Regulations were altered to make a certificate of registration apply to the whole country, instead of locally as hitherto. The time allowed for notification of change of abode was extended from 6 to 30 days. Commissioner Wohlmann to Minister of Justice, 3 Sep 1930; 'Notes on the amendment to Arms Act and Regulations (Proposed)' [undated, unsigned typed memo], P 2/4/-, part 2; *NZPG*, 1931, pp.373–5.

45. Arms Amendment Act 1930, sec.7: 'If any officer of police has reasonable grounds to suspect that any person has in his possession or under his control in any place any firearm, ammunition, or explosive, and that such person is of unsound mind, or is in a state of intoxication, or has attempted or threatened to kill or do serious bodily injury to himself or any other person, the officer may, without warrant, search that person or place, and may detain that person for the purpose of such search, and may seize any such firearm, ammunition, or explosive, and detain the same.'

46. Inspector Wohlmann, in charge of Hamilton District, in Annual Report, 1922, p.10.

47. E.g. receiving complaints; drawing up informations; issuing and serving summonses and warrants; entering details in charge books, summonses books, bail books, and criminal record books; collecting and 'paying over' fines and fees; providing quarterly returns of business to the Justice Department. Hence constables with prior experience as court orderlies in the cities could pick up the tasks more readily than others. Constables stationed at Kurow in the 1930s had no prior experience of court work and required 'considerable assistance and instruction' from the Clerk of the Magistrate's Court at Oamaru. H.W. Bundle SM to Under-Secretary for Justice, 5 Dec 1934; Inspector's report on Kurow Magistrate's Court, 5 Oct 1938; J 1, 1934/32/153.

48. Up to 50 or 60 criminal cases were transacted at Kurow annually in this period. Under-Secretary to Minister of Justice, 7 Jun 1939, J 1, 1934/32/153.

49. H.W. Bundle SM to Under-Secretary for Justice, 14 Mar 1935, J 1, 1934/32/153. The Kurow Magistrate's Court was closed from 1 Oct 1939.

50. *NZPD*, vol.222, 1929, p.194; J. Bitchener, MP for Waitaki, speaking on behalf of T.D. Burnett, MP for Temuka.

51. The dictum of Aporo Joyce, a highly regarded community constable at suburban Cannons Creek (Porirua) more than half a century later, captures well important influences on the local standing of suburban and country police: 'To do a job like this you need to be visible, you need to be available and you need to be credible'. *Dominion*, 5 Feb 1993.

52. R.S. Rusbatch to author, 30 Nov 1980; A.C. Strawbridge to author, 20 Jan 1981. When Rusbatch transferred to Cromwell in 1938 the 'large number of unemployed and road workers in the camp area' had made it 'difficult to fill the position'. Strawbridge was posted to the predominantly Maori district of Te Araroa near East Cape in 1933. According to Strawbridge, his predecessor had been transferred to Takapau when he was 'about to have a nervous breakdown' because of 'the Maoris behaviour towards him'. Later Strawbridge was told by 'the decent Maoris' that the constable 'had brought the worry on himself by not being firm with them.'

53. Eight Maori and two Pakeha attacked Constable Thom. Their cries of 'Kill him, kill him' were heard by other Pakeha residents who came to the constable's aid, quelling the 'unruly mob' with pick handles; Thom, 'Looking Backwards', p.9; *Press*, 26, 27 Apr 1929.

54. Connie Hayes to author, 12 Oct 1985. This is similar to other stories told about constables, or by retired men about their experiences at country stations, especially those that were remote, or had a high proportion of Maori in the locality, or a population of manual workers who looked askance at authority. For example, E.G. ('Ted') Carroll was remembered for 'mixing it' with miners at Runanga, and (as

Sergeant) knocking Maori riders off their horses in the main street of Ruatoria. Constable C.J. Halke of Waverley was 'remembered locally as a good fighter and after the first two or three brawls, found few wanting to tackle him'. Soon after Constable A.D. Knight arrived at Dargaville, 'one chap in a pub decided to have me on .... and after that I never had any trouble'. Similarly, at the Chatham Islands, 'there were about 30 locals on the bank watching me to see how long it was going to take to put the handcuffs on, and after that I had no trouble there either .... it depends on you and your size.' *RP*, 3 Sep 1955; Spicer, *Policing the River District*, p.153; A.D. Knight, interviewed by author, 6 Jan 1981.

55.   Thom, 'Looking Backwards', p.11.
56.   C.H. Reardon, interviewed by author, 8 Nov 1976.
57.   Charles Lovegrove to author, 25 Apr 1977. Lovegrove was rebuilding the Clive Hotel after the Hawke's Bay earthquake of Feb 1931. Constable G.W. Murray had been posted to Clive in 1910 and retired there in 1941.
58.   Rusbatch to author.
59.   Hodge told the Sergeant at Taumarunui that the prowler 'would not come back again as he had seen me, but I did not know who he was and he had bolted.' Hodge did country enquiries from the Taumarunui station for ten years from 1937. R.D. Hodge to author, 1 Mar 1977.
60.   E. Buckley to author, 12 Dec 1976.
61.   Thom, 'Looking Backward', p.10.
62.   Belton, *Outside the Law*, pp.197–8.
63.   Rusbatch to author. Also James Skinner, interviewed by author, 20 Jan 1981. While constable at Waitotara, Skinner called in a detective from Wanganui to investigate a theft within the family he was boarding with: 'I didn't like to get mixed up with it ... because I was pretty friendly with them ... [it was better to have] an outsider do the job'.
64.   For example: *NZPG*, 1926, p.330; 1931, p.422. Both Commissioners McIlveney and Wohlmann stressed that failure to observe Police Regulations 499 and 506 would be a disciplinary offence. Even so, George Rushton, for example, patrolled the rural Henderson district between 1927 and 1934 on horseback, dressed in leggings, waistcoat, sports coat and felt hat. Reputedly, he wore his uniform only when going into Auckland city. *Western Leader*, 31 Oct 1987, p.19.
65.   S.T. Allen (Kaponga Centennial Committee) to Inspector Sherwood Young, 11 Feb 1982 (in possession of author); Carr, *Policing in the Mountain Shadow*, p.102.
66.   Phillips, *A Man's Country?*, esp. pp.75–80.
67.   *Report of the Royal Commission on Licensing*, Wellington, 1946, pp.100–1, 168–70, 196–8. In 1945 there 1,104 licensed hotels in New Zealand, a countrywide ratio of 1,316 people per hotel. The lowest ratios of population to hotels were in the following licensing districts: Westland (248), Central Otago (266), and Buller (274).
68.   This expression, or a variant of it, was a common saying amongst retired police interviewed by the author.
69.   For example: W.G. Wood (at Winton from 1935), interviewed by author; George Baskin at Waverley (1938 to 1951), cited by Spicer, *Policing the River District*, p.155.
70.   For example H.H. Lowe, who resigned from Police in 1943 after eighteen years' service. While relieving at isolated country stations in the Wellington District, Lowe said, 'I more or less took the law into my own hands and allowed the licensees to indulge in a little after-hour trading .... so long as there was no reason for complaint.' At Tinui, 'On numerous occasions a group of local farmers and I have spent very enjoyable evenings in the tap-room of this hotel'; Notes of Proceedings, Royal Commission on Licensing, vol.11, pp.1595–6, J 61, box 3.
71.   Spicer, *Policing the River District*, pp.168–9. Conversely, Constable A.S. Ward seems to have responded to local opinion by being 'easy' at Kaeo between 1950 and 1953 and keeping no record of any hotel visits, and then 'strict' at Opunake in 1954

following requests by local notables to 'do something about the three Hotels in the district.' Second Interim Report of the Commission of Inquiry Appointed to Inquire Into Certain Matters Relating to the Conduct of Members of the Police Force, *AJHR*, 1954, H-16B, pp.28, 34–5; A.S. Ward, *Memories of Constable Ward*, Wellington, 1992, pp.30–4.

72.   This can be observed, for example, from the irregular pattern of visits and occasional breaches recorded in the Roxburgh Diary of Duty Book, 1 May 1920–29 Sep 1926, AG 189, Series 1/17, Hocken Library. During the same period Constable Claude Snow at Warkworth seems rarely to have visited the hotels at Puhoi and Waiwera. Warkworth Diary of Duty and Occurrences, 7 Nov 1921–22 May 1927, National Archives, Auckland Regional Office. The patterns of police visits to hotels observed in the 1950s by a Commission of Inquiry seem little different from those established 30 years earlier; see the Second Interim Report of Commission of Inquiry, 1954.

73.   Changes to the commissioned officer commanding the district could bring changes in the pattern of enforcement in Greymouth, most notably when Inspector Lopdell attempted to enforce six o'clock closing in 1932.

74.   Annual Report, 1922.

75.   Second Interim Report of Commission of Inquiry, 1954, pp.6–12, 29–35, 39–40, 49, 52–3.

76.   P. Treacy to author, 21 Nov 1980.

77.   Second Interim Report of Commission of Inquiry, 1954, pp.28, 40.

78.   Roxburgh Diary of Duty Book, 1 May 1920–29 Sep 1926.

79.   Second Interim Report of Commission of Inquiry, 1954, p.54.

80.   *Ibid.*, pp.56–7; *Report of the Royal Commission on Licensing*, 1946, p.175; see also *NZH*, 9 Nov 1923; *Press*, 8 Sep 1925; *Dominion*, 14 Feb 1930.

81.   *Report of the Royal Commission on Licensing*, 1946, p.174; Second Interim Report of Commission of Inquiry, 1954, pp.57–8. Strangers drinking in the bar after hours could be allotted to hotel lodgers who would claim them as their guests should the police appear. The 'guests' continued to pay for their own liquor.

82.   Constable Butler said in court that when he called at the hotel for his usual inspection he saw three men in the bar, but, knowing them to be personal friends of the licensee, regarded the position as quite legal. Butler, who said he had been up for two nights with a sick daughter and was not feeling well, accepted the offer of a drink from the licensee. The Whangarei magistrate, who had 'always regarded' Butler 'as a reliable witness', nonetheless convicted him for being illegally on licensed premises. However, this conviction was quashed on appeal to the Supreme Court. Butler went on to receive a third clasp on his long service and good conduct medal 22 years later. *NZH*, 17 Dec 1936; 6, 14 Jul, 6 Aug 1937.

83.   *PBH*, 30 Apr 1925.

84.   *Report of the Royal Commission on Licensing*, 1946, p.175.

85.   Until 1945 'no-licence' districts were coterminous with electorates; their boundaries changed with the periodical redrawing of electorate boundaries. Between 1918 and 1945 there were the following no-licence districts: (i) predominantly urban: Grey Lynn, Eden, Roskill, Wellington South, Wellington East (from 1928), Wellington Suburbs (until 1938, then Wellington West and Wellington East), Invercargill (until 1943); (ii) predominantly rural: Auckland Suburbs (from 1928), Ohinemuri (until 1925), Masterton, Ashburton (until 1928), Oamaru, Bruce (until 1922), Clutha, Mataura.

      Ohinemuri and Invercargill voted for the restoration of licences, and each became a licence district. Bruce and Ashburton were eliminated as electorates, with (particularly in the case of Ashburton) the former no-licence areas included in electorates which had been licence districts. However there was no provision for a vote on restoration, and thus no power to restore licences to sell liquor in areas which had formerly been included in no-licence districts. *Report of the Royal Commission on Licensing*, 1946, pp.33, 144–8, 197–8, 206–8. For the boundaries of the no-licence districts (electorates) see A. McRobie, *New Zealand Electoral Atlas*, Wellington, 1989, pp.74–93.

86. According to both the reminiscences of police and newspaper comment, sly-grogging was common in Oamaru in the 1930s; M. Thyne, Memoir, n.d., c.1978, copy in possession of author; Donald Scott, 'The Autobiography of Donald Scott', typescript, 1961, p.99; *Truth*, 9 Jun 1937. For images of the drinking patterns and sources of liquor in Invercargill in the 1930s, see Dan Davin, *Roads from Home* (ed. Lawrence Jones), Auckland, 1976, pp.34–47, 67–77.

87. For accounts of illegal whisky manufacture in the Hokonui Hills north-west of Gore, and attempts to detect it in the inter-war years, see Stuart Perry, *The New Zealand Whisky Book*, Auckland, 1980, especially ch.5; and David McGill, *The Guardians at the Gate*, Wellington, 1991, ch.7. Focusing on the activities of the Invercargill-based Collector of Customs, H.S. Cordery, and the McRae family, these published accounts do not fully describe the police activity in surveillance and the discovery of a number of 'stills' in various parts of Southland. Constables L.R.W. Nesbitt, J.A. Feely, and R.E.J. Brydon, amongst others, played important parts in detecting the illegal sale of spirits in Southland. Hokonui whisky was known to be available in places like Wyndham, Mataura, and Gore. R.E.J. Brydon to author, 4 Jul 1977; J.A. Feely to author, 31 Mar 1977; D.R. Sugrue to author, 23 Nov 1976.

88. *Report of the Royal Commission on Licensing*, 1946, pp.35–7, 212–27.

89. Annual Reports.

90. *Report of the Royal Commission on Licensing*, 1946, pp.146, 219–24; Evidence of Sergeant Theodore Campagnolo, Superintendent G.B. Edwards, and Senior Detective Patrick Doyle, in Notes of Proceedings, Royal Commission on Licensing, vol.6, pp.847–65, and vol.7, pp.908–19; Spicer, *Policing the River District*, esp. pp.234, 242–4, 259, 262–3; R.D. Hodge to author, 1 and 30 Mar 1977; M.E. Parker to author, 4 Mar 1977; D.R. Sugrue to author, 23 Nov 1976.

91. *Report of the Royal Commission on Licensing*, 1946, pp.35–7; J.H. Luxford, *Liquor Laws of New Zealand*, Wellington, 1938, pp.47–52.

92. Report of Constable W.H. Bradley, Tolaga Bay, 10 May 1945, P 1, 1944/901; 'Statement Submitted by the Under-Secretary of the Native Department ... to the Royal Commission on Licensing Law [contains the opinions of the Judges and Registrars of the Native Land Court on the operation of the Liquor Laws regarding Maori], in Notes of Proceedings, Royal Commission on Licensing, vol.3, pp.350–74; evidence of Chief Judge G.P. Shepherd, Sergeant T. Campagnolo, Superintendent G.B. Edwards, Senior Detective P. Doyle, Seton Henderson (member of Chatham Islands Licensing Committee), Constable W.A. Calwell, ex-Superintendent C.W. Lopdell, and Superintendent J. Sweeney, *ibid.*, vol.6, pp.817–42, 847–75, vol.7, pp.908–20, vol.10, pp.1397–1403, 1417–32, vol.20, pp.2963–3008, vol.21, pp.3078, 3116; *Report of the Royal Commission on Licensing*, 1946, pp.214–16, 219–27.

93. Reports of Constable F.K.H. Skerritt, 29 Sep 1950, Inspector W.J.K. Brown, 9 Oct 1950, P 25/4/-.

94. Annual Reports, 1911, p.10; 1912, p.8; 1914, p.11; 1915, p.12; 1917, p.11; 1918, p.8; 1920, p.10; 1921, p.11; 1923, p.10; 1932, p.10. In 1945, Commissioner J. Cummings echoed the prevailing opinion of his officers in pointing to the inadequacy of fines for Maori breaches of the Licensing Act and in seeking to make it an offence 'for a Native to be in possession of intoxicating liquor'. Notes of Proceedings, Royal Commission on Licensing, vol.4, pp.552–3.

95. Under the Maori Councils Amendment Act 1903, any person acting under the written authority of the Chairman of a Maori Council could seize liquor introduced or taken into a kainga or pa. The extent to which local police were given this authority is not clear. A.C. Strawbridge apparently exercised such authority as constable at Te Araroa between 1933 and 1938. He commented later: 'Some constables in Maori districts would go around the back of buildings or dark places to catch Maoris with bottles of beer or other intoxicating liquor .... I considered it would be contemptible to try and catch a Maori out in that way. The only time that I would take liquor from them

or prosecute them for that offence was when they exposed it to me in the streets, etc.' Strawbridge to author, 17 Feb 1981.

96. *Report of the Royal Commission on Licensing*, 1946, pp.226–7. The average annual rate of convictions for illegally supplying liquor to 'Natives' in these districts in this period was between 1 and 2 per 1,000 people.

97. Evidence of ex-Superintendent Lopdell in Notes of Proceedings, Royal Commission on Licensing, vol.20, pp.2967–8.

98. *Report of the Royal Commission on Licensing*, 1946, pp.224, 363.

99. Evidence of Chief Judge G.P. Shepherd, in Notes of Proceedings, Royal Commission on Licensing, vol.6, p.823.

100. As Senior Sergeant at Wanganui, Lopdell found Putiki Pa (near Wanganui) to be well controlled under the kaumatua Takarangi in the 1920s, in contrast to other marae he observed while Inspector at Hamilton during the 1930s. Native Land Court Judge H.E. Beechey pointed in 1945 to Ngaruawahia as a place where the local komiti marae enforced strict rules, by contrast to other marae. Notes of Proceedings, Royal Commission on Licensing, vol.3, p.363, vol.20, p.2988.

101. *Ibid.*, vol.20, p.2971.

102. This is a modification of Professor I.H. Kawharu's conclusion that 'for most tribal communities it is only since the Second World War that ... legal sanctions have come to take priority over those of kin.' I.H. Kawharu (ed.), *Conflict and Compromise: Essays on Maori Since Colonisation*, Wellington, 1975, pp.10–11.

103. James Belich, *The New Zealand Wars and the Victorian Interpretation of Racial Conflict*, Auckland, 1986, p.303; see also p.309. Belich's apposite metaphor is based on an analysis of charges laid against Maori, and on the conclusions reached by Alan Ward, *A Show of Justice*, Auckland, 1974, especially chs 16, 21; and by C. Lesley Andrews, 'Aspects of Development, 1870–1890', in Kawharu (ed.), *Conflict and Compromise*, pp.85–7.

104. *Statistics of New Zealand; Justice Statistics*. I have been assisted in my analysis of rates of charges laid against Maori by the research essay of Susan J. Thompson, 'Maoris and the Criminal Justice System, 1919–1939: A Preliminary Analysis', MA(hons) research essay, University of Canterbury, 1987.

105. The detail in this paragraph is based on an analysis of entries in the Te Araroa Watchhouse Charge Book.

106. Under-Secretary of the Native Department to Under-Secretary for Justice, 6 Apr 1936, J 1, 1936/31/28.

107. 'Magistrates Courts in North Auckland: Offences by Maoris: 1935', J 1, 1936/31/28; entries in Te Araroa Watchhouse Charge Book for 1935.

108. H.C. McQueen, *Vocations for Maori Youth*, Wellington, 1945, pp.83, 119, 148; Eileen Philipp, *Juvenile Delinquency in New Zealand: A Preliminary Study*, Christchurch, 1946, p.40.

109. Reports of Sergeant A.G. Beal, 24 Oct 1950; Senior Sergeant A.D. Buchanan, 3 Oct 1950; Sergeant W.H. Slater, 29 Sep 1950, P 25/4/-.

110. Northland contained 21% of the Maori population in the first half of the twentieth century. In both 1926 and 1945, Northland Maori are estimated to have had the highest Maori fertility rate, and the highest percentage of the Maori population under 15 years of age. Potentially, then, Northland had a Maori population with the highest risk of delinquency. Ian Pool, *Te Iwi Maori: A New Zealand Population, Past, Present and Projected*, Auckland, 1991, pp.121, 125–8.

111. Annual Report, 1935, p.7; see also *ibid.*, 1932, p.6.

112. H.C. Turbott, *Tuberculosis in the Maori, East Coast, New Zealand*, Wellington, 1935, pp.49–50. In 1940 Turbott wrote that 'Maori social life in our time is beset with problems. There is undoubtedly moral declension among the Maori people, as evidenced by intemperance, gambling, adultery and thriftlessness in sections of the race. This has resulted from the impact of western civilization upon Maori culture, from the unsettling of the race, the loss of tribal leadership and of the force of tribal

opinion.' Writing in the same volume of essays, Apirana Ngata saw 'allegiance to the tribal system' to be 'still strong' in North Auckland, Waikato, Rotorua, Bay of Plenty and the East Coast. He warned that *'Pakeha* students of the Maori are in danger of giving too much attention to the easily accessible and detribalized Maori and missing the characteristic and persisting patterns of Maori social life.' Apirana T. Ngata, 'Tribal Organisation', and H.B. Turbott, 'Health and Social Problems', in I.L.G. Sutherland (ed.), *The Maori People Today: A General Survey*, Wellington, 1940, pp.164, 170, 260.

113. In 1955 older Maori in Ahipara recalled public meetings called by kaumatua as attempts at social control. Similar memories came from older informants interviewed by Joan Metge in 1979 who had grown up and lived as adults in other Maori-speaking homes and communities. Joan Metge, *A New Maori Migration: Rural and Urban Relations in Northern New Zealand*, London, 1964, esp. pp.89–92; and *In and Out of Touch: Whakamaa in Cross-cultural Context*, Wellington, 1986, pp.7, 19, 95–8.

114. Reports of Sergeant A.G. Beal and Constable F.K.H. Skerritt, P 25/4/-.

115. Evidence of ex-Superintendent Lopdell in Notes of Proceedings, Royal Commission on Licensing, vol.20, p.2986.

116. A journalist commented on the 'unorthodox methods' of Maori policing at Waitangi in 1934, which included being 'tapped, not always gently, by staves'. Commissioner J. Cummings commented in 1945 on the use of marae police at important gatherings: 'they can do what we cannot do – tap them on the shins with a piece of manuka.' *NZH*, 6 Feb 1934; Evidence of Commissioner J. Cummings in Notes of Proceedings, Royal Commission on Licensing, vol.8, p.1173; O'Hara, *Northland Made to Order*, p.98. For similar Maori policing of big gatherings at Ruatoria, see Report of Senior Sergeant L.E.L. Wilson, 17 Oct 1950, P 25/4/-.

117. R.J. Walker, 'A Review of the Position of the Maori Warden', *Maori Wardens News*, vol.3, no.3, 1982, p.47; Augie Fleras, *From Village Runanga to the New Zealand Maori Wardens' Association: A Historical Development of Maori Wardens,* Wellington, 1980, pp.16–17.

118. Tuhi Karena was served a summons in the name of Sonny White, but spoke Maori in court and refused to answer to his English name. He said he had been given a certificate issued by T.W. Ratana which entitled him to keep order amongst members of the Church. The handcuffs were said to have been sold by the Police to Ratana for ceremonial purposes. The magistrate stated that the Ratana Church could not bestow the power to handcuff, and that 'they must do their work peaceably'. *PBH*, 15 Sep 1933; *Truth*, 20 Sep 1933. In 1950, Inspector Peter Munro (who was unsympathetic to Maori policing) commented that in Auckland 'during the last war, the Ratana Movement had several Policemen in uniform to deal with Maori conduct at dances and Maori functions. They proved a pest and a nuisance to the civil Police and were being continually assaulted by their own people.' Report in P 25/4/-.

119. Under the Maori Councils Act 1900 and its 1903 amendment, Maori Councils could make by-laws and impose fines for drunkenness, sly-grogging and the introduction of liquor. However these fines were reviewable by a magistrate and enforcable only by civil process in the Magistrate's Court. By statute at least, coercive authority seems to have been limited to the seizure of liquor introduced into a kainga or pa by any person authorised in writing to do so by the Chairman of a Maori Council. Luxford, *Liquor Laws of New Zealand*, pp.51–2. See also Augie Fleras, 'Maori Wardens and the Control of Liquor among the Maori of New Zealand', *Journal of the Polynesian Society*, vol.90, 1981, pp.495–513.

120. Fleras, *From Village Runanga to the New Zealand Maori Wardens' Association*, p.16; evidence of Police and Native Department officials generally to the Royal Commission on Liquor Licensing which reported in 1946.

121. *Report of the Royal Commission on Liquor Licensing*, 1946, p.215; Fleras, *From Village Runanga to the New Zealand Maori Wardens' Association*, pp.17–24; and

'Maori Wardens and the Control of Liquor'.

122.   Report of Senior Sergeant F. Taylor, 29 Sep 1950; see also reports of Constable
       F.K.H. Skerritt (Raetihi), Senior Sergeant C. McRae (Wairoa), Inspector W.J.K. Brown
       (Wanganui), Senior Sergeant E.E. Strawbridge (Kaitaia), Sergeant H. Sargent
       (Kaikohe), Senior Sergeant J.H. Greenlees (Dargaville), and Senior Sergeant J.
       Sutherland (Whangarei), P 25/4/-.

123.   The authority to physically remove a Maori from hotel premises remained with the
       Police. The warden at Ahipara in 1955 believed he lacked real power. Metge, *A New
       Maori Migration*, pp.87, 90.

124.   This is a point made by Metge, *ibid.*, p.92.

125.   Analysis of entries in Te Araroa Watchhouse Charge Book. When interviewed by the
       author in 1981, ex-Constable A.C. Strawbridge drew a distinction between the 'decent
       Maoris', the 'better class of Maori', and others he had encountered at Te Araroa.

126.   Entries in the Port Awanui Diary of Duty, e.g. 22 Aug, 8, 27 Oct, 1 Nov 1922; 16
       Jan, 26 Mar, 13 Apr, 15 May, 25 Jun 1923. In 1940 the economist H. Belshaw,
       discussing the Maori land development schemes of the inter-war years (especially on
       the East Coast), thought that a 'problem, the full implications of which do not appear
       to be realized even by the majority of [Maori] leaders themselves lies in the effects
       of individualized farming on community relations .... one cannot expect to fit Maori
       settlers into an individualist farm economy without weakening *existing* community
       relations and traditions.' H. Belshaw, 'Economic Circumstances', in Sutherland (ed.),
       The Maori People Today, p.212.

127.   Reports of Senior Sergeant J. Greenlees (Dargaville) and Sergeant H. Sargent (Kaikohe),
       3 Oct 1950; see also a similar comment by Senior Sergeant J. Sutherland (Whangarei),
       P 25/4/-.

128.   Metge, *A New Maori Migration*, pp.91–2; Belton, *Outside the Law*, pp.98–9.

129.   *NZH*, 31 Aug 1932. Entries in his Diary of Duty during the 1920s reveal that the Port
       Awanui constable found quite often that Maori he wished to interview were not at
       home, but said to be somewhere else within the Gisborne Police District.

130.   E. Buckley, interview with author, 5 Jan 1977.

131.   Te Whaiti Diary of Duty, entries for 23, 24 Oct 1933; 6, 7 Jan 1936.

132.   A.C. Strawbridge to author, 20 Jan 1981; Te Araroa Watchhouse Charge Book,
       entries for 27 and 30 Dec 1935.

133.   Philipp, *Juvenile Delinquency in New Zealand*, p.42.

134.   A.C. Strawbridge to author, 20 Jan, 17 Feb 1981.

135.   The importance of such cooperation was still evident in the experience of a constable
       in a remote northern North Island district in the late 1960s reported in Waters, 'The
       Role of a Rural Policeman', pp.79–81.

136.   An interpretation of entries in the Port Awanui Diary of Duty, 1922–1927.

137.   I owe this story, along with other information concerning East Coast policing, to John
       Robinson, a former Sergeant in the New Zealand Police, who has done considerable
       research on the history of the Gisborne Police District. See also John Robinson,
       Policing the Tairawhiti, Gisborne, 1995, pp.102–3, 115–16, 129–30.

138.   Report of Senior Sergeant R. Griffith (then at Taihape), 29 Sep 1950, P 25/4/-.

139.   The Native Constables were: Awanui (just north of Kaitaia) – Leopold Kaka; Rawene
       – John Beazley; Mangonui – Timoti Heteraka; Whangaroa – Pera Tamati; Matata –
       Topia Rotohiko; Te Kaha – John Pirini, 1922 to 1932; Rawiri Puhirake Hira, 1933
       to 1945. At Te Whaiti, A.M. Grant was appointed District Constable on 2 Mar 1900
       and died on 8 Jul 1923 as a result of injuries received in the crash of a passenger
       train at Ongarue. Grant, the storekeeper at Te Whaiti, was married to a Maori woman
       and spoke the language fluently. He was followed by his son-in-law, H.M. Macpherson,
       who served until his death (by suicide) on 16 Jan 1936. His successor, Louis Hekenui
       Bidois, a fluent Maori speaker, was first a District Constable and then a temporary
       constable at Te Whaiti. Details from PFDB, vol.2; and from Rorke, *Policing Two
       Peoples*, pp.108–12, 257–8, 262.

140. Te Araroa Watchhouse Charge Book, entries for 3 Aug 1934. Seven charges were laid.
141. Rorke, *Policing Two Peoples*, p.115.
142. A.C. Strawbridge to author, 17 Feb 1981.
143. *Waiuku News*, 20 Mar 1959; see also *NZH*, 18 Oct 1955.
144. Robinson, *Policing the Tairawhiti*, p.103.
145. *PBH*, 23 Mar 1935.
146. R.V. Petrowski, interviewed by author, 20 Dec 1980.
147. Claire Bibby, 'The Chatham Islands', in Young (ed.), *With Confidence and Pride*, p.390.
148. See *New Zealand Worker*, 24 Jun 1925, for a critical view of the perks of the local 'John Hops'; *NZPG*, 1927, p.80; A.J. Mills to author, 12 Dec 1976; W.G. Wood to author, 19 Apr 1977.
149. P 1, 1942/652; Belton, *Outside the Law*, pp.164, 201–2; Spicer, *Policing the River District*, p.156; G.C. Donnelly to author, 19 Jan 1977; E.F. Barry to author, 26 May 1977; A.T. Kelk to author, 22 Aug 1977.
150. George Innes, who relieved at Culverden in the early 1930s, was 'quite sure' that Sterritt's choice of drawing travelling allowances for staying in lodgings meant that 'the department would be out of pocket for their rigid adherence to the £52 limit for car allowance'. Innes to author, 31 Jan 1977; Thomson and Neilson, *Sharing the Challenge*, pp.174–5.
151. F.R. Henry to author, 10 Jun 1977.
152. *Gisborne Herald*, 7 Apr 1953.
153. Warkworth Diary of Duty, 10, 12 Jun 1922.
154. Port Awanui Diary of Duty, entries for 23 Apr, 1, 11 Jun 1926.
155. A rare example was a tribute to the work of policemen's wives paid by Superintendent D.J. Cummings on the retirement of Constable E.T. Bosworth after eighteen years at the Christchurch suburban station of Woolston; *LT*, 1 Jun 1933.
156. A.T. Kelk to author, 22 Aug 1977.
157. Innes to author, 31 Jan 1977; Thomson and Neilson, *Sharing the Challenge*, p.175.
158. Carson and Davison, *The Longest Beat*, p.127.
159. A.C. Strawbridge to author, 17 Feb 1981. See also Vibeke Wright, 'Hutt Valley and the Wairarapa', in Young (ed.), *With Confidence and Pride*, pp.227–34.
160. *PBH*, 23 Mar 1935. Similarly, at what was reckoned to be the 'largest gathering ever held' in Te Puka Hall, Tokomaru Bay, Mrs Carroll was farewelled along with her husband, the local Sergeant, in 1930. A member of the local county council declared: 'she had a heart of gold, always willing to help in anyway she could. She took an interest in sport, and appreciation of her many good qualities was indicated by the way in which people had been holding little farewell gatherings in [her] honour during the last few days.' *Ibid.*, 1 Apr 1930.
161. *NZH*, 7, 8 Sep 1933.
162. A. du Temple to author, 3 Mar 1977.
163. During a cold, damp winter in the Raurimu station house, for example, Mrs du Temple developed rheumatism which required her hospitalisation. *Ibid.* Constable H. Barrett's wife was also 'stricken with rheumatic fever' during his first year at Mangonui in 1938–39, and his younger daughter suffered lung trouble. Statement of Constable H.H. Barrett, 24 Jul 1942, P 1, 1942/652.
164. Port Awanui Diary of Duty, 15 Aug, 6 Oct 1926.
165. *Press*, 18 Oct 1927. E.L. Hargreaves was dismissed on 5 Jun 1927.
166. *Truth*, 6 Mar 1930; *NZH*, 26 Feb, 7 Mar 1930.
167. For example: Constable H.T. Smith of Kawhia was sentenced to three years' reformative detention for theft of money; Constable James Blakely of Tolaga Bay was sentenced to three months' imprisonment with hard labour on charges of forgery and theft. P 1, 1923/707; *PBH* 5, 13 Dec 1927, 7 Mar 1928.
168. Details on file P 1, 1942/652.

169. Commissioner to Inspector of Police, Whangarei, 25 Aug 1942, P 1, 1942/652.
170. P 1, 1942/652.
171. *New Zealand Census*, 1926, vol.9, 'Incomes'; *Ibid.*, 1936, vol.11, 'Incomes'.
172. Calculated from *New Zealand Census*, 1936, vol.11, 'Incomes'.
173. Carr, *Policing in the Mountain Shadow*, pp.69–70; A.J. Mills to author, 12 Dec 1976.
174. Along with the other references to farewells cited above, the public farewell to Sergeant E.J. Carroll and Mrs Carroll at Tokomaru Bay on 31 May 1930 contained this rhetoric. *PBH*, 1 Apr 1930.
175. *NZPD*, vol.266, 1944, p.371; *EP*, 7 Aug 1947.
176. H.C.D. Somerset, *Littledene: Patterns of Change*, Wellington, enlarged edn, 1974, pp.63–4.
177. Burdon, *Outlaw's Progress*, p.39.
178. Oliver Duff, *New Zealand Now*, Wellington, 1941, pp.103, 105. Note that both Burdon and Duff spoke of Sergeants at sole-charge stations. This seems to be a misconception, since Sergeants had charge of stations with at least one other constable. Nonetheless the portrayal of the local policeman as 'Sergeant' underscores his local standing and is an important element in the myth.
179. For example: pressing for a station at Ngatea (on the Hauraki Plains) rather than a proposed station at Kerepehi, and noting that Manutahi would be a better location than Tuparoa for an East Coast station, *NZPD*, vol.193, 1921–22, pp.790–1; provision of a police station at Port Moturoa, *ibid.*, vol.197, 1922, p.363; in Northland, *ibid.*, vol.249, 1937, p.811.
180. *ODT*, 17, 19, 23, 24, 28 May, 4 Jun 1928; Annual Reports, 1927, 1931.
181. Somerset, *Littledene*, p.64; Duff, *New Zealand Now*, p.30.
182. Press statement by the Minister of Police, 30 May 1952, and discussion on previous petitions, P 1, 1942/652.

Chapter 9: Supervision

1. O'Donovan, 'Address to the New Zealand Police Force', p.iv.
2. Ratios calculated from Annual Reports.
3. Rorke, *Policing Two Peoples*, p.60. Before the reorganisation of districts that was completed by 1921, the stations at Gisborne, New Plymouth, and Timaru were under the control of Sub-Inspectors. The stations at Whangarei and Nelson that were to become the headquarters of new districts were headed by Senior Sergeants in 1919.
4. Annual Reports.
5. *Ibid.*
6. *WN*, 24 Aug 1938.
7. It seems that only two Senior Sergeants in this period were passed over by others before being eventually promoted.
8. Data on careers derived from PFDB, vols 1 and 2, and *NZPG*.
9. Notably Superintendents A. Cruickshank, appointed Inspector at Greymouth in 1915, was promoted to Superintendent on 1 Jul 1921, at the age of 65, nine days before he retired. He then went to Western Samoa to succeed W.G. Wohlmann as Commissioner of Police. A.S. Bird, Inspector at Timaru, was promoted Superintendent on 1 Apr 1934, six months before he retired there; Superintendent James McIlveney, appointed to Dunedin on 1 Apr 1933, retired there on 9 Jul 1934; John Lander, appointed Superintendent on 17 Feb 1939 at Wanganui, retired there on 3 Feb 1940; J.K. Simpson, appointed Superintendent on 1 Sep 1930 at Palmerston North, retired there on 30 Nov 1931; Superintendent D.C. Fraser retired at Auckland after less than a year's service there.
10. In the case of D.J. Cummings, Prime Minister Peter Fraser later spelt out the key consideration: 'another capable man [Superintendent Stephen Till at Auckland], who

had about two years to go, was passed over in the interests of what he ... as Minister in Charge of the Police Department, felt was the efficiency of the Police Force. Mr Cummings had a much longer period to serve before retirement'. *NZPD*, vol.266, 1944, p.369.

11. A.H. Wright and C.R. Broberg, respectively. In Dec 1916, Wright had (potentially) over nine years' service remaining before he turned 65. Inspector (then Superintendent) Broberg acted as aide to Commissioners O'Donovan, Wright, and (for nearly two years) McIlveney. In Feb 1926, Broberg too had over nine years' service remaining, but he had not had command of a district and was in poor health. He eventually retired early, in Mar 1928.

12. *Truth*, 15 Sep 1923.

13. *Dominion*, 19 Aug 1919.

14. Lopdell also had his retirement deferred. He turned 65 on 15 Apr 1943, but did not retire until 1 Mar 1945.

15. *Dominion*, 15 Jan 1921.

16. *NZFL*, 28 Jun 1950.

17. *NZPG*, 1921, p.310.

18. Police Regulations 1919, nos 409 to 412.

19. *AS*, 21 Sep 1934; *Dominion*, 21 Nov 1935. Only one of those successful in 1935 was a Senior Sergeant. Commissioner Wohlmann's comment was that 'it was intended to make the examination ... hard. Positions for Sub-Inspector were limited and it was intended that only the best men should qualify.' Charles Belton details his preparation for the Sub-Inspector's examination, which he passed (while a detective) in the early 1930s, in *Outside the Law*, pp.153–4.

20. *AS*, 21 Sep 1934.

21. New Zealand was not alone in this: in Queensland, the first conference of the officers controlling the various police districts throughout the state was held in 1939. For this conference an agenda paper was prepared covering 'every phase' of police administration and a 'frank discussion took place on all items.' Queensland's Commissioner of Police saw the benefits of such a conference in terms of (i) more complete uniformity of action and greater coordination of effort; (ii) personal contact, facilitating discussion of problems peculiar to districts; and (iii) an exchange of experience. In view of these benefits, the Commissioner proposed that such conferences be held annually. Annual Report of the Commissioner of Police, Queensland, for 1939, p.4, held in Queensland Police Museum Library, Brisbane. In New Zealand the brief experiment of 'Co-ordinated Districts' in Auckland, Wellington, Christchurch and Dunedin between 1928 and 1930 should be noted. In Auckland, a Superintendent and two Inspectors, and in Wellington, Christchurch and Dunedin, a Superintendent and an Inspector, each had charge of a district and met daily to discuss common problems.

22. Notes of Conferences of North Island Officers in charge of Districts held 15 and 16 Oct 1940, and of South Island Officers, 22 Oct 1940, P 7/1/5–1940.

23. Governor-General to Secretary of State for Dominion Affairs, 19 Jan 1926, *AJHR*, 1927, A-1, p.2; Secretary of State for Dominion Affairs to Governor-General, 8 Nov 1926, *ibid.*, A-2, pp.49–50.

24. Regular, often annual, conferences of the Police Commissioners of the Australian states were held from 1903. However, the 1938 conference in Melbourne was the first for eight years. Following an invitation, Commissioner D.J. Cummings attended the 1939 conference at Brisbane at the request of the Minister in charge of the Police. Police war instructions were fully discussed, and consideration was given to national emergency regulations. Cummings commented that a 'great deal' was to be gained from attending such a conference. Though much of the discussion dealt with 'inter-State problems', Cummings thought that 'many of the points raised and discussed may arise in New Zealand'. After the conference, Cummings conferred with the Commissioners based in Brisbane, Sydney and Melbourne on 'all aspects of Police

administration'. Annual Reports of the Commissioner of Police, Queensland, for 1902, p.5; 1903, p.3; 1938, p.11; 1939, p.12; 1940, p.7; and Annual Report of the New Zealand Police Force, 1940, p.7.

25.   W.R. Murray, interview, 16 Feb 1978; see also *AS*, 21 Sep 1934. Charles Belton's recommendations for improvements in the Auckland Detective Office were not well received; *Outside the Law*, p.152. Ray Henry, a contemporary of Belton, commented that his colleague 'was an alert, active, and progressive type, and in those days any suggestion of innovations to systems, modus operandi, or facilities was frowned upon (really completely discarded). I think that those in a position to obtain some result in advocating them did not want the responsibility, and "just could not be bothered, or care less" '. Henry to author, 4 Dec 1977.

26.   An injury Hutton sustained when his horse lost its footing and fell on him during an inspection tour in 1922 later required an operation. *PBH*, 22 Apr, 21 Sep 1922, 22 Jun 1923, 11 Oct, 22 Dec 1924, 5 Jan 1925. Between 1922 and 1924, for example, Hutton visited Port Awanui station on 18 Apr and 31 Aug 1922, 17–18 Jun and 14 Nov 1923, 15 Jan, 8 Mar (with Superintendent Hendrey from Auckland), 15 May, 5 Aug, and 14 Oct 1924. Port Awanui Station Diary.

27.   *PBH*, 17 Jul 1934.

28.   Annual Report, pp.9–10.

29.   Auckland District Order, 11 Aug 1932, Remuera District Order Book.

30.   Greymouth District Order, 27 Mar 1924, Murchison Circular and Memorandum Book.

31.   Greymouth District Orders, 29 Sep 1922, 29 Jul 1926, *ibid.*

32.   This paragraph is based on newspaper and police reports, esp. Inspector C.W. Lopdell to Commissioner Wohlmann, 5 Oct, 1 Nov 1932, 12 Jan 1933; Senior Sergeant C.E. Roach to Lopdell, 1 Nov 1932; Detective Sergeant T.E. Holmes to Lopdell, 10 Jan 1933, in P 1, 1932/1279; and also on Ray O'Halloran, ' "Caesar's Ghost": A Policeman's Lot' (unpub. reminiscences about his father, Lott O'Halloran), 1981, pp.69–70; evidence of ex-Superintendent C.W. Lopdell to Royal Commission on Licensing, Notes of Proceedings, vol.20, especially pp.2975, 2980, 2993, 3004; *Dominion*, 20 Apr 1932; Annual Reports, 1933, 1934. See also Carson and Davison, *The Longest Beat*, pp.44–8, 72–4.

33.   Comments by Inspector R. Ward and Hollis himself at the latter's retirement. *NZH*, 23 Mar 1935.

34.   Evidence of Inspector Hollis in the Record of Proceedings and Depositions of Witnesses to the Commission of Enquiry into the conduct of members of the Police Force in relation to the disappearance and death of Elsie Walker, 22 Feb to 5 Mar 1929, p.60, P 1, 1928/1724, part 4.

35.   This role was defined by instructions to 'Sub-Inspectors assigned to Charge of Detective Offices', *NZPG*, 1930, p.241.

36.   *AS*, 18 Sep 1934. See also ch.3 for concerns regarding the efficiency of the Police, and Belton, *Outside the Law*, pp.150–4.

37.   Through either 'sheer incompetence or simple error', Sergeant Sweeney and Constable Culloty of Masterton had destroyed the evidence relating to a strychnine poisoning in 1923. When Sweeney was promoted to Inspector in Aug 1936, he was transferred to supervise the Uniform Branch in Wellington. Wright, 'Hutt Valley and the Wairarapa', in Young (ed.), *With Confidence and Pride*, p.273; *NZH*, 5 Aug 1936. See *NZH*, 27 Jul 1945, 21 Jan 1967, and also above, in ch.6, for comments on Ward.

38.   For details of his career, see the interview with Edwards reprinted in Thomson and Kagei, *A Century of Service*, pp.129–30.

39.   The Scottish-born Scott was a keen exponent of the bagpipes, which he played for Highland dancing at Oamaru and to mark the arrival of police rugby teams on the field in Wellington and Auckland. 'The Autobiography of Donald Scott, 1883–1962', typescript, dated Oct 1961.

40.   Unnamed, undated newspaper cutting on the eve of Scott's transfer to become officer in charge of the New Plymouth District in 1941, in Donald Scott, 'Autobiography'.

41. Scott, 'Autobiography', p.122.

42. Inspector Rawle to Commissioner McIlveney, 22 May 1930, W.B. McIlveney, personal file.

43. Evidence of Sergeant P. Geraghty, Inspector D. Scott, Sub-Inspector W. Pender, Sub-Inspector D.L. Calwell, and Superintendent J. Cummings to the Committee of Inquiry into the claim of Peter Geraghty for promotion to the grade of Senior Sergeant, 3 and 4 Feb 1941, New Zealand Police Museum. Note that Peter Harvey, who eventually became an Inspector, had had his promotion to Senior Sergeant blocked by adverse reports; *ibid.*, p.28.

44. Police Regulation 425. Note also Regulation 426, which provided that no constable or detective who had reached 50 years of age would be promoted to Sergeant or Detective Sergeant.

45. Constables on probation as Sergeants were still designated constables and paid a special allowance to bring their salary up to that of a Sergeant. For promotion to Sergeant, these acting Sergeants required a certificate of 'efficiency and good conduct' and a recommendation from the Superintendent; Circular 7/35, 27 Aug 1935. From Sep 1946, constables called up for duty as sectional Sergeants were promoted to the rank of Sergeant when they took up the duties of that rank. During their first six months on probation, they were reported on monthly by the officers under whom they served. Unfavourable reports could mean reversion to constable. Circular 7/46, 18 Sep 1946.

46. Austing, 'From Farm Hand to Assistant Commissioner'.

47. This was provided for in Police Regulations 422 and 423.

48. Waterson, interview with author, 26 Jan 1981.

49. *NZH*, 2 May 1928.

50. Others in the Auckland District were Sergeants J. Rock, at Newmarket from 1916 to 1928; J. Cowan, at Pukekohe from 1915 to 1936; and A.E. Rowell, who retired in 1932 after extended periods in charge at Devonport and Otahuhu.

51. Sugrue to author, 22 Nov 1976.

52. M.E. Parker to author, 4 Mar 1977.

53. Auckland District Order 5/28, 7 Jul 1928, Remuera District Order Book.

54. The phrase is that of retired Sergeant J.D. Walker, reflecting on the Sergeants in Dunedin during the early 1940s; J.D. Walker to author, 8 Mar 1977.

55. M. Thyne, 'Memoir' (copy of unpublished typescript in possession of author); H.S.S. Kyle (Riccarton), *NZPD*, vol.228, 1931, pp.36–7. Kyle referred to charges that had also been laid against Sergeants E.J. Rowe (who had subsequently left the Police) and D.B. Murray. In each of these cases, according to Kyle, appeals to an Appeal Board had been upheld: 'it looks as if there is something radically wrong with the superior officers in Christchurch – I repeat, radically wrong.'

56. This calculation is based on an analysis of often imprecise reports by officers in charge of districts in the Annual Reports.

57. In Sep 1929, Bonisch had passed the qualifying examination for Sub-Inspector, to which rank he would probably have been promoted but for his conviction and loss of seniority. James Bickerdike, a month older than Bonisch, and who had been sworn into the Force eleven days after him in Nov 1911, was promoted to Sub-Inspector according to seniority in Dec 1944 at the age of 60, while Bonisch remained a Senior Sergeant. Peter Fraser, when Minister in charge of the Police, commented: 'Sergeant Bonisch should not have been dismissed, but was culpable all the same'. Notes of interview of deputation from the Police Association to the Minister, 2 Apr 1938, P 13/1.

58. Report of Senior Sergeant W.J. Butler, 8 May 1930, W.B. McIlveney, personal file.

59. Police Regulation 31.

60. In 1935 only six stations had been controlled by Senior Sergeants, while 48 were controlled by Sergeants. See Annual Reports.

61. *PBH*, 10 Aug 1935; *ODT*, 17, 19, 23, 24, 27, 28 May, 4 Jun 1928.

62. District Office memorandum from Superintendent Wohlmann, 'Correspondence', 27 May 1926, Remuera District Order Book.
63. Ray Henry to author, 4 Dec 1977. Henry retired after ten years as Senior Sergeant at Newton between 1952 and 1962. The conditions he described had probably changed little since the 1930s.
64. In 1937 a Sergeant was appointed at the Wellington Central station to 'assist in the Senior Sergeant's office'. Annual Report, 1938, p.12.
65. The phrase is that of Superintendent P.J. O'Hara in his evidence to the Committee of Inquiry into the claim of Peter Geraghty for promotion to the grade of Senior Sergeant, 3 Feb 1941, Police Museum.
66. Inspector Donald Scott in his evidence to the Committee of Inquiry into the claim of Peter Geraghty for promotion to the grade of Senior Sergeant, 4 Feb 1941, Police Museum.
67. C.W. Kelly died in 1923 aged 56, T.J. Barrett in 1927, W.E. Lewis in 1928 aged 56, W.J. Quinn in 1930, J.J. O'Grady in 1931 aged 56, and H.H. Butler on 18 May 1933, aged 52.
68. Scott, 'Autobiography', p.94.
69. Neale, *The Nelson Police*, p.46; Rorke, *Policing Two Peoples*, p.59; *NZH*, 4 Jul 1930.
70. See Carter, *'Beyond the Call of Duty'*, pp.52–3.
71. At Invercargill, Senior Sergeant George Scandrett was in 1927 fined for breaches of regulations and transferred to Westport, where he was forced to resign; for the case of Senior Sergeant I.H. Mathieson, at Ashburton, in the same year, see below; Senior Sergeant A.E.J. Stark at Nelson was reduced to the rank of Sergeant in 1933.
72. The estimated populations in 1929 were: Ashburton, 5,290; Oamaru, 7,475; Masterton, 8,450; *NZOYB*, 1930, p.101.
73. *Justice Statistics*, 1921–30. See also 'No-License Districts: charges and convictions for drunkenness in, and quantity and kind of liquor sent into, during the year 1923', *AJHR*, 1924, H-37, pp.1–2.
74. Thomson and Kagei, *A Century of Service*, pp.110–11.
75. Scott, 'Autobiography', pp.97–9, 112, 129; Thomson and Kagei, *A Century of Service*, pp.112–13.
76. *Dominion*, 29 Nov 1922; *Truth*, 11 Oct 1933. For Chinese gambling and pakapoo more generally see Grant, *On a Roll*, especially pp.35–8, 72–4, 108, 144, 157–8.
77. *NZH*, 21 Mar 1923.
78. *Dominion*, 29 Mar 1919, 29 Nov 1922; *Truth*, 25 Mar 1922; *NZH*, 11 Sep 1922, 2, 14, 23 Jun 1923, 2 Jan 1924, 16 Feb, 16 Jul 1925, 24 Aug 1926, 12 Feb 1927, 16 Jan 1928, 19 Apr 1929, and references in the following footnotes.
79. *NZH*, 9 Jan 1926; *Dominion*, 13, 16 Feb, 12 Mar 1926; *Truth*, 15 Apr 1926; *New Zealand Worker*, 22 Jan 1930, 7 Mar 1934; *Press*, 21 Jan 1989. During at least two raids by detectives on pakapoo schools in Auckland's Grey Street, the large crowds which gathered demonstrated their 'sympathy' with 'the prisoners'. *NZH*, 14 Mar, 7 Apr 1932.
80. Joblin, 'The Breath of Scandal', pp.146–9; P. Law, 'Too Much "Yellow" in the Melting Pot? Perceptions of the New Zealand Chinese 1930–1960', BA (hons) thesis, University of Otago, 1994, pp.v, 14–17, 23–4, 38–44.
81. *NZH*, 19 Jul 1932.
82. See McGill, *Guardians at the Gate,* pp.81–91.
83. Note that the numbers of charges recorded in Police statistics are generally lower than those recorded in the *Statistics of New Zealand* (from 1921, *Justice Statistics*) for breaches of the Opium Prohibition Act and then the Dangerous Drugs Act. The Police statistics have been preferred because (i) there are inconsistencies in the presentation of the opium offences in the *Statistics of New Zealand*, with changes in 1912 (to arrests only) and in 1920 (to total charges); and (ii) the non-police series apparently records breaches prosecuted by the Customs Department as well as the Police.

84. This is the interpretation of R. Yska, *New Zealand Green*, Auckland, 1990, p.27.
85. *Report on traffic in opium and other dangerous drugs for 1930: Dominion of New Zealand*, cited by Yska, *New Zealand Green*, pp.27–8; *NZH*, 31 Mar 1931, 19, 20 Jul 1932.
86. In his reminiscences, he does not acknowledge following any instructions.
87. Scott, 'Autobiography', p.103.
88. *Ibid.*, pp.103, 107.
89. *Truth*, 11 Oct 1933.
90. Scott, 'Autobiography', pp.107–8. This was true also of raids in Auckland and Christchurch, as well as Wellington; see, for example, *NZH*, 21 Jan 1928, 9, 31 Mar 1931, 10, 14 Dec 1931, 19 Dec 1932; *CT*, 13 Jul 1931, 12 Apr 1932; *Dominion*, 25 Mar 1933; *Truth*, 29 Mar 1933.
91. *Dominion*, 20 Sep 1933.
92. Wellington District Order 2/1933, 9 Dec 1933, P-Wellington 14, p.16.
93. Scott, 'Autobiography', p.108. The occupier of premises received the heaviest fine (usually £50 or £100) for permitting opium to be smoked. There were additional fines (a minimum of £12 10s) for obstructing police, possessing opium, or being found on the premises.
94. *Dominion*, 30 Sep 1933.
95. *Truth*, 27 Sep 1933.
96. *EP*, 3 Aug 1964 (obituary).
97. *NZH*, 5 Apr 1935.
98. See Charles Belton's account of detecting and raiding an opium den in Auckland in the early 1930s in *Outside the Law*, pp.9–13.
99. Police Regulations 226–228; see also Belton, *Outside the Law*, pp.53–4, and comments above on 'detectives' work'. Note that in Auckland during the 1930s the Detective Sergeants would prosecute in the Magistrate's Court when there were too many cases for the Chief Detective to handle, or he was unavailable.
100. These points are made by Finnane, *Police and Government*, ch.4, esp. pp.76–7, 84–5. Finnane's discussion has influenced the argument of this paragraph.
101. Evidence of A.E. Currie and Detective Sergeant Thomas Kelly, in the Record of Proceedings and Depositions of Witnesses to the Commission of Enquiry into the conduct of members of the Police Force in relation to the disappearance and death of Elsie Walker, 22 Feb to 5 Mar 1929, pp.26, 119–22, 162–85, P 1, 1928/1724, part 4.
102. This comment, like others in this section on detectives, has been based on an analysis of detectives' careers derived from PFDB, vol.2, biographical details from newspapers, and the rank allocations in the Annual Reports. See also Belton, *Outside the Law*, p.156.
103. McHugh remained the only Detective Sergeant in Auckland until Mar 1935, when Detectives J. Walsh and A.B. Meiklejohn were promoted and transferred from Wanganui and New Plymouth respectively. When Sub-Inspector Sweeney was promoted Inspector and transferred to Wellington in Aug 1936, Senior Detective Hall became the Chief Detective, retaining this role when he was in turn promoted to Sub-Inspector in Auckland in 1940. *NZH*, 26 Mar, 10 Sep 1934, 4 Mar 1935, 17 Sep 1936; *AS*, 18, 19 Sep 1934.
104. Police Regulation 219.
105. See Finnane, *Police and Government*, esp. chs 4 and 9, for an Australian perspective.
106. Chief Detective Thomas Kemp became Sub-Inspector in charge of the Wellington Detective Office in Jul 1924, but this position lapsed when Kemp was promoted to Inspector and transferred to take charge of the Timaru District in Feb 1926. Senior Sergeants Reg Ward and Tom Gibson (who had both spent most of their careers as detectives) were promoted to Sub-Inspectors in charge of the Wellington and Auckland detectives, respectively, in Apr 1930. They became, in effect, the 'Chief Detective' in their office. *NZH*, 28 Jul 1924, 5 Apr 1930; *Dominion*, 1 Apr 1930. For the

'responsibility' of the Chief Detective at Auckland in 1929, see the evidence of Inspector J.W. Hollis in the Record of Proceedings and Depositions of Witnesses to the Commission of Enquiry into the conduct of members of the Police Force in relation to the disappearance and death of Elsie Walker, 22 Feb to 5 Mar, 1929, pp.60–1, P 1, 1928/1724, part 4.

107.   Circular 12/30, 28 Mar 1930, *NZPG*, 1930, p.241.

108.   Police Regulation 227.

109.   Evidence of A.E. Currie, Inspector J.W. Hollis, and Chief Detective A. Hammond in the Record of Proceedings and Depositions of Witnesses to the Commission of Enquiry into the conduct of members of the Police Force in relation to the disappearance and death of Elsie Walker, 22 Feb to 5 Mar 1929, pp.17–18, 66–9, 79, 84, 88–9, 99, 106–7, 113, P 1, 1928/1724, part 4. See also Belton, *Outside the Law*, pp.53–4.

110.   *NZH*, 18, 21 May 1927; *Truth*, 9, 30 Jun 1927.

111.   The author has found departmental material relating to only two cases: those of Sergeant G.F. Bonisch, whose disciplinary file was attached to the personal file of Commissioner W.B. McIlveney, and the disciplinary hearings of charges against Constables R.C. Hendren and H. Scandrett.

112.   Evidence of A.E. Currie, Inspector J.W. Hollis, and Chief Detective A. Hammond in the Record of Proceedings and Depositions of Witnesses to the Commission of Enquiry into the conduct of members of the Police Force in relation to the disappearance and death of Elsie Walker, 22 Feb to 5 Mar 1929, pp.23–4, 77, 116, P 1, 1928/1724, part 4.

113.   'Representatives of the press' also paid tribute, commenting that 'the happy relations which existed between the press and the police were in large measure due to Mr Cummings.' *ODT*, 30 Dec 1931.

114.   Inspector Lopdell commented on 'the fraternal associations of the Force which is different to outsiders' while discussing his relationship with Inspector Henry Martin during a disciplinary hearing concerning charges against Constables R.C. Hendren and H. Scandrett in Apr 1936 which is discussed below.

115.   R. Henry to author, 30 Nov 1977; G.C. Urquhart to author, 30 Nov 1976; R. Petrowski interview, 20 Dec 1980; G.C. Donnelly to author, 19 Jan 1977.

116.   W.G. Wood to author, 14 Mar 1977.

117.   Constable T. Cotter to J. Meltzer, 20 Sep 1955, Meltzer Papers. See also *RP*, 3 Sep 1955.

118.   A. Wilson to author, 25 Nov, 21 Dec 1976.

119.   J.D. Walker to author, 8 Mar 1977. George Donnelly noted that his relationships with his superiors changed through his service. When he joined in 1929 he had 'the impression that constables were a bit afraid of Sergeants, Sergeants of Senior Sergeants and so on through the ranks.' G. Donnelly to author, 19 Jan 1977.

120.   W.F. Pearce to author, 1 Dec 1976.

121.   G. Donnelly to author, 19 Jan 1977.

122.   R. Henry to author, 4 Dec 1977.

123.   D.R. Sugrue to author, 23 Nov 1976.

124.   W.S. Hammond interview, 16 Dec 1980.

125.   W.T. Thom to Editor, *NZPJ*, 25 Apr 1953, Meltzer Papers.

126.   Belton, *Outside the Law*, pp.150–6.

127.   Thom to Editor, *NZPJ*, 25 Apr 1953; Thom, 'Looking Backwards'.

128.   *LT*, 15, 23, 29 Sep 1927; *Press*, 27 Sep 1927; Thomson and Neilson, *Sharing the Challenge*, p.194.

129.   *PBH*, 17 Jul 1934. Announcing O'Halloran's transfer, the *Herald* had commented: 'During the comparatively long period in which Inspector O'Halloran has been chief officer of the force in this territory he has proved himself to be a police officer of outstanding ability and the utmost integrity, and regret will be general amongst his many friends'. *Ibid.*, 5 Jul 1934.

130.   Thomson and Kagei, *A Century of Service*, pp.32–3.

131. Annual Report, 1935, p.10.
132. O'Halloran, ' "Caesar's Ghost" ', p.85. This account is a retrospective one by Lott O'Halloran's son, who derived his information from his mother.
133. *NZPD*, vol.243, 1935, p.508 (Rev. C. Carr, MP for Timaru); O'Halloran, ' "Caesar's Ghost" ', p.85, comments: 'The men who were accused endeavoured to stir up stories against my father, mainly in connection with the woman who was largely responsible for the whole matter of the enquiry [into the alleged 'levy' on bookmakers].'
134. *Press*, 2 Oct 1935; *CSS*, 2 Oct 1935. Inspector Thomas Shanahan, who succeeded O'Halloran at Timaru, made no comment on these events in the next Annual Report, 1936, p.12. O'Halloran, ' "Caesar's Ghost" ', pp.85–6, comments that 'my father had a very painful last year of his service in Dunedin, severely crippled with arthritis and lumbago.'
135. A.C. Strawbridge to author, 17 Feb 1981. Mr Strawbridge was then stationed at Te Araroa and gave evidence at the hearing of charges against Constable R.C. Hendren.
136. *PBH*, 27 Nov 1936.
137. This account is based on an unnumbered police file relating to the disciplinary hearings concerning charges against R.C. Hendren and H. Scandrett; and *Press*, 1 Feb 1936; *PBH*, 10, 24 Feb, 22 Jul, 5 Sep 1936; *Dominion*, 1 Feb, 30 May 1936; *Truth*, 5 Feb 1936.

Chapter 10: Political Surveillance (1919–35)

1. Commissioner to [officers in charge, all districts], 29 Jan 1919, OPR 1/1/1.
2. Commissioner to [officers in charge, all districts], 3 Apr 1919; see also 10 Jul 1919; OPR 1/1/1.
3. Commissioner to [officers in charge, all districts], 10 Sep 1920, OPR 1/1/1.
4. See Hill, *Iron Hand*, pp.348–55.
5. High Commissioner to Prime Minister, 3 Dec 1919, AD 11/2/1, part 1.
6. In Apr 1919, Thomson (who had headed the Special Investigation Branch during the First World War) took the title of 'Director of Intelligence' and separated the Special Branch from the rest of the Criminal Investigation Department by moving from Scotland Yard to nearby Scotland House. This arrangement lasted until Oct 1921, when Thomson was forced to resign and the Branch was reabsorbed into the CID at Scotland Yard. From early in 1918 the Branch had issued a 'Fortnightly Report on Pacifism and Revolutionary Organisations in the United Kingdom and Morale Abroad'; from Apr 1919 this was superseded by weekly summaries presented to Cabinet, entitled 'Report on Revolutionary Organisations in the United Kingdom'. In Nov 1919, Thomson had asked the head of the recently established Investigation Branch attached to the Attorney-General's Department in Canberra for information on the 'growth of extreme movements' in Australia. R. Allason, *The Branch: A History of the Metropolitan Police Special Branch 1883–1983*, London, 1983, pp.74–7; S.R. Ward, 'Intelligence Surveillance of British Ex-Servicemen, 1918–1920', *Historical Journal*, vol.16, no.1, 1973, pp.179–80; Frank Cain, *The Origins of Political Surveillance in Australia*, Sydney, 1983, pp.191–2.
7. In Jan 1919, at the time of O'Donovan's first initiative regarding political surveillance, T.M. Wilford was Minister in charge of the Police. Massey became Minister following Wilford's resignation on 22 Aug 1919, and relinquished the portfolio to E.P. Lee on 18 Aug 1920.
8. Major-General Chaytor (General Officer Commanding New Zealand Military Forces) to Minister of Defence, 19 Dec 1919 (minute on file), AD 11/2/1, part 1.
9. Brigadier-General Richardson to Lieutenant-Colonel Smythe, 28 Aug 1919, AD 11/16/11.
10. See AD 11/16/11 for responses from military districts indicating lack of staff to carry out the necessary work, and the 'Note' on the file by Lieutenant-Colonel Smythe, 10 Oct 1919, recording that General Richardson 'said a new idea was growing in his

mind as to the way of dealing with Aliens and Bolshevists ie. by a secret agency working direct from GHQ'.

11. Notes of meeting, interview of Captain Campbell by General Richardson and Colonel Smythe, 16 Dec 1919, AD 11/16/11.

12. General Richardson to Commissioner O'Donovan, 2 Feb 1920, OPR 1/1/1.

13. Major-General Chaytor to Director of Intelligence, War Office, 12 Feb 1920, AD 11/16/11.

14. OPR 1/1/1, pencilled notes on file regarding a visit to both the Secretary of the Post and Telegraph Department and the Assistant Comptroller of Customs on 27 Feb 1920. O'Donovan secured Post Office support in approaching the Solicitor-General to extend the functions of the Censor to include the examination of newspapers, pamphlets, and other printed material addressed to individuals suspected by the police. (Such authority was not given, it seems, and the Police had to rely on less formal arrangements with the Post Office in their surveillance of those who received literature that might be seditious.) The Customs Department agreed to send any 'revolutionary literature' they found to the Police for perusal, 'providing it was returned'. (Such literature had to be submitted to the Minister of Customs.) Customs men would accept the names of suspects from detectives.

15. The Intelligence Committee would meet monthly to organise the gathering and appraisal of intelligence regarding aliens, 'extreme or revolutionary movements' and persons connected with them. Notes of meeting, 23 Jun 1920, and Richardson to O'Donovan, 28 Jun 1920, OPR 1/1/1 (also in AD 11/16/11).

16. OPR 1/1/1, handwritten 'Comments' (no date, authorship unclear). This could well have been written by Superintendent C.R. Broberg, who assisted O'Donovan with administration at Headquarters, and whose views were usually accepted by O'Donovan.

17. Allason, The Branch, pp.74–5; Ward, 'Intelligence Surveillance', pp.179–80.

18. OPR 1/1/1, handwritten 'Comments' (no date).

19. The Police relied on the Defence Department to supply information from MI5, which included mail intercepted in transit from New Zealand to Moscow, and its 'Suspect List'. Though detectives periodically checked the names of overseas travellers with lists held by Defence Intelligence staff, there seems to have been little high-level contact between Defence staff and Police Headquarters on intelligence matters. See Acting Secretary, Department of External Affairs to Commissioner of Police, 12 Nov 1930, OPR 26/8/43; and entries in OPR, Register of Secret Correspondence, vol.1: 1928/75, 1929/22, 1929/28, 1930/137, 1931/202, 1931/355.

20. In London, MI5 and the Special Branch had overlapping responsibilities, and it was not until 1931 that a clearer division of labour was established, with the Special Branch focusing on the Irish Republican Army and 'civil security', and MI5 on the Communist Party of Great Britain and 'defence security'; Allason, The Branch, pp.60–1, 95; OPR, Register of Secret Correspondence, vol.1, 1931/541. In Australia between the wars, the Investigation Branch attached to the Attorney-General's Department of the Commonwealth government (created in May 1919 to replace the Counter Espionage Bureau established in 1916) dominated the conduct of political surveillance. Cain, Origins of Political Surveillance, chs 6, 7.

21. 'Address to the New Zealand Police Force', pp.xiii–xiv.

22. See Basil Thomson, Queer People, London, 1922, esp. pp.273–8, 292–300; Cain, Origins of Political Surveillance in Australia, pp.176–9, 235–7; G.R. Kealey, 'The Surveillance State: The Origins of Domestic Intelligence and Counter-Subversion in Canada, 1914–21', Intelligence and National Security, vol.7, no.3, Jul 1992, pp.179–210; G.R. Kealey, 'State Repression of Labour and the Left in Canada, 1914–20: The Impact of the First World War', Canadian Historical Review, vol.73, no.3, 1992, pp.281–314; D. Williams, 'The Bureau of Investigation and its Critics, 1919–21: The Origins of Federal Political Surveillance', Journal of American History, vol.68, no.3, Dec 1981, pp.560–79. In both Britain and Australia, as in New Zealand, the military authorities as well as the Police were concerned about possible threats from

'revolutionary' action during 1919 and 1920.

23. R.C.J. Stone, 'The Unions and the Arbitration System', in Robert Chapman and Keith Sinclair (eds), *Studies of a Small Democracy*, Auckland, 1963, pp.207–10; H. Roth, *Trade Unions in New Zealand Past and Present*, Wellington, 1973, pp.43–5.

24. The War Regulations Continuance Act 1920 applied to 'seditious' strikes and lockouts in industries declared by Orders in Council on 16 Feb, 17 Apr, and 5 Jul 1917, in *NZG*, 1917, pp.700, 1291, 2761. As late as Oct 1929, Commissioner McIlveney drew attention to these provisions in the policing of industrial disputes; *NZPG*, 1929, p.695. See also more generally regarding the expansion and application of the concept of sedition during the period 1916 to 1918: John Anderson, 'Military Censorship in World War I: Its Use and Abuse in New Zealand', MA thesis, Victoria University College, 1952, ch.2; and Paul Baker, *King and Country Call*, Auckland, 1988, ch.6.

25. P.J. O'Farrell, 'The Russian Revolution and the Labour Movements of Australia and New Zealand, 1917–1922', *International Review of Social History*, vol.8, part 2, 1963, pp.181–6; Cain, *Origins of Political Surveillance*, pp.176–9, 194–6, 228.

26. Walter Kendall, *The Revolutionary Movement in Britain, 1900–21*, London, 1969, ch.10.

27. *LT*, 1 Mar 1919.

28. Town Clerk, Te Awamutu Borough Council to Minister of Defence, 25 Feb 1919, AD 11/2/1, part 1.

29. *NZPD*, vol.185, 1919, p.747 (Massey's words).

30. *Ibid.*, pp.826, 832.

31. H. Roth, 'The October Revolution and New Zealand Labour', *Political Science*, vol.3, no.2, Sep 1961, pp.45–55; R.P. Davis, 'The New Zealand Labour Party's "Irish Campaign", 1916–1921', *Political Science*, vol.19, 1967, pp.13–23.

32. F.W. Rowley to Commissioner O'Donovan, 10 Sep 1919, OPR 21/2/33. This is one of only a few unambiguous instances the author has found of the Commissioner responding to a direct political request for surveillance, possibly because the request was made in writing.

33. Report from Detective Sergeant W.E. Lewis regarding James Roberts, 11 Sep 1920. An Auckland detective reported that Roberts and James Purtell (the Secretary of the Sugar Workers' Union) 'are not good friends and that Mr Roberts is not in sympathy with the sugar workers' strike'; Report from Detective Sergeant A. Hammond regarding James Roberts, 16 Sep 1919, OPR 21/2/33.

34. Commissioner to [officers in charge, all districts], 10 Sep 1920, OPR 1/1/1.

35. Memorandum on 'Labour Disturbances', copy sent to Commissioner of Police on 23 Sep 1920, AD 11/2/1, part 1.

36. *Ibid.*

37. Commissioner of Police to General Richardson, 29 Nov, 4 Dec 1920, AD 11/2/1, part 1; Report of Detective Sergeant Lewis (Wellington), 20 Dec 1920, OPR 21/2/33.

38. See reports on OPR 21/2/33, 21/5/5.

39. Report of Detective Sergeant Lewis, 2 Aug 1921, OPR 21/5/5.

40. Crown Solicitor to Under-Secretary for Internal Affairs, 2 Oct 1931, referring to Crimes Act 1908, sec.118, IA 115/83.

41. The quotation is from a report in *NZH*, 18 Mar 1922. In an opinion of the Solicitor-General, W.C. MacGregor, which Massey submitted to his Cabinet, Liston's speech 'tends to incite His Majesty's subjects "to attempt to procure otherwise than by lawful means the alteration of" the Constitution and government of the United Kingdom, in the words of section 118(1)(b) of the Crimes Act.' Solicitor-General to Prime Minister, 23 Mar 1922, P 1, 1922/477. See also Rory Sweetman, *Bishop in the Dock: The Sedition Trial of James Liston*, Auckland, 1997. In 1921, by contrast, a Wellington magistrate dismissed a prosecution against the *Maoriland Worker* for publishing a pamphlet advocating Irish independence. The magistrate ruled that the pamphlet would have been seditious in Great Britain but was not in New Zealand; Davis, 'The New Zealand Labour Party's "Irish Campaign", 1916–1921', p.21.

Supporters of Sinn Fein and of the Self Determination for Ireland League were closely monitored between 1920 and 1922 (especially as they were backed by the various socialist groups). The formation in 1924 of a Wellington branch of the Irish Republican Association (which shared a small membership and rooms with the local branch of the Communist Party) led to concerns being expressed to the government by the New Zealand Welfare League and the Protestant Political Association, and thus to increased surveillance until at least 1927. OPR 26/8/92.

42.   See, for example, in OPR 21/2/40, the memoranda of the Solicitor-General, Arthur Fair, 17 Oct 1928, 29 Aug 1929; and the judgement of E. Page, SM, on literature seized from the Communist Party offices in Wellington, *Dominion*, 22 Nov 1929; and also cases and magistrates' comments cited in J.R. Powell, 'The History of a Working Class Party, 1918–1940', MA thesis, Victoria University College, 1949, pp.5–8, 26–8.

43.   Police Offences Amendment Act 1919, sec.2; Police Offences Act 1927, sec.34.

44.   Judgement of E. Page, SM, in the case of Police v. Martin, 26 Feb 1931. The possession of this pamphlet was submitted by the Commissioner of Police (along with other material relating to membership of the Communist Party) as evidence that another man, a Yugoslav, was 'disaffected and disloyal', and that his naturalisation should therefore be revoked. Commissioner of Police to Under-Secretary for Internal Affairs, 8 Oct 1931, IA 115/83. The naturalisation of Ivan Tomasevic was revoked in Nov 1933, after regulations allowing for this were issued in Dec 1932 and a court hearing was held in Sep 1933. He was not deported, and his application in Jun 1936 for the reinstatement of his naturalisation was successful. See Brian O'Brien, 'Tomasevic, Ivan', *DNZB*, vol.4, pp.531–2.

45.   See Andrew Moore, 'Policing the Enemies of the State: The New South Wales Police and the New Guard, 1931–1932', in Mark Finnane (ed.), *Policing in Australia: Historical Perspectives*, Kensington, NSW, 1987, ch.6; and Cain, *Origins of Political Surveillance*, pp.208, 213–22.

46.   'Police Narrative, New Zealand Government War History', n.d., typescript, pp.41–53, WA-II 21/43d; E.A. Stevenson interviewed by author, Feb 1978. Mr Stevenson was the detective who monitored the German Club.

47.   Reports of Detective Sergeant Lewis, 27 Dec 1920, 1 Feb 1921, in which he notes Labour, Socialist, Marxian, Communist, Anarchist, and Sinn Fein 'revolutionary organisations', OPR 21/2/33.

48.   See, for example, reports of Detective Young (Greymouth), 30 Oct 1920, Detective Beer (Dunedin), 31 Oct 1920, Detective Sergeant Ward (Auckland), 2 Nov 1920, OPR 21/2/33.

49.   Report of Detective Sergeant Lewis on the history and strength of the Communist Party in Wellington, 27 Sep 1921, OPR 21/5/5; Roth, 'The October Revolution and New Zealand Labour', pp.52–5; O'Farrell, 'The Russian Revolution and the Labour Movements of Australia and New Zealand, 1917–1922', pp.194–6.

50.   *Tablet*, 5 Aug 1920, cited by Davis, 'The New Zealand Labour Party's "Irish Campaign", 1916–1921', p.18.

51.   Kerry Taylor has argued that the Communist Party of New Zealand brought together elements of three revolutionary traditions which had emerged within the New Zealand Socialist Party during the period from 1910 to 1913. He comments that in 1921 'New Zealand's communists aligned themselves with the Bolsheviks emotionally but they were not Bolsheviks in terms of their political ideology or practice'. K. Taylor, " 'Our Motto, No Compromise": The Ideological Origins and Foundation of the Communist Party of New Zealand', *NZJH*, vol.28, no.2, Oct 1994, pp.160–77.

52.   Minister of Justice to Commissioner of Police, 21 Sep 1921. Commissioner O'Donovan replied on 28 Sep, enclosing a long report by Detective Sergeant Lewis which he described as 'the result of prolonged and intelligent attention on the part of the detective to the political, social, and industrial activities manifesting themselves in the city'. OPR 21/5/5.

53. Report of Detective Sergeant Lewis, 3 Jun 1921, OPR 21/5/5.
54. In Dec 1926, Commissioner McIlveney asked Auckland's Superintendent Wohlmann to refrain from including accounts of the Labour Party's Sunday night concerts where the subject of the lecture was unimportant. Commissioner to Superintendent, Auckland, 13 Dec 1926, OPR 1/1/1.
55. Report of Detective Sergeant Lewis, 3 Jul 1921, OPR 21/5/5.
56. Commissioner to all officers in charge of districts, 11 May 1926, OPR 26/8/90.
57. Minute by Superintent Till on report by Constable Laugeson, 5 May 1925. Commissioner Wright to Inspector [sic], Christchurch, 7 May 1925: 'The monthly reports are to continue'; OPR 21/2/33.
58. Commissioner to Superintendent, Auckland, 8 May 1926, OPR 26/8/90.
59. Superintendent Wohlmann to Commissioner McIlveney, 6 May 1926. This memorandum accompanied reports from detectives on surveillance work, including one of the same date by Detective J.K. Robertson, who made the suggestion that 'Bourbeau and a few of his communist and labour supporters are setting out to give moral support to the Strike at Home and make notoriety for themselves'. The next day Wohlmann sent a longer memorandum on 'Industrial Unrest', commenting that 'in view of the Industrial war in Great Britain ... we should know all that can be learned of what is going on inside the unions', and suggesting the use of a constable as a secret agent. The first report from such an agent was submitted on 11 May; OPR 26/8/90.
60. See, for example, the fears of the Auckland detective on surveillance duties early in 1927 that 'It may reasonably be expected, from the boldness lately displayed by the Communists in the "Hands off China" propaganda and the fact that there is an unusually large number of unemployed about the City at present, that these revolutionaries will attempt to create such a "mob" demonstration as will create disorder when the Royal Visitors are here' later in the month. Report of Detective Robertson, 3 Feb 1927, OPR 26/8/90.
61. Report of Detective Baylis, 27 Jul 1929, which contains a list of 544 people who had been, or were currently, subscribers to the Party newspaper. The list was compiled following a raid on CPNZ headquarters on 16 Jul 1929. OPR 21/2/40.
62. Powell, 'The History of a Working Class Party', p.34; S.W. Scott, *Rebel in a Wrong Cause*, Auckland, 1960, pp.52–6, 59. Griffin's return from the 6th World Congress of the Communist International marked the application in New Zealand of the 'new line' laid down by the Congress: a more complete break with the Labour Party, and (according to Scott) a more doctrinaire and inflexible approach.
63. Based on police reports on file OPR 21/2/40 for the period 18 May–2 Dec 1929.
64. Griffin was prosecuted and imprisoned again from Dec 1930 until 21 Feb 1931. See Powell, 'The History of a Working Class Party', p.38; Report of Detective Robertson, 22 Feb 1931, OPR 26/8/90. The following paragraph is based on police reports in file OPR 26/8/90 for 1930. Cf. R.T. Robertson, 'Isolation, Ideology and Impotence: Organisations for the Unemployed during the Great Depression, 1930–1935', *NZJH*, vol.13, no.2, 1979, pp.151–2.
65. *New Zealand Worker*, 28 May 1930.
66. This comment is based on comparisons, for example, of Acting Detective Waterson's report (23 May 1930) of a march to Parliament and a meeting of the unemployed with Acting Prime Minister Forbes with that of the *Dominion*, 24 May 1930; and of Waterson's report (14 Aug 1930) of another deputation whose leaders sought briefly to push through the lobby doors in Parliament and later sing the 'Red Flag' with the account in the *Dominion*, 27 Aug 1930; and of the reports by Detective Baylis (17 Sep 1930) and Sergeant Wilson (20 Sep 1930) with the *Dominion*'s account (17 Sep 1930) of a public meeting chaired by Wellington's mayor and its aftermath. Regarding accounts of 'disturbances' of the unemployed in Christchurch on 6 Dec 1930, Superintendent Eales commented in the report to Commissioner Wohlmann: 'The position looks more troublesome as recorded in the newspapers than it really is';

OPR 26/8/90.

67. Report of Inspector Cameron, 10 Dec 1930; he sought to distinguish the Communist leadership from the remainder of the unemployed in the Christchurch demonstrations. OPR 26/8/90.

68. Commissioner Wohlmann to Superintendent Emerson, Wellington, 21 Mar 1931, OPR 26/8/90.

69. This paragraph is based on police reports in OPR 26/8/90 for 1931, and also OPR, Register of Secret Correspondence, vol.1, entries for 1931, esp. 1931/101, /103, /104, /118, /205, /323, /375, /384, /389. See also Powell, 'The History of a Working Class Party', pp.38–45.

70. Commissioner Wohlmann to General Officer Commanding, NZ Military Forces, 24 Mar 1931, AD 11/2/1, part 2. See also OPR, Register of Secret Correspondence, vol.1, 1931/92 and /98, regarding 'preparations by the Chief Inspector of Explosives in the event of Industrial Trouble'; and Naval Secretary to Commodore Commanding NZ Station, 28 Mar 1931, with an instruction from the Minister of Defence that in view of the possibility of civil unrest, steps should be taken to safeguard arms and ammunition in naval charge, N 8/15/7.

71. *Dominion*, 28 Mar 1931. However, the next phrase in this article was underlined on the Police file, OPR 26/8/90, by the Commissioner: 'but ... there are a number of unions in key industries who may adopt such tactics'. This fear was further underscored by a report from Constable Adams, at Denniston, on 18 May 1931, that he had been informed that a national strike would soon be called in protest against the wage cut that was 'now under consideration'. The local miners' union had received instructions regarding the course of action to be taken. See OPR 40/18/10. The same rumour was publicised in the *CS* on 18 May 1931: 'Coal Strike on Coast is feared'. While the United Mineworkers' national executive saw the coal miners as providing militant leadership against wage cuts, the 'majority of pits were evenly divided' on the question of a national strike. Calls by the miners' leadership for continued resistance to the policy of wage reductions persisted through 1931 and into the early months of 1932. Richardson, *Coal, Class and Community*, pp.235–6.

72. Copies of search warrants issued on 21 and 24 Apr 1931 on the oath of Senior Sergeant H. Scott, who was in charge of the secret files at Police Headquarters. The warrants were executed on 24 Apr. The premises at Himatangi of Leo Sim, Literature Secretary of the Party, were also raided at the same time. In the first week of Apr, the house of a waterside worker which had been the meeting place of Auckland Communists was raided by detectives in search of literature 'inciting to lawlessness' (i.e. urging watersiders not to pay the unemployment levy). In May a letter was received by the Police 'from Secret Source (photograph and copied) alleging Communist plans for [the] overthrow of Governments in Australia and New Zealand', OPR 21/2/40. See also OPR, Register of Secret Correspondence, vol.1, 1931/147, 1931/182; Commissioner to Superintendent, Auckland, 20 Mar 1931, and minute by Inspector Hollis to Sub-Inspector Gibson, 24 Mar 1931, OPR 26/8/90; *AWN*, 8 Apr 1931 (a report of the Auckland raid).

73. Reports of Detective Jarrold, 27 Apr 1931, and Detective Tricklebank, 24 Apr 1931, OPR 21/2/40.

74. Report of Senior Sergeant H. Scott to Commissioner Wohlmann, 27 Jul 1931, OPR 21/2/40. This report, based on documents seized in the raids of 24 Apr 1931, provides the most detailed summary of the Police knowledge of (or beliefs about) the New Zealand Communist Party.

75. Commissioner Wohlmann to Solicitor-General, 17 Jul 1931, OPR 21/2/40.

76. Leo Sim was convicted in the Palmerston North Magistrate's Court of distributing seditious literature; OPR, Register of Secret Correspondence, vol.1, 1931/411.

77. OPR, Register of Secret Correspondence, vol.1, 1931/281, /323, /324, /415, /422. The 'front' organisations included the 'Labour Defence League', which was active in Auckland, and the 'No More War Movement' in Christchurch, whose organisers were

refused a permit to demonstrate on 1 Aug 1931 and, when they attempted to hold a procession, were involved in a clash with the Police; OPR, Register of Secret Correspondence, vol.1, 1931/268 and /286. It is not clear that Griffin, or his comrades, did follow the instructions of the Communist International. According to the report of an agent in Auckland on 18 Dec 1931, 'Griffin of Wellington decides Party tactics & ignores Communist International rulings'; see *ibid.*, 1931/560.

78. *Ibid.*, 1931/415 (pencilled note: 'Part file to Minister in support of proposed legislation re declaring C.P. illegal 3/10/32'); and OPR [packet], 'Communist Party: Documents in support of Legislation to declare Communism Illegal' (contains letters, Party material and press clippings, particularly for the years 1931 and 1932).

79. Commissioner to Solicitor-General, 27 Nov 1931, OPR 25/2/5. See also Scott, *Rebel in a Wrong Cause*, pp.56, 65, 80–5. 'Nellie' Scott had arrived back in Auckland from Leningrad on 16 Nov 1931; OPR, Register of Secret Correspondence, vol.1, 1931/185. In mid-1931, the 'communistic activities' of the Yugoslav Workers' Educational Club in Auckland came to the notice of the Commissioner; further evidence in Dec led him to seek the revocation of the naturalisation of one its members; *ibid.*, 1931/229, /570; also file IA 115. See also O'Brien, 'Tomasevic', *DNZB*, vol.4, pp.531–2.

80. Both the Solicitor-General and the Comptroller of Customs saw difficulties in drafting a regulation. Sec.3 of the Immigration Restriction Amendment Act 1931 allowed for an Order in Council to be made. In May 1931, after the passing of the Act, the Police had given the Customs Department a list of Australian 'undesirables' (Communists) who were to be denied entry permits. The long-standing practice of having passenger lists inspected by a detective before an overseas steamer berthed, which had been discontinued in 1926 as an economy measure, was reinstituted. Commissioner to Minister of Justice, 16 Dec 1931; Acting Comptroller of Customs to Minister of Customs, 18 Dec 1931, OPR 25/2/5; *ODT*, 13 Jan 1932.

81. Commissioner to Minister in charge of the Police, 9 Oct 1933; Minister of Customs to Minister in charge of the Police, 1 Nov 1933, OPR 25/2/5.

82. Wohlmann's memo submitting the draft legislation began: 'In view of the recent serious earthquake in Hawke's Bay and the still more recent exhibition of organised violence and disorder by crowds resulting in extensive damage to property and bodily injury to participants and the Police, I feel it is my duty to respectfully submit that the present inadequate legislative provision for dealing with these emergencies should now be remedied.' The legislation was modelled on similar South Australian legislation passed in 1930. Wohlmann had also secured a copy of Canadian legislation, and had before him an 'Emergency Powers' bill drafted at the instigation of Prime Minister Massey in mid-1921. OPR, Register of Secret Correspondence, vol.1, 1931/573; Commissioner to Minister of Justice, 15 Apr 1932, P 2/1/9.

83. OPR, Register of Secret Correspondence, vol.1, 1932/330, /335.

84. Robertson, 'Isolation, Ideology and Impotence', pp.156–7.

85. OPR, Register of Secret Correspondence, vol.1, 1932/225.

86. Reports on file OPR 26/17/9.

87. Minister of Justice to F.H. Grant, President, Unemployed Workers' Movement, Christchurch, 4 Jul 1932 (letter drafted by Wohlmann), in an unnumbered OPR file on the 1932 riots with letters of protest at the prosecutions and convictions of members of the Communist Party for publishing the *Red Worker*.

88. Reports in file OPR 21/2/40 and in OPR, packets 44 (file 33/333) and 51 (file 32/273).

89. Commissioner to Superintendent (Auckland), 14 May 1934, OPR 26/8/90.

90. Commissioner to Minister in charge of the Police, 28 Jun 1934, OPR 26/8/90.

91. The number of prosecutions for 'seditious offences' under the War Regulations Continuance Act 1920 peaked at 16 in 1932; there were 11 in 1933 and then none until 1940. Prosecutions for 'inciting violence, disorder, or lawlessness' under the Police Offences Act averaged 16 annually between 1918 and 1931; there were 143 in 1932, then an average of only 7 per year to 1939.

92.   Superintendent Norwood (Wellington) to Commissioner, 15 Sep 1920; Superintendent
        Dwyer (Christchurch) to Commissioner, 14 Sep 1920; Superintendent McGrath
        (Dunedin) to Commissioner, 15 Sep 1920; Superintendent Wright (Auckland) to
        Commissioner, 15 Sep 1920, OPR 1/1/1.
93.   Report of Detective Beer, 4 Jul 1921, OPR 21/2/33.
94.   Reports (for example) dated 1 Jan, 2 Mar 1921 (Beer); 3 Apr, 3 May 1921 (Ward),
        OPR 21/2/33.
95.   Report dated 1 Apr 1921, OPR 21/2/33.
96.   Report dated 2 Nov 1920, OPR 21/2/33.
97.   Report of Detective Robertson (Auckland), 13 Jun 1926: 'About 150 attended the
        unemployed meeting; while about ten yards away the Rationalists loudly spoke from
        their platform, and a religious meeting was conducted some ten yards further on, and
        motor buses frequently passed by, to add to the din of these three sets of speakers
        [in Quay Street] ... the Labour Party meeting and the Communist Party meeting
        (New Zealand section of the Australian Communist Party) held their meetings –
        being about ten yards apart .... The New Zealand Communist Party [an Auckland
        faction] did not hold a meeting'; OPR 26/8/90. Also Detective Robertson's report
        dated 22 Aug 1926, OPR 21/2/33.
98.   Report dated 3 Dec 1920, OPR 21/2/33.
99.   Sweetman, *Bishop in the Dock*, pp.146–54.
100.   Report dated 16 May 1926. Also Detective Robertson's reports of 28 Sep, 17 Nov,
        2 Dec 1925, 31 Jan 1926, OPR 21/2/33.
101.   Report of Detective Sergeant Lewis, 18 Apr 1921; Reports of Detective Sergeant
        Ward, 3 Mar, 4 Jun 1922, OPR 21/5/5. For prosecutions in 1921 see also Powell,
        'The History of a Working Class Party', pp.7–8, 14.
102.   Reports of Detective Sergeant Lewis, 1 Feb 1921, and of Senior Detective Cameron,
        2 Aug 1924, OPR 21/2/33; Reports of Lewis, 22 Jun, 3 Jul, 2 Aug, 27 Sep 1921,
        OPR 21/5/5; Reports of Senior Sergeant Butler, 15 Nov, 13 Dec 1930, OPR 26/8/90;
        Powell, 'The History of a Working Class Party', p.38.
103.   E.P. Lee, Minister of Justice, to T.L. Ley, Minister of Justice, New South Wales, 18
        Jul 1922, asking for copies of two bills proposed in New South Wales to 'deal with
        the dissemination of disloyal and revolutionary propaganda amongst children and
        aiming at the control of the Communist Sunday Schools'. The New South Wales
        initiatives were based on two English bills. OPR [packet], 'Communist Party:
        Documents in support of Legislation to declare Communism Illegal'.
104.   OPR, Register of Secret Correspondence, vol.1, 1931/386, 1932/22, 1932/94.
105.   *Ibid.*, 1931/455.
106.   Powell, 'The History of a Working Class Party', p.26. Report of Detective Sergeant
        Lewis, 18 Apr 1921: 'I am of the opinion that this party is not taken seriously. It is
        time that some steps were taken to deal with them, and to compel them to supply the
        information concerning their numbers, which at present has to be sought after under
        adverse circumstances. They are avowed revolutionaries, they are greatly in the
        minority, and they therefore have no right to practically undisturbed freedom for the
        purpose of talking revolution'; OPR 21/5/5.
107.   OPR, Register of Secret Correspondence, vol.1, 1932/109.
108.   *Ibid.*, 1931/183, 1932/250, 1932/343. J.C. Beaglehole commented on pressures for
        political conformity in the early 1930s: 'Only Otago, among the [university] colleges,
        effactually resisted the current, when it refused to consider the representations of the
        Commissioner of Police over an appointment to its staff' in 1934. J.C. Beaglehole,
        The University of New Zealand, Wellington, 1937, p.380.
109.   OPR, Register of Secret Correspondence, vol.1, 1931/43, /54, /71, /543.
110.   P.[eter] F.[raser] to Commissioner, minute dated 6 May 1936, OPR 21/2/40.
111.   OPR, Register of Secret Correspondence, vol.1, 1931/528. Cf. Powell, 'The History
        of a Working Class Party', pp.61–2. H.M. Smith, a seaman who became a prominent
        member of the Auckland group of Communists in the early 1930s, successfully sued

a Wellington detective for damages for assault in the Wellington Magistrate's Court. Smith was awarded £15, and the detective resigned from the Police. *NZH*, 15 Sep, 29 Oct 1927, 22 Oct 1931.

112. Report of Sergeant Paine, 5 Mar 1931, on an Unemployed Workers' Movement demonstration at the Wellington town hall: 'I offered to supply the necessary information if the council would prosecute, and I pointed out that if no prosecution is brought against these men they have had a moral victory and are sure to have more meetings of this nature, and probably at a time when the Police may not be available to keep them in check'. Inspector Rawle minuted to Superintendent Emerson, 9 Mar 1931: 'The attitude of the City Council serves to encourage the Communists to further breaches'. OPR 26/8/90.

113. OPR, Register of Secret Correspondence, vol.1, 1932/136.

114. Memoranda in OPR 25/2/5.

115. Report of Constable Hewitt, 20 Oct 1920, OPR 21/2/33.

116. *GRA*, 24, 29 Apr 1926, cuttings in OPR 1/12/1.

117. OPR, Register of Secret Correspondence, vol.1, 1932/198.

118. *Press*, 20 Oct 1920, cited by J. McAloon, 'Sedition, 1913–1925', MA(hons) research essay, University of Canterbury, 1983. McAloon notes that the prosecution of the *GRA* drew a sharp reaction from Harry Holland, who led a Labour Party campaign against political censorship during the next two years. Even so, by early 1921 (as noted above) the Labour Party 'did not aim to sell literature of a dangerous kind'. There were no further prosecutions of Labour Party publications. See also Powell, 'The History of a Working Class Party', pp.5–6, 10–11; and Stewart, *Sir Francis H.D. Bell*, pp.170–87.

Chapter 11: False Dawn (1936–39)

1. Belton, *Outside the Law*, p.210.

2. Specifically, to restore salaries to Mar 1931 levels; to guarantee the security of the public service superannuation funds; and to introduce a 40-hour, five-day working week; Henderson, *The Quest for Efficiency*, p.144; Roth, *Remedy for Present Evils*, p.91.

3. According to a contemporary Labour MP and critic of Fraser, John A. Lee, in his *The John A. Lee Diaries 1936–40*, Christchurch, 1981, p.20, entry for 3 May 1937.

4. See appendix.

5. This is the recollection of Ormond Wilson, a backbench Labour MP elected in 1935 who was a friend of Walter Nash. O. Wilson, *An Outsider Looks Back*, Wellington, 1982, p.144. See also K. Sinclair, *Walter Nash*, Auckland, 1976, p.119. B.L.S. Dallard, who was Under-Secretary for Justice from 1933 to 1949, later said that he had been told that Peter Fraser particularly wanted to take over the Police to (in Dallard's words) 'more or less tighten up control. There was a feeling that the Police were rather expressing themselves a little bit beyond their authority'. Dallard interview, 7 Feb 1977. One measure of the relative importance of Fraser's portfolios is given by James Thorn's biography, in which Fraser's administration of Education and Health is discussed in a separate chapter, while his role as Minister in charge of the Police is described in one paragraph; James Thorn, *Peter Fraser*, London, 1952, p.131, and ch.12. See also W. Renwick, 'Fraser on Education', in M. Clark (ed.), *Peter Fraser: Master Politician*, Palmerston North, 1998, ch.5. This volume of essays discusses Fraser's administration of neither Health nor the Police Force.

6. Fraser made this point in his address to the Police Association annual conference in 1938; *NZPJ*, 1938, 'Official Report', p.4. During the 1920s, as MP for Wellington Central, Fraser would speak on Friday nights at the corner of Taranaki Street and Courtenay Place. He kept his soapbox in the Senior Sergeant's office at the Taranaki Street station. W. Brown interview, 5 Feb 1977. He had been the most prominent of

the Labour MPs who commented periodically in Parliament on issues concerning police during the early 1930s. Sometime during 1931–32, E.R. Trask was a member of a delegation of ten Wellington police organised to approach Labour MPs 'to ascertain what action was contemplated to alleviate the then existing conditions.' The delegation was met by Fraser, 'who listened to voiced grievances in a placatory way and promised to being them before Parliament. He then gave each of the delegates a 2/- piece, but I managed to avoid receiving one by passing by quickly.' Trask to author, 3 Jul 1977. See also asides by James Thorn in *Peter Fraser*, pp.119, 131.

7.   See, for example, the comments of Labour MPs (including Fraser) in *NZPD*, vol.230, 1931, p.613; vol.234, 1932, pp.310–12, 721–6; vol.237, 1933, pp.558–60; vol.240, 1934, pp.241–4, 272–6, 841–9; vol.243, 1935, pp.148–9, 507–9.

8.   Henderson, *The Quest for Efficiency*, pp.144, 151. See also Roth, *Remedy for Present Evils*, p.91; Burdon, *The New Dominion*, pp.214–15.

9.   The view of Leslie Hobbs, the Christchurch *Press*'s representative in the parliamentary press gallery, on Fraser's relationship with the Police Force. Hobbs saw Fraser as having 'strong views on the need for good relations between police and public, especially in the big cities'; he took 'an almost morbid and quite unministerial interest in police work on murder cases'. Leslie Hobbs, *The Thirty-Year Wonders*, Christchurch, 1967, p.48.

10.   Hill, *Iron Hand*, p.291. For Fraser's early radicalism (and his personality and career more generally) see Tim Beaglehole, 'Fraser, Peter', in *DNZB*, vol.4, pp.182–6; and M. King, 'The Origins of Peter Fraser's Early Radicalism', in Clark (ed.), *Peter Fraser*, ch.1.

11.   Hill, *Iron Hand*, p.295, See also the references cited above in note 5. B.L. Dallard recalled Wohlmann telling him he was 'handing in my ticket' because he had heard that Fraser was to be the Minister in charge of the Police. Dallard interview.

12.   The Commissioner apparently took his new wife with him on this tour. Several retired men who were stationed at the time in Wellington recalled this as a 'honeymoon' at the Department's expense. Later, it seems, there was an inquiry, and Wohlmann was required to pay back the costs of using a police car on the tour. H.E. Campin to author, 11 Jan 1977; G.C. Urquhart interview, 8 Dec 1976; W. Brown interview, 5 Feb 1977; W.R. Murray, cited in McGill, *No Right to Strike*, p.46.

13.   The Police Department defrayed the costs of telephone calls during March between Wohlmann's home in Auckland and Police Headquarters in Wellington. P. Fraser to Commissioner Wohlmann, 25 Feb, 29 Apr 1936, Wohlmann, personal file; *Dominion*, 27 Feb 1936; *Press*, 27 Feb 1936; *NZH*, 27 Feb, 31 Mar 1936; *Truth*, 15 Apr 1936.

14.   *NZH*, 31 Jan 1936.

15.   Ray Henry to author, 29 May 1977.

16.   In response to a suggestion that a police federation on the English model be formed in New Zealand, Wohlmann circularised the officers in charge of districts on 19 Aug 1930 that: 'As the formation of such a Union as is proposed would be very detrimental to the interests of the Service and in breach of Police Regulation 172, it is desired that any tendency discovered to support a movement in this direction will be sharply discouraged.' Circular in P 13/1.

17.   *NZPD*, vol.244, 1936, p.861.

18.   The statutory authority for the appointment was not spelt out but was apparently sec.4 of the Police Force Act 1913, which provided that: 'In case of the illness or absence from New Zealand of the Commissioner, *or for any other cause*, the Governor may appoint the officer next in rank in the Force to the Commissioner, *or any other person whom he thinks fit*, to perform all or any of the duties imposed upon the Commissioner by this or any other Act' (author's emphasis).

19.   Superintendent O'Donovan, for example, acted for Commissioner Cullen; see Hill, *Iron Hand*, p.364. The evidence is more ambiguous for the period between 1924 and 1927, when Superintendent C.R. Broberg was at Headquarters.

20.   Madden was in Class One of the Clerical Division of the public service. His annual

salary in Mar 1936 was £566; that of a senior Superintendent was £523. *AJHR*, 1935, B-7, p.106. This relativity was maintained in subsequent increases in public service and police salaries. Madden continued to act as Deputy Commissioner when the Commissioner was absent until his retirement in May 1949. He was awarded an OBE in 1947. Annual Reports, 1947, p.2, 1949, p.2.

21. *Press*, 13 Mar 1936; *NZH*, 31 Mar 1936. A week after Madden's appointment as 'Deputy Commissioner' was formally acknowledged in May, the *Dominion* (and other morning newspapers) claimed that, while no official announcement could be made before the end of Wohlmann's retirement leave, the appointment of D.J. Cummings as the next Commissioner 'was assured'. The evening papers carried Fraser's denial that an appointment had been made. *Dominion, EP,* and *AS,* 13 May 1936. On 18 May, the Labour MP Archibald Campbell reportedly told Constable O'Halloran at the Christchurch police station that 'Mr Cummings of Wellington was to be the man'; Constable O'Halloran to Senior Sergeant D.L. Calwell, 20 May 1936, P 13/1. Between Dec 1909 and Mar 1912, Waldegrave, the Under-Secretary for Justice, was also Commissioner of Police; see Hill, *Iron Hand*, pp.256–73.

22. Fraser's background was Presbyterian. Of the three Auckland Ministers, neither W.E. Parry nor H.G.R. Mason were Catholics. Savage had been raised a Catholic, and returned to the faith in the late 1930s after professing to be a rationalist, according to Barry Gustafson. From 1935, critics in the Labour caucus accused Savage of favouring fellow Catholics. However, as Gustafson observes, A.H. Nordmeyer (a Presbyterian minister as well as Labour MP) believed that, 'although the Catholic bishops O'Shea and Liston had a minimal influence on Savage, it was certainly no greater than that exercised by the liberal Methodist Scrimgeour.' Four other Ministers of the fourteen in Savage's Cabinet were Catholics: P.C. Webb was not a churchgoer and M. Fagan had only recently returned to the church, while H.T. Armstrong was married to a Methodist and D.G. Sullivan to a Baptist. B. Gustafson, *From the Cradle to the Grave: A Biography of Michael Joseph Savage*, Auckland, 1986, pp.178, 212–13; C. van der Kroght, 'O'Shea, Thomas', *DNZB*, vol.3, p.375.

23. Archbishop O'Shea to Bishop of Auckland, 28 Feb 1936. Bishop Liston received the letter on 3 Mar and noted, 'During coming weekend will gladly do what is possible.' I owe this reference to Dr Rory Sweetman. Lord Trenchard, a forceful personality with a reputation based on having developed the Royal Air Force, sought to press a number of 'reforms' on the London Metropolitan Police – most notably, to recruit and produce 'officer material' through a scheme of direct entry for young men who were immediately given the new rank of Junior Station Inspectors, and by the creation in 1934 of a Police College. Trenchard also appointed senior officers who were military men. These measures were opposed by both the English Police Federation and Labour MPs, who denounced 'class measures' and 'militarism'. In 1939 there were major changes to Trenchard's scheme of recruitment and training. Critchley, *A History of Police in England and Wales,* pp.203–8; Emsley, *The English Police,* pp.143, 156–7; *NZPJ*, vol.3, no.4, Aug 1939, pp.338–43.

   Note also that former Brigadier-General T.A. Blamey was forced to resign in 1936 after a controversial decade as Chief Commissioner of the Victoria Police. Haldane, *The People's Force*, pp.194–215.

24. Peter Fraser looked to reform and revitalise the education system. Early in 1938 he asked C.E. Beeby, then aged 36 and Director of the New Zealand Council for Educational Research, to apply for the position of Assistant Director of the Education Department, with the intention that he would become Director. The Public Service Commissioner followed the established procedure in setting up an advisory body, which unanimously recommended Beeby. C.E. Beeby, *The Biography of an Idea: Beeby on Education*, Wellington, 1992, pp.108–11.

25. Following the forced resignation of an 'outsider', former Brigadier-General T.A. Blamey, as Chief Commissioner of the Victoria Police in 1936, the Victorian government recruited another 'outsider', Chief Inspector A.M. Duncan (aged 48)

from Scotland Yard to inspect and report on the Victoria Police. Duncan recommended wide-ranging changes and became Chief Commissioner on 7 Dec 1937. In May 1934, the Queensland government had appointed an 'outsider', C.J. Carroll (aged 46) from the Government Tax Office, as Commissioner. Carroll 'set about ... a thorough reorganisation of the whole Force.' Haldane, *The People's Force*, pp.217–20; W.R. Johnston, *The Long Blue Line: A History of the Queensland Police*, Brisbane, 1992, pp.210, 215, 218–19, 235.

26.   Superintendent Cummings was reported to have commented at a luncheon of the Napier Rotary Club that: ' "The way the citizens turned out and backed us up was marvellous" ... it was that which to a very considerable extent broke the back of the strike. "They are all back at work now, and sorry that the strike ever happened. As far as Canterbury and Christchurch are concerned there will be no further strikes." ' *Press*, 9 Jun 1932. After politicians both protested against and supported the remarks, Cummings claimed that the reporter had 'quite innocently put a different construction' on his brief answers to questions. J. McCombs to Minister of Justice, 9 Jun 1932; R. Macfarlane to Minister of Justice, 10 Jun 1932; H. Holland to Minister of Justice, 10 Jun 1932; Minister of Justice to H. Holland, 23 Jun 1932; Superintendent D.J. Cummings to Commissioner, 28 Jun 1932, P 1, 1932/521.

27.   *NZPD*, vol.234, 1932, p.723. On 8 Aug 1936, when Fraser met a deputation from the Police Force who brought a proposal to form a Police Association, he repeated that he had 'seen some of the Commissioner's work in Napier during the earthquake.' *NZPJ*, vol.1, no.1, Feb 1937, p.15.

28.   *NZPD*, vol.266, 1944, p.369. Fraser also told the President of the Police Association, W.R. Murray, and its General Secretary, I.D. Campbell, during an interview on 2 Apr 1938 that he had 'given the matter a great deal of thought before deciding on the appointment as, to appoint Mr Cummings, it had been necessary to supersede a man with seniority [Till], but he had never met a single officer of the Force who thought the decision was wrong.' Transcript of interview, 2 Apr 1938, p.8, P 13/1.

29.   Fraser's comment when expressing his confidence in the Commissioner to a deputation from the Police Force regarding the formation of a Police Association, on 8 Aug 1936. *NZPJ*, vol.1, no.1, Feb 1937, p.15.

30.   PFDB, vol.1, p.108; *Daily Telegraph* (Napier), 9 Jun 1932; *Press*, 10 Jun 1932; *Dominion*, 10 Dec 1935, 13 May 1936; *EP*, 1 Jul 1936; *NZH*, 2 Jul 1936; *Truth*, 8 Jul 1936; A. Gellatly to author, 26 Mar 1977; *NZPJ*, vol.1, no.1, Feb 1937, p.21. See also Hill, *Iron Hand*, esp. pp.230–3, 238, 249, 268, 341; Graeme Dunstall, 'Cummings, Denis Joseph', in *DNZB*, vol.4, pp.120–1.

31.   Sinclair, *Nash*, p.154, also p.174.

32.   Foss Shanahan, Secretary of Cabinet, to Sergeant A.M. Harding, 12 Apr 1955, Harding Papers, New Zealand Police Museum. Foss Shanahan became the assistant secretary of the Organisation for National Security and of the Prime Minister's Department, and then assistant secretary of the War Cabinet from 1940 to 1945. He was the son of Superintendent Tom Shanahan, who retired as the officer in charge of the Christchurch District in 1945.

33.   A. Gellatly to author, 26 Mar, 18 Apr 1977. Mr Gellatly joined the police staff at Headquarters in Nov 1940 as a shorthand typist. He commented also that the Commissioner 'would often alter 3 page letters for a single sentence. You would often type a letter, say 3 times and when it didn't appear for a retype after a while you would think "Thank God that letter's gone." Sometime later as much as 2 months it would again reappear for a retype.' See also comments about Nash's reluctance to make speedy decisions in Sinclair, *Nash*, p.261.

34.   Commissioner Cummings' address to the annual conference of the Police Association on 6 Sep 1938, *NZPJ*, vol.2, 1938, 'Official Report', p.3.

35.   At this point, Madden signed for the Commissioner of Police rather than as 'Deputy Commissioner'. The request was for information to update that received in response to the similar request made by Commissioner Wright in Feb 1922. Details of the

various Associations were sent to Fraser on 12 Jun 1936. See file P 13/1. Note that, unless otherwise indicated, the following discussion of the origins and development of the Police Association is based on reports in this large file and on material cited by McGill, *No Right to Strike*, part 2.

36. *EP*, 28 Mar 1936.
37. *Standard*, 29 Apr 1936. On 15 Apr, *Truth* reported that, when approached, Peter Fraser 'said nothing had been placed before him' regarding a Police Association. 'If any representations were made they would receive his consideration.'
38. Report in P 13/1.
39. Belton, *Outside the Law*, p.211; reports in P 13/1.
40. Constable T.F. Smith to Superintendent, Wellington, 12 May 1936, P 13/1, reprinted in McGill, *No Right to Strike*, p.30. Constable Smith later recalled that, one evening, he had gone to Parliament and asked to see Peter Fraser, who had listened to his case for a Police Association and 'advised me to make application which would reach him through the usual channels.' Thomas Frederick Smith, 'Reminiscences', Dec 1978 (typescript in possession of author).
41. Archibald Campbell had been secretary of the Port Chalmers Waterside Workers' Union since 1912, and was secretary of the combined Otago union. Elected in 1935, he spent one term in the House before being made a member of the Legislative Council.
42. Early in May, Ivan Levy of the *Standard* 'sounded out' Senior Sergeant J.A. Dempsey on the possible formation of a Police Association, and Constable R. Fletcher reported that he understood the Minister would receive a deputation. On 18 May Archibald Campbell spoke to Constable Walden and later in the day entered the library at the Christchurch police station and spoke to the constables there. According to Constable J. O'Halloran, Campbell said 'he was visiting on behalf of the Minister of Police all the main Police Stations in the South Island ... [to see] whether the members of the Force wanted to have a Union or an Association formed.' Reports of Senior Sergeant J.A. Dempsey, 14 May 1936; Constable Walden, 18 May 1936; Constable O'Halloran, 18 May 1936, P 13/1. See also comments in *Press*, 21 May 1936.
43. The other Labour MPs were: F.W. Schramm (Auckland East), W.J. Jordan (Manukau), E.L. Cullen (Hawke's Bay), A.H. Nordmeyer (Oamaru), D.G. McMillan (Dunedin West), and W.M.C. Denham (Invercargill). The order paper, on which the MPs were not named, erroneously gives Auckland West (M.J. Savage) rather than Auckland East. Schramm, an Auckland lawyer who had been deputy registrar of the Supreme Court, had previously asked questions concerning the working conditions of the police and supported the formation of an Association. It is unlikely that the Prime Minister, Savage, would have asked his Minister a parliamentary question. The press named Schramm. *Dominion* and *Press*, 21 May 1936. See also *Truth*, 20 May 1936.
44. Pencil marks in the margin against these passages of an editorial in *ODT*, 26 May 1936; see also similar comments in *Press*, 22 May 1936, P 13/1.
45. *NZPD*, vol.246, 1936, pp.390–1.
46. Every respondent in the Hamilton, New Plymouth, Napier, Palmerston North, Christchurch and Timaru districts was supportive. Only in Gisborne and Greymouth was support less than 90%. P 13/1.
47. Superintendent Till merely opened the meeting which followed the usual monthly pay parade and then retired. No other commissioned officers were present; Sergeant A. Bissett presided. Inspector G.B. Edwards and Sub-Inspector C.E. Roach were present at the Wellington meeting, but took no part in it. Detective W.R. Murray chaired the meeting. *AS*, 2 Jul 1936; Report of Constable W.S. Brown, 10 Jun 1936, P 13/1.
48. Rawle to Deputy Commissioner, 16 Jun 1936. Rawle was acting Superintendent. At Dunedin, Superintendent Allan Cameron remained in the library of the Central station, where the meeting was held, 'at the request of those present.' P 13/1.
49. Inspector Lander to Deputy Commissioner, 16 Jun 1936; Inspector Cummings to Commissioner, 2 Jul 1936, P 13/1.

50. Inspector T. Gibson, Invercargill, to Deputy Commissioner, 16 Jun 1936. Inspector
     Gibson was a member, 'ex officio', of a provisional local committee. Inspector T.
     Shanahan at Timaru felt an Association 'would be an asset' in bringing the views of
     the rank and file to the notice of the Commissioner; so did J. Powell at New Plymouth
     and J. Fitzgerald at Napier. It is noteworthy that these districts recorded high levels
     of response to the issue, and virtual unanimity, by contrast to Greymouth (for example),
     where Inspector Donald Cameron expressed ambivalence and noted that Regulation
     175 'at present gives a member ... an opportunity to state any grievance to the
     Commissioner or the Minister.' Reports to Deputy Commissioner from Inspectors
     Shanahan, 15 Jun 1936; Powell, 25 Jun 1936; Fitzgerald, 25 Jun 1936; and Cameron,
     17 Jun 1936, P 13/1.
51. Detective Sergeant Meiklejohn to Sub-Inspector J. Sweeney, 1 May 1936, P 13/1;
     NZPJ, vol.1, no.1, Feb 1937, p.23.
52. Constable Smith to Superintendent, Wellington, 12 May 1936, cited in McGill, *No
     Right to Strike*, p.30.
53. In this the police were not alone amongst public servants. In 1936, the annual
     conference of the PSA declined an invitation to affiliate with the Labour Party,
     deciding 'unanimously to continue the policy of political neutrality.' Roth, *Remedy
     for Present Evils*, p.94.
54. At a meeting on 6 Aug the Minister had instructed the deputation to draw up rules
     and a constitution for the Association, which was completed the next day. The
     chairman, J.B. Young, emphasised to the Commissioner that this was not 'perfect'
     and might not 'meet with the unanimous approval of all members.' To the delegates,
     the rule 'causing the most concern' related to the appointment of a general secretary.
     Sergeant T. Kelly led the delegation to its meeting with the Minister on 8 Aug.
     Reports in P 13/1. For J.B. Young's report, see also McGill, *No Right to Strike*, p.35.
55. *NZPJ*, vol.1, no.1, Feb 1937, pp.14–15. See also *NZPD*, vol.246, 1936, pp.390–1. On
     12 Aug, Commissioner Cummings sent a circular to officers in charge of districts
     giving permission for members of the Force to hold meetings from time to time 'in
     connection with the proposed formation of a Police Association.'
56. A clause in the rules first drafted on 6 and 7 Aug provided for compulsory membership.
     This was deleted before the rules were resubmitted to the Minister. After a delay
     while districts ratified the rules, the Minister again met representatives of the
     Association, led by W.R. Murray, on 21 Oct. Auckland District had been the slowest
     to respond, and its representative to the Association's first conference in Dec, A.B.
     Meiklejohn, submitted a complete set of new rules. Murray's motion to defer
     consideration of these was carried. McGill, *No Right to Strike*, pp.37–43; reports and
     draft rules in P 13/1.
         On its incorporation, the objectives of the New Zealand Police Association were:
     '(1) To promote the general welfare of members of the Police Force and to improve
     the conditions of its members;
     (2) To constitute the official channel of communication between its members and (i)
     the Minister in charge of the Police Department, (ii) the Commissioner of Police;
     (3) To foster a feeling of amity and good fellowship throughout the Police Service;
     (4) To provide assistance to members and their dependents in need thereof and where
     necessary to bring their claims before the Police Department.' *NZPJ*, vol.1, no.1, Feb
     1937, p.26.
57. This may be observed in the Commissioner's reaction to the publication of two
     articles in *NZH*, 14 Oct 1936 ('Police Working Conditions'; 'Policeman's Lot'),
     which were sent to him by Superintendent Till with the comment: 'I do not know
     where the press gets this information. Probably from a member of the Police
     Association.' On 23 Oct, Cummings instructed that 'Some effort should be made to
     trace the person responsible.' The source was not traced. P 13/1. Note that the
     wording of the amendments to the Police Regulations was suggested by Commissioner
     Cummings to the Minister on 1 Oct, and that they came into effect on 23 Oct.

58.   After chairing the first Wellington meeting on 9 Jun to canvass support for an Association, Murray had played a key role in its subsequent formation. Based in Wellington, he chaired the initial management committee, while T.F. Smith acted as General Secretary. When Murray and Smith both received 23 votes in the ballot for a Wellington delegate to join the Aug deputation to the Minister, Murray withdrew. He led subsequent deputations to both Commissioner and Minister. Reports of W.S. Brown, 10 Jun 1936, and Senior Sergeant J.A. Dempsey, 4 Aug 1936, P 13/1. For further discussion of Murray's role, see McGill, *No Right to Strike*, ch.6. When considering Murray's eligibility for promotion to Senior Detective in 1944, Commissioner D.J. Cummings commented that his presidency of the Police Association 'has not affected him one iota. There was never any trouble with him, he was always respectful and nice, and he could see [the] other side of the argument .... The Association has fallen a lot in grace since he resigned from the Presidency [in 1938]'; Report of Police Officers Conference, 1944, p.50, P 7/1/5.

59.   'For years he had stood for compulsory Unionism because he did not believe in some persons reaping the benefits of other men's labours without any contribution from themselves.' Fraser's comments to a deputation on 8 Aug 1936, *NZPJ*, vol.1, no.1, Feb 1937, p.15. He made similar comments to another deputation on 21 Oct 1936, when compulsory membership was strongly pressed; transcript of interview, P 13/1.

60.   *NZPJ*, vol.1, no.1, Feb 1937, p.23. The Queensland Police Union and the South Australia and Western Australia Police Associations had Arbitration Court awards covering wages and conditions. Deputy Commissioner to Minister in charge of the Police, 12 Jun 1936, P 13/1.

61.   Visiting the Hamilton District Headquarters before the Association's first conference in Dec 1936, Cummings told the men paraded before him that 'he would not allow it to dictate to him, and if it tried to dictate to him it would crash; and if control got into the wrong hands it would crash.' Within three weeks of being elected as the Hamilton District's delegate to the conference, the outspoken Detective Charles Belton received notice of his transfer to Gisborne. According to Association rules, a new delegate had to elected. (Later Belton became the delegate from the Gisborne District.) A.B. Meiklejohn, Auckland's delegate to the conference, was in 1937 transferred to Palmerston North. Between Aug 1936 and Feb 1937, 'Many capable association men on the management committee were also transferred out of Wellington.' Belton implies, and this was perceived by others at the time, that the Commissioner sought to neutralise by transfers those who could be seen as most strongly pressing for change. Belton, *Outside the Law*, pp.214–15. See also *NZH*, 15, 16, 19 Mar 1937; *NZPJ*, vol.1, 1937, no.1, Feb, p.45; no.2, May, pp.22–4; no.3, Aug, p.5.

62.   *NZPG*, 1936, p.677. Fraser commented that the government 'had not only recognized the Association, but has encouraged it', and was 'very anxious' that it be successful. A policeman had a 'duty' to join, out of 'loyalty to the Government, to the Service, and to his colleagues'.

63.   By 30 Jun 1937, there were 1,247 members; *NZPJ*, vol.2, no.4, Aug 1938, p.13.

64.   Detective Frank Sinclair, representing the views of the Christchurch District, 'New Zealand Police Association, Report of Proceedings. Conference of District Representatives, 8–11 December 1936', cyclostyled, pp.6–7, P 13/1.

65.   T.F. Smith, the acting General Secretary who represented the Wellington men's views, pressed for an 'outside secretary': 'It would be difficult for an inside man to say, for instance, to the Commissioner "I am sick and tired of waiting for a reply to my request – I am going to the Minister." ' This view was supported by W.R. Murray, the first President of the Association. Smith was not an applicant for the position of General Secretary. The issue of 'independence' was complicated by those like Meiklejohn, representing the Auckland and Whangarei districts, who wanted someone with police experience appointed as 'an outside general secretary'. A motion that the appointment be made from all applicants, including those with no police experience, was carried by 14 votes to 10. 'New Zealand Police Association, Report of Proceedings.

Conference of District Representatives, 8–11 December 1936', pp.5–9, P 13/1. For I.D. Campbell's background and activities as General Secretary, see McGill, *No Right to Strike*, ch.7.

66. On 6 Jun 1936 the *NZH* reported (three weeks before a meeting to canvass opinion was held in Auckland) that 'a section of the police force considered the mooted association would not fully meet the needs of the men', and that Archibald Campbell's inquiries in the South Island had indicated a 'strong desire' for a 'union'. It was rumoured that, if one was formed, there might be a move 'to appoint a secretary with Labour Party affiliations, but police officers desired a man thoroughly acquainted with the force, with a knowledge of the routine, and particular difficulties to be solved.'

That evening Campbell sent an urgent telegram to the watch-house keeper at Auckland Central station: 'Read comment in local paper about police union that is on the right lines[.] am prepared to organise all NZ free no cost to the union[.] I hope spread the gospel meeting here [Wellington] Tuesday'.

The telegram was forwarded to the Deputy Commissioner and then to Fraser, who minuted on 22 Jun: 'Deputy Commissioner, Mr Campbell acted without my knowledge or consent. He was obviously imbued with good intentions to help the men of the Force. I have informed him that his actions were detrimental instead of beneficial. Please keep me informed of any similar action by an MP or any other unauthorised person.' P 13/1.

67. Meiklejohn told the Auckland members: 'Your Association is now your voice, so remember to send your remits in plenty of time for the next conference .... Use the proper channel open to you, avoid newspaper articles such as you have recently experienced .... Also support your Journal'. *NZPJ*, vol.1, no.2, May 1937, pp.23–4. In his first address to an annual conference of the Association in Sep 1937, Commissioner Cummings declared that he objected very strongly 'to petty grievances being aired in the Press. I want to tell you very definitely that that absolutely defeats the object you have in view. If the men prefer to go to the Press instead of to the Department they will fail. It is obvious that they must fail. If we encouraged that sort of thing there is no telling where it would end.' 'Address of Commissioner of Police', typescript, P 13/1.

68. Fraser made this comment in replying to pressure for a right of appeal against dismissal by the Commissioner under the Police Force Act 1913, sec.9. Notes of interview of a Police Association deputation (W.R. Murray and I.D. Campbell) with the Minister (and the Commissioner present), 2 Apr 1938, p.7, P 13/1.

69. Roth, *Remedy for Present Evils*, pp.93–4; Thorn, *Peter Fraser*, pp.130–1. See also Wilson, *An Outsider Looks Back*, p.59, noting that Bob Semple, the Minister of Public Works, had 'electrified the country' on 13 May 1936 with an announcement of a 40-hour week at 2s an hour for employees on construction projects. Even with the restoration of the police pay cuts in Jul 1936, this hourly rate was higher than that received by a junior constable working a 56-hour week (or more).

70. *NZPD*, vol.246, 1936, p.769.

71. *NZPG*, 1936, p.768. Commissioner Cummings commented later: 'as soon as I was appointed Commissioner Mr Fraser asked me to go into the whole thing, that it was the policy of the Government to reduce working hours of everybody including the Police Force'; Report of Police Officers Conference, 1944, p.105, P 7/1/5.

72. Fraser's words; *NZPD*, vol.246, 1936, p.769.

73. The remit for a 40-hour week was moved by A.B. Meiklejohn. 'New Zealand Police Association, Report of Proceedings. Conference of District Representatives, 8–11 December 1936', pp.12–17, 25, P 13/1.

74. Reports of 'Delegation to the Commissioner and the Minister', *NZPJ*, vol.1, no.1, Feb 1937, pp.6–12. See also Belton, *Outside the Law*, p.214, for the views of the Commissioner and Association members at Hamilton. Later, Cummings commented: 'I went into the whole thing, and it took quite a lot of time, and I considered the 40

hour week was impossible .... it was far better to have a uniform system throughout the Service, and that is why I recommended a 48 hour week for everybody.' He tried to get an extra day's pay for all ranks to make up for the 'extra day' they had to work; the 'best I could get was 10/- per week'. If Peter Fraser had then 'been Prime Minister, there would have been no difficulty about it.' Report of Police Officers Conference, 1944, pp.105–6, P 7/1/5.

75. *NZH* and *Dominion*, 19 Apr 1937; *NZPD*, 1937, vol.248, pp.198, 433; vol.249, pp.374–5.

76. Between 1934/35 and 1937/38, expenditure on the Police increased by 38%; cf. Education 42%, Health 55%. Annual Financial Statements, *AJHR*, 1935–40, B-6. Allowances for the use of cars, rations and lighting were increased in 1937. For expenditure on buildings from the Public Works Fund, see below.

77. *NZH*, 19 Apr 1937; *Dominion*, 19, 20 Apr, 31 Jul, 2 Aug 1937; *NZPJ*, vol.1, no.2, May 1937, pp.3, 6–7.

78. *Ibid.*, p.9.

79. *Dominion*, 19 Apr, 12 Aug 1937; *Press*, 8 May, 21 Aug 1937; Annual Report, 1937, p.8.

80. Tait, *Never Back Down*, p.32.

81. F.A. Gordon to author, 11 Feb 1977; J.P. Larmer to author, 15 Nov 1976; H. McLean, interview, 17 Nov 1976; Tait, *Never Back Down*, pp.32–3; M.F. Gordon, 'Police Training', in S. Young (ed.), *With Confidence and Pride*, pp.99–100.

82. *NZH*, 31 Jul, 14, 19, 25 Aug, 16 Nov 1937; *Dominion*, 31 Jul, 12, 26 Aug 1937; *Press*, 8 May, 18, 21, 24 Aug, 9 Sep 1937; Annual Report, 1938, pp.7–8.

83. *Ibid.*, p.8; Commissioner to officers in charge of districts, 4 Jun 1937. This memorandum, which gave broad instructions as to how the 48-hour week was to be applied at the various types of stations and in the Detective Branch, and requested an indication of the number of men required, is reproduced in Thomson and Kagei, *A Century of Service*, p.34. See also Belton, *Outside the Law*, pp.216, 218–19, 243.

84. Indeed, the Victoria Police were not granted a weekly rest day until 1946. Two years later, however, the principle of a five-day/40-hour week was conceded to the Victoria Police, as it was to police in New South Wales in 1947 and Queensland in 1952. An eleven-day fortnight was not implemented in the New Zealand Police until 1957. Haldane, *The People's Force*, p.234; Annual Report of the Police Department for 1947, *New South Wales Parliamentary Papers*, 1947–48, vol.1; Johnston, *The Long Blue Line*, p.228.

85. By 1938, the principle of a five-day/40-hour week applied to most office workers within the public service and to all General Division staff, including institutional staff in prisons and mental hospitals as well as the Education, Health and Hospitals departments. In institutions such as prisons and mental hospitals, the hours worked were in theory reduced to 42 per week by the granting of additional leave. In Apr 1939, the *NZPJ* reprinted from the *Standard* (the Labour Party newspaper) the Minister of Labour's claim that more than three-quarters of the approximately 250,000 workers in 'industry' were then enjoying a 40-hour week, and that the government was going to give all workers the 40-hour week. *NZPJ*, vol.2, 1938, 'Official Report' of the third annual conference held 6 to 8 Sep, pp.16–24; vol.3, no.2, Apr 1939, p.141; 'Official Report' of the fourth annual conference held 25 to 27 Oct, pp.33–4; *Dominion*, 1 Nov 1939; Public Service Commissioner, T. Mark, to Private Secretary, Minister of Finance, 29 Jun 1939, re 'Improvements in Public Service under Labour Government', SSC 66/10/216.

86. Two detectives who returned early in 1936 from a period of observation and training in London commented in their report to the Commissioner in Apr (sent on to Peter Fraser in May) that: 'In all Police Forces in England, the longest period of service required of a Police Officer, irrespective of rank, is 30 years service and all officers are compulsorily retired on attaining that period of service, on a pension of two thirds of their pay.' They recommended that 'the present retiring age should be reduced

from 40 years to 35 years service for similar reasons that apply to the retirement of officers of the English Police Forces. These reasons have been the subject of submissions to the New Zealand Government from time to time, as the result of conferences [of police officers] held in New Zealand'. Report of [Detectives] William McLennan and Henry Murch Relative to Period of Training at Hendon Police College and New Scotland Yard, London, 22 Apr 1936, P 36/1.

87.   *NZPJ*, vol.1, 1937, no.1, Feb, pp.10–11, 33–4; no.3, Aug, pp.1, 43–4, 46; *Press*, 27 May 1936, 6 Aug 1937; I.D. Campbell to Commissioner, 2 Aug 1937, enclosing for his information a copy of letter sent to commissioned officers for their views on the retiring age; Inspectors O'Hara (Whangarei), Lander (Wanganui), and Lopdell (Hamilton) referred the letter to the Commissioner, P 13/1.

88.   Remits submitted to the Commissioner and the Minister, I.D. Campbell to Commissioner, 12 Nov 1937, P 13/1.

89.   Second Report of the Committee on the Police Service of England, Wales and Scotland (chaired by Lord Desborough) presented on 1 Jan 1920, clauses 28–31, P 13/1.

90.   During the five years to 31 Mar 1937, 92 men left the Force through death or retirement. Only 11 of them qualified for full superannuation (forty-sixtieths of salary); 26 were retired medically unfit, and 34 died. Of the latter, 14 died before completing 20 years' service, 13 died after between 20 and 30 years' service, and only 6 had more than 30 years' service. *NZPJ*, vol.2, no.1, Feb 1938, p.19. The totals for medical retirements and deaths have been recalculated by the author from the Annual Reports.

Data on police contributors to the Public Service Superannuation Fund in Mar 1936 painted a less pessimistic picture than that presented by the Association. Of the 1,166 contributors, 597 (51.2%) would qualify for retirement with 40 years' service *before* reaching age 65; 104 (8.9%) would qualify for retirement at age 65 with 40 years' service; 372 (31.9%) would qualify for retirement at age 65 with at least 35 years' service; 67 (5.7%) would have 34 years' service; and 26 (2.3%) who had joined the Police at ages ranging from 36 to 44 would have less than 30 years' service on reaching retirement age. Secretary, Public Service Superannuation Board to Minister in Charge of Public Service Superannuation Fund, 17 May 1939, P 13/1.

From the statistics supplied by the Public Service Superannuation Board, Campbell discovered that a general belief amongst police that those who retired on superannuation generally did not live long to enjoy their pension could not be sustained. Of 94 police superannuitants who had died before 31 Mar 1936, allowances had been paid to 22 for up to 5 years, 30 for 5 to 10 years, 18 for 10 to 15 years, 16 for 15 to 20 years, 6 for 20 to 25 years, and 2 for more than 25 years. The average age of death was 73.25 years.

Of police superannuitants still living on 31 Mar 1936, 18 had been drawing the allowance for 5 to 10 years, 26 for 10 to 15 years, 13 for 15 to 20 years, and 6 for over 20 years.

Campbell concluded that 'our argument should be directed to another angle, that is, that although those who did live until retiring age enjoyed their superannuation for a reasonable period, there are a great number who do not get to that stage.' *NZPJ*, vol.3, 1939, 'Official Report' of fourth annual conference held 25–27 Oct 1939, pp.9–10.

91.   Compulsory retirement at 55 was the norm for Sergeants and constables in English, Welsh, and Scottish police forces, and for constables in the Victoria Police.

92.   'Earlier Retiring Age: A Summary of the Case', *NZPJ*, vol.2, no.1, Feb 1938, pp.17–20.

93.   For an early sign of frustration see I.D. Campbell's 'In Lieu of Editorial', *NZPJ*, vol.1, no.4, Nov 1937, p.3.

94.   'The Commissioner Replies to Conference Remits' (transcript of an interview of Association delegates with the Commissioner on 3 Dec 1937), *NZPJ*, vol.2, no.1, Feb 1938, pp.9–10.

95.   The implications of a means-tested pension at age 60 (loosely termed 'superannuation'

in Apr 1938) concerned police and other public servants, as well as members of other occupational superannuation schemes. They would not be exempt from the proposed social security 'contribution', but they would be (as I.D. Campbell put it) 'debarred from benefit by the income restrictions' on the pension. Moreover, as Campbell observed, 'if the Government sees fit to introduce national superannuation at 60, police who are beyond that age and are still in the service may well wonder what is the obstacle to the 60-year retirement they are seeking.' Widespread dissatisfaction with the government's initial proposals led to the addition of a token universal national superannuation at 65 which would gradually increase in amount until it equalled the old-age pension. 'National Superannuation', *NZPJ*, vol.2, no.2, Apr 1938, pp.3–6; E. Hanson, *The Politics of Social Security*, Auckland, 1980, ch.7.

96.   Hanson, *Politics of Social Security*, ch.6; Sinclair, *Nash*, pp.160–5.

97.   Notes of interview of Police Association delegates with the Minister in charge of the Police, and Commissioner Cummings present, on 2 Apr 1938, P 13/1; Minister in charge of the Police Department to General Secretary, Police Association, 26 May 1938, reprinted in *NZPJ*, vol.2, no.3, Jun 1938, p.11.

98.   Sinclair, *Nash*, pp.169–71.

99.   *NZPJ*, vol.2, 1938, 'Official Report' of the third annual conference held 6 to 8 Sep, p.5.

100. W.R. Murray retired as President at the 1938 annual conference and was succeeded by Chief Detective J.B. Young from Dunedin. As the past President with considerable experience, Murray joined Young and I.D. Campbell in presenting the Association's remits to the Commissioner on 9 and 10 Dec 1938. Because Young was ill during 1939, Murray took his place in presenting the remits to the Minister.

101. Notes of interview of Police Association delegates with the Minister in charge of the Police, and Commissioner Cummings present, 8 May 1939, P 13/1.

102. On 10 May 1939 Fraser referred the Association's remits concerning superannuation to the Minister in charge of the Public Service Superannuation Fund, who in turn referred the matter to the Secretary of the Public Service Superannuation Board. The Secretary replied that a police member of the Fund entitled to retire with a full pension after 35 years' service would be receiving 'a gift of five years' service'. The Secretary pointed out that if the request was agreed to, 'demands would be made from other groups of public servants, for instance, prison warders, mental hospital attendants, for a similar concession and the effect on the stability of the Fund would be serious.' Secretary, Public Service Superannuation Board to Minister in charge of the Public Service Superannuation Fund, 17 May 1939, P 13/1.

103. Minister in charge of the Police to Secretary, New Zealand Police Association, 12 Oct 1939, P 13/1. Commissioner Cummings, who represented the Police Department on the Public Service Superannuation Board, drafted this letter. Though Fraser softened some phrases, he largely shared Cummings' views.

104. 'A Younger Police Force', *NZPJ*, vol.3, no.3, Jun 1939, pp.205–7; 'Official Report' of the fourth annual conference held 25–27 Oct 1939, p.14.

105. *Ibid.*, pp.8–16.

106. *Ibid.*, p.55. The emphasis on efficiency and public standing as well as working conditions was made by I.D. Campbell in his editorial, 'Police Buildings', *NZPJ*, vol.3, no.2, Apr 1939, pp.105–8.

107. Annual Reports, 1935, p.6; 1936, p.7.

108. *Ibid.*, 1937, pp.7–8, 14; 'Address of Commissioner of Police' [Sep 1937], typescript, P 13/1; *NZPD*, vol.248, 1937, p.433; *NZPJ*, vol.1, 1937, no.2, May, p.39; no.3, Aug, p.55; *Press*, 28, 31 May 1937; *ODT*, 29 May 1937; *NZH*, 31 May 1937. In May 1937, the *NZPJ* reported that a new two-storied building had been built in 1936 behind the old Invercargill station, making it one of the 'most up-to-date' police stations in the country.

109. Soon after Fraser's inspection an epidemic of German measles swept through the Auckland barracks. By 12 Oct 1937, ten constables were in hospital. *NZH*, 6 Jul, 12

Oct 1937, 6 Jun, 18 Aug 1938; *Press*, 28 Sep 1937; *NZPJ*, vol.1, no.4, Nov 1937, p.51; *NZPD*, vol.252, 1938, p.467.

110.   Annual Report, 1936, p.7; 'Address of Commissioner of Police' [Sep 1937], typescript, P 13/1; *NZPJ*, vol.2, 1938, 'Official Report' of the third annual conference held 6 to 8 Sep, p.2.

111.   Annual Reports, 1937, pp.7–8; 1938, p.8; 'The Building Programme', *NZPJ*, vol.3, no.4, Aug 1939, pp.352–3; *NZH*, 2 Jul, 18 Aug 1938; Carter, *'Beyond the Call of Duty'*, pp.48–9.

112.   *NZPJ*, vol.2, 1938, 'Official Report' of the third annual conference held 6 to 8 Sep, p.2; vol.3, no.6, Dec 1939, p.553, and 'Official Report' of the fourth annual conference held 25–27 Oct 1939, p.56; Draft report of Commissioner's address to 1939 annual conference, P 13/1; H. McLean, interview, 17 Nov 1976; E. Buckley to author, 12 Dec 1976. Ted Buckley commented that when he received the Public Works Department plan for a new house at Kaeo, he found it to be 'of an old type building. My wife redrew the plan, a modern home. I sent it back to the Commissioner who endorsed it'.

113.   *Dominion*, 20 Apr 1938; Carter, *'Beyond the Call of Duty'*, pp.48–50; Rorke, *Policing Two Peoples*, pp.64–5; *NZPJ*, vol.3, 1939, no.1, Feb, p.26; no.2, Apr, pp.108–9; 'Official Report' of the fourth annual conference held 25–27 Oct 1939, p.56. The local Inspector, detectives, Senior Sergeant, Sergeant and office staff were all consulted during the preparation of plans for the Palmerston North station.

114.   Unless otherwise indicated, this paragraph is based on the following sources: Annual Reports, 1938, pp.8–9; 1939, p.8; 1940, p.6; *NZPJ*, vol.2, 1938, 'Official Report' of the third annual conference held 6 to 8 Sep, p.2; vol.3, 1939, no.1, Feb, pp.26–7; no.2, Apr, pp.105–8; 'Official Report' of the fourth annual conference held 25–27 Oct 1939, pp.55–6; Draft report of Commissioner's address to 1939 annual conference, and notes of interview of the Police Association delegates with the Minister in charge of the Police, and Commissioner Cummings present, on 8 May 1939, P 13/1; *Press*, 18 May 1939; *NZH*, 15 Jun 1939; *Dominion*, 1 Nov 1939; R. Noonan, *By Design: A Brief History of the Public Works Department/Ministry of Works 1870–1970*, Wellington, 1975, ch.7; *NZOYB*, 1939, pp.449–50, 477–8.

115.   A constable submitted a report to the officer in charge of the district who (if he agreed) asked the local district engineer of the Public Works Department to submit an estimate of what was required. A Public Works inspector then prepared a report which went to the Commissioner for the authorisation of the work, which was carried out under the supervision of the Public Works Department.

116.   In 1938/39, £660,666 was spent on school buildings, £280,951 on post and telegraph buildings, and £216,939 on hospitals. Public Works Statement, *AJHR*, 1941, D-1.

117.   *NZPJ*, vol.3, no.2, Apr 1939, p.106.

118.   In his address to the 1938 conference, the Commissioner ridiculed remits that cloth be granted for uniforms every six months, that country constables receive loans to purchase cars for their work, and that there be a general increase in pay (to compensate for overtime) and in car and house allowances. 'Address of Commissioner of Police' [Sep 1937], typescript, P 13/1; *NZPJ*, vol.2, 1938, 'Official Report' of the third annual conference held 6 to 8 Sep, p.2.

119.   On these and other similar remits, Cummings responded positively to a deputation of delegates during the first annual conference of the Association in Dec 1936. *NZPJ*, vol.1, no.1, Feb 1937, pp.40–1.

120.   In response to a remit that the late leave regulations introduced in 1919 be amended to allow leave to 1 am, Cummings responded: 'the man who wants to be out till 1 o'clock and after that hour ... had better seek another job. I do not want him. I certainly will not give general leave until 1 o'clock.' When asked if he would consider a general extension to midnight, Cummings replied: 'I do not think I would even go that far. Eleven o'clock is certainly a bit early in certain circumstances.' *NZPJ*, vol.3, no.1, Feb 1939, p.20.

121.   Campbell made this assessment in promoting the improvements 'achieved' by the Police Association to non-members and 'any half-hearted members who have not yet given the Association their solid support.' *NZPJ*, vol.3, no.6, Dec 1939, pp.523–7.

122.   Such as the introduction of plain-clothes allowances for those doing such duty who were not attached to a Detective Office, a remote station allowance, and an extension of the clerical and typewriting allowances.

123.   *NZPG*, 1937, pp.384–5, for revised instructions on car allowances; *NZPJ*, vol.1, no.1, Feb 1937, pp.11, 40; vol.2, no.1, Feb 1938, p.13, and 'Official Report' of third annual conference, pp.1–2, 32–6; vol.3, no.1, Feb 1939, pp.25–6, and 'Official Report' of fourth annual conference, p.56; Remits submitted to Minister, I.D. Campbell to Minister in charge of the Police Department, 17 Apr 1939, P 13/1. The amount spent on motor-car allowances rose from £7,825 in the year ending 30 Jun 1936 to £10,510 in the year to 31 Mar 1939. The increase was essentially to cover the rising cost of fuel.

124.   *NZPJ*, vol.3, no.1, Feb 1939, p.6. See also letters to the editor regarding promotion in *ibid.*, vol.1, 1937, Feb, pp.16–17, May, pp.11–12, Aug, p.15; vol.2, no.1, Feb 1938, p.26; and Belton, *Outside the Law*, pp.220–3.

125.   Commissioner Wohlmann had also used sec.9, notably in the case of (then) Detective Studholme, who was subsequently reinstated. The case for repeal of sec.9 was made by A.B. Meiklejohn in *NZPJ*, vol.1, no.3, Aug 1937, pp.31–2.

126.   *NZPJ*, vol.1, no.1, Feb 1937, pp.11, 34, 37; vol.2, no.1, Feb 1938, p.15; vol.3, no.1, Feb 1939, p.27. Following Cummings' insistence on keeping this section at his meeting with an Association deputation in Jan 1937, the 1937 Association conference asked for a right of appeal for any member of the Force dealt with under sec.9 (which was again rejected by Cummings). This policy was reaffirmed by the 1938 and 1939 conferences.

127.   The member of the Police Association nominated by the Management Committee would replace a JP on the three-person Board, which also comprised a magistrate (as chairman) and a commissioned officer.

128.   *NZPJ*, vol.2, no.1, Feb 1938, pp.14–15; vol.3, no.1, Feb 1939, pp.27–8.

129.   The increased number of promotions (mainly to the ranks of Sergeant and Senior Sergeant) was due largely to the increased staff numbers that accompanied the introduction of shorter working hours and the raising of the status of some stations. In Apr 1938 Cummings claimed there had been 65 promotions. Notes of interview of Police Association delegates with the Minister in charge of the Police, and Commissioner Cummings present, on 2 Apr 1938, P 13/1. See also Annual Report, 1938, pp.7–8.

130.   *NZPJ*, vol.1, no.1, Feb 1937, pp.11, 39–40; vol.2, no.1, Feb 1938, p.11; vol.3, no.1, Feb 1939, pp.21, 27.

131.   'Notes of Deputation which waited on the Commissioner of Police', 15 Mar 1940, P 13/1. The deputation comprised Chief Detective J.B. Young, Detective Sergeant W.R. Murray, and the new General Secretary, J. Meltzer. The case of Sergeant Holt and others was the first remit from the 1939 Association conference to be discussed. A Committee of Inquiry, composed of commissioned officers, could be established by the Minister under sec.25(1) of the Police Force Act 1913, 'for the purpose of investigating and reporting to the Commissioner on the claim of any member or members of the Force with respect to their promotion ... or on any other matter connected with the Force.' See also *NZPJ*, vol.2, 1938, 'Official Report' of third annual conference, p.59; vol.3, no.1, Feb 1939, pp.5–7, 29, and 'Official Report' of fourth annual conference, pp.22–7; McGill, *No Right to Strike*, pp.56, 58, 61. J.B. Young succeeded Murray as President of the Police Association in Sep 1938 and held this position until he was promoted to Sub-Inspector and transferred to Christchurch in Apr 1943. In 1944 Cummings commented: 'He has got a "bug" about the Association, which is the only thing I saw wrong with him'; Report of Police Officers Conference, 1944, p.39, P 7/1/5.

132.   For example, Fraser observed in 1938 and 1939, when such issues were first put
        before him by Association delegates, that an Inspector hearing a case in which he had
        laid the charges seemed 'a bit invidious'; that 'a man should have the right of appeal'
        against dismissal; and that he was 'pleased' to consider whether vacancies should be
        advertised. Notes of interviews, 2 Apr 1938, 8 May 1939, P 13/1.

133.   In Holt's case, Fraser saw only an inconsequential 'alleged injustice' affecting an
        individual and not a 'general principle' affecting 'everybody'. He was thus 'surprised'
        that the Association had taken up the case when there was 'only a fear that he might
        have a grievance, and also recognition of the fact that other men who are equally
        good members of the Association as Holt is ... would be detrimentally affected.' His
        refusal of a Committee of Inquiry was strengthened when the Commissioner
        subsequently obtained a Crown Law Office opinion that was 'unable to see any
        merit' in Holt's claim that he was entitled to be listed on the Headquarters Seniority
        List provided for in Regulation 401 as senior to Sergeant Crowley. Notes of interview
        with Police Association delegates, 5 Sep 1940; C.H. Taylor, Crown Solicitor, to
        Commissioner, 30 Sep 1940, P 13/1.

134.   Notes of interview with Police Association delegates, 2 Apr 1938, P 13/1. In Mar
        1937, when newspapers reported that police in Auckland resented transfers which
        they saw as victimising prominent members of the Police Association, Fraser issued
        a strong statement (supported by the Management Committee of the Police Association)
        denying victimisation and asserting: 'To my personal knowledge he has been invariably
        fair and sympathetic in his dealings with the members of the force. It is, of course,
        his duty to see that discipline and efficiency are maintained, and he can be expected
        to carry out his duty with that end in view, regardless of adverse or unfair criticism.'
        ODT, 17, 19 Mar 1937. Fraser also asserted in Parliament that 'there had never been
        a Commissioner of Police who had been more anxious to deal fairly with the men
        than Commissioner Cummings, and that if there had been any cases of hardship he
        would undertake that the Commissioner would review them.' *NZPD*, vol.252, 1938,
        p.466. See also *ibid.*, vol.257, 1940, p.770; vol.266, 1944, pp.369, 376.

135.   *NZPD*, vol.244, 1936, pp.511, 521–2; *NZH*, 9 Jul 1936.

136.   Unless otherwise indicated, the sources for this paragraph are: Fraser's views expressed
        on 8 Aug 1936 to a deputation from the Police Force regarding a proposed Police
        Association, *NZPJ*, vol.1, no.1, Feb 1937, p.15; Minister in charge of the Police
        Department to the General Secretary of the Police Association, 26 May 1938, reprinted
        in *NZPJ*, vol.2, no.3, Jun 1938, pp.11–12; Notes of interviews of Police Association
        delegates with the Minister in charge of the Police, and Commissioner Cummings
        present, on 2 Apr 1938, 8 May 1939, and 5 Sep 1940; Minister in charge of the
        Police Department to General Secretary of the Police Association, 12 Oct 1939, 1
        May 1941, P 13/1.

137.   *NZPJ*, vol.1, no.1, Feb 1937, pp.14–15.

138.   *NZPJ*, vol.2, 1938, 'Official Report' of third annual conference, p.4.

139.   *NZPD*, vol.257, 1940, p.770. In his speech to the 1939 Association conference,
        Webb, unlike the more hard-headed Fraser, looked forward to a time 'when crime
        will virtually disappear' thanks to changes in the economic system. In future crime
        would 'only be the outcome of mental instability', and the police officer doing the
        'most good' would be 'one who has a good knowledge of psychology and of the
        impulses which drive people to transgress. After all, your job is not primarily to put
        people in cells but rather to prevent their reaching the stage when that is necessary.'
        NZPJ, vol.3, 1939, 'Official Report' of the fourth annual conference, pp.4–5.

140.   Commissioner W.J. MacKay of New South Wales had (as CIB Superintendent) spent
        eight months in Britain, Europe and the United States in 1929 studying police methods
        and operations, and had introduced administrative and operational changes (such as
        'modus operandi'). In 1936, as Commissioner, MacKay again visited Britain, Europe
        and the USA, and on his return made further changes in the organisation of detective
        work, introducing a new method of selection and a detective training course. He also

acquired new equipment for a 'police radio telephony system' which came into operation on 10 May 1937 with 14 cars, and established a Scientific Investigation Bureau with new equipment. In Victoria, Chief Commissioner A.M. Duncan, formerly of Scotland Yard, implemented similar changes in the same period, as did Commissioner C.J. Carroll of Queensland after observing the developments in Sydney and Melbourne. Annual Reports of the Police Department, 1931–39, *New South Wales Parliamentary Papers*, 1932–40; Annual Report of the Chief Commissioner of Police, 1946, *Victoria Parliamentary Papers*, 1947–48; *Annual Reports of the Commissioner of Police, Queensland*, 1934–39, held in the Queensland Police Museum Library, Brisbane.

141. *Truth*, 15, 29 Apr 1936, 3 Mar, 8 Sep 1937, 9 Feb, 20 Jul 1938.

142. Annual Report, 1937, p.9.

143. *Ibid.*, and notes of Commissioner's address to the 1937 Police Association conference, P 13/1.

144. The two detectives concluded that 'the training of New Zealand Police Officers in England is not of any particular advantage to the New Zealand Police and ... the cost of same is not justified' in 'Report of [Detectives] William McLennan and Henry Murch Relative to Period of Training at Hendon Police College and New Scotland Yard, London', 22 Apr 1936, p.40, P 36/1.

145. Annual Reports, 1937, pp.9, 16; 1938, p.7; 1939, p.7; notes of Commissioner's address to the 1937 Association conference, P 13/1. In Dunedin, Chief Detective J.B. Young began twice-weekly lectures on all aspects of criminal investigation for his detective staff during 1937. Men from the Uniform Branch also attended when 'room and time' permitted. Some of these lectures were subsequently published in the *NZPJ* during 1940 and 1941.

146. Circulars relating to 'Dress of Police' and 'Monthly Parade and Drill', *NZPG*, 1936, p.719.

147. *NZPJ*, vol.2, no.1, Feb 1938, p.12; vol.3, no.1, Feb 1939, pp.16–18. See also Belton, *Outside the Law*, p.243.

148. The Police Force Regulations 1919 nos 404 to 414 were superseded by Police Force Amendment Regulations 1938. Notes of Commissioner's address to the 1937 Association conference, P 13/1; Annual Report, 1938, p.8; *NZH*, 1 Jul 1938; E.R. Trask to author, 3 Jul 1977.

149. Commissioner Cummings saw 'Police and Detective Duties' as the 'stumbling block. It is entirely a matter for each District to give more attention to weak subjects. A lot depends on the man who goes up for the examination; he may not be ready for it'. To this Young commented: 'A man can go out and do practical work all right, but you put him in a room with a sheet of paper and he goes out.' Notes of interview Police Association delegates with Commissioner 15 Mar 1940, P 13/1.

150. *NZPJ*, vol.1, no.4, Nov 1937, p.36; vol.2, no.1, Feb 1938, pp.26–7; vol.3, 1939, 'Offical Report' of the fourth annual conference, pp.38–9.

151. The revision and consolidation of the Police Force Regulations was completed by staff under D.J. Cummings' successor, his brother James Cummings. The new Regulations came into effect on 1 May 1950, nearly three years after a new Police Force Act was passed in 1947. Annual Reports, 1948, p.1; 1949, p.1; 1950, p.1.

152. 'They want you to take a big stick to make me do it', Cummings told Fraser, who responded to the Association delegates, 'We all agree that if the job can be done it will be done.' Notes of interview of Police Association delegates with the Minister in charge of the Police, and Commissioner Cummings present, 5 Sep 1940, P 13/1. See also Notes of Commissioner's address to the 1937 Association conference, and Notes of interview Police Association delegates with Commissioner 15 Mar 1940, P 13/1; Annual Reports, 1937, p.9;·1938, p.8; *NZPJ*, vol.2, 1938, 'Official Report' of the third annual conference, p.40; vol.3, no.1, Feb 1939, p.29, and 'Official Report' of the fourth annual conference, pp.38–9.

153. Commissioner's Circular, 'Police Motor Transport, *NZPG*, 1937, pp.384–5; Annual

Reports, 1937, p.9; 1938, p.7; 1939, p.7.

154. In Christchurch, by May 1936, St John's had five motorised ambulances, while the police had an ancient prison van and two cars for commissioned officers, one of which was allocated sparingly to detectives. By 1939, St John's had seven ambulances and the Christchurch police three cars plus the van. G.W. Rice, *Ambulances and First Aid: St John in Christchurch 1885–1987*, Christchurch, 1994, pp.155–7; Thomson and Neilson, *Sharing the Challenge*, pp.236–7.

155. Annual Report, 1939, p.7.

156. This figure is an estimate, probably conservative, of the proportion of the 79 vehicles of the Victoria Police (including motorcycles and other vehicles besides cars) located in Melbourne in 1936; Annual Report of the Chief Commissioner of Police, 1946, p.24, *Victoria Parliamentary Papers*, 1947–48.

157. Unless otherwise acknowledged the sources for material in this and the preceding paragraphs are Annual Reports, 1935 to 1940; *Truth*, 29 Apr 1936, 3 Mar, 8 Sep 1937; *NZH*, 21 Feb 1936, 16 Jan 1937, 2, 9 Mar 1938; *Press*, 14 Mar 1936, 7 Aug 1937, 11 Mar 1939; reports regarding the fitting of sirens on six cars (2 each in Auckland and Wellington, 1 each in Christchurch and Dunedin) in 1939 in P 8/8/1; Roly T. Hermans, 'Wellington 1886–1992', in Young (ed.), *With Confidence and Pride*, pp.178–9; Thomson and Neilson, *Sharing the Challenge*, pp.236–7; Cherrett, *Without Fear or Favour*, pp.66–7; Annual Reports of the Police Department, 1928–39, *New South Wales Parliamentary Papers*, 1929–40; Annual Report of the Chief Commissioner of Police, 1946, *Victoria Parliamentary Papers*, 1947–48; *Annual Reports of the Commissioner of Police, Queensland*, 1934–42, held in the Queensland Police Museum Library, Brisbane; Haldane, *The People's Force*, pp.191–4, 227; Johnston, *The Long Blue Line*, pp.235–7.

158. Reports of the activities of the Auckland night patrol focused on them surprising burglars and detecting stolen cars. During the summer of 1938–39, there were two cars on night patrol in Auckland: one covering Remuera and especially the neighbourhood of Tamaki Drive (where a private night patrol had been organised in 1936), and the other covering a wide territory with a varying route which included Onehunga, Otahuhu and Papakura. *Truth*, 3 Mar 1937; *NZH*, 16 Sep, 7 Dec 1936, 21 Jul 1937, 30 Dec 1938; *AS*, 1 Nov 1939; *Press*, 7 Aug 1937, 5 Feb 1938, 29 Apr 1939.

159. Laugeson became a detective in Christchurch in 1927. He developed an expertise in radio communications and become Vice-President of the Amateur Transmitters' Society. In 1931 (in the wake of the Hawke's Bay earthquake) he suggested the creation of an emergency radio corps. This proposal was adopted by his society in 1932, and tested throughout the country. Laugeson also submitted a report to Commissioner Wohlmann recommending the adoption of the Melbourne police patrol car system using wireless telegraphy. In 1933 he resigned to become managing director of the New Zealand Radio Manufacturing Company, which he had formed with an associate ten months earlier and by then employed ten men. In 1936 he believed that the Melbourne system of two-way Morse communication between a central station and patrol cars could be readily established in the four main centres for £5,000. *CT*, 25 Jul 1933; *Press*, 30 Mar 1936; Conly, *The Shock of '31*, p.211.

160. In 1946 several patrol cars in Wellington and Auckland were fitted with standard broadcast radio receivers, modified to receive on a frequency of 1670 kilohertz, allowing one-way communication of messages from central stations via local base transmitters controlled by the Post Office. This technology had been available before the war. The Wellington base transmitter was on Tinakori Hill, which had been identified as the likely location in 1938. (In 1946, the Auckland base transmitter was at Musick Point.)

The one-way system introduced in 1946 was apparently less than Cummings had looked for in 1938 when he spoke of 'the transmission and receipt of messages' between the central police station and patrol cars. In 1939 he noted that the 'delay in finalising the installation of a [two-way] wireless plant' was 'due to the fact that it is going to be more difficult and expensive than was at first anticipated.' The development of a two-way radio system, first utilised at Christchurch in 1947 using a very high frequency band, followed wartime developments in communications.

In addition to sources cited for the preceding paragraph, this paragraph has been based on: Annual Reports, 1937, p.9; 1938, pp.7, 9; 1939, p.7; *Press*, 30 Mar, 3 Apr 1936, 3 Mar 1938, 3 Aug 1939; *NZH*, 2 Mar 1938; *NZPD*, vol.252, 1938, p.467; vol.255, 1939, p.623; vol.257, 1940, p.770; vol.266, 1944, p.369; 'Police Radio System of New South Wales', *NZPJ*, vol.3, no.3, Jun 1939, pp.214–16; 'Report of [Detectives] William McLennan and Henry Murch Relative to Period of Training at Hendon Police College and New Scotland Yard, London', 22 Apr 1936, pp.23–5, P 36/1; Critchley, *A History of Police in England and Wales*, pp.211–12; notes concerning the introduction of the one-way and two-way systems in 1946–47 supplied to author by E.R. Neal, Police telecommunications technician for the Wellington region, 2 Dec 1977.

161. Annual Reports, 1937, pp.6, 9; 1938, pp.6, 7; 1939, pp.6, 7; *Press*, 3 Mar, 15 May 1937, 2 Nov 1938; *NZH*, 2 Mar 1938; 'Report of [Detectives] William McLennan and Henry Murch Relative to Period of Training at Hendon Police College and New Scotland Yard, London', 22 Apr 1936, pp.14–17, 20, P 36/1; Critchley, *A History of Police in England and Wales*, pp.209–14; C. Billings, 'Policing Becomes a Profession', *NZPJ*, vol.3, no.4, Aug 1939, pp.322–5; Annual Reports of the Police Department, 1937–38, *New South Wales Parliamentary Papers*, 1938–39; Johnston, *The Long Blue Line*, pp.237, 239.

162. There was one officially unsolved murder in the period, that of E.N. Nelson, who was fatally shot at Waihou Valley, North Auckland, in 1936. In May 1938, the disappearance of the storekeeper Dalu Desai, who had lived with his brother at the isolated settlement of Taharoa, created police 'suspicions that he had been murdered.' However, three months of searching by a party of police failed to find his body, and thus 'no actual crime' could be established. Annual Reports, 1937, p.10; 1939, p.10; *AWN*, 8 Jun 1938; *NZH*, 27 Aug 1938.

163. *Press*, 28 Mar 1938.

164. *NZPD*, vol.252, 1938, pp.465–6.

165. In Nov 1937, Peter Fraser commented: 'it was hoped that, with the increased number of police constables, they might be able to do more towards checking minor offences such as drunkenness, sly-grog offences, and so on.' *NZPD*, vol. 249, 1937, p.375. The number of prosecutions for sly-grogging rose from 91 in 1935 to 360 in 1940, while those for breaches of prohibition orders rose from 357 in 1935 to 641 in 1938. The number of prosecutions for breaches of the Licensing Act affecting Maori increased from 152 in 1935 to 436 in 1939. Annual Reports.

166. The possession of liquor in the vicinity of dance halls was prohibited by the Statutes Amendment Act 1939, sec.59. This ban followed increasing concern expressed by officers in charge of the provincial police districts at the growing numbers of intoxicated drivers detected, and the recommendation by Inspector Lopdell of Hamilton for 'some legal machinery to control drinking at dances'. Annual Reports, 1937, pp.11–15; 1938, pp.10–15; 1939, pp.10–12; 1940, pp.7, 9–10; 1941, pp.7–8, 13.

167. The Arms Bureau was established following the Arms Amendment Act 1934, which provided that no firearms could be imported without a licence issued by a senior police officer. Its object was to minimise shooting accidents by eliminating unsafe firearms. Police were also given discretionary power to refuse or revoke licences according to their assessment of a person's fitness to have firearms. Commissioner Wohlmann recruited Kelly, who had urged the confiscation or compulsory repair of dangerous firearms, and had established his expertise in testing firearms and in assisting police in investigating fatalities caused by firearms. Kelly, *The Gun in the Case*, esp. pp.139–43, 151–2; Annual Reports, 1937, p.6; 1938, p.6; 1939, p.6; 1940, p.5; 1941, p.5. The annual number of reported accidents involving firearms

fluctuated between 30 and 60 in the decade from 1935, while the number of fatalities fell by half from a peak of 36 in 1936/37.

168. For instructions to police regarding reports on motor accidents involving death or personal injury see *NZPG*, 1937, p.200. Analysis of the first year's motor accident reports had implications for the patterns of police work in revealing, amongst other findings, that 39% of all accidents involving injury occurred between 4 and 8 pm; 52% occurred on Friday, Saturday or Sunday; a third occurred on country highways and rural roads; and one driver in every fourteen involved in accidents was unlicensed. In 1938/39 there were 4,402 reports, and in 1939/40, 4,147; *NZOYB*, 1939, pp.262–3; 1941, p.299.

169. Official Report of Police Association conferences, 1938, pp.41–2; 1939, pp.39–40. Fraser considered the Transport Department to be 'doing a fair job and we should leave them alone. One day it may be possible, after they reach the standard of efficiency they are aiming at, to amalgamate the two services.' Commissioner Cummings was 'very strongly in favour of giving Traffic Officers power to arrest because they are going to get involved in serious trouble one of these days.' Notes of interview of Police Association delegates with the Minister in charge of the Police, and Commissioner Cummings present, 8 May 1939, P 13/1/-. In fact those city traffic inspectors who had been sworn in as Special Constables already possessed the power to arrest; but not all traffic inspectors had this power, especially those appointed by county councils. *Press*, 1, 7 Jul 1938. During the 1930s there were periodical calls by representatives of the Automobile Association, local councillors, and a former Commissioner of Police for Washington DC, for the Police to take full responsibility for traffic control; see for example, *Truth*, 29 May 1930; *Press*, 2 Sep 1936, 19 Feb 1938.

170. While the authorised strength was increased by 25 to 1,462 for the 1938/39 financial year, insufficient police were trained to meet this target because of a higher rate of wastage through retirements, resignations and deaths; the Force was 1,439-strong in Mar 1939. Annual Report, 1939, pp.4, 8. Authorised strength calculated from Vote Police, *AJHR*, 1938, B-7, pp.117–18.

171. Mrs N.M. Molesworth in an address on 'Women Police' to members of the international circle of the Auckland Lyceum Club, *NZH*, 8 Aug 1937. To the Auckland Branch of the League of Nations Union eight months earlier she had asserted that in Auckland 'there is a crying need for women police. We have heard much about drinking among young people .... [which] is bringing along with it social problems I hardly dare speak about.' *Dominion*, 27 Nov 1936.

172. Elizabeth McCombs succeeded her husband, James, as MP for Lyttelton in 1933, and served until her death in Jun 1935. She was in turn succeeded by her son, Terence McCombs, who continued her advocacy of women police. See *NZPD*, vol.236, 1933, pp.160–1; vol.238, 1934, p.379; vol.243, 1935, p.148.

173. Janet Fraser's influence can only be surmised, since the author has found no direct evidence of her advocacy. In 1948, Commissioner James Cummings voiced a popular perception in asserting that 'The late Mrs Fraser was a strong advocate for the women police and she was really responsible for the establishment of the branch'. *EP*, 5 Apr 1948; see also *NZFL*, 14 Apr 1948. Janet Fraser was on the first list of women JPs appointed in Dec 1926, and was appointed a visitor of the Children's Court as well as being a founder member of the Women's Borstal Association. More generally, according to Hilary Stace, Janet had quite radical views regarding women's work in non-traditional spheres and was Peter's adviser on policies regarding women. Hilary Stace, 'Janet Fraser: Making Policy as Well as Tea', in Clark (ed.), *Peter Fraser*, ch.4, and personal communication.

174. *NZPD*, vol.246, 1936, pp.768–9. In response to deputations during 1934 and 1935, J.G. Cobbe had followed Commissioner Wohlmann's advice and argued that while women police might be 'a success in America', 'reports from Home were not so favourable.' Wohlmann pointed out in 1934 that the number of policewomen in

London had declined to 54 from 100 'three or four years ago.' In Feb 1936, however, it was reported that the London Metropolitan Police intended to increase its women police strength from 67 to 142. Also adding renewed impetus to lobbying for women police was the reception given by women's organisations in Wellington in Dec 1935 to Miss Kate Cocks (spelt 'Cox' in newspaper reports), who had been South Australia's first policewoman in 1915 and Principal of the Women Police Office until 1935. *Dominion*, 17 May 1934, 5 Dec 1935; *ODT*, 9 Oct 1935; *NZH*, 7 Feb 1936.

175. *ODT*, 3 May 1938. There had been renewed Wellington-based pressure for women police in Apr 1938; see letters and commentary in the *Dominion*, 13, 20, 26 Apr 1938.

176. Statutes Amendment Act 1938, sec.45: 'The powers conferred by the Police Force Act, 1913, to appoint members of the Police Force (including temporary members) are hereby extended so as to include power to appoint women to be members of the Force, and all references in the said Act to the Force and to the members of the Force shall be deemed to include the women members thereof.'

177. *NZPJ*, vol.2, no.2, Apr 1938, p.61. 'District notes' in each issue of the first three volumes of the *Journal* contain details of the origins and development of police social and sports clubs and their activities. For details on the New Zealand Police team sent to the NSW Police sports carnival in 1938 see vol.1, 1937, no.3, Aug, pp.17–18; no.4, Nov, p.55; vol.2, no.2, Apr 1938, pp.9–14; *AWN*, 15 Dec 1937; *NZH*, 24 Feb, 16 Mar 1938.

178. Belton's application in May 1938 for permission to stand as an independent candidate in the Gisborne electorate was refused too late for him to give the required month's notice of resignation in order to stand. As the Gisborne delegate to the Association's conference in Sep 1938, he was supported only by his Auckland counterpart in pressing for a 40-hour week to be introduced as soon as possible. He had only 'partial success' in gaining support for other changes, such as payment for overtime, keeping the weekly day off free from all duties except for urgent ones, straight (unbroken) shifts, more staff, lighter summer uniforms, increased car allowances, the advertising of vacancies, police taking over traffic control, the registration of bicycles, that Association conferences be held in July, and that the *NZPJ* give members 'freedom of expression' in a 'correspondence section'. Belton moved to Auckland and became a successful land agent. *Dominion*, 1, 2 Nov 1938; *ODT*, 13 Apr 1939; *Press*, 24 May 1939; *NZPJ*, vol.2, 1938, 'Official Report' of the third annual conference held 6 to 8 Sep, pp.8–59; Belton, *Outside the Law*, pp.208–55.

Chapter 12: Policing the Home Front (1939–45)

1. See Haldane, *The People's Force*, pp.220–31, and Johnston, *The Long Blue Line*, ch.26, for descriptions of the wartime activities of the Victoria and the Queensland Police respectively.

2. Minutes of Police conference, Christchurch, 22 Oct 1940, p.9, P 7/1/5–1940.

3. For a general account of the origins and work of the Organisation for National Security, see F.L.W. Wood, *The New Zealand People at War: Political and External Affairs*, Wellington, 1958, pp.86–9.

4. See Critchley, *A History of Police in England and Wales*, pp.224–7 for details on wartime police reserves in England.

5. *NZPJ*, vol.3, no.5, p.405. As the editor noted, the lack of training for air raid precaution duties, for example, probably reflected a belief that the possibility of such an attack was 'slight.' The Oct 1939 issue, the first after the outbreak of war, contains notes from a 'Civilian Anti-Gas Training Course' (between pp.448–9), but no other information regarding the war. The article was reprinted in 1942, when 'the possibility of bombs' was taken more seriously. *Ibid.*, vol.6, no.2, pp.90–6; no.3, pp.198–201; no.4, pp.269–72.

6. In Apr 1938, the then Detective Harding attended a meeting of the Combined

Intelligence Committee of the ONS; during 1938–39, he was the Police representative on the Aliens and Vital Points Committees. Harding was promoted to Detective Sergeant on 15 Jul 1940. He returned to the Uniform Branch on 1 Dec 1945, when he was posted as Sergeant to Feilding. In 1946 he was awarded an OBE for 'services to the Special Branch'.

Harding wrote the 301-page typescript 'Police Narrative' for the New Zealand government's official War History. This chapter relies heavily on the 'Police Narrative', largely because few Police files exist (or are accessible) for the wartime period. Police 'Special Branch' records were subsequently transferred to the Security Intelligence Service and have not been consulted; nor have the minutes of the various committees of ONS. Internal evidence (indicating considerable direct but unacknowledged citation from files), as well as evidence from other secondary sources which have used ONS files, and such files as have been consulted, suggest that Harding's narrative is an accurate account of the main decisions made by ONS committees, and of departmental thinking. Throughout the narrative, Harding signals (by a footnote, 'Narrator's comment') when he makes a personal observation.

7.   [A.M. Harding], 'Police Narrative, New Zealand Government War History' (hereafter cited as 'Police Narrative'), n.d., typescript, pp.34–5, WA-II 21/43d; P.J. Nalder to author, Jan and 27 Feb 1977.

8.   Though the Labour government did not repeal the War Regulations Continuance Act, the Comptroller of Customs was instructed in Oct 1936 to 'arrange for the restriction with regard to delivery of books on political, economic and other questions, to be removed'. R. Barrowman, *A Popular Vision: The Arts and the Left in New Zealand, 1930–1950*, Wellington, 1991, p.44.

9.   Stevens to Commissioner Cummings, 20 Apr 1938, OPR 1/1/1.

10. Minutes of the second and third meetings of the Combined Intelligence Committee of the ONS, 28 Apr, 4 May 1938; Lieutenant-Colonel Stevens to Chief of General Staff, 6, 14 Sep 1938; Minutes of meeting of Chiefs of Staff Committee, 19 Sep 1938, AD 11/16/14; 'Police Narrative', pp.35–6.

11. N. Taylor, *The New Zealand People at War: The Home Front*, Wellington, 1986, ch.19; McGill, *The Guardians at the Gate*, ch.8.

12. *Ibid.*, p.112.

13. Naval Secretary to Secretary, ONS, 14 Aug 1940, N 8/1/25.

14. *Ibid.*

15. Mawhood arrived in Australia from New Zealand in Dec 1940. His appointment by the Australian federal government in Jul 1941 to investigate both its newly established Security Service and the Army's Military Intelligence proved to be controversial. Cain, *Origins of Political Surveillance in Australia*, pp.281–6.

16. Folkes was promoted from Lieutenant to Major on his appointment as Director of the SIB.

17. In 1941 the SIB had an authorised establishment of 55 Army personnel, including 43 NCOs. In fact, two civilians were recruited to the Auckland bureau at the outset, and only 32 Sergeants had been enlisted by Jan 1942, ostensibly because the pay was 'unattractive' to the type of men Folkes wanted. Memorandum from Lieutenant-General Mawhood to Chiefs of Staff, n.d. [Nov 1940]; Chiefs of Staff Committee paper, 26 Nov 1940; Memoranda from Colonel Goss, General Staff, to District Headquarters, 14 Dec 1940, 7 Feb 1941; Chiefs of Staff Committee papers, 16 Sep 1941, 2, 12 Jan 1942, N 8/1/25.

18. Chiefs of Staff Committee paper, 2 Jan 1942; Director of Security Intelligence to Secretary, ONS, 14 Feb 1942, N 8/1/25.

19. Letters to the author from O. Power, 24 Feb 1977; G.C. Urquhart, 30 Nov 1976; and J.A. du Temple, 3 Mar 1977.

20. Navy Office Minute, 'Security Intelligence', 12 Mar 1941; Navy Secretary to Naval Officers in charge, 15 Jun 1941; ONS Minute, COS 96, Security Intelligence Bureau, 30 Sep 1941; Chiefs of Staff Committee paper, 2 Jan 1942; H.G.R. Mason to War

Cabinet, 18 Sep 1942, N 8/1/25. P.J. Nalder to author, Jan 1977; E.R. Trask to author, 3 Jul 1977; 'Police Narrative', pp.36–7; Wood, *Political and External Affairs,* p.161.

21. Ross was apparently assisted by Charles Remmers, who also had convictions for false pretenses. H.G.R. Mason, Memorandum for War Cabinet, 18 Sep 1942, N 8/1/25.

22. Detective Sergeants A.M. Harding, P.J. Nalder, and P. Doyle from Wellington, and J. Walsh from Auckland.

23. There are a number of brief accounts of this hoax. See especially: *Truth,* 29 Jul 1942; Wood, *Political and External Affairs,* pp.161–2; Taylor, *Home Front,* pp.884–5; D. Filer, 'The Great Spy Lie', *NZ Listener,* 25 Sep 1982, pp.18–19. Like those of Wood and Filer, this account draws particularly on H.G.R. Mason's report to the War Cabinet, 18 Sep 1942, a copy of which is in N 8/1/25.

24. H.G.R. Mason, Memorandum for War Cabinet, 18 Sep 1942, N 8/1/25.

25. Chiefs of Staff Committee paper, 22 Dec 1942, N 8/1/25.

26. On 24 Feb 1943, the day after James Cummings informed the Chiefs of Staff that he had taken over as Director of Security Intelligence, a meeting of their Committee agreed that a sub-committee (comprising Intelligence Officers of the armed forces and a Police representative) should meet to suggest 'the arrangements to be made in security matters in the future.' Two days later the sub-committee considered, for the first time, Mason's report of 18 Sep 1942 on the SIB. It recommended that the SIB be disbanded and Mason's scheme implemented. On 8 Mar the Vital Points Committee (usually composed of the Chiefs of Staff, the Commissioner of Police, and the Director of Security Intelligence) decided to defer consideration of the sub-committee's recommendations. It seems that no further decisions were formally taken. James Cummings to Chief of Naval Staff, 23 Feb 1943; Secretary, ONS, to Chiefs of Staff, 25 Feb 1943; Report of sub-committee meeting, 26 Feb 1943, 'Security Organisation'; Minutes of Vital Points Committee, 8 Mar 1943, N 8/1/25.

27. 'Police Narrative', pp.36–7.

28. In Feb 1944, for example, the Director of Security Intelligence joined with naval authorities in opposing the Commissioner's request that the Police be relieved of the duty of guarding gangways. *Ibid.,* pp.189–90.

29. Captain A.W. Yortt was Deputy Director of the SIB from 21 Jun 1943 to 16 Feb 1944, when he 'returned to civil life'. Director of Security Intelligence to Director of Naval Intelligence, 11 May, 23 Jul 1943, 17 Mar 1944, N 8/1/25. Letters to author from P.J. Nalder, Jan 1977; E.R. Trask, 3 Jul 1977.

30. Nalder had been appointed Deputy Director of Security on 17 Mar 1944, when Cummings visited Britain on security matters. J. Cummings to Director of Naval Intelligence, 17 Mar 1944, N 8/1/25.

31. 'Police Narrative', p.37; Nalder to author, Jan 1977; *Dominion,* 11 Sep 1945.

32. J.E. Cookson suggests that there is 'no reason to think that there was ever much above a thousand formally committed pacifists in the country.' According to Detective Sergeant Harding, the membership of the Communist Party 'did not exceed more than 700 or 800 persons' during the war. In 1936 there were some 450 Jehovah's Witnesses. J.E. Cookson, 'Pacifism and Conscientious Objection in World War II New Zealand', in P. Brock and T. Socknat (eds), *Challenge to Mars: Essays on Pacifism from 1918 to 1945,* Toronto, 1998; 'Police Narrative', p.212; Taylor, *Home Front,* p.234.

33. 'Police Narrative', p.216.

34. Wood, *Political and External Affairs,* pp.117–23; Sinclair, *Walter Nash,* pp.208–9; Hobbs, *The Thirty-Year Wonders,* p.49; D. Grant, *Out in the Cold,* Auckland, 1986, p.48; Thorn, *Peter Fraser,* pp.251–2. For Fraser's attitudes to dissent, war priorities and work habits, and the wartime political context more generally, see Clark (ed.), *Peter Fraser,* chs 3, 9, 10, 11.

35. Such files as exist (including those police records held by the Security Intelligence Service that the author was able to consult) contain no direct evidence of ministerial

direction of the Police. It is likely that specific matters of concern to Fraser, especially regarding subversion and industrial disputes, were communicated verbally to Cummings. The Commissioner's policies discussed below, and his directions to his officers, clearly reflect the government's priorities. This was especially noticeable in relation to industrial disputes which were monitored by police. According to a newspaper report, for example, a union organiser said to Manawatu cheese factory workers in 1942: 'Hello you slaves, still working for £4 or £5 a week? I can get you £10 a week in Wellington for half the work. Why don't you strike?' Fraser contacted Cummings immediately. Instructions were quickly issued, and detectives visited the cheese factory to make enquiries. *Press*, 17 Mar 1942.

36.   As when, for example, during the Pukemiro coal miners' strike in Sep 1942, Hamilton police banned a meeting of miners at a Huntly theatre (under the Public Safety Emergency Regulations) and refused to permit miners to speak at a mass meeting promoted by the mayor of Huntly to find a compromise. Note that this occurred two days before Fraser's return from overseas. *Press*, 16 Sep 1942; Richardson, *Coal, Class and Community*, pp.274–5; Taylor, *Home Front*, pp.414–15.

37.   Wood, *Political and External Affairs*, p.125; Taylor, *Home Front*, ch.19, esp. pp.976–8.

38.   'Police Narrative', pp.214–16; Taylor, *Home Front*, pp.886–7.

39.   Fraser stood surety for the three arrested so that they could be released on bail. Taylor, *Home Front*, pp.180–1; Grant, *Out in the Cold*, pp.48–9; E. Crane, *I Can Do No Other*, Auckland, 1986, pp.112–13.

40.   O. Burton, *In Prison*, Wellington, 1945, pp.10–12.

41.   'Police Narrative', pp.216–18; 'New Zealand Communist Party and the War' (hereafter cited as 'Communist Party Narrative'), n.d., typescript, pp.67–8, WA-II 21/63c; Taylor, *Home Front*, pp.181–93, 209–11; Grant, *Out in the Cold*, pp.49–74; Crane, *I Can Do No Other*, pp.114–31. An example of the controls on dissent that were exercised by J.T. Paul, the Director of Publicity, when the powers available to the Police were found wanting came in Jan 1940, when Fraser learnt of a meeting to be called by the Wellington Peace Committee in the town hall to establish a broad-based organisation to campaign for New Zealand's withdrawal from the war. Fraser instructed Paul to see what could be done to prevent the meeting. When Paul asked the Commissioner of Police 'what power could be exercised' to prevent the meeting 'if such a course were deemed necessary or desirable', Cummings said he did 'not know of any authority' to do so, but pointed out that the circular advertising the meeting seemed to be a breach of the Censorship and Publicity Emergency Regulations. Paul also had discussions with the town clerk, who consulted the mayor before informing the secretary of the Wellington Peace Committee on 10 Jan that his booking had been 'cancelled for reasons of a civic nature'. Two days earlier, a meeting at the Wellington Trades' Hall had formed the Wellington Peace and Anti-Conscription Council, which in turn called a public meeting in the Trades' Hall when the town hall booking was cancelled. After there was initial publicity for this meeting, Paul secured the agreement of the *EP* and the *Dominion* not to accept any further advertisements from the Peace and Anti-Conscription Council. Similarly, in May 1940, Oliver Duff, editor of the *NZ Listener*, agreed to Paul's request not to accept any 'publicity' from the Peace Pledge Union. Memoranda on file EA 1, 84/10/1.

42.   'Police Narrative', pp.206–12; 'Communist Party Narrative', pp.56–67 (note that this account states on page 56 that the NZCP had nearly 700 members by the end of 1939); Taylor, *Home Front*, pp.52–62, 211–12.

43.   'Police Narrative', pp.218–20. See also 'Communist Party Narrative', pp.68–70; H. Witheford, 'Censorship of the Press' (hereafter cited as 'Censorship Narrative'), 1948, typescript, pp.3–4, WA-II 21/3d; Taylor, *Home Front*, p.190.

44.   The Co-operative Press in Christchurch was seized in Jun, but no prosecutions to determine whether any of its pacifist publications was subversive followed. 'Police Narrative', pp.209, 223–4; 'Censorship Narrative', p.9; Taylor, *Home Front*, pp.191–

5, 894; Grant, *Out in the Cold*, pp.74–9.

45. In his annual report submitted on 16 Jul 1940, Commissioner Cummings declared that the 'position is now satisfactory'. Annual Report, 1940, p.7; 'Police Narrative', pp.219–24, 228–31; 'Communist Party Narrative', pp.70–1; 'Censorship Narrative', pp.4a–7, 9–12; Taylor, *Home Front*, pp.191, 212–16, 887.

46. Amendment no.2 to the Censorship and Publicity Regulations (1940/95).

47. Commissioner of Police to Superintendent, Auckland, 11 May 1940, OPR 1/1/1; 'Police Narrative', pp.229–32; 'Communist Party Narrative', pp.75–9; 'Censorship Narrative', pp.7–9; Taylor, *Home Front*, pp.104, 216–18, 892–4; Cain, *Origins of Political Surveillance in Australia*, pp.266–9.

48. Grant, *Out in the Cold*, pp.83, 87; Taylor, *Home Front*, p.195.

49. 'Police Narrative', pp.213–14, 233–7; Taylor, pp.234–43.

50. *Press*, 8 Oct 1940; Taylor, *Home Front*, p.219. In Christchurch, Superintendent Sidney Rawle carefully pasted the *Press* report of Semple's outburst into his scrapbook next to a faded newspaper clipping of his evidence, as a detective, in the prosecution of Semple for sedition in 1916.

51. Minutes of conference of North Island officers in charge of districts at Wellington, 15 and 16 Oct 1940, p.4. Cummings' comment is repeated in Minutes of Police conference, Christchurch, 22 Oct 1940, p.2, also pp.4, 5, P 7/1/5–1940.

52. Minutes of North Island conference, pp.2–6; Minutes of Christchurch conference, pp.2–8, P 7/1/5–1940.

53. 'Police Narrative', pp.243–4.

54. Inspector J.A. Dempsey, Wanganui, to Constable, Raetihi, 20 Oct, 3 Dec 1940 (copy in the author's possession).

55. Taylor, *Home Front*, p.220.

56. 'Police Narrative', pp.224–8; Grant, *Out in the Cold*, pp.87–95; Taylor, *Home Front*, pp.195–200. When Ormond Burton asked the government to allow the Christian Pacifist Society to hold a meeting in the Wellington town hall 'along the lines of' the Society's covenant, Fraser 'thought the Police would be inclined to refuse permission for such a meeting', having been 'given the power to stop any meeting if that meeting was likely to be subversive or inimical to the war effort.' Fraser added, however, that 'If any particular case were referred to the Government they give a direction.' Commissioner Cummings then 'stated the Police would definitely stop such a meeting.' Minutes of the meeting on 18 Nov 1940 between a deputation from the Christian Pacifist Society and the Prime Minister, Peter Fraser (together with the Attorney-General, the associate Minister of National Service, the Commissioner of Police, and the Directors of Publicity and of National Service), in C.L. Blaikie, 'Defaulters and Conscientious Objectors', 1948, typescript, WA-II 21/7c.

57. 'Police Narrative', pp.211–13, 238–41; 'Communist Party Narrative', pp.80–104; Taylor, *Home Front*, pp.223, 587–9.

58. The Aliens Committee was established by the ONS in 1937 and comprised representatives of the Army, Police, Internal Affairs, Customs, and Census and Statistics. 'Aliens Administration, 1939–1945' (hereafter cited as 'Aliens Narrative'), n.d., typescript, p.2, WA-II 21/63d.

59. 'Police Narrative', pp.39–66. The judgement regarding the extent of knowledge of the political loyalties of aliens in 1939 is that of the writer of the 'Aliens Narrative', p.60. See also accounts which draw on the 'Aliens Narrative': Wood, *Political and External Affairs*, pp.156–7; Taylor, *Home Front*, ch.18, esp. pp.856–7; M.M. Poole, 'The Treatment of Enemy Aliens in New Zealand During the Second World War', BA(hons) long essay, University of Otago, 1982, pp.1–4.

60. 'Aliens Narrative', p.6. The 'Police Narrative', p.68, also gives the date of Cabinet approval of the draft regulations as 29 Sep 1938, but on p.66 it cites ONS 108 of Nov 1938 in detailing the Aliens Committee's recommendations to Cabinet.

61. This became the main work of Constable J.P. Clements, for example, in the renamed Auckland Aliens and Arms Office; Clements to author, 16 Jun 1977.

62. *NZPJ*, vol.3, no.5, Oct 1939, p.487.
63. 'Police Narrative', pp.68–71, and part 2, schedule 4: Aliens Registered at 31 March 1944; and Taylor, *Home Front*, p.857. The 'Aliens Narrative', p.9, comments that 'about 7000 aliens' were registered, including some 1,600 Germans and 100 Austrians.
64. By 31 Mar 1944, only 11 Japanese were registered as aliens, by comparison with 1,196 Germans and 772 Italians; 'Police Narrative', part 2, schedule 4: Aliens Registered at 31 March 1944. Commissioner D.J. Cummings saw the definition of an 'alien' as the 'principal difficulty' in implementing the 1939 regulations. Minutes of conference of North Island officers in charge of districts at Wellington, 15 and 16 Oct 1940, p.2. In the first and fourth schedules of the 'Police Narrative', part 2, the number of 'German' and 'Italian' aliens registered at 31 Mar 1944 is less than the number in Aug 1940. This may reflect a reclassification of nationality, with a fall in the number of Germans and Austrians roughly balanced by an increase in those classified as Czechs. Some Germans and Italians classified as enemy aliens in 1940 may not have been so classified in 1944.
65. Calculated from A. Beaglehole, *A Small Price to Pay: Refugees from Hitler in New Zealand, 1936–46*, Wellington, 1988, p.146, Appendix 4c. The total number of refugees from these three countries in the period 1933 to 1940 was 1,015; *ibid.*
66. 'Police Narrative', pp.71–5; 'Aliens Narrative', pp.9–11; Taylor, *Home Front*, pp.857–8, 863–4; Poole, 'Treatment of Enemy Aliens', pp.12–13.
67. 'Police Narrative', p.69.
68. 'Aliens Narrative' pp.12, 57.
69. For details of the police surveillance of German organisations in New Zealand, see the 'Police Narrative', pp.41–55. The Deutscher Verein in Auckland was formed in Aug 1932 and its membership grew rapidly to a peak of about 220 in mid-1933. Following Hitler's consolidation of his power after becoming Chancellor in Germany, a rift developed in the German Club when Nazi sympathisers took control late in 1933. There were a large number of resignations, including some of the early office-holders and many of the British members. Membership had fallen to about 80 by Feb 1934, when Detective E.A. Stevenson, who had taken over local political surveillance from Detective P.J. Nalder, began monitoring the club. According to Stevenson, he initiated the surveillance and relied on informants. E.A. Stevenson interview, Feb 1978. The quality of the police pre-war surveillance was verified from records of the German Consulate-General which were examined after the war. Foss Shanahan, then Secretary of the Cabinet, informed A.M. Harding: 'You will be pleased to know that the Security Branch in its pre-war work identified correctly both [Nazi] Party branches [in Auckland and Wellington], office-bearers, the individual Party members and the main functions of the Party in New Zealand. This was a most creditable performance, particularly in view of the limited means at your disposal.' Foss Shanahan to Sergeant A.M. Harding, Devonport, 25 Mar 1955 (copy of letter in author's possession).
70. 'Police Narrative', pp.76–7; 'Aliens Narrative', pp.12–13, 17–18; Taylor, *Home Front*, pp.857–8, 865–6; Poole, 'Treatment of Enemy Aliens', pp.14–16.
71. 'Police Narrative', p.78; Wood, *Political and External Affairs*, pp.156, 158; 'Aliens Narrative', pp.13–14; Taylor, *Home Front*, pp.858–65; Poole, 'Treatment of Enemy Aliens', pp.13–15, 42–5.
72. 'Police Narrative', pp.78–81; 'Aliens Narrative', pp.18–20; Taylor, *Home Front*, p.866; Poole, 'Treatment of Enemy Aliens', pp.15–19.
73. Half of the Germans and two-thirds of the Austrians lived in either the Auckland or Wellington Police District. Half of the Italians and the Czechs lived in Wellington. 'Police Narrative', part 2, schedule 1.
74. Callan to Mason, 4 Sep 1940, cited by Poole, 'Treatment of Enemy Aliens', pp.24–5.
75. Three Aliens Authorities were appointed in the Auckland Police District, and one in each of the other districts, except Wellington, where the three members of the Appeal Tribunal acted as individual authorities. 'Police Narrative', pp.81–90; 'Aliens Narrative', pp. 21–4; Taylor, *Home Front*, pp.866–7; Poole, 'Treatment of Enemy

Aliens', pp.19–26.

76.   'Aliens Narrative', p.24. Comments on the work involved in 'aliens enquiries' in letters to the author from E.J. Gaines, 14 Mar 1977; F.A. Gordon, 11 Feb 1977; G.C. Urquhart, 8 Dec 1976; M.E. Parker, 7 Mar 1977.

77.   Annual Report, 1941, pp.7, 9, 12; 'Police Narrative', pp.82–4, part 2, schedules 1 and 2; 'Aliens Narrative', pp.24–5; Taylor, *Home Front,* pp.867–8; Poole, 'Treatment of Enemy Aliens', pp.29–38; Minutes of conference of North Island officers in charge of districts at Wellington, 15 and 16 Oct 1940, pp.9–12, P 7/1/5–1940.

78.   Poole, 'Treatment of Enemy Aliens', pp.29–33; Minutes of conference of North Island officers in charge of districts at Wellington, 15 and 16 Oct 1940, pp.11–12; Minutes of Police conference, Christchurch, 22 Oct 1940, p.9, P 7/1/5–1940.

79.   'Notes for the Guidance of the Aliens Authorities' issued by the Minister of Justice, cited by Poole, 'Treatment of Enemy Aliens', p.31; Callan, cited *ibid.,* p.34.

80.   Minutes of Police conference, Christchurch, 22 Oct 1940, p.2, P 7/1/5–1940.

81.   Poole, 'Treatment of Enemy Aliens', p.32, citing a memo from the Wellington Aliens Authority to the Minister in charge of Aliens, 8 Mar 1944. Detective Sergeant Harding found, in several cases he brought before the first tribunal in Aug/Sep 1940, that 'the person who recommended the alien did not even know the man.' Minutes of conference of North Island officers in charge of districts at Wellington, 15 and 16 Oct 1940, p.9, P 7/1/5–1940. Commissioner Cummings also believed that 'little trust' could be placed in 'guarantees given in respect of aliens'. Minutes of Police conference, Christchurch, 22 Oct 1940, p.10, *ibid.* See also 'Aliens Narrative', pp.25–33, regarding problems of classification and variations in decisions amongst the tribunals.

82.   Minutes of conference of North Island officers in charge of districts at Wellington, 15 and 16 Oct 1940, p.8; Minutes of Police conference, Christchurch, 22 Oct 1940, p.10, P 7/1/5–1940.

83.   Power to author, 24 Feb 1977.

84.   'Aliens Narrative', pp.33–4, 37–41; Taylor, *Home Front,* pp.869–72, 882–3; Poole, 'Treatment of Enemy Aliens', pp.25–6, 30, 38–40, 66.

85.   'Police Narrative', pp.244–5.

86.   Annual Report, 1942, p.3.

87.   Calculated from data in Poole, 'Treatment of Enemy Aliens', p.30; and in table 'Aliens Registered as at 31 March 1944', 'Police Narrative', part 2, schedule 4.

88.   Annual Report, 1943, p.3.

89.   Minutes of Police conference, Christchurch, 22 Oct 1940, p.11, P 7/1/5–1940 (typographical errors corrected).

90.   Annual Report, 1944, p.3; 'Police Narrative', pp.86–90, 96–9, 111–14; 'Aliens Narrative', pp.34–6; Poole, 'Treatment of Enemy Aliens', pp.19–22.

91.   'Police Narrative', p.121, and part 2, schedule 3.

92.   'Police Narrative', pp.114–23; Edna Pearce, recollections of her career supplied to author, Jan 1978.

93.   In 1940 the Department of Internal Affairs had opened a file on 'enemy aliens' along with a register of aliens. After the war it took over the role of registering aliens. Though the Commissioner of Police recommended the deportation of 29 enemy aliens in 1946, all ex-internees who applied for citizenship eventually received their certificates. M. Bassett, *The Mother of All Departments: The History of the Department of Internal Affairs,* Wellington, 1997, pp.116, 126, 149–51.

94.   'Aliens Narrative', p.58.

95.   'Police Narrative', pp.125–6, 156.

96.   Namely, the cable landings at Doubtless Bay, Harkness Point and Muriwai, the Lyttelton railway tunnel, the explosives magazine at Westport, the floating dock at Wellington, and bulk oil installations at Nelson and New Plymouth.

97.   'Police Narrative', pp.128–30, 158–9.

98.   See I.T. Clarke, *Deodar,* Auckland, 1994, ch.1, for Auckland's water police before 1919.

99.   A sub-committee comprising representatives of the three armed services and of the Police, Customs and Marine departments.
100.   'Police Narrative', pp.156–60, 202.
101.   *Ibid.*, pp.160–3, 202–3. For the allocation of police to wharves, see also Annual Report, 1941, pp.6, 9, 11–13. In response to a parliamentary question in Aug 1940, the Prime Minister commented that 'the question of water police, particularly in view of the war developments was receiving very close attention.' *NZPD*, vol.257, pp.769–70.
102.   J.V.T. Baker, *The New Zealand People at War: War Economy*, Wellington, 1965, pp.185, 373–4; McGill, *Guardians at the Gate*, pp.113–16. On 30 Nov 1940, F.P. Walsh, President of the Federated Seamen's Union of New Zealand, led a deputation to Peter Fraser (with Commissioner Cummings present) to complain that 'in Wellington in particular bad elements which had been expelled from the Union were continually going on to the wharves and stirring up trouble.' Fraser responded that 'If that was true there was a weakness in the Police supervision, and it must be tightened up .... The war was getting very close, and things had happened in other ports which showed quite clearly that there were people in the country who would commit sabotage.' Notes of deputation to the Prime Minister, 30 Nov 1940. A report from Sergeant J. Martin (in charge of constables on the Wellington wharves) 'emphatically' denied any 'justification' for Walsh's complaint; Sergeant Martin to Superintendent Lopdell, 6 Mar 1941, OPR 40/64/4.
103.   'Police Narrative', pp.16–17, 163–85. In Aug 1942, 160 additional police were on wharf duties, including 63 in Wellington and 39 in Auckland. *Ibid.*, part 4, schedule A.
104.   In Nov 1944, the *Tiromoana* was replaced at Auckland by the *Pirate*. Both boats had been chartered by the Navy. Clarke, *Deodar*, p.22.
105.   'Police Narrative', pp.198–205; Clarke, *Deodar*, pp.17–23; Cherrett, *Without Fear or Favour*, pp.251–2; Wayne Wilkey, 'The Waterfront', in Young (ed.), *With Confidence and Pride*, pp.348, 353–5; Thomson and Neilson, *Sharing the Challenge*, p.129.
106.   The 'some people' were apparently naval officers at the main ports and the SIB under Major Folkes. However, in 1944, both the Navy and the SIB (under the new leadership of Superintendent James Cummings) opposed Commissioner Cummings' request to withdraw from guarding ships' gangways because of the shortage of staff. The two agencies argued that because of their training and their prestige, the Police were better suited to the work. Report of Police Association Conference, 1942, p.28; 'Report of Deputation from Police Association ... [to] Commissioner of Police, 9 Dec 1942, p.7, P 13/1/-; 'Police Narrative', p.190.
107.   'Police Narrative', pp.186–91, 194–5; Taylor, *Home Front,* pp.442–5, 637. The difficulty of monitoring the hundreds of watersiders entering the wharves in the mornings had been apparent from 1940; Sergeant J. Martin to Superintendent Lopdell, 6 Mar 1941, OPR 40/64/4.
108.   By Mar 1943, Port Security Control comprised 14 Army personnel (Auckland 4, Wellington 7, Christchurch 3) responsible to the Director of the SIB; N 8/1/25. Comments on police resentment from Gordon Howes interview, 17 Aug 1978.
109.   Because of the shortage of police staff, the Army took over guarding the Wellington floating dock between 3 Mar 1942 and 23 Mar 1943; 'Police Narrative', p.137.
110.   *Ibid.*, pp.130–1, 135–7.
111.   Hamilton (3), Gisborne (2), Wanganui (4), Timaru (3), Invercargill (3); *ibid.*, p.141.
112.   *Ibid.*, pp.127–9, 131–5, 137–42.
113.   *Ibid.*, pp.142–50.
114.   Annual Report, 1943, p.3; 'Police Narrative', pp.150–3, 187–91, 195–7, 205.
115.   'Police Narrative', p.153.
116.   In Aug 1935, an Emergency Precautions Committee of the New Zealand Committee of Imperial Defence was formed with representatives from the Internal Affairs, Defence and Police (Sub-Inspector H. Scott) departments. This met periodically and became

part of the Organisation for National Security in 1937. Though the committee compiled reports, the drafting of an Emergency Precautions Scheme proceeded very slowly between 1935 and 1938. E.M. Rigg, 'Emergency Precautions Scheme: Civil Defence Organisation in New Zealand' (hereafter cited as 'EPS Narrative'), n.d., typescript, WA-II 21/96, [ch.1], pp.6–8.

117. 'Police Narrative', p.285; Taylor, *Home Front*, p.481; 'EPS Narrative', [ch.1], pp.8–9.

118. In Dec 1940, the Vital Points Committee of the ONS decided that vital points of a 'civilian and local character' (such as water supply reservoirs and gasworks) should be guarded by the appropriate committee of the local Emergency Precautions organisations. This responsibility was emphasised at an EPS conference in Jan 1941 at which local EPS committees were instructed to make immediate preparations in collaboration with the Police to provide men in an emergency. 'EPS Narrative', ch.9, pp.1–2. For the development of the Emergency Precautions Scheme, see Taylor, *Home Front*, pp.480–573.

119. At Wellington, the number of EPS auxiliary police rose from 297 in May to 540 in Nov 1941, remaining at just over 5% of the growing number of local EPS volunteers. At Christchurch, there were 200 EPS police by May 1941. On 22 Oct 1941 Emergency Reserve Corps Regulations which revoked the Emergency Precautions Regulations of 16 Aug 1940 provided for the establishment of emergency units, including Law and Order sections under Police control. *Press*, 11 Jan, 27 Feb, 1 Mar, 5 May 1941; *NZH*, 18 Dec 1941; 'Police Narrative', p.285; 'EPS Narrative', ch.14, p.1; Taylor, *Home Front*, pp.472, 482–3, 486–7, 491, 510–11.

120. 'Police Narrative', pp.286–9; *NZH*, 1 Mar 1941; *Press*, 5 Mar, 5 May, 27 Jun, 15 Jul 1941.

121. Besides adopting a standard syllabus and compiling a training manual, this course also clarified the respective roles of the police-controlled Law and Order units and those units controlled by the EPS wardens. It appears that cooperation between the Law and Order units and other EPS units had not been satisfactory. A conference in May 1943 (involving the Director of National Service, Regional Commissioners, the Director of Security Intelligence, representatives of the Police and Transport departments, and the Chief Traffic Inspectors of the four main centres) defined the functions of the Law and Order units and the authority of police more precisely. 'Police Narrative', pp.286, 289–90; *NZPJ*, vol.7, no.3, Jun 1943, pp.168–70; 'EPS Narrative', ch.14, pp.1–2; Taylor, *Home Front*, p.570.

122. Thom, 'Looking Backwards', pp.16–18; *Press*, 5 Dec 1941; R.E.J. Brydon to author, 4 Jul 1977. See also the activities of the EPS at isolated Te Whaiti in the Urewera, as described by Rorke, *Policing Two Peoples*, p.114.

123. As revealed by official statistics, at least. There is a gap in the *Judicial Statistics* for charges laid, convictions and sentences for specific offences for the period 1942 to 1945. Police statistics (in the Annual Reports) provide the only consistent wartime series of offences reported and prosecutions. They do not, however, record breaches of the wartime emergency regulations, except for subversion.

124. *Justice Statistics*, 1940 and 1941, p.16.

125. From 1942 to 1945, the three detectives at Hamilton made 310 prosecutions for acquisitive crimes and 108 for gaming offences, compared with 60 for breaches of the emergency regulations. W.R. Murray, typescript record of cases (copy held by author).

126. 'Police Narrative', pp.293–4; Annual Reports, 1942, p.3; 1943, p.3; 1944, p.3; 1945, p.3 (refers to police being 'very successful' in prosecuting people involved in 'black-market dealings'); Taylor, *Home Front*, pp.751–2, 793, 813, 821; Baker, *War Economy*, pp.473–4; *WT*, 11 Jun 1943. For wartime controls, including rationing, see also Bassett, *The State in New Zealand*, ch.8.

127. By 1942 the volume of motor spirits imported had fallen to two-thirds of the 1939 figure, and this level was broadly maintained until 1945, when it rose slightly; Baker,

War Economy, p.625, table 71. For petrol rationing for private cars, see Taylor, *Home Front*, pp.320–4, 743–8.

128. Philipp, *Juvenile Delinquency in New Zealand*, pp.15–17, 22, 29, tables 1 to 23; Taylor, *Home Front*, pp.1045–52.

129. *WT*, 19 Jun, 14 Aug 1942, 10 May 1943, 27 Jan, 16 Nov, 21 Dec 1944; and item dated 14 May 1944 regarding 8 servicemen charged with theft and handed over to the Air Force for disciplinary action, listed in W.R. Murray's record of cases.

130. The clear-up rate is a dubious measure as it depends on how much reported crime is recorded. Assuming police recording practices remained consistent, the declining trend seems significant.

131. Report of Police officers' conference, 1944, pp.8–9, P 7/1/5.

132. Taylor, *Home Front*, p.1045.

133. Magistrate's Court cases reported in the *Press* during the years 1940 to 1944 were analysed for the author by Bryan Daysh.

134. [B. Angus], 'War Narrative, Racing in Wartime', [1949], typescript, p.1, WA-II 21/48c; Baker, *War Economy*, pp.334–40, 474–5; Grant, *On a Roll*, p.124.

135. *WT*, 15, 16 Apr 1943.

136. Annual Reports, 1940–46.

137. See, for example, two Auckland homicides in which Americans were involved, cited by Taylor, *Home Front*, p.648.

138. Kelly, *The Gun in the Case*, p.110. Kelly was called into three fatal shooting cases involving American servicemen.

139. Then known as Koiterangi.

140. Unless otherwise acknowledged, this paragraph draws on the detailed and authoritative account by H.A. Willis, *Manhunt: The Story of Stanley Graham*, Christchurch, 1979. Other accounts can be found in R. Monigatti, *New Zealand Sensations*, Auckland, 1975; Kelly, *The Gun in the Case*, chs 17, 18; Rex Hollis, *Killer on the Coast: The True Story of Stan Graham and New Zealand's Deadliest Manhunt*, Wellington [1965]; A.H. McLintock (ed.), *An Encyclopaedia of New Zealand*, Wellington, 1966, vol.2, pp.397–8; and Carson and Davison, *The Longest Beat*, pp.74–9.

141. *NZH*, 22 Oct 1941.

142. Willis, *Manhunt*, p.181.

143. In his address to the Police Association conference on 29 Oct 1941, Commissioner Cummings commented: 'when I arrived there the responsibility was mine and I accepted it .... our main object was to capture Graham without any further loss of life .... So far as Constable Quirke is concerned he has nothing to worry about so far as the shooting is concerned. I gave specific instructions to everybody that if Graham was found approaching with firearms any of our men connected with the search he was to be shot on sight. We had already lost six men and I was anxious that there be no further loss of life. It was the only instruction I could give.' Typescript of address, P 13/1/-. Cummings had this passage deleted from the published copy of his address in *NZPJ*, vol.5, no.6, Dec 1941, pp.431–2. Fraser's comments, in his address to the conference on the same day, were published: 'no fairer order could have been given than to shoot on sight. There was nothing else to be done. It was an extreme order but 100% justified because no further risk could be taken. A man like Graham who was in a demented condition had to be shot down as one would shoot down a tiger.' *Ibid.*, vol.6, no.1, Feb 1942, p.10.

144. Kelly, *The Gun in the Case*, pp.92, 103.

145. *Truth*, 29 Oct 1941; Willis, *Manhunt*, pp.211–14.

146. Hollis, *Killer on the Coast*, p.44; Willis, *Manhunt*, p.212. Many years later, Quirke refuted any implication that he had been 'driven out' of the Police. He had remained in the Police nearly six and half years after returning to Auckland from Kowhitirangi, guarding a wartime vital point and doing relieving duty at various stations, as well as plain-clothes duty in Auckland. In 1947 he was transferred to Hamilton as a shift watch-house keeper. He did not like this transfer and resigned after fifteen months,

buying a private hotel and marrying 'an Auckland girl.' Copy of statement, 17 Jan 1981, in possession of author. See also Carson and Davison, *The Longest Beat*, p.78.

147. A portion of the ballad cited in Hollis, *Killer on the Coast*, pp.43–4. See also Willis, *Manhunt*, pp.215–17; *NZPJ*, Sep 1966, pp.155–6; Lawrence Jones, 'Stanley Graham and the Several Faces of "Man Alone" ', *Journal of Popular Culture*, vol.19, no.2, 1985, pp.121–36.

148. Baker, *War Economy*, pp.589–90, tables 12 and 13. Taylor, *Home Front*, pp.698–9, provides different figures indicating that mobilisation peaked in Jul 1942, with 154,549 men and women in the services, 52,651 of them overseas. Baker's figures, which relate to males alone, have been preferred in the context of this discussion of order.

149. For Blenheim, see the Second Interim Report of the Commission of Inquiry appointed to inquire into certain matters relating to conduct of members of the Police Force, *AJHR*, 1954, H-16A, pp.20–3.

150. Baker, *War Economy*, p.74; Taylor, *Home Front*, ch.14; H. Bioletti, *The Yanks are Coming: The American Invasion of New Zealand, 1942–1944*, Auckland, 1989, esp. chs 1, 3, 7.

151. Evidence of Sergeant J.L. Adams, in charge of detecting sly-grog offences at Auckland from Dec 1942 and of a Special Duty section established in Nov 1943, Notes of Proceedings, Royal Commission on Licensing, vol.19, p.2806, J 61.

152. 'Police Narrative', pp.291–5.

153. A further constable was stationed at Ohakea during 1942–43 to supervise the Public Works camp while the Air Force base was built. 'Police Narrative', p.296; Thomson and Neilson, *Sharing the Challenge*, p.212; Wright, 'Hutt Valley and the Wairarapa', in Young (ed.), *With Confidence and Pride*, p.228; Spicer, *Policing the River District*, p.205; Carter, *'Beyond the Call of Duty'*, pp.217–18.

154. Donnelly to author, 19 Feb 1977.

155. 'Police Narrative', p.293.

156. Commissioner to officers in charge of districts, 26 Apr 1940: Memorandum regarding 'Supply of Liquor to Soldiers in Uniform: Emergency Regulations, 1940', in author's possession.

157. *NZPJ*, vol.7, no.2, Apr 1943, pp.114–15.

158. 'Police Narrative', pp.275–84, 300–1.

159. See also Taylor, *Home Front*, pp.645–57.

160. C.W. Bowley to author, 7 Mar 1977.

161. *NZH*, 25 Nov 1941.

162. Letters to author from F.A. Gordon, 11 Feb 1977; A.J. Johnston, 28 Jan 1977; C.E.W. Black, 22 Mar 1977. See also informants cited by Bioletti, *The Yanks are Coming*, pp.67, 69, 87, 89, 108, 113–14, 123–4, 130, 140, 151–3.

163. Taylor, *Home Front*, pp.645–58; Bioletti, *The Yanks are Coming*, pp.87, 149–58.

164. An account of the 'Battle', based on recollections and apparently inaccurate, is given in A.H. McLintock (ed.), *An Encyclopaedia of New Zealand*, Wellington, 1966, vol.3, p.3. Taylor's account in *Home Front*, pp.646–7, uses elements of the version given by the *Encyclopaedia*, modified by sketchy contemporary newspaper information. In footnote 111, Taylor notes that a different account, based on an Army file (AD 1, 310/11/4), was given in *EP*, 31 Dec 1983. Bioletti, pp.149–50, cites both the *EP* account and a recollection from an informant whose version accords with that given in the *Encyclopaedia*. The following brief account is based on reports in the Army file.

165. Two arrests resulted from the disturbance on 3 Apr 1943: a civilian was subsequently convicted of being drunk and disorderly and a New Zealand serviceman was handed over to his officers. Reports on file AD 1, 310/11/4; *Press*, 10 Apr 1943.

166. J. Meltzer to Commissioner Cummings, 11 Aug 1943; Cummings to Meltzer, 17 Sep 1943, P 13/1/-. When recruitment was discussed at the Police officers' conference in Mar 1944, Superintendent R. Ward, in charge at Auckland, commented: 'What can

you do with men 18 or 19? They have no ideas. If I sent [sic] them down the street, the Americans go for them and take their batons from them. I do not want any men like that.' Report of Police Officers Conference, 1944, p.56, P 7/1/5. In Jan 1944, the Secretary of the Auckland RSA expressed to the Minister of Defence his committee's concern at 'reports of disturbances and actual cases of hooliganism committed in Auckland and other cities by American servicemen'. A recent dance at Avondale had been attended by a number of American servicemen, who came 'with bouquets of flowers which at a later stage they stripped and disclosed blackjacks, and with which they assaulted some of the young male civilians.' The Auckland RSA wanted the US authorities to 'adopt stronger and greater measures to put a stop to this hooliganism and particularly to prohibit the carrying and use of blackjacks and/or knives.' The Commandant of the Auckland Military District commented that after discussions with Commodore Jupp and military intelligence he doubted the accuracy of the report. AD 1, 310/11/4.

167. On 30 Jun 1939, the Under-Secretary for Justice recommended a Royal Commission of Inquiry. Notes of Proceedings, Royal Commission on Licensing, vol.1, pp.27, 35–45, J 61.

168. 'Police Narrative', pp.257, 260; *EP*, 6 Mar 1940, citing Inspector Scott reporting to the Auckland Licensing Committee on the practice of booking accommodation for large numbers of servicemen, which still continued at three overcrowded Auckland hotels early in 1945; Notes of Proceedings, Royal Commission on Licensing, vol.21, pp.3085–7, evidence of Superintendent Sweeney, J 61. See also Taylor, *Home Front*, p.1014.

169. 'Police Narrative', pp.259, 263. In Mar 1944, when the appointment of a Royal Commission on Licensing seemed imminent, Commissioner Cummings told his officers: 'I do not want any officer saying I think we ought to go back to 10 o'clock at night because from a policeman's point of view I would not vary one minute from 6 o'clock closing. From my point of view it is the best legislation we have got, but what we want is something done to stop the lodger and supposed lodger from supplying people coming in off the street.' Report of Police Officers Conference, 1944, p.104, P 7/1/5.

170. Annual Reports, 1940, p.7; 1941, p.7; 1942, p.3. See also Spicer, *Policing the River District*, p.263.

171. In 1938, Cummings suggested stricter enforcement of the laws regarding the unlawful supply of liquor to Maori for consumption off licensed premises, and the supply of liquor to them on licensed premises when they were intoxicated, especially on Saturdays. Memorandum from Commissioner Cummings to officers in charge of districts, 'Supplying of Liquor to Maoris', 19 Oct 1938. Inspector D.A. MacLean, in charge of the Gisborne District, declared in Mar 1944 that the 'position with Maoris to-day is deplorable. They are drinking to excess all over my district. They have taken advantage of utterances that have been made by the Prime Minister and Ministers of the Crown, and have been told there is equal right for the Maori and Pakeha. There are one or two bodies of religious people who object to liquor in any shape or form, but the rest of the Pakehas on the East Coast right through Whakatane to Bay of Plenty have been guilty of obtaining liquor for Maoris in large quantities.' Inspector J.A. Dempsey believed he had been 'fairly successful' in the Wanganui District, but conceded that in the King Country it was 'a simple matter for the Maori to get a Pakeha to pick up the liquor.' Inspector E.J. Carroll, with '54 years' experience in Maori districts, agreed that 'the law wants altering.' The 'only thing' that Commissioner Cummings could 'suggest is to keep hammering away as best you can.' Report of Police Officers Conference, 1944, p.100, P 7/1/5. The number of prosecutions for breaches of the Licensing Act relating to Maori increased from around 400 in 1939–41 to 679 in 1945. Annual Reports.

172. At the end of Apr 1942 extra duties were placed on wine and spirits, and on beer on the basis of its alcoholic content. The intention was to both encourage the drinking

of lighter beers and lessen overall consumption.

173. The Licensing Act Emergency Regulations 1942 gave authority to any constable to enter at any time any premises where it was suspected liquor was being sold and seize any such liquor, and placed the onus on the defendant to prove that an offence had not been committed where the prosecution could provide sufficient facts to constitute a reasonable suspicion that it had.

174. Except with meals in the dining room between 6 and 8 pm.

175. The Licensing Act Emergency Regulations 1942, no.2, were enacted on 22 Jun. 'Police Narrative', pp.258–64, 267; Taylor, *Home Front,* pp.1015–22.

176. Royal Commission on Licensing, Notes of Proceedings, vol.11, pp.1564–80, evidence of Detective Sergeant G.E. Callaghan (Wellington), vol.19, pp.2806–8, evidence of Sergeant J.L. Adams (Auckland); M.E. Parker to author, 7 Mar 1977; 'Police Narrative', pp.264–5; Taylor, *Home Front,* pp.1023–6.

177. Royal Commission on Licensing, Notes of Proceedings, vol.12, pp.2810–12; vol.19, p.2807, evidence of Sergeant J.L. Adams (Auckland); Commission of Inquiry into Police Conduct, 1954, Notes of Evidence, vol.6, p.1272, evidence of Sub-Inspector G.E. Callaghan (Wellington); 'Police Narrative', pp.265–6.

178. Before the 1943 election, Sidney Holland, leader of the Opposition, declared that a drastic overhaul was needed and promised that National would set up a Royal Commission to investigate the liquor laws. Fraser matched this promise, and a Royal Commission was eventually established in Jan 1945. Taylor, *Home Front,* pp.1026–9.

179. 'Police Narrative', p.266; Notes of Proceedings, Royal Commission on Licensing, vol.19, p.2808; *ODT,* 30 Oct 1943.

180. Sergeant G.E. Callaghan was in charge of the Wellington Special Duty section between Oct 1942 and Aug 1944. In that period, he prosecuted 150 people for sly-grogging and received rewards totalling a substantial £265 5s 4d. Sergeant J.L. Adams had charge of the Auckland Special Duty section (initially comprising four male constables and four women police) established in Nov 1943. Notes of Proceedings, Royal Commission on Licensing, vol.11, pp.1564–6, 1570; vol.19, p.2806; Commission of Inquiry into Police Conduct, 1954, Notes of Evidence, vol.5, pp.1093–7; vol.6, pp.1239, 1257–8, NZ Police College Library; 'Police Narrative', pp.273–4; *Press,* 5 Nov 1942.

181. The Police Offences Emergency Regulations, enacted on 23 Dec 1942, also contained provision for magistrates to order the detention for treatment of a convicted person suspected of having a venereal disease.

182. Notes of Proceedings, Royal Commission on Licensing, vol.19, p.2809; 'Police Narrative', pp.270–4; Taylor, *Home Front,* pp.1014–15, 1032–6, 1049–50. Twice as many women were imprisoned during 1942 (263) as in 1941; the increase was seen as being 'mainly due to the greater incidence of prostitution and the efforts of the authorities to combat venereal disease.' The same explanation was given for 1943, when the number of women imprisoned increased further to 293; *AJHR,* 1943, H-20, p.1; 1944, H-20, p.2. Similarly, the increase (from 92 in 1942 to 124 in 1943) in the number of girls charged under the Child Welfare Act with being 'not under proper control' was seen as being linked to the presence of American servicemen. Philipp, *Juvenile Delinquency in New Zealand,* p.16.

183. 'Night Clubs' was the first item on the agenda of the conference of officers held in Wellington in Mar 1944. Cummings sought opinions on the draft 'Places of Entertainment Emergency Regulations' which he had submitted to Fraser a week earlier. Report of Police Officers Conference, 1944, pp.5–7, P 7/1/5; Notes of Proceedings, Royal Commission on Licensing, vol.19, pp.2808–9; Annual Report, 1944, p.3; 'Police Narrative', pp.267–70; Taylor, *Home Front,* pp.1029–32; Baker, *War Economy,* p.591.

184. 'Police Narrative', pp.1–2.

185. Annual Reports, 1941–46.

186.   *Ibid.*, 1939, p.8, 1940, p.7.
187.   The Commissioner of Police between 1974 and 1978, K.B. Burnside, was appointed a temporary constable at Wellington on 6 Jun 1940; K.B. Burnside interview, 29 Jan 1980.
188.   Comment of Commissioner Cummings in 'Report of Deputation from the Police Association ... to Commissioner of Police', 9 Dec 1942, p.7, P 13/1/-.
189.   In Mar 1944, there were about 240 single men in the Police. Commissioner Cummings was concerned that the Force would be in a 'critical situation' if they were called up into the armed forces. Report of Police Officers Conference, 1944, pp.56, 95–6, P 7/1/5; Annual Reports, 1941, p.6; 1942, p.2; 1943, p.3; 1944, p.2; 1945, p.3; *NZPJ*, vol.7, 1943, no.3, Jun, pp.197–8; no.6, Dec, p.420; *NZPD*, vol.266, 1944, pp.377–8; 'Police Narrative', pp.10–15; Baker, *War Economy*, p.103; Taylor, *Home Front*, pp.699–705; *Dominion*, 21 Aug 1941; *Press*, 22 May 1943. Generalisations on the 1942 intake have been derived from an analysis of data gathered by Helen McLaughlin from 47 personal files, and from an analysis of entries in the PFDB, vol.2, by Constable Isla Jones.
190.   Annual Report, 1940, p.7.
191.   The experience of Ray Petrowski, who joined the Police at Wellington in Jun 1940 and recalled having 'approximately six weeks' intensive training' at the Wellington South Depot, seems to have been exceptional. R.N. Petrowski to author, 30 Nov 1980. The abandonment of formal training for male recruits at the Depot seems to have stemmed from the difficulties of recruiting, the need to get men on duty locally as soon as possible, and the imperative that it be used for the training of policewomen.
192.   Burnside interview, 29 Jan 1980. His induction into the Force was similar to the experiences of others who joined in smaller centres. Letters to author from A.E.K. Keown and A. Wilson (both joined at Greymouth, 1942), W.F. Pearce (Blenheim, 1942), and P.K. Treacy and J.D. Walker (both Dunedin, 1940). Information from these and other policemen provides the basis for general comments on working conditions in this and earlier sections of this chapter.
193.   The permanent appointments were made retrospective to a year after appointment as temporary constable. Annual Reports, 1941, p.6; 1942, p.3; 1943, p.3; 1944, p.2; 'Police Narrative', pp.15–16; Report of Police Officers Conference, 1944, pp.62–3, P 7/1/5; *NZPD*, vol.270, 1945, p.111. See also entries in PFDB, vol.2, for 1936 to 1945, analysed by Constable Isla Jones.
194.   Unless otherwise indicated, this paragraph is based on the following sources: 'Police Narrative', pp.2–10; Annual Reports, 1940, pp.7, 13; 1941, pp.6–7, 9; 1942, p.3; 1943, p.3; 1944, p.2; Reports of Police Association annual conferences, 1939, pp.40–2; 1940, pp.2, 13–14.
195.   The Police Association list of those who had resigned by Apr 1941 contains 31 names. The 'Police Narrative' records that by 12 Apr 1941, 34 members of the Force had resigned under sec.15 of the Police Force Act to join the armed forces. See 'Police Narrative', p.5; *NZPJ*, vol.5, 1941, no.3, Jun, p.172, no.4, Aug, p.265; Wills, *The New Zealand Police Medal*.
196.   *Press*, 7 Nov 1941; *NZPJ*, vol.5, no. 6, Dec 1941, p.409.
197.   *NZH*, 14, 18, 21 Aug, 18 Sep 1941.
198.   Ranging from a suspended sentence to a £10 fine. See *NZH*, 6 Feb, 5, 23 May 1942; *Press*, 21 Mar 1942. A Christchurch constable who had become disillusioned with the Police, bought a business and tendered his resignation was also fined £10. *Press*, 30 Jan 1942; *EP*, 21 Mar 1942. Delegates to the Police Association conference in Oct 1942 supported the reinstatement of those who had resigned to go war and had been convicted. Report of Police Association conference, 1942, pp.21–3.
199.   *NZPJ*, vol.6, no.4, Aug 1942, pp.275–6; vol.7, no.3, Jun 1943, pp.197–8.
200.   He was convicted and fined £10, and forfeited £55 in outstanding wages. *NZH*, 22 Dec 1945.
201.   This term, rather than 'policewomen', reflects contemporary parlance and also captures

their distinctive status and role in the 1940s.

202. By Sep 1939, for example, the Christchurch branch of the National Council of Women regarded the appointment of women police as 'urgent'; *Press*, 13 Sep 1939. In Jan 1940, the conference of the New Zealand League of Nations Union passed a remit urging the government to take immediate steps to appoint women police. *Press*, 1 Feb 1940.

203. Johnston, *The Long Blue Line*, pp.216–17, 289; B. Swanton, 'Women Police in NSW: The Formative Years', *Australian Police Journal*, Oct–Dec 1983, pp.142–3; Haldane, *The People's Force*, pp.163, 191, 226; P. Higgs and C. Bettess, *To Walk a Fair Beat: A History of the South Australian Women Police 1915–1987*, Adelaide, 1987, p.206. See also Finnane, *Police and Government*, pp.106–7; and T. Prenzler, 'Women in Australian Policing: An Historical Overview', *Journal of Australian Studies*, no.42, Sep 1994, pp.78–88.

204. *NZH*, 3 Nov 1939; Thorn, *Peter Fraser*, p.167.

205. Report of the fifth annual conference of the Police Association, 1940, p.1, Cummings' address.

206. *NZPD*, vol.257, 1940, pp.875–6, 904; *Press*, 1, 24 Aug, 23 Sep 1940.

207. In Mar 1941, Mrs C. Stewart (Labour) asked Fraser an urgent parliamentary question about the appointment of women police; *NZPD*, vol.259, 1941, p.231; 'Police Narrative', p.20; *NZH*, 1 May 1941; *Press*, 4 Jun 1941; *Truth*, 8 Oct 1941.

208. PFDB, vol.2, pp.311–14.

209. This was the view of Nora Crawford (who was in the third intake), interview, 11 Jan 1977. Perhaps the most notable example was Mae Kelly (in the second intake), whose father, W.T. Kelly, and brother, G.E.S. Kelly, were already in the Police.

210. *ODT*, 6 Oct 1941. The official view of the first intake of policewomen as an 'experiment, and at the time it was not known whether it would be successful or not', was reiterated by the acting Minister of Police, P. Webb, in Jun 1942; *NZPD*, vol.261, p.412. Details of training from Edna Pearce, a member of the first intake ('W8'), and from members of the second intake, Molly (Agnes Mary) Sim ('W13') and Mae Kelly ('W23'), supplied to the author. See also *Truth*, 8 Oct 1941; *NZFL*, 14 Apr 1948; Corallyn Newman (ed.), *Canterbury Women Since 1893*, Christchurch, 1979, pp.100–1.

211. Lilian Brocket, Margaret Holder and Edna Pearce to Auckland; Clara Berridge, Eileen O'Connor and Caroline Smith to Wellington; Nancy Aitchison and Mollie Speakman to Christchurch; Elizabeth (May) Callaghan and Vera McConchie to Dunedin. PFDB, vol.2, pp.311–12.

212. The wartime intakes apparently received no formal instructions on the clothing to be worn, except that it should be 'neat and tidy' and that hats and gloves were to be worn, especially in court. Nora Crawford interview, 11 Jan 1977; *NZH*, 4 Jun 1977.

213. 'Police Narrative', p.20.

214. Edna Pearce letter, Oct 1976; Mae Kelly letter, Mar 1977; Molly Sim letter, Feb 1977. All three remained unmarried and in the Police until their retirement at the age of 60.

215. One was a shoplifter, the other a 'girl who went around schools stealing raincoats'. Edna Pearce to author, Mar 1979; *Dominion Sunday Times*, 28 Jan 1990; *NZH*, 29 Nov, 1 Dec 1941, refuting a claim that Constable May Callaghan, at Dunedin, had made the first arrest, of a youth subsequently dealt with in the Children's Court.

216. *EP*, 2 Oct 1941; Molly Sim to author, Feb 1977. For the reception of the first policewomen in Auckland, see also Cherrett, *Without Fear or Favour*, p.140.

217. *NZPD*, vol.261, 1942, pp.411–13.

218. 'Police Narrative', pp.21–2; *NZH*, 22 Aug 1942; *NZPD*, vol.261, 1942, pp.412–13; vol.263, 1943, p.324.

219. Royal Commission on Licensing, Notes on Proceedings, vol.19, p.2806; cf. 'Police Narrative', pp.21–2; *Dominion*, 7 Oct 1942; *NZH*, 19 Feb, 24 Jul 1943, 4 Mar 1944; *ODT*, 6 Mar, 30 Jul 1943; *NZPD*, vol.263, 1943, p.323; *NZPJ*, vol.7, no.4, Aug 1943,

p.252; Annual Report, 1944, p.3. The month given by Sergeant J.L. Adams, the officer in charge, for the actual formation of the Special Duty section in Auckland (Nov) has been preferred to that given in the 'Police Narrative' (Sep), which is probably when the decision was made. The Maori recruit, Evelyn Tauroa Owen, was posted to Auckland in May 1944 and resigned there in Jan 1945; PFDB, vol.2, p.315.

220.   Letters from Mae Kelly, Molly Sim and Edna Pearce to author; Nora Crawford interview; Cherrett, *Without Fear or Favour*, p.140; *Gisborne Herald*, 30 Jan 1942; *NZH*, 4 Jun 1977; Taylor, *Home Front*, pp.674, 684–92, 1033–7, 1043–4.

221.   Inspector J. Carroll, speaking of his experience at Christchurch. Commissioner Cummings warned his officers in Mar 1944 that policewomen should be used 'very sparingly' for office duty 'because they were got for [the] special purpose of war, and if women's organisations get to know you are using them for offices there will be trouble.' He admitted, however, that he had a policewoman working in his office; she 'is doing wonderfully good work and is [a] great improvement on the man that was there, polite, quick, and can take messages in shorthand.' Report of Police Officers Conference, 1944, pp.92–3, P 7/1/5.

222.   This was apparent in the discussion amongst senior officers in Mar 1944, to which Commissioner Cummings responded: 'Where these women police are stationed it is the duty of officers and everybody with whom they are working to be sympathetic towards them and help them in every direction we can .... They are there to stay, and we must make the best of it.' Cummings envisaged that, after the war, half of the seventeen policewomen at Auckland, and some of those in Wellington, would be distributed to the smaller districts. They would probably continue to work in plain clothes, though the issue of uniforms had 'not been finally decided'. Report of Police Officers Conference, 1944, pp.58–60, P 7/1/5.

223.   A constable had to serve five years before sitting the Sergeant's promotion examination. Edna Pearce was not eligible to sit the examination until Jun 1946, when she would be 40.

224.   In Nov 1942, Commissioner Cummings told a journalist that when policewomen married they would have to resign. (He believed that they would 'have to be home, cooking their husband's dinner'.) In fact there was no legal requirement to do so, and neither D.J. Cummings nor James Cummings after him enforced resignation. *NZ Listener*, 6 Nov 1942; *Press*, 4 Jul 1991; PFDB, vol.2, pp.311–14.

225.   Cummings had refused Meltzer permission to address women recruits at the Depot, reversing a practice that had begun before the war with male recruits. His opposition to policewomen joining the Police Association was eventually overturned after Meltzer wrote to Fraser on the issue in Apr 1943. Cummings to Meltzer, 30 Jun 1941, P 13/1/-; Reports of Police Association conferences, 1942, pp.12–13; 1943, pp.29–30; McGill, *No Right to Strike*, pp.74, 241–6.

226.   Unlike that of the temporary male constables appointed during the war, the permanent appointment of policewomen in May 1947 was not made retrospective to a year after their appointment as temporary constables. Their seniority was thus affected. The 23 policewomen who were permanently appointed on 17 May 1947 were: N.H. Aitchison, C.M. Berridge, H.M. Day, R.M. Dudfield, V.P. Hayes, M. Hunter, M.B. Kelly, M.E. Malcon, K.H. McAlley, F. McDonald, J.C. McMath, R.M. McRae, R. Morrissey, E.M. O'Connor, K. Palmer, N.M. Parker, E.B. Pearce, A.M. Sim, C.M. Smith, J. Sneddon, H.M. Speakman, B.E. Sullivan, H.R. Weavers. PFDB, vol.2, pp.311–15.

227.   The concept of relative deprivation is 'based on the proposition that people's attitudes, aspirations, and grievances depend largely on the frame of reference in which they are conceived'. A difficulty with the concept is determining when deprivation becomes actual as well as relative 'hardship'. A. Bullock, O. Stallybrass and S. Trombley (eds), *The Fontana Dictionary of Modern Thought*, revised edn, London, 1988, p.736.

228.   Annual Report, 1942, p.3. For male factory workers, the annual average overtime worked per head reached 199 hours during 1943/44, over four times the immediate

pre-war level. Baker, *War Economy,* pp.156–7.

229. From Nov 1942, the American authorities paid men working on US Army and Navy vessels an extra shilling an hour above the award rates. Taylor, *Home Front,* pp.637–8; see also Baker, *War Economy,* pp.399–400, 448, 455–7, 477.

230. The police overtime allowance was calculated at 3/48ths of salary and backdated to 1 Oct 1942, when overtime payments had been introduced for other public servants at the rate of time and a half for over 44 hours, with double time on Sundays and public holidays. From 1 Dec 1943, all public servants other than police received payments at time and a half after 40 hours. After the introduction of the 'overtime allowance' for police, time in lieu was given more sparingly. In Mar 1944, a conference of senior police officers agreed with the Commissioner that as a 40-hour week was 'impractical', 'a full day's pay be granted to make up for the extra duty worked over the forty-hour week.' In the event, the Stabilisation Commission rejected the Commissioner's case. 'Police Narrative', pp.18–20; Reports of Police Association annual conferences, 1940, p.1; 1941, pp.32–3; 1942, pp.17–19; *NZPJ*, vol.6, no.2, Apr 1942, p.87; vol.7, 1943, no.1, Feb, p.5; no.3, Jun, pp.194–5; no.6, Dec, p.419; *NZPD*, vol.262, 1943, p.325; Henderson, *The Quest for Efficiency*, pp.167–8; Report of Police Officers Conference, 1944, pp.105–7, P 7/1/5. In Oct 1943, Cabinet agreed to offer wartime National Savings Bonds to public servants as compensation for any annual leave accumulated before 31 Dec 1941 that was still untaken. Police could elect to take these 'War Bonds' in exchange for arrears of leave. In the Police estimates for 1944/45, £4,715 was provided for payment in the form of War Bonds. *NZPG*, 1943, p.804; *NZPD*, vol.266, 1944, p.373.

231. Reports of Police Association conferences, 1940, pp.17–18, 1941, pp.30–1; Notes of a Police Association deputation to the acting Minister in charge of the Police, 17 Jun 1941, P 13/1/-; Baker, *War Economy,* pp.299, 616; Henderson, *The Quest for Efficiency*, pp.165–6; Roth, *Remedy for Present Evils*, pp.101, 103. Details of increases in constables' and NCOs' pay from *NZPJ*, vol.7, no.6, Dec 1943, p.411.

232. Constable F.X. Quin, delegate from Auckland, Report of Police Association conference, 1941, pp.31–2. Using the pseudonym 'Zave', Quin was an Auckland correspondent for the *NZPJ* during the early years of the war. He wrote two detailed articles on police pay: *NZPJ*, vol.5, no.1, Feb 1941, pp.31–2; vol.6, no.2, Apr 1942, pp.109–10. An article by 'Eureka' on 'A Policeman's Pay' also argued strongly from specific comparisons that police were 'very poorly paid' for the 'responsibility we have to carry and the hours we have to work.' *Ibid.*, vol.6, no.4, Aug 1942, pp.259–60. This article is reprinted in McGill, *No Right to Strike*, p.64.

233. *NZPJ*, vol.6, 1942, no.1, Feb, p.13; no.3, Jun, p.165; Minister in charge of the Police to J. Meltzer, n.d. [c.Jun 1942], P 13/1/-.

234. J. Meltzer to Commissioner Cummings, 7 Dec 1942; Report of Police Association conference, 1942, pp.18–19. On 23 Oct 1942, the Police Association had sent Fraser remits concerning payment for overtime, the payment of a War Bonus of at least 2s per day, a general increase in wages to meet the increase in the cost of living and compensate police for overtime worked, and a special payment for police on gangway duty; *NZPJ*, vol.6. no.6, Dec 1942, pp.428–9.

235. 'Representations on behalf of New Zealand Police Association for an Increase in Pay to Members', 18 Jan 1943 (copy in EA 1, 84/13/3); *NZH*, 9 Dec 1942, 12 Feb 1943; *ODT*, 2, 6 Jan 1943; 'Police Narrative', p.18; McGill, *No Right to Strike*, p.65.

236. In Mar 1943, a month after the police overtime allowance was sanctioned by the Stabilisation Commission, Fraser contended that the Police Force was 'well paid'. In Sep 1944 he maintained that police were 'adequately paid'. *NZPD*, vol.262, 1943, p.325; vol.266, 1944, p.373; Report of Police Officers Conference, 1944, pp.1–2, 105, P 7/1/5. Roth, *Remedy for Present Evils*, p.103; Baker, *War Economy,* pp.314–23.

237. Increases were sought in existing allowances for transfer and relieving duty, travelling, uniform and boots, wearing plain clothes, providing prisoners' meals, and housing;

new allowances were sought for visiting vital points, gangway duty, night duty, and performing the tasks of a higher-ranked officer.

238. The provision for allowances to police using their own cars on duty increased from £10,624 in 1939/40 for allowances for 242 police which varied from £17 to £58 10s per annum, to £14,112 in 1942/43 for allowances ranging from £18 to £78 for 269 police. In the same period the mileage payments to police using their own vehicles increased from £2,638 to £3,178. *AJHR*, B-7, 1940, p.107; 1942, p.101; 1943, p.93. The availability and cost of car tyres remained contentious.

239. In 1943, the right of temporary constables to a pay increment after three years was conceded, as was their right to join the Public Service Superannuation Fund. But anomalies still remained to be resolved. Reports of Police Association conferences, 1942, pp.26–7; 1943, pp.30–2.

240. Reports of Police Association conferences, 1942, pp.8–9; 1943, pp.12–13. In the 1942/43 year, £45,837 was spent on housing allowances for those 'unprovided with quarters' (an over-expenditure of £2,000), while 'free quarters' to the value of £22,323 were provided to 504 men. In 1943/44, £46,000 was provided for housing allowances, by contrast with £29,100 for the cost-of-living bonus and £34,000 for the overtime allowance, from a total vote of £795,164 in which the basic salaries of 1,400 male constables totalled £445,656. *AJHR*, B-7, 1942, p.101; 1943, pp.92–3.

241. Report of Police Officers Conference, 1944, p.106, P 7/1/5.

242. In 1941/42, for example, the expenditure on police transfer and removal costs was more than double the £5,000 voted, 'due to housing difficulties in connection with the appointment and transfer of married members.' *AJHR*, 1942, B-7, p.101.

243. Reports of Police Association conferences, 1940, p.2; 1941, pp.29–30; 1942, p.31; *NZPJ*, vol.5, no.4, Aug 1941, p.253; vol.6, no.5, Oct 1942, p.330; vol.6, no.6, Dec 1942, pp.410–11; vol.7, no.2, Apr 1943, p.88. Baker, *War Economy,* pp.242–3; Taylor, *Home Front,* pp.798–812.

244. This paragraph is based on 'Police Narrative', pp.25–30; J. Clements to author, 16 Jun 1977; Taylor, *Home Front,* pp.638–9; Cummings to Meltzer, 30 Apr 1942, P 13/ 1/-; *NZH*, 13, 16, 18, 26 Nov 1943; *EP*, 11, 16, 17 Nov 1943; *NZPJ*, vol.5, no.6, Dec 1941, p.418; vol.6, no.1, Feb 1942, p.30.

245. Less than two weeks after being sworn in, a temporary constable in Auckland pleaded guilty to being absent from barracks while working at the American Army Transport Service depot at Sylvia Park. Superintendent Ward commented that 'he followed the bad example of senior men.' Ward to Commissioner Cummings, 21 Oct 1943, P 13/ 1/-. In 1944, the Commissioner permitted police to take casual work in essential industries, such as harvesting, provided that this was approved by the officer in charge of the district, the hours were not excessive, staff remained fit for work, they did not join a trade union, and enough men remained available to deal with an emergency. Casual work by public servants on the waterfront, in wool and cool stores and in 'primary production' had been permitted by the Public Service Commissioner by 1943. 'Police Narrative', p.30; *NZPJ*, vol.7, no.4, Aug 1943, p.270.

246. Commissioner Cummings provided examples of what was unacceptable in justifying the Regulations to his officers: serving in a 'Greek restaurant', a 'waterside workers' restaurant', a tobacconist, as housemaid in the Waterloo Hotel. 'We want to look a bit higher than that …. We cannot have that.' Report of Police Officers Conference, 1944, p.90, P 7/1/5.

247. The words of Constable E.J.C. Hay, Christchurch delegate to the Police Association conference in 1942, who 'strongly objected' to a remit that Regulation 489 (prohibiting wives of policemen from engaging 'in business') be abolished. The Hamilton delegate who presented the remit 'saw no reason why a wife should not engage in business if she wishes to do so, without obtaining the permission of her husband's employer. He knew of no such restriction in any other walk of life.' Three other delegates besides Hay opposed the remit, which was lost by four votes to eleven. Report of the Police Association conference, 1942, p.20. For Cummings' view, see *NZ Listener*, 6 Nov 1942.

248. This paragraph is based on Address by Fraser to the Police Association conference on 4 Sep 1940, typescript, and notes of Police Association deputations to Minister in charge of Police, 5 Sep 1940, 13 Oct 1943, 19 Feb 1944, P 13/1/-; *NZPJ*, vol.5, no.3, Jun 1941, p.187; vol.7, no.6, Dec 1943, p.410; Reports of Police Association conferences, 1940, pp.19–21; 1941, pp.39–43; 1942, pp.24, 30; 1943, pp.5–7; Roth, *Remedy for Present Evils*, p.112; McGill, *No Right to Strike*, p.74.

249. Budget speech, 1941. Meltzer used this to argue that the war should not be 'used as an excuse to delay reforms that are overdue', such as earlier retirement and the repeal of sec.9 of the Police Force Act. *NZPJ*, vol.5, no.4, Aug 1941, p.247.

250. Cummings did not retire until 31 Oct 1944, fifteen months after he was due to; Lopdell was retained for twenty months beyond Apr 1943, and Carroll for six months after Apr 1944. By contrast, Inspector Henry Martin, Carroll's predecessor in charge at Invercargill, was allowed to retire in Aug 1943, aged 64 years, though there was 'not a fitter man of his age in the Service', according to the local Police Association delegate. Report of Police Association conference, 1943, p.6. Two Inspectors in charge of districts were promoted to Superintendent and retained in their positions (Inspector Donald Cameron at Napier, promoted in Apr 1943, became officer in charge at Wellington in 1946; Inspector G.B. Edwards at Hamilton, promoted in Apr 1944, became officer in charge at Wellington in Nov). At Auckland, Inspector James Sweeney had to wait until a vacancy occurred with the retirement of Superintendent R.R.J. Ward before he was promoted to take charge of the district in Sep 1944. Report of Police Officers Conference, 1944, pp.21–2, 55–7, P 7/1/5.

251. Unless otherwise acknowledged, this and the following paragraphs are based on correspondence between the General Secretary of the Police Association and the Commissioner and the Minister in P 13/1/-; and on addresses and correspondence by Cummings, Fraser and Webb, reprinted in either the Reports of the Police Association conferences (printed for circulation only to Association members) or the *NZPJ*.

252. For example, both Janet and Peter Fraser attended the Wellington Police Ball in Sep 1941, soon after arriving back from an extended period abroad, and also the funeral of Catherine Cummings, wife of Commissioner D.J. Cummings, in Apr 1943. *NZPJ*, vol.5, no.5, Oct 1941, p.381; vol.7, no.2, Apr 1943, p.138.

253. Fraser's formal reply to the remits of the 1939 conference, submitted in Jun 1940 and discussed with a deputation in Sep, was received in May 1941; remits of the 1940 conference submitted in Feb 1941 were discussed by Meltzer with Fraser in Mar and raised again by a deputation to Webb in Jun, but there was no formal reply. The Association was also slow in submitting its remits, notably in the case of the 1941 conference, the remits from which were not sent to the Commissioner and the Minister until May 1942. The frustration at delays was expressed in branch remits to the Police Association conference in 1942. Report of the Police Association conference, 1942, pp.23–4.

254. In the context of a discussion with his senior officers over whether temporary constables could be appointed acting detectives, Cummings commented: 'It does not matter what the Regulations say, these are extraordinary times, and we have got to [make] do with the best at our disposal, and I would not worry about the Regulations. There are many things I have done which the Regulations forbid, but still it is in the interests of the men in the Service. Why worry about Regulations in extraordinary times?' Report of Police Officers Conference, 1944, p.64; see also pp.5, 95, for comments indicating his caution, P 7/1/5.

255. While Fraser was 'quite prepared to look at the principle', he did not think sec.9 should be repealed in wartime. Notes of deputation from Police Association to Minister, 5 Sep 1940, P 13/1/-. Though Cummings never conceded to the Association that he had used sec.9, he did so twice in 1943, to avoid having constables charged with serious crimes appearing in the dock as constables: he secured their confessions (to attempted murder and burglary), then dismissed them. In Mar 1944, he gained the support of his senior officers for the retention of sec.9. Report of Police Officers Conference, 1944, pp.101–2, P 7/1/5.

256.   Report of Police Association conference, 1941, pp.47–8.
257.   According to Jack Meltzer, the right of those who resigned to join the armed forces
       before Jun 1942 to be reinstated, with their seniority preserved and their superannuation
       payments maintained from the War Expenses account, was granted in 1943. *NZPJ*,
       vol.5, no.5, Oct 1941, p.335; vol.7, no.3, Jun 1943, pp.197–8; Report of Police
       Association conference, 1942, pp.21–2. However, Cummings interpreted the concession
       more restrictively, telling his senior officers in Mar 1944 that 'Any man who walked
       out ['left without permission'] will not be taken back'; nor would any who could not
       pass a medical examination required by the Police Department or whose conduct in
       the armed services was not 'satisfactory'. Thus any who left after Apr 1941 would
       not be reinstated, nor would any who were disabled by war injuries. Report of Police
       Officers Conference, 1944, pp.95–6, P 7/1/5.
258.   Discipline was a recurring theme at the conference of commissioned officers called
       by Cummings in Mar 1944. The Commissioner believed that some NCOs did 'not
       enforce discipline for fear of becoming unpopular with the men', and was angered
       by some comments by NCOs at the Association's conference. On the other hand, he
       recognised that an NCO could have 'a restraining influence on some of those young
       hot heads of Constables.' Superintendent Lopdell agreed that there 'has been a slump
       in the authority of Sergeants over their men. There has been too much fraternising.'
       Cummings emphasised that 'there ought to be an Association ... it does a lot of good
       and gives them an opportunity of discussing things and giving us a hint .... [but] in
       the interests of discipline there should be a policeman secretary'. The resolution
       recommending a separate Association branch for NCOs and that a police constable
       should be Association Secretary was agreed to by 20 of the 21 commissioned officers
       present (the dissentient was Inspector J. Carroll). Report of Police Officers Conference,
       1944, pp.12–19, 79–85, P 7/1/5.
259.   This comment is based on correspondence in P 13/1/-. See also McGill, *No Right to
       Strike*, ch.8.
260.   Notes of a deputation from the Police Association to the acting Minister in charge
       of the Police, P.C. Webb, 17 Jun 1941; Cummings to Meltzer, 30 Jun 1941;
       Superintendent Lopdell to Cummings, 19 Aug 1941, P 13/1/-.
261.   Meltzer had scheduled the conference to open on 6 Sep; it commenced on 29 Oct.
       Meltzer to Webb, 30 Jul 1941; Cummings to Meltzer, 14 Aug 1941, 18 May 1942;
       Report of deputation from Police Association to Commissioner of Police, 1 Sep
       1941. Cummings commented later, reflecting on Meltzer's influence and abilities as
       an advocate: 'When they present Remits I insist on the President doing it. I will not
       allow the Secretary, who is stubborn, to submit anything to me .... When he gets up
       with the Minister he has a free go, which is a pity. If the President had to put there
       the same as he does here with me, it would have a big effect.' Report of Police
       Officers Conference, 1944, p.17, P 7/1/5.
262.   *NZPJ*, vol.6, no.1, Feb 1942, pp.11–12.
263.   'Report to Management Committee at Special Meeting Held at 7 pm on Wednesday
       23rd Dec 1942 By General Secretary', P 13/1/-. This cyclostyled report contains
       Meltzer's summary of his conversation with Fraser, who had telephoned him at 5.15
       pm the previous day. The report is to be found in the part of P 13/1/- dealing with
       the strains between the police administration and the Association in Sep/Oct 1953.
264.   *NZPD*, vol.262, 1943, p.324. See also telegrams and correspondence in EA 1, 84/13/
       3; 'Censorship Narrative', ch.10; Taylor, *Home Front*, pp.953–4.
265.   'Note for file: Police Association', Secretary, Police Department, 7 Dec 1954. This
       note refers to a statement by the Commissioner on 9 Dec 1943 relating to 'notes of
       a Conference called by the Minister in Charge of Police' on 19 Nov 1943 to discuss
       Meltzer's article and to 'general correspondence relating to Fraser giving consideration
       to the cancellation of the Police Association organisation.' P 13/1/-.
266.   *EP*, 17 Nov 1943; Director of Publicity to Commissioner of Police, 18 Nov 1943, EA
       1, 84/13/3.

267.   The first item on the agenda of the deputation of officers to Peter Fraser was 'Secretary of the New Zealand Police Association'; Report of deputation of commissioned officers, led by Commissioner Cummings, to the Prime Minister, 18 Mar 1944; Report of Police Officers Conference, 1944, p.84, P 7/1/5. In Sep 1944, Fraser repeated that 'if the formation of the Police Association, the recognition of which he had initiated and which he had assisted very substantially, would in any way militate against the discipline or efficiency of the Police Force, there would be a case for abolishing the association.' *NZPD*, vol.266, 1944, pp.370–1. For an account of the growing strain in the relationship between Meltzer and Cummings in 1943 and 1944, see McGill, *No Right to Strike*, ch.9.

268.   Correspondence between Meltzer and J.T. Paul, and between Paul and Commissioner D.J. Cummings and (from 1 Nov 1944) Commissioner J. Cummings, copies in EA 1, 84/13/3.

269.   Fraser said that it was 'far better to meet with the Commissioner as at present and discuss problems'. Notes of deputation by the Police Association to the Prime Minister, 27 Feb 1945, P 13/1/-.

Conclusion: A Policeman's Paradise?

1.   *EP*, 27 Sep 1928. The 'critic' was responding to earlier articles of 25 and 26 Sep 1928. The 'case-in-reply' (for a 'policeman's paradise') had been 'compiled' from 'particulars gathered in those Departmental circles opposed' to reducing the full-pension (superannuation) period from 40 to 35 years. Those in the Force most likely to be opposed to reducing the retiring age were the senior officers, as was the case in the late 1930s when the issue was again pressed. Unless otherwise acknowledged, the quotations in the following paragraphs come from this article.

2.   James Siddells, reported in *Wanganui Chronicle*, 5 Mar 1935.

3.   'Address to the New Zealand Police Force', p.v.

4.   *Wanganui Chronicle*, 5 Mar 1935. James Siddells addressed the Wanganui Rotary Club on 'New Zealand's Police'. He was Wanganui's Detective Sergeant when he retired in 1917 after 40 years' service.

5.   Calculated from tables showing length of service of members of the New Zealand Police and the New South Wales Police at 31 Dec 1928 in Senior Sergeant H. Scott and others to Commissioner, 26 May 1929, P 2/1/2.

6.   These changes are detailed in Dunstall, 'Police in New Zealand', Das (ed.), *Police Practices;* and will be the subject of the forthcoming fifth volume of the *History of Policing in New Zealand*.

Bibliography

A. UNPUBLISHED SOURCES

1. Archives and manuscripts

Auckland City Council: Town Clerk's Office
123/1926   Taking over traffic control from Police Department

National Archives
Army Department (AD)
Series 11
2/1   Aid to the civil power
16/11   Formation and functions of Intelligence Branch
16/14   Combined Intelligence Committee minutes

External Affairs (EA)
Series 1
84/10/1   Subversion – general
84/13/3   Censorship of New Zealand Police Journal

Internal Affairs (IA)
Series 1
115/83   I. Tomasevic
118/-   Royal Commission on Gaming and Racing (1946–49)
181/25/24 War Narrative: The Americans in New Zealand

Justice (J)
Series 1
1934/32/153 Kurow Magistrate's Court
1936/31/28 Convictions of Maori in Northland
1936/35/266 Protest re sentence of Thomas Curran

Series 61
Royal Commission on Licensing, 1945–46

Maori Affairs (MA)
Series 1, Accn W1369
26/3/2   Maori Councils: appointment of members
26/3/27   Maori Councils: appointment of native police constables

Navy Department (N)
Series 1
8/15/7   Intelligence: civil disturbances

Series 2
8/1/25   Intelligence, Intelligence Centres, Security Intelligence
              Organisation

Police (P)
Series 1
1919/1885   Death of Constable Dudding
1920/444   Dennis Gunn – murder
1920/1282   Murder of S. Eyre
1921/301   Murchison bank robbery
1921/1087   Murder of F.E. Jew
1921/1274   Murder of Constable James Dorgan
1922/477   Bishop Liston – sedition
1923/707   Constable H.T. Smith – theft
1923/1413   Murder of M.E. Oates
1925/189   G.W. Towns re murder of Constable Dorgan
1927/873   G.W. Boakes – murder of Miss E.G.I. Scarff
1928/498   Dr J. Hennesey – abortion
1928/1724   Elsie Walker case, including 'Report of and the Record of
              Proceedings and Depositions of Witnesses to the
              Commission of Enquiry into the conduct of members of the
              Police Force in relation to the disappearance and death of
              Elsie Walker', typescript, 1929
1929/1219   Himatangi fire tragedy
1929/1719   C.R. Gray and J.W. Gray – incendiaries
1931/301   Hawke's Bay earthquake
1932/521; 1932/616; 1932/628; 1932/654 re 1932 disturbances
1936/1   Report of detectives re visit to UK for training
1941/119   Bicycle stealing in Christchurch
1942/652   M.S. Urlich shot by Constable H.H. Barrett
1944/901   Royal Commission on Licensing, 1944–46
1944/1294   Commissioner D.J. Cummings
1947/1594   Restoration of death penalty for murder
1950/1802   Commissioner J. Cummings

1/1/26   Wrestling
1/1/57   Police Appeal Board (Disciplinary)

1/1/74	Boxing
1/1/149	Interviewing school children
2/1/2	Police Force Act
2/1/3	Emergency Regulations
2/1/9	Public Safety Conservation Act
2/4/-	Arms Act
4/1/9	Intoxicated motorists
7/1/5	Police Officers Conferences 1940 and 1944
8/8/1	Motor vehicles – sirens
13/1/-	Police Association
17/4/-	Police examinations policy
22/21/-	Women police
25/4/-	Recruitment of Maori
26/1/-	Police dogs

Series 38
personal files, 1909–28

Series 40: Indictable Offences

40/1	Detective W. Roycroft, 'The How, Why and Wherefore of an Indictable Case', 1928
40/2	Detective W. Roycroft, Collected papers re indictable offences, 1920–42

P-Wellington 31/1   City Sectional Reports – Taranaki Street, 1930

State Services Commission (SSC)

60/1/1	Economy in the Public Service 1918–20
60/3/32	Public Service Adjustment Act, 1922
60/10/28	National Expenditure Adjustment Act, 1932
60/10/39	Report of the Economy Committee, 1931
60/10/40	Report on National Expenditure Commission, 1932
60/10/49	Report of Economy Committee, 1921
66/10/49	Report and resolutions of the Economies Committee, 1921
66/10/216	Improvements in the Public Service, 1939

War Archives (WA-II)
Series 21: War History – Civilian Narratives

3d	Censorship of the Press
7c	Defaulters and Conscientious Objectors
43d	Police Department
48c	Racing in Wartime
63c	New Zealand Communist Party and the War
63d	Aliens Administration
96	Emergency Precautions Scheme

New Zealand Police
Dwyer, John, 'Fragments from the Official Career of John Dwyer, Superintendent of Police 1878–1921, typescript, 1 Nov 1934
Hickson, W.H., N.P. Saunders-Francis and I.N. Bird, 'New Zealand Police: Functional Review', 26 Aug 1982
Jackson, F., et al., 'CIB Activity Survey', Wellington, Apr 1985
Kerr, D.B., 'Powers of Executive to Direct Police', 16 Nov 1977
'Minutes of Evidence of the Committee of Inquiry', typescript, 1919
McIlveney, W.B., 'Scrapbook'
Monk, L.D., 'Notebook for Training School, Police Depot: Mt Cook Station', 3 Apr 1925
Notes of Evidence, Commission of Inquiry into Police Conduct, 1953–54
Personal files of W.B. McIlveney, W.G. Wohlmann
Police Force Description Book, vol.1 (1877–1920), vol.2 (1920–48)
Report of Committee of Inquiry into the claim of Peter Geraghty for promotion to the grade of Senior Sergeant, 3 and 4 Feb 1941

Police Station Books
Circulars and Memoranda Books: Darfield, Murchison
Diaries of Duty and Occurrences: Port Awanui, Mt Eden South, Roxburgh, Te Whaiti, Warkworth, Wellsford
District Order Books: Culverden, Remuera, Wellington
Summons Books: Ellerslie, Point Chevalier, Roxburgh
Watchhouse Charge Books: Darfield, Mt Eden South, Remuera, Te Araroa, Warkworth

Security Intelligence Service
Old Police Records (OPR), 1919–39
Register of 'Secret Correspondence', vol.1, 1920–32
parts of files: 1/1/1, 1/12/1, 21/2/1, 21/2/33, 21/2/40, 21/5/5, 21/7/5, 25/2/5, 26/8/43, 26/8/90, 26/8/92, 26/17/9, 40/18/1, 40/18/7, 40/18/10, 40/43/1, 40/62/1, 40/64/1, 40/64/2, 40/64/4, 40/74/1, 40/75/3, 40/75/27
packets: nos 44, 50, 51, and (not numbered) 'Communist Party: Documents in support of Legislation to declare Communism Illegal' (1931–32)

2. Personal papers (copies given or lent to author)
Almond, W.H., Scrapbook
Austing, G.S., 'From Farm Hand to Assistant Commissioner', typescript [1976]
Barling, E., Scrapbook
Beard, D.C.B., Scrapbook
Bevege, B., Notebook [1937]
Brady, F.J., Scrapbooks
Carter, Ray (comp.), 'Palmerston North Police District Register of Personnel', mimeograph, 1987

Craigie, W.S., Scrapbook
Davis, A.C., Scrapbook
Farquharson, B., Scrapbook
Hammond, W.S., Scrapbook
Harding, A.M., Letters
Lander, J., Scrapbook
Lewin, F., Scrapbook
MacDonald, C.H. (comp.), 'Police Staff: Napier Police District', mimeograph, 1986
McLean, J.B., Scrapbooks
Meltzer, J., Papers
Murray, W.R., 'Record of Cases' [1922–50], typescript
Murray, W.R., Scrapbooks and personal papers
O'Halloran, R., ' "Caesar's Ghost": A Policeman's Lot', typescript, 1981
O'Neill, D.J., Scrapbook
Rawle, S., 'Discuss the Advantages and Disadvantages of placing the various Police Forces in the United Kingdom under a Common Administration', essay submitted for the King's Police Medal Essay Competition [in London], 1935
Rawle, S., Scrapbook
'Ruawaro Murder Inquiry: Oct. 1933–Jan. 1934: Diary of Inspector Hollis and Inspector Rawle', typescript
Savage, R.C., 'Address to Cadet Wing Graduation [at New Zealand Police College]', typed speech notes, 14 Dec 1977
Scott, Donald, 'The Autobiography of Donald Scott', typescript
Simpson, D.G.M., Scrapbook
Smith, T.F., 'Reminiscences', typescript, 1978
Sterritt, Rosalie, 'Constable David Sterritt, DCM', typescript, 1979
Thom, W.T., 'Looking Backwards: A few personal observations of Forty Years Service with the New Zealand Police Force', typescript, 1953
Thyne, M., 'Memoir' [c.1978]
Wilson, H.A., Notebook [1930]
Young, J.B. (comp.), 'Notes on Criminal Investigation', typescript, 1937
Young, J.B., Scrapbooks

3. Miscellaneous reports held by author

Public Issues Committee, Auckland District Law Society, 'Never on Sunday', cyclostyled, 16 Jul 1975
Swanton, Bruce (comp.), 'Copspeak 1: A Glossary of Terms, Abbreviations and Phrases Employed by Police Officers Throughout Australasia', mimeograph, Philip, ACT, 1988

4. Theses and research essays

Anderson, John, 'Military Censorship in World War I: Its Use and Abuse in New Zealand', MA thesis, Victoria University College, 1952

Barton, B.J., 'Control of the New Zealand Police', LlB(hons) thesis, University of Auckland, 1978

Brown, W., 'Origins of the New Zealand Totalisator Agency Board', MA(hons) research essay, University of Canterbury, 1986

Clayton, Leo, 'The Angry Autumn of 1932: A Micro Study of the Collective Protest in Wellington on May 10 and 11, 1932', Hist 316 research essay, Victoria University of Wellington, 1998

Ewing, I.S., 'Public Service Reform in New Zealand, 1866–1912, MA thesis, University of Auckland, 1979

Green, J., 'The Society for the Protection of Women and Children: Dunedin Branch 1914–1945', BA(hons) long essay, University of Otago, 1982

Holland, K.J., 'Police Unionism in New Zealand', long essay for Diploma of Industrial Relations, Victoria University of Wellington, 1977

Joblin, Richard S.L., 'The Breath of Scandal: *New Zealand Truth* and Interwar Society, 1918–1939', MA thesis, University of Canterbury, 1990

Law, P., 'Too Much "Yellow" in the Melting Pot? Perceptions of the New Zealand Chinese 1930–1960', BA(hons) thesis, University of Otago, 1994

McAloon, J., 'Sedition, 1913–1925', MA(hons) research essay, University of Canterbury, 1983

McCahon, J., 'The Victorian Police Strike', BA(hons) thesis, University of Melbourne, 1962

Moores, H.S., 'The Rise of the Protestant Political Association: Sectarianism in New Zealand Politics During World War I', MA thesis, University of Auckland, 1966

Noonan, R.J., 'The Riots of 1932: A Study of Social Unrest in Auckland, Wellington, Dunedin', MA thesis, University of Auckland, 1969

Poole, M.M., 'The Treatment of Enemy Aliens in New Zealand During the Second World War', BA(hons) long essay, University of Otago, 1982

Powell, J.R., 'The History of a Working Class Party, 1918–1940', MA thesis, Victoria University College, 1949

Somerville, A., 'Moominpappa Got Away: The State and Child Welfare in New Zealand, 1925–30', BA(hons) long essay, University of Otago, 1982

Thompson, S.J., 'Maoris and the Criminal Justice System, 1919–1939: A Preliminary Analysis', MA(hons) research essay, University of Canterbury, 1987

Thynne, I.S., 'An Analysis of the Social Backgrounds, Educational Qualifications and Career Patterns of Permanent Heads in the New Zealand Public Service, 1913–73', PhD thesis, Victoria University of Wellington, 1978

Watson, James, 'Crisis and Change: Economic Crisis and Technological Change Between the World Wars, with Special Reference to Christchurch, 1926–36', PhD thesis, University of Canterbury, 1984

5. Letters and Interviews

Members of the Police Force between 1918 and 1945

T.W. Allsopp, A.J. Austin, G.S. Austing, E. Barling, E.F. Barry, C.J. Bell, C.E.W. Black, C.W. Bowley, F.J. Brady, McD. Brown, W.S. Brown, R.E.J. Brydon, E. Buckley, C.P. Burns, K.B. Burnside, H.E. Campin, A.S. Chiles, J.P. Clements, N. Crawford, J. Crowley, G. Diffey, G.C. Donnelly, A.L. Downes, J.A. du Temple, G.P. Dwan, J. Edwards, M.J. Elliot, J.A. Feely, W.R. Fell, A.A. Fraser, D.G. Fraser, E.J. Gaines, A. Gellatly, F.A. Gordon, W.S. Hammond, L.M. Hansen, L. Harrowfield, F.R. Henry, J.W. Hill, R.D. Hodge, S.B. Holder, C.W.S. Holmes, H.M. Holmes, E.V.B. Horne, E.J.G. Hotham, G.A. Howes, G. Innes, E.L. Jeffery, A.J. Johnston, P. Kearney, A.T. Kelk, M.B. Kelly, N. Kempt, A.E.K. Keown, A.D. Knight, J.P. Larmer, J.T. MacKenzie, H. McLean, J.B. McLean, R.K. Marley, J. Mathieson, T.J. Miles, A.J. Mills, W.R. Murray, P.J. Nalder, D.J. OCarroll, M.E. Parker, D.S. Paterson, E.B. Pearce, W.F. Pearce, H.E. Pearse, R.V. Petrowski, O.S.W. Power, J.H. Quartley, A.G. Quin, C.H. Reardon, D.F. Ross, R.S. Rusbatch, H.A. Sayer, W.H.A. Sharp, A.M. Sim, J. Skinner, A.H. Stapleton, E.A. Stevenson, W.A. Stock, A.C. Strawbridge, D.R. Sugrue, C.D. Taylor, E.R. Trask, P. K. Treacy, H.I. Tubman, E.S. Tuck, G.C. Urquhart, A.H.L. Valentine, J.D. Walker, E.G. Ward, R.H. Waterson, J. Watt, A. Wilson, H.A. Wilson, W.G. Wood

6. Others who provided information or assisted with research

F. Aplin, M. Boyd, P. Brewer, G. Burgess, I.D. Campbell, L.M. Clayton, E. Crosby, B.L. Dallard, J. Garner, D. Godfrey, C. Hayes, D. Hill, C. Hirst, R. Howarth, R. Jackson, I. Jones, W.D. McIntyre, C. Marr, D. Monigatti, E.R. Neal, A. Pond, J. Robinson, K. Rutledge, D. Smith, H. Stace, R. Sterritt, R. Sweetman, C. Swift, B.G. Thomson, D.A. Thomson, M. Thyne, J. Tucker, L. Waasdorp, J.D. Wills, D.H. Woodcock, B. Young, S.I. Young

B. PUBLISHED SOURCES

1. Official

New Zealand
Appendix to the Journals of the House of Representatives (AJHR)
A-3, 1948–49, Annual Reports of the Department of Island Territories: Cook Islands
B-1, 1911–20, Annual Public Accounts
B-4A, 1932, Final Report of the National Expenditure Commission
B-6, 1921–41, Financial Statement
B-7, 1921–41, Appropriations for Consolidated Fund Services

D-1, 1923 and 1941, Public Works Statement
G-11, 1934, Report of the Commission on Native Affairs
H-2, 1898, Report of the Royal Commission on the Police Force
H-11B, 1929, First Report of Committee on Unemployment in New Zealand
H-14, 1918–47, Annual Reports of the Public Service Commissioner
H-16, 1878–1955, Annual Reports of the Police Force
H-16A, 1954, First Interim Report of the Commission of Inquiry ... Into Certain Matters Relating to the Conduct of Members of the Police Force
H-16B, 1909, Report of, and Minutes of Evidence to, the Royal Commission on the Police Force of the Dominion
H-16B, 1954, Second Interim Report of the Commission of Inquiry ... Into Certain Matters Relating to the Conduct of Members of the Police Force
H-16C, 1955, Third and Final Report of the Commission of Inquiry Into the Conduct of Members of the Police Force
H-20, 1920–45, Annual Reports of the Prison Department
H-22, 1920–26, Annual Reports of the Department of Internal Affairs (Dominion Laboratory Reports)
H-23, 1948, Report of the Royal Commission on Gaming and Racing
H-28, 1929, Statement by the Minister of Justice regarding the Elsie Walker case
H-31A, 1925, Report of the Committee of Inquiry into Mental Defectives and Sexual Offenders
H-34, 1912, Report of the Commission of Inquiry into the Unclassified Departments of the Public Service of New Zealand
H-34, 1927–39, Annual Reports of the Department of Scientific and Industrial Research
H-37, 1924, No-License Districts
I-1, 1929, Report of the Public Petitions Committee
I-15, 1932–33, Evidence to the Government Superannuation Funds Bill Committee

Justice Statistics, 1921–42, 1945–46
New Zealand Census, 1921, 1926, and 1936
New Zealand Official Yearbook
New Zealand Parliamentary Debates
New Zealand Police Gazette
Statistics of New Zealand: Law and Crime, 1880–1920
The Police Force Act, 1913, Police Force Amendment Act, 1919, and Regulations made thereunder for the guidance of the Police Force of New Zealand, Wellington, 1920

Australia
Annual Report of the Chief Commissioner of Police, 1946, *Victoria Parliamentary Papers,* 1947–48
Annual Reports of the Commissioner of Police, Queensland, 1900–45

Annual Reports of the [NSW] Police Department, *New South Wales Parliamentary Papers*, 1921–48

2. Newspapers and periodicals

(those systematically examined, in addition to clippings cited from scrapbooks and archival files)
Dominion
Lyttelton Times (*Christchurch Times*)
New Zealand Herald
New Zealand Police Journal
New Zealand Truth
Otago Daily Times
Poverty Bay Herald
Press (Christchurch)

3. Articles and chapters

Arnold, T., 'Legal Accountability and the Police: The Role of the Courts', in N. Cameron and W. Young (eds), *Policing at the Crossroads*, Wellington, 1986, pp.67–85

Baker, F., 'Public Servants as Ministerial Advisers', in R.S. Milne (ed.), *Bureaucracy in New Zealand*, Wellington, 1957, pp.31–50

Barnett, S.T., 'The Limits of Decentralisation', in J.L. Roberts (ed.), *Decentralisation in New Zealand Government Administration*, Wellington, 1961, pp.17–34

Barton, G.P., 'Police Powers: Criminal Procedure', in K.J. Keith (ed.), *Essays on Human Rights*, Wellington, 1968, pp.30–44

Beaglehole, Tim, 'Fraser, Peter', *Dictionary of New Zealand Biography*, vol.4, Wellington, 1998, pp.182–6

Brampton, Lord, 'An Address to Police Constables on their Duties', in *Vincent's Police Code and General Manual of the Criminal Law*, 17th edn, London, 1931

Cain, Maureen, 'On the Beat: Interactions and Relations in Rural and Urban Police Forces', in Stanley Cohen (ed.), *Images of Deviance*, London, 1971, pp.62–97

Campbell, A.E., 'The Control of Primary Schools', in G.W. Parkyn (ed.), *The Administration of Education in New Zealand*, Wellington, 1954, pp.29–42

Chadwick, E., 'On the Consolidation of Police Force, and the Prevention of Crime', *Fraser's Magazine*, vol.77, 1868, pp.1–18

Chatterton, Michael R., 'The Supervision of Patrol Work under the Fixed Points System', in Simon Holdaway (ed.), *The British Police*, London, 1979, pp.83–101

Congalton, A.A., 'Social Grading of Occupations in New Zealand', *British Journal of Sociology*, vol.4, no.1, 1953, pp.45–60

Cookson, J.E., 'Pacifism and Conscientous Objection in World War II New Zealand', in Peter Brock and Thomas Socknat (eds), *Challenge to Mars: Essays on Pacifism from 1918 to 1945*, Toronto, 1998, pp.292–311

Cull, H.A., 'The Enigma of a Police Constable's Status', *Victoria University of Wellington Law Review*, vol.8, 1975–77, pp.148-69

Davis, R.P., 'The New Zealand Labour Party's "Irish Campaign", 1916–1921', *Political Science*, vol.19, no.2, Dec 1967, pp.13–23

Dunstall, Graeme, 'Cummings, Denis Joseph; Cummings, James', *Dictionary of New Zealand Biography*, vol.4, Wellington, 1998, pp.120–2

Dunstall, Graeme, 'Hammond, Walter Sydney', *Dictionary of New Zealand Biography*, vol.4, Wellington, 1998, pp.221–2

Dunstall, Graeme, 'McIlveney, William Bernard', *Dictionary of New Zealand Biography*, vol.4, Wellington, 1998, pp.311–12

Dunstall, Graeme, 'Murray, William Robert', *Dictionary of New Zealand Biography*, vol.4, Wellington, 1998, pp.367–8

Dunstall, Graeme, 'New Zealand Police, 1920–1980: An Isolated Occupational Community?', in S. Corcoran (ed.), *Law and History in Australia*, Adelaide, 1991, pp.77–87

Dunstall, Graeme, 'O'Donovan, John', *Dictionary of New Zealand Biography*, vol.3, Wellington, 1996, pp.370–1

Dunstall, Graeme, 'Police in New Zealand', in D.K. Das (ed.), *Police Practices: An International Review*, Metuchen, New Jersey, 1994, pp.285–418

Dunstall, Graeme, 'Wohlmann, Ward George', *Dictionary of New Zealand Biography*, vol.4, Wellington, 1998, pp.570–1

Dunstall, Graeme, 'Young, John Bruce', *Dictionary of New Zealand Biography*, vol.5 (forthcoming)

Fairburn, Miles, 'The Farmers Take Over (1912–1930)', in Keith Sinclair (ed.), *The Oxford Illustrated History of New Zealand*, Auckland, 1990, pp.185–209

Fairburn, Miles, and Stephen Haslett, 'Violent Crime in Old and New Societies: A Case Study Based on New Zealand 1853–1940', *Journal of Social History*, vol.20, Fall 1986, pp.89–126

Filer, D., 'The Great Spy Lie', *NZ Listener*, 25 Sep 1982, pp.18–19

Finnane, Mark, 'Police and Politics in Australia: The Case for Historical Revision', *Australian and New Zealand Journal of Criminology*, vol.23, no.4, Dec 1990, pp.218–28

Finnane, Mark, 'Police Corruption and Police Reform: The Fitzgerald Inquiry in Queensland, Australia', *Policing and Society*, vol.1, 1990, pp.159–71

Fleras, Augie, 'Maori Wardens and the Control of Liquor among the Maori of New Zealand', *Journal of the Polynesian Society*, vol.90, 1981, pp.495–513

Gatrell, V.A.C., 'The Decline of Theft and Violence in Victorian and

Edwardian England', in Gatrell, B. Lenman and G. Parker (eds), *Crime and the Law*, London, 1980, pp.238–370

Green, David, 'Bayly, William Alfred', *Dictionary of New Zealand Biography*, vol.4, Wellington, 1998, pp.41–2

Heal, K., 'The Police, Research and Crime Control', *Research Bulletin*, Home Office Research and Planning Unit, London, no.13, 1982, pp.16–19

Hill, Richard, 'An Uneasy Relationship: The Police and the PSA', *New Zealand Police Association Newsletter*, vol.17, no.1, Jan 1985, pp.4, 7

Hill, Richard, 'Cullen, John', *Dictionary of New Zealand Biography*, vol.3, Wellington, 1996, pp.125–7

Hill, Richard, 'Dinnie, Walter', *Dictionary of New Zealand Biography*, vol.3, Wellington, 1996, pp.134–5

Hill, Richard, 'Maori Policing in Nineteenth Century New Zealand', *Archifacts*, 1985, no.2, pp.54–60

Hill, Richard, 'The Rise and Fall of the First New Zealand Police Superannuation Scheme', *International Police Association (NZ Section) Journal*, vol.19, 1985, no.3, pp.79–83, no.4, pp.73–5

Hill, Richard, 'Tunbridge, John Bennett', *Dictionary of New Zealand Biography*, vol.2, Wellington, 1993, pp.551–2

Jones, Lawrence, 'Stanley Graham and the Several Faces of "Man Alone" ', *Journal of Popular Culture*, vol.19, no.2, 1985, pp.121–36

Kealey, G.R., 'State Repression of Labour and the Left in Canada, 1914–20: The Impact of the First World War', *Canadian Historical Review*, vol.73, no.3, 1992, pp.281–314

Kealey, G.R., 'The Surveillance State: The Origins of Domestic Intelligence and Counter-Subversion in Canada, 1914–21', *Intelligence and National Security*, vol.7, no.3, 1992, pp.179–210

Lange, R.T., 'The Tohunga and the Government in the Twentieth Century', *University of Auckland Historical Society Annual*, 1968, pp.12–38

McCarthy, L.J., 'Decentralisation in Educational Administration', in J.L. Roberts (ed.), *Decentralisation in New Zealand Government Administration*, Wellington, 1961, pp.56–73

McCarthy, Sir Thaddeus, 'The Role of the Police in the Administration of Justice', in R.S. Clark (ed.), *Essays on Criminal Law in New Zealand*, Wellington, 1971, pp.170–88

McCoy, A.W., 'Sport as Modern Mythology: SP Bookmaking in New South Wales 1920–1979', in R. Cashman and M. McKernan (eds), *Sport: Money, Morality and the Media*, Kensington, NSW, n.d., pp.34–67

McGibbon, Ian, 'Downes, Arthur Leonard', *Dictionary of New Zealand Biography*, vol.4, Wellington, 1998, pp.141–2

Macrae, J., and K. Sinclair, 'Unemployment in New Zealand During the Depression of the Late 1920s and Early 1930s', *Australian Economic History Review*, vol.15, no.1, 1975, pp.35–44

Marshall, J.R., 'Political Controls', in R.S. Milne (ed.), *Bureaucracy in New Zealand*, Wellington, 1957, pp.51–65

O'Brien, Brian, 'Tomasevic, Ivan', *Dictionary of New Zealand Biography*, vol.4, Wellington, 1998, pp.531–2

O'Connor, P.S., 'Sectarian Conflict in New Zealand, 1911–1920', *Political Science*, vol.19, no.1, 1967, pp.3–16

O'Farrell, P.J., 'The Russian Revolution and the Labour Movements of Australia and New Zealand, 1917–1922', *International Review of Social History*, vol.8, part 2, 1963, pp.177–97

Olssen, Erik, 'Depression and War (1931–1949)', in Keith Sinclair (ed.), *The Oxford Illustrated History of New Zealand*, Auckland, 1990, pp.211–35

Olssen, Erik, 'Towards a New Society', in G.W. Rice (ed.), *The Oxford History of New Zealand*, 2nd edn, Auckland, 1992, pp.254–84

Orr, G., 'Police Accountability to the Executive and Parliament', in N. Cameron and W. Young (eds), *Policing at the Crossroads*, Wellington, 1986, pp.46–66

Palmer, G., 'The Legislative Process and the Police', in N. Cameron and W. Young (eds), *Policing at the Crossroads*, Wellington, 1986, pp.86–106

Prenzler, T., 'Women in Australian Policing: An Historical Overview', *Journal of Australian Studies*, no.42, Sep 1994, pp.78–88

Richardson, Len, 'Class, Community, and Conflict: The Blackball Miners' Union, 1920–31', in Len Richardson and W. David McIntyre (eds), *Provincial Perspectives*, Christchurch, 1980, pp.106–27

Richardson, Len, 'Parties and Political Change', in G.W. Rice (ed.), *The Oxford History of New Zealand*, 2nd edn, Auckland, 1992, pp.201–29

Robertson, R.T., 'Government Responses to Unemployment in New Zealand, 1929–35', *New Zealand Journal of History*, vol.16, no.1, 1982, pp.21–38

Robertson, R.T., 'Isolation, Ideology and Impotence: Organisations for the Unemployed during the Great Depression, 1930–1935', *New Zealand Journal of History*, vol.13, no.2, 1979, pp.149–64

Rorke, Jinty, 'Skinner, Lewis', *Dictionary of New Zealand Biography*, vol.3, Wellington, 1996, pp.477–8

Roth, H., 'The October Revolution and New Zealand Labour', *Political Science*, vol.3, no.2, Sep 1961, pp.45–55

Simpson, Tony, 'Edwards, James Henry', *Dictionary of New Zealand Biography*, vol.4, Wellington, 1998, pp.154–5

Stone, R.C.J., 'The Unions and the Arbitration System', in Robert Chapman and Keith Sinclair (eds), *Studies of a Small Democracy*, Auckland, 1963, pp.201–20

Swanton, B., 'Women Police in NSW: The Formative Years', *Australian Police Journal*, Oct–Dec 1983, pp.142–3

Taylor, Kerry, ' "Our Motto, No Compromise": The Ideological Origins and Foundation of the Communist Party of New Zealand', *New Zealand Journal of History*, vol.28, no.2, Oct 1994, pp.160–77

Templeton, J., 'Rebel Guardians', in J. Iremonger, J. Merritt and G. Osborne (eds), *Strikes*, Sydney, 1973, pp.103–27

Thomson, Barry, 'The Police Uniform in New Zealand', *The Bulletin* [New Zealand Police], no.281, Oct 1983, pp.2–5

van der Kroght, C., 'O'Shea, Thomas', *Dictionary of New Zealand Biography*, vol.3, Wellington, 1996, pp.374–5

Walker, R., 'The New South Wales Police Force, 1862–1900', *Journal of Australian Studies*, no.15, 1984, pp.25–38

Walker, R.J., 'A Review of the Position of the Maori Warden', *Maori Wardens News*, vol.3, no.3, 1982, pp.47–53

Walsh, J., 'The Seamen on Strike, 1922–1923', in P. Walsh (ed.), *Trade Unions, Work and Society,* Palmerston North, 1994, pp.91–108

Ward, S.R., 'Intelligence Surveillance of British Ex-Servicemen, 1918–1920', *Historical Journal*, vol.16, no.1, 1973, pp.179–88

Waters, B.B., 'The Role of a Rural Policeman', *Auckland University Law Review*, vol.2, no.3, 1974, pp.75–86

Williams, D., 'The Bureau of Investigation and its Critics, 1919–21: The Origins of Federal Political Surveillance', *Journal of American History*, vol.68, no.3, Dec 1981, pp.560–79

Wilson, J.Q., and B. Boland, 'The Effect of Police on Crime', *Law and Society Review*, vol.12, 1978, pp.367–90

Young, Sherwood, 'Broberg, Charles Robert', *Dictionary of New Zealand Biography*, vol.3, Wellington, 1996, pp.67–8

Young, Sherwood, 'Wright, Arthur Hobbins', *Dictionary of New Zealand Biography*, vol.4, Wellington, 1998, p.574

4. Books

Allason, R., *The Branch: A History of the Metropolitan Police Special Branch 1883–1983*, London, 1983

Archer, Dane, and Rosemary Gartner, *Violence and Crime in Cross-National Perspective*, New Haven, Connecticut, 1984

Ascoli, D., *The Queen's Peace: The Origins and Development of the Metropolitan Police, 1829–1979*, London, 1979

Baker, J.V.T., *The New Zealand People at War: War Economy*, Wellington, 1965

Baker, Paul, *King and Country Call: New Zealanders, Conscription and the Great War*, Auckland, 1988

Barrowman, R., *A Popular Vision: The Arts and the Left in New Zealand, 1930–1950*, Wellington, 1991

Bassett, Michael, *The Mother of All Departments: The History of the Department of Internal Affairs*, Wellington, 1997

Bassett, Michael, *The State in New Zealand 1840–1984: Socialism Without Doctrines?*, Auckland, 1998

Beaglehole, A., *A Small Price to Pay: Refugees from Hitler in New Zealand, 1936–46*, Wellington, 1988

Beaglehole, J.C., *The University of New Zealand: An Historical Study*, Wellington, 1937

Beeby, C.E., *The Biography of an Idea: Beeby on Education*, Wellington, 1992

Belich, James, *Making Peoples: A History of the New Zealanders From Polynesian Settlement to the End of the Nineteenth Century*, Auckland, 1996

Belich, James, *The New Zealand Wars and the Victorian Interpretation of Racial Conflict*, Auckland, 1986

Belton, Charles, *Outside the Law in New Zealand*, Gisborne, 1939

Binney, J., G. Chaplin and C. Wallace, *Mihaia: The Prophet Rua Kenana and His Community at Maungapohatu*, Wellington, 1979

Bioletti, Harry, *The Yanks are Coming: The American Invasion of New Zealand 1942–1944*, Auckland, 1989

Boddy, Gillian, and Jacqueline Matthews (eds), *Disputed Ground: Robin Hyde, Journalist*, Wellington, 1991

Bottomley, Keith, and Clive Coleman, *Understanding Crime Rates: Police and Public Roles in the Production of Official Statistics*, Farnborough, England, 1981

Boyd, M.B., *City of the Plains: A History of Hastings*, Wellington, 1984

Bungay, Mike, and Brian Edwards, *Bungay on Murder*, Christchurch, 1983

Burdon, R.M., *Outlaw's Progress,* Wellington, 1943

Burdon, R.M., *The New Dominion: A Social and Political History of New Zealand, 1918–39*, London, 1965

Burton, O., *In Prison*, Wellington, 1945

Bush, G.W.A., *Decently and in Order: The Government of the City of Auckland 1840–1971: The Centennial History of the Auckland City Council*, Auckland, 1971

Cain, Frank, *The Origins of Political Surveillance in Australia*, Sydney, 1983

Cain, Maureen E., *Society and the Policeman's Role*, London, 1973

Campbell, M.D.N., *Story of Napier, 1874–1974: Footprints Along the Shore,* Napier, 1975

Carr, Margaret, *Policing in the Mountain Shadow: A History of the Taranaki Police*, New Plymouth, 1989

Carson, Kit, and Yvonne Davison, *The Longest Beat: A Social and Pictorial History of Policing on the West Coast*, Greymouth, 1990

Carter, Ray, *'Beyond the Call of Duty': A History of the Palmerston North Police District*, Palmerston North, 1988

Chandler, E.C., *Waiuta Ghosts: The Meanderings of a Quartz-miner*, Christchurch, 1962

Cherrett, O.J., *Without Fear or Favour: 150 Years Policing Auckland 1840–1990*, Auckland, 1989

Clark, M. (ed.), *Peter Fraser: Master Politician*, Palmerston North, 1998

Clarke, I.T., *Deodar: The Story of Auckland's Water Police*, Auckland, 1994

Clarke, R.V.G., and J.M. Hough (eds), *The Effectiveness of Policing*, Farnborough, England, 1980

Coatman, J., *Police*, London, 1959

Commemorating Traffic Safety: 55 Years 1937–1992, Land Transport Division, Ministry of Transport, Wellington, 1992

Conly, G., *The Shock of '31: The Hawke's Bay Earthquake*, Wellington, 1980

Cox, B., J. Shirley and M. Short, *The Fall of Scotland Yard*, London, 1977

Crane, E., *I Can Do No Other: A Biography of the Reverend Ormond Burton*, Auckland, 1986

Critchley, T.A., *A History of Police in England and Wales*, 2nd edn, London, 1978

Dalley, Bronwyn, *Family Matters: Child Welfare in Twentieth-Century New Zealand*, Auckland, 1998

Davin, Dan, *Roads From Home* (ed. Lawrence Jones), Auckland, 1976

Dixon, D., *From Prohibition to Regulation: Bookmaking, Anti-gambling and the Law*, Oxford, 1991

Duff, Oliver, *New Zealand Now*, Wellington, 1941

Dyne, D.G., *Famous New Zealand Murders*, Auckland, 1974 edn

Edwards, J., *Break Down These Bars*, Auckland, 1987

Emsley, Clive, *Policing and its Context 1750–1870*, London, 1983

Emsley, Clive, *The English Police: A Political and Social History*, Hemel Hempstead, Hertfordshire, 1991

Fairburn, Miles, *The Ideal Society and its Enemies: The Foundations of Modern New Zealand Society, 1850–1900*, Auckland, 1989

Field, Michael J., *Mau: Samoa's Struggle for Freedom*, Auckland, revised edn, 1991

Finnane, Mark, *Police and Government: Histories of Policing in Australia*, Melbourne, 1994

Finnane, Mark (ed.), *Policing in Australia: Historical Perspectives*, Kensington, NSW, 1987

Fleras, Augie, *From Village Runanga to the New Zealand Maori Wardens' Association: A Historical Development of Maori Wardens: A Paper to be Presented to the Maori Wardens*, Wellington, 1980

Fosdick, R.B., *American Police Systems* (1st edn 1920), Montclair, New Jersey, 1969 reprint

Fosdick, R.B., *European Police Systems*, New York, 1916

Gardner, W.J., *The Amuri: A County History*, Culverden, 2nd edn, 1983

Gee, David, *Poison: The Coward's Weapon*, Christchurch, 1985

Grant, David, *On a Roll: A History of Gambling and Lotteries in New Zealand*, Wellington, 1994

Grant, David, *Out in the Cold: Pacifists and Conscientious Objectors in*

New Zealand During World War II, Auckland, 1986

Gurr, T.R., P.N. Grabosky and R.C. Hula, *The Politics of Crime and Conflict: A Comparative History of Four Cities*, Beverly Hills, California, 1977

Gustafson, B., *From the Cradle to the Grave: A Biography of Michael Joseph Savage,* Auckland, 1986

Haldane, R., *The People's Force: A History of the Victoria Police*, Melbourne, 1986

Hanson, E., *The Politics of Social Security: The 1938 Act and Some Later Developments,* Auckland, 1980

Hare, A.E.C., *Report on Industrial Relations in New Zealand,* Wellington, 1946

Hatch, Elvin, *Respectable Lives: Social Standing in Rural New Zealand*, Berkeley, California, 1992

Hawke, G.R., *The Making of New Zealand: An Economic History*, Cambridge, 1985

Hawke's Bay 'Before' and 'After' the Great Earthquake of 1931: An Historical Record, Napier, 1931, facsimile edn with additional chapters by D.G. Conly, 1981

Henderson, Alan, *The Quest for Efficiency: The Origins of the State Services Commission,* Wellington, 1990

Hermans, R.T., *Capital Coppers: An Illustrated Review of the Wellington Police District, 1840–1986*, Wellington, 1985

Higgs, P., and C. Bettess, *To Walk a Fair Beat: A History of the South Australian Women Police 1915–1987*, Adelaide, 1987

Hill, Murray, *In the Line of Duty: 100 Years of the New Zealand Police*, Auckland, 1986

Hill, Richard S., *Policing the Colonial Frontier: The Theory and Practice of Coercive Social and Racial Control in New Zealand, 1767–1867*, Wellington, 1986

Hill, Richard S., *The Colonial Frontier Tamed: New Zealand Policing in Transition, 1867–1886*, Wellington, 1989

Hill, Richard S., *The Iron Hand in the Velvet Glove: The Modernisation of Policing in New Zealand, 1886–1917*, Palmerston North, 1995

Hobbs, D., *Doing The Business: Entrepreneurship, the Working Class, and Detectives in the East End of London*, Oxford, 1989

Hobbs, Leslie, *The Thirty-Year Wonders*, Christchurch, 1967

Hodge, W.C. (ed.), *Doyle Criminal Procedure in New Zealand*, Sydney, 2nd edn, 1984

Hollis, Rex, *Killer on the Coast: The True Story of Stan Graham and New Zealand's Deadliest Manhunt*, Wellington, [1965]

Holt, Betty, *Women in Council: A History of the National Council of Women of New Zealand*, Wellington, 1980

Horse Racing, Trotting and Dog Racing in New Zealand: Report of Royal Commission of Inquiry, Wellington, 1970

Hunn, J.K., *Not Only Affairs of State*, Palmerston North, 1982

Ingram, Wallie, *Legends In Their Lifetime*, Wellington, 1962

Johnston, W. Ross, *The Long Blue Line: A History of the Queensland Police*, Brisbane, 1992

Joseph, George, *By a Person or Persons Unknown: Unsolved Murders in New Zealand*, Sydney, 1982

Kawharu, I.H. (ed.), *Conflict and Compromise: Essays on Maori Since Colonisation*, Wellington, 1975

Keenan, N.J., *The History of a Small Town Police Station*, Hawera, 1982

Kelly, G.G., *The Gun in the Case*, Christchurch, 1963

Kendall, Walter, *The Revolutionary Movement in Britain, 1900–21: The Origins of British Communism*, London, 1969

Leary, L.P., *Not Entirely Legal*, Christchurch, 1977

Lee, John A., *The John A. Lee Diaries 1936–40*, Christchurch, 1981

Lipson, Leslie, *The Politics of Equality: New Zealand's Adventures in Democracy*, Chicago, 1948

Luxford, J.H., *Liquor Laws of New Zealand*, Wellington, 1938

Lynch, P.P., *No Remedy for Death: The Memoirs of a Pathologist*, London, 1970

McCoy, A.W., *Drug Traffic: Narcotics and Organized Crime in Australia*, Sydney, 1980

MacDonald, C.H., *The Story of the Napier Police District*, Napier, 1986

McGill, David, *No Right to Strike: The History of the New Zealand Police Service Organisations*, Wellington, 1992

McGill, David, *The Guardians at the Gate: The History of the New Zealand Customs Department*, Wellington, 1991

McIntyre, W.D., *New Zealand Prepares for War: Defence Policy, 1919–39*, Christchurch, 1988

McQueen, H.C., *Vocations for Maori Youth*, Wellington, 1945

Mark, Sir Robert, *In the Office of Constable: An Autobiography*, London, 1978

Mark, Sir Robert, *Policing a Perplexed Society*, London, 1977

Marlborough Police History Committee, *The Strait and Narrow: A History of Policing in Marlborough*, Blenheim, 1998

Martin, J.P., and G. Wilson, *The Police: A Study in Manpower: The Evolution of the Service in England and Wales, 1829–1965*, London, 1969

Martin, John E., *Holding the Balance: A History of New Zealand's Department of Labour 1891–1995*, Christchurch, 1996

Mason, L.B., and M.F. Gordon (eds), *Trentham in Retrospect: 25 Years of Police Training*, Featherston, 1982

Meredith, V.R., *A Long Brief: Recollections of a Crown Solicitor*, Auckland, 1966

Metge, Joan, *A New Maori Migration: Rural and Urban Relations in Northern New Zealand*, London, 1964

Metge, Joan, *In and Out of Touch: Whakamaa in Cross-cultural Context*, Wellington, 1986

Miller, W.R., *Cops and Bobbies: Police Authority in New York and London, 1830–1870*, Chicago, 1977

Monigatti, Rex, *New Zealand Sensations*, Auckland, 1975 edn

Monkkonen, Eric, *Police in Urban America, 1860–1920*, New York, 1981

Morris, G. (ed.), *Waiuta, 1906–1951: The Gold Mine, the Town, the People*, Reefton, 1986

Mukherjee, Satyanshu K., *Crime Trends in Twentieth-Century Australia*, Sydney, 1981

Mulgan, E.K., and A.E. Mulgan, *The New Zealand Citizen: An Elementary Account of the Citizen's Rights and Duties and the Work of Government*, Christchurch, 1914

Mulgan, John, *Man Alone*, Auckland, 1972 edn

Neale, June E., *The Nelson Police: The Story of the Nelson Police District 1841–1986*, Nelson, 1986

New Zealand Department of Justice, *Crime in New Zealand*, Wellington, 1968

Newman, Corallyn (ed.), *Canterbury Women Since 1893*, Christchurch, 1979

Noonan, R., *By Design: A Brief History of the Public Works Department/ Ministry of Works 1870–1970*, Wellington, 1975

O'Hara, C.R., *Northland Made to Order*, Whangarei, 1986

O'Hara, J., *A Mugs's Game: A History of Gaming and Betting in Australia*, Kensington, NSW, 1988

Olssen, Erik, *A History of Otago*, Dunedin, 1984

Pearson, David, *Johnsonville: Continuity and Change in a New Zealand Township*, Sydney, 1980

Pearson, D.G., and D.C. Thorns, *Eclipse of Equality: Social Stratification in New Zealand*, Sydney, 1983

Perry, Stuart, *The New Zealand Whisky Book*, Auckland, 1980

Philipp, Eileen, *Juvenile Delinquency in New Zealand: A Preliminary Study*, Christchurch, 1946

Phillips, Jock, *A Man's Country? The Image of the Pakeha Male, A History*, Auckland, 1987

Polaschek, R.J., *Government Administration in New Zealand*, Wellington, 1958

Pool, Ian, *Te Iwi Maori: A New Zealand Population, Past, Present and Projected*, Auckland, 1991

Pratt, John, *Punishment in a Perfect Society: The New Zealand Penal System, 1840–1939*, Wellington, 1992

Punch, M., *Conduct Unbecoming: The Social Construction of Police Deviance and Control*, London, 1985

Reiner, Robert, *The Blue-Coated Worker: A Sociological Study of Police Unionism*, Cambridge, 1978

Reiner, Robert, *The Politics of the Police*, Brighton, 1985

Report of Commission of Inquiry into Possible Illegal Activities and Associated Police Misconduct (Fitzgerald Inquiry), Brisbane, 1989

Report of the Committee on the Employment of Women on Police Duties, London, 1920

Report of the Departmental Committee on Employment of Policewomen, London, 1924

Report of the Royal Commission on Licensing, Wellington, 1946

Report of the Trial of Dennis Gunn for the Murder of Mr Augustus Edward Braithwaite, Postmaster at Ponsonby, Auckland, on Saturday 13th March 1920: Held Before the Honourable Mr Justice Chapman at Auckland on 24th, 25th, 26th, and 28th May 1920, Wellington, 1921

Report of the Trial of Samuel John Thorne for the Murder of Mr Sydney Seymour Eyre, a Farmer at Pukekawa in the Auckland District on 25th August 1920. Held Before the Honourable Mr Justice F.R. Chapman at Auckland on the 29th and 30th November, and the 1st, 2nd, and 3rd December, 1920, Wellington, 1925

Review of Firearms Control in New Zealand: Report of an Independent Inquiry Commissioned by the Minister of Police, Wellington, 1997

Rice, G.W., *Ambulances and First Aid: St John in Christchurch 1885–1987: A History of the St John Ambulance Association and Brigade in Christchurch, New Zealand*, Christchurch, 1994

Richardson, Len, *Coal, Class and Community: The United Mineworkers of New Zealand, 1880–1960*, Auckland, 1995

Robinson, H., *A History of the Post Office in New Zealand*, Wellington, 1964

Robinson, John, *Policing the Tairawhiti: The Gisborne Police District 1769–1995*, Gisborne, 1995

Rorke, Jinty, *Policing Two Peoples: A History of Police in the Bay of Plenty, 1867–1992*, Tauranga, 1993

Roth, B., and J. Hammond, *Toil and Trouble: The Struggle for a Better Life in New Zealand*, Auckland, 1981

Roth, Bert, *Remedy For Present Evils: A History of the New Zealand Public Service Association from 1890*, Wellington, 1987

Roth, H., *Trade Unions in New Zealand Past and Present*, Wellington, 1973

Salaman, Graeme, *Community and Occupation: An Exploration of Work/Leisure Relationships*, London, 1974

Scott, Sir Harold, *Scotland Yard*, London, 1954

Scott, K.J., *The New Zealand Constitution*, Oxford, 1962

Scott, S.W., *Rebel in a Wrong Cause*, Auckland, 1960

Sellwood, A.V., *Police Strike, 1919*, London, 1978

Sinclair, K., *Walter Nash*, Auckland, 1976

Singe, Miles, and David Thomson, *Authority to Protect: A Story of Policing in Otago*, Dunedin, 1992

Skolnick, Jerome H., *Justice Without Trial: Law Enforcement in Democratic Society*, New York, 1966

Smith, Max, *Champion Blokes*, Christchurch, 1964

Smithies, Edward, *Crime in Wartime: A Social History of Crime in World War II*, London, 1982

Somerset, H.C.D., *Littledene: Patterns of Change,* Wellington, enlarged edn, 1974

South Auckland Police Development Plan, Wellington, 1984

Spicer, Charles E., *Policing the River District, 1886 to 1986: The First Hundred Years of the Wanganui Police,* Wanganui, 1988

State Services in New Zealand: Report of the Royal Commission of Inquiry, Wellington, 1962

Stewart, W.D., *Sir Francis H.D. Bell: His Life and Times*, Wellington, 1937

Sutch, W.B., *The Quest for Security in New Zealand, 1840 to 1966*, Wellington, 1966

Sutherland, I.G.L. (ed.), *The Maori People Today: A General Survey*, Wellington, 1940

Swain, Evan, *Unsolved Murders in New Zealand*, Auckland, 1972

Sweetman, Rory, *Bishop in the Dock: The Sedition Trial of James Liston,* Auckland, 1997

Taylor, N., *The New Zealand People at War: The Home Front*, Wellington, 1986

Thomson, Barry, and Robert Neilson, *Sharing the Challenge: A Social and Pictorial History of the Christchurch Police District*, Christchurch, 1989

Thomson, Basil, *Queer People,* London, 1922

Thomson, David A., and Hendrik Kagei, *A Century of Service: A History of the South Canterbury and North Otago Police,* Timaru, 1987

Thorn, James, *Peter Fraser: New Zealand's Wartime Prime Minister*, London, 1952

Tonry, Michael, and Norval Morris (eds), *Modern Policing,* Chicago, 1992

Treadwell, C.A.L., *Notable New Zealand Trials*, New Plymouth, 1936

Turbott, H.C., *Tuberculosis in the Maori, East Coast, New Zealand*, Wellington, 1935

Walker, S., *A Critical History of Police Reform: The Emergence of Professionalization*, Lexington, Massachusetts, 1977

Walker, Trevor, *Slain on Duty: An Account of New Zealand Police and Traffic Officers Killed on Duty, 1886–1996,* Wellington, 1996

Ward, Alan, *A Show of Justice: Racial 'Amalgamation' in Nineteenth Century New Zealand*, Auckland, 1974

Ward, Alex S., *Memories of Constable Ward*, Wellington, 1992

Webb, L., *The Control of Education in New Zealand*, Wellington, 1937

Webb, L., *Government in New Zealand*, Wellington, 1940

Webb, P.M., *A History of Custodial and Related Penalties in New Zealand*, Wellington, 1982

Welch, Dave, *The Lucifer: A Story of Industrial Conflict in New Zealand's 1930s*, Palmerston North, 1988

Whitaker, Ben, *The Police in Society*, London, 1979

Willis, H.A., *Manhunt: The Story of Stanley Graham*, Christchurch, 1979

Wills, John D., *The New Zealand Police Medal: The Police Long Service and Good Conduct Medals of New Zealand, Her Dependencies and Mandated Territories, 1886–1976*, Auckland, 1990

Wills, John D., *To Guard My People: Honours and Awards to the Police in New Zealand, 1861–1995*, Auckland, 1995

Wilson, H.J. (ed.), *The Bayly Case*, Wellington, 1934

Wilson, J.Q., *Thinking About Crime*, revised edn, New York, 1983

Wilson, J.Q., *Varieties of Police Behaviour: The Management of Law and Order in Eight Communities*, New York, 1971

Wilson, Ormond, *An Outsider Looks Back: Reflections on Experience*, Wellington, 1982

Wood, F.L.W., *The New Zealand People at War: Political and External Affairs*, Wellington, 1958

Woolston, Alan, *Equal to the Task: The City of Auckland Traffic Department, 1894–1994*, Auckland, 1996

Young, Sherwood, *Guilty on the Gallows: Famous Capital Crimes of New Zealand*, Wellington, 1998

Young, Sherwood (ed.), *With Confidence and Pride: Policing the Wellington Region, 1840–1992*, Wellington, 1994

Yska, Redmer, *New Zealand Green: The Story of Marijuana in New Zealand*, Auckland, 1990

Zehr, Howard, *Crime and the Development of Modern Society: Patterns of Criminality in Nineteenth Century Germany and France*, London, 1976

Index

The index includes references to information in the text, the footnotes, the figures and the illustrations. References to figures are 'italicised'. References to the illustrations are given as ill.1, ill.2, etc. References to the footnotes give the page number and note number, e.g. 378n10.

Gartly, James, 192
Garvey, J., 370n19
Gellatly, A., 454n33
George, Wally, 105
Geraghty, P., 233, 439n43
Gibson, J., 186
Gibson, Thomas, 265, 404n5, 441–2n106, ill.55
Gillard, Benson, 146
Gillespie, J., ill.105
Gilligan, W.P., 202, 214
Gillum, A.T., 82, 156
Gisborne Police District, 230, 237, 249–50
Gourlay, Michael, 156, 182, 420n73
Graham, Stanley, 150, 329–31, ill.115
Grant, A.M., 434n139
Great Britain, beat work in, 140–1
    crime in, 131
    fingerprinting, 168
    intelligence work, 253–5
    NZ police train at Scotland Yard, 99, 229, 294
    police in, 6–7, 18, 23, 73
    Second World War security liaison, 304–6
    working conditions, 43, 285
    see also London Metropolitan Police
Gregory, William, ill.4
Gribben, F., 371n34
Griffin, Kenneth, 169, 410n78
Griffin, R.F., 261, 263, 264, 268
Griffith, Roy, 213
Gunn, Dennis, 50, 165, 169, 370n7, ill.56, ill.58

Halke, C.J., 429n54
Hall, S.G., 243, ill.121
Hamilton, R.J., ill.55
Hamilton Police District, 70, 72, 224, 230
Hammond, Alfred, 245
Hammond, Wally S., 141, 142, 143, 145, 148, 247–8, ill.35, ill.40, ill.46
    awarded medal, 403n84, ill.54
    dismissed, 154
Hampton, W.J., 425n12
Hanan, J.R., 71
Hansen, L.M., 104
Harding, Arthur M., 204, 305, 317, 320, 470n6
Harrison, F.C., 235
Harvey, Peter, 439n43
Hasselberg, D., 370n19
Hastings police station, 29, 224

Hawera, ill.79
Hayes, J., ill.55
health, of police, 113–14, 161, 162
    at country stations, 218
    of NCOs, 238
    sick leave, 291
    see also death, stress
health patrols, 123, 394n156, ill.42
Heeps, Thomas, murdered, 98, 113, 126, ill.37
    funeral, ill.38
Henare, Tau, 120
Henderson, P.S., ill.78
Hendren, R.C., 249–50, 396n182
Hendrey, C.W., 68, 375n71
Henry, F. Ray, 104, 141, 156, 237, 386n23, 440n63
Herdman, Alexander L., 12, 14, 16, 41, 164
    and women police, 121, 122–3
Hicks, H.E., 370n19
Hill, J.W., 156
Hira, Rawiri Puhirake (Dave), 120, 213, 394n146, 434n139, ill.41
Hodge, Reese, 103–4, 104–5, 200
Holder, Margaret, 483n211, ill.118
Holland, Harry, 88, 259, ill.87
Hollis, J.W., 75, 88, 170, 171, 227, 232, 245
Hollis, R.T., 145
    funeral, ill.39
Holmes, Henry, 107, 399n12
Holmes, James, 193
Holt, G., 292, 463n131, 464n133
homicides, 3, 4, 26, 50, 74, 131, 166–8
    convictions in court, 19
    fingerprinting and, 165
    numbers of, 83, 97, 298
    serial killers, 166–7
    Second World War, 327, 329
    unsolved, 172, 412n97, 467n162
    see also specific homicides, e.g. Lakey, Scarff, Walker
Hona, Henry, 98, 388–9n84, ill.37
Horry, George, 170
horses, and police work, 151, 215–16, 296
    see also mounted police
Hotham, Ted, ill.47
hours of work, 42, 43, 65, 71, 374n30
    beat shifts, 392n130
    country police, 214–15
    detectives, 66–7, 375n43
    during Second World War, 344–5
    leisure pursuits and, 118

41, 292–3, 348, 364n70, 365n80, 464n134
relationships with Public Service Commissioners, 11–12
salary, 361n27
work of, 54
see also individual Commissioners, e.g. Cummings, McIlveney, O'Donovan
police districts, 1, 51–3, 82, 372n59
hierarchy, 223–5
maps of, ix–xii
staff numbers, *24*, 75–6
see also specific districts, e.g. Auckland, Christchurch, Hamilton
Police Force Acts and Amendments, 14–15, 20, 47, 79, 81
Police Headquarters (Wellington), 1, 53–4, 360n1, ill.6
Police Matrons, 121, 123, 124–5
see also women police
police officers, 52–3, 223–51
career paths of, 225–9
first conferences of, 229, 437n19, ill.121
Police Association and, 229–30
relationships with men, 245–51
training for, 228–9
work of, 229–32
see also Inspectors, non-commissioned officers, Police Commissioners, Superintendents
police stations, 1, 10, 11, 42
construction of, 54–6, *55*, 69, 288–90
description, 61
inspections of, 230
NCOs and, 236–7
rural stations, 191–3
see also individual stations
policemen, authority of, 199–201, 352
background of recruits, 102–8
career paths, 126–8, 189–94
characteristics of, 35–7, 107–8
discretion used by, 10, 13–20, 183–4, 191–201
image of, 106, 112, 219–21, 293, 352
military organisation of, 9, 12, 223, 361n27
moonlighting by, 346–7, 486n245
nature of work, 131–7
numbers of, 1, 2, 7, 8, *24*, 28–32, *44*, 45, 49, 65, *135*, 351–2
occupation of, 101–2, 112–17, 125–8
professionalisation, 2, 8, 19, 102

Second World War, 303–4, 323–4, 336–9
as separate community, 117–19
see also constables, country police, detectives, police officers, urban police
political surveillance, 4, 7, 33–4, 161, 253–69
in Second World War, 303, 304–14
of German organisations, 474n69
see also aliens, communism, industrial unrest, New Zealand Labour Party, pacifists, sedition
Port Awanui police station, 211, 213, 214, 215, 216, 218, ill.74–6
ports, security of, 321–4, 476n102
Post Office, 10–11, 269, 305
Potter, V.H., 186
Power, Orme, 107, 156, 318
Prater, R.A., 387n63
preventive policing, 20–37, 136–7
measurement of, 132
social conditions and, 351–3
professionalisation, 2, 8, 19, 102
promotion practices, 8, 126–8, 291–2, 396n185
and women police, 343
to NCO, 233–4, 396–7n189, 439n45
to commissioned officer, 225–8
see also examinations
prostitutes, and police, 147
Second World War, 335–6, 342–3, 481n182
Protected Places Emergency Regulations, 325
public attitudes, and police, 19, 32–7, 106, 112, 219–21, 293, 352
town and country, 353–4
Public Safety Conservation Act, 92
Public Safety Emergency Regulations, 311, 312
public service, 7–9, 11–12
police as agents of government departments, 10–11, 21, 194–6, 219
role of police within, 8, 9–20, 35, 47, 59
see also state and police; statistics
Public Service Association, police membership of, 42–3, 49, 63–4
police resign over salary cuts, 63, 277, 280, ill.10
public works camps, 84, 150, 193

Quartermain, A.G., 246
Quinn, W. Joseph, 144, 238
Quirke, J.D., 330, 478n143, 478–9n146

Index